Arsenale
Tintori
Fortuny

CADOGANguides

Venetian Gothic
Lombard Renaissance
Palladio
17th. Baroque Longhena
& Rococo

VENICE

DANA FACAROS AND
MICHAEL PAULS

D0358405

About the authors

Dana Facaros and **Michael Pauls** have written over 30 books for Cadogan Guides, including all of the Italy series. They lived in Umbria for three years, but have now moved to a farmhouse surrounded by vineyards in the Lot Valley.

About the contributor

Trained as a professional musician, **Nicky Swallow** has lived in Italy for 20 years. During that time, her enthusiasm for all things Italian has led to an in-depth knowledge of the country and an ongoing search for its less obvious attractions.

Cadogan Guides
Highlands House, 165 The Broadway,
London SW19 1NE
info.cadogan@virgin.net
www.cadoganguides.com

The Globe Pequot Press
246 Goose Lane, PO Box 480, Guilford,
Connecticut 06437–0480

Text design: Andrew Barker
Series cover design: Sheridan Wall
Art direction: Sarah Rianhard-Gardner
Photography: OLIVIA, © Olivia Rutherford
Additional Photography: Front Cover Gondolas at night ©
W.Bibikow/jonarnold.com, p.16 © Wolfgagn Kaehler/CORBIS,
p.17 © Mark Stephenson/CORBIS
Thanks to Gran Caffè Lavena for permission to use the images
on the front cover and p.22
Maps © Cadogan Guides, drawn by Map Creation Ltd
Additional cartography: Angie Watts

Series Editor: Christine Stroyan
Editors: Linda McQueen and Rhonda Carrier
Proofreading: Molly Perham
Indexing: Isobel McLean
Research assistance: Jacqueline Chnéour
Production: Navigator Guides Ltd
Printed in Italy by Legoprint
A catalogue record for this book is available from the
British Library
ISBN 1-86011-822-4

Entertainment p.281

Festivals p.299

The Guide p.71

Eating Out p.263

Where to Stay p.251

Shopping p.286

Sports and Green Spaces p.292

Nightlife p.281

A Grand Canal Tour p.233

Contents

Introducing

Introduction 1
The Neighbourhoods 2
Days Out in Venice 13
Roots of the City 27
Art and Architecture 55

The Guide

01
Travel 71

Getting There 72
Tour Operators 75
Entry Formalities 76
Arrival 76
Getting Around 77

02
Practical A–Z 81

Admission Prices and
   Discount Cards 82
Climate and When to Go 83
Crime and the Police 83
Disabled Travellers 84
Electricity, Weights and
   Measures 85
Embassies and
   Consulates 86
Etiquette 86
Gay and Lesbian Venice 86
Health, Emergencies
   and Insurance 86
Internet 87
Lost Property 87
Media 87
Money, Banks and Taxes 88
Opening Hours and
   Public Holidays 89
Packing 89
Photography 89
Post and Fax 90

Religious Affairs 90
Smoking 90
Students 91
Telephones 91
Time 91
Tipping 91
Toilets 92
Tourist Information 92
Women Travellers 93
Working and Long Stays 93

03
Piazza San Marco 95

St Mark's Basilica 98
Palazzo Ducale
   (Doge's Palace) 108
Piazzetta San Marco 115
Piazzetta dei Leoncini 116
The Procuratie and
   Museums 117
Museo Correr 118

04
San Marco 121

North of Piazza San Marco:
   The Mercerie 124
San Zulian 124
La Fenice and Around 126
La Fenice 126
San Moisè 127
Santa Maria Zobenigo 127
North of La Fenice 128
Museo Fortuny 128
Santo Stefano
   and Around 130
San Samuele 132

05
Castello 133

Santi Giovanni e Paolo
   and Around 136
Around Campo
   Santa Maria Formosa 141

Fondazione Querini-
   Stampalia 141
San Zaccaria and Around 142
Between Rio dei Greci and
   the Arsenale 144
La Pietà 144
Scuola di San Giorgio
   degli Schiavoni 146
The Arsenale
   and Around 148
Naval History Museum 149
Eastern Castello 151
Isola di San Pietro 152
Giardini Pubblici 154
Isola Sant'Elena 154

06
Dorsoduro 155

The Accademia
   and Around 158
Raccolta d'Arte
   Vittorio Cini 162
Peggy Guggenheim
   Collection 163
La Salute and Around 163
Northern Dorsoduro 165
Ca' Rezzonico 165
Campo Santa
   Margherita 166
San Sebastiano
   and Around 167
Angelo Raffaele 168
Along the Zattere 169
Campo di San Trovaso 171
Gesuati 172

07
San Polo and
Santa Croce 173

The Frari and Around 176
Scuola Grande
   di San Rocco 179
Casa Goldoni 182

Scuola Grande di San
  Giovanni Evangelista 182
San Polo and Around 184
Rialto 184
North of the Fondamenta
  del Vin 186
Ca' Pésaro and Around 187
San Stae 188
Fondaco del Turchi/Natural
  History Museum 189
San Giacomo dell'Orio 190
Western Santa Croce 190

08
Eastern
Cannaregio 193
Ca' d'Oro and Around 196
Santi Apostoli
  and Around 197
Two Renaissance
  Churches 198
Santa Maria dei Miracoli 198
San Giovanni
  Grisostomo 198
Campo dei Gesuiti 199
Fondamenta Nuove 200

09
Western
Cannaregio 201
Around Madonna
  dell'Orto 204
San Marcuola
  and Around 207
The Ghetto 209
Canale di Cannaregio
  to the Station 210
Scalzi 213

10
The Lagoon 215
South Lagoon 217
San Giorgio Maggiore 217

The Giudecca 220
The Lido 222
From the Lido
  to Chioggia 223
North Lagoon 225
San Michele 225
Murano 226
Burano 229
San Francesco
  del Deserto 230
Torcello 230
Cavallino and Jesolo 232

11
Grand Canal Tour 233

12
Day Trips 241
Veneto Villas 242
Padua 244
Verona 247

Listings
Where to Stay 251
Eating Out 263
Nightlife and
  Entertainment 281
Shopping 286
Sports and
  Green Spaces 292
Children's
  and Teenagers'
  Venice 295
Festivals 299

Reference
Language 302
Index 308

Maps
Unmissable Venice
  inside front cover
The Neighbourhoods 2–3
Piazza San Marco 96–7
St Mark's Basilica 105
San Marco 122–3
Castello 134–5
Santi Giovanni e Paolo 137
Eastern Castello 152–3
Dorsoduro 156–7
San Polo and
  Santa Croce 174–5
I Frari 177
Scuola Grande di
  San Rocco 180
Eastern Cannaregio 194–5
Western
  Cannaregio 202–203
The Lagoon 217
The Giudecca 220–21
The Grand Canal 234–5
The Veneto 242
Padua 245
Verona 248
Hotels 254–5
Restaurants 268–9
Colour Street Maps
  end of guide
Venice Transport *final page*
Off the Beaten Track
  inside back cover

Introduction

Venice may sit proud on its laurels as the most beautiful and romantic city in the world, but it is also one of humanity's most inspiring examples of what people can create, from literally nothing: the first Venetians, fleeing into the lagoon from Attila the Hun, didn't even have land to build on. Protected by impregnable 'walls' of water, they evolved into an amphibian race of sea folk – merchants, pirates and plunderers with a keen eye for the main chance. *Serenissima*, they fashioned themselves, but they played a bold hand, sailing uncharted waters to the court of Kublai Khan, leading the sack of Constantinople to take 'a quarter and a half of the Roman empire' and standing up defiantly to the popes, even when they threatened eternal Hell.

And yet they also made Venice. They invented the strange and beautiful fabric of their mermaid city, and decorated it with their own school of rich, luminous painting by the likes of Bellini, Giorgione, Titian, Tintoretto and Tiepolo. They invented a unique form of government that abhorred tyranny and made the majority of its citizens happy for a thousand years; and they managed their unusual environment with exemplary wisdom and forethought. They made their city the richest in the world and, when the jig was up, they burned the candle at both ends in a riotous farewell party that lasted for much of the 18th century.

Venice, ever sparkling, defiantly holding her head above water, is their great monument, preserved as she was in the days of the doges in the formaldehyde of her lagoon; she is famous for her canals, but she is also a last, precious fragment of a pre-car world built on a human scale. Retired from her role as a vital trading city for merchants from east and west – 'the market-place of the Morning and Evening lands' – Venice now exists to delight; an incomparable art city preening in the mirror of her waters, a museum city, perhaps, but one full of panache rather than pedantry, always ready to throw a good party (Carnival, the Redentore, the Biennale, the film festival, to name a few) as well as supply, like no other city in the world, the stuff that dreams are made on.

The Neighbourhoods

In this guide, the city is divided into the five central neighbourhoods outlined on the map below, each with its own sightseeing chapter. A further chapter covers the Lagoon and Venice's less central islands. This map also shows our suggestions for the Top Ten things to see and do in Venice. The following colour pages introduce the neighbourhoods, explaining the distinctive character of each.

Cannaregio

San Polo and Santa Croce

Dorsoduro

San Marc

The Lagoon

3 Scuola Grande di San Rocco, p.179

7 The Frari, p.176

5 The Accademia, p.158

4 A gondola trip, p.79

Quiet canals in western Cannaregio, p.201

The Lagoon

8 Shopping for glass in Murano, p.226

6 Rialto Bridge and markets, p.184

Castello

1 St Mark's Basilica, p.98

10 The view from the campanile of San Giorgio Maggiore, p.219

2 Palazzo Ducale, p.108

San Marco

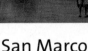

La Serenissima concentrated its soul, brains, nerves and juices in San Marco – and, because this is Venice, the juices sparkle like a glass of *prosecco*. The city's incomparable parlour, Piazza San Marco, with its glittering basilica and frothy Doge's Palace, has been everyone's first stop since Venice began. But there's plenty more to bring you back time and time again – the Museo Correr, a treasure trove of things Venetian; Sansovino's beautiful library and archaeology museum; the fancy medieval shopping streets of the Mercerie; a handful of endearingly quirky churches; handsome *palazzi*; and, perhaps coming soon, operas at glorious La Fenice, finally rising from the ashes.

Clockwise from top left: St Mark's Basilica, Hotel Danieli, Bridge of Sighs, Piazza San Marco nightlife.

Clockwise from top left: Piazza San Marco, Palazzo Contarini del Bovolo, gondolas at dusk in the Bacino San Marco, Doge's Palace.

San Marco
Piazza San Marco chapter p.95
San Marco chapter p.121
Hotels p.252 Restaurants p.266 Bars p.283

Castello

The eastern *sestiere* of Castello was for centuries the working end of the city, where in the high-walled Arsenale Venice cranked out warships and merchants' galleys in a medieval proto-assembly line that made her the mistress of the seas – a story told in the nearby Naval Museum. The rest of Castello is characterized by little lanes where the Arsenale workers and Venice's Greek and Dalmatian residents lived. Their churches nearly all house great works of art – the majestic tombs of the doges in Santi Giovanni e Paolo, the charming Carpaccios in the Scuola di San Giorgio degli Schiavoni, Bellini in San Zaccaria, Palma Vecchio in Santa Maria Formosa, and many more. Castello also offers the city's one and only big park, the Giardini Biennale, scene of the summer art competition.

Clockwise from top left: washing lines, San Zaccaria ceiling, Castello bridge.

Castello
Castello chapter p.133
Hotels p.256 Restaurants p.270 Bars p.283

Dorsoduro

Wedged between the Grand and Giudecca Canals, with the splendid church of Santa Maria della Salute as a landmark, Dorsoduro is a seriously arty *sestiere*, where Bellini, Titian and Tintoretto glow in the Accademia; Picasso, Max Ernst and Jackson Pollock spark and squiggle in the Peggy Guggenheim Collection; and Veronese puts on an impressive one-man show in his parish church of San Sebastiano. Browning lived here in the Ca' Rezzonico, which now serves as a wonderful museum of 18th-century Venice. But lurking around the next little canal are colourful corners: the market in Campo Santa Margherita, the Squero di San Trovaso boatyard, and

From the top: façade on the Zattere, Ca' Rezzonico, Dogana di Mare.

the Ponte dei Pugni, where rivals from either side of the Grand Canal duked it out over the drink. And if Venice begins to feel a bit claustrophobic, take a stroll down the wide, rarely crowded Zattere.

Clockwise from top: Santa Maria della Salute, Grand Canal, Palazzo Salviati.

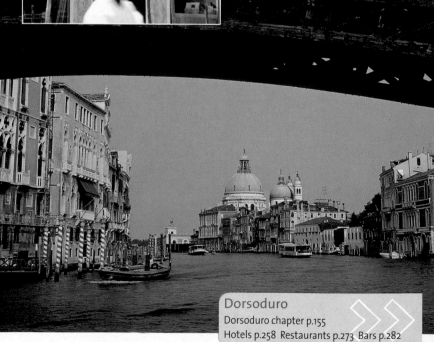

Dorsoduro
Dorsoduro chapter p.155
Hotels p.258 Restaurants p.273 Bars p.282

San Polo and Santa Croce

These two *sestieri* make up the bulk of Venice's Left Bank, embracing the Rialto, the Wall Street of the wealthy Republic, where you can still buy anything from a tomato to a gold bracelet. Although much of Santa Croce has been sacrificed to the demands of the 20th century (the huge car park of Piazzale Roma and freight yards), its intact part and San Polo are great territory for aimless wandering: each micro-neighbourhood, with a *campo* and church, has its own personality. Much of the high art is concentrated in Venice's magnificent Franciscan church, the Frari, home to Titian's celebrated *Assumption*, and in the nearby Scuola Grande di San Rocco, where the ever-daring Tintoretto exceeded even himself to create Venice's 'Sistine Chapel'.

Clockwise from top left: Rialto markets, Scuola Grande di San Rocco, Rialto Bridge, the Frari, Campo San Giacomo.

San Polo and Santa Croce
San Polo and Santa Croce chapter p.173
Hotels p.259 Restaurants p.274 Bars p.282

Cannaregio

Clockwise from top left: quiet canal, gondola ride, Campo del Ghetto.

Cannaregio, the biggest *sestiere*, is home to some of the most intense tourist activity in Venice (along the Lista di Spagna, by the train station) but also to wonderfully atmospheric canals and lanes where few foreigners ever venture, where cats prowl, kids play basketball, and laundry flaps overhead. It offers dozens of secret nooks and crannies for those with time to explore. Cannaregio has its share of Venetian essentials – the now-silent Ghetto, Marco Polo's home in the Corte del Milion, the lavish Ca' d'Oro (now an excellent museum), one of the grandest ballrooms in Italy (in Palazzo Labia), the lovely Gothic church of Madonna dell'Orto and a perfect jewel of a Renaissance church, Santa Maria dei Miracoli.

Cannaregio
Eastern Cannaregio chapter p.193
Western Cannaregio chapter p.201
Hotels p.260 Restaurants p.276 Bars p.282

Clockwise from top: Torcello, Lagoon reflections, Santa Maria Assunta.

The Lagoon

A waterscape of many moods, the Lagoon made Venice, and over the centuries Venetian engineering did much to make the Lagoon. Its 39 islands are part and parcel of the city. The nearby curl of the Giudecca is mostly residential except for Palladio's masterful Redentore, a counterpart to his San Giorgio Maggiore, one of the city's best-known landmarks, on its own islet. Modern holiday Venice was born in

the early 1900s in the fabulous hotels on the Lido, where the beach is as lovely as ever. Then there are the three northerly islands – Torcello, where the ancient pre-Venetians first took refuge from Attila the Hun and left exquisite mosaics in the cathedral; Murano, the fabled island of glass, still very much in business; and Burano, the rainbow-coloured island of fishermen and lacemakers.

Clockwise from top left: island window, Torcello archways, lacemaking, Burano.

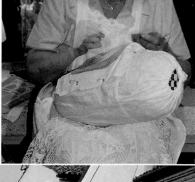

The Lagoon

Lagoon chapter p.215
Hotels p.261 Restaurants p.278 Bars p.282

Days Out in Venice

Renaissance Venice p.16

Medieval Venice p.14

Baroque and Rococo Venice p.18

Indoor Venice p.20

Pigeon Venice p.24

Decadent Venice p.22

MEDIEVAL VENICE

Venice was late out of the starting gate by Italian standards, emerging (literally) out of the mud only in the Dark Ages to become, by the early 10th century, the greatest and wealthiest city in Christian Europe. Some canny relic-snatching gave the city the holy juju it needed, and Doge Dandolo's diversion of the Fourth Crusade to Constantinople in 1204 gave it the hitherto unimagined wealth to build the gorgeous treasure-filled *palazzi* and churches that remain its glory to this day.

One

Start: Ca' d'Oro *vaporetto* stop.
Breakfast: Buy a delicious pastry from **Puppa**, just back from the canal.
Morning: The **Ca' d'Oro**, Venice's loveliest Gothic *palazzo* and a fine museum, then visit the **Corte del Milion** (Marco Polo's home base), and the **Rialto**, the city's medieval business centre.
Lunch: At animated **Alla Madonna**, for a fishy lunch by the Rialto.
Afternoon: Cross back over and follow the medieval shopping streets, the **Mercerie**, to **St Mark's Basilica** (*photo top*), the soul of Venice and one of the crown jewels of medieval art. Inside, don't miss the Treasury, Pala d'Oro, and Museo Marciano.
Dinner and Evening: Tipple and snack your way through the evening at **Al Volto**, a lovely wine bar.

Two

Start: Giardini *vaporetto* stop.

Breakfast: Take a *cornetto* into the Giardini Biennale, or sit on the top floor of **Caffè Paradiso** in the yellow pavilion just south of the *vaporetto* stop, for the classic view of Venice's front door.

Morning: Escape the tourist throngs to see the former cathedral, **San Pietro di Castello**, then learn the secrets of Venice's success at the **Arsenale** and **Naval History Museum**.

Lunch: From San Zaccaria *vaporetto* stop, take the 52 *motoscafi* to Fondamenta Nuove, then *vaporetto* no.12 out to Torcello island, and dine at **Al Ponte del Diavolo**.

Afternoon: Visit **Santa Maria Assunta** (*photo below*) and the museum on **Torcello**, where it all began, then stop at **Murano** on the way back, home of Venice's glassmakers since 1291 (*photo below left*). Watch how they do it, and if there's time, visit the museum, and the medieval churches of **Santi Maria e Donato** and **San Pietro Martire**.

Dinner: **Le Bistrot de Venise**, for a feast of historic Venetian dishes.

Evening: Lose yourself in the evocative back lanes of the city, where the only sound is the soft lapping of the canals.

Food and Drinks

Le Bistrot de Venise, p.266
Caffè Paradiso, p.272
Alla Madonna, p.275
Al Ponte del Diavolo, p.279
Puppa, p.278
Al Volto, p.267

Sights and Activities

Arsenale, p.148
Ca' d'Oro, p.196
Corte del Milion, p.199
Mercerie, p.124
Murano, p.226
Naval History Museum, p.149
Rialto, p.184
St Mark's Basilica, p.98
San Pietro di Castello, p.152
San Pietro Martire, p.227
Santi Maria e Donato, p.229
Torcello, p.230

RENAISSANCE VENICE

Unlike Florence, the Most Serene Republic can claim few of the artistic innovations that led to the Italian Renaissance, but its painters, sculptors and architects, infatuated with colour and splendour, evolved a rich sensual school that didn't mind breaking the rules for sumptuous effect. And Venice, above all, had the money to pay for it, thanks to its new possessions on the *terra firma*. Much of what you see today in the city dates from the 15th and 16th centuries, so Renaissance Venice is fairly unavoidable, but the following itineraries will make sure you see the highlights, on top of all the Giorgiones, Titians, Carpaccios, Bellinis, Veroneses and Tintorettos in the Accademia (*see* 'Indoor Venice', p.20).

Three

Start: Campo San Luca.

Breakfast: A traditional *zaleto* (polenta cake) at **Rosa Salva**.

Morning: Head down Calle dei Fabbri to Piazza San Marco for the splendiferous art-filled **Doge's Palace (Palazzo Ducale)** (*photo top*) and the Secret Itinerary through its workaday bits, to appreciate how well run Venice really and truly was in its heyday.

Lunch: Venetian specialities at **Al Mascaron**.

Afternoon: **Santa Maria Formosa** for Palma Vecchio's buxom Santa Barbara, **Santi Giovanni e Paolo** (*photo on p.17*) for a big Renaissance sculpture and painting feast, and the Carpaccios in the **Scuola di San Giorgio degli Schiavoni**.

Dinner: **La Caravella**, excellent food served in a reproduction 16th-century Venetian galley.

Evening: Work off all those calories at the **Sound Code** disco in Mestre.

Four

Start: San Tomà *vaporetto* stop.
Breakfast: Grab a *doppio espresso* at **Caffè dei Frari**.
Morning: The great barn of the **Frari** (*photo on p.16*), chock-a-block with Renaissance art, and the nearby **Scuola Grande di San Rocco** (*photo on p.9*), Tintoretto's masterpiece.
Lunch: Take the 82 *vaporetto* to Giudecca (stop Zitelle) for scrumptious sandwiches and cakes at **Cips**.

Afternoon: Spend it with Palladio, at two of his greatest churches, **Il Redentore** and **San Giorgio Maggiore**, then take the 82 back over to San Basilio stop to see Veronese's frescoes in **San Sebastiano**.
Dinner: At **Da Fiore**, for Venice's finest gourmet feast.
Evening: Walk along café-lined **Fondamenta del Vin** (*photo on p.16*), for a night view of Renaissance *palazzi* and a *caffè corretto*.

Food and Drinks
Caffè dei Frari, p.276
La Caravella, p.266
Cips, p.278
Da Fiore, p.274
Al Mascaron, p.271
Rosa Salva, p.270

Sights and Activities
Doge's Palace, p.108
Frari, p.176

Il Redentore, p.221
San Giorgio Maggiore, p.218
San Sebastiano, p.167
Santa Maria Formosa, p.141
Santi Giovanni e Paolo, p.136
Scuola Grande di San Rocco, p.179
Scuola di San Giorgio degli Schiavoni, p.146

Nightlife
Fondamenta del Vin, p.186
Sound Code, p.283

BAROQUE AND ROCOCO VENICE

With its love of effect and wealth of ornament, Baroque would seem to have been ideal for Venetian sensibilities. But the style was invented in Rome, and, as Rome's enemy, the Venetians rarely dabbled in it. Baroque's light-hearted successor Rococo, however, found a warm welcome in a city ready to party away its twilight years, when Vivaldi composed his concertos and Giambattista Tiepolo became the leading painter in Europe, and Canaletto and Guardi provided views for Grand Tourists.

Five

Start: San Silvestro *vaporetto* stop.
Breakfast: Sample a strudel at **Rizzardini**, a delightful *pasticceria* dating back to 1742.

Morning: See Giandomenico Tiepolo's excellent *Stations of the Cross* in **San Polo**, the ceiling of **San Pantelon** and the Rococo wonders in the Museo del Settecento, in the **Ca' Rezzonico** (*photo on p.19*).
Lunch: A meaty feast at **L'Incontro**.
Afternoon: Great paintings – the Tiepolo in the **Carmini**; the Guardi in the **Angelo Raffaele**; more Tiepolo in **Santa Maria del Rosario**; plus Longhena's Baroque masterpiece, **Santa Maria della Salute** (*photo above left and on p.19*).
Dinner: Immerse yourself in Venice's culinary past with steak cooked with coffee at **Osteria San Marco**.
Evening: *Settecento* Venetian comedy at the **Teatro Goldoni**, then a hot chocolate at **Florian's**, with its nostalgic 18th-century décor.

Six

Start: Ponte Guglie *vaporetto* stop.
Breakfast: Down a *ristretto* at the bar of **Caffè Costarica**, one of Venice's oldest coffee-houses.
Morning: A Baroque church stroll: the **Scalzi**, **San Simeone Piccolo**, and **San Nicolò da Tolentino**; then wander over to **San Stae**. Cross the Grand Canal in a *traghetto* at Santa Sofia to visit **Santi Apostoli**.
Lunch: A pizza at **Casa Mia**.
Afternoon: Visit the **Fondazione Querini-Stampalia** for Pietro

Longhi's delightful genre scenes; then walk down to the **Riva degli Schiavoni** to see Vivaldi's church, **La Pietà**. Next, hop on the *accelerato* to Santa Maria del Giglio to see **Santa Maria Zobenigo** (*photo left*), **Palazzo Pisani** and the outrageous **San Moisè**.
Dinner: Delightful **Antico Martini**, in a former 18th-century coffee-house.
Evening: A Baroque concert at **La Pietà**, or at **Palazzo delle Prigioni**.

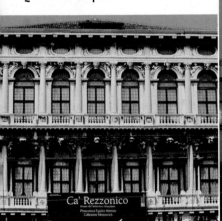

Ca' Rezzonico
Pinacoteca Egidio Martini
Collezione Mestrovich

Food and Drinks
Antico Martini, p.266
Caffè Costarica, p.278
Casa Mia, p.277
L'Incontro, p.273
Osteria San Marco, p.267
Rizzardini, p.276

Sights and Activities
Angelo Raffaele, p.168
Ca' Rezzonico, p.165
Carmini, p.167
Fondazione Querini-Stampalia, p.141
Palazzo Pisani, p.131
La Pietà, p.144
Riva degli Schiavoni, p.144

San Moisè, p.127
San Nicolò da Tolentino, p.191
San Pantalon, p.181
San Polo, p.184
San Simeone Piccolo, p.190
San Stae, p.188
Santa Maria del Rosario, p.172
Santa Maria della Salute, p.163
Santi Apostoli, p.197
Santa Maria Zobenigo, p.127
Scalzi, p.213

Nightlife
Caffè Florian, p.267
Palazzo delle Prigioni, p.284
La Pietà, p.284
Teatro Goldoni, p.284

INDOOR VENICE

As one of the most beautiful cities in the world, Venice has the kind of looks that distract visitors from museums that would be major attractions anywhere else; outside of the great and unmissable Accademia and the blockbuster exhibitions at the Palazzo Grassi, visitors who duck indoors may find themselves surprisingly alone. If you come out of season, when Venice is at its most atmospheric (even at the risk of cold and showers), these indoor charms become even more attractive.

Seven

Start: Accademia *vaporetto* stop.

Breakfast: Be an early bird with the locals at **Bar da Gino**, open from 6.30am.

Morning: Get there first thing, ahead of the crowds, to linger over the beauties of the Venetian school in the **Accademia** (*photo left*) .

Lunch: Sup steaming hot soup in tiny **Trattoria ai Cugnai**.

Afternoon: After the Accademia, be shocked by the new at the nearby **Peggy Guggenheim Collection**, and risk total art glut at the **Palazzo Cini** (*open part of the year only*). Revive your flagging senses with an *ombra e cicheti* at **Da Codroma**.

Dinner: Fresh tuna *'in saor'* at **Ai 4 Feri**.

Evening: Check out **Margaret Duchamp**, a designer 'disco bar'.

Eight

Start: San Stae *vaporetto* stop.

Breakfast: In or near your hotel – there's not much just around the museum and you won't want to be walking too far.

Morning: Head over to Longhena's massive **Ca' Pésaro**, on the Grand Canal, to visit its Museum of Oriental Art and Museum of Modern Art.

Lunch: Forget the weather with the civilized service at **Vecio Fritolin**.

Afternoon: Hop on the *accelerato* line 1 at San Stae and pick up our **Grand Canal tour** (*photo top*) at point 13, alighting at San Marco. Get the lowdown on Venice in the wonderful **Museo Correr**, and then visit Sansovino's **Biblioteca** to see the priceless treasures in the library and the lovely (if often neglected) gems in the **Museo Archeologico**.

Dinner: **Alle Testiere**, for delectable fish and warming puddings.

Evening: A post-prandial drink with the Venetians at the **Taverna l'Olandese Volante**.

Food and Drinks

Ai 4 Feri, p.273
Bar da Gino, p.273
Da Codroma, p.273
Alle Testiere, p.271
Trattoria ai Cugnai, p.273
Vecio Fritolin, p.274

Sights and Activities

Accademia, p.158
Biblioteca Nazionale Marciana, p.119

Ca' Pésaro, p.187
Grand Canal tour, p.233
Museo Archeologico, p.119
Museo Correr, p.118
Palazzo Cini, p.162
Peggy Guggenheim Collection, p.163

Nightlife

Margaret Duchamp, p.282
Taverna l'Olandese Volante, p.283

DECADENT VENICE

Few cities know more about decadence, and how to go about declining in style. The witty Rococo was the last bloom of the thousand-year-old Serene Republic, and, rather than mourn for past glories and its lost Mediterranean empire, Venice pleasured the world (or the part of the world that could afford to do the Grand Tour) with a six-month carnival, casinos (both gambling- and love-nests), and Casanova, along with the Tiepolos, father and son, the greatest painters of the day in Europe.

Nine

Start: Piazza San Marco.
Breakfast: Sleep late, then indulge in a leisurely espresso in the *piazza* at **Gran Caffè Quadri**, **Caffè Florian**, or **Caffè Lavena** (*photo above*).

Morning: Take a water taxi (or cheaper *vaporetto*) to the **Lido** and find a beauty to ogle *Death in Venice* style while soaking up the rays on a sun-lounger.
Lunch: Splash out on elegant seafood at **La Favorita**.
Afternoon: Go back to Venice and spend the afternoon shopping in the designer boutiques of Frezzeria and the Mercerie (*photo opposite*) – at **Trois** for Fortuny silks, at **Mondonovo** for a carnival mask, and **Jade Martine** for sensual lingerie. When your feet start to hurt, stop to watch the celebrities over a chilled Bellini at **Harry's Bar**.
Dinner: Slip over to Giudecca on the clients-only hotel boat for a romantic meal in the incomparable main dining room of the **Hotel Cipriani**.
Evening: Splash out on a leisurely private gondola down the **Grand Canal** (*photo on p.23*).

Ten

Start: In front of your hotel.

Morning: Have the concierge order you a private chauffeured *moto-scafo* for the day, and visit canals few other visitors ever see.

Lunch: Head across the lagoon to Torcello to lunch at idyllic **Locanda Cipriani**.

Afternoon: Buzz over to the Lido for a round at the **Alberoni Golf Course**.

Dinner: Dine like a doge on Venetian classics at the rooftop terrace of the **Danieli Hotel** (*photo top left*).

Evening: In true Venetian style, risk what remains in your bank account at the **Casinò di Venezia**, in Ca' Vendramin-Calergi.

Food and Drinks

Caffè Florian, p.267
Danieli Terrace, p.271
La Favorita, p.278
Gran Caffè Lavena, p.267
Gran Caffè Quadri, p.270
Harry's Bar, p.266
Hotel Cipriani, p.278
Locanda Cipriani, p.278

Sights and Activities

Alberoni Golf Course, p.293
Gondola hire, p.79
Grand Canal, p.233
Lido, p.222
Shopping, p.286

Nightlife

Casinò di Venezia, p.208

PIGEON VENICE

The lion, symbol of St Mark, is the official totem creature of Venice, and you'll see lions everywhere. But now that the Republic is a mere provincial capital, the lion has lost his roar and the humble pigeon, who knows the quiet, secret places, seems more appropriate. Unlike most city-dwellers, the amphibious Venetians are quite fond of them; they even have their own little water trough next to St Mark's in the Piazzetta dei Leoncini. This is the gritty Venice of back streets and deserted squares, where you and the birds leave the tourist throng behind.

Eleven

Start: Piazza San Marco (*photo above*).
Breakfast: Buy a large brioche (and scatter plenty of crumbs!).
Morning: Get to know the statues and crannies of the big square in pigeon detail, then climb the **Campanile** for the bird's-eye view (*photo top left*). Visit the **Museo Diocesano** in a Romanesque cloister, where pigeons are your only company.
Lunch: **Al' Aciugheta**, to peck at a good light lunch.
Afternoon: Walk to the Fondamenta Nuove by way of Santi Giovanni

e Paolo for the **Colleoni statue**, a favourite pigeon roost; then take the *vaporetto* to Burano and a *sandolo* to isolated **San Francesco del Deserto**, where bird-loving St Francis founded a peaceful chapel.

Dinner and Evening: Join the mixed crowd flocking to relaxed, bohemian late-night bar-restaurant **Paradiso Perduto**.

Twelve

Start: Rialto.

Breakfast: Prop up the bar at **All'Arco**, a tiny authentic *bacaro* in the lanes around the markets.

Morning: Venice's fruit and vegetable market, the **Erberia** (*photos above*), and the fish market at the **Peschiera**, are nearly as fun as the smelly rubbish boats that take the leftovers away. Stop for an *ombra* at **Ai Do Mori** and visit the church and *campo* of **Santa Maria Materdomini** and **San Giacomo dell'Orio**. Follow the signs to the Stazione, and head along the **Lista di Spagna** and up into the quiet outer reaches of Cannaregio (*photo on p.24*).

Lunch: Eat kosher at characterful **Gam-Gam**.

Afternoon: Explore the piquant **Ghetto** (*photo on p.26*) and its

museum, **Sant'Alvise** (with Ruskin's 'Baby Carpaccios'), the Campo dei Mori and **Madonna dell'Orto**, then take a *vaporetto* out to wistful **San Michele**, the cemetery island.
Early dinner: Nibble *cicheti*, pigeon-style, washed down with glasses of wine at **Al Bottegon**, a wonderfully old-fashioned wine shop near the San Trovaso boatyard.
Evening: Hang out in buzzy **Campo Santa Margherita** and eat ice-cream till late at **Il Doge**.

Food and Drinks

Ai Do Mori, p.275
Al' Aciugheta, p.271
All'Arco, p.275
Al Bottegon, p.273
Il Doge, p.274
Gam-Gam, p.277
Paradiso Perduto, p.283

Sights and Activities

Campanile, p.114
Colleoni statue, p.139
Ghetto, p.209
Lista di Spagna, p.213
Madonna dell'Orto, p.204
Museo Diocesano, p.120
Rialto markets, p.185
San Francesco del Deserto, p.230
San Giacomo dell'Orio, p.190
San Michele, p.225
Sant'Alvise, p.207
Santa Maria Materdomini, p.187

Nightlife

Campo Santa Margherita, p.166

Roots of the City

THE INVENTION OF VENICE 28

568–810: A CANDLE IN A DARK AGE 29

810–1032: THE FIRST CITY OF MODERN
EUROPE 30

1032–1204: CRUSADES AND A
CONSTITUTION 34

1204–1310: A QUARTER AND A HALF OF THE
ROMAN EMPIRE 35

1310–1453: GENOESE WARS AND THE
MAINLAND EMPIRE 37

1453–1571: *SERENISSIMA* IN SPITE OF
EVERYTHING 42

1573–1796: A DECLINE TO REMEMBER 46

1797 ONWARDS: JUST ANOTHER
PROVINCIAL CAPITAL 51

For you live like sea birds, with your homes dispersed, like the Cyclades, across the face of the waters ...
    letter to Venetian tribunes by Cassiodorus, prefect of King Theodoric; AD 523

Venice (*Venezia*, in Italian, and *Veneixia* to the Venetians of long ago) is 3ft above sea level on good days and stands on the same latitude as Ottawa and Dalandzadgad in Mongolia; it's almost due south of Oslo and north of Luanda, Angola.

The raw facts of the city lend some credence to Chateaubriand's opinion that this is a '*ville contre nature*': it rests on 118 islands, the average consisting of a cake of hard clay (10–15ft thick) iced by 100ft of mud. These are separated by 200 canals, and reunited by 400 bridges. Its shape has been compared to that of a dolphin; or the Yin and Yang, separated by the Grand Canal; or perhaps to the gloves of two boxers shaking hands before a fight – an appropriate image, for the city was divided into two cross-canal factions, the Nicolotti and Castellani, who would settle their differences with annual punch-ups.

Between 697 and 1797 Venice was an independent republic – a record for longevity that may never be broken. Its once great land and sea empire is confined now to a small *comune*, including the lagoon islands and Lido, and Mestre and Marghera on the mainland, with a total population of 340,873. The mere 66,000 souls in the historic centre today complain that they are outnumbered by the pigeons.

The Invention of Venice

Long before anyone ever dreamed of gondolas or plates of liver and onions, an Indo-European people called the **Venetii** (or Henetii, or Enetii) occupied most of northeast Italy. They probably came from Illyria or Asia Minor about 1000 BC, a trading nation, who also produced very good wine. Rome gradually developed colonies in their territory, and the Venetii settled in comfortably as Roman provincials in the 2nd century BC.

The Invention of Venice
Attila's Seat, the Hun's legendary temporary resting place, p.232
Magazzini del Sale, where the precious commodity was stored, p.172
Museo Archeologico, to find out more about Venetian prehistory, p.119
Torcello Island, recipient of waves of immigration from Altinum, p.230

Roman Venetia, with its wealthy cities – Aquileia, Padua, Verona and Altinum – was one of the favoured corners of Italy. Many of the islands of the Lagoon were already inhabited; besides fishing, salt-pans furnished the most important element of the coastal economy. Several busy Roman roads passed through Venetia on their way across the mountains to Illyria or Pannonia, convenient for trade – and also, as Rome decayed, for invaders. **Alaric the Goth** began the troubles, sacking Aquileia in 401. **Attila the Hun** repeated the performance in 452: the Scourge of God, and a figure who has passed into legend in the Venetian chronicles. His destruction of Aquileia, one of the greatest cities of the Empire, started the first flight of population into the lagoons. Apparently, it was no picturesque flight of woebegone refugees – rather a planned migration, a refounding of cities that had no chance of survival on the mainland. The first generations brought their furniture, and later returned to the old towns to bring back stone for new buildings.

Small communities grew up around the lagoons: the Aquileians settled mostly in Grado, the Altinese on Torcello and Burano. The Paduans sent a colony to the island of Rivo Alto – *Rialto*, the centre of the Venice that was to be, traditionally founded on 25 March, in the year 425.

Everyone needs salt, even during the fall of empires. And the new settlements had a near monopoly on it, enough to support them through the worst troubles. With trade disrupted, they had to fall back on their own resources to ship it and to protect the ships: right from the start, necessity led them to their first steps in their ordained vocation, as a commercial nation and a naval power. Necessity also taught them to work together. As early as 466, the 12 lagoon settlements were electing their own tribunes to coordinate common actions and policy. Already in the 500s, both the Gothic kings and the eastern emperors had to treat them with kid gloves: sovereignty over them could be pretended but not easily enforced.

In the **Greek-Gothic Wars** that began in 539, so destructive for the rest of Italy, the Venetians fortuitously chose the winning side. Their fleet aided the Byzantines in taking the Gothic capital, Ravenna, and in return they received their first trading privileges in the East.

In gratitude for Venetian aid, Narses the Eunuch, Justinian's victorious general, built a church to St Theodore where St Mark's stands today. More importantly, he invited the **Lombards** over the Alps to assist in his campaigns as mercenaries. These most unpleasant of all Teutonic barbarians soon overran an impoverished and exhausted Italy, and delivered the *coup de grâce* to the surviving cities of the Venetian mainland. Another, still larger, wave of refugees fled to the Lagoon. In these darkest of times it was clear that any future lay here.

568–810: A Candle in a Dark Age

Through the tinted Venice glass of the Republic's later historians, this early period was a golden age. One chronicler called the Venetians 'a lowly people, who esteemed mercy and innocence, and above all religion, rather than riches. They affected not to clothe themselves with ornaments, or to seek honours, but when need was, they answered to the call.' The towns scattered across the islands were as yet only wood and thatch, interspersed with gardens, each house with its little boat 'tied to posts before their doors like horses on the mainland'.

But beneath the surface some embryonic political troubles were already taking shape.

To prevent the settlements from sliding into anarchy, a Patriarch of Grado named Christopher called an assembly of citizens and convinced them of the need for a single authority. In 697, a certain Paoluccio Anafesta was supposedly elected as the **first Doge** (from *dux*, the common title of Byzantine provincial governors), though there is some doubt that such a person ever existed. More likely, the decisive events occurred during the **Iconoclast struggles**, beginning in 726. Emperor Leo III's war on religious images was intensely unpopular in Italy; Pope Gregory II and his new allies, the Lombards, quickly exploited the discontent. There were revolts in Ravenna, the seat of the Byzantine exarch (viceroy). A doge, Orso Ipato, elected in 726, seems to have helped the exiled exarch retake the city.

What happened next is unclear. Some reports say there was civil war in Venice between the partisans and opponents of Byzantium. However the process evolved, Venice must have been master of its destinies after 752, when the Lombards took Ravenna and effectively ended any Byzantine pretensions to rule over northern Italy.

If the Venetians were now free, their 'Golden Age' was definitely a thing of the past. Nearly all the early doges tried to turn the office into a family dynasty. Not many of them died in bed; one Patriarch was thrown off the top of his palace's tower. Factionalism continued unchecked in a stream of intrigues, rebellions and assassinations. And the Venetians discovered a commodity even more profitable than salt – slaves, mostly

568–810

Campo Santi Apostoli, site of one of the first Rialtine islets to be colonized in the 7th century, p.197

The **Lagoon waters**, to see the channel markers that protected Venice from invasion since its earliest days, p.216

Museo dell'Estuario, for the story of the Lagoon in the Dark Ages, p.232

Santa Maria Assunta, Torcello's basilica, founded in 639, p.230

Christian Slavs destined for the flesh markets of North Africa and Spain. The new state started its career with few friends. Even without slave-trading, Venice's wealth and the essential difference of its society were enough to earn it distrust in the narrow-minded world of feudal Europe. A 10th-century official in Pavia wondered: '... these people neither plough nor sow, but can buy corn and wine everywhere'.

The slave trading earned the Venetians one formidable enemy, the righteous Charlemagne. Since 752, the **Franks** had been the leading power in Italy, thanks to Charlemagne's father, Pepin, who delivered the peninsula from the Lombards. They claimed dominion over all northern Italy, including the lagoons, and relations were tense until 810, when amid another factional struggle the Doge, Obelario de'Antenori, actually invited the Franks to send in their army. Charlemagne's son, another Pepin, was not long in arriving.

Facing real danger, the Venetians responded with decision. The treacherous Doge was expelled, and defences rapidly organized. The channel markers and buoys were removed, making the shallow lagoon impassable to anyone not familiar with it. Malamocco, the capital, was abandoned as indefensible (unlike the present Malamocco, this island was east of the Lido), and the new Doge, **Angelo Participazio**, concentrated the defences around the Rialto. Pepin besieged them for six months, but could not penetrate the lagoon before the summer heat and disease took their toll. In the end, the Venetians had to concede a tribute, but they had survived their greatest trial so far. A treaty was signed recognizing the sovereignty of Constantinople, the convenient legal fiction under which Venice would grow and prosper for centuries to come, but also a tie that would confirm its isolation from the rest of Italy. Doge Participazio, the hero of the hour, presided over the reconstruction. The momentous decision was made to move the capital to the **Rialto** – Participazio's home, but also a central, defensible site. The fight

against Pepin had made the Venetians a united people, and from that time they combined to build Venice.

810–1032: The First City of Modern Europe

Very soon, Participazio erected the **first Doge's Palace** for himself. The pieces were falling into place; all that was needed was the right corpse. In retrospect, the embroidered legends can be disregarded: there can be little doubt that the **theft of St Mark from Alexandria** in 828 was a calculated and brilliant manoeuvre of Venetian policy. Of the 55 holy cadavers abstracted from around the Mediterranean by Venice (see p.222, 'The Lagoon', 'The Invasion of the Bodysnatchers'), this is the one that mattered. To underscore the tradition of Mark's founding of the see at Aquileia, a legend was concocted that Mark had landed in Venice, where an angel appeared to him, saying, 'Peace to you, Mark, my Evangelist; here your body shall lie.' To medieval Italy, an Evangelist in your crypt was as good as an Apostle, maybe better. Besides giving the city a powerful protector in Heaven, Mark could intervene in more mundane affairs, allowing it to counter the theological and political pretensions of both Constantinople and Rome.

The body was Venice's Declaration of Independence. The Venetians wasted no time in stitching Mark's lion symbol to their banners; their newly adopted battle-cry, 'Viva San Marco!', would be heard around the Mediterranean for nearly a thousand years. Finding a home for the priceless relic became the first priority, and a Basilica was dedicated four years later – significantly, Mark was to rest in the shadow of the Doge's new palace, and not in the cathedral on the distant island of Olivolo.

Despite the new foundation, Venice still conducted internal affairs with anarchic contentiousness. The Participazio family continued its near-monopoly over the dogeship, although after 887 they had to share their dominance with the Candiani. One of these, **Pietro Candiano IV** (959–76), proved catastrophic. Vain and ambitious, Pietro conducted himself more like a feudal auto-crat than a republican prince of merchants. His marriage with Waldrada, sister of the Marquis of Tuscany, brought him towns on the mainland, and he soon began to treat Venice as just another of his possessions. Coercing the Venetians to help him subdue rebellious Ferrara touched off a revolt to remember in 976: a mob stormed the Doge's Palace and set it on fire, and before long the flames engulfed the still-wooden city. When the smoke cleared there were no Candiani left standing, and very little of Venice. The Orseoli became the new dynasty, until another revolt put an end to them in 1032.

Trouble came not only from within. In the 830s Arab corsairs appeared to plague Venetian shipping from their bases in Apulia and Sicily. In 899, the rampaging Magyars overran northern Italy. Once more the Lagoon saved the city, but just to sleep better the Doge built fortifications, stretching from the castle on Olivolo to the Grand Canal. Great stretches of lagoon must have been filled for it – part of the gradual process that was converting the Rialto islands into modern Venice.

The Arabs were not the only pirates. Beginning in the late 800s, Slavic **'Narentine' pirates**, so-called for their bases around the Narenta river, would lie in wait among the maze of islands on the Dalmatian coast, posing a continuous threat to Venice's trade lifeline with Constantinople. After alternately fighting the pirates and paying them tribute, the Venetians felt strong enough to decide the issue by the year 1000. **Doge Pietro Orseolo II**'s naval expedition turned into a triumphal procession through Dalmatia, as town after town swore fealty to the Republic, and the worst strongholds of the pirates were burned. Soon the Doges were affecting the title 'Duke of Dalmatia', as another show-piece of Venetian folklore was evolving – the Marriage with the Sea.

In the 9th century, drawing the line between pirates and non-pirates would have been difficult. The difference comes later, when the histories are written. Most likely Venice preyed on her neighbours as much as they preyed on her, and her pretended monopoly over Adriatic shipping kept other towns from making an honest living on the sea. Croatian pirate historians, had there been any, would have noted that Venetians were still snatching off their countrymen for sale as slaves. Towards legitimate competi-tion, Venice reacted in much the same way. Comacchio, a rival trading town on the Po, was sacked by the Venetians in 866 and completely destroyed in 932. Further afield, Amalfi, Gaeta, Bari and, more ominously, Pisa and Genoa were testing seas and markets that Venice already regarded as her own.

One summer night in 998, a small boat silently entered the Lagoon. At the island of San Servolo it picked up a passenger and headed for the city, where its occupants made a moonlight tour of the quiet canals. In that boat was Otto III, the young and impetuous Emperor of the Germans, and his passenger was the Doge himself. Otto had arranged this secret visit to see the city as it was, without the stifling protocol. Already, Venice had to be seen: the greatest city of western Europe (excepting perhaps Moslem Cordoba and Seville) was an inconceivable marvel to any sleepy feudal soul. On the threshold of medieval civilization, it was also a sign of things to come.

810–1032

Museo Correr, to see early Venetian coins, p.118

Naval History Museum, for the model of a *Bucintoro*, the galley used by the Doge in the Marriage to the Sea ceremony, p.151

St Mark's Basilica, founded in 892 to house the stolen relics of the saint, and *The Translation of the Body of St Mark*, the painting that tells the story, p.100

San Giorgio Maggiore, to visit the Benedictine monastery founded in 982, p.218

San Polo and **Sant'Eufemia**, examples of 9th–11th-century churches, pp.184 and 221

Timeline

401	Alaric the Goth's sack of Aquileia.
425	Venice founded on 25 March; first settlement on the Rivoalto (Rialto).
452	Attila the Hun plunders Venetia; people seek safety in the Lagoon.
466	The 12 Lagoon communities elect their own tribunes.
560	Venetians assist Narses the Eunuch and are rewarded with Church of San Teodoro on the Rivoalto.
568	Lombards invade; inhabitants of Altinum flee to Torcello.
697	Election of the first doge.
726	Iconoclast struggles in Byzantium: first documented use of the title of *Dux* or Doge.
737	Rule of the Six Maestri de Militi.
742	Capital established at Malamocco.
810	Pepin (Charlemagne's son) unsuccessfully besieges the Lagoon. Charlemagne and Byzantine Emperor Nicephorus sign a treaty recognizing Venice as subject to Constantinople.
828–9	St Mark's body stolen by Venetian merchants.
932	Venice sacks salt rival Comacchio and removes its population to create a salt monopoly in the Adriatic.
960	Dalmatians raid Venice.
998	Emperor Otto III visits Venice.
1000	The Doge leads Venice's fleet in crushing the pirates of Dalmatia, beginning conquest of the Adriatic.
1095	First Crusade preached.
1098	Crusade expedition, first naval battles with Pisa.
1102	Venice establishes trading quarter in Sidon.
1104	Founding of the Arsenal.
1106	Great flood destroys Malamocco.
1123	Siege of Tyre.
1128	First street lighting in the city.
1166	Zara and Dalmatia rebel.
1171	Venice's trading colony in Constantinople, 200,000 strong, is arrested and its goods confiscated by the Emperor, on the instigation of trading rivals, the Genoese; Doge declares war on Empire, and leads Venice into a humiliating setback; six *sestieri* are established to facilitate tax collections.
1172	Doge Vitale Michiel II killed, after returning home, defeated by plague; establishment of self-electing Great Council limits the Doge's power.
1173	First bridge at the Rialto.
1204	Taking charge of the Fourth Crusade, 90-year-old Doge Dandolo subdues Dalmatia, Zara and captures Constantinople; Venice controls the Adriatic, Aegean, seaports of Syria and major East–West trade routes.
1253	First war with Genoa.
1261	Greeks retake Constantinople; merchants Nicolò and Matteo Polo make first visit to Kublai Khan.
1271	Polos return to Mongolia, with Nicolò's son Marco.
1284	First minting of the golden ducat.
1291	Glass furnaces moved to Murano; Muslims retake Tyre.
1297	*Serrata*, or closing, of the *Maggior Consiglio*, limiting membership to patricians.
1298	Genoa defeats Venice at Curzola.
1300	The disenfranchised people of Venice rebel; ringleaders are beheaded.
1308	First papal interdict against Venice.
1310	Nobles led by Tiepolo conspire to seize power; Council of Ten established; constitution takes form that will endure until 1796.
1325	The 'Golden Book' begun.
1338	Church of the Frari begun.
1346	Santi Giovanni e Paolo begun.
1348	Black Death halves the population.
1353	Venice defeats Genoa at Alghero.
1358	Revolt in Dalmatia.
1363	Revolt in Crete.
1373	Arrival of Jews in Venice.
1380	Genoa defeated at Chioggia.
1400	Birth of Jacopo Bellini.
1402	The death of Milan boss Gian Galeazzo Visconti leaves most of northern Italy up for grabs.

1405	Venice picks up its first mainland possessions: Padua, Verona, Bassano and Belluno.	1539	Council of Three established.
		1569	Three hundred Arsenal workers burst into the Ducal palace with axes.
1406	Angelo Correr, Patriarch of Venice, becomes Pope Gregory XII.	1570	Turks take Cyprus.
1420	Venice weasels Udine and the Friuli from the King of Hungary.	1571	Battle of Lepanto, great naval victory over the Turks in the Gulf of Patras.
1429	Birth of Gentile Bellini.	1576	A vicious outbreak of plague carries off 60,000, including Titian.
1431	Birth of Giovanni Bellini.		
1450	Birth of Carpaccio.	1577	Fire in Doge's palace.
1453	Mehmet II captures Constantinople; Venice quickly signs trade agreement with Sultan.	1580	Birth of Longhena.
		1606	The Great Interdict: Pope Paul V excommunicates Venice.
1454	Expansion on the mainland includes Treviso, Bergamo, Friuli, and Ravenna.	1630	Venice decimated by the most deadly plague of its history.
1456	Venetian Alvise da Mosto discovers Cape Verde islands.	1631	Santa Maria della Salute begun.
		1640	The Republic introduces coffee (as a medicine) to Europe.
1464	First Turkish war; Venice loses Negroponte and part of the Morea (Peloponnese).	1669	Venetians surrender Candia (Herakleon), Crete, to the Turks.
1469	First books printed in Venice.	1685	Francesco Morosini reconquers the Morea for Venice.
1478	Birth of Giorgione.		
1484	Venice wins Rovigo and the Polesine from Ferrara, completing a *terra firma* empire that is to last until Napoleon.	1693	Birth of Tiepolo.
		1697	Birth of Canaletto.
		1709	Lagoon frozen solid.
		1712	Birth of Guardi.
1485	Titian born.	1718	Venice loses the Morea to the Turks.
1488	Caterina Cornaro 'cedes' Cyprus to Venice.	1790	Construction of La Fenice.
1493	Aldus Manutius prints his first book.	1797	Napoleon abolishes Venetian Republic: apathy is replaced by anger when he sells it to the Austrians.
1494	Italy invaded by Charles VIII of France; Venice allies with other states to fight the French.	1806	Napoleon visits Venice.
		1836	Cholera plague strikes the city.
1498	Vasco da Gama's voyage around the Horn to India – the end of Venice's old trade monopolies with the East.	1846	Railway bridge ends Venice's isolation.
		1848	Daniele Manin's heroic uprising against the Austrians.
1508	Birth of Palladio. League of Cambrai formed against Venice by jealous rivals.	1866	Venice is joined to the new Kingdom of Italy; becomes provincial capital.
1510	League of Cambrai defeats Venice at Agnadello.	1912	Publication of Mann's *Death in Venice*.
1512	Birth of Tintoretto.	1928	New port of Marghera completed.
1516	Jews confined to the Ghetto.	1931	Mussolini builds road causeway.
1527	Sack of Rome: artists, architects and scholars flee to Venice, bringing the High Renaissance in tow.	1960	Venice gets an airport.
		1966	4 November, terrible flood.
1528	Birth of Veronese.	1993	Venice elects a mayor, Masso Cacciari, from the Partita Democratica della Sinistra (PDS), the former Communist Party.
1537	Turkish wars, territorial losses in Greece.	1996	La Fenice fire.

1032–1204: Crusades and a Constitution

The Orseolo clan lost control of the doge-ship in 1026, but their faction at home, and their alliances with the emperors, kept the pot boiling for another six years. When their last feeble attempt to seize power was crushed, the Venetians resolved to find a more efficient form of government. A new doge, **Domenico Flabanico**, oversaw a complete reform. A senate was elected, along with dogal councillors, and doges were required, not requested, to seek their advice. Finally, the system by which a doge would 'associate' a kinsman with his rule as a desig-nated successor was forbidden, eliminating the monarchical tendency once and for all.

It was a perfect time to give the ship of state an overhaul, for the Adriatic was becoming a busy place. In northern Italy the reviving towns were asserting their inde-pendence against emperor and pope, and embarking on commercial careers of their own. In the south, the big noise was being made by the **Normans**, carving out their own empire in Apulia, Calabria and Sicily. Their ambitions towards Byzantium crossed

---

1032–1204

Arsenal, built in 1104, the world's first 'assembly line' and testament to ruthless 12th-century Venetian efficiency, p.148

Doge's Palace, especially the Sala del Maggior Consiglio, in the Doge's Palace, the room where the council met; and the Sala del Scrutinio, where votes for a new doge were counted, p.108

Hotel Danieli, originally Palazzo Dandolo; its lobby was the site of the murder of Doge Vitale Michiel by a mob in 1172, p.256

Pala d'Oro, the altar screen in St Mark's, a product of the collaboration between Greek and Venetian goldsmiths, p.106

Rialto Bridge, first built in 1173, p.184

San Francesco del Deserto, to visit the monastery and chapel founded where St Francis ran aground in 1220, p.230

Venice's, and battles around the Apulian coast were waged between 1081 and 1085, with the Venetians usually winning. Most importantly, this war permitted Venice to extort even greater trading concessions out of the demoralized Greeks, who had recently lost almost all Asia Minor to the Seljuk Turks. Venice attained virtual control over all Byzantine commerce, making the ancient empire a sort of gilded dependency.

Just coincidentally (and if you believe that, we have some genuine relics of St Nicholas we'll sell you), the **First Crusade** was preached 10 years later in 1095. It was clear that a major power vacuum had appeared in the eastern Mediterranean, and the Venetians were not alone in seeing the opportunity. Pisa and Genoa made their fortunes ferrying crusaders, and both soon became important players in the region. Venice, possessing little of the crusading zeal of the murderous Franks and rather resentful of being forced to share its new windfall, kept aloof from the conflict, fleecing the Franks where possible and grabbing economic control of Levantine cities such as Sidon (1102) and Tyre (1123).

Back home, the city was beginning to look more like the Venice we know. The **Basilica of St Mark** was consecrated in 1094. The city's scattered shipyards and foundries were consolidated in one place, the **Arsenal** – for centuries the backbone of Venetian power and the biggest industrial establishment in the world. There was one notable subtrac-tion: the island of Malamocco, Venice's first capital, obliterated by a terrific storm in 1106. Two more great fires in the same year finally convinced Venice of the necessity of building in brick and stone.

For the first time in centuries, Venice was forced to look towards the mainland. In the 1140s she obtained control of much of Istria. In the 1150s, there were the Wars of the Lombard League, in which Venice aided the northern Italian cities against **Emperor Frederick Barbarossa**. The real action, however, still lay over the sea. In 1172 Venice met a startling setback as the humiliated

Greeks sought to take their revenge on their insatiable creditors; in a concerted action they imprisoned the entire Venetian trading colony in Constantinople (which numbered in the tens of thousands) and seized its property. An enraged Venice, already heavily in debt from its other ventures, raised a forced loan from its citizens and sent a large fleet eastwards under **Doge Vitale Michiel II**. Clever Byzantine diplomacy stalled the Venetians until plague ravaged their force in the Aegean.

It was a disaster that could have done permanent damage to Venetian ambition. In its wake, the returning Doge was assailed by a mob (in what is now the lobby of the Hotel Danieli) and murdered, resulting in a political crisis and another wave of constitutional adjustment. 'Reform' would not exactly be the right word, for the new measures took the relatively democratic state that had evolved since 697 and turned it into a tightly controlled oligarchy. No longer were doges to be elected by the popular assembly, but by a Great Council, the *Maggior Consiglio*, entirely dominated by the richest merchants. The Doge himself was forced to take an oath, the *promissione ducale*, vowing to be little more than a figurehead; and upon the death of each an inquisition was to be held to see if any new provisions were necessary to keep future doges in check. The élite club of the *Maggior Consiglio* assumed control of every aspect of government, filling each state office from among its own members. To discourage factionalism, it made all its choices through complex procedures involving selection by lot or indirect election through several layers of committees.

The first doge selected under the new rules, **Sebastiano Ziani** (1172), happened to be the richest man in Venice. He served well, and under the new system Venetian prosperity made a strong comeback. In 1177, all Europe watched as Venice orchestrated the reconciliation between Barbarossa and Pope Alexander III. The visitors would have crossed the first Rialto Bridge (1173), and seen the columns of Saints Mark and Theodore

recently erected in the Piazzetta. Venice largely sat out the Third Crusade; while Cœur-de-Lion and Saladin slugged it out, the *Maggior Consiglio* freshened up their fleets and their bank balances. They might have thought they had a score to settle.

1204–1310: A Quarter and a Half of the Roman Empire

Enrico Dandolo, who accepted the silly cap and umbrella of the dogeship in 1193, was 90 years old and blind. Legend has it he lost his sight in Constantinople, either in a street brawl or at the hands of the imperial torture-masters. If he indeed held a personal grudge, he found his opportunity for revenge with the beginning of the **Fourth Crusade**. In 1201, an embassy under Geoffroi de Villehardouin came to discuss the ferrying of crusaders in Venetian ships. The following spring, some 33,000 men were to be transported to the Holy Land, at the cost of about one and a third pounds of silver each. For a kicker Venice asked for only one-half of all territories conquered.

The Venetians cleverly leaked a detail of the arrangement: instead of Palestine, the destination of the Crusade was to be Egypt, the leading Moslem sea power, and Venice's biggest trading partner. This was strategically a sound move, but bad for crusading propaganda. The next spring, as a result, only one-third of the expected number of crusaders assembled in Venice. The Venetians refused to lift an anchor; they wanted the full package price, and they saw no reason to waste money feeding their guests until the agreed sum was raised. The starving crusaders passed the hat round but came up some 34,000 silver marks short. No problem, Enrico Dandolo said: simply make a stop on the way to deliver us the rebellious city of Zara (modern Zadar, Yugoslavia) on the Dalmatian coast.

Zara was taken, amidst bloodshed. About the same time, events in Constantinople took an interesting turn – one tyrannical usurper had been tossed out by another. The deposed tyrant's son, **Alexius IV**, cried out for vengeance. Whether or not the Venetians had planned it all along, the idea was now obvious: restore the pretender Alexius to Constantinople, and perhaps pick up a bit of booty on the side. Venice's Egyptian embarrassment was solved, while providence had supplied the thickheaded French knights to square accounts with the Byzantines.

To a medieval mind it was a breathtaking deed: divert the Crusade and attack the fabulous city, the heir of Rome. The assault was quick and merciless; Dandolo himself, disembarking under the very walls under constant fire, led the Venetians and French to the attack, and Constantinople fell for the first time in its 900-year history. Alexius was crowned, but during several months of uncertainty a Greek reaction threw him out again. Now the Westerners decided that only a complete sacking would repay their expenses. On 9 April 1204, the allies attacked again. The Greeks, although grievously outnumbered, fought bravely for three days until the Theodosian walls were breached. The carnage was frightful, and was followed by history's all-time biggest daylight robbery. After the traditional three days' sack (during Holy Week, as chance would have it) and months of more methodical looting, 900 years' accumulation of imperial spoils was packed into the holds of Venetian galleys.

Historians, inexplicably misty-eyed over corrupt, useless Byzantium, often exaggerate the crime of Dandolo and his allies – as if they were responsible for the triumphs of the Turks two centuries later; as if they had done anything more than liquidate a bankrupt concern. The Venetians got all the best (like the famous bronze horses of the Hippodrome), and in the division of the Empire that followed they showed their cleverness again. They let the French keep the city and most of its mainland provinces, impoverished and hard to defend (their 'Latin Empire' was a disaster, and lasted less than 60 years), contenting themselves with the

1204–1310

St Mark's Basilica, its Museo Marciano and the Treasury, to see the loot brought back from the sack of Constantinople, including the bronze *quadriga*, p.102

Teatro Malibran, the family home of the exploring Polo family, p.199

Rialto markets, to buy and sell in the footsteps of the medieval traders, p.185

Secret Itinerary of the Doge's Palace, especially the Sala del Consiglio dei Dieci and the Torture Chamber, to find out more about the feared Council of Ten, p.112

The Old Woman with a Mortar, the relief on the Mercerie that commemorates the Tiepolo uprising, p.124

islands and strong points that lay along their trade routes. Still it was a considerable prize, 'a quarter and a half' of Byzantium, as the treaty quaintly put it, and a manageable little empire that wouldn't get in the way of doing business.

Venice, now a European power in her own right, lacked experience in such matters and farmed her new colonies out to her nobles to be run as feudal possessions. Politically and religiously, it was an oppressive rule, though perhaps no worse than any of the other states of the region. Venice's spectacular success, and her stranglehold over the Eastern trade, had also earned her a new supply of enemies. Of these, the most bitter and dangerous was **Genoa**. Genoese trading concessions often existed next to those of the Venetians in the cities of the Levant, and conflict was inevitable. Fighting broke out in 1253, over Acre; Venice won, but it was only the beginning of a war that lasted 127 years.

In 1261, the Greeks recaptured Constantinople from the Franks. The new Emperor, **Michael VIII Palaeologus**, was understandably anxious to be avenged on the Venetians: he gave the Genoese the Quarter of Galata in Constantinople for a base and encouraged them to seize the Black Sea and Aegean trade. Also in 1261, and not entirely coincidentally, **Marco Polo**'s father and uncle began the first of their voyages to the distant East; if there were any new trade possibilities avoiding Constantinople, Venice's merchants meant to find them.

Altogether, the 13th century was not the best of times for Venice. Business was still booming, and goods flowed into the markets of the Rialto, as one contemporary noted, 'like water from the fountain'. The city continued to deck itself with new glories: most conspicuously the churches of San Zanipolo and the Frari. But the expense of defending its new possessions put the Republic under heavy strain. Besides the wars with Genoa, the collapse of the last crusader states in the 1290s hurt trade and forced Venice into uneasy alliances with the Moslems. At home, the lower classes felt pinched, politically as well as economically. During the course of the century the *Maggior Consiglio* gradually tightened its hold over the Republic, giving the Venetian constitution the rough form it was to keep for the next 500 years.

With the famous *Serrata* (locking) of the *Consiglio* in 1297, the Venetian élite turned itself into a hereditary caste. The only qualification for an inscription in its **'Golden Book'** was to have had an ancestor in an elected office. 'Locked' out were the overwhelming majority of Venetians, with no chance of ever taking part in public life. Locked in were not only the wealthy, but also some poor people with illustrious ancestry. This new caste enforced very strict codes of conduct for itself; as soon as he turned 25, a patrician had to pay heavy taxes and was duty bound to the State for life, liable at any time to be selected for an office that probably would cost more money than it paid. The motivation for these reforms was perhaps more fear of revolution from above than from below. All over Italy, city republics were falling under the rule of strongmen *signori*, taking over where merchant élites could not resist factionalism or restrain their appetites. The Venetian élite were remarkably clear-sighted: if their ship of state was to avoid foundering, they must remain at the helm. And if they were to have absolute privilege, they had to accept absolute responsibility.

Not that all Venetians accepted the new order of things. The first revolt among the disenfranchised occurred in 1300 and was brutally suppressed. A more serious disruption came in 1310, the Tiepolo uprising. **Baiamonte Tiepolo**, the '*Gran Cavaliere*', came from a noble family that had produced two doges. But Baiamonte's supporters were nearly all noblemen, and their attempted coup found no support among the common people, who apparently had already decided that the political monopoly of one class was preferable to a tyrant. One important innovation came about as a result of the revolt, as expressed in an old song:

In the year one thousand three hundred
*   and ten*
In the midst of the month for harvesting
*   grain*
Baiamonte passed over the ponte
and so was formed the Council of Ten.

The Council of Ten, originally an emergency body formed to root out Baiamonte's supporters, was to become the most powerful part of the state machinery. More powerful than the doge, the Ten guarded Venice's internal security, looked after foreign policy, and, with its sumptuary laws and sententious taboos, still found time to look after the moral conduct of the Venetians.

1310–1453: Genoese Wars and the Mainland Empire

Meanwhile, the struggle with Genoa proceeded fitfully. A particularly exhausting round in the 1290s had seen battles from Liguria to Constantinople before the Genoese victory at Curzola (1298) and mutual exhaustion brought peace again. Once more, though, Venice had to concern itself with problems on the mainland, where ambitious tyrants such as the **Visconti** of Milan and the **Scaligeri** of Verona were posing a new threat.

The next decades were relatively quiet – **Dante** visited in 1321 and got a cold reception as an emissary from Ravenna. In 1341, the

Black Death in Venice

Whenever the 21st century leaves a bad taste in your mouth, give some consideration to the 14th. Things were bad all over Europe then, but in Italy they were so rotten that historians speak of a collective death wish in the 1340s. Calamities of every kind befell the peninsula – earthquakes, floods and some of the worst weather on record; wars raged everywhere (Venice was locked in its death struggle with Genoa) and upheavals and disorder were a constant threat. Bankruptcies wrecked the economy; in 1346–7 the crops were so poor that thousands of people died of starvation. Even the wine went off.

The Italians were exhausted, and resigned to disaster. As if on cue, the worst epidemic of all, the Black Death, arrived on the scene in October 1347 – brought from the Crimea on Venetian galleys (though the Venetians blame it on the Genoese). As usual Venice suffered the most: as the densely populated chief port of entry from the East, the city had a dire record of 70 major epidemics in 700 years. No wonder the Venetians lived so intensely, when life itself was so precarious.

On 20 March 1348, Doge Andrea Dandolo set up a council to deal with the plague. The dead were taken on special barges to be buried at San Erasmo on the Lido and at a new cemetery at the long-lost San Marco Boccacalme, or simply sunk into the waters of the Lagoon. Beggars were forbidden to exhibit corpses (an old custom) to raise alms. Strict immigration controls were ordered, and all travellers were obliged to spend 40 days in quarantine at Nazarethum Island (its name, later elided to Lazzaretto, became widely used for all such places).

All the measures were too late. At its worst the Black Death killed 600 Venetians a day; the total dead numbered an almost incredible 100,000 (about half the population). Helpless against the epidemic, most doctors in Venice either died or fled in horror. There was one exception, a health officer named Francesco da Roma, who received an annuity of 25 gold ducats as a reward for remaining in Venice during the Black Death. When asked why he stayed when everyone else fled, he replied: 'I would rather die here than live anywhere else.'

Doge's Palace was completed in the form we see today. In the 1330s, Venice checked the ambitions of Verona, and found it expedient after a victorious conclusion to keep the city of Treviso to guard its increasingly important land trade routes over the Alps to Germany: like it or not, the city that had always turned its back on the land now found itself an actor on that stage, in the midst of all the intrigues and petty wars of that era at the dawn of the Renaissance.

The **Black Death** hit Italy in 1347 – Venice's fault, in a way, since a Venetian ship transported the disease from the Crimea where it had ravaged the Mongol *Golden Horde*. In Venice, as in many other cities, it carried off some three-fifths of the population. Genoa suffered too, but both sides were in shape to resume hostilities only three years later. Again the conflict was conducted on an epic scale. After victories and defeats on both sides, Genoese Admiral Paganino Doria

ambushed an idle Venetian fleet at Portolungo, in the Peloponnese, in 1352, capturing 56 ships.

The subsequent peace gave few advantages to Genoa, but for Venice more reverses waited in store. **Marin Falier**, the splenetic 54th Doge (1354–5), attempted with the aid of disaffected Arsenal workers to stage another coup, making himself a true prince free of the constitutional burdens. The Council of Ten got wind of the plot and before most Venetians knew what was happening their Doge was missing his head and his co-conspirators were dangling from the columns of the Doge's Palace. Dalmatia was gobbled up by the King of Hungary, and in 1363 a revolt in Crete, joined by some local Venetian barons, gave the Ten a three-year headache.

The last war with Genoa, the **War of Chioggia**, began in 1378. At first the Venetians, under Admiral **Vettor Pisani**, defeated the Genoese fleet near Rome; in a repeat of 1353, though, they let the Genoese surprise them in winter quarters at Pola, in Istria. Only six ships made it back to Venice, and Pisani was tossed into the Doge's prisons – the common fate of Venetian commanders who permitted such things to happen. But Venice was in desperate straits, undefended, with a huge enemy fleet speeding towards the Lagoon. As in Pepin's time, the channel markers were pulled up and the Lagoon entrances blocked. The entire population mobilized itself just in time to receive the Genoese fleet. The Genoese believed Chioggia, on the southern edge of the Lagoon, to be the key to capturing all. With their Paduan allies they stormed it in August 1379, and Venice was under siege. The Venetians, high and low, responded to the threat with their accustomed resolve, but they had a demand that even the Doge and the Ten could not withstand. They wanted Vettor Pisani for their leader, and no other. The old Admiral's chains had to come off, and, back in command, he produced the inspired plan of blockading the blockaders. In a fierce fight on the longest night of the year, he dragged out old hulks full of rocks and sank them in the channels, cutting off the occupying force from its fleet and from the Paduans on the mainland. The Venetians knew they could not keep it up for long. The success of their gamble depended on the chance that their other fleet, under the mercurial Admiral Carlo Zeno, would return in time before the larger Genoese force could assert itself. At the beginning of the war, Zeno had been sent out to harass Genoese shipping. He was a year overdue, and no one even knew if his fleet still existed, or where it might be.

Providence was evidently in a poetic mood, and now the city that had lived so long by fabricating legends and miracles found its reward. On New Year's morning, the sails were sighted. It was **Carlo Zeno**, and Venice was saved. After a year of sweeping Genoese shipping off the seas, he had come with an enormous load of booty and a fleet in

fighting trim. The counter-siege continued until June, but it ended in the total annihilation of the Genoese army and fleet. Both sides were now completely exhausted. Venice, its commerce and navy intact, would recover quickly; Genoa would soon drop from the ranks of the major powers in a maelstrom of civil war and economic decline.

One lesson learned from the war was the danger of allowing the hinterlands to be in enemy hands. The Paduans, in cutting off the city's food supply, had given Venice a greater fright than all the galleys of Genoa. In addition, economic forces now made clear the need for an assured market for Venetian goods and guaranteed access to the markets of the north. Despite the dangers, Venice held her nose and plunged head first into the confusing, sordid world of Italian power politics. Treviso, lost in the War of Chioggia, was retaken in 1382. After a perilous involvement in the wars of **Gian Galeazzo Visconti** of Milan, who nearly gained control of all northern Italy before his death in 1402, Venice learned about the necessity of maintaining the Italian balance of power. She also emerged with two very gratifying prizes, old enemies Padua and Verona.

Mostly by diplomacy – not surprisingly for a nation that had learned subtlety from the Byzantines themselves – Venice's new career

---

1310–1453

Dogana di Mare, the customs house where from 1414 all goods were unloaded and taxed, as commerce continued unabated by war, p.164

I Frari and **Santi Giovanni e Paolo**, the two great churches built in reaction to the religious revivals of the late 13th century by Saints Francis and Dominic, pp.176 and 136

Tomb of Vettor Pisani, the unfortunate admiral, in Santi Giovanni e Paolo, p.138

Lazzaretto Vecchio, the plague quarantine island that gave its name to all such future locations, p.224

Piombi, the prisons in the Doge's Palace where Pisani was thrown, to imagine his dismay and that of countless others, p.114

Doges

697	Paoluccio Anafesta	1043	Domenico Contarini
717	Marcello Tegalliano	1071	Domenico Selvo
726	Orso Ipato	1085	Vitale Falier
742	Orso Deodato	1096	Vitale Michiel I
755	Galla Gaulo	1102	Ordelafo Falier
756	Domenico Monegario	1117	Domenico Michiel
764	Maurizio Galbaio	1130	Pietro Polani
787	Giovanni Galbaio	1148	Domenico Morosini
804	Obelario de' Antenori	1156	Vitale Michiel II
811	Angelo Participazio	1172	Sebastiano Ziani
827	Giustiniano Participazio	1178	Orio Malipiero
828–9	Giovanni Participazio I	1193	Enrico Dandolo
836	Pietro Tradonico	1205	Pietro Ziani
864	Orso Participazio I	1229	Giacomo Tiepolo
881	Giovanni Participazio II	1249	Marin Morosini
887	Pietro Candiano I	1253	Ranier Zeno
888	Pietro Tribuno	1268	Lorenzo Tiepolo
912	Orso Participazio II	1275	Jacopo Contarini
932	Pietro Candiano II	1280	Giovanni Dandolo
939	Pietro Participazio	1289	Pietro Gradenigo
942	Pietro Candiano III	1311	Giorgio Marin
959	Pietro Candiano IV	1312	Giovanni Soranzo
976	Pietro Orseolo I	1329	Francesco Dandolo
977	Vitali Candiano	1339	Bartolomeo Gradenigo
978	Tribuno Memmo	1343	Andrea Dandolo
991	Pietro Orseolo II	1354	Marin Falier
1008	Otto Orseolo	1355	Giovanni Gradenigo
1026	Pietro Centranico	1356	Giovanni Dolfin
1032	Domenico Flabanico	1361	Lorenzo Celsi
		1365	Marco Corner

went from success to success. By 1420, she had regained Dalmatia from the Hungarians and acquired Vicenza, Friuli and most of the Veneto, a natural frontier that perfectly suited her modest ambitions.

Some Venetians wanted more, and in 1423 a growing war party secured the election of its leader, **Francesco Foscari**, as doge. At the time, Venice was at her height, the richest city in Europe, and probably the largest, with the biggest and best fleet. Her trade – increasingly a state-run affair, too costly and complex to be managed by the old merchant adventurers – dominated the Mediterranean, and her efficiency and fair-dealing earned her the grudging respect even of competitors. Some historians see 1423 as a turning

point for Venice. The old Doge, **Tommaso Mocenigo**, had made a rouser of a deathbed speech, warning the Venetians not to elect Foscari in his place and not to turn their backs on the sea for adventures on land, and his words are always recalled by those who would claim that it was with Foscari that Venice went wrong.

Doge Foscari had some problems of his own, particularly a corrupt waster of a son (see Byron's The Two Foscari). He tried twice to resign, was refused, then finally (1457) had to be removed by the Ten on grounds of senility. But he hardly deserves the reproaches he gets from the more superficial histories. The wars of his time were only a continuation of those that had won Venice

1368	Andrea Contarini	1612	Marcantonio Memmo
1382	Michele Morosini/Antonio Venier	1615	Giovanni Bembo
1400	Michele Steno	1618	Nicolò Donà/Antonio Priuli
1414	Tommaso Mocenigo	1623	Francesco Contarini
1423	Francesco Foscari	1624	Giovanni Corner I
1457	Pasquale Malipiero	1630	Nicolò Conurini
1462	Cristoforo Moro	1631	Francesco Erizzo
1471	Nicolò Tron	1646	Francesco Molin
1473	Nicolò Marcello	1655	Carlo Contarini
1474	Pietro Mocenigo	1656	Francesco Corner/Bertuccio Valier
1476	Andrea Vendramin	1658	Giovanni Pésaro
1478	Giovanni Mocenigo	1659	Domenico Contarini
1485	Marco Barbarigo	1674	Nicolò Sagredo
1486	Agosino Barbarigo	1676	Alvise Contarini
1501	Leonardo Loredan	1683	Marc'Antonio Giustinian
1521	Antonio Grimani	1688	Francesco Morosini
1523	Andrea Gritti	1694	Silvestro Valier
1539	Pietro Lando	1700	Alvise Mocenigo II
1545	Francesco Donà	1709	Giovanni Corner II
1553	Marcantonio Trevisano	1722	Alvise Mocenigo III
1554	Francesco Venier	1732	Carlo Ruzzini
1556	Lorenzo Priuli	1735	Alvise Pisani
1559	Girolamo Priuli	1741	Pietro Grimani
1567	Pietro Loredan	1752	Francesco Loredano
1570	Alvise Mocenigo	1762	Marco Foscarini
1577	Sebastiano Venier	1763	Alvise Mocenigo IV
1578	Nicolò da Ponte	1779	Paolo Renier
1585	Pasquale Cicogna	1789	Ludovico Manin (d. 1802)
1595	Marino Grimani	1797	Napoleon abolishes Venetian Republic
1606	Leonardo Donà		

her land empire and they were certainly unavoidable. And Venice hardly turned her back on the sea; in that direction there simply was nothing left to achieve. The wars, rather genteel after the conventions of the age, were almost continuous from 1425 until 1454. And they were colourful enough. Venice employed famous mercenary captains such as **Carmagnola**, the greatest soldier of his generation, **Gattamelata** (the 'Honey Cat' from Umbria) and **Francesco Sforza**. The first turned traitor, and ended up hanging between the Piazzetta columns; the second stayed true and got a famous equestrian statue in Padua; and Sforza played his own game and finished as Duke of Milan. In the end Venice came out ahead, gaining the

metal-working towns of Bergamo and Brescia to round out her borders and her new continental economy.

As the events of the next two centuries were to demonstrate, the land empire was a sound investment despite all the trouble it took to keep it. It would pay for Venice's retirement; she in turn would rule it (unlike her colonies elsewhere) with justice and sympathy – often, when an invader seized one of the mainland towns, he would find himself up against a popular insurrection bellowing '*Viva San Marco!*'. This is part of the developing 'Myth of Venice' that commanded the world's admiration: stability, continuity and impartial justice under its unique constitution. No state in Europe planned its economic affairs more intelligently or took better care of its own people. Perhaps it was only Venice's head start that made it a society more highly evolved than any in Europe – the Venice of Foscari was already a thousand years old.

1453–1571: *Serenissima* in Spite of Everything

Pride, for your average imperialist, is supposed to come before a fall. And, directly upon digesting her new land empire, Venice's luck began to change. Soon things turned really bad, then worse, and then worse still. The dislocations in trade should have been fatal to such a strictly mercantile city, as earlier trade shifts had been to Amalfi, and Pisa. They were not. The rabid crusade of the great powers of Europe against her should have finished her off. It didn't. Politically, the 16th century was one of the ghastliest periods in European history. For Venice, it featured a murderers' row of bitter enemies – ferocious, berserk Pope Julius II; the megalomaniac Charles V, with half of Europe in his pocket; and worst of all the invincible Turk, with a million men, a thousand galleys and nothing better to do than beat on the Venetians. So how did Venice survive? In grand style, thank you, with masques and pageants, and an artistic achievement unequalled by any city of the Renaissance save Florence.

In Istanbul's Military Museum, you can see the sword of Attila the Hun, leader of one of the 'twelve historical Turkish empires'. No Venetian would have been surprised to hear that their esteemed founding father had been a Turk, their foe. Even without him, the Venetians had been trading with Turkish emirates for centuries around the coasts of Anatolia. The Ottoman Turks, who by 1400 controlled much of Greece, the Balkans and eastern Anatolia, were more of a problem.

Their talents at warfare, combining great resources with a steady discipline and the most up-to-date technology, were well known to the courts of Europe. The bad news for Venice was that they were also discovering the joys of sailing. In 1352, when the Ottomans first crossed the Dardanelles, they had to pay Catalan mercenaries to ferry them over. A hundred years later they had built a fleet of galleys. The Emir then was Mehmet II, **Mehmet the Conqueror**, and in 1453, he used his new navy to help realize the old Ottoman dream of the **conquest of Constantinople**. The pitiful force that defended the metropolis to the end included almost as many Venetians as Greeks.

The end of this peculiar symbiosis, of seven centuries of trade between the merchants of Venice and the decadent empire, did not at first seem irreparable. Mehmet signed a liberal commercial treaty, and Venice sent Gentile Bellini to paint the Conqueror's portrait. But the Turks were just taking a rest. In the 1460s they seized the mainland Peloponnese and made inroads in Albania and Bosnia. An exhausting war of 15 years, from 1464 to 1479, lost Venice the important island of Euboea. No assistance was available from the rest of the Italian states; engrossed

1453–1571

Biblioteca Nazionale Marciana, to find out why Fra Mauro's 1459 *Mappa Mundi* offended the Senate, p.118

Colleoni Statue, to admire one of Venice's most celebrated *condottieri*, p.139

The Ghetto, where Venice's Jews were confined after they fled from Padua during the War of Cambrai, p.209

Ponte delle Tette, the most notorious bridge in Venice in the heydey of prostitution; and **Santa Maria del Soccorso**, where poet-courtesan Veronica Franco founded an asylum for whores, pp.184 and 168

San Giuseppe di Castello, to spot the mistakes in the relief depicting the Battle of Lepanto, p.154

Scuola degli Albanesi, centre of the Albanian community, built in 1531 by refugees from Ottoman imperialism, with its façade showing Sultan Mehmet II, p.128

Tomb of Caterina Cornaro, humiliated queen of Cyprus, in San Salvatore, p.125

in their own petty wars, they were in fact happy to see Venice's pride taken down a peg. In 1478, the Turks staged raids deep into Friuli; the fires they set could be seen from the Campanile of St Mark's.

After signing a humiliating peace treaty, Venice gained a short breathing space. Mehmet died in 1481, succeeded by his scholarly son Bayezit II, who abhorred warfare. As if on cue, the princes of Italy stepped in to square off with Venice once more. In 1483, a trifling argument over salt pans with the Duke of Ferrara escalated into a war with Milan, Florence and Naples. Pope Sixtus IV put Venice under an interdict in May, which was politely disregarded. Four months later half the Doge's Palace burned down when someone left a candle burning. But by the following August, while work on the rebuilding was under way, the Italian allies sued for peace. Venice picked up the city of Rovigo and some other small territories; the Pope was incensed on hearing the news, and died the next morning.

Another minor success came with the **acquisition of Cyprus** in 1488. This island was a curious relic of the Crusades, governed by kings of the French house of Lusignan. The Venetian **Caterina Cornaro** had married King James back in 1468, and when the King died five years later she gained the throne. The Venetians lost no time and insinuated their men into all the important positions of the kingdom. Poor Caterina found herself effectively a royal prisoner. In 1488, threatened with intrigues on all sides, Venice easily convinced the Queen to give up her crown and proclaim the annexation of Cyprus by the Republic. Caterina earned in return a toy kingdom at the pretty town of Asolo, with plenty of entertainments to while away boredom until the War of the League of Cambrai chased her back to Venice in 1509.

For Venice, exasperating popes and snatching up islands were child's play, but further disasters were in store. Another bogey of the *Serenissima*'s history, one wearing neither turban nor tiara, appeared in 1498: none other than an honest Portuguese captain, **Vasco da Gama**, who c[...] first voyage around the Horn of [...] India. Venice's monopoly of the E[...] gone for ever. The disaster was neither immediate nor fatal, but a steady decline in receipts was recorded over the next century. Venice responded with her accustomed energy, even proposing to the Sultan of Egypt that a canal be dug across the Suez, but there was little the Republic could do.

In 1501, Venice elected a doge of substance, the first since Foscari. **Leonardo Loredan** might have passed into history with as little notice as his predecessors. It was his fate, however, to be Doge during the greatest trials Venice would ever undergo. The **Wars of Italy** had already been going on for seven years, with the consequent intrusion of foreign powers that would put an end to both Italian liberty and the Italian Renaissance. In 1494, Duke Lodovico of Milan started the commotion by inviting the King of France, **Charles VIII**, to give him a hand against his arch-enemy, Naples. Charles could not resist and marched his army down the peninsula and took Naples with surprising ease. The Italians, who had lackadaisically watched Charles' parade, now finally became alarmed. Venice took most of the initiative in forming a defensive league against the French and Venice supplied most of the money and men for the League's army, attempting to block Charles' return to France. When the League failed to do so, at the **Battle of Fornovo** (1495), it was clear to all that plenty of Italian real estate was available to any power bold enough to snatch it.

Throughout the 1490s and 1500s, the wars continued, with another invasion by Charles' successor, Louis XII, resulting in the conquest of Milan, and the retaking of Naples by the Spanish. Venice, scheming to expand towards the south and perhaps even to the Tyrrhenian coast, could not help becoming involved. Under the Borgia Pope Alexander VI (1492–1503), Cesare Borgia had created a little empire for the family in central Italy. He lost it to his father's fiery and determined successor, **Julius II**, in 1504, and Venice took advantage of the confusion to grab Rimini and other towns of the Romagna, the property of the Papal States. That was a mistake.

Giuliano della Rovere, the story goes, won his papal election by pretending to be meek and pliable. Once enthroned as Julius II, however, he moved ruthlessly to reassert papal control over towns that had slipped away. Julius' constant appeals to foreign princes for support kept the Wars of Italy boiling, and ultimately condemned the nation to foreign rule. In 1508, Julius decided it was time to deal with Venice, the only state strong and determined enough to keep the foreigners out. Thanks to the diplomatic situation of the time, he easily arranged an alliance with the Holy Roman Empire and Austria, France, Spain and Naples, Ferrara and Mantua. This '**League of Cambrai**' intended nothing less than the partition of the Venetian empire. Julius placed Venice under another futile interdict, but much more damaging was a tremendous explosion and fire in the Arsenal in March 1509, a grave blow to the city's preparations for defence. The next month, the League declared war and French troops invaded from Lombardy.

The Venetians had few illusions about the danger they were in, but disaster struck more quickly than anyone could have guessed. As usual, Venice depended on a mercenary army, led by *condottieri* whose careless tactics allowed the French to separate and defeat their forces utterly at the **Battle of Agnadello** on 14 May 1510. Most of the discouraged mercenary companies simply went home. Venice, without an army, had lost its entire land empire at a single blow. The League wasted little time in dividing the spoils; only Treviso and Ùdine remained under the banner of St Mark.

Some of the lost towns, hardly overjoyed at the thought of replacing Venetian rule with that of greedy foreign princes, produced spontaneous revolts. In Venice itself, the government was in fearful disarray. But just as the Pope was the author of Venice's calamity, he would soon become Venice's saviour. Julius now decided that the French

were the real foes of Italy and Christianity. In a typically impulsive move, Julius betrayed his allies. He made a severe peace with the frightened Venetians, requiring their ambassadors to indulge him in a double helping of the grovelling and foot-kissing so dear to Renaissance pontiffs. Not long after, he asked them to join a new League against France. After a few years of complicated changes of alliance and fortune, conflicting ambitions cancelled out and Venice, by diplomacy and the good will of its former possessions, saw nearly all of them return to the fold by 1517.

Diplomacy and luck also helped Venice stay clear of the final stage of the Wars of Italy, the deadly struggle between Emperor Charles V and King Francis I. In 1529, when the treaties of Barcelona and Cambrai set up Spanish-Imperial control across Italy, Venice lost only Ravenna and her last few port towns in Apulia. She was fortunate to be alive – the only Italian state not under the heel of Spain or the Pope. The Turks, who had providentially been busied with eastern conquests during the Italian Wars, now returned in force. Under Sultan **Suleiman the Magnificent**, Ottoman power reached its zenith: Rhodes was taken in 1522, and the great, unsuccessful siege of Vienna took place seven years later. Naval campaigns against Venice occupied most of the 1530s. Corfu, the key to the Adriatic, withstood a tremendous siege in 1537, but for the Aegean islands and Peloponnese there was no hope.

The Turks also fostered another menace that hit Venice much closer to home. The **Uskoks**, an unsavoury band of Dalmatian Slavs, repeated the story of the Narentine pirates of the 900s. Supported by the sultans, they annoyed Venetian shipping for decades. In 1570, the Turkish Wars began anew when Sultan Selim II ('the Sot', the first of the decadent Ottomans) attacked Cyprus. For once, Venice was not alone. Four years earlier, the Turks' unsuccessful attack on Malta had betrayed their ambition of dominating the entire Mediterranean, and Spain was alarmed enough to send a fleet to the East. That year, the effort came to naught when the Spanish Admiral, Gian Andrea Doria of Genoa, refused to attack or cooperate in any way with the Venetian fleet. (His father, the famous Andrea Doria, had twice pulled similar tricks on the Venetians; the shameless treachery of the Dorias and indeed of all Genoese is a recurring motif in Venetian history).

Cyprus, just off the Turkish coast, had no chance of surviving. The climax of the campaign was the siege of Famagusta, where a small force under **Marcantonio Bragadin** distinguished itself in a hopeless defence. For his trouble Bragadin was flayed alive by the Turkish commander. The following year, the embarrassed Spaniards sent a larger force under the more trustworthy Don John of Austria, a bastard son of Charles V. More help came from the least likely of naval powers, the Papal States, and the allied fleet sailed straight for Greece. The Turks were waiting in the Gulf of Patras, and on 7 October 1571, lines of galleys four miles long joined what was perhaps the biggest sea battle ever fought in the Mediterranean, the **Battle of Lepanto**.

It lasted less than six hours, and at the end (despite the collapse of the allies' right wing, thanks to Venice's old friend Gian Andrea Doria) the Turkish fleet was scattered. A hundred of their galleys were sunk and 130 captured, and some 15,000 Christian slaves were liberated. When the ships brought the news to Venice and pyramids of captured turbans and banners were piled in the Piazzetta, Venice celebrated for four days. Ironically, the victory of Lepanto changed little in the Mediterranean. Two years after, when it was clear that Spain would provide no further aid – Philip II was more concerned with the Low Countries and England – Venice felt itself compelled to sue for peace. Abandoned by her allies, Venice did not regain Cyprus or anything else – only an increase in the tribute demanded by the Sultan for the last few Venetian enclaves in the East.

Venice's century of trials was almost over. The peace with Turkey would last fifty years. The Ottomans, under an unbroken line of wretched sultans, were well on their way to becoming the 'Sick Man of Europe'. Venice, her trade declining every year, realized with a merchant's perspicacity that there was nothing to be done – no prospects, no risks worth taking, no chance of earning an honest sequin by land or sea. Throughout the century, the *Nobil Homini* had been doing what any wealthy class would do under the circumstances: investing in real estate. As always, they did it with a flourish. The scores of **Palladian villas** across the Veneto, the last word in High Renaissance refinement, are the monuments of diminished expectations and of the Venetian businessman's supremely enjoyable retirement.

Historians of a century ago tended to interpret this great turning point differently. To the virtuous Victorians, too much art and too many parties had sapped the city's will to outfox her rivals. The evidence, to the morally minded, is not lacking. There is the little matter of 11,654 registered **prostitutes** (13% of the female population) for example, and the directory of them published for visitors. Venice's *cinquecento*, for all the wars and troubles, was conducted as one long festival. In no century were more palaces and churches built, or more beautiful ones. While keeping their enemies at bay, the Venetians had added the Rialto Bridge, San Giorgio Maggiore and the great palaces of the Grand Canal, along with the paintings of Carpaccio, Giorgione, Tintoretto and Veronese.

In 1573, the Venetians received another sovereign, **Henry III of France**. The King entered in a procession of gilded gondolas, entertained along the way by floating tableaux, firework shows and a barge on which the glassmakers of Murano turned out crystal goblets for him on the spot. The Doge gave him an album of miniatures to peruse; the one he liked best was of the celebrated courtesan-poetess **Veronica Franco**, and she soon arrived to keep him company and write him a sonnet. The King met Veronese and Tintoretto, who did his portrait in pastels; he bought a diamond sceptre from a jeweller on the Rialto, who always kept a few on hand in case a king should visit his shop. There was a dinner party at the Doge's Palace. Earlier in the day the King had visited the Arsenal and seen the keel of a new galley being laid. At the end of the dinner, after 1,200 different dishes and an opera (one of the first ever performed) he saw the completed galley sailing under the palace windows. Like many visitors to Venice, it is recorded that after his return Henry was never quite the same again.

1573–1796: A Decline to Remember

In Browning's words, 'Venice spent what Venice earned'. Not only Venice, but the entire Mediterranean world was declining in the last decades of the 16th century. Trade was contracting and politics were subverted by the twin vampires of Rome and Madrid. Venice had the resources to survive, but not enough to break free from the constraints of the new era. Her policy of neutrality and her centuries of diplomatic experience kept her afloat with little difficulty, but the grandchildren of the Venetian merchants and warriors found they had to resign themselves to a very different life: they could enjoy themselves, and weren't averse to it, but beyond that opportunities were limited.

For the next two centuries, history would be largely limited to vignettes: a fire in the Doge's Palace in 1577, occasioning Tintoretto's gigantic *Paradise* and the rebuilding of the Palace. The first state-run banks appeared in 1587. The wars against the Uskoks continued until diplomacy induced the Austrians in 1617 to stop supporting them.

Along the way a really serious issue came up, one that would reflect brilliantly the maturity and decency of the Venetian state. By 1606, the Papacy was greatly weakened by its own excesses but still a dangerous power in Italian affairs. In 1606, Pope Paul V chose to make an issue over two Venetian priests, a rapist and a child molester, indicted by the Ten. Despite centuries of practice, the popes still maintained the fiction that clerics were

immune to civil justice in Venice. Although this trivial affair was part of a much larger struggle, the Pope used it as a stick to beat Venice, and for the fourth time the hated city was placed under interdict and its leaders excommunicated.

But Venice had a secret weapon. A scholarly Servite friar named **Paolo Sarpi**, devoted to Venice and to religious tolerance, was employed by the State to refute the papal arguments, which he did with an astuteness that attracted the attention of all Europe, Protestant and Catholic. The Ten, with their accustomed waggishness, took care of any recalcitrant priests. One who refused to say mass woke up one morning to find a gallows erected in front of his church. Another, claiming that he would act as the Holy Spirit moved him, was told that the Holy Spirit had already moved the Ten to hang all traitors. Sarpi and Venice won: the interdict was lifted in 1607, and it was the last time the popes would ever try such a thing against anyone. Rome knew how to bear grudges in those days – three times the Roman Curia sent assassins after Sarpi, though they bungled each attempt.

Venice could still wage a war when required. The Turks gave her one of 25 years that began in 1645 and ended with the loss of Crete, Venice's last important overseas possession. And after 1683, when the last attack on Vienna failed, exposing the Turks' real weakness, Venice found it in her to go back on the offensive. In 1685, **Francesco Morosini** led a brilliant expedition that regained many of the lost territories in Greece. Most of these, however, slipped away again in Venice's last war with Turkey, between 1714 and 1718.

As in the rest of Italy, the 17th century had been a disaster economically for Venice. The city had responded well to the changes of the 16th century, developing new industries in glass and textiles. Now even these were forced off the market by northern competitors, while the Dutch and English took over much of the dwindling Mediterranean trade. In its decline, both the strengths and the weaknesses of Venice's unique state revealed themselves clearly. The decomposing nobility, mincing between casino and ball-room, still kept its stranglehold over politics, and to the end prevented any reforms that would bring new blood into the government. On the other hand, the uncanny machine of the constitution continued to sputter on: stability and justice were maintained, the provinces were happy, and despite rampant corruption the State finances remained perfectly solid right up until 1797.

After the last Turkish war, Venice let her fleets and armies rot. Undefended, she depended on her diplomacy and neutrality to keep the world at bay. The rest of Europe, which had come to enjoy the city as a sort of adult fun-fair, was glad to leave her alone. This gayest and most cosmopolitan of all cities became a necessary stop for north-erners on the Grand Tour. Besides the opera and the casino and the legendary promis-cuity, they came for the sense of unreality, a vacation for the mind. For the first and only time in her long history, sensible Venice succumbed completely to the sensual promise of her sea-borne home. The passing years were named for the appearances of sopranos at the opera. The first hot-air balloon in Italy ascended in 1784 from in front of St Mark's. The Ten's ridiculous spies marked it all down, but no one gave a fig. New churches were built with garish façades glorifying not God, but minor Venetian fami-lies. Spectacle became an end in itself, and with its millennium of practice the machinery of Venetian pomp and ceremony trundled around the calendar as brilliantly as ever. Venice was full of impoverished noblemen, still forced by law to dress in silks and keep up a good front: they somehow scraped up some pennies to rent a servant for the night if someone were to call.

'*Esto perpetua*', may it last forever – as Paolo Sarpi had said on his deathbed. But the end was closer than anyone knew. First, though, comes a last surprise echo of the old spirit: **Angelo Emo**, the last admiral of Venice on Venice's last expedition. In 1790 he

1573–1796

Ca' Rezzonico (Museo dei Settecento), with its reconstruction of an 18th-century phar-macy and its painting of the *salon* held by the naughty nuns of San Zaccaria, p.165

Calle del Ridotto, No.1332, the building that used to be the Ridotto or state-controlled gaming house, p.127

La Fenice, the opera theatre that housed the swansong of the Republic, p.126

Florian's and **Quadri**, the new coffee-houses flocked to for gossip, intrigue and dalliance, p.117

Fonzazione Querini-Stampalia and **Palazzo Mocenigo**, two museums offering a revealing picture of the frippery and decadence of 18th-century Venetian noble and bourgeois life, pp.141 and 189

Museo Correr, to marvel at the extraordi-nary shoes worn by the tattered nobility, p.118

Naval History Museum, to see the monu-ment to Angelo Emo, last admiral of Venice, p.151

La Pietà, where Vivaldi concerts are still performed today, p.144

Santa Maria della Salute, 'St Mary of Health', built in thanksgiving for Venice's deliverance from the 1630 plague, p.163

Statue of Carlo Goldoni and **Casa Goldoni**, for the dialect playwright who documented everyday Venetian life, pp.125 and 182

Statue of Paolo Sarpi, the scholar who saved Venice, p.208

chastised the Barbary pirates while everyone else, including the English, was paying them tribute. Six years later, **Napoleon**'s Army of Italy was marching into the Veneto. Before he ever reached the city, Napoleon destroyed Venice in a war of nerves, alternating threats and accusations while the Venetians fretted and trembled. Neither the miserable last Doge, Ludovico Manin (who had fainted when he heard of his election in 1789), nor the Ten, nor anyone else could summon up the courage to organize a defence – while ironically their people were staging revolts and conducting guerrilla warfare across

A Day in 18th-century Venice

It is already the sixth hour when Cecilia Contarini wakes to a new day in the family palazzo on the Grand Canal; her eyelids have scarcely fluttered when her cavalier servente, Rodrigo Sagredo, is at her side. 'Good morning, bellissima,' he murmurs, even though Cecilia's face is covered with strips of milk-soaked veal.

As Cecilia steps into a steaming bath, Rodrigo entertains her with a recital of the morning's gossip, much of it concerning her own husband. Giancarlo is a senator, but one whose slumming in the sestiere's malvasie has more than once attracted the attention of the Ten and their spies. None of this bothers Cecilia as much as the news that Giancarlo's older brother was threatening to cut back their weekly allowance again.

While Cecilia lingers over her morning chocolate, flicking through the engraved visiting cards left by friends (there's one she nonchalantly slips into the pocket of her dressing gown), the tutor announces the children, who file in for morning dress inspection. Cecilia gives each tot a big hug and kiss before the tutor shuffles them out again. It's time for the main business of the morning: hairdressing. Seeing that his charge is in good hands for the next six hours, Rodrigo ducks out to tend to some pressing business of his own at the convent of San Zaccaria, where his sister, a nun, can always get him a loan. 'And which patch will La Signora choose today?' asks the hairdresser, primping the last blonde curl in place. Cecilia reflects for a moment, and remembers the note. 'Assassina,' she whispers.

It's November, 1770, in the reign of Doge Alvise Mocenigo IV. Although it's the sixth hour, Cecilia, like most patricians, is not up early. Like every Venetian lady, noble or bourgeois, Cecilia has a *cavalier servente*, a kind of auxiliary husband who belonged to the same social class as she; more extravagant women had several. Rodrigo's role was to squire Cecilia about town, and to provide for her every little need. No husband would be caught dead with his own wife. Like most *cicisbei* Rodrigo was even written into

Cecilia's marriage contract. On the surface at least, all was accepted and respectable.

After all, there was no such a thing as a love marriage in Venice. In most patrician families, one brother would be chosen to marry and produce heirs. The others, who remained in the family *palazzo*, followed careers in politics, the priesthood, or, very rarely now in the 1700s, in the military. Each brother would be given an allowance, augmented if he were elected to an important office; Venetian officials were expected to pay their own expenses. Besides these burdens, most noble families would rustle up a considerable dowry to marry off their eldest daughter, in the interests of a political alliance; extra daughters were sent off to convents. These unwilling nuns were a major source of Venetian scandal, but their convents played banker to noble families, giving them loans that were rarely repaid. When Napoleon suppressed the convents half the nobles were forced into bankruptcy.

The Council of Ten's spies shadowing Cecilia's wayward husband could safely be ignored. The Ten's power had so eroded at the end of the Republic that they did little more than issue stern warnings to be studiously read and studiously ignored. Giancarlo caused concern because the *malvasie* (named after malmsey, the Greek wine they peddled) were used as common brothels and no place for a patrician. But they were popular nonetheless: some 20 streets are still called Calle di Malvasia.

In the 18th century Venetian women began a sexual revolution that makes the 1960s look prudish. Every traveller remarked on the beauty of the women – and the fact that it was hard to tell a noble lady from a prostitute. Every palace had several discreet entrances, and every gondolier, if he wanted to keep his job, was committed to complete secrecy. No one took them very seriously. If Venetian women cut loose, it was partly as a reaction to the lives of their foremothers. Ever since the founding of the city, its women had been treated like Byzantine chattels forced to live such reclusive lives that all we know about them is that they spent half their time on their *altane* or rooftop terraces bleaching their hair. Cecilia, too, was a Venetian blonde, but with the aid of the hairdresser's dyes that red-gold colour was much easier to obtain. A lot of women had opted for wigs (in 1797 there were 850 wigmakers in Venice) but Cecilia was vain about her thick hair, which could hold so many fashionable fruits and flowers.

The average noble woman spent hours on her appearance every morning. Although the bulk of the hairdresser's work was on the tower of hair, he was also responsible for make-up on the face and breasts. This was never extreme in Venice and the ideal was to look as natural as possible, except for the artificial moles, or patches. The wearer used these as a code: a mole placed in a dimple meant she was feeling coquettish, if placed on the nose she was feeling rather forward. The *assassina*, by the corner of the mouth, was the most daring of all.

Her toilette over, Cecilia sends the hairdresser off with a note for her admirer, then dresses for church. It is Saturday and the orphan girls at La Pietà are performing a new mass. Rodrigo appears with Cecilia's prayer book to escort her, and the family gondola is waiting. But they are late, and some English milords, in town for Carnival, have taken Cecilia's favourite seat. A comical row breaks out, silenced only when the music begins.

Cecilia and Rodrigo leave church and call at a friend's house to don the traditional Carnival disguise: white beaked masks, or bautte, *tricorne hats and concealing, long cloaks, or* tabarri. *By the time they reach the Piazza, it is heaving with other masqueraders, dancing bears, soothsayers, dentists, and Irish weight-lifters. The cafés are overflowing.*

Seeing her opportunity, Cecilia quickly sets a time for Rodrigo to meet her for the theatre, then loses him in the crowd to slip down a back alley off the Mercerie. On her way, she passes Giancarlo and his friends, masked as Tartars and Red Indians and singing racy songs to all passers-by. Cecilia manages to slip past, but even if Giancarlo had somehow

recognized his wife, they would have pretended not to know each other.

In the aftermath of the Great Interdict, the Church had less of a role to play in Venice than anywhere in Italy. The Senate had always maintained that its citizens were Venetians first and Christians second. By the 18th century mass for many Venetians was just another social occasion. Throughout the service they behaved appallingly, chatting, flirting and quarrelling. Prostitutes hung about in the side chapels. The priest only stood a chance of being heard if he had a good voice; although Rome disapproved, many priests were *castrati*, because the lagoon folk couldn't resist a soprano. Indeed the Venetians, of every walk of life, had an 'unbelievable infatuation' for music. Visitors wrote that there was simply no escape from singing; the narrow streets and canals offer excellent acoustics. Nearly everyone played an instrument or sang; the gondoliers were famous for singing passages from Tasso across the night lagoon. Orphan girls at La Pietà, Ospedaletto and the Incurabili were formed into orchestras of renown (Vivaldi wrote most of his compositions for them).

Carnival in Venice was more than the traditional 10-day celebration before Lent: it meant the licence to go about masked in total anonymity. In the 18th century the wearing of masks became legal for six months of the year to bring in more tourists and to let impoverished patricians go about the streets without shame. Carnival in Venice also meant gambling and the freedom to commit any indiscretion. It was extremely bad form ever to show any sign of recognizing a masked person: everyone from doge to scullery maid was simply addressed as *Sior Maschera*, or Mr Mask.

It is getting dark as Cecilia meets Claudio, her gondolier, at the back entrance of her lover's casino. Claudio is such a model of discretion that he, too, wears a costume over the telltale colours of the family livery, to the confusion of the snoops and informers hanging out the windows.

Tonight is the gala opening at the Teatro San Samuele, where Cecilia has a box. Although the Inquisitors insist that women wear the bautta and tabarro to the theatre, no one takes heed. Cecilia dons a glittering satin gown; she drips jewels, and her hair is laced with pearls. Rodrigo arrives, looking just as elegant in white knee-breeches and stockings, a pink and green embroidered waistcoat, a coat covered with stitches of gold and a tricorn hat over his wig.

As usual, Cecilia and Rodrigo gossip with their neighbours through the entire performance, pausing only when a brawl breaks out in the pit below, as the customers, dressed in their own costumes, try to steal the show. The villain of the play is so evil that the audience pelts him with stewed pears. Cecilia and the other ladies amuse themselves by dropping their ices and candle ends on the heads of the most obnoxious people below. At the end, one of the actresses sings a moving farewell that silences the audience and causes a veritable paroxysm of rapturous howls at the end. Cecilia begins to swoon from emotion, but Rodrigo, never at a loss, is ready with a spoonful of triaca, or treacle, a panacea made from a recipe of 60 ingredients that dates back to the time of Nero. As always it works a treat, and the bloom returns to her cheeks.

The night is coming alive; music and laughter drift down the Grand Canal, from the streets, from the palaces. Cecilia lets Rodrigo take his fair share of liberties in the gondola, behind the blinds of the cabin, or felze; at supper with friends at their casino he feeds her the best titbits by hand. Everyone chatters and laughs at the same time and they drink too much, all in preparation for the principal excitement of the evening at the Ridotto. Here the laughter stops, as Cecilia and Rodrigo manage to squeeze into the silent throng gathered around the biribissi table – the ancestor of roulette. Cecilia feels lucky and wins, once, twice, before losing once, twice, a dozen times. Rodrigo gently touches her elbow; Giancarlo is standing behind her, stoically watching. Neither he nor Rodrigo can cover her losses. 'Perhaps we could sell that old

Bellini Madonna in the family chapel?' she whispers. Giancarlo smiles sadly, and kisses her hand for response: his own losses make hers look like child's play. They are close to ruin, but he's too much of a gentleman to tell her, especially when she looks so beautiful.

Cecilia pleads a headache and when Rodrigo offers to escort her home, she convinces him he should stay at the Ridotto, where their luck would be sure to change. Once in her gondola, however, she gives Claudio an address far from home, and toujours gaie, she ends up at dawn, forgetting all discretion on the arm of the French ambassador, as they wander among the morning-after crowd at the Rialto vegetable markets.

Perhaps Fellini is the only one who could do justice to Venetian theatre in the 18th century. It was the rage: for a population of 130,000 there were six active theatres, and this was before the construction of La Fenice. Goldoni, who put a mirror to the Venetians and their foibles, was a great success. But the audience, who enthusiastically identified with the actors, always demanded novelty, celebrity actors or singers and scantily clad ballerinas.

Gambling was the national vice. The patricians, no longer able to gamble their fortunes at sea, squandered them every night during Carnival at the state-run casino, or Ridotto. So many patricians like Giancarlo met bankruptcy there that the government closed it in 1774. But the Venetians had gambling in their blood: immediately the casini (informal flats or love nests, where the patricians could relax, as they were unable to do in their museum-palaces) brought out card tables to take the Ridotto's place, and hence our English word, 'casino'. When the famous Giacomo Casanova was young, he would gladly have joined Cecilia in the dawn pageant of the debauched and ravished at the Rialto's Erberia. But when he was old and a secret agent for the Ten, he sent in scandalized reports. Still, he failed to make much impact. And when the Ten sacked him, he left Venice for good, with a broken heart.

the occupied Veneto against their revolutionary 'liberators'.

Some Venetians too were ready to fight. When a French frigate, chased by the Austrians, took refuge in the Lagoon, the harbour patrol opened fire and took her, giving Napoleon the pretext for a final ultimatum. The thousand-year Republic ended in a shameful note of *opera bouffe*: at the last meeting of the *Maggior Consiglio*, the *Nobil Homini* were frightened out of their pantaloons by the sound of gunshots – only the farewell fusillade of a loyal Dalmatian battalion on their way home. In panic, they voted for their own extinction and scuttled off to their palaces before the counting was even finished. In the empty chamber, Manin is reported to have handed his doge's cap to an attendant, saying: 'You may have this, I won't be needing it any more.'

1797 Onwards: Just Another Provincial Capital

I will have no more Inquisition, no more Senate. I will be an Attila to the Venetian state.

Napoleon

What was it about Venice that made the little fellow so mad? Was it the brute's contempt for weakness or his basic instinct to vandalize things he did not understand – or was it simply that Napoleonic types cannot stand the idea of people who refuse to drill and salute and who insist on the right to enjoy themselves? Whatever the reason, Napoleon went after Venice and its symbols with a greater relish than he showed for any of his other conquests: contractors were paid to chop down all the evangelical lions (in Venice itself they took the money but never did the work); the horses of St Mark's were removed to Paris; the French even burned the doges' state barge, the glorious *Bucintoro*. Philistine that he was, Napoleon only visited the city once – his men looted tons of paintings and sculptures just the same, and it is

frightening to think how much Napoleon would have fancied had he ever seen it.

For all his ideological posturing, Napoleon had few scruples about handing Venice over to Austria in the Treaty of Campoformio only five months after he had taken it. During the rest of the Napoleonic wars, Venice remained a sullen, forgotten backwater under the Austrians and later under the French again. No more carnivals and intrigues, no more masked balls, only the despair of a city from which ambitious men had wrung the last drops of pride and gaiety. When the 1815 Congress of Vienna made its decisions over post-Napoleonic Europe, Venice's rightful independence was naturally forgotten. She was to be an Austrian province, and as such she found little to do but serve as a curiosity to entertain foreigners.

To the Venetians, the English were their 'swallows', because they always came back with the season. After Napoleon, they flocked to Venice in even greater numbers – Byron swimming down the Grand Canal (*see* box, p.53), Shelley neglecting his children, and later John Ruskin, climbing ladders to scrutinize Gothic arches. The visitors must often have been the best show in town, for Venice, under the leaden rule of the Austrians, could never regain anything of its accustomed gaiety. Though not particularly oppressive, neither were the Austrians very sympathetic: high taxes and dreary censors were Venice's lot, along with an administration largely manned by Germans or Slavs who often knew no Italian. Business dwindled to almost nothing, as the Austrians consciously favoured the port of Trieste. But while Venice was perfecting its touristic vocation, packaging romantic melancholy for northerners, another invasion was plotted: modernity mounted its attack in 1846, when an Austro-Italian syndicate built the railway causeway over the Lagoon to the city. Along with its independence, Venice's beloved sense of separateness was gone for ever.

Gone, though not forgotten, and there was a chance for a heroic interlude, a last '*Viva*

San Marco!' before the city finally surrendered to history and old age. In March 1848, when revolts convulsed Europe, Venetian patriots seized the Doge's Palace and the Arsenal, and declared the Republic reborn. Their leader, who had been stewing in the Doge's old dungeons for anti-Austrian activities, was a Jewish lawyer named **Daniele Manin**. Though ironically sharing the surname of the last, disgraceful Doge, this Manin would help redeem Venice's honour, in a brave defence that lasted long after the other revolts around Italy had been crushed. Towns and villages in the Veneto sentimentally raised money and sent soldiers. In Venice itself, Manin organized a democratic government, and some of the old noble families sold their treasures and even their palaces to help finance the cause.

The Venetians blew a hole in the new causeway, and the Austrians were reduced to mounting a blockade and bombarding the city from the mainland. British shipping, of course, ignored the blockade, and there was a hope that Lord Palmerston's sympathetic government might intervene – Venetians later blamed the failure to do so on the British consul in Venice, a friend of the Austrians named Dawkins, who wrote back to London deriding the revolutionaries as 'unprincipled adventurers'. Along with Kossuth and the Hungarians, Venice was the last to hold out in the great year of failed revolutions. Hunger, and a raging epidemic of cholera, forced Manin to surrender in August 1849.

When the Austrians returned, they did their best to behave, though with Italian unification reaching its climax, they knew their days were numbered. Still, Venice and the Veneto remained one of the last bits to join the new Italian kingdom. That came courtesy of the Prussians, when they defeated Austria in 1866.

Under Italian rule, business began to improve. A new port was begun at **Marghera**, a prelude to the industrial areas, the oil port and the road causeway, all built between the wars when Venice was in a mood to catch up with the modern world. In 1945, Venice was not liberated until the final German collapse. Legends have grown up about it: one has it that the British forces arrived in gondolas, as the various Allied contingents raced to get in first, to have their pick of the best hotels. The New Zealanders won: as they sped their tanks over a bridge in Mestre they passed the entire German occupation force, marching out beneath them.

After the war, the earlier improvements began to have some unforeseen consequences for the city. Venetians moved into less expensive, newer housing close to their jobs on the mainland, and Mestre and Marghera grew into huge toadstool suburbs while their industries fouled the air and water of the lagoon. The city that had 170,000 people in 1936 is now down to 66,000, and the metropolitan area of which it is the centre has developed a unique and troubling split personality: on the shore, a dull Italian anytown, rather unsympathetic towards Venice and fond of initiating referenda to secede from it (the last one failed in

---

1797 on

Ala Napoleonica and **Giardinetti Reali**, to judge Napoleon's contribution to Piazza San Marco, pp.117 and 116

Daniele Manin – his tomb on St Mark's north façade, his statue in Campo Manin, and the floor devoted to him in Museo Correr, pp.102, 129 and 118

Fondamenta Zattere ai Gesuati, where on a clear day you can see the oil port of Marghera on the skyline, p.172

Giardini Pubblici, created in 1895, with its 1920s Biennale exhibition pavilions, p.154

The Lido, to follow in the footsteps of the Grand Tourists, p.222

Mulino Stucky, the late 19th-century flour mills on the Giudecca, p.221

Naval History Museum, to find the display on Venice in the Second World War, p.151

Palazzo Mocenigo, where Byron lived, loved and composed, p.189

Strada Nuova, bulldozed through Venice from the Rialto to the new station, p.196

Byron Goes Swimming

Like lime (or linden) blossoms, Venice tends to relax the mind, or at least the logical centres; this is especially true in the minds of those who, like the rascally Aretino, 'live by the sweat of their ink'. Many have written their worst books about the city (the most recent culprits are Hemingway and Muriel Spark). Legions of other writers have been unable to resist the challenge of describing Venice; they strive to leave their mark on the city with the persistence of spraying tomcats. Some are mercifully content to settle for vignettes or epigrams. DH Lawrence, who loved the dry desert of Arizona, called Venice 'an abhorrent, green, slippery city'; for Boris Pasternak Venice was 'swelling like a biscuit soaked in tea'. In the end perhaps all descriptions meet in a soft centre, as Italo Calvino's Marco Polo commented to Kublai Khan in a lovely book called *Invisible Cities*: 'Every time I describe a city I am saying something about Venice.'

But, on certain metabolisms, linden blossoms have the opposite effect, stimulating rather than relaxing the brain. Doctors of literature could call it the 'Byron syndrome' and can study the symptoms from the poet's arrival in 1816, his heart full of romance as he rented a villa on the Brenta to compose the last canto of his *Childe Harolde's Pilgrimage*. Venice checks in here with a rather tepid 'fairy city of the heart'. Its canals at least afforded him the personal advantage of being able to swim anywhere (his limp made him shy); on one occasion he swam a race from the Lido to the Rialto bridge and was the only man to finish.

It wasn't long before the emotional polish of *Childe Harolde* began to crack. To Byron's surprise, romantic Venice didn't aggravate his romantic temperament, but cured him of

it; the ironic detachment and mock heroics of the city's own *ottava rima* tradition made him question all his previous assumptions. He went to live in the Palazzo Mocenigo on the Grand Canal, in the company of 14 servants, a dog, a monkey, a wolf, a fox and a passionate, garlicky baker's daughter who stabbed him in the thumb with a table fork (which so angered Byron that he ordered her out, whereupon she threw herself off the balcony into the Grand Canal). Under such circumstances, all that had been breathless passion reeked of the ridiculous, as he himself admitted:

And the sad truth which hovers o'er my desk
Turns what was once romantic to burlesque.

Venice and its women and its noble Armenian monks and its love of liberty galvanized Byron and set his mind free to write first *Beppo: A Venetian Story*, spoofing Venice's *cavalieri serventi* (escort/lovers – even the nuns had them), balls, and Titians and its gondolas, while celebrating the freedom of its people. He wrote two bookish plays on Venetian themes, *Marino Faliero* and *The Two Foscari*, and most importantly began his satirical masterpiece, *Don Juan*.

Meanwhile too much sex was beginning to take a toll: an English acquaintance in 1818 wrote home: 'His face had become pale, bloated, and sallow, and the knuckles on his hands were lost in fat'. Byron became infatuated with the Contessa Teresa Guiccioli and left Venice to move in with her and her husband in Ravenna. But, having tasted freedom in Venice, Byron began to chafe; the Contessa was 'taming' him. He bundled up the manuscript of *Don Juan* and left for Greece, only to die of fever at the age of 36 in its war of independence. His last moments were soothed by his faithful gondolier Tita Falsieri, who for love had followed him to Greece.

1990). Over the causeway, there is the fabulous invalid herself, with international legions of planners, restorationists and bureaucrats constantly checking her pulse and X-raying her tissue. Postwar Venice has seen one little plague after another: the

great flood of 1966, the scare that the city was sinking, the disgusting **algae** invasions of the 1980s, the Pink Floyd concert of 1989 that trashed Piazza San Marco, and of course the indispensable **tourists** themselves, without whom Venice would be an empty

Life in Venice 2003

The mere 66,000 souls in the historic centre complain that they are outnumbered by the pigeons. More than a third – some 28,000 Venetians – are more than 60 years old. According to the last census, there are only 3,768 children in the entire city (about the same number as the stone and painted lions), and exactly 19 fishermen, one of whom is a woman. Half the people employed in Venice are involved directly or indirectly in the tourist trade, handling an estimated three million visitors a year; a 'pendular Venetian' is one who lives in a modern apartment in Mestre but works or studies in the city and joins in the busy trail of ants who descend on Piazzale Roma each morning to bring the city back to life. Venice has the lowest per capita income of any city in the wealthy Veneto, although consumer prices are the highest in Italy, about 1 per cent higher than Milan and 3 per cent higher than Rome.

shell. Proposals have been made to charge admission at the causeway and limit the number who come in daily.

Probably more restoration work has been done here than in any other Italian city – although the need for more is still greater here than anywhere else. Troubles caused by neglect in the walls, canals and general infrastructure since the Second World War and the disastrous dredging of canals in the lagoon for oil tankers are coming home to roost. All debates are so highly politicized that action of any kind is extremely difficult, but current environmental paranoia, largely justified, has reached the stage where some action may result: already two new **aqueducts** to the mainland have ended the need

for Mestre and Marghera to take so much water out of the Lagoon, thus stabilizing it and saving Venice's foundations from sinking. 'Moses', the huge new sea gate that is supposed to protect against further disastrous floods, is in place – although some doubt if it will work at all. For all that, the city may be doomed by one of the very few things that can't be blamed on the Italian disdain for long term planning: global warming. A 27-inch tide is enough to flood Piazza San Marco, which happened only seven times in 1990, and 99 times in 1996. Not only are the floods or *acque alte* more frequent, they are deeper and more severe. Nearly everyone who has remained in the city has abandoned their ground floors.

Otherwise, the Queen of the Adriatic sits well scrubbed and pretty, still entertaining her many admirers but with half a mind to try and seek some more honourable employment. The doomed 2000 Expo, a proposal withdrawn at the last minute by the Italian government, was supposed to have served as a catalyst for economic reconstruction, with such extravagant but potentially useful proposals as an underground to unite the city with the mainland. Other ideas are in the air: a free-trade zone, or a headquarters city for international organizations. The recent political changes in central Europe may have a surprising effect. As the region's logical window on the Mediterranean (a role that thanks to the Austrians she must now share with Trieste), there may be some new chances for trade or as a cultural meeting-place for a vast part of Europe growing every day closer together. Venice's experience should not be wasted, and in the decades to come it may be that the *Serenissima* may find some real work to do once again.

Art and Architecture

VENETO-BYZANTINE ART:
THE 'PROTO-RENAISSANCE' 57

LINGERING GOTHIC IN THE 14TH
AND 15TH CENTURIES 58

THE EARLY RENAISSANCE OF
THE *QUATTROCENTO* 60

HIGH RENAISSANCE 61

BAROQUE (17TH CENTURY) 63

AN 18TH-CENTURY ROCOCO REVIVAL 63

THE 19TH AND 20TH CENTURIES 65

HISTORICAL, ARTISTIC
AND ARCHITECTURAL TERMS 64

DIRECTORY OF ARTISTS AND ARCHITECTS 66

Their untrammelled genius is not over-burdened with thought, nothing about them reveals any anxiety as to the interior life, and finally, as goes without saying, they did not trouble themselves about historical accuracy. The truth they sought to attain was that of colour, reflection, light, and shade, bold foreshortening, transparency of atmosphere, and the power of contrast.

Pompeo Molmenti, *Venice*, 1926

If you had to pick out what sets Venetian art and architecture apart it would have to be its sensual immediacy: it demands little from the intellect, but everything from that tremulous bridge between the eye and the heart. Light is its ruling deity. Giovanni Bellini and Titian pre-Impressionistically smeared oil paints with their fingers to diffuse the light in their canvases. Seascapes by Guardi dissolved into pure light. Even the architects took account of the light reflecting off the water when designing a church or palace.

After Florence, Venice was Italy's most inspired and original art city. But, as rich as it is, modern Venice offers only hints of its past glory: Venetian art was always popular abroad, and much of the best was sold to foreigners. The worst blow to Venice's heritage came when Napoleon 'relocated' some 20,000 works of art to France, including so much gold and silver that it took the French 15 days to plunder it all.

Building Venice

STREETS COVERED WITH WATER STOP
PLEASE ADVISE STOP

So Robert Benchley cabled home to his New York publisher in the 1930s. An awareness of Venice's obvious difference is only the beginning of understanding how this city is made. How would you build a city on a sheet of water? The Venetians started with a collection of tiny islands, the Realtine archipelago, including the sites of San Marco, the Rialto, and San Pietro di Castello. Over the centuries, they gradually filled up the spaces in between; Sant'Elena, on the eastern tip of the city, is one of the newest additions.

On a map, you can see how the city is split into roughly uniform 'blocks' divided by the canals. On each of these is one or perhaps two squares (*campi*) containing the parish churches. This is the basic unit of Venice; in each *campo* you will see a well, often beautifully made from ancient architectural fragments. Collecting fresh water was crucial in this city, and here the medieval Venetians show their cleverness. They sloped the *campi* to catch all the rainwater from surrounding streets and roofs; as the water trickled in it was filtered through layers of sand before arriving in the huge cisterns beneath the wells. On your first walk around, you'll notice that neither the streets nor the canals seem to have any firm intention of leading anywhere. The canals are as much boundaries as traffic routes, and the streets are meant only to connect each part of the block with its *campo*.

The design, where facilitating movement was thought less important than establishing a sense of place, and identity, gives Venice a peculiar cellular quality; it was inspired by the Greek and Arab cities of the early Middle Ages. There are many echoes of Constantinople in Venice's layout. The Grand Canal mirrors the famous Meze of the imperial capital, a great street neatly dividing the city in two; at the foot of each city is the all-important square, with a view over the water on one side – Piazza San Marco in Venice or the Golden Square in Constantinople, containing both the religious centre (St Mark's, Hagia Sophia) and the symbol of the state (Doge's Palace, Imperial Palace).

Piazza San Marco is, by popular acclaim over the centuries, the finest square in Europe. It is so not only for the sumptuous buildings around it, but for their arrangement, the textbook example of medieval urban design. The key to it is the integration of the main buildings, St Mark's and the Palace, into their surroundings, instead of leaving them isolated and open as a modern planner would do. Their intrusion into the

Although some of the most famous pictures and statues were later returned, Venice's art and architecture continued to bleed away throughout the 19th century, as bankrupt families and suppressed churches, convents and scuole sold off their Titians. The Austrians knocked down scores of *palazzi* when their owners fell behind in taxes, and in the First World War they dropped 620 incendiary bombs on the city for good measure. If you take into account losses from neglect, pollution and the damp, it is estimated that only four to ten per cent of Republican Venice's movable treasures remain in the city.

Think of that when your eyeballs begin to swim.

Veneto-Byzantine Art: the 'Proto-Renaissance'

Although Byzantium dominated Venice's first politics and art, the oldest surviving buildings in the Lagoon, the **Cathedral** and **Baptistry** at **Torcello** (rebuilt in 1008) were inspired by forms closer at hand: the Early Christian basilicas of Ravenna, and their ancient Roman antecedents. The basic plan consisted of a nave and side aisles, with the triumphal arch over the chancel: Murano's **San Donato** (1125), **San Nicolò dei Mendicoli** and the Giudecca's **Sant'Eufemia** were built along these lines. But other early churches were designed In the centralized Greek-cross

square creates smaller, complementary spaces – the two *piazzette* – and a subtle three-dimensional composition that offers differing, equally exciting prospects from a multitude of viewpoints. Instead of infantile symmetrical geometry, the composition is a carefully considered artistic whole. You can see other variations on this theme at Campo Santa Maria Formosa, at Santa Maria dei Miracoli, Santi Giovanni e Paolo, and around the Frari. (If you're interested, you can learn more about what's right with Venice, and wrong with your home town, in the classic *The Art of City-Building* by Camillo Sitte (1889), well known everywhere on the Continent and even in America, but never published in Britain.)

Consider also the Venetian house and what it takes to keep one standing – a solid platform of wooden piles, driven into the mud. Some of these have stood their ground for almost a thousand years. In the old merchants' palaces, the windows give a clue to the plan inside. On the ground floor, there was always one large hall running the length of the building, where business was transacted; directly above it, where the Byzantine-Gothic fenestration is at its loveliest, was another hall, the main room of the *piano nobile*, where the family lived. The most impressive façade always overlooked the

water, and the main door would always be the water door, often marked by gaily painted mooring poles, or *pali*; Venetians lived in their boats the way modern city dwellers live in their cars. On top, you'll often see surviving *altane*, the sun terraces of the women, along with a few of the old top-heavy chimneypots, designed to limit the risk of fire, a characteristic feature that the city's Renaissance artists loved to incorporate in their paintings.

One thing you won't often see is a family coat of arms over a palace: the Republic usually forbade such displays of vanity. There will be stone winged lions instead, several thousand of them in all, and also plenty of unexpected and random decoration: a haughty Byzantine emperor, probably stolen from Constantinople in 1204, frowning over a tiny courtyard, a duck, a griffin, a pair of 6th-century capitals, a shrine to Persephone erected by a scholarly Renaissance humanist.

There aren't many stone plaques, at least compared to Rome, but if you look carefully you'll find water-level markers from historic floods, a score of indignant memorials to Austrian bombs from the First World War, and a few notices from the slapstick days of the 18th century warning you against spitting or gambling or otherwise making a spectacle of yourself.

style, such as the 11th-century **Santa Fosca**, built next to Torcello Cathedral, and the original of **Santa Maria Formosa**. The most important example, however, was the first: the **Basilica of San Marco**, built in the 830s, a copy of Constantinople's five-domed church of the Apostles – a form kept through all subsequent rebuildings.

Constantinople's other great contribution to the young city was in mosaic decoration. The dazzling mosaics of Ravenna's basilicas begun by the last Roman emperors were finished by the new Romans of the Byzantium, who imported artists from Constantinople. These artists soon found additional work in Torcello and St Mark's. Their stiff, 'hieratic' portraiture of highly stylized, spiritual beings who live in a gold-ground paradise, with no need of shadows or perspective or other such worldly tricks, was to remain prominent in Venetian pictorial art until the 13th century. The third important artistic cross-current from Constantinople was in gold-work, namely the spectacular **Pala d'Oro** (altar screen) in St Mark's, ordered by Doge Ordelafo Falier in 1105, and in its final form a collaborative effort between Greek and Venetian craftsmen.

The great looting of Constantinople's treasures in 1204 did much to prolong the Byzantine influence in the Lagoon. Although most of the fabulous riches were devoted to embellishing St Mark's, marble columns, mosaic icons and carvings were incorporated into other churches as well. A new wave of Greek mosaicists emigrated to Venice to sheath St Mark's domes in gold, in images straight from the 5th century. For, curiously, the loot from Constantinople sparked a retro fashion for Early Christian art (sometimes called the 'Proto-Renaissance') that lasted through the 12th and 13th centuries. The Venetians had the style down so pat that no one will ever know if some of the works date from the 6th or 13th century (St Mark's alabaster columns, for example). As Rome, the upstart, had Virgil's *Aeneid* to give the city an ancient and noble lineage, Venice (a much later upstart) has the mosaics in

St Mark's to anchor it to the hallowed traditions of the Early Christian church. But on the façade of St Mark's the Venetians took iconographic pains to show they could also claim an ancestor as illustrious as Hercules. The anonymous 13th-century sculptors of the pseudo-antique reliefs of Hercules and the basilica's side portals formed Venice's first workshop. They had hardly begun when their work was overshadowed by the far livelier, more natural figures of the **Labours of the Months** on the central portal, carved by Lombard stonemasons trained by the great Benedetto Antelami of Parma.

Venice's oldest palaces (such as the **Ca' da Mosto**, **Ca' Farsetti** and the **Fondaco dei Turchi**) date from the 13th century, and show a similar taste for Byzantine and Islamic designs, especially in their arches. In them you can already see the classic form of the Venetian palaces: main façade on a canal, where waterborne arrivals entered the *androne*, a long hall running through the centre of the ground floor (*see* also box, pp.56–7). This is where Venice's merchant princes conducted their business, with their store rooms off to the sides and their offices on the *mezzanine*. The same floor plan is repeated in the living quarters on the first floor, or *piano nobile*, where the long room is called the *portego* or *salone*. In later palaces this would be the ballroom, and the family moved up to the next floor, or *secondo piano nobile*. But the basic structure remained the same throughout the centuries, leaving fashion to change only the surface decoration, and the shape and patterns of the windows and arches.

Lingering Gothic in the 14th and 15th Centuries

In many ways this was the most exciting and vigorous phase in Italian art, an age of discovery when the power of the artist was almost like that of a magician. Great imaginative leaps occurred in architecture, painting and sculpture, especially in Tuscany – nor was it long before Tuscan masters

Finding Venice's Architecture

Byzantine/Early Gothic Churches: St Mark's Basilica, p.98; San Giacomo dell'Orio, p.190; San Giacomo di Rialto, p.186; San Nicolò dei Mendicoli, p.169; Santa Fosca, p.232; Santa Maria Assunta, p.230; Santa Maria e Donato, p.229; S. Stefano, p.130; Sant'Eufemia, p.221

Byzantine/Early Gothic Palaces: Ca' Farsetti, p.130; Ca' da Mosto, p.197; Corte Corner, p.131; Fondaco dei Turchi, p.189; Palazzo Falier, p.197; Palazzo Sagredo, p.238

Late Gothic Churches: Frari, p.176; Madonna dell'Orto, p.204; Santi Giovanni e Paolo, p.136

Late Gothic Palaces: Ca' Foscari, p.239; Ca' d'Oro, p.196, Palazzo Agnusdio, p.187; Palazzo Ariani, p.168; Palazzo Ducale, p.108; Palazzo Erizzo, p.235; Palazzo Foscari, p.238

Early Renaissance Churches: San Giovanni in Brágora, p.144; San Giovanni Grisostomo, p.198; San Michele, p.226; Santa Maria Materdomini, p.187; Santa Maria dei Miracoli, p.198; San Zaccaria, p.142

Early Renaissance Palaces and Other: Arsenal Gateway, p.148; Palazzo Corner-Spinelli, p.238; Palazzo Vendramin-Calergi, p.235; Scuola Grande di San Giovanni Evangelista (courtyard and stair), p.182

High Renaissance Churches: Il Redentore, p.221; San Francesco della Vigna, p.147; San Fantin (dome), p.126; San Giorgio Maggiore, p.217; San Salvatore (interior), p.125; San Zulian, p.124

High Renaissance Palaces and Other: Biblioteca Marciana, p.118; Ca' Grande, p.240; Loggetta, p.114; Palazzo dei Camerlenghi, p.185; Palazzo Soranzo, p.235; Procuratie Vecchie, p.117; Rialto Bridge, p.184

Baroque Churches: Gesuati, p.172; San Marziale, p.206; San Moisè, p.127; Santa Maria Zobenigo, p.127; Santa Maria della Salute, p.163; Scalzi, p.213

Baroque Palaces and Other: Ca' Pésaro, p.187; Ospedaletto, p.140; Palazzo Foscarini-Giovanelli, p.235; Palazzo Moro-Lin, p.239; Palazzo Pisani, p.131; Procuratie Nuove, p.117; Scuola dei Carmini, p.166

Rococo Churches: Gesuiti, p.199; La Pietà, p.144; San Simeone Piccolo, p.190; San Stae, p.188; Santa Maria della Fava, p.142

Rococo Palaces: Palazzo Diedo, p.234; Palazzo Labia, p.212; Palazzo Venier dei Leoni (Peggy Guggenheim Collection), p.240

19th/20th Century: Ala Napoleonica, p.117; Biennale Pavilions, p.154; La Fenice, p.126; Mulino Stucky, p.221; Palazzo Patriarcale, p.116; Palazzo Salviati, p.240; Ponte degli Scalzi, p.234; San Maurizio, p.128; Stazione Santa Lucia, p.234

---

introduced the new style to the Veneto. In Padua's **Cappella degli Scrovegni** (1308) (*see* p.244) Giotto used all he knew about intuitive perspective, composition and a new, more natural way to render figures in natural settings. It was revolutionary in its day, the masterpiece of an artist who inspired the first painters of the Renaissance. But the Venetians didn't want to know. Although Byzantine influences lingered into the 14th century, Venice by that time was ready to go Gothic in its half-oriental, flamboyant way. The once-stiff Byzantine figures cautiously begin to sway in dance-like movements, including the famous *Salome* mosaic in St Mark's Baptistry (1340s) and the marble statues on the basilica's rood screen, by **Jacobello** and **Pier Paolo dalle Masegne** (1394). The real break with the past came

with the completion of the **Palazzo Ducale**, decorated with exquisite sculptural groups, capitals and lacy Gothic tracery that had nothing to do with Byzantium. Venetian architecture in that period had more openwork than anywhere else – walls were built to define voids as well as solids: the **Ca' d'Oro** (1420–40s) by **Giovanni Bon** is the most effervescent example. Bon, with his son **Bartolomeo**, also designed the Porta della Carta (1430s), the grand entrance to the Doge's Palace and the flowery pride of Venice's late Gothic period.

The religious revivals of the 14th century saw in Venice the building of two giant brick Gothic churches to hold the crowds – **Santi Giovanni e Paolo** and the **Frari**. This being Italy, the architects were not interested in towering verticals but in creating immense spaces; this being Venice, there was always the danger of such large structures shifting on their foundations, no matter how many piles were driven into the slime. One of the distinctive features of Venetian Gothic was the use of tie beams to add support to their aisles and arches. Another danger was weight, but Venice was able to draw upon the experience and talents of its Arsenal shipwrights: many smaller churches, such as Santo Stefano and San Giacomo dell'Orio, were given lightweight wooden ship's keel roofs in the 1300s.

In painting, not only Giotto's innovations but also the more natural style of the Palazzo Ducale sculptors were ignored. The first Venetian painter to make a name for himself was **Paolo Veneziano**, who flourished in the 1330s: although still heavily Byzantine, his delight in brilliant colour was a harbinger of the Venetian school. In the 1350s, **Lorenzo Veneziano** (no relation) took another step away from Byzantium with his graceful line and soft shading to suggest three dimensions. But the strongest influence on local painters was the colourful, fairy-tale style called **International Gothic**. Two of its greatest masters, Gentile da Fabriano and Pisanello, painted frescoes (now lost) in the Palazzo Ducale at the beginning of the 15th century; you can see the highly decorative gilded panels by their Venetian followers (most notably **Jacobello del Fiore** and his pupil **Michele Giambono**) in the first room of the Accademia. International Gothic continued to have its adherents long into the 15th century thanks to the glowing polyptychs of **Antonio Vivarini**, father of a dynasty of painters from Murano, and his collaborator **Giovanni d'Alemagna**.

The Early Renaissance of the *Quattrocento*

Although the Venetians were slow to give up Gothic and join the Renaissance, the art and architecture produced in the transition period of the early 15th century was often crystalline in its freshness. Greek artists continued to arrive, taking refuge from the Turks (El Greco was to be one of these), but it was other Italians who intrigued the Venetians now – the great Florentine sculptors **Donatello** and **Verrocchio**, whose bronze equestrian statues left lessons in human form and expression, and painters such as **Andrea del Castagno** and **Paolo Uccello**, who helped design mosaics in St Mark's.

The advent of Renaissance painting in Venice can be fairly concentrated on the careers of two men, father and son: Jacopo and Giovanni Bellini. **Jacopo Bellini** was a Gothic student of Gentile da Fabriano, but also collaborated with **Andrea del Castagno** in St Mark's Cappella della Madonna dei Máscoli; he painted two major cycles for the *scuole* of San Marco and San Giovanni Evangelista (both destroyed). But Jacopo's best surviving work is in his sketchbooks, in London and the Louvre – lovingly meticulous drawings from nature that had a major influence on his sons. **Gentile Bellini**, the elder, picked up on the meticulousness in his photo-like paintings of narrative historical scenes, while **Giovanni Bellini** inherited his love for nature. Like many other painters and sculptors of his time, Giovanni was also heavily influenced by his brother-in-law, **Andrea Mantegna** of Padua, whose powerfully drawn sculptural figures exist in startling perspectives, drawn with a keen interest in antiquity. **Antonello da Messina**'s visit to Venice in the 1470s introduced Giovanni to the luminous oil-painting techniques he learned in a Flemish workshop. Lastly, **Cima da Conegliano** came to Venice from the rural Veneto and set his shimmering religious scenes against his own native hills, instructing Bellini in one of the tenets of the early Renaissance: that heaven is here on earth.

Giovanni Bellini combined all these new influences and techniques to create some of the most lyrical, sensually poetic art of the Renaissance. Throughout his long career, he never stopped experimenting, seeking new responses to nature and light and colour and atmosphere. His Madonnas and Saints are at once ideal and human, noble and tender, warmed by the liquid sun, never striving to outdo or out-scale nature. And it is this very empathy and sense of human measure that makes Bellini's angels divine. His follower, **Vittore Carpaccio**, took this empathy with nature and actuality to a more earthly level, and painted some of the most charming narratives of all time, with enough literal detail to make his canvases important historical records (especially the Sant'Ursula and San Giorgio degli Schiavoni cycles).

The classical calm and natural nobility of Donatello's work in Padua was a formative influence on sculptors in Venice in the 1400s. **Antonio Rizzo** of Verona spent much of his career in Venice as master architect of the Ducal Palace. Two of his works, the Palace's statue of *Eve* and the Frari's Tron tomb, are Early Renaissance works in the most classic sense, harmonious and confident. **Pietro Lombardo**, his contemporary from Cremona, refined Rizzo's style in his pure Renaissance tomb of Doge Pasquale Malipiero, in Santi Giovanni e Paolo. In his exquisite little church of **Santa Maria dei Miracoli** and the façade of the **Scuola di San Marco**, Pietro Lombardo created an architectural style known as the Lombardesque, inspired by St Mark's basilica: decorated with marble sheathing, rounded arches, sculptured friezes, Corinthian capitals and coloured discs. Pietro's sons and assistants, **Tullio** and **Antonio Lombardo**, supplied most of Venice's best reliefs and statues from the 1480s on.

The busiest architect of the period was **Mauro Codussi** (or Coducci), a native of Bergamo, who in 1469 built the first Renaissance church in Venice, **San Michele in Isola**. Like Pietro Lombardo, Codussi adapted former Venetian styles, especially Byzantine, to Renaissance forms and proportions, borrowing the plans, silhouettes and decorative elements from older buildings. Yet he was also capable of great originality (see the staircase in the Scuola di San Giovanni Evangelista). His palaces on the Grand Canal (Palazzo Corner-Spinelli and Ca' Vendramin-Calergi), with their delightful synthesis of Veneto-Byzantine elements with Tuscan (double-arched windows, rusticated ground floors, etc.), became the models for many others in the next two centuries.

High Renaissance

The 16th century is often called the 'Golden Age' of Venetian Art. While the rest of Italy followed the artists in Rome in learning drawing and anatomy, the Venetians went their own way, obsessed with the dramatic qualities of light and atmosphere. The elusive, short-lived **Giorgione** of Castelfranco, a pupil of Giovanni Bellini, was the seminal figure in this new manner. In his most famous painting, the *Tempest*, the mysterious subject matter is subordinate to its tense, brooding atmosphere. Giorgione invented '**easel painting**' – art that served neither Church nor State nor the vanity of a patron, but stood on its own for the pleasure of the viewer. Giorgione was also the first to paint freely, without preliminary sketches, beginning the Venetian trend away from drawing – much to the disdain of their Tuscan contemporaries.

Giorgione's brief career was linked with two fellow Bellini students and collaborators, whose works are sometimes confused with his. The first, **Sebastiano del Piombo**, left for Rome the year after Giorgione died, while the second, **Titian**, stayed in town to become a major transitional figure in Venetian art, though 95 per cent of his works were sent abroad to a host of foreign clients, or lifted by Napoleon. Emperor Charles V held him in such respect that during a sitting he bent over to pick up one of his fallen brushes. In Titian's 90 or so years, he went from a style so imitative of Giorgione that it's virtually impossible to tell who painted some canvases, to dramatic religious compositions full of vibrant colour (most famously, the Frari altarpiece), through a series of ripe, barroom nudes and portraits of big shots, to his last style, epitomized in the Accademia's *Pietà*, the paint literally smeared on with his hands, and left unfinished at his death.

In spite of his achievements, Titian's artistic vision seldom rose above the obvious; with his work, true imagination and virtuosity have parted ways. Nor are his contemporaries especially riveting, with the exception of **Lorenzo Lotto**, who, as a potential rival, was forced out of Venice by Titian's clique to spend the rest of a lonely career painting the most psychologically penetrating portraits of his generation. Another contemporary, **Palma Vecchio**, specialized in beautiful women, from courtesans to his famous *Santa Barbara* in Santa Maria Formosa, in an intellectually undemanding style echoed by his prolific followers, **Bonifazio Veronese** and **Jacopo Bassano**. The latter was also influenced by the exaggerated poses and extreme lighting

effects of the Mannerists (the main appeal for **El Greco**, whom he also influenced), although in the end Bassano and his two artist sons are best remembered for their night-time nativities set in Italian barnyards.

Some 35 years younger than Titian, **Tintoretto** entered the Venetian scene of beautiful light and colour like a comet from outer space, reuniting virtuosity and imagination in his dynamic first canvases. Light and colour, or the lack of them, became the means and not the end to his feverishly visionary canvases, painted with fast, furious brush strokes. The inspiration to paint was so strong in him that he would offer his services for free, or resort to tricks to get a commission, as in the case of his magnificent cycle in

Finding Venice's Art

Accademia, for a chronological tour of the greatest masterpieces of Venetian art, p.158

Angelo Raffaele, to see Guardi's *Tobias and the Angel*, p.168

Ca' d'Oro, the 'House of Gold', for the impressive Franchetti collection, p.196

Ca' Pésaro, with its two galleries: modern art and oriental art, p.187

Ca' Rezzonico, to wallow in a Tiepolo ceiling, Rococo furniture, Rosalba Carriera's pastel portraits, and Canaletto and Guardi scenes of 18th-century Venetian life, p.165

Fondazione Querini-Stampalia, to mourn the 18th-century 'age of trivialization', p.141

I Frari, to see why Titian's *Assumption of the Virgin* caused a revolution, p.176

Madonna dell'Orto, Tintoretto's parish church, and crammed with his art, p.204

Museo Correr, for the best collection of paintings outside the Accademia, including three *Pietàs*, Canova models, frescoes, and Barbari's etching, *Aerial View of Venice*, p.118

Museo di Icone, to understand century Byzantine influence on Venice, p.144

Palazzo Ducale, for sculpture, Tiepolo, Tintoretto and Veronese, and the biggest oil painting in the world, p.108

Palazzo Labia, to look up at Tiepolo's *Life of Cleopatra* on the ballroom ceiling, p.212

Peggy Guggenheim Collection, for superb modern art including Max Ernst, Matisse, Picasso, Braque, Klimt, Kandinsky, Rothko and other glories of the 20th century, p.163

Raccoltà d'Arte Vittorio Cini, for delicate, less well known Renaissance works, p.162

St Mark's Basilica, for 13th-century mosaics and reliefs, sculptures, paintings, Byzantine gold and silver and the Pala d'Oro, p.98

San Francesco della Vigna, which has a good selection of early Renaissance art, p.147

San Salvatore, with Titians, and the famous *Supper at the House of Emmaus*, p.125

San Sebastiano, Veronese' parish church, which he decorated throughout, p.167

San Zaccaria, mainly to see Giovanni Bellini's gorgeous *Madonna and Saints*, p.142

Sant'Alvise, to decide if Ruskin was right about the 'baby Carpaccios', p.207

Santa Maria Formosa, for Palma Vecchio's unmatched *Santa Barbara*, p.141

Santa Maria della Salute, for Titians and more, p.163

Scuola dei Carmini, for another bright Tiepolo ceiling, p.166

Scuola Grande di San Rocco, Venice's Sistine Chapel, with its awe-inspiring Tintoretto-lined Chapter House, p.179

Scuola di San Giorgio degli Schiavoni, to view the extraordinary Carpaccio cycle, p.146

the Scuola di San Rocco. Unlike Giovanni Bellini, however, he was a baleful influence on his followers, who would fit Yeats' gibe, 'The best lack all conviction and the worst are full of passionate intensity.' **Palma Giovane** was only the most prolific. Fewer painters tried to follow the act of Tintoretto's elegant and urbane contemporary, **Paolo Veronese**, who arrived in Venice in the 1550s to paint lavish canvases in jewel-like colours that are the culmination of all that Venice had to teach in interior decoration.

The most important architect, and one of the greatest sculptors in 16th-century Venice, was **Jacopo Sansovino**, who adapted his training in Tuscany and Rome to create a distinctive Venetian style, richly decorated with sculpture and classical motifs that create patterns of light and shadow (especially in the Libreria and Loggetta). His most famous pupil, **Alessandro Vittoria**, broke away from Sansovino's graceful classicism in favour of a more emotional Mannerist style. But the lovers of antiquity were to dominate, especially in the work of the most influential architect produced by the Veneto, **Palladio**. Palladio's greatest talent was in adapting classical models to modern needs: his famous villas not only fitted his client's desire to look the part of a Roman patrician in the country, but were also functional as working farm centres. His ecclesiastical buildings (San Giorgio Maggiore, the Redentore, San Francesco della Vigna) are concentrated in Venice – sleek, white, minimally adorned temples.

Baroque (17th Century)

As an art designed to induce temporal obedience and psychical oblivion, Baroque's effects are difficult to describe. On the whole, however, little of the most excessive brand of Baroque made it to Venice. In short, the 17th century saw more of the same Venetian palaces and churches, only inflated into Baroque. The age does provide some exceptions to the rule that in art, less is more: see **Baldassare Longhena**'s magnificent church

of the **Salute** on the Grand Canal. Longhena, deeply indebted to both Sansovino and Palladio, was Venice's only Baroque architect of note, and his palette ranged from the massive but exuberant Ca' Pésaro to the grotesque in the Ospedaletto façade and the lugubrious in the Scalzi. Baroque frosting, most of it gone a bit rancid, is the keynote to Longhena's mediocre successors, **Alessandro Tremignon** (San Moisè) and **Giuseppe Sardi** (Santa Maria del Giglio). The best 17th-century sculptors came from elsewhere: the Genoese **Nicolò Roccatagliata**, the Flemish sculptor **Juste Le Court**, and Bernini's pupil from Rome, **Filippo Parodi**.

Meanwhile, Venetian painters, wallowing in the muddy aftermath of Tintoretto, darkened the city's churches with one diagonal, shadow-bound composition after another, reaching a hypnotic extreme in **Gian Antonio Fumiani**'s *trompe l'œil* ceiling for San Pantalon. Most of the fresh inspiration was to come from outsiders, many of whom arrived in Venice as pilgrims desiring to learn more about light and the free handling of paint: the short-lived German **Johann Lys** stands out, along with two inspired if somewhat eccentric Italians, **Francesco Maffei** of Vicenza and **Sebastiano Mazzoni**.

An 18th-century Rococo Revival

Venice bloomed like Camille on her deathbed, with a revival of talent to ease her political decline. Someone once called the 18th century the 'vegetable period' in art, but if everyone else made turnips, Venice created a charming, elegant style that became the international fashion of its day. The transition to iridescent light and graceful forms began with **Sebastiano Ricci** of Belluno, in his ceiling of San Marciliano (San Marziale). His foil was **Giambattista Piazzetta**, who disdained colour for *chiaroscuro* and dramatic zigzagging compositions.

Both proved fertile inspiration for the celebrity decorator of the rococo era,

Historical, Artistic and Architectural Terms

altana: roof terrace of a Venetian house, where the ladies would repose and bleach their hair blonde in the sun

atrium: entrance court of an ancient Roman house or early church

baldacchino: baldachin, a columned stone canopy over an altar

basilica: a rectangular building, usually divided into three aisles by rows of columns. In ancient Rome this was the common form for law courts and other public buildings; Roman Christians adopted it for their early churches

bocca dei leone: 'lion's mouth'; boxes for anonymous denunciations of traitors and criminals

ca': *casa*, a word the Venetians preferred to *palazzo* for even the grandest mansions

chiaroscuro: monochrome painting using only light and shade, always more popular in Venice than elsewhere in Italy

ciborium: a tabernacle; a construction on or behind an altar containing sacramental host

confraternity: a religious lay brotherhood, often serving some specific charitable work; in Venice they are called *scuole*

contrapposto: the dramatic but rather unnatural twist in a statue, especially in a Baroque work

cornu: peculiar 'horned' cap worn by doges

cupola: a dome

etoimasia: in Byzantine symbolism, the 'preparation of the Throne' for Christ at the Last Judgement

exedra: (It. *esedra*) a semicircular recess

ex-voto: an offering (a terracotta figurine, painting, medallion, silver bauble or whatever) made in thanksgiving to a god or Christian saint; the practice has always been present in Italy

graffito: originally, incised decoration on a building façade; only lately has the word come to mean casually scribbled messages

Greek cross: in the floor plans of churches, a cross with equal arms. The more familiar plan, with a long nave and shorter transepts, is called a Latin cross

grotesque: decoration with carved or painted faces, used by the Etruscans and Romans, and back in fashion in the Renaissance

iconostasis: a transenna (*see* below) in a Byzantine church, though often more elaborate and decorated

Giambattista Tiepolo, a virtuoso master of theatrical, buoyant ceilings, narrative, heroic frescoes set in illusionist (*quadrata*) backgrounds (as in the Palazzo Labia) and dazzling altarpieces (Sant'Alvise). He often worked with his son **Giandomenico Tiepolo**, who had no heart to continue his father's heroic style, but instead painted some highly original genre scenes (as in Ca' Rezzonico). This was also the period of the precise **Antonio Canaletto** and the more impressionistic brothers **Francesco** and **Gian Antonio Guardi**, whose countless views of Venice were the rage among travellers on the Grand Tour; even today the majority of their works are in Britain and France. Equally popular was **Rosalba Carriera**, whose flattering rococo pastel portraits were the rage among Europe's nobility. Another painter of the era,

Pietro Longhi, devoted himself to genre scenes that are most interesting as a documentary of Venice some 200 years ago.

Meanwhile Venetian architect **Giorgio Massari** translated their rococo sensibility into stone, especially in the lovely church/concert hall of **La Pietà**, while architect/sculptor **Domenico Rossi** defied gravity and reason for the Jesuits at the **Gesuiti** church, and in his loop-the-loop façade for **San Stae**. One of the most memorable figures of the early 1700s was a furniture-carver, **Andre Brustolon**, a student of Parodi, who set his imagination loose to create Italy's most densely populated furniture. The greatest sculptor to work in Venice in the late 18th century was the neoclassical master, **Antonio Canova**, although he spent much of his career in Rome.

intarsia: inlay work in wood or stone

loggia: an open-sided gallery or arcade

lunette: semicircular space on a wall, above a door or under vaulting

matroneum: the elevated women's gallery around the nave of a church. Segregating women at Mass was a Byzantine practice that spread to Italy in the 6th–7th centuries

narthex: the enclosed porch of a church

orders: architectural systems of proportion, based on the widths of a building's columns, ranging from the squat, plain Doric to the slender Ionic and the Romans' favourite, the even more delicate Corinthian. Codified by the classical writer Vitruvius, and rediscovered in the Renaissance

palazzo: not just a palace, but any large, important building (the word comes from Rome's *Palatium*)

paterae: exterior plaque or rondo often carved with reliefs

pendentives: four curved, triangular pieces, springing from four piers, that help to support a dome

piscina: a swimming pool, tank or reservoir

portego: the main hall of a Venetian house.

predella: smaller paintings on the panel below main subject of a painted alterpiece

putti: (or *amoretti*) flocks of painted or plaster cherubs with rosy cheeks and bottoms, derived from ancient decoration, that infested much of Italy in the Baroque era

quadriga: chariot pulled by four horses

quattrocento: the 1400s, in the Italian way of referring to centuries (*trecento, quattrocento, cinquecento, seicento, settecento*, etc.)

rio terrà: a Venetian street replacing a filled-in canal

salizzada: a paved street in Venice

scuola: Venetian word for a confraternity or its headquarters (*see* above)

tenebroso: the contrast of darkness and illuminated subjects used with such effect by Caravaggio and his followers

tessera: one of the stone or glass cubes, or enamelled chips, used in mosaics (pl. *tesserae*)

transenna: marble screen separating the altar from the rest of an early church

trompe l'œil: art that uses perspective effects to deceive the eye – for example, to create the illusion of depth on a flat surface, or to make columns and arches painted on a wall seem real

veduta: view

The 19th and 20th Centuries

Whatever artistic spirit remained at the end of the 18th century evaporated after Napoleon. More was demolished than built in the 19th century – 49 churches bit the dust, and the splendid art that adorned them was dispersed to various galleries or simply destroyed. One of the few names to drift down is that of **Gian Antonio Selva**, designer of La Fenice opera house and the façade of San Maurizio. Foreigners such as Turner drifted in to paint the city, while John Ruskin wrote his *Stones of Venice*, which to his dismay didn't educate his readers in the glories and pitfalls of architecture as much as begin a trend for ogival arches in Manchester. But thousands were inspired to come and see the real thing, and when sea bathing became popular, the Lido was developed with its outrageous eclectic hotels. Another attraction was the great international art exhibits of the **Biennale**, inaugurated in 1895, and still one of the most prestigious in Europe (*see* p.300). Holding international exhibitions has become big business in Venice today; many are excellent, and bring visitors back over and over again.

In the 20th century the local scene has been grim, though not for lack of trying. The Italian movements of the age – Futurism with its emphasis on speed, and the Metaphysical School with its emphasis on stillness – had little response from Venice. In 1946 Renato Guttuso and Emile Vedova founded an avant-garde group, the Fronte Nuova, with more talk than notable results.

Again the main input has come from abroad, particularly the USA, which has always had empathy with Venice. **Peggy Guggenheim**'s collection of contemporary art arrived in Venice like a breath of fresh air, but misplaced atavism prevented the construction of Frank Lloyd Wright's palace on the Grand Canal (though when the authorities vetoed a hospital designed by Le Corbusier, even Le Corbusier agreed they were right).

In short, preservation has pretty much pre-empted creation in fragile, delicate old Venice. Saving the city and its art has become a major preoccupation of Italians and foreigners alike. The British **Venice in Peril Fund**, begun after the flood in 1966, is one of the most active of the 32 international organizations, and Americans and Italians have contributed buckets of money to keep the old girl afloat, most of it now spent in cooperation with the local UNESCO office, **Amici dei Musei e Monumenti Veneziani**. But will any new artists ever swim against the tides of municipal embalming fluid?

DIRECTORY OF ARTISTS AND ARCHITECTS

Antonello da Messina (c. 1430–79), a Sicilian painter who visited Venice. Antonello was one of the first Italians to perfect the Van Eyckian oil painting techniques of Flanders; his mastery of light, shadows and the simplification of forms was a major influence on Giovanni Bellini (see the great but damaged Pietà in the Museo Correr).

Barbari, Jacopo de' (d. 1515), precise pupil of Alvise Vivarini whose most famous work is the bird's-eye-view plan of Venice in the Museo Correr.

Basaiti, Marco (1470–c. 1530), student and collaborator of Alvise Vivarini (Accademia).

Bassano, Jacopo (da Ponte; 1510–92), pater-familias of a clan of artists working mainly from Bassano del Grappa. Jacopo began by

painting in the monumental Central Italian style but is better known for churning out a whole succession of religious night scenes in rustic barnyards. His son **Francesco** (1549–92) was his most skilled assistant and follower; the more prolific **Leandro** was less talented (Return of Jacob, in the Palazzo Ducale).

Bastiani, Lazzaro (c. 1420–1512), probably Carpaccio's master, and the painter responsible for the 'baby Carpaccios' (Sant'Alvise).

Bella, Gabriel (1730–99), Venice's charming naïve painter of city scenes, a valuable source of information about the 18th century despite his technical ineptitude (Palazzo Querini-Stampalia).

Bellini, Gentile (1429–1507), elder son of Jacopo, famous for his detailed depictions of Venetian ceremonies and narrative histories (Procession of the Relic of the True Cross, Accademia) and his portrait of Sultan Mehmet II, now in the National Gallery in London, painted during a sojourn in Istanbul. (The latter presented him with the head of a freshly decapitated criminal, to help him paint a scene of St John the Baptist. At this point Gentile asked to go home and, showing no hard feelings, the Sultan sent him back to Venice with a beautiful gold chain.)

Bellini, Giovanni ('Giambellino', c. 1431–1516), the greatest early Renaissance painter of northern Italy, an innovator who kept experimenting even into his 80s and greatly influenced (and was influenced by) pupils Giorgione and Titian. No artist before him painted with such sensitivity to light, atmosphere, colour and nature; none since has approached the magical tenderness that makes his paintings transcendent (masterpieces in the Accademia, San Zaccaria, the Frari, and San Pietro Martire, on Murano).

Bellini, Jacopo (1400–70), father of Giovanni and Gentile, father-in-law of Mantegna, all of whom were influenced by his beautiful drawings from nature. In Venice his best works are his natural and lifelike Madonnas (Accademia).

Bon, Bartolomeo (d. 1464), prolific Venetian sculptor and architect, designer of the Porta della Carta, Palazzo Ducale.

Bon, Giovanni (d. 1444), late Gothic sculptor and architect of great refinement, designer of the Ca' d'Oro.

Bonifazio de' Pitati (Bonifazio Veronese; 1478–1553), the most talented follower of Palma Vecchio (Accademia).

Bordone, Paris (1500–1571), student and imitator of Titian; best work in the Accademia.

Brustolon, Andrea (1662–1732), maker of proto-kitsch rococo furniture (Ca' Rezzonico).

Calendario, Filippo (d. 1355), master architect of the Doge's Palace (disputed), and probably the inventor of its unique top-heavy design. Executed for his part in the Falier conspiracy.

Canaletto, Antonio (1697–1768), master of meticulous Venetian *vedute*, or views, though the best place to see his paintings is in Britain – there's just one in the Accademia, and two in the Ca' Rezzonico.

Canova, Antonio (1757–1822), of Possagno, Europe's neoclassical celebrity sculptor, the favourite of Napoleon and Benjamin Franklin (Museo Correr, Frari).

Carpaccio, Vittore (c. 1465–1525), the most charming of Venetian artists, with fairy-tale paintings full of documentary details from his life and times (major cycles at the Scuola di San Giorgio degli Schiavone and the Accademia; his *Two Women* in the Museo Correr is Venice's first genre painting).

Carrà, Carlo (1881–1966), started out as a Futurist but changed gears to the Metaphysical School in Ferrara with de Chirico (Peggy Guggenheim).

Carriera, Rosalba (1675–1758), a Venetian portraitist and miniaturist, and perhaps the first woman to make a good living as an artist: her soft, pastel portraits were the rage of the powdered wig set in Venice, Paris and Vienna (Accademia and Ca' Rezzonico).

Castagno, Andrea del (1423–57), a Tuscan master of striking form and precise drawing, who visited in 1445 and left the city food for thought in St Mark's and San Zaccaria.

Chirico, Giorgio de (1888–1978), a Greek-Italian who was one of the founding fathers of the Metaphysical School in Ferrara (1916–18), best known for his uncanny urban landscapes dotted with classical odds and ends and mannequins (Peggy Guggenheim).

Cima da Conegliano, Giovanni Battista (1459–1518) painted luminous autumnal colours and landscapes inspired by Bellini – as Bellini was inspired by several of his compositions (Madonna dell'Orto, Accademia and Carmini).

Codussi, Mauro (c. 1420–1504), architect from Bergamo, who worked mainly in Venice; a genius at synthesizing traditional Venetian styles with the classical forms of the Renaissance, and the first to use Istrian stone for façades (San Michele, San Zaccaria, staircase at the Scuola di San Giovanni Evangelista, Palazzo Vendramin-Calergi).

Crivelli, Carlo (c. 1435–95), Venetian painter keen on luminous, almost 3D perspective, crystalline forms, garlands and cucumbers; spent most of his time in the Marches (Accademia).

De Pisis, Filippo (1896–1956), Ferrara neo-Impressionist who spent a long period in Venice (Peggy Guggenheim).

Donatello (1386–1466), of Florence, was the best Italian sculptor of the *quattrocento*, if not of all time, never equalled in technique, expressiveness or imaginative content. He spent a long period in Padua, casting his Gattamelata statue and altar for the Basilica di San Antonio (also a statue in the Frari).

Francesco di Giorgio Martini (1439–1502), Tuscan architect, sculptor and painter of grace and symmetry (Carmini).

Gambello, Antonio (d. 1481), generally credited for bringing Renaissance architecture to Venice in the form of the Arsenal Gate, though he's also responsible for the northern Gothic elements of San Zaccaria.

Giambono, Michele (c. 1420–62), painter and mosaicist, one of the princes of Venetian retro; while everyone else moved on to the Renaissance, Giambono was still churning out rich paintings in graceful International Gothic (Accademia, altarpieces in St Mark's).

Giorgione (Giorgio Barbarelli, c. 1478–1510), got his nickname 'Great George' not only for his height but for the huge influence he had on Venetian painting. Although he barely lived past 30 and only several paintings are undisputed, his poetic evocation of atmosphere and haunting ambiguity were echoed not only by his followers, Titian (who assisted him in the lost Fondaco dei Tedeschi frescoes) and Sebastiano del Piombo, but by his master Giovanni Bellini (Accademia).

Giotto di Bondone (c. 1267–1337), one of the most influential painters in Italian art, the first to break away from stylized Byzantine forms in favour of a more 'natural' and narrative style. Although associated with Florence and Assisi, he painted his masterpiece in Padua: the Cappella degli Scrovegni.

Guardi, Francesco (1712–93), younger brother of Gian Antonio, with whom he often worked, making some attributions difficult. Favourite subject was Venice, but his views, unlike Canaletto's, are suffused with atmosphere; some approach Impressionism (Ca'd'Oro, Accademia, Angelo Raffaele).

Guariento (14th century), a Paduan follower of Giotto whose greatest work, a massive fresco of *Paradise* in the Palazzo Ducale, was lost in a fire – only fragments remain.

Jacobello del Fiore (c. 1370–1439), Venetian master of International Gothic, very fond of raised gold embossing (Accademia).

Le Court, Juste (1627–79), Flemish sculptor who spent many years in Venice; main work is the theatrical *Plague* altarpiece (Salute).

Leopardi, Alessandro (d. 1522), classicizing sculptor responsible for completing Verrocchio's Colleoni monument and casting the ornate flagstaffs in front of St Mark's.

Lombardo, Antonio (c. 1458–c. 1516), a major figure in the Venetian High Renaissance, though most of his surviving works are now in St Petersburg's Hermitage.

Lombardo, Pietro (c. 1435–1515), founder of Venice's greatest family of sculptors and architects, strongly influenced by Donatello's work in Padua (Santi Giovanni e Paolo, San Giobbe, San Francesco delle Vigna, and Santa Maria dei Miracoli).

Lombardo, Tullio (c. 1455–1532), son of Pietro, with whom he often worked; Tullio was an exquisite marble sculptor, best

known for his tombs (Santi Giovanni e Paolo) and classical reliefs (Ca' d'Oro).

Longhena, Baldassare (1598–1682), Venetian architect, a student of Scamozzi; his best work was one of his first: the church of the Salute (also Ca' Pésaro).

Longhi, Pietro (1702–85), 18th-century Venice's dutiful society portraitist (Ca' Rezzonico, Accademia, Querini-Stampalia).

Lorenzo Veneziano (active 1356–79), disciple of Paolo Veneziano and painter in a luxurious, golden style presaging International Gothic (Accademia).

Lotto, Lorenzo (c. 1480–1556), a native Venetian and pupil of Giovanni Bellini; best known for intense portraits that seem to catch their sitters off-guard, capturing the painter's own restless energy. Run out of Venice by Titian and Aretino (Accademia).

Lys, Johann (1595–1630), a German painter of verve whose career was tragically cut short by plague (San Nicolò da Tolentino).

Maffei, Francesco (c. 1600–60), a somewhat dissonant and unorthodox painter from Vicenza inspired by Lys; the *Guardian Angel* in Santi Apostoli is his masterpiece.

Mansueti, Giovanni (c. 1465–1527), underrated student of Giovanni Bellini and a talented painter of narrative histories (Accademia).

Mantegna, Andrea (c. 1420–1506), a remarkable painter and engraver born near Padua, whose interest in antiquity, sculptural forms as hard as coral, and unusual perspectives dominated art in the Veneto until the rise of his brother-in-law Giovanni Bellini (Accademia and Ca' d'Oro).

Dalle Masegne, Jacobello and Pier Paolo, 14th-century Venetian sculptor brothers influenced by Tuscan sculptor Nicolò Pisano, creator of a new realistic, classically inspired style (San Marco).

Massari, Giorgio (1687–1766), Venetian architect who collaborated with G. Tiepolo and Vivaldi to produce some of Venice's most delightful rococo (La Pietà and Gesuati).

Mazzoni, Sebastiano (1611–78), Baroque painter after Lys and Maffei who marched to a different drum (San Benedetto); also designed the Palazzo Moro-Lin.

Morandi, Giorgio (1890–1964), an heir of the Metaphysical school; naturally austere, his still lifes invite a subtle meditation on form (Ca' Pésaro).

Palladio (Andrea di Pietro della Gondola, 1508–80), the Veneto's most influential architect, not only for his buildings but for his books and drawings reinterpreting Roman architecture to fit the time (San Giorgio Maggiore and the Redentore).

Palma, Giovane (1544–1628), the most prolific painter of his day in Venice; the great-nephew of Palma Vecchio and a follower of Tintoretto, specializing in large but usually vapid narrative paintings (every church in Venice seems to have at least one; best in the Oratorio dei Crociferi and Querini-Stampalia).

Palma Vecchio (Jacopo Negreti, c. 1480–1528), a student of Giovanni Bellini who successfully adopted the new sensuous style of Giorgione, and is best known for his beautiful paintings of women – courtesans and saints (Santa Maria Formosa, Accademia).

Paolo Veneziano (c. 1290–1360), the leading Venetian painter of the day, whose colourful Byzantine style is reminiscent of the Pala d'Oro (Accademia).

Parodi, Filippo (1630–1702), sculptor who adapted his master Bernini's late, flowing style (San Nicolò da Tolentino).

Piazzetta, Giambattista (1683–1754), Venetian Baroque painter extraordinaire, who went to dramatic extremes in his use of light and dark; was first president of the Accademia (Accademia, Santa Maria della Fava and Santi Giovanni e Paolo).

Piero della Francesca (c. 1420–92), a Tuscan painter who wrote two theoretical books on perspective, then illustrated them with a life-time's work, reducing painting to the bare essentials: mathematics, light and colour (Accademia, Vittorio Cini Collection).

Pisanello (Antonio Pisano, c. 1415–c. 1455), originator of the Renaissance medal and one of the leading International Gothic painters in Italy (medals in the Ca' d'Oro).

Ponte, Antonio da (1512–97), designer of the Rialto Bridge and new prison building.

Pordenone (Giovanni de' Sacchis, 1484–1539), always wore a sword in case he should happen upon his chief rival, Titian. Had a more monumental, Roman style, quick brushstrokes and a tendency to the bizarre (San Giovanni Elemosinario, Ca' d'Oro).

Ricci, Sebastiano (1659–1734), Mazzoni's pupil, who combined a bright-coloured palette with the scenographic monumen-tality of Roman Baroque (San Marziale).

Rizzo (Bregno), Antonio (c. 1445–99), pure Renaissance sculptor and architect from Verona, who worked in Padua and Venice (Tron monument, Frari, Scala dei Giganti and courtyard of the Palazzo Ducale).

Roccatagliata, Nicolò (fl. 1593–1636), sculptor of elegant early Baroque bronzes (San Giorgio Maggiore, San Moisè).

Rossi, Domenico (1657–1737), hyper-rococo architect and sculptor; created the apsidal altars of the Gesuiti and façade of San Stae.

Sammicheli, Michele (1484–1559), refined Venetian Renaissance architect, though best known for his fortifications, most notably in Venice – the Forte di Sant'Andrea by the Lido (also Palazzo Grimani).

Sansovino, Jacopo (Jacopo Tatti, 1486–1570), sculptor and architect who took his name from his Tuscan master, sculptor Andrea Sansovino. Fled the Sack of Rome in 1527 and came to Venice, where he became chief architect to the Procurators of St Mark's and a good friend of Titian and Aretino, who promoted his career. Used his Tuscan and Roman periods to create a new decorative Venetian High Renaissance style – the rhythmic use of columns, arches, loggias and reliefs, with sculpture playing an integral role in the building (major works include Libreria Marciana, Zecca, dome of San Fantin, sculptures in the Palazzo Ducale and St Mark's).

Santi, Andriolo de' (14th century), Paduan sculptor whose 1336 tomb of Duccio degli Uberti in the Frari was probably the proto-type of the Venetian tomb: a sarcophagus topped by an arch, holding an effigy of the deceased. Son Giovanni de' Santi carved the unwieldy *Virgin* in Madonna dell'Orto.

Sardi, Giuseppe (1620–99), muddly Baroque architect responsible for the façades of the Scalzi and Santa Maria del Giglio.

Scamozzi, Vincenzo (1552–1616), architect from Vicenza and Palladio's closest follower, taking his ideas to classicizing extremes, as in the Procuratie Nuove. Spent most of his Venetian career finishing Sansovino's library.

Sebastiano del Piombo (1485–1547), colleague of Giorgione and rich autumnal colourist. Went to Rome and became chief notary of the Vatican; a painter after Raphael until he made enough money to stop painting altogether (S. Giovanni Grisostomo).

Selva, Gian Antonio (1751–1819), architect of La Fenice, precocious believer that form should follow function (also façade of San Maurizio).

Tiepolo, Giambattista (1696–1770), Venice's greatest Baroque painter, and an excellent draughtsman, a pupil of Piazzetta, though he had little use for chiaroscuro. His subjects, many mythological, live in the delightful warm afterglow of Venice's decline. In 1762, when he was 66, the Senate, wanting to ingratiate itself with the king of Spain, ordered him against his will to go to paint ceilings in Madrid (Palazzo Labia, Scuola dei Carmini and Gesuati).

Tiepolo, Giandomenico (1727–1804), son of Giambattista, with whom he frescoed Villa Valmarana. Giandomenico's work is more introspective and often haunting, especially his masquerades in Ca' Rezzonico and his stations of the cross at San Polo.

Tintoretto (Jacopo Robusti, 1518–94), was given his name, 'little dyer', after his father's profession. His ideal was to combine Michelangelo's drawing with the colouring of Titian, but his most amazing talent was in his visionary, unrestrained and totally original composition (Scuola di San Rocco series; the world's largest painting, in the Palazzo Ducale; Accademia and S. Giorgio Maggiore).

Titian (Tiziano Vecellio, c. 1480s–1576), came from Pieve di Cadore in the Dolomites to become 16th-century Venice's most popular painter, the favourite of princes, popes and emperors. Made his reputation with the monumental altarpiece in the Frari, a bold handling of form and colour that would prove a pivotal influence on Tintoretto. Although Titian spent most of his life in Venice, his international reputation saw most of his canvases scattered around the courts of Europe: his fine portrait of *Philip II* convinced Mary Tudor that she should marry him. (Besides the Frari altarpieces, Venice keeps his works in San Salvatore, the Accademia and the Salute.)

Tura, Cosmè (c. 1430–95), of the Ferrara school, whose singularly craggy and weirdly tortured style is an acquired taste (Museo Correr, Accademia).

Veronese (Paolo Caliari, 1528–88), the most sumptuous and ravishingly decorative painter of the High Renaissance, fond of striking illusionism, shimmering colours and curious perspectives set in pale Palladian architectural fantasies (Accademia, Palazzo Ducale and San Sebastiano).

Verrocchio, Andrea del (1435–88), painter, sculptor and alchemist, a follower of Donatello and teacher of Leonardo da Vinci. Considered the greatest bronze sculptor of the day, and hired by the Senate to create the dynamic equestrian statue of Colleoni in front of Santi Giovanni e Paolo.

Vittoria, Alessandro (1525–1608), Venetian sculptor, a student of Sansovino and famous for his bronze statuettes and portrait busts (San Francesco della Vigna, Frari, Ca' d'Oro).

Vivarini, 15th-century family of painters from Murano, the chief rivals of the Bellini workshop, noted for their rich, decorative style. **Antonio** (c. 1415–c. 1480), a follower of Jacobello del Fiore, collaborated with Giovanni d'Alemagna to paint lavish golden altarpieces (San Giobbe and San Zaccaria); brother **Bartolomeo** (1432–99) played an influential role in Venetian art through his use of colour and rhythm (Santa Maria Formosa, Frari); **Alvise** (1446–1503), son of Antonio, was influenced by Antonello da Messina (Frari, San Giovanni in Brágora).

Travel

GETTING THERE 72
By Air 72
By Train 73
By Sea 74
By Coach 74
By Car 74

TOUR OPERATORS 75

ENTRY FORMALITIES 76

ARRIVAL 76

GETTING AROUND 77
Addresses, and Finding your Way in Venice 77
By Water 78
By Bus 80
Car Hire 80
Guided Tours 80

GETTING THERE

By Air

From the UK

The two national airlines of Britain and Italy operate direct **scheduled flights** from the UK to Venice's Marco Polo airport; any others may involve a change in Milan or even Rome. **Low-cost airlines** fly either to Venice, or to Treviso, 35km north. The flight takes about 2hrs.

The cost of fares varies wildly, depending on season; travellers under 26 and students under 32 can pick up discounts from specialist travel agencies, and keep an eye out for the many special offers.

Flights on the Internet

The best place to start looking for flights is the Internet – just about everyone has a site where you can compare prices (see the airlines listed below), and booking online usually confers a 10–20% discount.

In the UK and Ireland

w www.airtickets.co.uk
w www.cheapflights.com
w www.expedia.co.uk
w www.flightcentre.co.uk
w www.lastminute.com
w www.skydeals.co.uk
w www.sky-tours.co.uk
w www.trailfinders.com
w www.travelselect.com

In the USA

w www.airhitch.org
w www.expedia.com
w www.flights.com
w www.orbitz.com
w www.priceline.com
w www.travellersweb.ws
w www.travelocity.com
w www.smarterliving.com

In Canada

w www.flightcentre.ca
w www.lastminuteclub.com
w www.newfrontiers.com

Airline Offices in Venice

The airline offices at the airport do not take phone bookings: for that you have to call the general numbers of each airline.

Alitalia, *Marco Polo Airport, Tessera,* **t** *041 260 6431/848 865 642.*

British Airways Marco Polo Airport, *Tessera,* **t** *199 712 266.*

easyJet *(no office),* **t** *848 88 77 66.*

Ryanair, *Treviso airport,* **t** *0422 315 331.*

Scheduled Flights

Alitalia, **t** *08705 448 259,* **w** *www.alitalia.it.* Two flights daily from London Gatwick.

British Airways, **t** *08457 733 377,* **w** *www.britishairways.com.* Daily flights from London Gatwick from around £110 Apex (14 days' notice).

Both airlines also offer good-value city break packages with a selection of hotels. Brochures are available in travel agents and from the airlines directly.

Low-cost Airlines

EasyJet and Ryanair flights average about £80–100 return, but, depending on when you book and/or special offers available at the time, they can be much higher or much lower. It pays to have flexible dates.

easyJet, **t** *0870 600 0000,* **w** *www.easyJet.com.* Has picked up the old Go route, from London Stansted, Bristol and East Midlands airports to Venice Marco Polo.

Ryanair, **t** *0871 246 0000,* **w** *www.ryanair.com.* Flies from Stansted to Treviso.

Charter Flights

These can be incredibly cheap, and offer the added advantage of departing from local airports.

Italy Sky Shuttle, *227 Shepherd's Bush Road, London W6 7AS,* **t** *(020) 8748 1333,* **f** *8748 6381,* **w** *www.travelshop.com.* Specializes in flights to Italy.

Ciao Travel, *New Bond St, W1,* **t** *(020) 7629 2677,* **f** *7629 4853,* **w** *http://ciaotravel.co.uk.*

Student and Youth Travel

CTS Travel, **t** *(020) 7290 0620,* **w** *www.cts travel.co.uk.*

Europe Student Travel, *6 Campden St, London W8,* **t** *(020) 7727 7647.*

STA Travel, **t** *08701 600599,* **w** *www.sta travel.co.uk.* Agents for STA travel are based at many university campuses.

Trailfinders, **t** *(020) 7938 3939,* **w** *www.trailfinders.com.*

usit Campus, **t** *0870 240 1010,* **w** *www.usit campus.co.uk.*

usit NOW, *Dublin* **t** *(01) 602 1600,* **w** *www.usitnow.ie.*

From Ireland

There are no direct flights from the Republic of Ireland.

From the USA and Canada

From the United States, Delta has direct scheduled flights to Venice from New York, costing between $350 and $800. Other major carriers fly direct only to Rome and Milan. Your travel agent may be able to find you a much cheaper fare from your home airport to Venice via London, Brussels, Paris, Frankfurt or Amsterdam. From Canada, you will need to fly via Rome, Milan or Paris.

Scheduled Flights

Air Canada, **t** *888 247 2262,* **w** *www.air canada.ca.* From Montreal and Toronto.

American Airlines, **t** *800 433 7300,* **w** *www.aa.com.* From Boston, Chicago, Dallas, JFK and Miami.

Continental, *USA* **t** *800 525 0280,* **w** *www.continental.com.* From Houston and Newark.

Delta, **t** *800 241 4141,* **w** *www.delta.com.* From Atlanta, Boston, Chicago, Cincinnati and Los Angeles International.

Northwest Airlines, **t** *800 447 4747,* **w** *www.nwa.com.* From Detroit.

United Airlines, **t** *800 538 2929,* **w** *www.ual.com.* From Chicago, Los Angeles, Miami, New Orleans and Seattle.

Charter, Budget and Discount Flights

For discounted flights, try the small ads in newspaper travel pages (e.g. *New York Times, Chicago Tribune, Toronto Globe & Mail*). Travel clubs and agencies also specialize in discount fares, but may require a membership fee.

Air Brokers International, **t** *800 883 3273,* **t** *415 397 1383,* **w** *www.airbrokers.com.*

Air Courier Association, **t** *800 282 1202,* **w** *www.aircourier.org.* Members club.

Airhitch, *224 West 35th Street, New York, NY 10001,* **t** *1800 326 20 09,* **w** *www.airhitch.org.* Last-minute stand-by fares, just over half the scheduled price.

CIEE, **t** *800 223 7402.* Can get you as close as Rome or Milan from New York and connect you with domestic flights.

Now Voyager: **t** *212 431 1616,* **w** *www.nowvoyagertravel.com.*

It is also possible for North Americans to take advantage of the explosion of cheap inter-European flights, by taking a charter flight to London, and booking a London–Italy budget flight on the airline's website. This will need careful planning: you're looking at an 8hr flight followed by a 3hr journey across London and another 1½–2hr hop to Italy; it can be done, and you may be able to sleep on a night flight, but you may prefer to spend a night or two in London.

Student and Youth Travel

Council Travel, **t** *1 800 2COUNCIL,* **w** *www.counciltravel.com.* Specialist in student and charter flights; branches across the USA.

CTS Travel, **t** *877 287 6665,* **w** *www.cts travelusa.com.*

STA Travel, **t** *1 800 781 4040,* **w** *www.statravel.com.* Branches at most universities.

Travel Cuts, *USA* **t** *1 866 246 9762, Canada* **t** *416 979 2406,* **w** *www.travelcuts.com.* The largest student travel specialists, with branches in most big towns.

By Train

Of course, you can wallow in romantic splendour, Grand Tour style, on the luxurious vintage **Venice Simplon Orient-Express** from London to Venice via Paris, Innsbruck and Verona.

Fares start at about £1,270 (USA $2,050) one-way, return £1,790 ($2,975). The Orient Express runs most Sundays and Thursdays from March to November.

Venice Simplon-Orient-Express Tours Ltd, *Sea Containers House, 20 Upper Ground, London SE1 9PF, t (020) 7928 6000, w www.orient-express.com.*

Abercrombie and Kent, *1520 Kensington Rd, Oakbrook, Illinois 60521, t (708) 954 2944, f 954 3224.* From the USA, contact this main booking office.

Trains arrive at Venice's **Stazione Santa Lucia** (*see* p.77; C2–D4). There are frequent connections to Padua (half-hourly), where the budget-conscious visitor may prefer to stay (*see* p.246). All trains from Santa Lucia stop in Mestre, where you may have to change. The information offices in the station itself are nearly always very crowded.

By Sea

This is the most thrilling way to approach Venice in all her majesty, although it's only practical if you're coming from the east.

Adriatica Lines, *Zattere 1412, Venice, t 041 520 4322 or t 041 522 8018.* Connections every 10 days in June–Sept with Split (15hrs) and Dubrovnik (24hrs).

Minoan Lines, *2 Vass. Konstantinoú, 15125 Athens, t 010 751 2356, f 010 752 0540, e info@minoan.gr.* Daily car ferries between Venice, Corfu and Patras, Greece (2 days); Heraklion, Crete (2½ days); and Alexandria, Egypt (3½ days).

An easier way to approach Venice in style would be to follow the path of Portia in *The Merchant of Venice*, by travelling as far as Padua to pick up the *Burchiello* and sailing up the Brenta Canal to Piazza San Marco.

Burchiello, *t 049 660 944, March–Nov Tues–Sun.*

By Coach

Usually more expensive than a budget flight, the coach is the last refuge of aeroplane-phobic bargain-hunters. The journey from London to Venice is around 28hrs, changing in Paris and Milan.

Eurolines, *t 08705 143219 (daily 8am–10pm), w www. gobycoach.com.*

By Car

Taking your car on a **Eurotunnel** train is the most convenient way of crossing the Channel between the UK and mainland Europe in order to drive south through France to Italy. It takes only 35mins to get through the tunnel between Folkestone and Calais, and there are up to four departures an hour every day. Peak-time tickets for a car and passengers cost around £300 return in the low season, rising to £350 return in the high season. Prices are per car less than 6.5m in length, plus the driver and all passengers.

Eurotunnel, *t 08705 353 535, w www. eurotunnel.com.* Information and bookings.

Venice is the best part of three days' driving time from the UK, even if you stick to fast toll roads.

To bring a UK-registered car into Italy, EU citizens need a vehicle registration document, full driving licence and insurance papers (these must be carried at all times when driving). If your driving licence is an old-fashioned one without a photograph, you are also strongly recommended to apply for an international driving permit (available from the AA or RAC). Non-EU citizens should have an international driving licence, preferably with an Italian translation. Your vehicle should display a nationality plate indicating its country of registration. Red triangular hazard signs and headlight converters are obligatory; also recommended are a spare set of bulbs, a first-aid kit and a fire extinguisher. Spare parts for non-Italian cars can be difficult to find, especially Japanese models. **Insurance** should be taken out before leaving – your own insurance company will provide information on the documents needed. **Seat belts** are now compulsory in Italy.

AA, *t 0990 500 600, t 0800 444 500, w www.theaa.com.* '5-star' breakdown cover.

RAC, *t 0800 550 550, w www.rac.co.uk.* A similar service to the AA.

AAA, *(USA) t 407 444 4000, t 800 222 5000, w www.aaa.com.* The American Automobile Association.

TOUR OPERATORS

In the UK

Artscape Holidays, *P.O. Box 1605, Salisbury SS2 7XD 0SA, t (01722) 743 163, e sallyg. reygan@virgin.net.* 'Lighthearted' cultural tours with painting tuition included.

Citalia, *Marco Polo House, 3–5 Lansdowne Road, Croydon, Surrey CR9 ILL, t (020) 8686 5533.* Probably has the widest range of general good-value Italian city breaks.

Fine Art Travel, *15 Savile Row, London W1X 1AE, t (020) 7437 8553, w www.bellinitravel. co.uk.* Tours in the Veneto, with excellent lecturers and access to many things that are normally closed.

Italia 2000, *8 Timperley Way, Up Hatherley, Cheltenham, Glos GL51 5RH, t (01242) 234215, e iancook@italia2000.co.uk.* Golf on the Lido.

Italian Journeys, *European Travel Centre, 216 Earl's Court Rd, London SW5 9QB, t (020) 7370 6002, e italy@italianjourneys.com.* Specialists in package and tailored holidays to Italy, with upmarket, stylish hotels.

Liaisons Abroad, *Chenil House, 181–3 King's Road, London SW3 5EB, t (020) 7376 4020, w www.liaisonsabroad.com.* Will tailor-make holidays for any number of people for opera, Carnival, museums and other themes.

Martin Randall Travel, *10 Barley Mow Passage, London W4 4PH, t (020) 8742 3355, f (020) 8742 7766, e info@martinrandall. co.uk, w www.martinrandall.com.* Cultural tours accompanied by a lecturer.

Page and Moy, *135–40 London Road, Leicester LE2 1EN, t 0870 010 6212, w www. page-moy.co.uk.* Escorted city trips.

Prospect Music and Art Tours, *36 Manchester St, London W1M 5PE, t (020) 7486 5705, f (020) 7486 5868.* Fully accompanied tours of Venice's museums and galleries.

Swan Hellenic, *Richmond House, Terminus Terrace, Southampton SO14 3PN, t 0845 3555 111, e reservations@swan-hellenic.co.uk, w www.swanhellenic.co.uk.* One- or two-week cruises around the Mediterranean including stops in Venice.

Travel for the Arts, *12–15 Hanger Green, London W5 3EL, t (020) 8799 8350, e tfa@ stlond.com, w www.travelforthearts.com.* Opera and classical music tours.

In the USA and Canada

Archaeological Tours Inc, *Suite 904, Madison Avenue, New York, NY 10016, t (212) 986 3054/866 740 5130, e archtours@aol.com, w www.archaeologicaltrs.com.* Tours to Venice and the Veneto focus on the city's history, such as Byzantine and Baroque monuments of the region. All tours are led by an expert in the field.

CIT (North America) Ltd., *15 West 44th St, New York, NY, t (212) CIT-TOUR, w www.cit-tours.com.* Several Italian tours each year that visit Venice, ranging from 8 to 15 days, some escorted ('Italian Treasures').

CIT (Canada) Ltd., *80 Tiverton Ct, Suite 401, Markham, Ontario L3R 0GA, t 800 387 0711, w www.cit-tours.com.* The Canadian contact address for CIT, see above.

Italiatour, *666 5th Avenue, New York, NY 10103, t 800 845 3365 (USA) and t 888 515 5245 (Canada), w www.italiatourusa.com.* Straightforward city breaks organized by Alitalia, with sightseeing excursions that can be booked separately.

Kesher Tours, *347 Fifth Avenue, Suite 706, New York, NY 10016, t (212) 481 3721, t 800 847 0700, f (212) 481 4212, w www.keshertours. com.* Fully escorted kosher tours.

Maupintour, *1421 Research Park Drive, Kansas 66049, t 800 255 4266, w www. maupintour.com.* Escorted city breaks, including Venice Carnival and 'Treasures of Italy' trip.

Specialty Travel Index, *305 San Anselmo Ave, Suite 313, San Anselmo, CA 94960, t (415) 459 4900, e info@specialtytravel.com, w www.specialitytravel.com.* Try the website for various art and architecture and culinary tours to Venice and the Veneto region.

Trafalgar Tours, *11 East 26th Street, New York, NY 100107, w www.trafalgartours.com.* Their 'European Spectacular' 11-day trip includes Venice.

ENTRY FORMALITIES

Passports and Visas

For EU citizens, a visa is not necessary; a valid passport or national ID card is sufficient and the length of stay is unrestricted.

Full passports are needed for non-EU citizens, and nationals of the United States, Canada, Australia and New Zealand need visas for stays of longer than three months.

By law, you are supposed to register with the police (at the Questura, Santa Croce 500) within three days of your arrival (if you check into a hotel or campsite this is done for you automatically). However, few people bother to go through the bureaucracy involved (and checks are rare) unless they plan to stay for more than three months. In this case, it is necessary to apply for a *permesso di soggiorno* or residents' permit.

Customs

Duty-free allowances have been abolished for journeys within the European Union. Up to 10 litres of spirits, 90 litres of wine, 110 litres of beer and 3,200 cigarettes – bought locally and provided you are travelling between EU countries, can be taken through customs if you can prove that they are for private consumption only. Shops at ports, airports and the Channel Tunnel continue to sell other products, such as perfume and cosmetics, at reduced prices.

Non-EU citizens visiting the EU can buy duty free on their way home, but face restrictions on how much they can take back. Americans over the age of 21 can take 1 litre of alcohol, 200 cigarettes and 100 cigars home with them. They can take $400 worth of goods duty-free, and pay 10% tax on the next $1,000 worth of goods. .

US Customs: *PO Box 7407, Washington, DC 20044, t (202) 927 6724, w www.customs. ustreas.gov.* For more detailed information, look at the website or call the office and request the free booklet *Know Before You Go*.

Canadians can bring back 200 cigarettes, 50 cigars, 200 tobacco sticks, 220 grams of manufactured tobacco, 1.5 litres of wine or 1.14 litres of spirits or 8.5 litres of beer. They have a $750 duty-free limit if they have been away for more than 7 days ($200 for trips between 2 and 6 days long).

Revenue Canada: *2265 St Laurent Blvd., Ottawa K1G 4KE, t 800 461 9999, t (613) 993 0534, w www.ccra-adrc.gc.ca.* The free booklet, *I declare*, gives further information.

ARRIVAL

Arriving by Air

Marco Polo, Venice

General information, t 041 260 6111, w www.veniceairport.it. Recorded flight information *in English and Italian, t 041 260 9260.* **Arrivals, t 041 260 9240; departures, t 041 260 9250; lost property, t 041 260 6436.**

Marco Polo airport, 12km from the city centre, handles up to 6.5 million passengers a year. The full facilities include shops, tourist information centres, a post office, banks, car hire, left luggage, a bar and restaurants.

The airport is linked with Venice by water-taxi (SOC Marco Polo, **t** 041 966 170, or Cooperativa San Marco, **t** 041 523 5775), the most expensive option (€45 for up to four passengers to the Centro Storico, €55 to the Lido, prices negotiable for more people and depending on amount of luggage); or by *motoscafi* to Piazza San Marco roughly every hour, although connecting with most flights between March and Oct (€10).

Less romantic but considerably cheaper, the direct ATVO bus zips to Piazzale Roma every half-hour (**t** 041 520 5530; €2.70); and, cheapest of all, the local ACTV city bus no.5 (€0.77) passes by twice an hour, taking only 25 minutes, also finishing at Piazzale Roma.

San Giuseppe, Treviso

Airport information, t 0422 230 393.

Treviso's San Giuseppe airport lies 35km southwest of the town. There are trains every

15mins to Venice's Santa Lucia station (€1.80). ATVO buses (**t** 041 520 5530, **w** *www.atvo.it*; €4.30) run between Piazzale Roma and Treviso airport to coincide with flights.

Arriving by Train

Venice's **Stazione Santa Lucia** (C2–D4), the name a consolation prize to the saint whose church had to be bulldozed for the station), normally referred to simply as the **Ferrovia** within Venice, is the terminus of the Orient-Express and numerous other less glamorous trains from the rest of Europe and Italy. There are especially frequent connections to Padua (half-hourly), where the budget-conscious visitor may prefer to stay.

Water-taxis, *vaporetti* and gondolas (*see* below) wait in front of the station to sweep you off into the city. If you've brought more luggage than you can carry, one of Venice's infamous **Cooperativa Trasbagagli** (porters distinguished by their badges; **t** 041 713 719) will lug it to your choice of transport and, if you pay his fare on the water-taxi, will take it and you to your hotel (the official price for two pieces of luggage is €20.66 between any two points in the historic centre, extra bags are €7.75) – or, less likely, you can try to track down a porter once you disembark at one of the main landings or the Lido. Since rates for baggage-lugging are unregulated every-where other than at the station, be sure to negotiate a price in advance.

Left-luggage office, *near the tracks, €2.58 per bag for each 12hrs.*

Arriving by Car

All roads to Venice end at the monstrous municipal parking towers in **Piazzale Roma** (C5) or its cheaper annexe, **Tronchetto** (**t** 041 520 7555, **w** *www.veniceparking.it*), nothing less than the largest car park in all Europe, which may take up the entire Lagoon before it's finished. You can leave your car here, for €18 (there's a 20% discount for stays of longer than two days if you pay in advance). In summer, at Easter and Carnival, when the causeway turns into a solid conga-line of cars waiting to park, consider the **Italian Auto Club**'s three alternative and less expensive car parks (*open to non-members*):

Fusina, *t 041 547 0160; vaporetto 16 to Venice.* With a shady, year-round campsite, located at the mouth of the Brenta Canal south of Marghera.

Punta Sabbioni, *t 041 530 0455; vaporetto 17 from San Marco.* Between the Lido and Jesolo.

San Giuliano, *Mestre; bus service to Venice.* Near the causeway.

GETTING AROUND

Addresses, and Finding Your Way in Venice

An interesting phenomenon, peculiar to Venice, is the street numbering. Venice may well have been the first city to possess such a thing, and the system they invented has an archaic charm. The numbering isn't by street, but by the entire *sestiere*. Each of the 'sixths' of the city has one number 1; from there the numbers wind up and down the ancient alleys in no particular pattern, terminating with a flourish as San Marco's does, near the main post office, with a huge painted sign proclaiming to all the world: 5562. THE LAST NUMBER OF THE *SESTIERE* SAN MARCO.

Venetians get by with a little book called the ***Indicatore Anagrafico***, which matches numbers with street names (*see* below). But even knowing the street name affords little comfort when a *sestiere* has several lanes of the same name, or when the names on the street signs fail to correspond with either the *Indicatore* or your map. Venetians are as accomplished at spelling as they are in the kitchen; the height of this orthographical madness comes in Campo San Biagio, or Blasio, or Biasio – you can take a souvenir photo of three signs on one wall, with three different spellings.

Before you start navigating around Venice, you'll need to get acquainted with some specifically Venetian street talk. At first you may think you're in Spain: why 'street' and 'canal' in Venetian dialect should be *calle* and *rio* is a linguistic mystery. There is of course only one *piazza* in Venice – St Mark's, along with two *piazzette* (adjacent to it), and one *piazzale* (Roma, the car park). All the rest are properly called *campo*. A small one may be a *campiello. See* 'Language', pp.306–307, for a further list of the various Venetian street names that may differ from the usual Italian.

Maps

No two maps of Venice ever agree, either in the actual street names and their dialect spellings, or where the back alleys actually end up. Among the first-rate maps of Venice that make a game effort to include every puny *corte* and *ramo* of every street are *Touring Club Italiano*'s 1:4500 atlas format, complete with a directory of street names; the yellow *Studio FMB Bologna* 1:5000 map with street index on the back; or the *Hallwag* 1:5500. For something a little more fun and surprisingly accurate, with pretty drawings of the main sights, every *palazzo* along the Grand Canal marked and named, and a key for shops and restaurants, try *The Illustrated Venice Map* (published in the UK by Magnetic North). But even the best maps aren't very much help in finding the typical Venetian address that lists only the *sestiere* and street number (see above): for these you need the *Indicatore Anagrafico*, available in most bookshops. If you get desperate, find a postman.

By Water

Vaporetti and *Motoscafi*

Public transport in Venice means by water: by chugging, grinding **vaporetti** (the all-purpose water-buses) or the faster but more enclosed **motoscafi** run by the ACTV, **t** 041 528 7886, **w** www.actv.it. The only canals served by public transport are the Grand Canal, the Rio Nuovo, the Canale di Cannaregio and Rio dell'Arsenale. Other stops are all on the edge of the city or on other islands, which means most of the time you'll be on your own two

Tickets and Passes

Single tickets (a flat rate of €3.10) should be purchased and validated in the machines at the landing-stages (random inspections aren't very frequent, but if you get caught without a validated ticket you'll have to pay a fine of €23 plus the cost of the ticket on the spot). You can buy tickets on board at no extra cost, but tell the boatman immediately. When you buy a single ticket at a booth, they are automatically stamped with the date and time and are only valid for that journey.

If you intend to do some intense scouting that involves being on a boat at least three times in a given day, purchase a **24-hour tourist pass** (€9.30), valid for unlimited travel on all lines, or the **3-day pass** (€18.80).

If you plan to spend more than three or four days in Venice, the cheapest option is to buy a **tesserino di abbonamento** from the ACTV office at Piazzale Roma (€5.16 and a photo machine mugshot – there's a machine at the Ferrovia) which is valid for three years and entitles you to buy monthly season tickets (€23.24) or single tickets at greatly reduced rates.

For younger travellers and students, there are also **Rolling Venice** cards (*see* p.82).

feet – not the gruelling prospect it sounds, as Venice is so small that you can walk across the whole city in an hour.

Lines of interest to visitors are listed below, the first five being the most central and frequently used; most run until at least midnight. Precise schedules are listed in the tourist office's free fortnightly guide, *Un Ospite di Venezia* or the ACTV's *Orario*. During the summer season, three additional lines with slightly changing routes, nos.**3**, **4** and **23**, help to increase the links between the most popular tourist hotspots.

Line 1 runs from Piazzale Roma and the Ferrovia (train station) down the Grand Canal to San Marco and the Lido, and vice versa, calling at every stop; around the clock, every 10mins (20mins after 10pm). The entire one-way journey takes an hour.

Line 82 covers a good deal more water between stops and does a similar grand circular tour from San Zaccaria (near San Marco), taking in the Grand Canal, the station, Giudecca and so on, though it stops less often. Every 10mins during the day, approximately once an hour at night.

Line 52 (green) is a *motoscafo* running between the Lido and all stops to S. Zaccaria, Zattere, Piazzale Roma, Ferrovia, Fondamenta Nuove and Lido. Every 20mins.

Line 6 (*diretto motonave*) is the large steamer from San Zaccaria to Lido (every 20mins).

Line 11 (the 'mixed' line) begins at the Lido on a bus to Alberoni, from where you catch a boat for Pellestrina, then another boat for Chioggia, or vice versa (about once an hour, sometimes more often).

Line 12 Fondamenta Nuove (on northern shore of Venice) to Murano, Torcello, Burano and Treporti (about once an hour).

Line 13 Fondamenta Nuove to Murano, Vignole and Sant'Erasmo (about once an hour).

Line 14 San Zaccaria to Lido and Punta Sabbione (every half-hour).

Line 17 A car ferry that cuts its way from Tronchetto (Piazzale Roma) through the Giudecca Canal to Lido and Punta Sabbione (every 50mins).

Line N (*servizio notturno*) runs all night (every 20mins from about 11pm), doing a sweep that includes the Lido, S. Zaccaria, Accademia, S. Toma, Rialto, Piazzale Roma, Zattere, Zitelle and S. Giorgio Maggiore.

See the transport map opposite the inside back cover of this guide for more routes.

Excursion Boats

At S. Marco you can also find a number of **excursion boats** to various points in the Lagoon. They are more expensive than public transport but may be useful if you're rushed.

Water-taxis

The de luxe way to get around the city at de luxe prices. These jaunty motor-boats can hold up to 15 passengers and you catch them from stands at the station, Piazzale Roma, Rialto, San Marco, the Lido and the airport. **Fares** are based on a rate of €73 per hour, with set fees for destinations beyond the historic centre. Within the centre, the minimum fare for up to four people is €73; additional passengers cost €4, and there are surcharges for baggage, holiday or nocturnal service (after 10pm), and for using a radio taxi, **t** 041 522 2303 or **t** 041 723 112. As a rule of thumb, a ride from one end of the Grand Canal to the other is likely to cost about €75, a city tour €73 an hour.

Watch out for launches posing as water-taxis without a number (this is their licence) clearly marked in yellow and black. They won't be controlled by any pricing policy and you could get heartily ripped off, especially when arriving at Tronchetto (Piazzale Roma).

Gondolas

Gondolas (*see* p.170) have a stately mystique that commands all other vessels to give way. Shelley and many others have compared them to funeral barks or the soul ferry to Hades, and not a few gondoliers share the infernal Charon's expectation of a solid gold tip for their services. Though they once numbered more than 10,000 and were used by all and sundry like carriages, while noblemen had private fleets at their beck and call, there are now only 400 gondolas in Venice and most Venetians have never been in one. They are the exclusive domain of tourists (up to six per gondola) who can pay the official €62 for a 50min ride (€77.50 after 8pm), plus €31 for every extra 25mins. Before setting out, do agree with the gondolier on where you want to go and how long you expect the journey to take, thus avoiding any unpleasantness later on. Remember that the above prices are the official tariff, but that

---

Useful Numbers

Lost property (*municipio*), t 041 274 8225
Lost property (trains), t 041 785 238
Lost property (*vaporetti*), t 041 272 2179
Train information, t 848 888 088
***Vaporetto* information, t** 041 528 7886

most gondoliers, particularly in high season, will wish to negotiate a premium.

Convenient places to hire a gondola include the stretch of water south of Piazza San Marco, on Riva degli Schiavoni, e.g. in front of the Danieli (J8) or at the Vallaresso *vaporetto* stop (H–I8); on the Riva del Carbon by the Rialto bridge (H6); and near the station, by Piazzale Roma bus terminus (C5).

Gondola Traghetti

Gondolas retired from the tourist trade are used for eight *gondola traghetti* services helpfully crossing the Grand Canal in the long stretches between its three bridges – your chance to enjoy a brief but economical gondola ride across the canal for €0.40.

For appearance's sake you'll have to stand up for the short but precarious experience: only sissies ever sit down on *traghetti*.

1 Fondamenta de Santa Lucia–Giardini Papadopoli (i.e. Ferrovia–Piazzale Roma).
2 Fondaco dei Turchi–S. Marcuola.
3 Pescheria–S. Sofia.
4 Fondamenta del Vin–Riva del Carbon.
5 S. Tomà–S. Angelo.
6 Ca' Rezzonico–S. Samuele.
7 S. Gregorio–S. Maria del Giglio.
8 Punta della Dogana–S. Marco.

These routes are also shown on the transport map opposite the inside back cover of this guide.

Hiring a Boat

Perhaps the best way to spend a day in Venice is to bring or hire your own boat – a small motor-boat or a rowing-boat – although beware of the local version of the oar, which requires some practice to use.

You may have to be persistent even to find a boat (the Venetians are tired of rescuing tourists stranded in the Lagoon), but ask in the tourist office for suggestions.

Motoscafi for hire are easier to find, especially with chauffeurs:

Cooperativa San Marco, *San Marco 4267, Campo San Luca, t 041 523 5775; H6.*

Narduzzi & Solemar, *San Marco 2828, Fondamenta Barbaro, t 041 520 0838; F8.*

Serenissima Motoscafi, *Castello 4545, Calle de la Rasse, t 041 522 4281; J7.*

Veneziana Motoscafi, *San Marco 4179, Calle del Carbon, t 041 716 000; H6.*

By Bus

Piazzale Roma is Venice's bus terminus. There are frequent city buses from here to Mestre, Chioggia, Marghera and La Malcontenta; regional buses run every half-hour to Padua and less frequently to other Veneto cities and Trieste.

Piazzale Roma tourist information office, *t 041 528 7886; C5.* Friendly and helpful.

Car Hire

If you want to explore the mainland by car, there are hire firms with offices in Piazzale Roma, the airports or Mestre.

Avis, *Marco Polo airport, t 041 541 5030, w www.avisautonoleggio.it.*

Europcar, *Piazzale Roma, t 041 523 8616, w www.europcar.it; Treviso airport, t 042 222 807.*

Hertz, *Piazzale Roma, t 041 528 3524.*

Maggiore, *Marco Polo, t 041 541 5040, w www.maggiore.it; Mestre, t 041 935 300.*

Guided Tours

Apart from the guided tours of individual churches and museums, several companies organize guided city tours. The tourist office also has **recorded tours** – you rent a handset and it takes you on a route, explaining as you go along at your own pace (1hr €3, 2hrs €5, 4hrs €7, whole day €10).

Associazione Guide Turistiche, *San Marco 750, Calle Morosini de la Regina, t 041 520 9038, e guideve@tin.it, w www.guidevenezia. it; I7.* Two-hour tours, suitable for small groups.

City Sightseeing by Gondola and On Foot, *San Marco 1471, Salizzada San Moisè, t 041 520 0844; run March–October; H8.* A walk and then a gondola trip, with explanations in English, lasting 2½hrs and costing around €30 per person.

Practical A–Z

Admission Prices and Discount Cards 82
Climate and When to Go 83
Crime and the Police 83
Disabled Travellers 84
Electricity, Weights and Measures 85
Embassies and Consulates 86
Etiquette 86
Gay and Lesbian Venice 86
Health, Emergencies and Insurance 86
Internet 87
Lost Property 87
Media 87
Money, Banks and Taxes 88
Opening Hours and Public Holidays 89
Packing 89
Photography 89
Post and Fax 90
Religious Affairs 90
Smoking 90
Students 91
Telephones 91
Time 91
Tipping 91
Toilets 92
Tourist Information 92
Women Travellers 93
Working and Long Stays 93

Admission Prices and Discount Cards

Museums are free for Venice residents, children under five and disabled people 'with escort'. Otherwise, entry fees vary enormously; state-owned museums are free for EU members with proof that they're under 18 or over 60; where relevant we have indicated the normal fee and the reduced rate for **students** (e.g. €4/€2.50). Some places, such as the Peggy Guggenheim, are real sticklers for student cards, so always carry proof.

The 'Settimana dei Beni Culturali' is a nationwide **week of free admittance** to all state museums. This is usually held sometime in the spring; ask at the tourist office for exact dates nearer the time (dates are often decided at the last minute).

There are **joint tickets** you can buy purely for museums, which saves money: the Piazza San Marco museums (Palazzo Ducale, Museo Correr, Museo Archeologico, Biblioteca Marciana; €9.50/€5.50); the museums of 18th-century culture (Ca' Rezzonico, Palazzo Mocenigo, Casa Goldoni; €8/€4.50); and the island museums (€6/€4). Reductions are given for EU students 15–29 years, EU residents over 65, EU residents aged 6–14, and holders of Rolling Venice cards.

Discount Cards

There are various discount schemes for visitors to Venice. For €12.91, people between the ages of 14 and 29 can buy a **Rolling Venice** card, giving discounts on the city's attractions, from films at the Film Festival to museums, hostels, shops and restaurants (and free access to the university canteen in Palazzo Badoer, Calle del Magazen 2840). It also allows you to buy a special reduced price ticket for travelling on the *vaporetti*. Apply at:

Agenzia Arte e Storia, S. Croce 659, Corte Canal, t 041 524 0232; *vaporetto* Riva di Biasio; E4. **Open** Mon–Fri 9–1 and 3–6.15.

Assessorato alla Gioventù, San Marco 1553, Corte Contarina, t 041 274 7653; *vaporetto* San Marco; H7–8. **Open** Mon–Fri 9.30–1, Tues and Thurs 3–5.

Associazone Italiana Alberghi per la Gioventù, San Polo 3101, Calle del Castelforte, t 041 520 4414; *vaporetto* San Tomà; E6. **Open** Mon–Sat 8.30–1.30.

Take a photo and your passport. It's also available at **VELA** ticket offices (*see* box).

The **Blue Venice** card, which is valid for one day, three days or a week and costs €7/€11, €17/€23 and €39/41 respectively, depending on whether you are under or over 29, offers unlimited travel on all *vaporetti*, *motoscafi* and buses in Venice, Mestre and the Lido and to the islands, plus free admittance to public toilets (*see* p.92). Similarly, the **Orange Venice** card is valid for one day, three days or a week and costs €16/€26, €30/€42, €51/€58 depending on whether you are are under or over 29. This offers the same as the Blue card, plus it also includes admission to all civic museums in Venice, including the San Marco museums, the 18th-century museums and the island museums. The cards must be booked (**t** 899 90 90 90 within Italy, **t** 041 271 4747 from abroad, **w** *www.venicecard.it*) at least 48 hours in advance of when you want them to begin. You will be given a booking reference number and a pick-up point (they vary), and you must pay cash.

Many churches now belong to an association called **Chorus** (**t** 041 275 0462, **w** *www.chorus-ve.org*), and a collective ticket

VELA

The commercial branch of the ACTV transport company acts as a ticket office not only for bus and boat tickets but also for some concerts, operas, dance events (including La Fenice's programme) and the Biennale, and sells Rolling Venice and Blue and Orange Venice cards too.

All are available from main *vaporetto* stops (Accademia, Ferrovia, Rialto, Tronchetto, Vallaresso, San Zaccaria, Lido) and VELA agencies (Calle dei Fuseri, **t** 041 241 8029, *open* 7.30–7, and Piazzale Roma, **t** 041 272 2249; *open* 8.30–6.30).

For information, call **t** 899 90 90 90 (**t** 041 271 4747 from outside Italy and for info in English) or see **w** *www.velaspa.com*.

for all these churches costs €8 (individually, each church costs €2). All Chorus churches have the same opening times (*Mon–Sat 10–5 and Sun 1–5*). Tickets are available from the churches, from VELA ticket offices (*see* box), from the Venice Pavilion tourist office (*see* p.92), and from travel agents.

Climate and When to Go

> *Obviously things have to smell of whatever they smell of, and obviously canals will reek in the summertime, but this really is too much.*
>
> Burgundian president, Charles de Brosses, 18th century

But pungent canals keep Venice from getting too bijou. In no other city will you be so aware of the light: on a clear, fine day no place could be more limpid and clear, no water as crystal-bright as the Lagoon. The rosy dawn igniting the domes of St Mark's, the cool mist of a canal dulling the splash of an oar, the pearly twilit union of water and sky are among the city's oldest clichés.

If you seek solitude and romance with a capital 'R', go in November or January. Pack a warm coat, wellingtons and an umbrella and expect frequent fogs and mists. It may even snow, a rare and beautiful sight – in 1987 you could ski-jump down the Rialto Bridge. Roughly once a century the canals and lagoons freeze up enough to skate or roast an ox. But there are also plenty of radiant diamond days, brilliant, sunny and chill; any time after October you take your chances. If there's an *acqua alta* (high water) while you're in town, don't miss the sight of Piazza San Marco submerged.

As spring approaches there is Carnival, a flamboyantly touristy attempt to revive a piece of old Venice. Lent is fairly quiet, although there's an expectant undercurrent as the Venetians build up for their first major invasion of sightseers at Easter. By April the tourism industry is cranked up to full operational capacity: all the hotels, museums and galleries have reopened: the gondolas

Climate Statistics

Average Temperatures in °C (°F)

Jan	April	July	Oct
6 (43)	15 (60)	25 (77)	15 (60)

Average Rainfall in mm

Jan	April	July	Oct
58	77	37	66

are un-mothballed, the café tables have blossomed in the Piazza. In June even the Italians are considering a trip to the beach.

In July and August elbow-room is at a premium. Peripheral camping grounds are packed, queues at the tourist office's room-finding service stretch longer and longer, and the police are kept busy reminding the hordes that there's no more sleeping out and no picnicking in Piazza San Marco. The heat can be sweltering, the canals pungent, the ancient city gasping under a flood of cameras, shorts, sunglasses and rucksacks. Scores head off to the Lido for relief; a sudden thunderstorm over the Lagoon livens things up, as do the many festivals. In autumn the city and the Venetians begin to unwind, the rains begin to fall and you can watch them pack up the parasols and beach huts on the Lido with a wistful sigh.

Crime and the Police

Venice is a very safe place, even for lone women (though the dark, narrow alleyways can be a bit disconcerting when there's no one else about). However, while bag- or camera-snatching from the back of a passing motorbike is not an option here, pickpockets are always a danger in crowded places (including *vaporetti*).

Any crime (violent or otherwise) should be reported to the police, either the light blue and grey clad **Polizia di Stato** (state police) or the black clad and red trimmed **Carabinieri** (the military arm of the police). Though it is unlikely that a stolen camera will turn up, you will need an official report for insurance purposes – go to the nearest police station (*questura* or *commissariato; see* p.84) and this '*denuncia*' will be typed up (you will be

Police Stations

Polizia di Stato

Castello 50/56, Fondamenta San Lorenzo, **t** 041 270 5511; **vaporetto** San Zaccaria; K6–7.
Santa Croce 500, Piazzale Roma, **t** 041 271 5511; **vaporetto** Piazzale Roma; C3.

Carabinieri

Cannaregio 4876, Campo dei Gesuiti, **t** 041 277 0714; **vaporetto** Fondamenta Nuove; I3.
Castello 4693A, Campo San Zaccaria, **t** 041 520 477; **vaporetto** San Zaccaria; K7.
Piazza San Marco, **t** 041 277 0984; **vaporetto** San Marco; I7. In 2002 this office was set up in the inner courtyard next to Caffè Florian in Piazza San Marco expressly to deal with thefts and the like from tourists.

required to state exactly when, where and how the crime happened) and stamped, and a copy will be given to you. If, by some miracle, your stolen property is dumped by the thief and then found again by an honest citizen, it may turn up at one of the lost property deposits in the city, so it's worth checking the numbers below.

Lost or stolen passports should also be reported to the consulate and credit cards to the relevant emergency numbers.

Police, **t** 113
Carabinieri emergency number, **t** 112
Lost property (Municipio), **t** 041 274 8225
Lost property (trains), **t** 041 785 238
Lost property (vaporetti), **t** 041 272 2179

Disabled Travellers

Thanks to the efforts of Venice's Institute for Architecture and its Veneziapertutti (Venice For All) campaign launched several years ago, the labyrinth opened up a little for visitors with disabilities or limited access. The agency for the promotion of tourism, the APT, has now taken over, with continued efforts to build ramps and install lifts all over the city.

There are four bridges in Venice with **chair lifts**: Ponte Goldoni, Ponte Manin, Ponte del Teatro a San Luca and Ponte dei Frati a Sant' Angelo. To obtain a key for the lifts (which

you can keep after you leave; they work for all chair lifts in Italy), go to the Informahandicap office (see below), the URP office of the comune (San Marco 4137, Ca' Farsetti, **t** 041 274 8080, open Mon, Wed and Fri 9–1, Tues and Thurs 9–1 and 3–5), or any of the tourist offices listed on p.92.

The city's other 407 bridges still present the major obstacle in getting around, but by judicious use of the vaporetti a good proportion of the city becomes accessible. With the exception of Lines 52 and 13, all the boat transport listed on pp.78–80 is wheelchair-friendly; as a rule the vaporetti are accessible and the smaller motoscafi are not.

The tourist office's **Venice–Lido** map no.1 indicates the parts of the city easily accessible by wheelchair (shaded in orange).

Total wheelchair accessibility is listed for the main sights in this guide, but of course many churches and museums have one or two small steps up, so accessibility depends very much on your personal circumstances. Venice's tourist offices have lists of accessible hotels, churches, monuments, gardens and public offices, and toilets with facilities for the disabled; you can write ahead for free copies (see 'Tourist Information', p.92).

For further information on accessibility on buses and vaporetti, call the ACTV on **t** 041 528 7886; for trains, call **t** 041 785 570. There are free parking places for holders of a valid disabled badge in the council car park at Piazzale Roma. The new Marco Polo airport is fully accessible for wheelchair users, both in arrivals and departures. If you need particular help, call **t** 041 260 3620, but it is normally the airline that arranges assistance.

Informahandicap is a helpful council-run organization providing information for disabled people on the accessibility of Venice's museums, monuments, hotels and the like. Staff freely admit that this information has never been thoroughly checked so be prepared for surprises, but its guide to all the museums and monuments in the city, published in Italian by the **AIAS** is extremely detailed and accurate (it will tell you how to get, for example, to the Accademia from the *vaporetto*, what steps, bridges and narrow *calle* you will encounter on the way, how many steps there are into the gallery, which parts of it are accessible, whether there is an adapted WC, etc.).

AIAS (Italian Spastics Association), *Viale Viareggio 42, 33038 Spinea, VE, t 041 991 520, e giamlav@tin.it, w www.aiasnazionale.it*.

Informahandicap, *Mestre, Viale Garibaldi 155, t 041 534 1700, f 041 534 2257, e informa handicap@comunevenezia, w www.comune. venezia.it/handicap*.

The public toilets listed on p.92 are accessible to wheelchair users and cost €0.50.

Organizations in the UK

Access Travel, *6 The Hillock, Astley, Lancashire M29 7GW, t (01942) 888 844, f (01942) 891 811, e info@access-travel.co.uk, w www.access-travel.co.uk*. Travel agent for disabled people: special air fares, car hire, etc.

Can Be Done, *7–11 Kensington High St, London W8 5NP, t (020) 8907 2400, f (020) 8909 1854, w www.canbedone.co.uk*. Tailored city breaks.

Holiday Care Service, *2nd Floor, Imperial Buildings, Victoria Rd, Horley, Surrey, RH6 7PZ, t (01293) 774 535, f (01293) 784 647, Minicom t (01293) 776 943, e holiday.care@virgin.net, w www.holidaycare.org.uk*. Provides up-to-date information on travel.

RADAR (Royal Association for Disability and Rehabilitation), *12 City Forum, 250 City Rd, London ECIV 8AF, t (020) 7250 3222, f (020) 7250 0212, Minicom t (020) 7250 4119, w www.radar.org.uk*. Information and books on all aspects of travel.

Organizations in the USA

Accessible Journeys, *35 West Sellers Av, Ridley Park, PA 19078, t 800 846 4537, f (610) 521 6959, w www.disabilitytravel.com*. Group tours and independent travel.

Mobility International USA, *PO Box 10767, Eugene, OR 97440, USA, t/TTY (541) 343 1284, f (541) 343 6812, e info@miusa.org, w www. miusa.org*. Information on international educational exchange programmes and volunteer service overseas for the disabled.

Rollaround Travel, *239 Commercial Street, Malden, MA 02148, t (781) 322 8197, f (781) 322 3031, w www.rollaround.org*. Specialist travel agency with contacts all over Europe.

SATH (Society for Accessible Travel and Hospitality), *347 5th Av, Suite 610, New York, NY 10016, t (212) 447 7284, w www.sath.org*. Travel and access information.

Other Useful Contacts

Access Ability, *w www.access-ability.co.uk*. Information on travel agencies catering specifically to disabled people.

Access Tourism, *w www.accesstourism.com*. Pan-European website.

Australian Council for Rehabilitation of the Disabled (ACROD), *PO Box 60, Curtin, ACT 2605, Australia, t/TTY (02) 6682 4333, w www.acrod.org.au*. Information and contact numbers for specialist travel agents.

Disabled Persons Assembly, *PO Box 27-524, Wellington 6035, New Zealand, t (04) 801 9100, w www.dpa.org.nz*. All-round source for travel information.

Emerging Horizons, *e horizons@emerging horizons.com, w www.emerginghorizons. com*. International on-line travel newsletter for people with disabilities.

Electricity, Weights and Measures

The **voltage** in Venice is 220 AC, and outlets take two round prongs; try to pick up an adaptor before you leave or at the airport as they are hard to find in the city.

Italy uses the **metric** system.

1 centimetre = 0.394 inches
1 metre = 3.094 feet
1 kilometre = 0.621 miles
1 kilogramme (1,000g) = 2.2 pounds
1 litre = 0.264 gallons (1.76 pints)
1 inch = 2.54 centimetres
1 foot = 0.305 metres
1 mile = 1.6 kilometres
1 pound = 0.454 kilogrammes
1 ounce = 25 grammes
1 liquid pint = 0.473 litres
1 gallon = 3.785 litres

Embassies and Consulates

There are no embassies and few consulates in Venice; you will need to contact Rome embassies or Milan consulates.

In Italy

Australia: *Via Alessandria 215, Rome,* *t 06 445 981.*

Canada: *Via GB de Rossi 27, Rome,* *t 06 68 30 73 16.*

Ireland: *Piazza Campitelli 3, Rome,* *t 06 697 9121.*

New Zealand: *Via Zara 28, Rome,* *t 06 441 7171.*

UK: *Palazzo Querini, Accademia, Dorsoduro 1051,* *t 041 522 7207;* ***vaporetto*** *Accademia.*

USA: *Via Vittorio Veneto 119, Rome,* *t 06 46741.*

Abroad

Canada: *275 Slater St, Ottawa, Ontario K1P 5HG,* *t (613) 232 2401,* *f (613) 233 1484,* *e ambital@italyincanada.com,* *w www.italy incanada.com.* Consulates in Toronto, Montreal and Vancouver.

Ireland: *63/65 Northumberland Road, Dublin 4,* *t (01) 660 1744,* *f (01) 668 2759,* *e italianembassy@eircom.net.*

UK: *14 Three Kings Yard, London W1Y 4EH,* *t (020) 7312 2200,* *f (020) 7312 2230,* *e emblondon@embitaly.org.uk,* *w www. embitaly.org.uk.* Consulates in Edinburgh, Manchester and Bedford.

USA: *3000 Whitehaven St, NW Washington DC 20008,* *t (202) 612 4400,* *f (202) 518 2154,* *e stampa@itwash.org,* *w www.italyemb.org.* Consulates in most major cities.

Etiquette

A no bare shoulders, no bare knees code is strictly enforced at St Mark's. Respectful attire while visiting other churches will reflect well on you. Large hats should be removed, mobile phones switched off, and smoking, kissing, eating and loud talking avoided. Venetians tend to be both more charming and more assertive than British people, who should be prepared to adjust their style a little to get along and to get served in shops, restaurants and the like.

Gay and Lesbian Venice

Although the Gay Jubileum Day was not part of the Vatican's Holy Year 2000 programme, the Pope at one point conceded that homosexuals are all God's children, too – as long as they remain chaste. Straight Italians tend to be of two minds about the gay community. In the most general sense, in Italy as elsewhere, left-wingers tend to support gay rights, and right-wingers do not.

On top of this, Venice is certainly not a city with a thriving gay or lesbian culture, and you will find no clubs or places specifically for gays. There are a couple of evening cruising areas: the Muro del Pianto between the Accademia and San Marco and Alberoni beach at the south end of the Lido.

Arcigay Dedalo, *Mestre, Via A. Costa 38A,* *w www.gay.it/arcigay, www.women.it/ arciles.* Meetings are held in this centre on the first Tues of each month, 9–11pm.

Gay helpline, *t 041 538 4151. Open Mon 7–9pm and Thurs 9–11pm.*

Italy's gay website, *w www.gay.it.* Look under the Veneto region.

Il Lato Azzuro, *Via Forti 6, Sant'Erasmo,* *t 041 523 0642.* Gay-friendly hotel on this quiet island; Venice is a boat-ride away.

Metro Venezia, *Mestre, Via Cappuccina 82b,* *t 041 538 4299,* *w www.metroclub.it.* ***Open*** *2pm–2am.* Gay club with sauna and massage rooms.

Palazzo Pompeo, *Castello 6113, Borgoloco P. Molmenti,* *t 041 277 8544.* Gay-friendly hotel.

Health, Emergencies and Insurance

Ambulance, *t 041 523 0000*
Medical emergencies, *t 118*

If you have an accident or become seriously ill, go to the casualty (first aid), or *Pronto*

Soccorso (Accident and Emergency) department of these hospitals.

City Hospital, *Campo Santi Giovanni e Paolo, Castello,* **t** *041 529 4516;* **vaporetto** *Ospedale Civile; J5.*

Ospedale del Mare, *1 Lungomare d'Annunzio, Lido, Pronto Soccorso* **t** *041 529 4111, central switchboard* **t** *041 529 4111;* **vaporetto** *Lido; off maps.*

If you need a doctor at night or on public holidays ring the Guardia Medica, **t** 041 529 4060.

If it's not too serious, go to a **chemist** – Italian pharmacists are trained to diagnose minor ills and can give you prescription drugs (although you'll pay full price for the remedy). Several *farmacie* are open all night on a rotating basis: the addresses are in the window of each, or you can ring **t** 041 531 1592 for a list, or find them in *Un Ospite di Venezia* (*see* p.92).

National medical coverage in the UK and Canada covers their citizens while they're travelling in Italy (in Britain, pick up form E111 from a post office or your local office of the Department of Health and Social Security before you leave). Nationals of other countries may want to take out **travel insurance** if their current policy fails to cover them while abroad. Travel agents offer policies that cover not only health, but stolen or lost baggage, and cancelled or missed flights.

Internet

The concept of the Internet or Cyber Caffè is not widely diffused in Italy. Most Internet points in Venice are just that: offices where you can use a computer and access the Internet but not buy food or drink.

The following Internet points offer all the usual services, but there are many more all over town.

Café Noir, *Dorsoduro 3805, Crosera,* **t** *041 710 925;* **vaporetto** *San Tomà; E6.* **Open** *daily 10am–2am.* Busy, studenty café with computers in the back room.

Crearte, *San Polo 1083, Calle del Luganegher,* **t** *041 241 1100;* **vaporetto** *San*

Silvestro, G5–6. Also offers graphic and web page design services.

The Netgate, *Dorsoduro 3812A, Crosera,* **t** *041 244 0213;* **vaporetto** *San Tomà; E6.*

Net House, *San Marco, Campo Santo Stefano,* **t** *041 2771190;* **vaporetto** *Sant'Angelo/San Samuele/Accademia; F7–8.* **Open** *daily 24 hours.* Serves coffee and drinks.

Venetian Navigator, *S. Marco 676, Spadaria,* **t** *041 241 1293;* **vaporetto** *San Marco; I7.*

Lost Property

Depending on where you lose an item, contact one of the following:

ACTV, *Piazzale Roma,* **t** *041 272 2179; C3.* **Open** *daily 8–7.30.* Buses or boats.

Comune, *San Marco 4136, Riva del Carbon,* **t** *041 274 8225; H6.* **Open** *Mon and Wed 8–12.30 and 2.30–4.20, Tues, Thurs and Fri 8–12.30.* Streets, restaurants, public places.

Stazione S. Lucia, **t** *041 785 238; D4.* **Open** *Mon–Fri 8–4.* On trains or at the station.

Media

Most of the main news-stands sell British **newspapers** (which arrive the same evening in the summer months) and British and American glossy mags (*Vogue, Elle, Harpers* and the like), but they come at a high price—the *Sunday Times* costs about€3.80. The only American paper available is the *Herald Tribune*, which has an *Italy Daily* insert. The same insert also comes with the Italian language *Corriere della Sera*. Smaller news-stands stock *Time* and *Newsweek*. For Italian-speakers, *Panorama* and *L'Espresso* are good weekly current affairs magazines with some excellent journalism (in Italian).

Of the national dailies, *La Repubblica*, a reliable centre-left bet, has a 'Venezia' insert. Venice's most popular dailies are *Il Gazzetino* and *La Nuova Venezia*. Both are good sources of what's on listings. Local listings magazines include the monthly *Venezia News* in both English and Italian. *Boom* and *Aladino* are weekly free small ads papers that include job and accommodation ads.

Italian **television** is pretty dire, and even the more 'serious', state-owned RAI channels (1, 2 and 3) are dominated by game and quiz shows and by appalling 'variety' shows featuring an amazing amount of almost bare bums and cleavage. Many hotels, at least those of two stars and up, now have satellite TV, which includes Sky, CNN and BBC World.

You can get the BBC's schedule of **radio** broadcasts to Italy by writing to Auntie at Casella Postale 203, Roma 00100 (though you can nearly always find the BBC if you fiddle with the dial long enough). The US Armed Forces radio comes in after sunset at 1107AM, with major league baseball games nightly during the season beginning around 2am local time.

Money, Banks and Taxes

On 1 January 1999 the **euro** became the official currency of Italy (and 10 other nations of the European Union) and lire notes were no longer accepted after 17 February 2002. The euro is divided into 100 cents. Notes come in denominations of 5, 10, 20, 50, 100, 200 and 500 euros; coins come in denominations of 1, 2, 5, 10, 20 and 50 cents, and 1 and 2 euros. At the time of writing, the euro was worth UK£0.65, US$0.94 and C$1.47.

Traveller's cheques are the safest way of carrying money, but the wide acceptance of **credit and debit cards** and the presence of ATMs (*distributeurs de billets*), at banks and post offices, make using a card a convenient alternative. The types of card accepted are marked on each machine, and most give instructions in English. Check with your bank before you leave whether your debit/cash cards can be used in Italy. Credit-card companies charge a fee for cash advances, but rates are often better than those at banks.

Nearly every hotel accepts at least Mastercard and Visa (though you would be prudent to check in advance with one- and two-star hotels), while those with three stars or more accept most cards. Most shops and restaurants in the main tourist paths accept credit cards; others, frequented mostly by

Banks and Bureaux de Change

Head offices of major banks in Venice are all clustered in the *sestiere* of San Marco (*vaporetto* San Marco).

Banca Commerciale Italiana, *Via XXII Marzo 2188, t 041 529 6811; vaporetto San Marco; H8.*

Banca Nazionale del Lavoro, *Bacino Orseolo 1188, t 041 667 511; vaporetto San Marco; H7.*

Banco di Roma, *Merceria dell'Orologio 191, t 041 662 411; vaporetto San Marco/Rialto; I7.*

Banco San Marco, *Calle Larga S. Marco 383, t 041 529 3711; vaporetto San Marco/Rialto; I7.*

Credito Italiano, *Campo S. Salvatore, t 041 522 6330; vaporetto Rialto; H6.*

Deutsche Banca, *Via XXII Marzo 2216, t 041 520 0766; vaporetto San Marco; H8.*

Places that exchange money outside normal banking hours include:

American Express, *San Moisè 1471, t 041 520 0844, vaporetto San Marco; H8. Open Mon–Sat 9–7.45 (winter 9–5).*

CIT, *Piazza S. Marco 1261, t 041 241 1922, vaporetto Vallaresso, I7. Open Mon–Sat 8–6.*

Thomas Cook, *San Marco 5126, Riva del Ferro, t 041 528 7358, vaporetto Rialto; H6. Open Mon–Sat 9–6, Sun 9.30–5.*

Venetians, probably don't. The listings chapters of this guide state 'No Cards' whenever cards are not accepted.

Banking hours are Mon–Fri 8.30–1.30 and 2.35–3.35.

Lost/Stolen Cards

American Express, *(international collect) t 06 336 668 5110.*

Visa/Eurocard, *(freephone) t 800 018548.*

Diners Club, *(freephone) t 800 864 034.*

VAT Refunds

Value-added tax (VAT, or IVA in Italy) is charged at 20 per cent on clothing, wine and luxury goods. On consumer goods it is already included in the amount shown on the price tag, whereas on services it may be added later. Non-EU citizens are entitled to a VAT refund on certain items under the Retail Export Scheme. You cannot get a refund on hotel and restaurant bills.

To get your refund, shop with your passport and ask for an invoice itemizing the article, price and tax paid. When you depart Italy, take the goods and invoice to the customs office at the point of departure and have the invoice stamped. You need to do this at your last stop in the EU. Once home, and within 90 days of the purchase date, mail the stamped invoice (keeping a copy) to the shop or store, which is legally required to send you a VAT rebate. You'll get around 16.5 per cent back once post and admin are deducted. Shops that do not advertise tax-free services may be reluctant to get involved with official invoices, but the law entitles you to a refund.

For anyone who spends more than €150 at a go, many stores participate in the Tax Free Shopping scheme – you'll recognize the sign displayed in shop windows – which will do all the admin for you for a small fee. Get your invoices stamped at customs as above, then take them to one of the counters conveniently located at airports and your money will be refunded in cash on the spot, or as a refund to your debit or credit card.

Opening Hours and Public Holidays

General opening hours for **shops** and offices are Mon–Sat 8 or 9–1 and 4–7.30, although many tourist shops stay open during the siesta, and even on Sundays and holidays. Many shops (except grocers) are closed Monday morning and on 21 November for the *Festa della Salute*; markets and grocers tend to close on Wednesday afternoons.

No two **museums** keep the same hours, so consult the listings. Many **churches** take a lunch break, generally between 12 and 4; again, we've noted their hours wherever possible. Many museums close on Christmas Day, New Year's Day and 1st May. Some **hotels** close for a break some time in winter; check the individual listings for information. **Restaurants** often close for a couple of weeks in early January and in August; again, this has been noted where relevant.

> ### Public Holidays
> **1 Jan** New Year's Day (*Capo d'Anno*)
> **6 Jan** *La Befana*
> **Mar/April** Easter Monday
> **25 April** Liberation Day and St Mark's Feast Day
> **1 May** Labour Day
> **15 Aug** Assumption of the BVM
> **1 Nov** All Saints' Day (*Tutti Santi*)
> **21 Nov** *Festa della Salute*
> **8 Dec** Immaculate Conception of the Blessed Virgin Mary
> **25–26 Dec** Santo Stefano

For bank and post office opening hours, *see* 'Money' and 'Post and Fax'.

Shops, banks, offices and schools in Venice are also closed on official national holidays (*see* box). Some places also take the festival of Il Redentore (third Saturday and Sunday in July) as a public holiday.

Packing

Venetians, like all Italians, love to dress up and won't venture out unless they look as they always have: elegant slaves to fashion. They are also historically accustomed to seeing oddly costumed foreigners and except in churches rarely bat an eyelid at halter-tops, shorts, T-shirts and ridiculous hats. Comfortable shoes are absolutely essential: the city on the water demands a great deal of walking. Bring rain gear or an umbrella unless you're travelling in the height of summer. Be warned that film and books in English cost twice as much as at home. Opera glasses or binoculars and a small torch may come in handy in gloomy churches, or to find your way home along the side canals on a moonless night.

Photography

Film and developing are much more expensive than they are in the USA or UK. You are not allowed to take pictures in most museums or in some churches.

Post and Fax

The Italian postal system is the worst in Europe, and if you're only spending a week or two in Venice, you'll almost certainly be home before your letters and postcards. However, **Posta Prioritaria** and the more expensive **Postacelere** are new special-delivery services from the post office that guarantee delivery within 24 hours in Italy and 3–5 days abroad. Light letters and post-cards up to 20g sent as Posta Prioritaria to the USA and Canada cost €0.82, to anywhere in the EU €0.62. Make sure you buy the special gold PP stamps.

If it matters when your post arrives, or if you want to send a package and avoid the incredibly fussy Posta Italiana red tape, try one of the international couriers such as **DHL, t** (800) 345 345.

Post Offices

The central Venetian branch of the postal service is at Fondaco dei Tedeschi, near Ponte Rialto (*open Mon–Sat 8.15–7.25; I5*). If you're having mail sent *poste restante* to Venice, have it addressed *Fermo Posta*, Fondaco dei Tedeschi 80100 and pick it up with your passport.

There are other post offices at the foot of Piazza San Marco (Calle dell'Ascensione) and at western end of the Zattere, although you can purchase stamps at any tobacco shop.

Faxes

There are fax machines in many *cartolerie* (stationers' shops). Most hotels will also be happy to send a fax for you.

Religious Affairs

Venetians have always liked to go to church, some for piety's sake, some for the music, and some to flirt. The average Mass was drowned in chatter until the priest raised the Host, when all dropped to their knees in silence, only to continue as rowdily as ever afterwards. Today Venetians are among the most pious Italians, and when you want to visit a church, chances are a

Church Services
Catholic

St Mark's, t *041 522 5697; **vaporetto** San Marco; I7.* Mass in Latin, Sun 11.30am, 12.30pm and 6.45pm.

San Giorgio Maggiore, t *041 528 9900; **vaporetto** Salute; J10.* Mass with Gregorian chant, Sun 11am.

San Moisè, t *041 528 5840; **vaporetto** Vallaresso; H8.* Readings in English, Sun 7pm.

Non-Catholic

Anglican: *St George's, Campo San Vio 870, Dorsoduro, t 041 520 0571; **vaporetto** Accademia; F8.* Sun, sung Eucharist 10.30am; Evensong 6pm.

Evangelical Waldensian and Methodist: *Campo Santa Maria Formosa 5170; **vaporetto** Rialto; J6.* Sun 11am.

Greek Orthodox: *San Giorgio, Ponte dei Greci 3412, t 041 522 7016; **vaporetto** San Zaccaria; K7.* Sun 9.30am and 10.30am.

Jewish: *Campo del Ghetto Vecchio, t 041 715 012; **vaporetto** Ponte delle Guglie; E2.* Sat 9.30am.

Lutheran Evangelical: *Campo Santi Apostoli 4443; **vaporetto** Ca' d'Oro; I4.* 2nd and 4th Sun of month, 10.30am.

Mass will be going on that you ought not to interrupt. Persevere, and bring a handful of coins for the lights. *See* box above for service times.

Smoking

Italy is still a great nation of smokers, although recent legislation has banned smoking in public offices (post offices, banks, etc.), on public transport (although trains have smoking compartments) and in any public places with inadequate air filtering. However, these rules are frequently ignored, and you are unlikely to get much sympathy if you ask someone to stop blowing smoke in your face in a restaurant or in a non-smoking railway carriage. Non-smoking rooms in Italian hotels are rare, as are non-smoking sections in bars and restaurants (although

Venice itself has a surprising number of restaurants that ban smoking altogether).

Tobacconists (*tabacchi*) display a blue and white 'T' sign outside the shop; they and some bars sell cigarettes, which are cheaper than in the UK.

Students

For information about student discounts, see p.82. Studenty areas of Venice are Campo Santa Margherita, the bars and cafés along the Fondamenta della Misericordia and the area around the university at Ca' Foscari. See p.93 for information about long stays.

Courses for Students

Benedict School, *Frezzeria 1688,* **t** *041 522 4034;* **vaporetto** *San Marco; H7.* Language classes by the month.

Dante Alighieri Institute, *near the Arsenale,* **t** *041 528 9127;* **vaporetto** *Arsenale; L7.* Morning language classes, 10–12.

European Centre for Training Craftsmen, *in the Conservation of the Architectural Heritage, Isola di San Servolo,* **t** *041 526 8546.* Design workshops and architecture courses.

Fondazione Giorgio Cini, *on the islet of San Giorgio Maggiore,* **t** *041 528 9900,* **w** *www.cini.it;* **vaporetto** *San Giorgio; J10.* Europe's only school of comparative music, financed by UNESCO, holds forth during April–September with lectures, concerts, lessons and workshops.

Istituto Superiore di Architettura e Disegno, *Palazzo Papafava, Cannaregio 3762,* **t** *041 522 4414.* Design workshops.

Italian Institute, *39 Belgrave Square, London SW1X 8NX,* **t** *(020) 7235 1461; or 686 Park Ave, New York, NY 10021,* **t** *(212) 879 4242.* For information, and possible scholarships.

Università degli Studi di Venezia, *Ca' Foscari, Dorsoduro 3246,* **t** *041 234 8111,* **w** *www.unive.it;* **vaporetto** *Accademia; E7.* Literature, philosophy and languages.

Università Internazionale dell'Arte, *Palazzo Fortuny, San Marco 3780* **t** *041 524 0616;* **vaporetto** *Sant'Angelo; G7.* Courses in art restoration and stage design, October–April.

Venice Institute, *Dorsoduro 3116A, Campo Santa Margherita* **t** *041 522 4331;* **vaporetto** *Ca' Rezzonico; D7.* Language classes by the month.

Telephones

Beware: there's no uniformity in the number of digits for Italian phone numbers; since they range from nine to 11, it's easy to think you're a digit short. The Venice code (041) must be dialled even from within the city.

Venice is fairly well supplied with public telephones, along the pavements, in bars and in most other public places. Some call boxes accept €0.10, €0.20, €0.50 and €1 coins (€0.10 should be enough for a short, inter-city call), but most now work with phonecards instead: *Scheda Telefonica* are available from tobacconists for €2.58, €5.16 and €7.75. Once you call long-distance the telephone becomes a real hog so don't even try it for international calls: get a pre-paid international phonecard (also available from tobacconists) that uses a toll-free number.

The telephone **country code** for the UK is 00 44, for the USA and Canada 00 1; for Australia 00 61. To call Italy before you leave, dial the country code of 00 39. For information (in English) on international calls, dial 176; on calling with your credit card, or to reverse the charges (*reversibile*), 170.

Time

Italy is always one hour ahead of Greenwich Mean Time and generally six hours ahead of Eastern Standard Time in the USA.

Tipping

Refreshingly, there is not a lot of pressure in Italy to leave major tips. It is customary to round restaurant bills up to the nearest euro or two; less in modest places.

A few coins are sometimes expected in public toilets for the caretaker. In hotels, the usual kinds of 'rules' apply: 10–15%, but it should reflect your general satisfaction with the service offered.

Toilets

Public ones do exist in Venice, but they are usually impossible to find without asking someone or getting a special map (published by the Azienda Multiservizi Ambientali Veneziana) from the tourist office. Around Piazza San Marco there's one in the **Giardinetti Reali** and in the **Albergo Diurno**, just on the other side of the Ala Napoleonica (Ramo Primo a Ascensione, signposted, open 8am–10pm; also showers, barbers, left luggage, etc.); other pay toilets (€0.50) are in **Calle della Bissa**, off Piazza San Bartolomeo; at **San Leonardo**; just north of the **Rialto Bridge**; right in front of the Accademia; at **Bregora** in Castello; in **Piazzale Roma**, in Santa Croce; and in **Campo San Bartolomeo** in San Marco.

They are open from 7 or 8am to 8pm and are all wheelchair accessible.

You can also find nice hygienic facilities in most museums, at Piazzale Roma, and at the railway station (though here it will cost you €1). Otherwise, duck in a bar, as most Italians do, although in main tourist nodes you're likely to see signs saying there are no toilets, or that they're for the use of customers only (in most places, you aren't obliged to buy anything, although it's good form to do so).

Tourist Information

The main source in English for current events is *Un Ospite di Venezia*, a small fortnightly magazine distributed free at tourist offices (*see* also website, in box)

Abroad

Australia: *Level 26–44 Market Street, NSW 2000 Sydney, t (02) 92 621666, f (02) 92 621677, e lenitour@ihug.com.au.*

Canada: *175 Bloor Street East, Suite 907, South Tower, Toronto M4W 3R8 (ON), t (416) 925 4882, t 925 3725, f (416) 925 4799, w www. italiantourism.com.*

New Zealand: *c/o Italian Embassy, 34 Grant Road, Thorndon, Wellington, t (04) 736065.*

UK: *Italian State Tourist Board, 1 Princes Street, London W1R 8AY, t (020) 7408 1254,*

Useful Websites

www.actv.it. Public transport (boats and buses) in Venice.
www.comune.venezia.it. The council site.
www.comune.venezia.it-museicivici. The official site of the municipal museums.
www.jewishvenice.org. For Jewish info.
www.regione.veneto.it/cultura. Information on events in the Veneto region.
www.trenitalia.it. The official website of the Italian State Railways
www.turismovenezia.it. The official tourist board site.
www.unospitedivenezia.it. Website of the listings and info magazine produced by the hotel concierge association.
www.venice-carnival.com. Carnival info.

f (020) 7493 6695, w www.enit.it, w www. italiantourism.com; **Italian Embassy**, *14 Three Kings Yard, Davies St, London W1Y 2EH, t (020) 7312 2200, f (020) 7312 2230, w www.embitaly. org.uk.*

USA: *630 Fifth Avenue, Suite 1565, New York, NY 10111, t (212) 245 5095/4822, f (212) 586 9249; 500 N Michigan Avenue, Suite 2240, Chicago, IL 60611, t (312) 644 0996, f (312) 644 3019; 12400 Wilshire Boulevard, Suite 550, Los Angeles, CA 90025, t (310) 820 1898/9807, f (310) 820 6357, w www.italiantourism.com.*

In Venice

Opening times for the following vary throughout the year and from year to year, but on the whole they are open from 9 or 10am to 6pm daily.

Palazzina dei Santi, *in the Giardini Reali, by Piazza San Marco, t 041 522 5150/529 8730;* **vaporetto** *Vallaresso; I8*. The main office.

The branch offices at **Venice Pavilion** (t 041 529 8730; *vaporetto* San Marco); at **Santa Lucia train station** (t 041 529 8727; *vaporetto* Ferrovia) and the bus station in **Piazzale Roma** (t 041 2411499; *vaporetto* Piazzale Roma) offer accommodation services.

There are also offices on the **Rotonda Marghera** (t 041 937 764), at **Marco Polo Airport** (t 041 541 5887) and on the **Lido** at Gran Viale 6 (t 041 526 5721).

Women Travellers

Italy is a relatively safe country for women travelling alone, although you may find yourself hassled by men. This is rarely threatening, but it can be annoying and persistent; the best way to deal with such advances is to ignore them and walk away.

Venice is safe at night, although it's prudent to avoid the station area and the car parks.

Working and Long Stays

Whether you're coming to Venice to work, study, retire, or just live for more than three months, you will save yourself a lot of trouble by getting the appropriate visa before you arrive. If you're an EU citizen, this may not even be necessary, but do check.

Studying in Venice

Students (see p.91) will require a declaration from an Italian consulate certifying that they have been accepted to study in Italy, and will have to prove that they've taken out health insurance. (British nationals need only the E111 form that entitles them to medical coverage in Italy, see p.87).

Living in Venice becomes much easier if you hone your Italian and take a course: see p.91 for a list of language schools in Venice. Your school may be able to help you with lodgings, or you can try for one of a handful of **furnished rooms** in the city (tourist offices have up-to-date listings).

Registration and Residency

Upon arrival in Venice, anyone who plans to live in the city or stay for more than three months should go to the police station (*Questura*) in Marghera (Via Nicolodi 21, **t** 041 271 5767), where the *Ufficio Stranieri* will issue a *permesso di soggiorno*. Once you have your *permesso* you can go to the *Ufficio Anagrafe* or Municipal Registry Office (**t** 041 270 8111) to get your residence certificate. This document entitles you to move household goods and vehicles into Italy within six months without

paying duty or taxes. If you are coming to Venice to work, your employer may require you to take up residency to keep things nice and legal. The problem comes if you're looking for a flat to rent. Because of rent control many landlords will only let to foreign non-resident tenants.

Finding Accommodation

One unavoidable fact is that Venice is expensive; the main reason is the cost of transporting goods from the mainland by boat and porter.

Renting

Rents for a one-bedroom flat in reasonable condition in a 'nice' area range from about €750 to €900 per month. Nearly all business is done through estate agents, though check the papers and ask around in local bars.

Estate agents who deal in rentals include:

Cannavò, *Via S. Gallo 5/a, Lido,* **t** *041 526 0071; **vaporetto** Lido SME; off maps.*

Ferro, *Via Cerigo 7, Lido,* **t** *041 526 0006; **vaporetto** Lido SME; off maps.* Also seasonal lets.

Giaretta, *Calle degli Orbi 5212, Castello,* **t** *041 520 9747; **vaporetto** San Zaccaria; J6.*

House Deal Consulting, *Castello 5274/a,* **t** *041 520 9352, **f** 528 9671; **vaporetto** San Zaccaria; J6.*

Narduzzi Immobiliare, *Campo S. Luca 4578,* **t** *041 520 8111; **vaporetto** Rialto; H6.*

S. Angelo, *Campo S. Angelo 3818, S. Marco,* **t** *041 522 1505; **vaporetto** Sant'Angelo; G7.*

If you're renting, most landlords insist on a **deposit** of two, and sometimes three months, in advance, and it can be the devil to get it all back when you leave, even if you give the required three months' notice (note: *contessa*-landladies are especially bad about it). If you find your flat through an estate agent, commission is usually 10% of the first year's rent. Rental leases are signed through a *commercialista* who represents both you and the landlord and is paid to know all the complicated legal niceties. The lease (usually for one year) may very well specify that you are not to become a resident.

Buying

The current rate for an unrestored property in a 'nice' area is about €3,615; for a restored property it is about €5,165. This means that a three-bedroom place measuring about 12 m square might cost about €380,000/€610,000 unrestored/restored.

Chances are what you find is going to need some major restoration (for instance, nearly half the houses lack decent bathrooms, and many have subsided to some degree) and it doesn't come cheaply, especially if you want to have it done properly, by Venetians who have a feel for the unique quirks and materials of their watery home town. Before buying, have an independent estimate done on how much the repairs will cost. Then, if you still want to buy, make an offer, and if the seller accepts it, you'll be expected to pay 10–15% on signing an agreement called the *compromesso*, which penalizes either you or the seller if either party backs out. The paperwork is handled by a *notaio*, who works for you and the seller, though many people also hire a *commercialista* to look after their affairs. A payment schedule is worked out; Italian mortgages are usually for 50% of the selling price, payable over a 10-year period. Foreigners pay 10% more than Italians, but never have to pay rates. *Buying a Property: Italy* (Cadogan Guides, 2002) is an excellent source for all the details.

Finding a Job

Finding a job in Venice is probably harder than in any city in Italy. EU residents may register at the *Ufficio di Collocamento* (employment office) at Calle del Megio, San Stae; it occasionally publishes a list of available jobs in *Il Gazzettino* (look under the heading *Taccuino*, which lists events, night pharmacies, etc.). Both *Il Gazzettino* and *La Nuova Venezia* carry a few wanted ads. English-teaching jobs, the usual standby, are harder to find in Venice than anywhere else in Italy. English-speaking au pair, catering or secretarial jobs sometimes come up, though for the latter you won't get far without some Italian.

Finding a School

State schools in Italy offer a good, rounded education free to all children living in Italy (after you get all the proper documents translated into Italian and stamped, that is). Sending a young child to a *scuola elementare* (primary school) or *asilo* (nursery school/ kindergarten, run by the *comune* or nuns) will have him or her fluent in Italian in a matter of months. Foreign children adapt amazingly fast because the teachers and their peers are irresistibly helpful.

Translations: You never know when the Italian bureaucracy is going to demand an official translation of some fiddly bit of paper. Try **TER Centro Traduzioni**, Cannaregio 1076/c, Ramo San Zuane, **t** 041 524 2538 (*vaporetto* Ferrovia).

Piazza San Marco

ST MARK'S, PALAZZO DUCALE
AND AROUND 98
St Mark's Basilica 98
Palazzo Ducale (Doge's Palace) 108
The Campanile 114

PIAZZETTA SAN MARCO 115
The Two Columns 115
On the Waterfront 116

PIAZZETTA DEI LEONCINI 116
Torre dell'Orologio 116

THE PROCURATIE AND MUSEUMS 117
The Procuratie 117
Museo Correr 118
Biblioteca Nazionale Marciana 118
Museo Archeologico 119
Museo Diocesano 120

Piazza San Marco

There are few city squares in the world where you can easily spend an entire day exploring, or just dawdling as the rest of world goes by dressed in funny hats. But then again, few cities have so much psychologically concentrated in one place. The quay in Piazzetta San Marco is Venice's front door to the Lagoon and the East, its traditional lifeline and heartline; around

the rim stand not only the palaces of government and religion – the residence of the Doge, the mint, the state library, the prisons and place of public execution – but also St Mark's Basilica, which is not so much a church as a compact made between Venice and God. Arrive as early as you can to avoid the armies of Babylon, or linger late, to see the *piazza* as a masterpiece of urban design rather than a phenomenon of natural crowd control.

1 Lunch

Osteria San Marco, *S. Marco 1610, Frezzeria*, *t 041 528 5242*. *Open Mon–Sat 12.30–2.30 and 7.30–10.30*. *Expensive*. Plain, stylish *enoteca* with interesting food, not at all touristy.

2 Coffee

Caffè Florian, *Piazza San Marco, t 041 520 5641*. *Open daily 10am–midnight*. The essential nostalgic coffee stop, though expensive.

3 Drinks

Harry's Bar, *San Marco 1323, Calle Vallaresso*, *t 041 528 5777*. *Open daily 12–3 and 7–10.30*. *Very expensive*. For a classic Bellini.

Highlights

Medieval Venice: St Mark's Basilica, in particular its mosaics and Pala d'Oro, p.98

Renaissance Venice: The Doge's Palace, with its seriously big art, p.108

Baroque/Rococo Venice: Florian's and the Quadri, the last two 18th-century coffee-houses in Venice, p.117

Indoor Venice: Uncovering the secrets of the Council of Ten in the Secret Itinerary, p.112

Decadent Venice: The astonishing platform shoes in the Museo Correr, p.118

Pigeon Venice: Absolutely everything in Piazza San Marco, especially grazing tourists

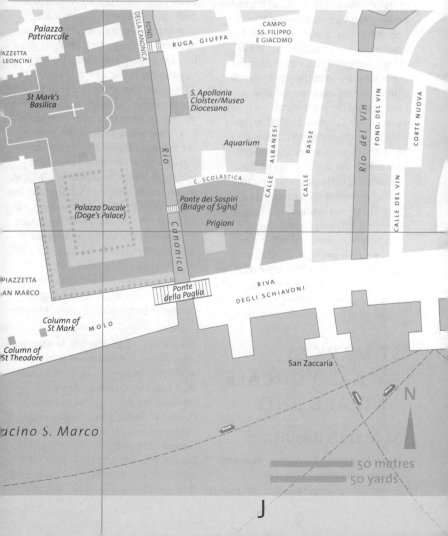

The World's Drawing Room

Piazza San Marco is the only square digni-fied enough to merit the title '*piazza*' in Venice, though this pickiness over names seems quaint now that the square has been co-opted by the rest of humanity. It isn't merely 'the world's heritage' but 'the world's drawing room' (Alfred De Musset), the only one 'worthy of having the sky for its roof'. The Venetians themselves joined in the act after the Second World War by dedicating their only *piazza* to peace; all the political parties unanimously voted never to hold rallies or demonstrations here. The tourist office estimates that about half the throng milling about the square will visit nothing else in Venice, and when their heads or cameras bob incessantly in your line of vision, as they invariably do, you might reflect that the *piazza* has been swarming with Venetians and foreigners alike since the 12th century. The world's nations may debate their ceasefires in New York, but to Venice and St Mark's Square they come, as they have for the past 500 years, for delight.

Whatever sensations of *déjà vu* most people bring to Piazza San Marco after seeing so many pictures never last for very long. The Venetians who walk through it day in and day out never tire of its magic, in all weathers or at any hour, whether the autumn *acque alte* have turned it into a gigantic looking-glass (they often do, as the *piazza* is the lowest point in the city); or in a winter fog, when everything – the pavement, the wings of the Procuratie, the pigeons, and even the mosaics of St Mark's – dissolve into pearly grey and white *sfumato* shadows; or in the summer, when it's filled with a chat-tering, jaunty, fun-fair crowd from the four corners of the globe. The café orchestras grind away, swinging out old jazz tunes the way only Europeans in starched shirts and bow ties can, while the huge banners flutter and the Basilica's golden mosaics catch the sun, and children bombard waddling pigeons with little bags of corn.

The *piazza* proper is flanked by two smaller squares, the Piazzetta dei Leoncini to the left of the Basilica, and the Piazzetta San Marco on the right, by the Lagoon. What regularity these spaces may appear to possess is dispelled by a single glance at the plan: the *piazza* is Italy's biggest trapezoid, 180 yards long and 60 yards wide before the Ala Napoleonica, 85 yards in front of St Mark's.

The square took a thousand years to evolve into this interesting shape, beginning in the 9th century, when the seat of government was moved to *Rivo Alto* from Malamocco, and the seaward islet of Morso used to support a new castle for the doge and a lighthouse (site of the Campanile). The islet already had two churches, San Theodore and San Geminiano, built by Justinian's general, the eunuch Narses, in the 550s in gratitude for Venice's support of Byzantium against Totila and the Goths. But most of Morso in the 9th century was planted with the vegetable gardens and orchards of San Zaccaria convent, and when the abbess donated these to the doge in 829 (when the

ST MARK'S, PALAZZO DUCALE AND AROUND

St Mark's Basilica 17

Piazza San Marco, t 041 522 5205; vaporetto San Marco; wheelchair accessible from Piazzetta dei Leoncini. Open Mon–Sat 9.30–5, Sun and hols 2–4.30; adm free. As is the case when visiting all Italian churches, men must wear a shirt and long trousers and women must have their shoulders covered, a minimum of décolletage, and no shorts. Queues can be diabolically long in season.

St Mark's Basilica crowns the head of the *piazza*; it's the most irresistible church in Christendom and national shrine of the Venetian state. Squint at it, and imagine the three great banners in front as sails, the first chapel of St Mark's was built) the *piazza* was born. It attained its current dimensions in the second half of the 12th century, thanks to the vision of the fabulously wealthy 'architect doge' Sebastiano Ziani, who filled in the canal that once traversed it, demolished Narses' church of San Geminiano, and transformed what had been a crenellated wall into porticoes for the Procurators of St Mark (now the Procuratie Vecchie). The *piazza* that evolved from the doge's foresight so pleased the Republic that later doges were forbidden to order even the least tinkering without the consent of the *Maggior Consiglio*.

As the only open space of any size in the city, the *piazza* quickly became the centre of Venetian social life, of religious processions and the great Sensa fair (*see* p.150), and of the triumphs of newly elected doges, who would be carried around the *piazza* on the shoulders of the Arsenal workers, tossing out handfuls of gold to the people. Inter-city sports and neighbourhood rivalries filled the *piazza* with crowds to watch death-defying feats like the human towers called 'the *forze* of Hercules', or 'the Turkish tightrope' where daredevils walked down a wire stretched from the top of the Campanile to a boat halfway to San Giorgio Maggiore, or the ghastly Renaissance sport of binding a cat to a post to see who could butt it to death with a shaven head. Jousts and tournaments were held here, one attended by Petrarch, who declared Venice 'a nation of sailors, horsemen and beauties'. The second seems surprising, for the Venetians in the saddle were a

standing joke. But it is a fact that one of the bells in the Campanile was named the 'Trotter', warning senators that the council session was about to begin and they ought to spur their mounts to a trot, and it's another fact that Doge Michele Steno had a stable of 400 horses dyed saffron-yellow. In later centuries, jousts were replaced with bullfights; the last *corrida* was run in 1782, in honour of the heir to the throne of Russia. A few years later Napoleon erected a Tree of Liberty here, an event that went down the average Venetian's throat as smoothly as the Pink Floyd concert in 1989, when 200,000 rockers left a mess that took the army three days to tidy up.

Though now bull-less, the *piazza* holds exactly 13 lions, and 200 times that many pigeons, Venice's totem bird; according to a poetic tradition, when a bird feels death approaching it flies off towards the magical East until it drops into the sea. One tale has it that St Mark's pigeons are descended from a pair given by an oriental potentate to relieve the melancholy of a *dogaressa*; another that pigeons were released each Palm Sunday from St Mark's to re-enact Noah's release of a dove from the Ark, and as such were holy and protected from urban poachers. The birds have returned Venice's favour with tons of droppings; ironically, pigeon-coated stones better endure the air pollution wafting over from Mestre and Marghera. Your odds of becoming a target while crossing the Piazza are 2004 to one. Just be thankful all those winged lions stay put.

Campanile tall and straight like a mast, the ship's exotic cargo wrapped in fairy domes splashed by a roofline, where, as Ruskin wrote, 'the crests of the arches break into a marble foam, and toss themselves far into the blue sky in flashes and wreaths of sculptured spray...', while the four bronze steeds breast the waves, like figureheads, or like sea horses themselves – the ideal temple for a seafaring people with a marked inclination towards piracy.

The first St Mark's was a wooden chapel hastily erected in 828 to house the Evangelist's relics just in from Alexandria. It was a decision of major importance to make his shrine the ducal chapel: not only did it declare an official move away from Venice's former (and Greek) patron saint, Theodore, but it also established the special relationship between St Mark's relics and the doge, his vicar and *patronus et gubernator*. The official hierarchy of the Roman Catholic church had almost no say in the Basilica, where the doge served a role similar to the pope in St Peter's. For St Mark's was the core and vortex of Venetian religious-state; the glory of 'Messer San Marco' was the glory of the Republic and vice versa.

The first wooden chapel burned, along with the ducal palace, during the bloody insurrection of 976, when Doge Pietro Candiano IV was assassinated at the church door. Both the chapel and palace were immediately rebuilt in the same form, but the chapel was soon regarded as inadequate, and torn down in 1063, under Doge Domenico Contarini who sent out the order: 'make the chapel the most beautiful ever seen'. Each merchant was to bring back some embellishment; each doge was to donate large sums to its perfection. A Greek architect from Constantinople was hired to design the new church, asking in payment that the Republic erect a statue of him. But when the Senate criticized the result as a botched job, the poor architect fell from the scaffolding in dismay. And so, the legend goes, the Venetians carved his likeness over the main door, leaning on his crutches, ruefully biting his fingers.

His model for St Mark's was the no longer extant Church of the Holy Apostles in Constantinople, the imperial mausoleum of Byzantium, where Constantine and the first emperors were buried (it also inspired the ruined Basilica of St John at Ephesus, and St Front in France). It is in the form of a Greek cross with cupolas over the centre crossing and over each of the arms, with a narthex wrapped around the front to the transepts (though the right narthex is now closed), and five doorways, doubled by the arches over the *loggia*. Originally these were brick (like the rest of the church) and pointed in the Gothic style, but after the conquest of Constantinople, when Venice became the ruler of its proud fraction of the Roman empire, it yearned to look the part. So the arches were rounded off, the brickwork sheathed in pillaged rare marble and stone, in the grand old Roman

tradition. And could anything look more Roman than the triumphal arch of the central door, with the famous gilded horses of an ancient *quadriga* pawing the air?

The Exterior

The only jarring notes in the Basilica's millennial collage are the gaudy Technicolor mosaics in the arches, all cocky, painterly 17th–19th-century replacements of the originals – one of which was by Paolo Uccello. Sansovino, who in 1529 became St Mark's *Proto Magister* (in charge of maintaining the church) had to remove them to reinforce the structure.

The only mosaic to survive is the 13th-century lunette over the **Porta di Sant'Alipio** (the far left door) representing the *Translation of the Body of St Mark*, which not only tells the story of the relics' arrival in Venice, but features the earliest known representation of St Mark himself. The bas-relief, wedged between this arch and the next, is a 3rd-century Roman one, of *Hercules and the Erymanthean Boar* (Hercules was the traditional tribal hero of the Venetii people); in the 13th century, Venetian sculptors carved an imitation *Hercules and the Hydra* to fill in the space between the right-hand arches. Between the inner portals are a Byzantine figure of St Demetrius (left) and another Venetian imitation of St George (right) – both Christian warrior saints – while the relief in the centre is of the *Annunciation*, depicting the traditional protectors of the doge: the Virgin and the Angel Gabriel.

Best of all are the three bands of 13th-century reliefs around the central arch and its ungainly 19th-century mosaic of the *Last Judgement*. The carvings, however, are among Italy's finest, uniquely flowing, complex compositions; even the Corinthian columns that support them seem to sway in the breeze. The outermost band of reliefs shows Venetian trades, from shipwright to fisherman (including the finger-biting architect on the left). The middle arch is devoted to the **Labours of the Months** (February for example has nothing to do but warm himself by the fire), signs of the zodiac, and the Virtues and Beatitudes. The order of the months is especially interesting: note that the astrological signs are a month off, as they were (correctly) in classical times, proving either that the Venetians were better scholars than astronomers, or that their obsession with imitating the Romans was perfected to an extreme. The innermost arch is dedicated to chaos, including a vineyard filled with battling beasts and the favourite medieval fancy of a lady suckling a serpent.

The **upper loggia** of the façade, with its unique horses (or rather, their copies), is crowned by statues of the saints, standing just out of reach of the late 14th- and 15th-century tidal froth and frills that so delighted Ruskin. Nor does any other church have so much loot embedded in its surface, picked up around the Mediterranean like exotic stickers on an old-fashioned travelling trunk: on the right corner of the loggia, you can see an 8th-century Syrian (or Alexandrian) porphyry bust of Byzantine Emperor Justinian III Rhinotometus ('of the cut-off nose'); several *aquarii* with water pots on their shoulders serve as gargoyles.

But the **Piazzetta San Marco façade** (the one most visitors used to see first) was the Republic's main trophy case, bristling with a kind of *braggadocio* that in the 20th century seems almost charmingly naïve: there's the Pietra del Bando, a stump of porphyry pinched from the Genoese in Syria in 1256, and used as a stand for the reading of proclamations, and every now and then as a pedestal for the heads of traitors until they began to smell. In 1902 it was the hero of the hour for safeguarding the Basilica when the Campanile collapsed. Near this are two free-standing pilasters from Acre, decorated with rare Syrian curly carving. These were pilfered from the Genoese in 1256, and put here to get their goat, for the medieval Genoese treasured them as much as the Venetians treasured their *quadriga* of shining horses. Four porphyry Moors, generally thought to

be 4th-century Egyptian work, huddle on the corner; according to legend, they were changed into stone for daring to break into St Mark's Treasury (the protruding part of the façade, believed to have once been part of the original ducal castle). The odds are that they're really a pair of caesars and a pair of emperors, or the *tetrarchs*, established with Diocletian's attempt to divide the dying Roman empire into more governable sections, the better to persecute the Christians and overtax everyone else.

Below is a crude sculpture of two *putti* coming out of dragons' mouths, with the earliest known inscription in Venetian dialect: 'Man can do and must think – and must beware what may result'. This profoundly banal dictum is seconded by the legend of the 'Little Baker's Madonna' (a 13th-century mosaic of the Virgin in the upper lunette), whose pair of votive lamps are popularly said to be a reminder of the unjust execution of a young lad for murder – a true story, though the records attribute the lamps to the vow of an old sea captain lost at sea and saved by the Virgin.

Among the other pretty things here are the colourful *paterae* like artists' palettes of coloured marbles and onyx, the 12th-century griffons supporting the columns of one of the arches, and the 6th-century Byzantine columns on the upper part of the façade, with capitals carved in the form of baskets overflowing with fruit.

The north or **Piazzetta dei Leoncini façade** suffered from a band of rogue restorers in the 1860s, who decided that its sheath of polychrome marbles didn't look quite as fine as the dingy grey stone – only an international campaign spared the main façade from their handiwork. Especially note the two bas-reliefs on the right: the Twelve Apostles symbolized by lambs, worshipping the *etoimasia*, the empty throne prepared for the Last Judgement, either a rare Byzantine work made during the Iconoclasm (7th or 8th century) or – as slippery as most of St Mark's dates – by a 13th-century school of ancient art imitators. Nearby is a charming 10th- or 12th-century relief of Alexander the Great transported to heaven in a car pulled by two griffons, lured by pieces of liver dangled on spears over their heads – the moral of the story, of course, being that he failed, and you can't get to Heaven on a piece of liver. Beyond the 13th-century **Porta dei Fiori** is the tomb of Daniele Manin, who last revived the Republic of Venice in 1848.

Some of the most vivid mosaics are in six shallow domes of the **narthex**, or porch. These, mainly Old Testament scenes, are from the 13th century, made by Greek-trained Venetian artists, who learned their lessons well. The story unfolds from the right to left, beginning with the epic of the Creation and the story of Noah (who like any Venetian has a soft spot for the lion). The Creation scene is currently being restored and will be covered up for the foreseeable future.

Note the door on the right; the bronze **Portal of San Clemente** is an 11th-century Byzantine work, a gift to Venice from Emperor Alexis Comnenos. The narthex floor's geometrical marble mosaic dates from the 11th and 12th centuries; by the main entrance, a lozenge marks the spot where Emperor Frederick Barbarossa knelt and apologized 'to St Peter and his Pope' – Alexander III in 1177. Barbarossa had tossed Alexander out of Rome and installed an antipope sympathetic to the imperial cause, but when his armies were disastrously defeated by the Lombard League he was forced into reconciliation, stage-managed by Venetian diplomacy – one of the few gold stars Venice ever earned with the papacy.

To the right is the oldest tomb in Venice, that of the doge who consecrated the Basilica, Vitale Falier (d. 1096) 'King of kings, corrector of laws' – an epitaph that would give an 18th-century doge a heart attack. On the left behind an Islamic-inspired grille is the Tomb of the Dogaressa Felicità Michiel (d. 1101); her exceptional piety earned her a last resting place in the Basilica. The central door into the church retains the rare, original 11th-century mosaic of the *Madonna and Saints*.

Museo Marciano and Loggia

Open 9.30–5; adm €1.05.

Just to the right of this door, a sign invites you up a steep stone stair to the gallery, with the Museo Marciano and Loggia dei Cavalli. At the top of the stairs are a couple of rooms housing evocative fragments of the original mosaics and odds and ends, including a 16th-century double bass, which once accompanied St Mark's famous choir.

The **Loggia** offers a mesmerizing pigeon-eye view of the *piazza*, and lets you take in some of the rich sculptural and decorative details of the Basilica itself. The four replica horses on the façade, paid for with much fanfare by Olivetti, don't bear close examination after you've seen the originals, restored and regilded in 1979, only to be imprisoned inside – one of the saddest sights in Venice, for they were made to glint in the sun and shimmer in the light of the moon. This, after all, is the only bronze *quadriga* (four horses that once pulled a triumphal chariot) to survive from antiquity, though no one is sure whether the Greeks or Romans cast them, or when – suggested dates range from the 3rd century BC to the 2nd century AD. Constantine, himself no greenhorn in the plunder department, picked them up perhaps on the Greek island of Chios or in Rome, to embellish his new capital, and the Byzantine emperors put them out to pasture in Constantinople's Hippodrome until the Venetians snatched them in 1204. Originally they stood by the Arsenal, until someone had the extraordinary idea of putting them on the terrace of the Basilica, where they soon became one of Venice's best known symbols. Napoleon took them to Paris and installed them in the Place du Carrousel, where they stayed for 18 years, until sculptor Antonio Canova persuaded the French to return them to Venice. During the First and Second World Wars they were packed off to Rome for safe keeping.

The other treasures of the **Museo Marciano** aren't always on display: Paolo Veneziano's painted *Cover for the Pala d'Oro* (1345) and a series of early 15th-century tapestries on the

Life of Christ, woven after designs by Nicolò di Pietro.

From the **Gallery** inside the Basilica there's a wonderful view into the shadowy golden interior, and your best chance to get a close view of its mosaics.

A Tour of the Interior

The interior of St Mark's is if anything even more lavish than the exterior. Its lofty arches, shadowy walls, dizzy catwalks and swollen domes are covered with over 4,000 square yards of golden mosaics, a golden sheath that seems to breathe like a living thing when caught in the sun – gold that shimmers in ancient mystery in the evening shadows. On a high feast day, when all the candles and lamps were lit, the splendour would be overwhelming: the rich robes of the clergy, the heady fragrance of incense, the music of six orchestras of a hundred musicians each accompanying the celebrated Marciana choir, once directed by Monteverdi himself.

After the pagan glories of the façade and the Old Testament theme of the narthex, the mosaics here are all based on the New Testament (*see* plan, over); begun in the 11th century, they have been constantly repaired and replaced ever since, a year-round, full-time job. The peculiar catwalks over the aisles were once the women's galleries, chopped up to admit a bit of light when the side windows were covered up for more mosaics. When your neck begins to ache from gazing up into the domes, take a look at the intricate **pavement** of richly coloured marbles and porphyry and glass, its swirling geometric patterns subsiding into rolling waves and tidal pools.

The first dome, the early 12th-century **Pentecost dome**, was also the first to be decorated, with mosaics representing the nations whose languages were given to the Apostles on Pentecost Sunday. Especially note the arch between this and the central dome and its exceptional 12th-century scenes of the *Crucifixion, Descent into Limbo* and *Doubting Thomas*. In the upper wall of the right aisle is another early 12th-century

mosaic masterpiece, *The Agony in the Garden*, where the artist took no chances on portraying the correct posture of Christ – he kneels, falls, and falls on his face, according to the differing descriptions in the Gospels.

Just below this mosaic, to the right, a door leads to the **Baptistry**, which with any luck may be reopened by the time you get there. This was one of Ruskin's favourite places, and the Gothic Tomb of Doge Andrea Dandolo (d. 1354), by Giovanni de' Santi, in front of the door, was his favourite Venetian monument. Dandolo, a man of refined tastes and a friend of Petrarch, was the last doge to be buried in the Basilica; among the mosaics he commissioned: charming, anecdotal scenes on the *Life of St John the Baptist*, with swivel-hipped Salome in a red dress, dancing in triumph with the Baptist's head on a platter. Also buried in the baptistry are, to the right, Doge Giovanni Soranzo, Dandolo's predecessor (d. 1329), and, under a slab in the pavement, Jacopo Sansovino, whose remains were brought here in 1929, to lie near the giant **font** he designed. The mighty block of granite by the altar was part of the booty picked up in Tyre in 1126, lugged into this holy place on the chance that Christ stood on it when he fed the multitude.

A door from the baptistry leads into the **Cappella Zen** (*also currently closed*). The affluent Cardinal Giambattista Zen, like the *condottiere* Colleoni (*see* p.139), left the Republic his fortune on the condition that he be posthumously recognized at St Mark's – though the Cardinal was more specific, and to get the money the Senate ordered that the *piazzetta* entrance and narthex be closed in to make him a chapel, and hired Tullio Lombardo to design it. The doorway, decorated with a pair of 11th- or 12th-century mosaic angels flanking a *Madonna* (a 19th-century copy), has mosaic niches with small but expressive statues of the prophets; in the vault overhead are mosaic *Scenes from the Life of St Mark* (13th century). Antonio Lombardo carved the high altar's classical goddess with a child, the *Madonna of the Shoe* in 1506.

1 *Translation of the Body of St Mark* (1270)

2 *Venice Venerating the Relics of St Mark* (1718)

3 Central door, with magnificent 13th-century carvings in arches

4 *Venice Welcoming the Relics of St Mark* (1700s)

5 *Removal of St Mark's Relics from Alexandria* (1700s)

6 Pietra del Bando, stone from which the Signoria's decrees were read

7 *Scenes from the Book of Genesis* (1200) and 6th-century Byzantine door of S. Clemente

8 *Noah and the Flood* (1200s), tomb of Doge Vitale Falier (d. 1096)

9 *Madonna and Saints* (1060s); red marble slab where Emperor Barbarossa submitted to Pope Alexander III (1177); stair up to the Loggia and Museo Marciano

10 *Death of Noah and the Tower of Babel* (1200s)

11 *Story of Abraham* (1230s)

12 *Story of SS. Alipius and Simon, and Justice* (1200s)

14 Tomb of Doge Bartolomeo Gradenigo (d. 1342)

15 *Story of Joseph*, remade in 19th century

16 Porta dei Fiori (1200s); Manzù's bust of Pope John XXIII

17 *Christ with the Virgin and St Mark* (13th century, over the door)

18 Pentecost Dome (the earliest, 12th century)

19 On the wall: *Agony in the Garden* and *Madonna and Prophets* (13th century)

20 Baptistry, *Life of St John the Baptist* (14th century) and the tomb of Doge Andrea Dandolo

21 Cappella Zen, by Tullio and Antonio Lombardo (1504–22)

22 On the wall: *Christ and Prophets* (13th century)

23 In arch: *Scenes of the Passion* (12th century)

24 Central Dome, the *Ascension* (12th century)

25 Tabernacle of the Madonna of the Kiss (12th century)

26 On wall: *Rediscovery of the Body of St Mark* (13th century)

27 Treasury

28 Dome of S. Leonardo; Gothic rose window (15th century)

29 In arch, *Scenes from the Life of Christ* (12th century)

30 Altar of the Sacrament; pilaster where St Mark's body was rediscovered, marked by marbles

31 Altar of St James (1462)

32 Pulpit where newly elected doge was shown to the people; entrance to the sanctuary

33 Rood screen (1394) by Jacopo di Marco Benato and Jacobello and Pier Paolo Dalle Masegne

34 Singing Gallery and Cappella di S. Lorenzo, sculptures by the Dalle Masegnes (14th century)

35 Dome, *Prophets Foretell the Religion of Christ* (12th century); Baldacchino, with Eastern alabaster columns (6th century?)

36 Pala d'Oro (10th–14th century)

37 Sacristy door, with reliefs by Sansovino (16th century)

38 Sacristy, with mosaics by Titian and Padovanino (16th century) and Church of St Theodore (15th century), once seat of the Inquisition and now part of the sacristy: both are rarely open

39 Singing Gallery and Cappella di S. Pietro (14th century): note the Byzantine capitals

40 Two medieval pulpits stacked together

41 *Miracles of Christ* (16th century)

42 Dome, with *Life of St John the Evangelist* (12th century)

43 Cappella della Madonna di Nicopeia (miraculous 12th-century icon)

44 Cappella di S. Isidoro (14th-century mosaics and tomb of the Saint)

45 Cappella della Madonna dei Máscoli: *Life of the Virgin* by Andrea del Castagno, Michele Giambono, Jacopo Bellini

46 On wall: *Life of the Virgin* (13th century)

47 Greek marble stoup (12th century)

48 *Virgin of the Gun* (13th century – rifle ex-voto from 1850s)

49 Il Capitello, altar topped with rare marble ciborium, with miraculous Byzantine Crucifixion panel

St Mark's Basilica

Note how crooked it is!
In the Middle Ages symmetry
was synonymous with death.

Captions in italics refer to mosaics.

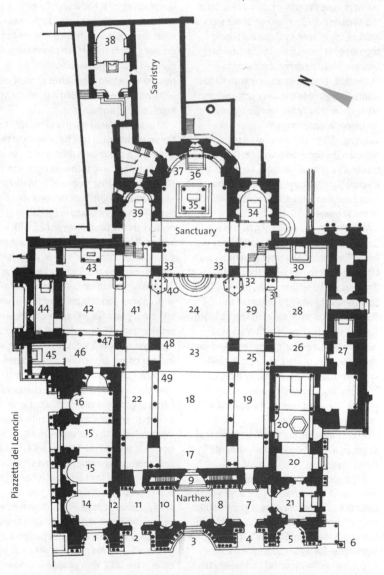

Go back to the main basilica. The central **Ascension dome** has concentric circles of heavenly notables around the main event, above allegories of the Four Rivers of Paradise, spilling over, as most Venetians probably thought, right into their own lagoon of manifest destiny. Towards the right transept, note the 12th-century bas-relief of the *Madonna dei Bacci* on one of the piers, a work nearly effaced by thousands upon thousands of kisses from the faithful over the centuries. The dome, dedicated to St Leonard, is relatively austere with its four saints, though note the lively 12th-century *Scenes from the Life of Christ (Entry into Jerusalem, Temptations, Last Supper and Washing of Feet)* shimmering on the arch between the dome and nave. On the transept's right wall mosaics, known as the *Inventio* (13th century), show events that happened across the transept at the **altar of the Sacrament**.

After the disastrous fire of 976, it was commonly believed that St Mark's body was lost in the flames. This blow to Venice's prestige was exacerbated when the merchants of Bari beat the Venetians to the relics of St Nicholas of Myra (the patron of sailors). Something had to be done, and on 24 June 1094, as the new church of St Mark was being consecrated and everyone prayed for the rediscovery of Mark's relics, the good saint was made to miraculously reappear, his arm breaking through the wall of the left pilaster (the exact spot indicated with a marble inlay and mosaic).

On the nave pier, to the left, is the **altar of St James**, a lovely work in the Lombardo family style.

At the end of the right transept is the door, now locked, through which the doge would enter the basilica, topped by a giant Gothic rose window. The door with the ogival arch to its right leads into **St Mark's Treasury** (*open Mon–Sat 9.30–5, Sun 1.30–5; adm €2.07*), housed in a room of immensely thick walls, believed to have been a 9th-century tower of the original ducal castle.

The capture of Constantinople by the so-called Fourth Crusade, and its subsequent pillage and sack, was perhaps a tragic loss of art and beauty to civilization. With equal equanimity the rough Franks smashed and melted down the treasures of the ancient Greeks and Romans as well as Byzantine; the Venetians at least had an eye for beauty as well as for the main chance. They salvaged what they could and shipped it home to the greater glory of their Messer San Marco. Five hundred years later Napoleon and his henchmen helped themselves to most of what was left – and melted it down for 55 ingots of gold and silver.

All in all, this lends a sense of wonder to the small collection that has managed to survive. But the objects displayed are beautiful and magical in their own right: the 6th-century marble throne of St Mark carved in Alexandria, a gift from Emperor Heraclius to the Patriarch of Grado in 630; a 4th-century crystal lamp, embellished with a crab and what looks like a piranha; a Byzantine glass bucket with chase scenes; an Egyptian vase of porphyry and feldspar, perhaps as old as 3500 BC; an 11th-century icon of *St Michael*, with enamel portraits and Venetian filigree; a 1st-century AD onyx and agate chalice; a votive crown of Emperor Leo III, adorned with rock crystal (*c.* 900); a golden rose bush; an incense burner shaped like a five-domed Byzantine church; a turquoise bowl sent from the Shah of Persia in 1472; chalices of intricate gold embroidery studded with thumb-sized gems; a magnificently decorated dish of alabaster and enamels. Nowhere will you see a better collection of 12th-century Byzantine gold and silver.

To the right of the high altar is the large odd-shaped ceremonial pulpit, where a newly bonneted doge would show himself to the people; here too is the entrance to the **Sanctuary and Pala d'Oro** (*open Mon–Sat 9–5, Sun 2–4; adm €1.55*). Straight on as you enter is the little alcove **Cappella di San Clemente**, with sculpture by the Dalle Masegne brothers and a pretty Gothic tabernacle on the side pier to the left. Eight bronze reliefs by Sansovino line the singing gallery of the chancel.

Take a close look at the four columns supporting the *baldacchino* over the high altar. These are the subject of another Venetian mystery: made of oriental alabaster, and sculpted with worn and murky New Testament scenes, these may be Byzantine works of the early 500s, or 13th-century Venetian retro art; or perhaps, as legend has it, they were brought to Venice from Dalmatia by Doge Pietro Orseolo II in the year 1000. Under a bronze grating in front of the altar is the crypt containing the supposed relics of St Mark. Overhead, the dome is another brilliant work of the 12th century, its subject *The Religion of Christ Foretold by the Prophets*, with the typically Byzantine *Christ Pantocrator*, blessing the congregation from the apse.

Under this, between the windows, are four of the oldest mosaics to be seen in the Basilica, the 11th-century *Saints Nicolas, Peter, Mark and Hermagorus*; in the central niche is an altar with translucent alabaster columns. The left-hand niche has the sacristy door, with bronze reliefs by Sansovino of the *Entombment* and *Resurrection*; in the frame, Sansovino sneakily included busts of himself and his closest friends, Titian and the roguish Aretino (*see p.129*).

But the highlight, of course, is the dazzling and incomparable **Pala d'Oro**, the masterpiece of generations of medieval Byzantine and Venetian goldsmiths and the most precious treasure in the basilica. Measuring 10ft by 4ft, it consists of beautifully worked gold, set with sparkling gems: 300 sapphires, 300 emeralds, 400 garnets, 100 amethysts, 1,300 pearls, not to mention handfuls of rubies and topazes to accompany 157 enamelled rondels and panels. The original altar screen was ordered from Constantinople by Doge Pietro Orseolo I in 976, and it was revised and enriched in 1105, again in Constantinople. In 1209, the Venetians enlarged it with some of the jewels and gold

they had plundered, and it was reset in its final state in 1345 by Gian Paolo Boninsegna. The miniature enamelled scenes are microscopically intricate and well crafted, but tend to get lost in the razzle-dazzle: the large figure on top is St Michael, encircled by rondels of saints and six larger panels with New Testament scenes. Below, the dominant figure is Christ Pantocrator; this and the 39 niches filled with saints are 12th-century Byzantine, while the small square panels that run along the top and sides of the lower screen, with scenes from the lives of the Evangelists, are thought to be from the original 10th-century Pala; in the one in the upper right-hand corner, an angel greets St Mark from the future city of Venice.

Before leaving the sanctuary, take a look at its magnificent rood screen of eight columns of twilit marble, holding the silver and gold *Cross* (1394) by the Venetian goldsmith Marco Benato and marble statues by Jacobello and Pier Paolo Dalle Masegne, perhaps the brothers' finest works. On the left side is a second pulpit, built on another pulpit, made of columns of rare marbles and parapets of *verde antico*.

Just within the left transept, vaulted by the 12th-century dome of St John, is the busiest chapel in St Mark's, the **Chapel of the Madonna di Nicopeia**, festooned with hanging red lamps and candles glimmering in the permanent twilight. The chapel is named after the prodigious 12th-century icon of *Our Lady, Bringer of Victory*, which Byzantine emperors would carry into battle. Part of the haul of 1204, it has been venerated ever since as the Protectress of Venice. At the end of the transept is the **Cappella di Sant'Isidoro**, built by Doge Andrea Dandolo in 1355 to house the relics of St Isidore, stolen from Chios in 1125; and in the beautiful, pristine mosaics on the upper walls and barrel vault that tell the saint's life story he seems glad to go, grinning as the Venetians kidnap him. Behind the altar his sarcophagus bears a 14th-century reclining effigy; by the door there's a delightful holy water stoup.

The next chapel in the left transept, the **Cappella della Madonna dei Máscoli** ('of the males', after a 17th-century masculine confraternity). This chapel not only has confessionals in four languages, but lovely mosaics on *The Life of the Virgin* (1450s). Based on cartoons by the Tuscan Andrea del Castagno and probably Jacopo Bellini, and carried out by Michele Giambono, this chapel was one of the seeds of the Renaissance in Venice; the scenes are set in the kind of fantasy architecture beloved by the Tuscans. A Gothic altar of 1430 is embedded in a wall of rich marbles, and the figures of the Madonna and St John and St Mark are by Bartolomeo Bon. Before leaving the transept, take in the Romanesque carvings on the Greek stoup in the centre and, on the pier, a relief of the *Madonna and Child*, with perhaps the most curious and unexplained ex-voto in Italy: a rifle. And on the first pier in the left aisle is **Il Capitello**, a tiny chapel constructed entirely of rare marble and agate to house a painted wooden *Crucifix*, believed to have once belonged to the Byzantine Emperor; abused by a blasphemer in 1290, it miracuously bled, and has been tucked in here to prevent further mishaps.

Palazzo Ducale (Doge's Palace) 17–8

*Piazzetta San Marco, t 041 528 3524; **vaporetto** San Zaccaria; partly wheelchair accessible.* ***Open** April–Oct daily 9–7; Nov–March daily 9–5; **adm** €12.50 incl. Itinerari Segreti **tour** (see p.112), or €9.50 ('biglietto accumulativo', also including Museo Correr, Biblioteca Nazionale Marciana and Museo Archeologico). **Entrance** and **tickets** on Riva degli Schiavoni.*

The gravity-defying Palazzo Ducale is Europe's most dazzling secular building of the Middle Ages, a synthesis of the Romanesque, Gothic and Islamic, wrapped in a diapered pattern of white Istrian stone and red Verona marble. No building of its period is as open and defenceless to the point of topsyturvydom as the Palazzo Ducale, Its

massive top-heavy upper floor like a straw-berry cake held up by its own frosting – a form that echoes the basic structure of the city itself, of palaces supported by millions of piles. But this fairy confection was all business, the nerve centre of the Venetian empire: the residence of the doge, seat of the Senate and a score of councils, of the Serenissima's land and sea governments and and their bureaucracies, courts, and even the state prisons. For Ruskin it was 'the central building of the world'. The Venetians, more unassumingly, think of it as the valve of a rather large seashell.

The original palace was a typically walled and moated citadel, begun shortly after the city's consolidation on the Rialto in 810. It only began to assume its present shape in 1309, as the government evolved into its final form with the *Serrata del Consiglio*. In 1340 the massive hall for the *Maggior Consiglio* was begun on the seaward side – a task that took until 1419. This new building made the older sections of the palace, facing the *piazzetta*, look decrepit, but the Senate had decreed that any doge who even *proposed* any changes to it faced a thousand-ducat fine. Doge after doge suffered in a silent waiting game until a fire in 1419 caused severe damage. Doge Tommaso Mocenigo couldn't bear any more, and paid the fine, with which the Senate voted to build a 'more noble edifice'. Work began on 27 March 1422, 'the first act of the period properly called the "Renaissance",' groaned Ruskin. 'It was the knell of the architecture of Venice – and of Venice herself.'

To the Venetians, however, their decline was not immediately apparent: in 1438 Doge Francesco Foscari commissioned the florid **Porta della Carta** in line with his pride in Venice's land expansion, and the city's greatest painters were hired to fresco the interior – all destroyed in the fires of 1574 and 1577. So much damage was done that there were serious moves to tear the remaining bits down and let Palladio start again *à la* classical High Renaissance. Fortunately, however, you can't teach an old doge new tricks, and it was rebuilt as it was – a rather extraordinary decision for the time. Who else in the 1570s would reconstruct a Gothic building?

The Exterior

The theme behind the Palazzo Ducale's exterior decoration is moral instruction and justice (and, naturally, the glory of Venice). Beautiful sculptural groups adorn the corners, most notably the *Judgement of Solomon* (c. 1410, by Jacopo della Quercia of Siena, one of the greatest early Renaissance sculptors) on the corner nearest the Porta della Carta, with a statue of the *Archangel Gabriel* overhead. On the Piazzetta San Marco corner are *Adam and Eve*, tempted by the serpent, while the *Archangel Michael* stands overhead with his sword to guard humanity from temptation. On the Ponte della Paglia corner is a group portraying *The Drunkenness of Noah*, an allegory on the frailty of humanity, with the *Archangel Raphael* overhead, helping to guide the tiny Tobias down the straight and narrow.

Less benign are the two red pillars in the loggia (on the *piazzetta* façade), according to legend dyed by the blood of Venice's enemies, whose tortured corpses were strung out between them; one of the palace's master builders, Filippo Calendario, was hung and quartered here for his role in the Marin Falier conspiracy. On Maundy Thursday the doge would stand between the columns to preside over a tongue-in-cheek ceremony celebrating Venice's victory over the Patriarch of Aquileia and his 12 prelates – marked by the baiting and decapitation of a bull and 12 pigs.

The rising water level over the centuries has forced the pavement to be raised the equivalent of two steps, making the 36 columns of the ground floor colonnade seem low and squat. But these are crowned with some excellent medieval sculpture, depicting a few sacred and many profane subjects – animals, guildsmen, Turks and Venetians, each telling a story for the benefit of the

patricians strolling in the shade. One of the most beautiful is the seventh column from the basin (facing the *piazzetta*), carved with a Romeo and Juliet scene of courtship, marriage, the first night, the birth of the first child, and then, after all that happiness, the child's death.

Inside the Palace

The new ticket office on the Riva degli Schiavoni leads you straight into the big **courtyard**, which you can visit immediately or leave until the end of the tour. This delightful arcaded 'Cortile', designed by Antonio Rizzo after the fire of 1483, contains two of Venice's finest well-heads.

First on the tour is the **Museo dell'Opera**, with its rooms full of vast bits of stone capitals, columns, chunks of stonework from the upper loggia, and models of the palace. Then you go back into the courtyard and begin the tour proper by ascending the **Scala dei Censori** to the first floor, or *primo piano nobile*, once the private apartments of the doge and now often used for special exhibitions (separate admission), although its stripped-down unfurnished state offers few clues as to how the doge lived in this gilded cage of pomp and ritual, leading public and private councils and rites as grand as the 'Marriage to the Sea' and as absurd as the one involving 17 women from Poveglia, who on Easter Tuesday had the right to give him a big kiss before sitting down to a ducal dinner.

Turn right, and Sansovino's **Scala d'Oro** (1580s, with gilded stuccoes by Vittoria) leads you up to the *secondo piano nobile*, from where the Venetian state was governed. After the fire that destroyed its great frescoes, Veronese and Tintoretto were employed to decorate the newly remodelled chambers with mythological themes and scores of allegories and apotheoses of Venice – a smug, fleshy blonde in the eyes of these two. These paintings, most of them beaverishly over-restored into a flat, soulless paean of dead glory, are the *palazzo*'s chief interest. The first room, the **Sala delle Quattro Porte** (where ambassadors waited to be summoned

A Doge's Life: Gormenghast with Canals

Senator in Senate, Citizen in City were his titles, as well as Prince of Clothes, with a wardrobe of gold and silver damask robes, and scarlet silks; and it's not surprising the most lavish room is **Sala degli Scarlatti**, or dressing room, with gilded ceiling, a chimney by Tullio and Antonio Lombardo, and a relief of the *Virgin* and *Doge Leonardo Loredan* by Pietro Lombardo. Once the doge was dressed, the rest of his procession would fall in line, including all the paraphernalia of Byzantine royalty: a naked sword, six silver trumpets, a damask umbrella, a chair, cushion, candle, and eight standards bearing the Lion of St Mark in four colours symbolizing peace, war, truce and allegiance. Yet for all the glamour this was the only man in Venice not permitted to send a private note to his wife, or receive one from her, or from anyone else; the only gifts he could accept were flowers or rose-water. He could not go to a café or theatre; he could not engage in any activity to raise money, but was expected to pay out of his own pocket for his robes, banquets, donations, taxes and gifts to St Mark's. Nor could he abdicate, unless requested.

The office was respected, if not the man. When a doge died he was privately buried in the family tomb before the state funeral – which used a dummy corpse stuffed with straw and a wax mask, a custom originating with Doge Giovanni Mocenigo's funeral in the early 16th century, during a plague. An 'Inquisition of the Defunct Doge' was held over the dummy, to discover if the doge had kept to his *Promissione* (the oaths made before his coronation) or if his heirs owed the state any money; and it ascertained if any amendments to the *Promissione* were in order to further limit the powers of the new doge. Then the dead doge's dummy was taken to St Mark's to be hoisted in the air nine times by sailors, to the cry of '*Misericordia!*', and then given a funeral service at Santi Giovanni e Paolo.

before the doge) is typical, not even redeemed by the lavish ceiling stuccoes by Palladio and frescoes by Tintoretto.

Some of the best works, however, are in the next waiting room, the **Anticollegio**. On the walls are four mythological subjects by Tintoretto, designed to plant ideas of concord and harmony in the viewer: his powerful *Bacchus and Ariadne Crowned by Venus* and *Vulcan's Forge*, and less remarkable *Minerva Dismissing Mars* and *Mercury and the Graces*. Other paintings here are Veronese's *Rape of Europa*, one of his finest mythological works, and Jacopo Bassano's *Jacob Rejoins his Family*.

After digesting these paintings, visiting ambassadors would finally be admitted into the **Sala del Collegio**, or seat of Venice's inner council of 25 members, presided over by the doge. As if all the previous glitter hadn't made its point, this room is decorated with Veronese's sublimely confident and colourful ceiling, with its centrepiece of *Venice Triumphant*, and behind the throne, his equally sanguine *Doge Sebastian Venier Thanking Christ for Victory at Lepanto*.

Less attention was given to the decoration of the **Sala del Senato**, since the only ambassadors admitted here were Venetians serving abroad. But because of their reports many of the most important decisions were made in this room, by the doge and the Senate, a nucleus chosen from the *Maggior Consiglio* that over the years varied from 60 to 300 members. The stale paintings are mainly by Tintoretto's school, with only a touch or two by the master.

Back through the **Sala delle Quattro Porte**, past Giambattista Tiepolo's *Neptune Paying Homage to Venice* (on the easel), the next stop is the **Sala del Consiglio dei Dieci**, headquarters of the dread, secret Council of Ten. The main panel of the ceiling, by Veronese, was pinched by the French and still hangs in the Louvre, but they left behind Veronese's oval *Old Man in Eastern Costume with a*

Young Woman, now the star work of the room. Under this the Council of Ten (a misnomer, as the Ten were always complemented by the doge and six councillors to make 17) deliberated and pored over the accusations deposited in the *Bocche dei Leoni* – the lions' mouths, the insidious boxes spread over the city – there's one next door in the Ten's waiting room, the **Sala della Bussola**. Although no unsigned accusations without the support of two witnesses were considered (and accusers knew they themselves would be given the punishment of the crimes if they falsely reported), the procedure had such an evil reputation that when someone joked to Montesquieu that he was being watched by the Ten, he immediately packed his bags and left town. And woe indeed to anyone whose alibi refused to satisfy the Ten; a door in the Sala della Bussola passes through the office of the Three Heads of the Ten, in charge of investigating cases of treason – and from there bang, into the torture chamber.

From here steps descend to the old **Armoury** (*Sale d'Armi*), housing a fine collection of medieval and Renaissance armour, most of it showpieces that were rarely dented by halberd or sullied by guts, like the suit presented by Venice to Henry IV of France in 1603. A small stair takes you down to the small **Sala del Guariento** and the remains of Guariento's enormous fresco of the *Coronation of the Virgin* or *Paradise* (1365–7), damaged in the 1577 fire and discovered under Tintoretto's *Paradiso* in the Sala del Maggior Consiglio. Here, too, are Rizzo's original *Adam* and *Eve*.

To the right is the magnificent **Sala del Maggior Consiglio**, originally built in 1340 and almost as large as a football field, capable of holding all 2,500 patricians of the lower house of the Senate, or Great Council. Before the fire of 1577, it was beautifully decorated by Gentile da Fabriano, Giovanni Bellini, Carpaccio and Titian, but at least one of the replacement paintings – nothing less than the biggest oil painting in the world

(23ft by 72ft) – will give you pause: Tintoretto's awesome, recently restored *Paradiso*, which he painted free of charge, beginning the task at the age of 72. This replaced Guariento's fresco and follows the same subject, Canto XXX of Dante's *Paradiso*, listing the hierarchy of angels, saints, and Old Testament figures, and others of the heavenly vortex, 500 figures circling Christ crowning the Virgin, the Queen of Heaven. William Blake would have appreciated it, and probably also the story of how some nosy patricians came to watch Tintoretto painting it, and commented, 'But other painters take more time and draw the figures more carefully.' To which the short tempered artist snapped, 'Because they don't have to put up with fools watching them!'

On the ceiling is the *Paradiso*'s secular counterpart: Veronese's magnificent, vertiginous *Apotheosis of Venice*, its pride and confidence, even in allegory, probably very irritating to visitors, and embarrassing to behold in May 1797, when Napoleon's troops were at the gate and the Council in wimpish terror voted to accept all Napoleon's demands, obliterating Venice's thousand years of independence and its own existence.

The frieze on the upper wall, by Domenico Tintoretto and assistants, portrays the first 76 doges, except for the space with a black veil that would have held the head of Marin Falier (1355) had he not been deprived of it for treason in a conspiracy to take sole power ('*Hic est locus Marini Falethri decapitati pro criminibus*' reads the dire inscription).

The portraits of the last 44 doges, each painted by a contemporary painter, continue around the **Sala dello Scrutinio**, where the votes for office were counted. Elections for doge were Byzantine and elaborate – and frequent; the *Maggior Consiglio* preferred to chose doges who were old and wouldn't last long enough to gain a following. Even the most straightforward election took only five days of lots drawn to form a committee to elect a committee to elect a committee to elect a committee to elect a doge; the longest election, Giovanni Bembo's in 1615, took 24 days.

From the Sala dello Scrutinio, you have to go back through the Sala del Maggior Consiglio to get to the **Ponte dei Sospiri** (Bridge of Sighs), across which is the 17th-century **Palazzo delle Prigioni**, mostly used for petty offenders. The real rotters were dumped into uncomfortable *Pozzi*, or 'Wells' in the lower part of the Palazzo Ducale, while more illustrious offenders like Casanova were lodged in the *Piombi* or 'Leads' just under the roof (which you can visit on the Secret Itinerary). The horrible rumours of these cells, rumours encouraged by the State, made the French think they would find hundreds upon hundreds of innocent victims of the Ten rotting away inside them. With a flourish they burst in, only to have a bad case of *déjà vu*. The Bastille had had only three prisoners waiting to be liberated; Venice managed to have four, but one was so fond of his cell he incessantly begged the French to let him go back. Further embarrassment was averted when he died from an overdose of chocolate and rich cakes.

The tour of the prison area has been extended and you can now descend into the very bowels of the building, following a labyrinth of corridors past endless gloomy cells. At the end is a room containing various relics of prisoners' lives backed up by vivid descriptions of living conditions (which included a '*taverna da vin*' open to prisoners and public alike – just imagine that in Wormwood Scrubs).

You exit the palace via the long, triumphal Arco Foscari with the **Scala dei Giganti**, Antonio Rizzo's elaborately sculpted grand stairway, behind you. The latter was named after the gargantuan statues of *Neptune* and *Mars* by Sansovino (1566); among the details, see if you can find the basket of medlars, meant to symbolize cultivated but still unripe young patricians. At the top of this stair the newly elected doge would be crowned with a special Phrygian cap studded with gems, called the *zogia*, the 'jewel of

independence', which he could only don again at Easter Mass in San Zaccaria.

The **Arco Foscari**, which stands at the end of the entrance passage, was built by the Bons for Doge Foscari and finished by Rizzo, and is decorated with bronze copies of his statues of *Adam* and *Eve* (originals now inside; the wonderfully self-assured *Eve* so captivated the Duke of Mantua in the 16th century that he offered Venice the statue's weight in gold in exchange for it, a deal that the Venetians refused).

Go out through the **Porta della Carta** (Paper Door), a florid Gothic symphony in stone by Giovanni and Bartolomeo Bon (1443); its name may derive from the clerks' desks that once stood near here. Originally brightly painted and gilded, it has been thorough scoured, so that it's hard to tell that the figures of *Doge Francesco Foscari* and the lion are 19th-century replacements.

The Secret Itinerary

*Guided tour, 20 people only; **reserve** a place at least a day in advance with the secretary in the Director's office on the first floor, or call t 041 522 4951. **Tours** 10am and 12 noon; **tickets** €12.50. Usually, after the tour, you can walk through the **state rooms** on the same ticket, so be sure to do the Secret Itinerary first.*

Besides the gilded state rooms created to be seen by visitors, both in the days of the Republic and now, the Doge's Palace contains the chambers where the nitty-gritty business of running the state took place. In 1984 this latter section of the palace was restored and opened to the public, but because many of the rooms are tiny, the guided tour, or *Itinerari Segreti* is limited. This 'secret' tour is one of the most fascinating things to do in all Venice – it lasts an hour and a half and the only reason why more people don't know about it is because the tour commentary is in Italian. But if Italian isn't your language, read on.

The tour begins at the top of the Scala d'Oro, but instead of turning right into the state rooms the guide takes you left into the tiny wooden ship-shape offices of the

Chancellery on the *mezzanine*, which could easily fit aboard a fat Venetian galley – designed not only to be snug in the winter, but to make the average Venetian feel at home. The 18th-century **Hall of the Chancellery** is an elegant wooden room lined with cupboards for storing treaties, each bearing the arms of a chancellor, though Napoleon intervened before the last six cupboards could be decorated. Like most civil servants, chancellors were recruited from the *cittadini originarii* – native-born Venetians, preferably at least of three generations, and rich enough not to have to engage in manual labour. Three chancellors managed to be elevated to the nobility (after paying the equivalent of €500,000), but as usual good service was expected and not singled out, while anything less than the best meant trouble. If a chancellor lost a document he had three days to find it or face the death penalty; one chancellor who secretly consorted with foreigners was slipped a poisoned cup of coffee (as was, more recently, Michele Sindona, the Vatican-related swindler).

Outside are the narrow stairs down which Casanova and his friend the renegade priest escaped when they broke out of the Leads (*see* p.114). The two passed the night in an office, then calmly walked unnoticed out of the Porta della Carta in the morning, when the offices were unlocked. A gondola was waiting for them; Casanova, however, stopped first for a morning coffee at Florian's café, which according to legend still has a copy of his bill.

Beyond the stair are the rooms of the justice department linked to the Council of Ten, especially the **torture chamber** where the three *Signori della notte dei criminali* (judges of the night of the criminals) would 'put to the question' their suspects, hanging them by the wrists by the rope still dangling ominously in place. Because the victim's screams would make the civil servants next door nervous, such torture was done at twilight, and the chamber was so arranged

that the light of the dying sun would fall in the victim's eyes, so that the three inquisitors would be invisible in the darkness. The two cells on either side of the rope were for the next suspects to be questioned, who, hearing the proceedings, might be encouraged to talk without all the messy rigamarole.

For psychology was one of the Republic's chief weapons even before there was a word for it, and as Venice grew old she relied far more on her bark than her bite, encouraging 'police state' rumours of torture and assassination and the relentless Council of Ten to make Venetians toe the line. For the most part, it worked. The stories were so good that nearly every visitor to Venice still believes them, when in truth few states were as humane and progressive: prisoners had a legal right to a lawyer as early as the 970s; a prisoner had to be brought to trial in a month and no more; house arrest was invented for a sick prisoner in 1572; no one could be arrested without sufficient evidence; search warrants could only be issued by committee, and not by a single man; and along with Tuscany, the Republic abolished torture before anyone else, in the early 1700s.

The tour continues to the ornate **Sala dei Tre Capi**, the chamber of the three heads of the Council of Ten, who served as guardians of Venetian legality, and had to be present at all state meetings, at all appeals trials, and at every function attended by the doge, to make sure he kept to his coronation oath. As this chamber might be visited by some foreign dignitary or ambassador, it was given a lavish ceiling by Veronese, a fireplace carved by Sansovino, a luminous *Pietà* by the School of Antonello da Messina, and three paintings by Hieronymus Bosch: the peculiar *Santa Libertà*, a crucified woman, a *Paradise and Inferno* and *St Jerome*, with the usual Boschian rogue's gallery of monsterettes. Another curiosity of the room is the secret passageway built into the wall; the palace has quite a network of these, including one for busybodies that passed right behind the ducal bed; the state wouldn't even let sleeping doges lie in peace.

From here it's up to the notorious **Piombi**, or 'Leads', so named because the cells are just under the leaded roof. In spite of their evil repute, as prisons go they are downright cosy – as good as some one-star hotel rooms, at least, with wooden walls, dry, and not too hot or cold, or crowded, with never more than two prisoners in a 7½ft square cell. The doors seem to be covered with at least seven different locks, but open with only one key. Casanova's cell is pointed out, where he lived comfortably enough, inviting his fellow prisoners in for the odd macaroni and cheese, and the guide offers an elaborate explanation of his escape that began through a hole in the roof. You can read more about it in his memoirs. There are wonderful views of the *piazza* and Lagoon from the Leads' porthole windows.

The tour continues past a display of weapons to one of the engineering marvels of Venice: the **attic** above the grand **Sala del Maggior Consiglio**, where you can see exactly how the shipwrights from the Arsenale made such a vast heavy ceiling float unsupported over the room below; built in 1577, it is so well made it has yet to need any repairs. Part of the reason why was the care taken to produce the right wood. Venice's forests in the northern Veneto were planted scientifically to ensure that the trees grew tall, strong and straight for masts or beams like these; anyone who cut one down faced the death penalty. Next comes the palace attic, which like most attics contains both the obsolete and nostalgic – old wooden toilets, three swords (one for heads, one used in bullfights, and one that fell into a canal and was fossilized in the mud – 'Nowadays,' the guide remarks drily, 'it would dissolve.'), a collar with spikes inside, two *Bocche dei Leoni*, one for denunciations against thieves, and the other for those against spies and traitors. The latter saw relatively little use, for most Venetians believed, as Marin Sanudo wrote in the 1500s, that, 'Anyone who wishes to dissent must be mad.'

The Campanile I7

Piazza San Marco, t 041 522 4064; vaporetto San Zaccaria/San Marco. Lift open 9–7 daily, adm €6.

In front of St Mark's, supporting three huge flags on holidays, or whenever the city feels like flying them, are Alessandro Leopardi's bronze **flagstaff bases** (1505), swarming with a mythological *misto del mare* of tritons and nereids. Overlooking them, and everything else in Venice, is the *Golden Archangel of the Annunciation* shining like a beacon atop the 325ft red brick Campanile.

Although Venice looks strikingly canal-less from the exalted height of the Campanile, the secretive *Serenissima* was always very picky about who was permitted to enjoy the view, fearing that spies would peek into the Arsenal, or map the Venetians' canals through the Lagoon, easily visible at low tide. After all, when begun in 912, the tower doubled as a lighthouse, and even afterwards the function of its five bells was entirely civic. Besides the aforementioned *Trottiera*, the largest, the *Marangona*, signalled the beginning and end of the working day; the *Nona* announced noon; the *Mezza Terza* the opening of the Senate; and the small but ominous *Maleficio* rang for an execution.

The elegantly classical **Loggetta** at the base, designed by Sansovino, though intended as a *Ridotto dei Nobili* (a noblemen's club) was soon given over as a guardroom to the *Arsenalotti*, 50 of whom showed up as volunteer (and apparently, totally unnecessary) policemen whenever the *Maggior Consiglio* met. In the 18th century, it became the centre of the state lottery.

The Campanile has looked the same since 1515, only what now stands is an exact replica, made after the original one considerately warned everyone out of the way by opening a big crack, then genteelly collapsed into a pile of dust on 14 July 1902 (the only casualty was the keeper's cat, who had run in to check its bowl). You can buy postcards of a cleverly rigged photo that looks as if it were taken as the Campanile falls; others show what the *piazza* looked like without this lumbering landmark. The fact that it looked much better, St Mark's and the Palazzo Ducale no longer obscured and outscaled, had no bearing at all on the decision made, the very evening of the Campanile's demise, to construct it *dov'era e com'era* ('where it was and as it was'), only this time several tons lighter, and stronger. The whole world chipped in, and the Campanile was officially reopened in 1912. Although the *Pietra del Bando* diverted the cascading rubble from St Mark's, the Loggetta was completely smashed; like a jigsaw puzzle it was pieced back together, along with Sansovino's allegorical statues and reliefs; as the Loggetta was built during Venice's brief tenure over Cyprus, this includes a marble relief of *Venus* on the attic, keeping company with *Justice* (Venice's favourite persona) and *Jupiter*, a native of another Venetian possession, Crete.

PIAZZETTA SAN MARCO

The Piazzetta San Marco is Venice's traditional foyer, where visitors from overseas would disembark at the Molo under the sleepless eye of the state bureaucracy. A few hundred years ago, one section of it was reserved for patricians, politicking in their trailing robes. This was known as the *Broglio* (or 'kitchen garden'), for it once grew the turnips for the nuns at San Zaccaria. Long before modern politicians had smoke-filled rooms, the Venetians had their *Broglio* for making deals, and for soliciting votes whenever an election was up; a number of visitors remarked on the quaint sight of a grand patrician from one of the oldest families, bowing so low to kiss the edge of an elector's sleeve that his neck stole scraped the ground. The very Byzantine intrigues, entanglements and machinations that went on here, some say, gave Italian and then English the word *imbroglio*.

The Two Columns 18

Piazzetta San Marco; vaporetto San Zaccaria.

The *piazzetta* holds one of Venice's oldest symbols: the Two Columns. Take a look at these first thing in the morning, before the forests of tourists plant themselves on the steps and hide their curious medieval carvings. It's hard to tell what many of these once were, so eroded have they become from centuries of weather and bottoms, though superstitious Venetians never sit here, or walk between the columns.

These granite pillars were part of the loot the Venetians picked up at Tyre in 1170. Originally there were three, but such was the difficulty in unloading them that one went overboard into the Bacino di San Marco and still keeps the fish company there. Even thornier was the problem of getting them to stand upright, and during the reign of the 'architect doge' Ziani the proclamation went out that whoever succeeded would be granted any *grazia onesta*. No one could until a Lombard named Nicolo Barattieri managed the feat with wet ropes (a story suspiciously similar to the 16th-century tale of the raising of the Vatican obelisk in Rome) and asked, as his reward, for permission to set up gambling tables between the two columns, thus making the area Venice's first casino. This idea was also about half a millennium ahead of its time and scandalized the government; the last thing they wanted in their municipal parlour was a gambling den. Unable to renege on the *grazia onesta*, the artful doge decreed at the same time that all public executions should henceforth take place 'between the two red columns' (though one is really grey), and the heads of criminals be put on display there – which, as had been suspected, succeeded in driving away so many potential gamblers that Barattieri's games were soon run out of business. Most unfortunates were hanged or decapitated; on one memorable occasion in 1405, however, the Venetians woke up to find three traitors buried alive here, with only their legs sticking out of the ground.

The Venetians had not only a knack for converting their booty into self-serving symbols, but a precocious ability to create art from *objets trouvés*. The figure on one column is the obscure St Theodore with his crocodile or dragon, or fish. Venice's first patron (made redundant with the arrival of St Mark's relics, and not restored to his post until the late 13th century) was made from a Parian marble head of Mithridates of Pontus and a Roman torso, and other ancient bits, now all replaced by a copy. The second column's Lion of St Mark is actually a bronze chimera from Syria or China; the Venetians simply added wings, and slid a book under its paw.

On the Waterfront

Vaporetto San Marco/San Zaccaria.

The **Molo** (I–J8), the waterfront of Piazzetta San Marco, is solid with bobbing gondolas and excursion boats to Murano and beyond. Behind the Zecca and a row of booths offering good prices on plastic light-up gondolas are the **Giardinetti Reali** (I8), not much as 'royal' gardens go, but a rare patch of green (and an even rarer public WC) in the capital of stone and water. Eugène de Beauharnais created it when he knocked down the *Fontegheto della Farina*, or state granary, to create a view of the Lagoon from the Ala Napoleonica (*see* p.117). He also added the pretty neoclassical pavilion called the **Casino da Caffè** (1807), now a tourist information office (*Palazzetto Selva, t 041 529 8730*).

Down the Molo, past the Palazzo Ducale, is the **Ponte della Paglia** (J8; straw bridge, named after the loads of straw unloaded here for the garrisons of the Palazzo Ducale and prisons), invariably crowded with people all taking identical photos of the famous Istrian stone **Ponte dei Sospiri** (J7; Bridge of Sighs), built in 1600 by Antonio Contino, to link the Palazzo with the **Prigioni** (J7–8; prisons, 1560–1614, and suitably grim, at least by Venetian standards). The legendary sighs were emitted by prisoners on their way to the State Inquisitors' office and built-in torture chamber.

Across the Ponte della Paglia is the **Riva degli Schiavoni** (J8), or 'Dalmatians' Quay', long one of the city's favourite promenades, now a tourist trinket trap, lined with *vaporetto* landing stages. In the old days this stretch of quay would be lined with ships from all corners of the Mediterranean; in 1782, when it is commonly thought that Venice was about to drop dead of exhaustion, the Riva did such thriving business (no longer in silks and spices from the Orient, perhaps, but as the major transit port for goods from the Adriatic gulf and Ionian islands) that the Riva had to be widened; the white marble strip in the pavement marks its original size.

PIAZZETTA DEI LEONCINI

On the north side of St Mark's Basilica is its other *piazzetta*, named for a handsome pair of **porphyry lions** presented to the city by Doge Alvise Mocenigo III on his accession in 1722 and especially endowed with some special child magnetism that proves irresistible to any crumbsnatcher who walks by. The east end is closed off by the 19th-century **Palazzo Patriarcale** (I–J7), where John XXIII, John Paul I and all the other Venetian patriarchs have resided since the rational Napoleon made St Mark's a cathedral. Incorporated within is the dining hall where the doge hosted his legendary state banquets for notables and official guests; a corridor that once connected it directly to the Palazzo Ducale has been demolished. Also in the *piazzetta* is the deconsecrated church of San Basso, used for exhibitions.

Torre dell'Orologio I7

Piazzetta dei Leoncini; vaporetto San Marco/San Zaccaria; currently being restored, with a view to reopening in 2004.

Horas non numero nisi serenas: 'I only number happy hours,' says the legend, but it doesn't always number them accurately, and gets especially muddled at the phases of the moon and signs of the zodiac. Still, it is such a fine clock, built by Mauro Codussi in 1499, with works by Paolo and Carlo Rainieri of Reggio Emilia, that other Italian cities maliciously circulated the rumour that the Venetians tore out the eyes of the Rainieri brothers to prevent them from ever building a similar one. In reality they were given a fat pension.

Like all exotic characters in Venice, the time-darkened bronze men on top of the tower are called the 'Moors', proto-Morris dancers in hairyman dress. Their task of sounding the hours is complemented at Epiphany and during Ascension Week (*La Sensa*) when figures of the three Magi and an angel roll out to pay homage to the Madonna.

THE PROCURATIE AND MUSEUMS

The Procuratie I7–8

Piazza San Marco; vaporetto San Marco.

The Procuratie that run along the two long sides of Piazza San Marco were originally built as offices for the nine procurators, whose positions were elective but permanent, and whose princely status was second only to the doge. Three were responsible for the upkeep of the Basilica and six for the city on either side of the Grand Canal.

The buildings are not identical; the one adjoining the Clock Tower, the **Procuratie Vecchie**, was begun by Mauro Codussi in 1500 and finished by Sansovino some 30 years later. The **Procuratie Nuove** opposite were designed by Scamozzi and Longhena between 1582 and 1640. But they are close enough in appearance to continue the city's motif of looking-glass reflections, which,

Coffee Culture

Two hundred years ago Piazza San Marco had 27 coffee-houses, with names like the 'Queen of the Sea', the 'Coach of Fortune', the 'Matter of Fact', and, most famously, 'Venice Triumphant', now called **Florian's** after its founder (*see* p.267). They were open around the clock, lit with 'a dazzle of everlasting day' – the best places in Venice for a gossip or intrigue, where checks on fidelity were very lightly kept. If expenses be damned, you may agree with an Austrian writer, who reasoned that 'since Europe is the most beautiful continent in the world, and Italy the most beautiful country in Europe, and Venice the most beautiful city in Italy, and Piazza San Marco the most beautiful square in Venice, and Florian's the most beautiful café in the Piazza, I can sit and have my coffee in the most beautiful place in the world.'

Besides the pretty mirrored and painted Florian's, the only surviving 18th-century café is the **Quadri** across the *piazza* (with its elegant and outrageously priced restaurant upstairs; *see* p.270), while the **Lavena** (*see* p.267), favourite of the composer Wagner, in Piazzetta San Marco, is a 19th-century 'newcomer'. All three have cacophonous bands or piano players and, if they're pumping out the schmaltz, will add another €1.50 to a tab that already threatens cardiac arrest, even for the tiniest espresso.

when the *piazza* is flooded, becomes surreal, and you feel as if you're inside a magic box. Nowadays the city rents out the Procuratie as shops.

Linking the Procuratie together is a similar arcaded building known as the **Ala Napoleonica**, which the French built in 1810 to replace the last incarnation of San Geminiano (by Sansovino) out of an urge for symmetry and the crying need for a ball-room. It is a copy of the Procuratie Nuove, except for the attic, crowned by a cast of Roman emperors, minus a would-be title holder from Corsica.

Museo Correr 18

*Piazza San Marco, t 041 522 5625; **vaporetto**
San Marco; wheelchair accessible. **Open**
April–Oct daily 9–7, Nov–March daily 9–5
(last tickets 90mins before closing time); **adm**
€9.50 ('biglietto accumulativo', also including
Palazzo Ducale, Biblioteca Nazionale
Marciana and Museo Archeologico).*

Founded by Teodoro Correr (d. 1830), this
museum holds the city's vast historical and
art collection. It runs hot and cold like any
attic, but not in any chronological order. In
the first rooms is an interesting collection of
books, manuscripts, prints and maps, old
models of ships, navigational instruments
and globes, describing the history of Venice
and its relationship to the sea. This is all now
clearly labelled.

The neoclassicism of the Napoleonic ballroom, dining room, throne room, etc. houses
works from the period, including plaster
models by Canova and frescoes by Giovanni
Carlo Bevilacqua.

Other rooms on this side of Piazza San
Marco (affording a great bird's eye view of
the square) are filled with Venetian memorabilia – the robes, ducal bonnets and old-
maidish nightcaps of the doges; a copy of the
statue of Marco Polo from the Temple of Five
Hundred Genies in Canton; musical instruments; arms and armour; and an interesting
section called 'Venetian Civilization' with all
sorts of objects from Venetian domestic life –
pots and pans and other domestic artefacts.
There are also some antique games – a
roulette wheel, playing cards, a draughts set,
jigsaw, children's games (a yo-yo), a bingo set,
dominoes – all are from the 18th century.
Among the bric-a-brac, note the pair of
20-inch-high platform shoes called *zoccoli*
or *ciapine*, the Renaissance rage among
Venetian ladies, because their increased
height allowed them to wear more lavish
gowns, even though the wearers could
hardly walk (a fact apparently much appreciated by their husbands, as it kept down the
risk of infidelities).

Upstairs, the **picture gallery** holds the best
collection of Venetian paintings outside the
Accademia, including Carpaccio's *Two
Venetian Ladies* (an essay in total boredom,
often called *The Courtesans*, though in fact
all Venetian ladies dressed that way – note
their shoes) and his *Young Man in a Red
Beret*, with an archetypal Venetian face.

Three of the most important paintings are
on the subject of the *Pietà*, one by Antonello
da Messina, painted during his Venetian
sojourn in the 1470s, and despite its
damaged state, still offering hints of the
luminosity that seduced Venetian painters.
Another is by Giovanni Bellini and a third by
the wiry Ferrarese painter Cosmè Tura.

Another section of this floor (*often closed*)
is dedicated to the Risorgimento and Daniele
Manin, who led the revolt against Austria in
1848; another holds the minor arts – small
bronzes made expressly for collectors by
Tullio Lombardo and Il Riccio, lace, household
items, and the outstanding *Aerial View of
Venice* by Jacopo de' Barbari, engraved in
1500, the most accurate view of the city
from the period and shown here with the
original blocks.

Biblioteca Nazionale Marciana 18

*Piazzetta San Marco; **entrance** via Museo
Correr (see p.118), t 041 522 4951; **vaporetto**
San Marco; wheelchair accessible. **Open**
April–Oct daily 9–7, Nov–March daily 9–5
(last tickets 90mins before closing time); **adm**
€9.50 ('biglietto accumulativo', also including
Palazzo Ducale, Museo Correr and Museo
Archeologico).*

On the west side of Piazzetta San Marco is
the building that Palladio thought was the
most beautiful in the world since the
temples of yore: Sansovino's **Biblioteca**,
begun in 1536 and finished by Vincenzo
Scamozzi in 1591. Made of white Istrian
stone, the Biblioteca is the key High
Renaissance building in Venice, notable not
only because it recalls ancient Roman

structures with its Doric and Ionian orders, frieze, and statues on the balustrade, but for the play of light and shadow in its arcades. Sansovino's training as a sculptor didn't always prepare him for some of the finer points of architecture, and in 1545 the vaulted ceiling in the main hall came crashing down (it has now been carefully reconstructed). The Council of Ten, who were never very tolerant of error, tossed poor Sansovino in the clink, and he was only released after Titian and his other pals pleaded for him.

The Biblioteca's **Sala Grande** is filled with ornate manuscripts and globes. Fra Mauro's magnificent 1459 *Mappa Mundi* ('Map of the World'; *see* 'San Michele', p.226) in the adjacent antechamber is hidden behind a curtain to protect it from the light; ask one of the custodians to open it. This *anticamera* was once the public statuary and is still filled with statues, among them some important pieces such as a 5th-century BC *Persephone*, called the '*Abbondanza Grimani*', an *Attilio* and a *Leda and the Swan*. These are on either side of the door above the grand staircase., elaborately stuccoed by Vittoria, which you can view from above.

Despite the grand treatment, the Biblioteca Nazionale Marciana didn't have the most auspicious of starts. A far-sighted official in the 14th century made a deal with Petrarch in his old age, that the Republic would take care of the poet if he would leave Venice his library. He did, in 1362, and the books were placed in some attic until a place was found for them. Another major library bequest in 1468, this time from Cardinal Bessarion (*c.* 1403–72), a native of Trebizond who did much to promote Greek scholarship and humanism in Italy, roused the Senate to found the Biblioteca Nazionale Marciana – but when it came to adding Petrarch's books, no one remembered where they were.

Still, displayed in some small rooms off the main hall are treasures any library would be proud of, most beautifully the **Grimani Breviary**, illuminated in 1501 by Flemish artists (though this is rarely exhibited), a 14th-century illuminated Dante, codices of Homer, and Marco Polo's will.

La Zecca I8

*Piazzetta San Marco; **vaporetto** San Marco/San Zaccaria. Not currently **open** to the public.*

Part of the Biblioteca, the Zecca or mint stands out as one of the very few buildings in Venice made of solid stone. Another of Sansovino's creations, this rusticated Doric building, finished in 1547, replaced the 12th-century mint where the first golden ducat had been produced in 1284. Ducats (after the 16th century, the gold coin was called the *zecchino*, hence our word for sequin, while the name *ducat* was used for a silver coin) were a major currency in Europe's exchanges, like the dollar today; unlike the dollar, they were worth their weight in 24-carat gold – between 1284 and 1797 the amount of gold in the coin never varied. Over a million gold and silver coins were minted each year – three times the wealth of the entire kingdom of France.

Museo Archeologico I7–8

*Piazzetta San Marco; **entrance** via Museo Correr (see p.118) and Biblioteca, **t** 041 522 4951; **vaporetto** San Marco; wheelchair accessible. **Open** April–Oct daily 9–7, Nov–March daily 9–5 (last tickets 90mins before closing time); **closed** 25 Dec and 1 Jan; **adm** €9.50 ('biglietto accumulativo' also including Palazzo Ducale, Museo Correr and Biblioteca Nazionale Marciana).*

Back through the Biblioteca's Sala Grande is this excellent but still relatively unknown museum, which re-opened in 1999 after major renovations. The itinerary here is a bit confusing, but the useful brochures in English, French and German will help. It was founded in 1523, when Cardinal Domenico Grimani left the State his impressive collection of Greek and Roman sculpture. It gets a few points for being one of the few museums to be heated in the winter.

A set of colossal 4th-century AD marble toes in the first room is followed by an extensive Roman coin collection, some massive pieces guaranteed to put holes in a toga pocket. Among the Roman works are three fine copies of *Gallic Warriors*, presented by Attalos of Pergamon to Athens, also a votive relief to Cybele, and a winsome bust of a boy from the 2nd century BC. Among the busts there's one of Pompey looking troubled, Caligula as an all-American football hero, the kind of boy you might bring home to meet your mother, though perhaps most memorable of all is the bust of the bloated Emperor Vitellus, antiquity's most legendary trencherman. Other highlights include a 2nd-century sarcophagus with a naval battle, a 5th-century AD ivory casket, and a scene of the god Mithras, whose cult challenged Christianity in its early days, complete with his bull, dog, snake and scorpion; a porphyry bust of the priest Isaac that looks quite modern, and a couple of mummies in the small Egyptian collection.

Museo Diocesano J7

Ponte de la Canonica, t 041 522 9166; vaporetto San Zaccaria. Open Mon-Sat 10.30–12.30; adm free.

Sant'Apollonia's Romanesque cloister – the last one remaining in Venice – has become a safe and remarkably tranquil haven for Venice's religious trappings and art orphaned by the demolition of churches.

Among the more notable paintings are two by Luca *fa presto* ('quick draw') Giordano of Naples from Sant'Aponal, Titian's *San Giacomo*, A. Pellegrini's *Allegory on the School of the Crucifixion*, the spooky *Transport of a Drowned Man* and a series of portraits of the *Primiceri* (head chaplains of St Mark's).

Other works include a harrowing *Crucifixion* without a cross, and a wide array of reliquaries, missals, vestments, silver – and the cardinal's beret that Pope John XXIII wore as Patriarch of Venice.

San Marco

NORTH OF PIAZZA SAN MARCO: THE MERCERIE 124
San Zulian 124
Campo San Salvatore 124
Campo San Bartolomeo 125

LA FENICE AND AROUND 126
La Fenice 126
Campo San Fantin 126
San Moisè 127
Around San Moisè 127
Santa Maria Zobenigo 127
Campo San Maurizio 128

NORTH OF LA FENICE 128
Museo Fortuny 128
Campo Manin 129
Palazzo Contarini del Bovolo 129
San Luca 130
Riva del Carbon 130

SANTO STEFANO AND AROUND 130
Campo Santo Stefano 130
San Vitale 131
Palazzo Pisani 131
Campo Sant'Angelo 131
A Detour North to Corte Corner 131
San Samuele 132

04

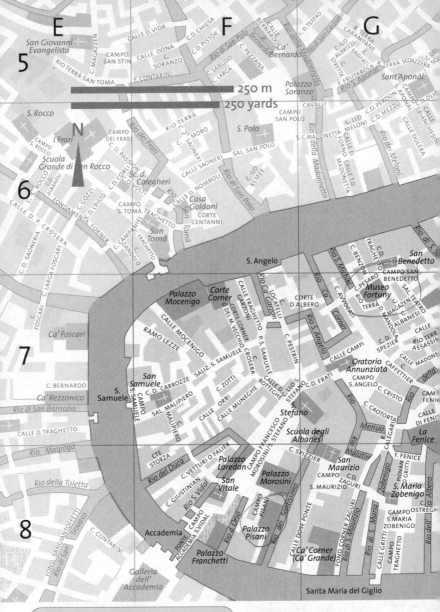

1 Lunch

Antico Martini, *Campo San Fantin*, **t** *041 522 4121*. **Open** *Thurs–Mon 12–2.30*. **Very expensive**. Classic, elegant, traditional, *see p.266*.

2 Coffee and Cakes

Marchini, *San Marco 676, C. Spadaria*. **Open** *Mon–Sat 9–8*. Delicious cakes, *see p.270*.

3 Drinks

Bacaro Jazz, *Sal. del Fontego dei Tedeschi*. **Open** *Thurs–Tues 11am–2am*. See *p.282*.

Highlights

Medieval Venice: Campanile Santo Stefano, Vencie's most alarming leaning tower, p.131

Renaissance Venice: San Salvatore's art, p.125

Baroque/Rococo Venice: The gooey, bizarre façade of San Moisé, p.127

Indoor Venice: Early 20th-century arty atmosphere at the Museo Fortuny, p.128

Decadent Venice: Designer shopping along the Mercerie, p.124

Pigeon Venice: Carlo Goldoni's statue, p.125

San Marco

The *sestiere* of San Marco, west of Piazza San Marco to the Grand Canal, manages to be both the most pedestrian and the most glitzy quarter of Venice: local institutions such as La Fenice are here, among designer shops and swish hotels, but culture vultures will find meagre pickings – relatively, that is, since any city would give its eye-teeth for a few of its *palazzi* or works of art.

NORTH OF PIAZZA SAN MARCO: THE MERCERIE

From under the magic clock tower of Piazza San Marco, you leave the city's centre stage to enter another world: the winding lower gut of golden consumption, the **Mercerie** (or *Marzarie* in Venetian dialect and on the street signs). It has five transformations, from the **Merceria dell'Orologio** (I7) to the **Merceria 2 Aprile** (H–I6), strung together like brightly lit sausages to form the shortest route from San Marco to the Rialto Bridge.

For a long time the *mercerie* were the only streets in Venice paved with marble blocks; they have always been lined with shops, probably offering the same kind of status economic surplus as they do now – precious silks and spices, Lacoste shirts and Opium

---

The Old Woman with a Mortar

It was a dark and stormy night, 15 June 1310, and the atmosphere was tense with conspiracy. No one was more displeased with the *Serrata* of the *Maggior Consiglio* than the noblemen who were shut out, and under the banner of Baiamonte Tiepolo they rode through the Mercerie towards Piazza San Marco intending to overthrow the Republic.

The old woman who lived over the Sottoportego, Giustina Rossi, was unable to sleep, and looked out of her window, only to see Baiamonte's insurgent army approaching underneath. Thinking quickly, she prised a stone from her windowsill and dropped it, scoring a direct hit on the skull of the standard-bearer. In the rain and thunder, the army panicked and retreated in confusion, failing to meet the other rebel contingent in the *piazza*. Thanks to Signora Rossi's aim, the revolt was foiled, and the grateful *Signori* granted the reward she requested: the right to fly the banner of St Mark from her window on every feast day – and a promise never to raise her rent.

---

perfume. But no one's ever accused the Venetians of offering anything but the shrewdest of bargains for their wares.

If the throngs aren't too pressing (or depressing) you can pause to pick out one of the Mercerie's landmarks: the relief of the **Old Woman with a Mortar** (*see* box, below), over the arch of Sottoportego del Nero Cappello (first left after the clock tower).

San Zulian I7

*Campo San Zulian, on the Mercerie; **vaporetto** San Marco. **Open** daily 8.15–10.15 and 11–3.45; **adm** free.*

Rebuilt in 1553 by Sansovino, San Zulian's most remarkable feature is the figure over the door of Tommaso Rangone with all his favourite books and globes. Rangone, like many Venetian benefactors, had no modesty when it came to reminding posterity exactly who it was who paid for the church, though he is the only one who wished to be remembered for his scholarship, never a Venetian forte (and Rangone was from Ravenna). He is buried inside, under Palma Giovane's ceiling of *St Julian in Glory*; on the first altar on the right is a grimy Veronese: the *Pietà* with saints Rocco, Girolamo and Marco, a late work. Even better is Giovanni da Santacroce's *Coronation of the Virgin* with three saints, a detached altarpiece on the left wall.

Campo San Salvatore H6

***Vaporetto** San Marco.*

This busy crossroads has a memorial column to the abortive revolt of 1848, and a more memorable iron dragon, over a luggage and umbrella shop, holding up a coloured globe made of glass umbrellas. Its major buildings both wear safe, nondescript Baroque façades by Giuseppe Sardi: the **Scuola di San Teodoro**, now an exhibition hall, and the church of **San Salvatore**. The adjacent **monastery of San Salvatore**, now occupied by the phone company, has a cloister attributed to Sansovino, which the phone folks will let you see.

San Salvatore (San Salvador) H6

Campo San Salvatore, on the Mercerie;
vaporetto *Rialto.* **Open** *daily 10–12 and 5–9;*
adm *free.*

San Salvatore has a remarkable
Renaissance interior, begun in 1508 by
Giorgio Spavento and completed by Tullio
Lombardo and Sansovino. Its unique design
imaginatively fuses a long basilican nave
with two aisles and a central Greek cross
plan, by stringing together three Greek
crosses, three domes and three transepts,
and tying them together at the corners with
pilasters and mini-cupolas. The clean lines
and lack of decorative encrustations let the
eye enjoy the interplay of space and light.

Sansovino also contributed the **Tomb of
Doge Francesco Venier** (d. 1556), sculpting the
fine figures of Hope and Charity at the age of
80. But Venice was known as a city of old
men; the *Maggior Consiglio* even devised a
special committee for patricians over 80 to
keep them occupied with the State until they
dropped dead. At the age of 89, Titian
painted the *Annunciation* by the next altar,
an unusual work that he signed with double
emphasis *Titianus Fecit.* ('Fecit' because, it is
said, his patrons refused to believe that he
had really painted it.) The right transept
contains the **Tomb of Caterina Cornaro**
(d. 1510), queen of Cyprus, at least for a little
while, before the Republic convinced her of
her duty as a good Venetian to cede the
island to direct Venetian rule. In exchange for
Cyprus Caterina got Asolo, where luxurious
ennui was first distilled into a fine art, and
when she died she got a funeral fit for a
queen and this better-than-middling tomb,
with reliefs by Bernardo Contino.

On the high altar, Titian's *Transfiguration* is
in the way of a more impressive work of art: a
14th-century silver gilt **reredos** made by
Venetian goldsmiths and, after the Pala d'Oro
in St Mark's, their greatest masterpiece. The
reredos is exposed only during Holy Week;
otherwise ask the sacristan to push the
button that lowers the Titian – a charming
device that takes some of the glitz off the
cinquecento's Mr T. To the left is another
painting that upstages Titian, *The Supper at
the House of Emmaus* by the school of
Giovanni Bellini. In front of the high altar, a
glass circle set into the floor permits you to
see a recently discovered merchant's tomb,
with damaged frescoes by Titian's brother,
Francesco Vecellio. The third chapel on the
left has statues of the two major plague
prevention saints, *Santi Rocco* and
Sebastiano, by Vittoria.

Campo San Bartolomeo H–I6

Vaporetto *Rialto.*

One of the social hubs of Venice, this long
and narrow and almost invariably crowded
campo has for its centrepiece a wonderfully
benign bronze **statue of Carlo Goldoni**,
whose comedies in Venetian dialect still
make the Venetians laugh. Goldoni (1707–93)
(like Hemingway, nicknamed 'Papa'), used to
wander Venice in his three-cornered hat,
eavesdropping on conversations; often, he
claimed, a mere turn of phrase would inspire
his next play. By the smile on his jolly face he
still finds his fellow citizens amusing, and if
he needed fresh material, he'd find plenty
every evening around seven. But perhaps 120
plays is enough for anybody.

Salizzada Pio X leads from here to the
Ponte Rialto, with views over the Grand
Canal that may be more tempting than its
trinket and jewellery shops. Long gone,
however, is the sign 'It is Forbidden to Spit on
the Swimmers'. In the snowy winter of 1987,
it briefly took on a new role: Venice's only ski
slope. For more on the bridge, *see* p 184.

San Bartolomeo H6

*Campo San Bartolomeo, entrance on
Salizzada Pio X;* **vaporetto** *Rialto.* **Closed** *for
restoration.*

The church of San Bartolomeo turns its
back on the *campo*, with its entrance around
the corner. This was formerly the German
church in Venice (the Fondaco dei Tedeschi,
now the post office, is nearby) but few of its
old parishioners would recognize it since the

pedestrian rebuilding of 1723. Today it is used for the occasional exhibition; some day it may get its most famous work of art, Sebastiano del Piombo's *Organ Shutters*, back from the Accademia. Don't miss the funny face, sticking its tongue out at you from the foot of the campanile. It's a good job Ruskin didn't see this one.

LA FENICE AND AROUND

La Fenice G7

Campo San Fantin, **w** *www.teatrolafenice.iy;* **vaporetto** *Santa Maria del Giglio. Due to* **reopen** *2004.*

Calle Larga XXII Marzo, which extends in front of San Moisè, is named after Daniele Manin's revolt against the Austrians of 1848, and is dotted with designer boutiques and banks. Take it and turn right into Calle delle Veste and into Campo San Fantin.

At the time of writing, this *campo* is rather spooky and uninviting, since the whole theatre is shrouded in scaffolding after the terrible fire which ripped it apart in 1996. However, the arguments and long delays seem to be over now that a new building contractor has taken over. Progress is being made, and the theatre is due to open early in 2004 (with an inaugural concert – by invitation only – planned for late 2003).

Designed by Gian Antonio Selva in 1792, Venice's opera house was the swansong of the Republic, a last burst of fun before Napoleon. It also proved true to its name (the 'Phoenix'), rising up from the ashes of an earlier devastating fire in 1835 in the same design, by Selva's pupils – neoclassical understatement outside, and, within, enough Late Empire excess to match all comers in the *bel canto* league. It's hard to believe, but Selva was lampooned and criticized for his precocious functionalist design for the interior, which was not at all in the balanced, symmetrical fashion of the day. The Sala

Apollinea, the banqueting rooms, and especially the oval 1,500-seat auditorium with its gilded boxes were the highlights; new, inexpensive seats had been added, to give casual visitors to the city more chance to attend a performance in one of Europe's prettiest theatres.

To an Italian opera maven, La Fenice suffered comparison only with the Teatro San Carlo in Naples for 'genuine operatic tradition' (Milan's La Scala is a mere upstart) – a tradition that began with two decades of *castrati*, immensely popular though forbidden to don female attire 'to the disappointment of many interested gentlemen'. La Fenice had its low notes as well: the première of Verdi's *La Traviata* in 1853 was so bad that the composer himself described it as a 'fiasco', though an improved performance redeemed the opera the next year. But Verdi could never stay unpopular for long, if not for his music, but for the rallying note he sounded in the *Risorgimento*. Under the Austrians, when official public life was denied to the Venetians, they would flock here, join in the patriotic choruses, and do all they could to niggle their overlords behind the cover of music. In the 20th century La Fenice rejoined the musical vanguard with premières of Stravinsky's *The Rake's Progress* (1951) and Britten's *The Turn of the Screw*.

Campo San Fantin H7

Vaporetto *Santa Maria del Giglio.*

The square in front of the opera house is named after the plain and crumbling 1507 church of **San Fantin** by Scarpagnino, with a perfect Renaissance dome over the sanctuary by Sansovino.

Nearby, behind an Istrian stone façade, was the home of the former Scuola della Buona Morte, a confraternity that comforted prisoners who were condemned to death (Michelangelo belonged to the branch in Rome). The building is now occupied by the mouldering **Ateneo Veneto**, whose members might let you in to see some mediocre paintings by Veronese – or they might not.

San Moisè H8

*Campo San Moisè; **vaporetto** San Marco.*
***Open** Mon–Sat 3.30–7, Sun 9–12 and 3.30–7;*
***adm** free.*

Venetians who regularly have to face the
façade of San Moisè (1668) have developed a
self-willed blind spot for Italy's most
grotesque church – although casting their
glance in the direction of the nearby Bauer-
Grünwald hotel isn't much of an
improvement. Blame Alessandro Tremignon
and sculptor Heinrich Meyring, but not too
much: at the time of construction their
grotesqueries fitted well into surroundings
that included the state casino, or Ridotto
(*see* box, below), where nearly all the players
wore masks, and the Teatro San Moisè
(demolished in 1876), which opened in
1639 with the première of Monteverdi's
opera *Arianna*.

Meyring also created the extraordinary
high altar, or rock pile, of *St Moses on Mount
Sinai*. But also look in the sacristy for the
elegant 1633 bronze altar of the *Dead Christ
and Angels*, by Nicolò and Sebastiano
Roccatagliata, and over the left door for the
leering skeletons on the Hallowe'en tomb of
one Canon Ivanovich. And if anyone on earth
still plays trivia games, you can probably

stump your opponents by asking where the
great Scottish financier John Law (1671–1729)
ended up, after killing a man in a duel in
London and fleeing to France, where he
single-handedly took over the national
economy until his bubble burst in the
Mississippi Scheme. The answer to this
teaser is in the floor of San Moisè, after
spending his last years in Venice living by
what he made at cards. There's an inscription
on a slab near the entrance.

Around San Moisè

Behind San Moisè and to the left is the
Frezzeria (H7), Venice's scarcely noticeable
red light district. A right on Calle del
Selvadego leads to the **Bacino Orseolo** (H7),
always filled with gently bobbing gondolas.

Santa Maria Zobenigo G8

*Campo Santa Maria Zobenigo; **vaporetto***
*Santa Maria del Giglio. **Open** Mon–Sat*
*10–5.30, Sun and hols 3–5.30; **adm** €1.*

A quirky blossom, Zobenigo isn't the
Venetian attempt to pronounce 'lily', but
'Jubanico', the family who erected the church
in the 9th century. This long memory is a rap

Gambling

Off Salizzada San Moisè, at Calle del
Ridotto, San Marco 1332, with its grand *piano
nobile* windows, was Venice's celebrated
Ridotto, or state-controlled gaming house,
ancestor of the modern Casino Municipale.
Gambling seems to have been inbred in
Venice, especially in its decline, when the
wealthy, no longer able to stake their
fortunes in shipping, had a chronic need to
risk them in some other way. Cards took the
place of ships, and the State, seeking to take
advantage of this, founded the Ridotto in
1638. Open only during the six months of
Carnival, it guaranteed fair play in exchange
for a percentage of the proceeds. The
State got rich, while everyone else slowly or
spectacularly went bankrupt, patricians and

commoners alike (the only requirement to
enter was that one wore a mask); tourists
like John Law made a fortune there, though
others fared less well, like composer
Domenico Scarlatti of Naples, who picked up
a gambling habit that became the cancer of
his career. In 1774 the Senate could no longer
ignore the scandal and held a vote on closing
the Ridotto. To encourage the members to
vote according to their conscience, the vote
was secret; when the votes were counted the
Senate discovered to its dismay that it had
voted to abolish one of its principal sources
of income. But, as an observer wrote,
'Evidently, no state can keep going without
the aid of vice,' and over 100 illegal *casini*
('little houses'), or social clubs, soon came to
take on the meaning they have today.

on the knuckles of the Barbaro family, who in rebuilding the church in the 1680s devoted its entire façade to themselves, without even a nod to religion. The four heroic statues are of the Barbaro brothers, no-accounts as far as Venetian history is concerned. Above, allegorical figures of *Venice, Virtue, Wisdom, Honour* and *Fame* are forced to accompany the clan, while, below, reliefs depict maps of the towns where they gained their supposed triumphs and war trophies; you can learn quite a bit about the topography of Rome, Corfu and Padua, while Zara, Spalato and Candia are inexplicably unfinished, imposing walls with nothing inside.

Art of a more pious nature clutters the interior, chiefly a pair of *Evangelists* by Tintoretto behind the altar and the *Stations of the Cross* along the nave, a memory of an 18th-century competition; each artist contributed two scenes, though no one remembers who won.

Campo San Maurizio G8

Vaporetto Santa Maria del Giglio.

This is the headquarters of Venice's antiques dealers, who often turn the square into an open-air market. The bland church of **San Maurizio**, rebuilt in 1806 by Gian Antonio Selva, is a prime candidate for Venice's most wilted wallflower, saved only by some vigorous neoclassical reliefs on the façade.

A door down from the church is the **Scuola degli Albanesi**, built in 1531 as the centre of Venice's Albanian community, refugees from Ottoman imperialism who settled in this neighbourhood in the 1400s; the Lombardesque reliefs on the façade include a scene of Sultan Mehmet II studying the castle of Scutari. The Albanians hired Carpaccio to paint a series on the *Life of the Virgin*, and in the 1700s, when the Albanians were too few to keep up the confraternity, it was taken over, art and all, by the bakers' guild; two of the paintings are now in the Ca' d'Oro (*see* p.196) and the others hidden somewhere in the back rooms of the Museo Correr (*see* p.118).

NORTH OF LA FENICE

Museo Fortuny G7

Campo San Benedetto, t 041 520 0995; vaporetto Sant'Angelo. Open only for special exhibitions (due to reopen entirely in 2004); adm to be decided.

The 15th-century brick **Palazzo Pésaro degli Orfei** was long the home of Catalan artist Mariano Fortuny (1871–1949), fashion designer, photographer, inventor (he designed a model for a mobile dome) and all-round Renaissance man. One of the most charming things about the palace has been its unrestored condition, its rickety wooden stair and balcony in the courtyard, though if there was a popular show, this fragile state would limit the access to a few people at a time. It's also something the current restoration work will put paid to.

The large rooms of Fortuny's home and studio are jammed full of paintings of nymphs, nymphs, and more nymphs. Other rooms are hung with the pleated silks to which he owes his fame today, which once tickled the backs of Sarah Bernhardt, Isadora

Aldus

The founder of the Aldine Press, Aldus – whose first love was Greek – played a major role in preserving, printing, developing a Greek typeface (he also invented italics) and diffusing authoritative editions of nearly every classical text to the general reading public at affordable prices. He had a unique editorial board that featured some of the greatest scholars of the Renaissance, including Pico della Mirandola and in 1508 Erasmus, who helped print his own *Adages*, a best-seller in its day. Another of Aldus' publications, Francesco Colonna's beautifully illustrated philosophical romance, *Hypnerotomachia Polifili* (or *The Dream of Polyphilus*, 1499) inspired the design of Longhena's Santa Maria della Salute.

Aretino – Scourge of Princes

A native of Arezzo in Tuscany (like Sansovino), Aretino was the first man to run a literary protection racket – princes and cardinals paid him *not* to write about them. Like Sansovino, he came to Venice as a refugee from Rome, after a career smearing the reputations of cardinals (for Giulio de' Medici, when he wanted to be elected pope), publishing erotic sonnets, and surviving an assassination attempt by a bishop.

With Venice as a secure base, he began his new career of publishing brilliant letters, flattering and satirizing public figures from Emperor Charles V on down, using well-informed sources; he also had a keen eye for art, and did much to increase the reputation of his friend Titian, while annoying Michelangelo so successfully that the artist painted him in the Sistine Chapel *Last Judgement* as St Bartholomew, holding the skin of Michelangelo, whom he had 'flayed' (Titian, perhaps in response, used Aretino as a model for Pontius Pilate). Besides getting under the skin of public figures, he wrote comedies and dialogues, mostly about brothels, poking fun at the erudition of the day. His prurient interests kept his reputation in the hands of the same kinds of academics he mocked, and not only earned him an anonymous burial in this church, but lent a certain truth to the story that he died from laughing too hard at a dirty story told about his own sister.

Duncan, Eleonora Duse, and the loony Marchesa Casati. The museum nearly always includes a photography or design exhibition.

Around the Museum

Sharing the palace's boxy little Campo San Benedetto is one of Venice's more obscure churches, **San Benedetto** (G6), containing Baroque paintings by Sebastiano Mazzoni, Giambattista Tiepolo, and Bernardo Strozzi.

Southwards from San Benedetto, Salizzada della Chiesa e Teatro has, at No.3998, a Byzantine-style **mosaic** in a shrine of the *Madonna and Child*, smothered in necklaces.

Campo Manin H7

From the Museo Fortuny, take Rio Terrà della Mandola and turn left on to Calle della Mandola to reach Campo Manin, with a statue of the fiery patriot, lawyer **Daniele Manin**, who led the revolt against the Austrians in 1848 (and ended up as a schoolmaster, teaching Italian in Paris). His statue looks towards his house by the little bridge on the left. The **Cassa di Risparmio** bank (1964) is by Pier Luigi Nervi, Italy's most acclaimed postwar architect – and the only one to get a chance to build on a conspicuous spot in Venice. On this same site

in 1490, **Aldus Manutius** (Teobaldo Pio Manuzio), a humanist teacher from Rome, founded his famous Aldine Press, with its imprint of the anchor and dolphin (*see* box, opposite).

Palazzo Contarini del Bovolo H7

Calle dei Risi (south of Campo Manin), t 041 270 2464; vaporetto Rialto. Open April–Oct daily 10–6, Nov–March Sat and Sun 10–4; adm €2.50.

From Campo Manin, Calle della Vida (under the sign for the Hotel Centauro) will take you on a short detour to the Palazzo Contarini del Bovolo ('of the spiral stair') tucked in a tiny courtyard. Perhaps only one in a thousand visitors ever tries to find this, but those who do are abundantly rewarded with Giovanni Candi's flamboyant external **spiral stair** (*c.* 1500), its ranks of arches curling up five storeys like an architectural ice cream *parfait*. The collection of medieval **well-heads** in the garden, thrones for a motley collection of stray pussies, is equally whimsical.

The view from the top is much more localized than the one from the campanile in Piazza San Marco, and in many ways rather more illuminating.

San Luca G–H6

Vaporetto Rialto.

From Campo Manin, the Ramo di Salizzada leads in a few steps to the church of San Luca, an ungainly 19th-century reconstruction, though light and airy inside. None of the paintings is worth a second glance, though there is a very damaged altarpiece by Veronese and the unmarked grave of **Pietro Aretino** (1492–1556), the century's most lively vernacular writer (*see* box, p.129).

Facing the side entrance of the church in Campo Chiesa is the **Casa Magno**, with an exceptionally fine early Gothic doorway, a masterpiece of brickwork.

Riva del Carbon H6

Vaporetto Rialto.

From Campo Chiesa, Calle Cavalli leads up to the Grand Canal; the first palace to your right is **Palazzo Farsetti** (H6), now Venice's *Municipio*, or City Hall. The next, the **Palazzo Loredan** (H6), was as the plaque says the home of Elena Lucrezia Corner Piscopia, who in 1678 became the first woman to receive a university degree (from Padua, in philosophy).

Beyond is **Riva del Carbon** (the coal docks), one of the rare walkways along Venice's 'Champs-Elysées of the Water God' as the French like to call the Grand Canal. The Riva changes name several times on its way to the Rialto *vaporetto* stop and bridge.

SANTO STEFANO AND AROUND

Campo Santo Stefano F7–8

Vaporetto Accademia.

This large *campo* near the Accademia bridge was home to bear-baiting until 1802, when the crush of spectators on the seats caused a tragic collapse. The bulls have been replaced by a statue of Risorgimento scholar Nicolò Tommaseo (1802–74), watched over by the peering eyes of several palaces: **Palazzo Morosini** (F8) on the east side (No.2802), home of the battling Doge Francesco Morosini and, across the *campo*, the long classical façade of **Palazzo Loredan** (F8) (now the Veneto Institute of Science, Letters and Art), with its seaworthy door-knocker by Alessandro Vittoria. Opposite San Vitale on the southern side of the *campo* are the high iron fences of the **Palazzo Franchetti** (F8), ornately restored in the 19th century, and one of the few palaces on the Grand Canal to have its own gardens.

Santo Stefano F–G7

*Campo Santo Stefano (Campo Francesco Morosini); vaporetto Accademia. **Open** Mon–Sat 10–5, Sun 1–5; **adm** to sacristy €2.*

Early Gothic Santo Stefano (S. Stin), with its grandly florid Gothic door has a couple of distinctions: it's the only church built directly over a canal and, more dubiously, it has had to be reconsecrated the most often – six times, because of the repeated murders that occurred within its walls. The interior, however, is most serenely Gothic, with harmoniously patterned walls and wooden ship's-keel roof. On the wall by the door is the pretty equestrian **Tomb of Giacomo Surian** (d. 1493), decorated with skulls, garlands and griffons; a bombastic bronze seal in the middle of the nave marks the grave of Doge Francesco Morosini, conqueror of the Morea.

The **sacristy** is rendered slightly claustrophobic by the large stretches of canvas on its walls, among them three late, shadowy Tintorettos: *The Washing of the Feet*, the *Last Supper*, composed at the extraordinary angle the artist favoured, and *The Agony in the Garden*. Off the left aisle a door leads into the cloister, now government offices, though still containing the **Tomb of Doge Andrea Contarini** (d. 1382). Less fortunate were the hundreds of victims of the plague of 1630, buried in trenches in Santo Stefano's graveyard (now Campiello Nuovo, off Calle del

Pestrin facing the façade); for 200 years it was strictly off-limits.

Outside, the **bell tower** has a dangerous-looking lean, best viewed from Campo Sant'Angelo over the canal to the northeast (*see* later this page).

San Vitale F8

Campo Santo Stefano/Campo San Vidal;
*vaporetto Accademia. **Open** only for concerts and exhibitions; **adm** free.*

At the southernmost end of Campo Santo Stefano is the deconsecrated church of San Vitale (or Vidal), with a pseudo-Palladian façade, now used for exhibitions.

In its day San Vitale was the site of an unusual ceremony, celebrating the anniversary of the execution of Doge Marin Falier; the current Doge would attend Mass, followed throughout by a priest bearing a phial of red liquid symbolizing the traitor's blood, a humiliating reminder of the consequences of independent action.

Of the paintings, Carpaccio's *San Vitale* on a white horse with two pedestrian saints survives *in situ* over the high altar, while Sebastiano Ricci's *Immaculate Conception*, a study in blue and white draperies, is on the left. Note the ancient Roman inscription embedded in the foot of the campanile (to the left of the façade), itself a survivor of the original 11th-century church.

Palazzo Pisani F8

*Campo Pisani; **vaporetto** Accademia. **Closed** to the public, except courtyards.*

Off Campo Santo Stefano, Palazzo Pisani is tucked into its own little *campo*. The tycoons of the Pisani family suffered from the most lingering case of 'stone fever' or *mal della pietra* in Venice. You could land a Concorde in their villa at Strà, and this town palace of theirs, begun in 1614, would have reached similar proportions – or at least the Grand Canal – if the government hadn't ordered them to stop building during the mid-18th century. The palace, now the

Conservatory of Music, has courtyards, linked by a loggia – popping into to see the wall of po Pisani busts.

Campo Sant'Angelo G7

Vaporetto Sant'Angelo.

A large dusty square (as much as a Venetian *campo* can ever be large and dusty), this is adorned on one side by the former Convent of Santo Stefano, two Gothic *palazzi* (the Duodo and the Gritti) and the best view of Santo Stefano's jauntily leaning tower, just to the southwest.

As perilous as it looks, it was spared the fate of the campanile that once accompanied the long gone church of Sant'Angelo, which tilted so dangerously in the 15th century that a specialist was brought in from Bologna to try to right it. He succeeded magnificently, making the leaning tower plumb-straight – until the day after the scaffolding was removed and it collapsed in a pile of rubble.

A Detour North to Corte Corner

If you take Calle delle Botteghe from the northwest corner of Campo Santo Stefano (opposite and to your left as you leave the church of Santo Stefano), and take the first right, and then the first left, you'll find a lovely street called **Piscina San Samuele** (F7). Here you'll pass the most wistfully Venetian of **plaques**. It honours Francesco Querini, who left in 1904 'to try and explore the unknown paths of the Arctic, but who did not return victoriously...'

Turn left into Ramo della Piscina. The next corner offers a choice of short digressions: on the right, Calle Corner o del Magazen Vecchio leads to the charming **Corte Corner** (F7), with a Gothic palace and Veneto-Byzantine well-head, while to the left, on Calle Crosera, you can see the curious **shoe** (high heel, of course) carved in the old Scuola of the Shoemakers at No.3127.

San Samuele F7

Campo San Samuele, on the Grand Canal; vaporetto San Samuele. Open Mon–Sat 9.30–12.30 and 3–6; Sun 3–6; adm free.

An ancient church rebuilt in 1685, San Samuele still retains its fine old campanile; and is often called upon to take some of the cultural overflow of the Grassi's shows. Of its original decoration, only some 15th-century frescoes by Paduan artists remain; little of the church recalls the reputation it had as Venice's naughtiest, recorded in a dialect doggerel:

> Contrada piccola, grande bordel;
> Senza ponti, cattive campane,
> Omini becchi e donne puttane.
>
> (A small parish, but a big bordello;
> Without bridges, with wicked bells
> Its men are cuckolds and its women whores.)

It just figures that San Samuele was Casanova's parish church; the self-styled 'Cavalier de Seingalt' was born nearby in 1725, in Calle Malipiero (with a plaque), near the long gone Teatro di San Samuele, where his theatrical parents once performed. As little Giacomo demonstrated a certain precocious ability, his parents destined him for the priesthood, and at San Samuele he took minor orders, before discovering his real vocation in the bedrooms of Europe.

Campo San Samuele F7

Campo San Samuele on the Grand Canal has fine views across to the Ca' Rezzonico. On the right of the church is the **Palazzo Grassi**, purchased by Fiat and used for some of Venice's blockbuster exhibitions.

Pestrin facing the façade); for 200 years it was strictly off-limits.

Outside, the **bell tower** has a dangerous-looking lean, best viewed from Campo Sant'Angelo over the canal to the northeast (*see* later this page).

San Vitale F8

Campo Santo Stefano/Campo San Vidal; vaporetto Accademia. Open only for concerts and exhibitions; adm free.

At the southernmost end of Campo Santo Stefano is the deconsecrated church of San Vitale (or Vidal), with a pseudo-Palladian façade, now used for exhibitions.

In its day San Vitale was the site of an unusual ceremony, celebrating the anniversary of the execution of Doge Marin Falier; the current Doge would attend Mass, followed throughout by a priest bearing a phial of red liquid symbolizing the traitor's blood, a humiliating reminder of the consequences of independent action.

Of the paintings, Carpaccio's *San Vitale* on a white horse with two pedestrian saints survives *in situ* over the high altar, while Sebastiano Ricci's *Immaculate Conception*, a study in blue and white draperies, is on the left. Note the ancient Roman inscription embedded in the foot of the campanile (to the left of the façade), itself a survivor of the original 11th-century church.

Palazzo Pisani F8

Campo Pisani; vaporetto Accademia. Closed to the public, except courtyards.

Off Campo Santo Stefano, Palazzo Pisani is tucked into its own little *campo*. The tycoons of the Pisani family suffered from the most lingering case of 'stone fever' or *mal della pietra* in Venice. You could land a Concorde in their villa at Strà, and this town palace of theirs, begun in 1614, would have reached similar proportions – or at least the Grand Canal – if the government hadn't ordered them to stop building during the mid-18th century. The palace, now the **Conservatory of Music**, has two interior courtyards, linked by a loggia – worth popping into to see the wall of pouting Pisani busts.

Campo Sant'Angelo G7

Vaporetto Sant'Angelo.

A large dusty square (as much as a Venetian *campo* can ever be large and dusty), this is adorned on one side by the former Convent of Santo Stefano, two Gothic *palazzi* (the Duodo and the Gritti) and the best view of Santo Stefano's jauntily leaning tower, just to the southwest.

As perilous as it looks, it was spared the fate of the campanile that once accompanied the long gone church of Sant'Angelo, which tilted so dangerously in the 15th century that a specialist was brought in from Bologna to try to right it. He succeeded magnificently, making the leaning tower plumb-straight – until the day after the scaffolding was removed and it collapsed in a pile of rubble.

A Detour North to Corte Corner

If you take Calle delle Botteghe from the northwest corner of Campo Santo Stefano (opposite and to your left as you leave the church of Santo Stefano), and take the first right, and then the first left, you'll find a lovely street called **Piscina San Samuele** (F7). Here you'll pass the most wistfully Venetian of **plaques**. It honours Francesco Querini, who left in 1904 'to try and explore the unknown paths of the Arctic, but who did not return victoriously...'

Turn left into Ramo della Piscina. The next corner offers a choice of short digressions: on the right, Calle Corner o del Magazen Vecchio leads to the charming **Corte Corner** (F7), with a Gothic palace and Veneto-Byzantine well-head, while to the left, on Calle Crosera, you can see the curious **shoe** (high heel, of course) carved in the old Scuola of the Shoemakers at No.3127.

San Samuele F7

Campo San Samuele, on the Grand Canal;
vaporetto San Samuele. Open Mon–Sat
9.30–12.30 and 3–6; Sun 3–6; adm free.

An ancient church rebuilt in 1685, San
Samuele still retains its fine old campanile;
and is often called upon to take some of the
cultural overflow of the Grassi's shows. Of its
original decoration, only some 15th-century
frescoes by Paduan artists remain; little of
the church recalls the reputation it had as
Venice's naughtiest, recorded in a dialect
doggerel:

> *Contrada piccola, grande bordel;*
> *Senza ponti, cattive campane,*
> *Omini becchi e donne puttane.*
>
> *(A small parish, but a big bordello;*
> *Without bridges, with wicked bells*
> *Its men are cuckolds and its women whores.)*

It just figures that San Samuele was
Casanova's parish church; the self-styled
'Cavalier de Seingalt' was born nearby in 1725,
in Calle Malipiero (with a plaque), near the
long gone Teatro di San Samuele, where his
theatrical parents once performed. As little
Giacomo demonstrated a certain precocious
ability, his parents destined him for the
priesthood, and at San Samuele he took
minor orders, before discovering his real
vocation in the bedrooms of Europe.

Campo San Samuele F7

Campo San Samuele on the Grand Canal
has fine views across to the Ca' Rezzonico.
On the right of the church is the **Palazzo
Grassi**, purchased by Fiat and used for some
of Venice's blockbuster exhibitions.

Castello

SANTI GIOVANNI E PAOLO AND AROUND 136
Santi Giovanni e Paolo 136
Colleoni Statue 139
Scuola Grande di San Marco 140
Ospedaletto 140

AROUND CAMPO SANTA MARIA FORMOSA 141
Santa Maria Formosa 141
Fondazione Querini-Stampalia 141
Santa Maria della Fava 142

SAN ZACCARIA AND AROUND 142
San Zaccaria 142
Riva degli Schiavoni 144

BETWEEN RIO DEI GRECI AND
THE ARSENALE 144
La Pietà 144
San Giovanni in Brágora 144
San Giorgio dei Greci 145
Museo di Icone 145
Scuola di San Giorgio degli Schiavoni 146
San Francesco della Vigna 147

THE ARSENALE AND AROUND 148
The Arsenale 148
South of the Arsenale 149
Naval History Museum 149

EASTERN CASTELLO 151
Isola di San Pietro 152
Giardini Pubblici 154
San Giuseppe di Castello 154
Isola Sant'Elena 154

1 Lunch

La Corte Sconta, *Castello 3866, Calle del Pestrin*, **t** *041 522 7024; **vaporetto** Arsenale.* **Open** *Tues–Sat 12.30–2 and 7–9.45*. **Expensive**. *Book*. Superb seafood: fishy antipasti, *taglioni* with lobster, *gnocchetti* with fresh anchovies, and John Dory. The rustic but uncluttered décor is a breath of fresh air.

2 Coffee and Cakes

Rosa Salva, *Castello 6779, Campo Santi Giovanni e Paolo*, **t** *041 522 7949; **vaporetto** Fondamenta Nuove.* **Open** *daily 8.30–8.30.* The best *pasticceria* in Venice, with a wonderful old-fashioned feel, quiet tables and excellent coffee, pastries and ice cream.

3 Drinks

Alla Mascareta, *Castello 5183, Calle Lunga Santa Maria Formosa*, **t** *041 523 0744; **vaporetto** San Zaccaria/Rialto.* **Open** *Mon–Sat 6pm–1am*. Enoteca with an exceptional wine list (400 labels) and wonderful choice of cheeses, hams and salamis.

Castello

Castello, named after the long-gone fortifications on the island of San Pietro, stretches from Piazza San Marco out to the easternmost quarters of the city. One of the older, and now poorer *sestieri*, it contains famous monuments and churches like Santi Giovanni e Paolo, the Colleoni statue, San Zaccaria, and the magical Carpaccios in San Giorgio degli Schiavoni, as well as the mighty engine that made Venice tick for so many centuries: the Arsenale. Eastern Castello is still the site of many of Venice's boatyards, littered with the rusting hulks of bygone *vaporetti* and often stinking of varnish. It is an area refreshingly devoid of your fellow tourists; here you'll find Venice's largest park, its most impressive display of laundry billowing overhead, and relatively few canals – ideal little neighbourhoods that could perhaps exist in many other Italian cities, made metaphysical by the total lack of traffic.

Highlights

Medieval Venice: The Arsenale and nearby Naval History Museum, the secret of the city's medieval success, p.148

Renaissance Venice: Santi Giovanni e Paolo, the pantheon of the doges and an art gallery in its own right, p.136

Baroque/Rococo Venice: Longhena's vertiginous Ospedaletto, or La Pietá if there's a concert, pp.140 and 144

Indoor Venice: The intimate guildhall of San Giorgio degli Schiavoni, and its delightful Carpaccios, p.146

Decadent Venice: See how the 18th-century Venetians declined in style, in the Fondazione Querini-Stampalia, p.141

Pigeon Venice: The big trees of the Giardini Pubblici, in Venice's peaceful east end, p.153

SANTI GIOVANNI E PAOLO AND AROUND

Santi Giovanni e Paolo

J–K5

Campo Santi Giovanni e Paolo; vaporetto Fondamenta Nuove. Open Mon-Sat 8–12.30 and 3–6, Sun 3–5.30; adm free.

The huge Gothic church of Santi Giovanni e Paolo, better known in Venice as **San Zanipolo**, is the most important church on the right bank after St Mark's.

Every now and then, Venice left its splendid isolation to join the Italian mainstream. One such occasion came during the great 13th-century religious revival begun by Saints Francis and Dominic, whose minor orders sought to bring the faith directly to the people by preaching and works of charity. Rather than dwell in self-absorbed monasteries, the Franciscans and Dominicans built jumbo utilitarian churches in the cities to bring their message to the biggest possible congregations. Every Italian city, Venice included, has one impressive example from each order; the Franciscans built Venice's Frari church, and this one is the Dominicans'. Their first church on this site, erected in 1246, was on land donated by Doge Giacomo Tiepolo, but it soon proved too small, and in 1333 work began on the present cavernous basilica. The design is simple, vast and functional. The unfinished façade, next to the Scuola di San Marco, would be invisible but for a handsome doorway attributed to Bartolomeo Bon, with marble columns from Torcello and two Byzantine reliefs; a third one, of *Daniel in the Lions' Den*, stands by itself in the right corner of the wall.

San Zanipolo's steep and prodigious space, hemmed together by tie beams, braced by 10 massive Istrian stone columns and lit by a beautiful crescent of Gothic windows in the choir, was put to good use as a **pantheon of doges**; all their funerals were held here after 1430, and some 25 of them lie here in splendid Gothic and Renaissance tombs. The west wall belongs to the Mocenigo family [1], who gave the church three dead doges, the first interred in the celebrated, classical **Tomb of Doge Pietro Mocenigo** (to the left of the door) by Pietro Lombardo, assisted by his sons Tullio and Antonio (1476–81). Recently scrubbed, it is as beautiful as it is haughty, the culmination of Venice's Renaissance style, a stage for statues representing the *Three Ages of Man* and other assorted warriors, standing over a pair of reliefs of the *Labours of Hercules*. Religion is relegated to a relief at the top, but it too is suitably heroic: a triumphant *Resurrection*. An inscription proudly remarks that the tomb was paid for by the Doge's enemies (not willingly, mind you). Over and around the portal is the huge **Tomb of Doge Alvise Mocenigo I and Wife** (1577), while on the right is Tullio Lombardo's classically inspired **Tomb of Doge Giovanni Mocenigo** (d. 1485), with a fine relief of *St Mark Baptizing Annianus*.

The first item on the right wall, in the shadow of Pietro Mocenigo's mighty tomb, is a 13th-century Byzantine sarcophagus, all that remains of the tomb of Doge Ranier Zeno (d. 1268). Note the flying angels supporting the *Throne of Christ*: a conventional Byzantine symbol, and a remarkable example of artistic continuity – in Augustus' day the same angels in the same poses were holding the civic crown of the caesars over public buildings.

After the first altar in the right aisle is the **Monument to Marcantonio Bragadin** [2], the commander of Famagusta (Cyprus) in 1570, who had withstood a Turkish siege for nearly a year when, outnumbered ten to one, he was forced to surrender (*see* p.138). The adjacent chapel contains Giovanni Bellini's fine polyptych of *St Vincent Ferrer*, a fire-eating preacher who helped incite Spain's religious persecutions. *Vincent Ferrer* is accompanied by a charming *St Christopher* and rather uncomfortable *St Sebastian*, while under the polyptych is an effigy of the Blessed

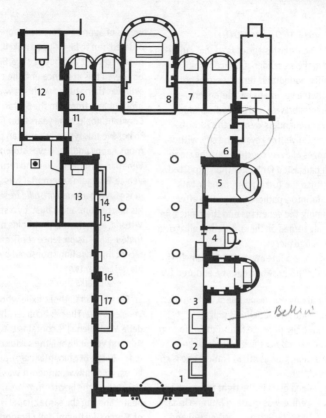

1   Tombs of the Mocenigo family
2   Bragadin monument
3   Tomb of Ludovico Diedo
4   Chapel of the Madonna della Pace
5   Chapel of St Dominic
6   Tomb of Nicola Orsini
7   Capella della Maddalena
8   Tombs of Doges Michele Morosini
    and Leonardo Loredan
9   Tombs of Doges Andrea Vendramin
    and Marco Corner
10 Tomb of Doge Giovanni Dolfin
11 Tomb of Doge Antonio Venier
12 Chapel of the Rosary
13 Sacristy
14 Tomb of Palma Giovane
15 Tomb of Doge Pasquale Malipiero
16 Tomb of Doge Tommaso Mocenigo
17 Tomb of Doge Nicolò Marcello

Tommaso Caraffini, confessor of St Catherine of Siena. In the floor of the nave, near the next chapel, is the niello-work **Tomb of Ludovico Diedo** [3] (1460s), with a bizarre relief with a dragon contemplating an orrery. The next chapel, the Addolarata, was lavishly Baroqued in the 17th century, while the next, the **Chapel of the Madonna della Pace** [4], is named after a miraculous Byzantine icon brought to Venice in 1349, but the flamboyant 1708 tombs of the Valier doges,

Bertucci (d. 1658) and Silvestro (d. 1700) steal the show. Giambattista Piazzetta painted the ceiling of the next chapel, the **Chapel of St Dominic** [5], with the *Glory of St Dominic* (1727), where the hero-saint is sucked up in a luminous vortex, accompanied by a small floating orchestra. The six bronze reliefs on scenes from the *Life of St Dominic* are the masterpieces of Bolognese sculptor Giuseppe Mazza (1720). Next comes a shrine containing the **foot of St Catherine of Siena**,

The Defeat of Bragadin

After the Turkish siege of 1570 that culminated in the surrender of Marcantonio Bragadin, honourable terms were negotiated, for the Venetians had defended themselves bravely, and Bragadin and his fellow commanders went to the Turkish camp to deliver the keys of the city, with exchanges of every courtesy. But the siege, which had lasted far longer than expected, had turned the Turkish commander, Lala Mustafa, into a pathological sadist; after welcoming the Venetians and their allies, he suddenly turned on them, ordering all 350 to be hacked to pieces.

Even worse a fate awaited Bragadin: first relieved of his nose and ears, he endured two weeks of agonizing torture before the pasha ordered him to be stripped naked, tied to the public scaffold, and flayed alive. Bragadin bore even this in silence until he expired. His skin was then stuffed with straw and brought as a trophy to the Sultan in Constantinople. Nine years later (if you care to believe this typically Venetian posthumous happy ending) it was stolen by a Venetian prisoner of war and returned to Venice. Bragadin's memorial was set up here in 1596, with a faded *grisaille* fresco depicting his martyrdom, and a bust, by a student of Vittoria, atop the urn that holds his neatly folded skin – its presence confirmed by a recent investigation sponsored by one of his descendants.

black and tiny, and resplendent in its golden Gothic reliquary. Catherine's skill in convincing the popes to return to Rome from Avignon earned her the gratitude of an entire nation; along with St Francis, she is co-patron of Italy.

The stained glass in the **right transept**, the finest in Venice, was made in Murano in 1473, from cartoons by Bartolomeo Vivarini and Girolamo Mocetto. Here, too, are first-rate paintings by Alvise Vivarini (*Christ Bearing the Cross*, 1474), Cima da Conegliano and/or Giovanni Martini da Udine's *Coronation of the Virgin*, and Lorenzo Lotto's newly restored and richly coloured *St Antonine Distributing Alms* (1542), to beggars whose faces reveal their anxious need. The usually tight-fisted Signoria paid for the two monuments in this transept, in gratitude for service rendered during the War of the League of Cambrai: the gilded equestrian **Tomb of Nicola Orsini, Prince of Nola** [6], who earned it for his brave defence of Padua, and, over the door, the **Tomb of Dionigi Naldo di Brisighella**, with a second-rate statue by Lorenzo Bregno of the *condottiere* who led Venice's infantry and died in action in 1510.

In the first of five transept chapels (starting from the right), are several works by Alessandro Vittoria: a *Crucifixion* and the grand tomb of Sir Edward (*Odoardo*) Windsor, an Elizabethan Catholic exile who died in Venice in 1574. The next chapel, the **Cappella della Maddalena** [7], contains the **Tomb of Admiral Vettor Pisani**, the saviour of Venice in the Battle of Chioggia (1380), during which he was mortally wounded; it was reconstructed on the 600th anniversary of his death. Sharing the same chapel is the **Tomb of Marco Giustiniani della Bragora** (d. 1346), held up by a quartet of primitive heads.

Double lancet windows with Gothic tracery light the polygonal **chancel**: on the right wall is the splendid **Tomb of Doge Michele Morosini** [8] (d. 1382), a marriage of Gothic design and Byzantine mosaics possible only in Venice, with carvings attributed to the dalle Masegne, and the more lavish **Tomb of Doge Leonardo Loredan** [8] (d. 1520), decorated with bronze reliefs by Danese Cattaneo. On the left wall, the **Tomb of Doge Andrea Vendramin** [9] is a fine work by Tullio and Antonio Lombardo (1478) that nevertheless earned a quart of poison ink from the pen of Ruskin, the king of cranks. He caused the Venetians some alarm by ordering a ladder to clamber all over the tomb and prove that, just as he suspected, the sculpture was a sham because the sculptors hadn't bothered to finish off the parts no one would ever see, a sign of 'an extreme of intellectual and moral degradation'. To fit it in, the earlier **Tomb of Doge Marco Corner** [9] (d. 1368) took a few chops, but still preserves its fine statues by Nino Pisano of Pisa.

The chapel to the left of the high altar has some mediocre paintings by Leandro Bassano, while the next contains **two sarcophagi** suspended on the walls: the first is of Jacopo Cavalli (d. 1384) with an effigy by Pier Paolo Dalle Masegne and a large fresco background; the other contains the mortal remains of Doge Giovanni Dolfin [10] (d. 1361). In the **left transept**, the Dalle Masegne brothers were also responsible for the pink and white **Tomb of Doge Antonio Venier** [11] (d. 1400) and his wife and daughter, an effort that became the model for Venice's lingering transition from Gothic to the full bloom of the Lombardesque Renaissance. A door in the left transept leads to the **Chapel of the Rosary** [12], built to celebrate the victory at Lepanto. Burned in 1867, with all of its art and fine paintings by Giovanni Bellini and Titian, temporarily lodged there, it underwent a half-century of restoration, and re-opened in 1959 with a ceiling by Veronese.

Another string of monuments lines the left aisle, though the first work is a fragment of *Three Saints* from a polyptych by Bartolomeo Vivarini. Over the door of the **sacristy** [13] is the **Tomb of Palma Giovane** [14], with busts of Titian, Palma Vecchio and himself (beyond the 18th-century organ). Pietro Lombardo, nearly as prolific as Palma Giovane, contributed the next work: the 1462 **Tomb of Doge Pasquale Malipiero** [15], one of the first and purest Renaissance works in Venice. The next batch of tombs includes an equestrian model for Pompeo Giustiniani, the **Tomb of Doge Tommaso Mocenigo** [16] (d. 1423), by Pietro di Nicolo Lamberti and Giovanni di Martino, and Pietro Lombardo's **Tomb of Doge Nicolò Marcello** [17] (d. 1474). The last altar on the left has a *St Jerome* by Vittoria (1576).

Walk around the flank of San Zanipolo; the small building near the apse is the **Ex-Scuola of St Ursula**, now a permanently closed chapel, containing the tombs of Giovanni and Gentile Bellini.

Colleoni Statue J5

Campo Santi Giovanni e Paolo.

Few statues have had such a rocky history. When celebrated *condottiere* Bartolomeo Colleoni (*see* p.139) died it was discovered that, in gratitude for the Republic's goodness towards him, he would leave it the princely sum of 100,000 ducats on the condition that it erect an equestrian monument to him '*super platea San Marco*'. After all, Colleoni's predecessor, the *condottiere* 'Honey Cat' Gattamelata, had got a fine one by Donatello in Padua (paid for by the Republic). Greedy for the money, but gagging at the thought of erecting a statue in the sacred Piazza San Marco to anybody on this planet, much less a mercenary warlord, the Senate came up with

Condottiere Colleoni

Born into a war-like aristocratic family, and always proud of his emblem of *coglioni* ('testicles' – a play on his name), Bartolomeo Colleoni (1400–76) began his mercenary career at the age of 19, in Naples, and first worked for Venice under Gattamelata in 1431. After a period of wavering between Milan and Venice, he decided to stick to the latter, but only when Milanese ambitions for north Italian domination were laid to rest (1454) was Colleoni appointed commander-in-chief of the Venetian forces. He was one of the celebrity military commanders of his day, who well served Venice's claims on the Terra Firma – both by leading the Republic's mercenary army and by not taking up the many other offers he had to fight against Venice – Venice ensured his loyalty by making him incredibly wealthy. The lack of subsequent wars and enforced idleness made this an amazingly cushy job (he only had to fight one battle in his last 20 years); to kill time, he ran his castle at Malpaga as a mixed court of artists and army pals, even entertaining the King of Denmark. Yet along with ducats he left Venice a warning: never to give any other military commander as much power as it had given him.

the wily solution of erecting the statue in the *campo* of the Scuola di San Marco.

But the cheat ended there. In return for his ducats, Venice gave Colleoni one of the greatest equestrian statues of all time. Andrea Verrocchio, sculptor, alchemist and the master of Leonardo da Vinci and Botticelli, won the competition to make the monument in 1479, and was on the point of casting the horse when he heard a rumour that the Venetians doubted his ability to make the rider and were looking for another artist. Furious, Verrocchio broke the cast and went back to Florence. The Venetians banned him from Venice, and by the time the two parties were reconciled, and Verrocchio went back to work, he only had time to make the casts for the horse and rider before his death. The Republic then entrusted Alessandro Leopardi to cast Verrocchio's figures and the plinth beneath them, and the monument was unveiled, at last, in 1496.

Compared to the powerful dynamics of Verrochio's Colleoni, Donatello's Gattamelata looks like the pussycat of his nickname; in fact, it's hard to avoid noting Colleoni's striking resemblance to the late Klaus Kinski. And it is fitting, for if Werner Herzog ever wanted to make a film about a Renaissance *condottiere*, Colleoni would fit the bill.

Scuola Grande di San Marco J5

Campo Santi Giovanni e Paolo, t 041 529 4313; vaporetto Fondamenta Nuove. Open Mon–Sat 8.30–1; adm free.

Founded in 1260 and one of the six *Scuole Grandi* or guild halls (*see* p.183), the original Scuola di San Marco (now the main entrance to the Ospedale Civile) burned in 1485 and was replaced with one of those unique buildings of distilled Venetian fantasy, an asymmetrical, sumptuously decorated Renaissance confection. Pietro Lombardo designed this replacement, with help from his sons and Antonio Buora; in 1495 Mauro Codussi was summoned to design its upper level of six curved crowns, a rolling motif that

echoes not only Tullio and Antonio Lombardo's charming shallow relief arches with lions on the ground floor, but also the domes of the other St Mark's and the city's arched bridges. The façade is vertically divided in two; the loftier left-hand section once held the Scuola's **Great Hall**, drastically rearranged by the Austrians. Just within the door is the **Lower Hall**, and in the morning you can usually visit Scamozzi's 17th-century San Lazzaro dei Mendicanti, incorporated into the hospital as its funerary chapel, with a *St Ursula* by Tintoretto and a *Crucifixion* by Veronese. Better still, ask to see the **medical library**, formerly the Scuola's chapter room, with the most ornate coffered ceiling in Venice (16th-century).

Ospedaletto K5

Barbaria della Tole; vaporetto Fondamenta Nuove. Open Thurs–Sat 3.30–6.30; adm free.

Longhena was having a bad day when he designed this nervous wreck of a Baroque façade; the cumulative effect of all the strong men, lions and giants hovers some-where between a circus poster and low-calorie nightmare – a fair reflection of the low ebb of everyday life in the declining 1670s. Also known as Santa Maria dei Derelitti ('of the waifs', or 'orphans'), it belonged to a hospital and school for orphans founded in 1527; like La Pietà, its female students became internationally famous for their music (its elegant **concert chamber**, frescoed in the 18th century, may be seen on request).

Longhena also redesigned the interior (entered by a side door of the hospital), deco-rated with some fairly vertiginous ceiling frescoes, including a *trompe l'œil* organ zooming out over the altar. There is a sampling of 18th-century Venetian paintings, including a dramatic early Giambattista Tiepolo, *Abraham's Sacrifice of Isaac*, a small vignette over the fourth arch on the right. All the little scenes over the arches are good, though hard to see; some on the right side are also sometimes attributed to Tiepolo.

AROUND CAMPO SANTA MARIA FORMOSA

This lively *campo* has a market, several bars and *pizzerie*, and a handful of noble palaces: the **Ca' Malpiero Trevisan** (No.5250, with marble discs) by Tullio's son, Sante Lombardo, the Veneto-Byzantine **Palazzo Vitturi** (No. 5246, with Byzantine carvings; J6), and the 16th-century **Palazzo Priuli** (J6), next to the PDS (Communist Party) headquarters.

Santa Maria Formosa J6

*Campo Santa Maria Formosa; **vaporetto** San Zaccaria/Rialto. **Open** Mon–Sat 10–5, Sun 1–5; **adm** €2.*

In 639, during his exile on the Rialto, Magno, Bishop of Oderzo, had a vision of the Virgin, where she appeared as a very buxom and beautiful (*formosa*) matron and ordered him to build a church wherever a little white cloud settled. It was the first Rialtine church dedicated to Mary, and when it was rebuilt in 1492 by Mauro Codussi he maintained its original Greek cross shape. The Austrians dropped an incendiary bomb through it in 1916 (you can see a bas-relief of the bomb just outside the right transept door).

The church has two **façades**, both to the greater glory of the Cappello clan; the one facing the canal is a military triumph dedicated to Vincenzo Cappello (d. 1541), with never a religious symbol in view; and the one facing the *campo* honours even more Cappellos (and the Virgin Mary) built in 1604. Over a door in Santa Maria's Baroque campanile leers the most hideous face in Venice, a grotesque mask added in 1688: 'in that head is embodied the type of the evil spirit to which Venice was abandoned', wrote Ruskin, who didn't share Venice's sense of the absurd. If that head is the ugliest, many consider that of Palma Vecchio's *Santa Barbara* (1524) in the Chapel of the Bombardiers (in the right transept) the most

beautiful in the city, the perfectly ripe Venetian Renaissance beauty – modelled on the artist's daughter. George Eliot saw her as 'an almost unique presentation of a hero-woman', and indeed, in her life, Barbara was so heroically stubborn that her own father had her locked in a tower and then martyred. She became patroness of artillerymen and bombardiers when her father was struck dead by lightning on his way home.

The other major painting inside is Bartolomeo Vivarini's 1473 triptych of the *Madonna della Misericordia* in the first chapel on the right, the parishioners under the Virgin's protective mantle having earned their place there by paying for the painting. To the right of the main door you can take in the shrine to Pius X, the Venetian patriarch who became the last pope to be canonized, while on the left is an icon of the *Virgin*, carried on the admiral's flagship during the Battle of Lepanto. The last work of art is Codussi's grey and cream interior itself, a complex variation on the Brunelleschian Renaissance archetype, with chapels divided by double open arches.

Fondazione Querini-Stampalia J6

*Campo Santa Maria Formosa, **t** 041 271 1411, **w** www.provincia.venezia.it/querini/gallery; **vaporetto** San Zaccaria; wheelchair accessible. **Open** Tues–Thurs and Sun 10–6, Fri and Sat 10–10; **adm** €6. There is a **café/restaurant** (**open** Tues–Sun 12–3 and 7.30–10) run by Florian and serving snacks and lunch, and an interesting **book/gift shop. Concerts** are sometimes held here (see p.284).*

At the southern end of Campo Santa Maria Formosa, the little Campiello Querini is resplendent with window boxes and the 16th-century Palazzo Querini-Stampalia, home of the library and gallery founded in 1869 by Count Giovanni Querini. The Querini-Stampalia collection features a handful of masterpieces and bushels of the not-so-masterful, but works fascinating to anyone with a spark of curiosity about Venice in the

18th century. This was the grand age of trivi-alization for the aristocracy throughout Europe, but nowhere pursued so feverishly as in Venice, where the spirit of adventure that had created the mighty Republic of yore had evaporated like perfume; patricians spent their days frittering away their ancestors' huge heritage and doing their best to look like poodles. You can see them here in the childlike paintings of Gabriel Bella and in room after room of Venetian *Biedermeiers* by the indefatigable Pietro Longhi.

The bright stars of the collection are scat-tered randomly among the sleepers, beginning with an exquisite *Coronation of the Virgin* (1372) by Donato and Caterino Veneziano. There are some not too pene-trating portraits of Venetian senators by Palma Giovane, as well as his excellent unfin-ished marriage portraits of *Francesco Querini* and the lovely *Paola Priuli Querini*; there's a *Bacchanale* complete down to the grape-stained teeth by Nicolò Frangipane. Don't miss the room of brittle counter-Reformation hallucinations, with paintings by Pietro Liberi (1614–87; a *Man Fallen through Vice* being kicked by a midget and a whore) and Matteo dei Pitocchi 'of the beggars' (1626–89; alarming rustic scenes full of ugly brutes and menacing skies – genre painting gone haywire). Further along you are rewarded with a pretty but damaged *tondo* of The *Virgin, Child and St John* by Lorenzo di Credi (a follower of Leonardo da Vinci), and Giovanni Bellini's *Presentation at the Temple*, an early painting inspired by his brother-in-law Mantegna that haunts with its stillness. And then, a bit further along, there's an uncannily modern *Christ Bearing the Cross* by an anonymous follower of Pordenone, and the startling *Judith*, holding Holofernes' head as if it were a trophy, by the great amateur Vincenzo Catena.

Around the Museum

There's a pretty corner to see just to the west of the museum: the **Fondamenta di Rimedio** (J6–7) with its little iron bridges over an extremely narrow canal.

Santa Maria della Fava I6

Campo della Fava; vaporetto Rialto. Open Mon–Sat 8.30–11.45 and 5–7.30, Sun 8.30–11.30; adm free.

St Mary of the Fava Bean is the more popular name for Santa Maria della Consolazione; in the old days a pastry shop in the neighbourhood was renowned for its *fave dolci*, the sweets eaten on All Souls' Day. Built in the 18th century, it was decorated by some of the most popular artists of the period: Giambattista Tiepolo (*Education of the Virgin*), first altar on the right; the second chapel on the left holds Giambattista Piazzetta's *tenebroso* masterpiece, *The Virgin Appearing to St Philip Neri* (1727), an intense, zigzagging composition of reds and browns. This church is also dedicated to that saint, the 16th-century Roman who helped invent modern sacred music. The statues along the nave are from the chisel of Torretto, perhaps best known as the Master of Canova.

San Lio I6

Salizzada San Lio; vaporetto Rialto. Open rarely; adm free.

Near Santa Maria della Fava is the neigh-bourhood's other little church, **San Lio**; if it's open, stop in to see the chapel to the right of the altar, with some fine sculpture by Pietro and Tullio Lombardo, including a relief of the *Pietà*; on the restored ceiling is Giandomenico Tiepolo's *Apotheosis of St Leo*.

SAN ZACCARIA AND AROUND

San Zaccaria K7

Campo San Zaccaria; vaporetto San Zaccaria. Open Mon–Sat 10–12 and 4–6, Sun 4–6; adm free, €1 for chapels and light.

The present church was begun in retro-Gothic by Antonio Gambello in 1444 and finished in the Renaissance style of Mauro

Codussi in 1515, who is responsible for the distinctive Istrian stone façade above the level of the door (oddly, the only church front visible from the top of St Mark's campanile), its lunettes and delicate seashell reliefs disguising Gambello's Gothic naves. Inside, Codussi converted the original plans for a rib-vaulted ambulatory into an elegant ring of elliptical cupolas, lit by long narrow windows – a northern Gothic inspiration, the only one of its kind in Venice.

The star attraction is Giovanni Bellini's recently restored Madonna and Saints (1505) in the second chapel on the left. Large, riveting and luminous, the perspectives of the painted columns and arch are continued into the design of the frame to create a unique sense of depth, directing the eye towards a rare visual equivalent of the music of the spheres. The saints on either side of the Madonna's throne, and the angel musicians below, are posed symmetrically, in a spiritual, self-absorbed dance; Bellini was one of the few artists capable of giving even the most common subject and composition new meaning – don't expect as much from the 17th- and 18th-century artists whose canvases decorate the nave. At the end of the left aisle is the tomb and a self-portrait bust of Alessandro Vittoria (1528–1608), who also sculpted the headless figure of San Zaccaria over the main door, and the two saints of the holy water stoups.

The original San Zaccaria was founded in the 9th century to house the relics of St Zacharias, father of John the Baptist, whose body still lies in the right aisle. Near this is the entrance to the **Cappella di Sant'Atanasio** and **Cappella di San Tarasio** (adm €1, light machine inside €0.50); the first contains an early Tintoretto, the Birth of St John the Baptist, while San Tarasio chapel, actually the chancel of the original church (with fragments of its Byzantine mosaic paving) houses three ornate ancone by Antonio Vivarini and Giovanni d'Alemagna, painted in the 1440s. The one in the centre, a hyper-Gothic gilt extravaganza, features carved wooden saints with expectant faces, set into the frame as if seated in theatre boxes. In the fan vault are frescoes by the Tuscan Andrea del Castagno of the same period, which, though sadly damaged, hint at how atavistic the Venetians were in the early Renaissance.

A stair leads down into the murky old **crypt**, under whose flooded floor and pygmy vaults moulder the remains of eight doges. San Zaccaria and its nuns enjoyed special ducal favours after the 12th century, when the abbess donated the convent garden to Doge Sebastiano Ziani; the nuns embroidered the ducal bonnets, and the Doge attended a special Easter Mass here.

Campo San Zaccaria J7

This quiet campo, with its little garden of trees and cats, only dimly recalls the two doges who were assassinated here: Pietro Tradonico (864) and Vitale Michiel II in 1172. As ordered on the old plaque at the entrance to the campo, you can't gamble, argue, curse or fight here, and you had better not throw any litter under the trees either.

To the right of San Zaccaria is the brick patterned façade of its 13th-century predecessor, used in winter by an Anglo-Venetian society for lectures; left of the church, part of its 16th-century **cloister** has homes built into the arches. At the southern end of the *campo*, in Sottocalle San Zaccaria, is a William-Morris-style *palazzino* with an eclectic relief of St George.

If you leave the *campo* by way of Campo San Provolo and Salizzada San Provolo, look back to see the pretty **bas-relief** over its arch.

Riva degli Schiavoni J–L8

Vaporetto San Zaccaria.

People with children, in the winter, will inevitably be pushed southwards to Riva degli Schiavoni, where a modest but noisy **funfair** operates on the Lagoon's edge in January. The rest of the year there's nothing to see on the Riva but cafés and trinket shops – and the fierce **Vittorio Emanuele II monument**, a humdinger commemorating Italy's first king, with winged lions ripping off the chains of Austrian domination.

BETWEEN RIO DEI GRECI AND THE ARSENALE

La Pietà K7–8

Riva degli Schiavoni, t 041 523 1096, w www.vivaldi.it; vaporetto San Zaccaria. Open only for concerts, see p.284.

The Venetians like to call this 'Vivaldi's church', as its predecessor was attached to a charity hospital for orphan girls (founded in 1346) where Vivaldi was chorus-master and violin teacher between 1704–38, composing some of his greatest *concerti* for star pupils. Thanks to him, the hospital's fame increased so much that the authorities had to put up the plaque you can still see on the south

wall, threatening lightning bolts and excommunication upon any parent who tried to palm their child off as an orphan. It was fashionable for visitors to attend one of La Pietà's concerts, and leave a suitably large donation towards the good work.

As churches did double duty as concert halls, Giorgio Massari designed La Pietà in 1739 in an elegant oval shape, with acoustics as well as God in mind – if you do get in, note the rounded angles, the choir stalls along the back and sides, and the high vaulted ceiling. The oblong vestibule served to dampen street noise, a feature that may well have been suggested by Vivaldi himself. Decorated in luscious cream and gold, with Giambattista Tiepolo's *Triumph of Faith* on top, La Pietà is just like being inside a Fabergé Easter egg. The white façade was stuck on only in 1906. Climb the steps of the bridge near La Pietà for the best view of San Giorgio dei Greci's crazy campanile (*see* below).

San Giovanni in Brágora L7

Campo Bandiera e Moro; vaporetto San Zaccaria/Arsenale. Open Mon–Fri 9–11 and 3.30–7, Sat 3.30–5.30, Sun–9–11; adm free.

San Giovanni in Brágora ('in the marketplace') was rebuilt in 1475, with a simple, lobed brick façade. San Giovanni's simple interior, which retains its original ship's keel roof, contains treasures for all tastes: for relic-mongers, the body of St John the Almsgiver in a glass case; plus a pretty 13th-century Byzantine relief over the sacristy door, flanked by Alvise Vivarini's *Resurrected Christ* (1498) and Cima da Conegliano's *Constantine and St Helena*. Cima also contributed the church's chief treasure, the high altar's *Baptism of Christ* (1494), an excellent painting restored to its original brilliant colours. In the last chapel on the left, the 15th-century *Life of St Nicholas* is a reminder of how late Byzantine influences lingered in Venetian art; also note the **baptismal font**, where in 1675 Mrs Vivaldi's red-headed son was christened Antonio.

Campo Bandiera e Moro L7

San Giovanni's church square is named after three Venetian officers in the Austrian Navy who plotted a revolt in Calabria for Italian unily In 1844 and were betrayed by the English government, in whom they had confided; so noble was their effort that for 60 years this *campo* was dignified with the title of *'piazza'*. It is also the address of the lovely Gothic **Palazzo Gritti Badoer**, now La Residenza *pensione* (*see* p.257).

San Giorgio dei Greci K7

Fondamenta dei Greci, t 041 523 9569; vaporetto San Zaccaria. Open Mon and Wed–Fri 3.40; closed Tues and Sat; Orthodox services Sun at 10.30; adm free.

In the 1530s, the Greeks were given permission to build an Orthodox church in Venice, and hired Sante Lombardo to design their San Giorgio dei Greci, with a very fine Renaissance façade and a lovely clock on its perilously listing campanile, which ever since its construction in 1592 has hung like a diver about to leap into Rio dei Greci.

Some of the finest paintings, by the 16th-century Cretan artist Michele Damaskinos, are part of the golden *iconostasis*; the older icons were brought over after the fall of Constantinople.

Museo di Icone K7

Ponte dei Greci; vaporetto San Zaccaria. Open Mon–Sat 9–12.30 and 2–4.30, Sun 10–5; adm €4.

The **Scuola di San Nicolò dei Greci** (1678, by Longhena) is now part of the Hellenic Centre for Byzantine and Post-Byzantine Studies. Its collection, mostly from the 16th–18th centuries, points up both the glories and the limitations of late Byzantine art as artificially preserved in Venice. Most conspicuous is its iron-clad conservatism – the Orthodox Church, after all, never looked upon its icons as art but as objects of devotion that reflect the spirit of heaven, and one of the tenets of Orthodox faith is that fashion or style never

The Greeks in Venice

The Scuola di San Nicolò dei Greci and the Orthodox church next door were the heart of a thriving Greek community that began with a handful of artists invited in to make the mosaics at Torcello and which numbered 15,000 in its heyday – according to the Greeks, who now number exactly 10. 'So where did they all go?' you might ask, and the Greeks will reply, 'Some went back to Greece, some to Padua, but most fell in love with Venetians.'

The links between Greece and Venice were so close throughout history that some linguists claim much of the modern Greek language is directly derived from Venetian dialect (for example, a 'fork' in Italian is a *forchetta*, but in Venetian it's a *piroun*, similiar to the Greek *pirouni*; the utensil was introduced into western Europe by the Greek wife of an early doge, though at first its use was condemned as effete). Many Greeks, especially merchants, courtesans and artists, came to Venice in the 15th and 16th centuries when the Turks conquered Constantinople and Greece; most celebrated of these was a school of painters from Crete known in Venice as the *'Madonneri di Rialto'*.

changes up there. But their conservatism goes farther than that; in a corner of one rare and remarkable 15th-century *Nativity*, there is a girl pouring water from an amphora who could have stepped off an ancient Greek vase. Some lively *Last Judgements* show how powerful and visionary this art could be even in its decay; even better is a 16th-century *Jesus and the Samaritan Girl*, set in a dream-like landscape of purple, gold and green, and a fairytale *Noah's Ark*. Although some of the later icons show that the Greeks weren't totally immune from the west, none bristles with the energy of the Cretan-Venetian school's chief rebel, El Greco, who spent a few years by the lagoon studying Tintoretto and the Bassanos before moving to Spain.

Restoration of the entire collection was begun in 1998, and some pieces are still undergoing work.

More than 101 Dalmatians

In their long history abroad, the Venetians won more minds than hearts, but they did build up an affectionate relationship with the Dalmatians. This is in spite of a chequered history dating back to the 9th century, when Venice's merchants were harassed by Dalmatian pirates. The Venetians retaliated by capturing the Dalmatians and selling them as slaves, and colonizing Dalmatian ports. For centuries Venice fought the Hungarians, the Turks and the Dalmatians themselves over the region. Off and on it went, but by the 15th century Venice's Dalmatian community had enough interests to protect to found a *scuola*, and enough sense to hire Carpaccio to decorate it with a series on their patron saints, George, Tryphon and Jerome.

The relationship lasted down to the very end. Dalmatian troops served as the Republic's tiny standing army, and in 1797 they were ordered home to comply with Napoleon's ultimatum. As they departed, they inadvertently played a last bitter joke on the terrified Doge and Great Council, who were holding their last session in the Palazzo Ducale to vote on the democratic government Napoleon demanded. All of a sudden shots rang out across Riva degli Schiavoni. The patricians broke off the debate, hurled their cowardly ballots in the box and fled in disguise – only later discovering that the shots they had heard had been fired by the Dalmatians as a farewell salute to Venice. Enough Dalmatians remained behind to look after the *scuola*, and, like the Greeks at San Nicolò dei Greci, they still own it.

Scuola di San Giorgio degli Schiavoni L7

Calle dei Furlani; **vaporetto** *San Zaccaria/ Arsenale.* **Open** *Tues–Sat 9.30–12.30 and 3.30–6.30, Sun 9.30-12.30;* **adm** *€3.*

Schiavoni was the Venetian word for the Dalmatians, and this was their confraternity headquarters – little bigger than Dr Who's police box, but, thanks to Vittore Carpaccio, a Tardis ready to transport you to a world of storybook delight.

Carpaccio's cycle, painted between 1502 and 1508, was originally intended for the hall upstairs. Removed to the ground floor in 1551, it has had the rare fortune to stay there ever since, cosy, warm, glowing with colour, and filled with the exact, literal details that bring the story of the *scuola* to life – the bits of undigested maidens by the dragon in the painting of *St George*, just to the left of the door, or the monster brought to heel in *The Triumph of St George*. Next is *St George Baptizes the Pagan King and Queen*, followed by an altar of the *Virgin and Child* by Carpaccio's son Benedetto. Then Vittore again, with the legend of the obscure Dalmatian Saint Tryphon, *St Tryphon Exorcizing Emperor Gordianus' Daughter*,

whose demon is a pouty little basilisk, followed by *The Agony in the Garden* and *The Calling of St Matthew* (which takes place in the Ghetto) and *St Jerome Leading his Lion into a Monastery*, a creature who wouldn't harm a fly but causes much comical consternation among the monks. *The Funeral of St Jerome* is followed by perhaps the best loved painting in the city: *St Augustine in His Study*, showing the good saint thoughtfully gazing out of the window, watched by his little white dog – the story follows a passage in St Augustine, who describes how he was writing to St Jerome, not knowing he had died, when a heavenly light streamed down and a voice warned him it was too late. Although none of the subjects has anything to do with Venice, they are as infused with the city as if Carpaccio soaked them with a Venetian tea bag.

Around San Giorgio

From San Giorgio degli Schiavoni, you can dip down Fondamenta dei Furlani to see if the 17th-century church of **Sant'Antonin** (L7) is open (*years of restoration continue*). It contains a *Deposition* by Carpaccio's master Lazzaro Bastiani. Some 600 years ago you would have probably been molested by a pig; in honour of St Anthony Abbot, the monks used to keep a herd of free-ranging swine with bells around their necks who visually, orally and olfactorally made such a nuisance of themselves that the Senate ordered them to be penned up in 1409.

Calle dei Furlani, right next to the Scuola di San Giorgio, leads back to the **Campo delle Gatte** (L7), 'of the female cats', though *gatte* was actually Venetian for 'legate', or Apostolic Nuncio. But nowadays the feline connotations better fit the bill: nearly every shop, no matter how incongruous, sells tins of cat food, and in some of the smaller alleys you can see little improvised kitty shelters and litter boxes (obviously a problem for the Venetian cat).

Yet another little diversion from the Scuola di San Giorgio is to plain brick **San Lorenzo** (K6; *closed for restoration*) – on Calle dei Furlani, walk west over the canal, and then immediately turn right up the Fondamenta S. Giorgio degli Schiavoni, and turn left in Calle di San Lorenzo. San Lorenzo is one of the oldest churches, founded in the 6th century; it was the last resting place of Marco Polo, only the great traveller's sarcophagus was misplaced in its 16th-century restoration. The church was damaged in the First World War, deconsecrated, used as storage space, and every now and then hosts an exhibition.

Retrace your steps to the Fondamenta San Giorgio degli Schiavoni and continue to its end. Cross the canal again for **Corte Nuova** (L6), where there's a quaint, home-made chapel with a painted ceiling and shrines to the war victims in the archway to Calle Zorzi.

San Francesco della Vigna L6

Campo San Francesco della Vigna, t 041 520 6102; vaporetto Celestia. Open daily 8–12.30 and 3–7; adm free.

This slice of the Renaissance seems lost in a remote, graffiti-filled square, with the rusty skeletons of gasworks for company. Its south flank is skirted by a ghostly *campo*, with a campanile, a Gritti palace (1525) – long the residence of the Papal Nuncio, the Oratory of the Holy Stigmata – and a lofty 19th-century neoclassical portico.

According to hoary tradition, the first church on this site commemorated the spot where the living St Mark the Evangelist came closest to Venice; while sailing from Aquileia to Egypt, he fell asleep, and as his boat sailed past he had his famous '*Pax tibi...*' dream. Named after the vines planted on this site in 1253 when it was donated to the Franciscans, the present church was begun in 1534 to a design by Sansovino, its foundation stone laid by Sansovino's friend, Doge Andrea Gritti. In 1572 it was given a temple façade by Palladio in bright Istrian stone, which seems a bit sad and extravagant without the flickering play of water and light that brings its whiteness to life elsewhere.

Sansovino's interior was reshaped according to designs by Fra Francesco Zorzi, a keen student of Renaissance philosophy, proportions and geometry, into a spacious Latin cross with five chapels along its single nave – a dry, academic design more Tuscan than Venetian. The art is much better than the building itself: by the door, bronze statues of *SS. Francis* and *John the Baptist* by Vittoria and a triptych by Alvise Vivarini. The third chapel on the right sports a pair of tombs of *Contarini* doges; the fourth chapel, belonging to the Badoer family, has a recently restored *Resurrection* attributed to Veronese, but better still is Antonio da Negroponte's 1450 shimmering *Madonna and Child Enthroned* in the right transept, a golden-robed Virgin in a merry spring bower full of roses and orange trees – one of Venice's hidden gems from the early Renaissance, when artists were still content to imitate nature rather than improve on it.

Doge Gritti is buried in the chancel, but there is more art in the marble-clad **Giustiniani chapel** to the left of the altar, a survivor from the original church. Designed by the Lombardos, its row of prophets are by Pietro and helpers, while the four *Evangelists* and altar are by Tullio and Sante. On the left side of the nave, perhaps the best work is Gerolamo da Santacroce's *Martyrdom of St Laurence* under the pulpit.

Veronese's *Sacra Conversazione* (1562) is in the fifth chapel on the left; the third, with a bright frescoed ceiling lit by an oculus, is decorated with a quirky combination of *chiaroscuro* by Giambattista Tiepolo and sculpted garlands; while the second has a fine altarpiece by Alessandro Vittoria, with statues of *SS. Sebastian*, *Roch* and *Anthony Abbot*. A door in the left transept leads out into the simple but lovely 15th-century cloisters, full of flowers and lined with tombs. Near the entrance, a chapel contains a *Madonna and Child* by Giovanni Bellini and assistants. Have €2 for the lights – a bargain for one of Venice's sweetest Madonnas. The main cloister leads into another, larger one, now used as a garden nursery; it has what might be Venice's only vineyard.

THE ARSENALE AND AROUND

The Arsenale L–M7

Campo dell'Arsenale; vaporetto Arsenale.
Open various hours depending on exhibitions.

The public can finally see inside parts of the Arsenale now that the Biennale has taken over a vast section of its empty shipyards as a year-round space for exhibitions, arts events, music and the like. The massive new premises, with its timbered ceilings and crumbling brickwork, involves various old (mostly 16th-century) adjacent buildings – the **Gaggiante** (attributed to Sansovino), the huge **Corderie** (rope works), the **Artiglierie** and the **Tese** (four enormous hangars with open-air slipways). The space also incorporates two theatres, including the vast **Teatro alle Tese**, which opened in 2000 and can be adapted for all sorts of performances.

This first of all arsenals was founded in 1104, and is believed to have derived its name from the Venetian pronunciation of the Arabic *darsina'a*, or artisans' shop. In later centuries the Arsenale was enlarged to occupy 80 acres, surrounded by a forbidding 2-mile-long wall. Within this protected naval base, Venice's fleet was built, maintained and refitted for each voyage; all provisions and equipment were stored here, as was the artillery, in an area nicknamed the Iron Garden.

Torri dell'Arsenale M7

Campo dell'Arsenale; vaporetto Arsenale.

The **Great Gateway of the Arsenale** used to be all the Italian military allowed you to see of what the Senate called 'the heart of the Venetian state'.

Touted as Venice's first Renaissance structure, it was built by Antonio Gambello in 1460 (better late than never, the Venetians say) who assembled his work out of older bits – four Greek columns, Byzantine capitals, entablature and floral reliefs. After the Battle of Lepanto, two new statues were added; and in 1682 the present terrace was introduced in front to replace a drawbridge. This over the years became an honoured retirement home for old Greek lions: the two on the right, one bald and skinny with a silly toothless grin, and the other aged into an innocent Easter lamb, are originally from the Lion Terrace on the holy island of Delos, brought to Venice after the rescue of Corfu in 1718. The larger two on either side of the entrance were brought back from Greece by Francesco Morosini after his troops blew the top off the Parthenon: the one to the right, a dead ringer for the Cowardly Lion of Oz, may once have stood on the sacred road to Eleusis, while the other, sitting upright with an expression like the decayed Errol Flynn in *The Sun Also Rises*, was the famous Lion of Piraeus; if you look very closely at his haunches, you can make out the runes scratched in 1040 by a member of the Byzantine Emperor's Varangian Guard led by Harald Hardrada, future king of Norway. The most ridiculous lion of all, however, is the bellicose Venetian feline over the gateway,

The Arsenale Assembly Line

Venice's Arsenale holds a unique place in the prehistory of the Industrial Revolution. Though Henry Ford sometimes gets credit for inventing the assembly line, the Venetians were using the same methods 500 years earlier to produce not only more and better ships than anyone else, but fat galleys and long tapered galleasses (the bane of the Turks at Lepanto) that were as identical as Model Ts.

As a result, all Venetian ships used uniform spare parts, which were available at any Venetian port; all ships could quickly be adapted to either war or trade ('trade war' in the Middle Ages being more than mere metaphor); all ships could be boarded by any Venetian crew, who would i 'know the ropes', so to spea the last speech of Doge Mo the Arsenale employed 16,000 men, by far the most ever employed in one place before the 19th century. During the most intensive fighting with the Turks it cranked out a ship a day; on special occasions, to impress visitors like Henry III, King of France, the *arsenalati* produced a beautiful galley between the antipasto and dessert courses of a State feast. Dante visited this great complex twice and, as Blake would later do with his 'Dark Satanic Mills', relegated it to the *Inferno*, where its cauldrons of boiled pitch came in handy to poach crooks who sell public offices.

jealously guarding a closed book (so as not to reveal the pacific *'Pax tibi Marce'* phrase), whose parents must have been a winged poodle and a warthog.

South of the Arsenale

To the left of the gate, down the Fondamenta di Fronte, **San Martino** (L7; *open Mon–Fri 4–7*), is yet another church designed *c.*1540 by Sansovino; the most impressive thing about its heavily decorated Greek cross interior is the false octagonal cupola, painted with 17th-century *trompe l'œil* architectural perspectives, a style that the Italians called *quadratura*.

You can get a good view of the Arsenale's walls along the Fondamenta Penini in front of San Martino, by following the Rio delle Gorne ('rain gutter'); at its end, Sottoportico d'Angelo is named after the **statue of the angel** on its low tiny archway, flanked by the only hedgehogs in Venice.

Also from Campo dell'Arsenale, take Calle della Pergola and Calle dei Forni to the Lagoon-front Riva Ca'di Dio. The building with the ornate frieze is the 1473 **Forni Pubblici** (L8), where the ships' biscuit for Venice's fleet and garrisons was baked to last (some Venetian hardtack discovered in Crete was still edible after 150 years).

Just before the next bridge is the **Ca' di Dio** (L8), a 13th-century pilgrims' hostel used by the Crusaders, and later expanded by Sansovino. This is one of the busier parts of Venice's shore, where tugboats and ferries dock and tired ACTV *vaporetti* rest for the night.

Naval History Museum M8

*Campo San Biagio, t 041 520 0276; **vaporetto** Arsenale. Open Mon–Fri 8.45–1.30, Sat 8.45–1; **adm** €1.55.*

If any citizen of the *Serenissima* worth their salt could come back to contemporary Venice, the first place they'd visit is this museum. Without the right stuff displayed here, there would have been no St Mark's, no doges, no Bellinis or Titians, and indeed no Venice. The low admission price makes this museum one of the best deals in town, and as a bonus there are explanations in English.

On the **ground floor** you can learn all about Italy's one outstanding success in the Second World War: the 'nautical pigs' or manned torpedoes, invented by Prince Valerio Borghese. Not as kamikaze as they sound, these were operated by two divers, who would guide the weapon to its target, set the

La Sensa

The name comes from Ascension Day, a movable feast that takes place 40 days after Easter. For 795 years of Venetian history, it meant much more: it was Venice's own symbolic apotheosis as the husband, lord, and master of the sea. It was on Ascension Day in the year 1000 when Doge Pietro Orseolo II began his campaign against the Dalmatians – Venice's first foreign conquest and the source of immense civic pride. Whatever ceremony ensued was given a boost by Pope Alexander III in 1177, who gave the doge a ring in gratitude for his help in securing the submission of Emperor Barbarossa: 'Let posterity remember that the sea is yours by right of conquest, subject to you as a wife to her husband,' said the Pope.

What really got under the skin of Venice's many rivals was her joyously excessive arrogance, much of it concentrated in *La Sensa*, an astute mix of politics and religion and trade fair that followed the city's maxim: *prima di tutto Veneziani, poi Cristiani* (Venetians first of all, and Christians second).

The day began with the procession of the Arsenale workers from the church of San Martino to the Piazzetta San Marco, where the ducal barge, the *Bucintoro*, waited, a 100ft floating centrepiece of gilded statues and flame-coloured velvet. There the *Arsenalotti* would be joined by the doge, playing his usual role as high priest, accompanied by his insignia – eight banners, six long silver trumpets and an umbrella (gifts from Alexander III) – and along with his retinue he would board the *Bucintoro* and be rowed out to the Lido, accompanied by a fleet of other vessels, all lavishly decorated with carpets, garlands, banners and flowers. At the church of Sant'Elena, the doge would meet the ship of the Patriarch and Papal Nuncio and sail to the port of San Nicolò del Lido, where the choir of St Mark's would sing as the Patriarch boarded the *Bucintoro* to sail to the lighthouse, where he would bless the *Serenissima* and pour holy water into the sea (the *benedictio*), after which the doge would toss a golden wedding ring into the waves (the *Deponsatio*), declaring: 'With this, we wed thee, O Sea, in sign of our true and perpetual dominion'. This was the most exciting part of the festival, not only because horns would blast and bells would peal and everyone cheered, but because the *Bucintoro* was so flimsy that there was always a chance of the doge falling in the sea.

Afterwards the doge would visit the chapel of San Nicolò to pay homage to the phoney relics of the patron of the sea, then preside over two banquets that the public was invited to watch. After this, everyone would dress in their finery for the opening of the *Sensa* fair in the *piazza* – a market that lasted for a week, and later 15 days, where the latest silks and spices from the East would be displayed, along with the finest things the city could make, from glass and gold to works of art – Canova's *Orpheus and Eurydice* was first shown in the *Sensa* fair of 1778. Most important was a large tyrannical doll called the 'Piavola da Franza' dressed in the latest French fashions, who determined what Venetian women would wear during the next season. A crucial feature of *La Sensa*'s success was the liberty to wear masks. And at midnight, candle-lit orchestras playing love songs floated down the Grand Canal.

---

explosive and swim away. They sank 16 ships, nearly all of them British anchored in the port of Alexandria; after they had sunk HMS *Valiant* on 19 December 1941 the Admiral of the Fleet very sportingly decorated the divers for their courage. Also on this floor are reliefs of the citadels captured by the Venetian fleet, a monument by Canova to Venice's last admiral, Angelo Emo (d. 1792), mighty cannons, and the great three-branched lantern from Morosini's galley.

The **first floor** has earlier mementoes: two wooden figures of chained Turks who sailed with Morosini, and Morosini's prayer book (with a pistol fitted in the back cover); 17th-century sea charts and plans of the Arsenal; nautical instruments; models of Venice's ancient bridges and gates; elaborate, carved

and painted decorations salvaged from a
17th-century Venetian galley; rooms full of
ships' models – of Caligula's ships recovered
from Lake Nemi (near Rome) in the 1930s,
only to be burned by the Nazis, of galleys and
triremes hung with cobwebs and moth-
eaten sails – these owe their amazing detail
not to the fond hobby of some old sailor, but
to the fact that they were used by the ship-
builders in the Arsenal, who preferred them
to drawings. Most splendid of all is a huge
model of the last *Bucintoro* (1728; *see* box,
opposite), which Napoleon, in his role of
'Attila of the Venetian state' had burned in
1798, all the better to remove its 60,000
sequins' worth of gilding; one of the few
things to survive was the doge's throne,
on which he would ride in state to marry the
sea with a ring big enough to fit King Kong.
The *Bucintoro* was grand but scarcely
seaworthy; one Turkish sultan, who thought
the whole marriage of the sea thing quite
ridiculous, predicted that it wouldn't be
long before the marriage was actually
consummated.

The **second floor** (models of gunboats,
lagoon craft, etc.) lacks the poetry of the first,
but the **third floor** has a colourful room of
rare models of ancient junks and 18th-
century Chinese silk panels, donated to the
museum in 1964 by Jacques Sigaut, a French
expert in oriental naval affairs and admirer
of Marco Polo; other rooms contain charm-
ingly naïve ex-votos painted by mariners to
the Madonna dell'Arco in Naples. The **fourth
floor** is dedicated to the Vikings and the
Swedes, whose lions had much sharper teeth
than Venice's; exhibits include a copy of the
runes in dragon scroll, from the lion in front
of the Arsenal, and a slightly self-righteous
display claiming that it wasn't Morosini, the
conqueror of the Peloponnese, who blew up
the Parthenon in Athens, but a Swedish
admiral named Otto Wilhelm von
Königsmark working in his employ.

Last of all is a beautiful, iridescent **shell
collection** donated by Giuliana Coen-
Camerino, alias the Venetian designer
Roberta di Camerino.

EASTERN CASTELLO
Along Via Giuseppe Giribaldi M–N9

Vaporetto Arsenale.

Broad and busy Via Giuseppe Garibaldi was
a wide canal before the Napoleonic government filled it in. Near the western end of the
street, note the **plaque** set up on the right,
marking the home of Giovanni and
Sebastiano Cabot, natives of Genoa who
remained long enough in the city to become
Venetian merchants and citizens, before
moving to the Venetian community at
Bristol. In 1496 John and Sebastian sailed off
in the service of King Henry VII and claimed
Nova Scotia and Newfoundland for the
crown (though on landing they planted not
the Union Jack, but the Lion of St Mark). Their
explorations inspired England to seek the
fabled Northwest Passage to the Orient, and
led to the settlement of Canada.

Continuing east down Via Garibaldi, take
the sixth left (Calle del Forno, a very narrow
street between a food store and a jeweller's)
to the **Fondamenta della Tana** (M8), facing
the high wall of the great rope factory (or
Tana), 1,000ft long. The houses along the
Fondamenta are a survival of perhaps the
world's first public housing, built by the state
from medieval times on for workers in the
Arsenale. Walk down to the Fondamenta's
east end; this used to be a market, as you can
see from the ancient stone plaque setting
minimum sizes for fish. Turn right on Calle
Loredan and left on Fondamenta
S. Gioacchino, a part of Via Garibaldi that still
has its canal; the market moved here long
ago, and in the morning this area is a
convivial jumble of ragged awnings and fruit
crates, red-nosed market ladies and furtive
tomcats, the most old-fashioned and least
touristy corner of all Venice.

Follow Fondamenta S. Gioacchino east
(left) over a bridge. Turn left at the next
bridge, down Calle S. Gioacchino; this leads
into the charming little canal, **Rio Riello** (O8).

Isola di San Pietro O8–P9

At the end of Via Garibaldi, a bridge crosses to the remote Castello island of San Pietro, surrounded by boatyards. Excavations have revealed the foundations of a late Roman/early Venetian settlement; its long-gone castle lent its name to the entire *sestiere*.

San Pietro di Castello P8

*Campo San Pietro; vaporetto Giardini. **Open** Mon–Sat 10–5; Sun 1–5; adm €2.*

This was Venice's cathedral from the 11th century until 1807, when the rationally minded Napoleon made the ducal chapel of San Marco the seat of Venice's Patriarch. Its lonely, distant site is no small comment on the Republic's hostile attitude towards the Papacy. In practice the Venetians were (and still are) more church-going than the Romans, but when it came to popes trying to assert any degree of temporal authority, the Venetians firmly drew the line. Their Patriarch, a position assumed in 1451 from the ancient see of Aquileia, Grado and Udine, with the same status as a cardinal, was appointed by the Venetian Senate instead of the Pope; and whenever a church problem was discussed by the Senate it was always

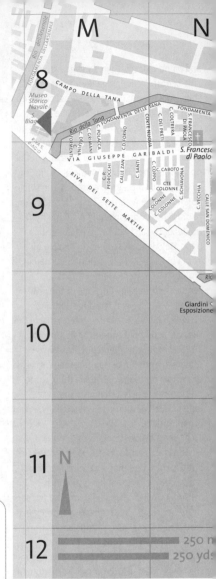

The Feast of the Marys

Tradition has it that in 944 a mass wedding of brides from all over the city was being held at San Pietro when a band of Dalmatian freebooters swooped down and carried off both girls and dowries. The young men from the parish of Santa Maria Formosa set off in pursuit and saved the day, catching the pirates before they got far. This evolved into a major Venetian holiday known as the Feast of the Marys that lasted until the fall of the Republic, celebrated with a wedding of two couples from each *sestiere* at San Pietro; eight days of parties followed, and ended at Candlemas with the doge's visit to Santa Maria Formosa, where he was ceremoniously presented with a straw hat and a glass of wine – in 944, Doge Pietro Candiano III had hesitated to make the journey for fear of rain and thirst.

noted at the head of the official minutes: '*Cazzadi i papalisti*' ('The supporters of the Pope have been removed').

Retired from its cathedral status, San Pietro is as relaxed as any pensioner could be, nursed by a pretty if tipsy **campanile** in white Istrian stone built by Mauro Codussi; neighbourhood ladies pull up their deckchairs and knit in its shadow. The first church on this site was last replaced in 1550 by a white and spacious pseudo-Palladian design, recently restored by a Los Angeles committee. In the right aisle there's a

O P Q

Rio san Daniele
C. LARGA S. PIETRO
SAL. STRETTI
C. DETTO RIELLE
CAMPO SAN PIETRO
✠ S. Pietro
di Castello
Isola di
San Pietro

C. S. GIOVANNI
ALL FOND. PIELLO
C. D. TERCO
C. ZULIAN
CAMPO DI RUGA
C. RUGA
C. MARATONI
C.D. OLE
C. CAMPANILE
C. SALAMON
FONDAMENTA QUINTAVALLE
CTE NUOVA
C. QUINTAVALLE
C. MEZZO

della Trina
C. RIZIER
C. BASSA
C. MASCELLI
TANA
C. LOREDAN
C. S.ECCHINO
C. CAPROZZOLA
FOND. SAN GIOACCHINO
Rio di Sant'Anna
FONDAMENTA SANTANNA
CORTE D. BIANCO
C. CROTTERA
S. ANNA
PONTE DI QUINTAVALLE
C. ILO POMORI
C. FARI
FOND. CASTEL OLIVOLO

CANALE DI SAN PIETRO
Rio di Quintavalle

C. SARESIAN
ONELLA
C. SCO MARINA
CORTE SARESIN
CALLE DELL'ANCORE
CORRERA
CALLE
CALLE TIEPOLO
CALLE CATTANAO
CORTE S. MARIA NOVELLA
MARINA
RAMO DI NICOLI
C. SECCO MARINA
CORTE SARESIN E TERRA
LESINA
FORNER
SECCO
SABBIONELLI
FONDAMENTA
C. PRETI
Rio di San Giuseppe
CORTE CASE NUOVE

San Giuseppe
S. Giuseppe
di Castello
CAMPO S. GIUSEPPE
RIO TERRA DI SAN GIUSEPPE
PALUDO SAN ANTONIO

VIALE TRENTO
Giardini
CALLE DIETRO IL GIARDINO

DEI GIARDINI PUBBLICI
BIENNALE D'ARTE
RAMO MONTELLO
VIALE 24 MAGGIO

DARSENA
DI
S. ELENA

V. LE TRIESTE
VIALE TRENTO
Pubblici
VIALE DEI GIARDINI PUBBLICI
Rio dei Giardini
CALLE DEL MONTELLO
CALLE PASUBIO
C.D. CINGIA
C.D. FORNER
C.D. PUZZO
C.D. CONGREGAZION
CALLE DEL PASUBIO
ASINO
CAMPO D. GRAPPA
MONTE SANTO
C.S. MICH.
C. HERMADA
C. OLIVIA
LONGHI
C. PODGORA
Rio di Sant'Elena
VIALE SANT'ELENA
Campo Sportivo
CAMPO CHIESA SANT'ELENA

CALLE D. CARSO
SMOTINO
CALLE CANTORE
C. CHINOTTO
CAMPO STRINGARI
C. ZUGNA
RAMO ZUGNA
VIALE PIAVE
CALLE BAINSIZZA
CALLE GORIZIA
CALLE DUCA D'AOSTA
CALLE ROVERETO
CALLE CARNARO
C. BUCARI
C. ZUGNA

Parco delle Rimembranze
VIALE VITTORIO VENETO
VIALE 4 NOVEMBRE
✠ Sant' Elena
S. Elena
Isola di
Sant'Elena

marble **throne** with an eight-shaped back, two Stars of David and an inscription from the Koran, part of a 13th-century Muslim tombstone. The belief that this was St Peter's throne from Antioch (note the old inscription above it) probably grew up when some shrewd prankster sold it to an ignorant crusader. The **sanctuary** was built to an elegant design by Longhena, to enshrine relics of San Lorenzo Giustiniani – Venice's first patriarch (d. 1456) and the one consecrated body the Venetians didn't have to steal. Most essentially for the Venetians, he

had some influence in Heaven during plagues, as can be seen in the painting on the right wall; it was his intercession in 1630 that earned him the fancy altar, ordered by the Senate, even though he wasn't canonized until 1690. Most compelling of all is the little **Cappella Lando** in the left aisle, with a 5th-century Roman mosaic fragment of a vase of flowers, a marble *pluteus*, stylized Byzantine-Veneto capitals on the columns, and a bust of *San Lorenzo Giustiniani*, whose sunken cheeks, tight lips and lines of care betray him as a true son of Venice.

Giardini Pubblici N10–O11

Viale dei Giardini Pubblici; vaporetto Giardini.

This rare green oasis in the city of stone and water was planted by Eugène de Beauharnais in the name of Napoleon at the expense of four churches and two monasteries, which no one mourned too deeply. Though the garbage bins could be emptied a bit more often, the public gardens are respectable enough, and a cool place to lounge away a hot afternoon. As one of Venice's few open spaces, they have become a repository for forgotten and bizarre memorials – a crabbed bit of concrete and rusty steel mesh labelled: 'From the Veneto to her *partigiani*' – among others. There's also a small **children's playground** with swings and the like. If you come in an even-numbered year you can explore the offerings in the national pavilions of the Biennale (*see* p.300) mostly built in the 1920s; (in odd-numbered years they're usually locked up, though exceptional exhibitions occasionally bring it out of its bi-annual darkness).

San Giuseppe di Castello O9–10

Campo San Giuseppe; vaporetto Giardini.
Open Mon–Sat 9.20–12.30 and 3–6, Sun 3–6; adm free.

One of Venice's most obscure churches, this was rebuilt in the 16th century and given a simple, classical façade. Within, the most prepossessing monument is the left aisle's **Tomb of Doge Marino Grimani** (d. 1605), designed by Scamozzi with figures and good reliefs (a *Nativity* with angel musicians) sculpted by Gerolamo Campagna. Its altar was dedicated in honour of the victory of Lepanto and has a relief of the battle. The battle order as shown isn't quite right – the Turks had their ships in a crescent as shown, but the Christians attacked in a straight line, with the five big galleasses in the centre leading the charge (in the relief the god Neptune seems to be cheering them on). In the **sanctuary**, a Grimani who served as a

procurator is remembered with a monument and bust by Vittoria.

Isola di Sant'Elena P9–Q12

Vaporetto *Sant'Elena.*

This is Venice at its remotest. The lack of little canals winding in and out and the recent date of most of its buildings make it seem like an Italian 'Anywhere' miraculously delivered of the national plague of automobilitis. Long an open meadow in front of a church and convent, Sant'Elena was a fashionable 19th-century retreat for Sunday picnics and promenades until the Austrians began to expand it for a military parade ground, and blocks of flats took over all of the meadow, except for the crescent of the **Parco delle Rimembranze** (P12).

Sant'Elena Q11

Campo di Chiesa Sant'Elena; vaporetto Sant'Elena. Open summer Mon–Sat 4–7, Sun 5–7, winter Mon–Sat 4–6, Sun 5–6; adm free.

At the very eastern end of the island, Sant'Elena is hemmed in by the walls of a sports field and a naval college. Venice picked up the body of Constantine's mother Helen in the great 13th-century haul of Eastern booty. As one of the chief saints of the Eastern church, Helen's relics merited their own church; the present Gothic version was built in 1435 by Olivetan monks. Although one of Venice's chief religious shrines, it was deconsecrated by Napoleon in 1807; the Austrians added insult to injury by using it as a foundry. In 1928 it was restored and reconsecrated, and you can see its finest work of art right in front: Antonio Rizzo's monumental *Doorway Dedicated to Comandante Vittore Cappello, Kneeling Before St Helen* (1470s), celebrated for the natural realism in the Comandante's expression. In contrast to the doorway, the rest of Sant'Elena's façade is severe but handsome, its narrow elevation relieved by the chapels on the right and the cloister on the left. The paintings that once adorned the interior are mostly in the Accademia and other museums.

Dorsoduro

THE ACCADEMIA AND AROUND 158
Galleria dell'Accademia 158
Raccolta d'Arte Vittorio Cini 162
St George 162
Peggy Guggenheim Collection 163

LA SALUTE AND AROUND 163
Santa Maria della Salute 163
Dogana di Mare 164

NORTHERN DORSODURO 165
Ca' Rezzonico 165
Campo San Barnaba 166
Campo Santa Margherita 166
Scuola dei Carmini 166
Carmini 167

SAN SEBASTIANO AND AROUND 167
San Sebastiano 167
Angelo Raffaele 168
Palazzo Ariani 168
Santa Maria del Soccorso 168
San Nicolò dei Mendicoli 169

ALONG THE ZATTERE 169
Campo di San Trovaso 171
Santa Maria della Visitazione 171
Gesuati 172
Rio Terrà Antonio Foscarini 172
The Eastern Zattere 172

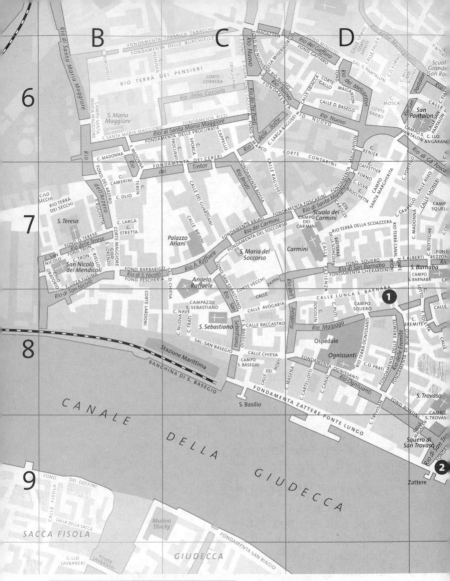

1 Lunch

Ai 4 Feri, *Calle Lunga San Barnaba*, **t** *041 520 6978*; **vaporetto** *Ca' Rezzonico*. **Open** *Mon–Sat 12–2.30*. **Cheap**. A new *osteria* with excellent *cicheti* or good-value, tasty meals, *see* p.273.

2 Coffee and Ice Cream

Nico, *Fond. Zattere*; **vaporetto** *Zattere*. **Open** *daily 8am–9.30pm*. Best ice cream in town!

3 Drinks

Al Bottegon, *Fondamenta Nani*; **vaporetto** *Zattere*. **Open** *Mon–Sat 8.30–2.30 and 3.30–8.30*. Wine by the glass in this old-fashioned shop near the San Trovaso boatyard.

Highlights

Medieval Venice: The wonders of the medieval art in the Accademia, p.158

Renaissance Venice: San Sebastiano, decorated by local parishioner Veronese, p.167

Baroque/Rococo Venice: Longhena's great masterpiece, La Salute, p.163

Indoor Venice: Peggy Guggenheim's delightful art museum/*palazzo*, p.163

Decadent Venice: The splendours of Venice's twilight, at the Ca' Rezzonico, p.165

Pigeon Venice: Campo Santa Margherita, one of the nicest little market squares in Venice, p.166

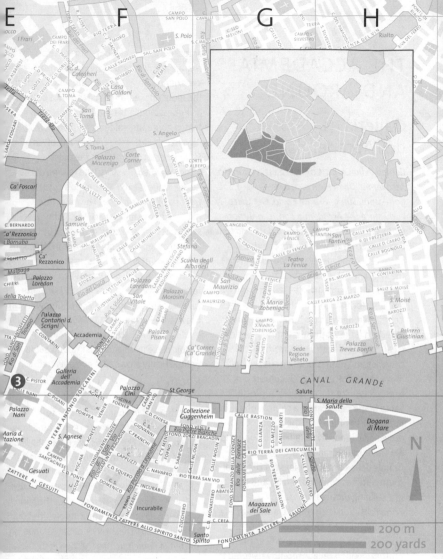

Dorsoduro

Dorsoduro, 'the hard-back', stands on tougher clay than the rest of Venice, perhaps the added smidgeon of security that encouraged the Venetians to entrust some of their most elaborate palaces and finest art to this neighbourhood. Its eastern 'hook', tipped by the Dogana di Mare, is the city's most exclusive area, where the palaces, many bought up by the insatiable Milanese, are in very good nick; others contain small galleries and shops selling art supplies. The Zattere,

running the length of Dorsoduro along the Giudecca Canal, is a favourite promenade, with a large selection of watering holes and even a touch of rare Venetian nightlife. The northern reaches, around Campo Santa Margherita, have a mix of students and plain folk, of corner bars and shops selling plastic buckets and potatoes instead of glass harlequins and carnival masks.

THE ACCADEMIA AND AROUND

Galleria dell'Accademia E8–F9

Campo della Carità, t 041 522 2247; vaporetto Accademia. Open Mon 9–2, Tues–Fri 9–9, Sat 9am–11pm, Sun 9–8; adm €6.50. Get there early, since the Accademia admits only 300 visitors at a time, or pre-book a date and time on t 041 520 0345, which costs €1 extra.

Venice's art academy was founded just as the Republic's inspiration was petering out, in 1750, with Giambattista Piazzetta as its first director. In 1807, Napoleon, art's biggest 'centralizer', decreed that the Accademia's collection (at least those paintings he didn't steal, combined with works from the churches and monasteries he suppressed) be moved to the large religious complex he expropriated for the purpose. This included **Santa Maria della Carità**, a church rebuilt In 1451 by Bartolomeo Bon, the adjacent convent designed by Palladio, **the Convento dei Canonici Lateranensi**, and the **Scuola Grande della Carità**, the oldest of the 'great' confraternities, founded in 1260 and housed in a building dating from 1343.

The collection is arranged chronologically, beginning in the former refectory of the Scuola (Room I) under a magnificent 14th-century wooden ceiling, recently restored to reveal ranks of cherubic faces smiling down.

Room I

On the entrance wall, Jacobello del Fiore's golden *Justice and Two Angels* is a lovely expression of the Republic's favourite virtue. The other subjects in the room are all religious, and most of them depict the *Coronation of the Virgin*, a theme straight from the twilight of chivalry and the Crusades. Although Paolo Veneziano's early 1300s *Coronation of the Virgin*, magnificent in its almost Islamic patterns, is not far removed from its Byzantine icon

antecedents, you can begin to sense a change a few decades later in Lorenzo Veneziano's great *Annunciation* polyptych, in the more relaxed, almost dance-like poses of its figures, and in the worldly interest in things gorgeous, golden, and blonde. Michele di Matteo's early 15th-century *Polyptych of St Helen and the Cross* has the most intriguing *predella* story (the finding of the Cross), while Jacopo Alberegno's 1390s *Scenes from the Apocalypse* has the most fascinating iconography; in Scene XX, the skeletons look as if they're reading dirty jokes to each other. The first real smile in Venetian art appears in Nicolò di Pietro's 1394 *Madonna, Child, and Donor*, when Venice had recovered from the Black Death, the Marin Falier conspiracy and the War of Chioggia. On the left wall is one last *Coronation of the Virgin*, a mid 15th-century International Gothic piece by Michele Giambono, set in an optimistically crowded scene of Paradise.

Room II

Giambono sets the stage for the stupendous changes in Room II, changes so remarkable that it's easy to understand how the painters of the Renaissance seemed like magicians in the 15th century. All the works here are large altarpieces: the most sublime, Giovanni Bellini's *Sacred Conversation*, is also called the *Pala di San Giobbe*, after the church where it was orginally hung. Its architectural setting repeats the interior of San Giobbe; on the left *St Francis* invites the viewer to contemplate the scene, accompanied by the timeless music of the angels at the Madonna's feet. Carpaccio strikes radically different moods in two paintings: a sweet *Presentation of Jesus at the Temple* and a *Crucifixion and Apotheosis of 10,000 Martyrs on Mount Ararat*, full of languid youths suffering a variety of martyrdoms at the hands of Turks in fancy dress. Marco Basaiti's *Christ Calling the Sons of Zebedee* (1510) is brilliantly coloured, with a watery fantasy background, while Cima da Conegliano's *Madonna of the Orange Tree* has a softer light, and more subtle atmosphere.

Room III

The highlights of Room III are Cima's *Pietà* and Bartolomeo Montagna's beautifully coloured *Madonna and Saints*.

Room IV

Room IV has some of Giovanni Bellini's loveliest melancholy and tender brown-eyed *Madonnas*, with the Child on the table before them, a composition that his patrons never tired of, and one that he managed constantly to vary; outstanding are the *Madonna and Child between St Catherine and the Magdalen*, wonderfully lit with its dark background, and the *Madonna with the Blessing Child*, perhaps the sweetest and saddest of them all. Other works include Jacopo Bellini's *Madonna and Child*, which looks like an icon next to his son's paintings; Hans Memling's *Portrait of a Youth*, Cosmè Tura's typically wiry and lumpy *Madonna and Child*; and Andrea Mantegna's *St George*, set amid antique pillars and garlands of fruit. The only Tuscan in the room is Piero della Francesca's youthful study in perspective, *St Jerome and Devotee*, brown, dry, and austere company for the Venetians; yet the expression on St Jerome's face couldn't be better (he looks at the donor, as much as to say 'It's all very well to pay Piero to put you here, but it won't get you any points in the Bank of Grace!').

Room V

Room V contains the most famous painting in the Accademia, Giorgione's *The Tempest*, unfortunately hard to see behind a plate of reflective glass. One of the few paintings all art historians agree in ascribing to 'Big George', it was innovative for the importance given to atmosphere over detail. The inexplicable relationship between the soldier and mother in the foreground, the whole air of ambiguity and mystery, are revolutionary in the fact that they were painted without preliminary drawings, and that they exist only for the sake of the pleasure they give. This is one of the first (and best) 'easel paintings', serving neither Church nor State nor a patron's vanity. Giorgione's other painting in the room, *Col Tempo* ('with time'), has a more

obvious message with its slightly sinister old woman and her all-too-true warning. Yet both pictures are uncanny; it is said that Giorgione invented easel painting to delight the bored patricians of Venice's decline, but the two paintings here would seem to reflect rather than lighten their restless *ennui*.

Also in Room V are Giovanni Bellini's five mysterious *Allegories*, and three more of his *Madonnas*, including the softly coloured *Madonna degli Alberetti*. In his *Pietà*, the same Bellini *Madonna* is poignantly alone in an empty brown landscape.

Rooms VI–VIII

Here the lushly coloured Venetian High Renaissance makes its first appearance, with fine works by Palma Vecchio (*Holy Family with Saints*) and his pupil, Bonifazio Veronese (*Dives and Lazarus*); and Paris Bordone – his masterpiece, *Fisherman Presenting St Mark's Ring to Doge Bartolomeo Gradenigo*, is based on the legend of a fisherman given the ring by the saint, as an amulet to guard the city from a hurricane brewed by Satan himself. Psychologically light years away is Lorenzo Lotto's *Gentleman in his Study*, a remarkably candid portrait of a pale and anaemic fellow caught off-guard with his book, his lizard, and what appear to be torn petals of some 16th-century *fleurs du mal*.

Room IX

This is the bookshop, which also sells the usual museum shop range of derivative artefacts, including scarves, ties and jewellery.

Room X

The Venetian High Renaissance reaches a climax in Room X, not only in art but in size, in Veronese's masterpiece, *Christ in the House of Levi* (1573), painted for the refectory of Santi Giovanni e Paolo. The setting, in a Palladian loggia with a ghostly white imaginary background, almost a stagedrop, is in violent contrast to the rollicking life and lush colour of the very Venetian feast in the foreground. With its Turks, cat, big Veronese hounds, midgets, Germans and artist's self-portrait (in the front, next to the pillar on the left), it could be a scene from a Renaissance

Fellini film. Instead, the original title was *The Last Supper*, and as such it fell foul of the Inquisition, which took umbrage at the animals, dwarfs, drunkards, buffoons – and especially at the Germans, the evil spirits of the Reformation. Veronese was cross-examined, and in the end was ordered to make pious changes at his own expense; the artist, in true Venetian style, saved himself the time and expense by simply changing the title.

Other Veroneses in the room include a *Crucifixion*, where, in a typically Venetian manner, the clothes and pageantry tend to overwhelm the main event, which is shunted off into the left-hand corner involving only a handful of figures, while prancing horsemen and ladies go about their business; and an *Annunciation*, Veronese-style, in another Palladian setting, the Virgin gorgeously dressed for the occasion. His *Battle of Lepanto*, painted shortly after the event, has the Virgin and saints deciding the outcome in the clouds, just as the gods in Homer watched over the battle of Troy.

In the same room Tintoretto checks in with his first major painting, *St Mark Freeing the Slave* (1548). Inspired by Michelangelo's handling of form and composition, Tintoretto would often make small wax models of his figures and arrange them in a box, experimenting with lighting and poses. In this painting depicting St Mark's miraculous delivery of a slave who visited his shrine, St Mark doesn't walk into the scene, but nose-dives in a dramatic loop-the-loop from the top of the canvas. Even more compelling is Tintoretto's *Translation of the Body of St Mark*, one of the strangest paintings in Venice. The subject is the 'pious theft' from Alexandria, complete with an obligatory nonplussed camel, but what are those pale figures on the left, fleeing into a row of doorways, and who are those people sprawled on the ground? The eye is drawn past them all to a boiling orange and black sky. The two other Tintorettos in the room are slightly more traditional, *St Mark Rescuing the Saracen* in a dark and stormy whirlpool, and *St Mark's Dream* painted with son Domenico

(the famous '*Pax tibi*, etc.' scene, with a dark, wet embryonic Venice in the background).

The last great painting in Room X, *La Pietà*, was Titian's last, which he was working on in his 90s (probably for his own tomb) when the tough old man was felled, not by old age but by the plague. Dark and impressionistic and more moving than 10 other Titians put together, it was left uncompleted at his death and, as the inscription states, finished by Palma Giovane.

Room XI

Room XI has more by Tintoretto: his *Madonna dei Camerlenghi* ('of the Treasurers'), populated by prosperous-looking Venetians, bringing the Virgin a sack of money; Old Testament scenes of *The Creation of Animals* (some of these not in any known book of zoology), *Adam and Eve* and *Cain and Abel*. *Il Ricco Epulone*, by Bonifazio de' Pitati, is imbued with Veneto melancholy, none of which is present in the curved *trompe l'œil* ceiling panels by Giambattista Tiepolo, all that survived the 1915 bomb that fell on the church of the Scalzi (*see* p.213).

Rooms XII–XVI

In the long corridor of **Room XII**, the colours take on the sombre tones of the murky 17th century, with landscapes by the likes of Giuseppe Zais and Marco Ricci. **Room XIII** is devoted to portraits by Tintoretto; **Room XIV** has more from the 17th century, most of it from foreigners living in Venice, and **Room XVI** features mythological scenes gone sour after a couple of centuries of respectability, beginning with Sebastiano Ricci's *Diana and Actaeon*, a joyless subject to begin with, here frozen, sickly and bored – even the nymphs are homely. Giambattista Tiepolo's *Rape of Europa* is slightly more endearing, with its nonchalant bull and urinating cherub. The star of **Room XVIa** is Piazzetta's weird *Fortune Teller* (1740), the most memorable work to come from the brush of the first director of the Accademia.

Room XVII

Room XVII contains more paintings from the 18th century, a time when Venice proved one of the few bright spots in Italian art. But, as technically brilliant and innovative as the great painters of the day were, it isn't hard to sense a loss of the old Venetian spirit: the buildings that featured in the backgrounds of Veronese and Tintoretto are now under scaffolding, or crumbling; the bold confidence of the past has dwindled into views, interiors, genre scenes, and an obsession with the picturesque. There are works by the brothers Guardi (*Fire at San Marcuola*), a Canaletto with nuns, and portraits by Rosalba Carriera, whose soft pastels flattered her sitters, though her best piece is a *Self-portrait*, painted in her old age, with ivy woven through her grey hair. Longhi contributes his genre scenes, one called *L'Indovino*, with a fortune-teller speaking through a tube.

Rooms XVIII–XIX and XXIII

In **Room XVIII** (with neoclassical architectural scenes) is the entrance to the upper level of the 15th-century church of the Carità (**Room XXIII**), where you can take in some first-rate early Renaissance works by Gentile Bellini, including his earliest signed work, the 1445 *Portrait of the Blessed Lorenzo Giustiniani* – which may have been a processional banner (hence its weathered state) – and four triptychs from the workshop of his brother Giovanni. Their Vivarini rivals get their say here, especially Bartolomeo (*Polyptych of the Nativity* and *Saints*) and his nephew Alvise (*Santa Chiara*). There are also paintings by Lazzaro Bastiani and Carlo Crivelli, a painter of exquisitely drawn *Madonnas* who left little behind in his native Venice. **Room XIX** has more Renaissance art from Marco Basaiti (a beardless *Dead Christ*, with *putti*) and Marco Marziale (the very decorative *Dinner at the House of Emmaus*).

Room XX

This room is given over to a series of large paintings from the Scuola di San Giovanni Evangelista, depicting the *Miracles of the True Cross*, all fascinating for their meticulously accurate depictions of late 15th-century Venice. You have to look hard to find the

miracle in Carpaccio's bustling view of *The Patriarch of Grado Curing the Lunatic*, set by the old wooden Rialto drawbridge, in a forest of chimney pots and an exotic crowd of Venetians, foreigners and festive gondolas. The main event in Gentile Bellini's famous dry, almost photographic view of Piazza San Marco in the *Procession of the Relic of the Cross* (with St Mark's original mosaics on the façade) is the man kneeling at the relic to implore Christ to cure his son's fractured skull. Gentile's other painting here, *The Recovery of the Relic from the Canal of San Lorenzo*, chronicles a mischance that occurred during the Relic's annual rounds – it fell in the canal, but floated to the surface to be recovered by the Grand Guardian of the Scuola; Caterina Cornaro, ex-Queen of Cyprus, looks on from the extreme left, and Gentile Bellini himself joins the group in the right foreground (fourth from the left). Giovanni Mansueti's *Healing of a Sick Child* shows the interior of a Venetian palace, while his *Miracle of the Relic in Campo San Lio* demonstrates just what happens to members of the confraternity who dare to disparage the Relic – it refuses to enter the church for their funerals – and, worst of all, everyone in the neighbourhood knows it.

Room XXI

Room XXI is entirely devoted to Vittore Carpaccio's delightful *Legend of St Ursula* series (*see* box, p.162), painted in 1490–96 for the ex-Scuola di Sant'Orsola and recently restored to its original fairytale colours.

Room XXIV

Last of all, Room XXIV, the former *albergo* of the Scuola della Carità, preserves its original panelling and 15th-century ceiling with the four evangelists, and a Titian – the *Presentation of the Virgin*, which he painted for this very room (1538). It's a charming scene set before Titian's native Cadore in the Dolomites, with the child Mary walking alone up the great flight of steps to the temple, while her relatives stand anxiously below. Also painted for this room is a triptych by Antonio Vivarini and Giovanni d'Alemagna,

Ursula – a Martyr's Life

The story behind Vittore Carpaccio's paintings is that of Ursula, daughter of King Maurus of Brittany. Carpaccio had considerable scope in interpreting the events, distant in both place and time, and went about it with his customary verve for the narrative and the literal, though naturally most of the details are from the Venice of his day. In the first scene, *The Arrival of the English Ambassadors*, the ambassadors are asking for the hand of Ursula for Hereus (Erero), son of the English King Conon; its very Venetian background contains a centrally planned octagonal Renaissance temple. To the right we see Princess Ursula dictating the conditions of marriage to her father; marry she will, but on the condition that she be allowed three years to make a pilgrimage to Rome, and that Hereus convert to Christianity. *The Return of the English Ambassadors* shows the Englishmen presenting the conditions to King Conon, a formal scene rounded out with a triumphal arch and a monkey on the steps.

Good egg that he is, Hereus accepts Ursula's conditions, and even offers to accompany her to Rome. In the next painting he meets Ursula and together they depart for Rome in a 15th-century Venetian galley. But then comes *The Dream of Ursula*, in which the princess has a dream of an angel foretelling her martyrdom – Carpaccio has the saint tucked in her little bed, slippers tidily arranged underneath, her crown at the foot of the bed, while the angel, like any mortal, comes in the door. Despite the dream warning, Ursula, Hereus and some fellow travellers – 11,000 virgins – continue to the Eternal City in the next painting: *The Pilgrims Meet Pope Ciriaco before the Walls of Rome*. There are almost as many bishops as virgins, and their crocodile hats make a surreal pattern. Together with the Pope, the pilgrims travel to Cologne (*Arrival at Cologne*), badly timing their arrival to coincide with a siege by the Huns, who send the 11,000 to their reward in the *Martyrdom of Pilgrims and Funeral of Ursula*.

and a portrait of Cardinal Bessarion, the famous Greek scholar whose collection formed the nucleus of the Biblioteca Nazionale Marciana (*see* p.118).

Raccolta d'Arte Vittorio Cini F8–9

Piscina del Forner, t 041 521 0755; vaporetto Accademia. Closed for restoration until end of 2003.

Palazzo Cini was the residence of Count Vittorio Cini (1884–1977), who loved and collected Tuscan art.

There are some beautiful works here, by the very first, and often anonymous, wizards of the Renaissance: a splendid *Maestà* of the early 14th century, by the Master of Badia a Isola, a *Crucifixion* by Bernardo Daddi, and a *Madonna Enthroned* by the Master of the Horne Triptych. Rooms III and IV are devoted to the 15th century, with a *Judgement of Paris* by Botticelli and his workshop; a lovely, luminous *Madonna, Child, and Two Angels*, by Piero di Cosimo; *Madonnas* by Filippo Lippi and attributed to Piero della Francesca; and a double portrait by Pontormo. Ivories, china, manuscripts, books and a 14th-century Tuscan marriage chest round out the collection.

St George F8–9

Campo San Vio; vaporetto Accademia. Open irregularly, but generally 8–12 and 4–6; adm free.

Venice's Anglican church appropriately has the tombstone of the consul Joseph Smith (1682–1770), recently moved here from the Lido. Smith lived in Venice for 70 years, and was the foremost collector of his day. An early patron of Canaletto, he acted as an agent between the painter and the English 'Grand Tourists' who snapped up his works, leaving Venice itself only three canvases. Smith's personal collection and library were among the most fabulous of the day, and greatly enriched the royal collections when King George III purchased them in 1770.

Peggy Guggenheim Collection G9

*Fondamenta Venier dei Leoni, **t** 041 240 5411, **w** www.guggenheim-venice.it; **vaporetto** Accademia/Salute. **Open** Wed–Mon 10–6 (1 April–2 Nov also Sat 10–10); **adm** €8. **Café/restaurant**, expensive.*

After the Accademia, this is the most visited museum in Venice, and deservedly so; it's the freshest breath of air in Doge City.

The museum is one of the oddballs on the Grand Canal, in the ranch-style Palazzo Venier dei Leoni, better known as the Palazzo Non Finito (begun in 1749 and never finished past the first floor). From 1910 it was the stage for the antics of the Marchesa Casati of Milan, glittering queen of decadence and folly, the Futurists' Gioconda, who held parties here with an artificial lilac jungle populated by apes, ocelots, Afghan hounds, and torch-bearing naked slaves painted with gold (who later died), until 1919 when she packed her bags to become the mistress of Gabriele D'Annunzio. Thirty years later the Palazzo Non Finito was purchased by another arty lady, American copper heiress Peggy Guggenheim (1898–1979), who had an irresistible smile and an irrepressible love for modern art, even marrying into it (her second husband was Max Ernst). She filled it with her treasures and, when she died, left it to the Guggenheim Foundation in New York.

The setting, the back garden (where Peggy and several of her dogs are buried) and the homey atmosphere add much to the quirky charm of the collection, which includes representative examples from the major movements of this century and a whole room of Jackson Pollocks (including his great 1942 *Moon Woman*). From husband Max Ernst there's *The Robing of the Bride* (an offbeat tribute to Peggy?). Other works include Picasso's 1937 *La Baignade*, with the mysterious face on the horizon watching the two Cubist girls on the beach; Brancusi's *Bird in Space*, de Chirico's *Nostalgia del Poeta*; Dali's hysterical *Birth of Liquid Desires*;

Kandinsky's *Landscape with Church*; five box constructions by Joseph Cornell; and much more by Arp, Rothko, Motherwell, Magritte, Tanguey, Severini, Moore, Malevich, Chagall, Braque, Balla, Mondrian, de Kooning, Giacometti and others. The **bedroom** has a mobile and bedstead by Alexander Calder, and bright paintings by Peggy's daughter Pegeen, who inherited some of her mother's *joie de vivre*. It must have been this same spirit of fun that led Mrs Guggenheim to erect something besides a palace outside on the Grand Canal – take a look at Mariano Marini's joyously obscene equestrian statue, the *Angel of the Citadel*.

LA SALUTE AND AROUND

Santa Maria della Salute H9

*Campo della Salute, **t** 041 522 5558; **vaporetto** Salute. **Open** daily 9–12 and 3–5.30; **adm** free, sacristy €1.05.*

At the entrance to the Grand Canal, with a perfect sense of theatrical timing and spacing (in the City of Water, the two begin to merge) stands this magical white pavilion erected in honour of St Mary of Health.

The plague of 1630–31 was the most heinous since the Black Death of 1348, taking some 95,000 people to early graves. In October of 1630 the Senate offered Mary a church if she would intervene and spare the city. Mary delivered, and the Senate did too, choosing in a competition the design of the 26-year-old Baldassare Longhena, who would just live to see his life's masterpiece completed in 1682.

The ideal of a centralized domed temple was a favourite of the Renaissance, but Longhena was the first architect since the early Middle Ages to centralize his temple in the form of an octagon surrounded by an ambulatory. This unique shape is made obvious from the exterior, marked by the smaller Palladian-style façades of the chapels and the wonderful scrolls, tightly spun party streamers ready to shoot off across all Venice; without their festive touch the exterior of the Salute would be almost severe. The main door, framed by a triumphal arch, is only open on the Salute's Feast Day, 21 November, when a pontoon bridge is laid across the Grand Canal for the grand procession, and a fine sight it is, especially as you can see into the interior of the church as Longhena intended, the eye drawn in through a series of receding arches.

Stand in the centre of the octagon and this same play of arches makes the seven chapels and high altar seem even deeper than they really are (the inscription here: *Unde Origo, Inde Salus* – 'From the origins comes Salvation' – refers to the official date of Venice's founding, 25 March 425, which coincides with the Feast Day of Mary). One of the many debts Longhena owed the Renaissance tradition and his immediate mentor Palladio was the white and grey colour scheme of the interior, though Longhena is far more manipulative, using the grey not to outline the structure, but as an optical device.

The **sanctuary**, reached by steps, is almost separate from the main body, and owes much to Palladio's Redentore. A great arch, supported by four ancient Roman columns from Pola, spans the **high altar**, with its large remarkable sculptural group of *The Queen of Heaven Expelling the Plague*, designed by Longhena and sculpted by Juste Le Court (1670). Venice kneels as a suppliant before the Virgin in the clouds, whose look of disdain is enough to send the horrid old hag of plague on her way, while St Mark and St Lorenzo Giustiniani look on. In the centre is a 13th-century Byzantine *Madonna and Child*, picked up by the light-fingered Francesco Morosini in Crete. This piece of Baroque theatre is made more effective by the shadowy rectangular choir behind the altar, visually united to the rest of the composition by its tier of three more arches.

In this church Longhena provided 17th-century Italy with a stimulating if insubstantial alternative to the Baroque masters of Rome, and its influence was felt throughout the peninsula, though,, surprisingly, the octagon never caught on. The art in the chapels fails to match the confection that surrounds them (the three on the right are by the over-talented Neapolitan Luca '*fa presto*' (do it quickly) Giordano, and the third altar on the left is by Titian) but there are some treasures in the **sacristy**, to the left of the high altar, where the authorities brought Titian's paintings from the suppressed church of San Spirito: over the altar, an early work, *St Mark Enthroned between SS. Rocco and Sebastiano and SS. Cosma and Damian* (the surgeon saints), a votive for the liberation of a previous plague; and on the ceiling three restored canvases of Old Testament scenes in violent perspective: *Cain and Abel*, *David and Goliath* and *Abraham and Isaac*, all from the 1540s. Titian also painted the eight *tondi* of the Doctors of the Church. Next to the altar is Padovanino's *Madonna with Angels* and a model of the Salute; the *Marriage at Cana* is a 1561 work by Tintoretto.

The Salute is one of Venice's marvels, built under genuinely pious auspices. Yet, less than a hundred years after its completion, a notice appeared near the entrance: 'In honour of God and His Holy Nature, please do not spit on the floor!' And if the celebrant of mass were good-looking, another note would be attached, expressing the hope that the parishioners would limit their contributions in the collection baskets to money (and not love letters!).

Dogana di Mare (Customs House) H9

Fond. Dogana alla Salute; vaporetto Salute.

Set on the point of Dorsoduro's promontory, this is its landmark, a customs house topped with a bright golden ball supported by two Atlases, and topped with a circus acrobat figure of Fortune, who serves as a weathervane with her pointer and rudder; a charming conceit though it's hard not to notice that all three figures are sectioned like cuts of meats in a buther's diagram. Beginning in 1414, all goods brought into Venice by sea were unloaded here and assessed for customs duty, but the main reason for visiting now is to take in the view.

NORTHERN DORSODURO

Ca' Rezzonico (Museo dei Settecento) E7

Fondamenta Rezzonico, t 041 241 0100; vaporetto Ca' Rezzonico. Open Wed–Mon 10–5; adm €6.50. Bookshop and café.

This is the house where Robert Browning died in 1889 while visiting his son Pen, but if his ghost wanders these salons devoted to 18th-century Venice, it is a discreet phantom, one remembered only with a plaque visible from the Ca' Rezzonico *vaporetto* stop:
Open my heart and you will see Graved inside of it 'Italy'.

It could be that Browning's shade doesn't feel comfortable among all the stuff that the city has stowed here since purchasing the palace in 1934, arranging it so that the average sumptuous Venetian of the *settecento* would feel at home. One of the most charming objects stands on Giorgio Massari's Grand Stair leading up to the *piano nobile* – a droll *putto* dressed in a Russian hat and coat, by Juste Le Court. At the top is the lavish **ballroom**, with a ceiling by Giambattista Crosto and a mind-boggling collection of rococo furniture by Andrea Brustolon of Belluno (1662–1732), whose chisel knew no bounds, either in craftsmanship or taste. The ceiling of the second room (on the right) was frescoed by Giambattista Tiepolo, celebrating an event of consummate social importance to the *nouveau riche* Rezzonici: the 1758 marriage of Ludovico Rezzonico to a Savorgnan bride (of such exalted status that she is driven by Apollo and Cupid in the chariot of the Sun). In the middle of the floor is the upper half of an old

gondola, with window slats that close for complete privacy. One room is devoted to Rosalba Carriera's pastel portraits of nobles; the library, with a display of books published in Venice, has ceiling frescoes by Francesco Maffei.

The **second floor** offers more paintings, including two views by Canaletto (1697–1768), among the only ones left in Venice; scenes by Francesco Guardi (including the Ridotto and the famous salon held by the pretty nuns of San Zaccaria, *see* p.143), and 34 of Pietro Longhi's most endearing scenes of *settecento* Venice, populated by dwarfs, masked merrymakers, friars, invalids, lap dogs, plates of doughnuts (Carnival *frittelle*), charlatans, alchemists, the 'giant Magrat', washerwomen, tailors, hairdressers, and the famous rhinoceros that visited Venice in 1779 (which seems to have lacked a horn, but made a prodigious amount of rhino poo). Giambattista Piazzetta contributes a major piece of Venetian kitsch (*The Death of Darius*), and there's a candy-coloured *Interior of St Peter's* by Giampaolo Panini. The 18th-century interiors nearly all have authentic furnishings – the bedroom, boudoir and the Green Drawing Room, with lacquered Venetian chinoiserie.

The last set of rooms on the second floor are the most delightful, with frescoes by Giandomenico Tiepolo taken from the Tiepolo family home, Villa Zianigo, near Mestre. Painted in 1791, they are perhaps the last carefree hurrah before Venice's dotage, but show no forebodings: in *The New World* the audience dresses up to see scenes from America; Commedia dell'Arte figures, acrobats, centaurs and satyrs sport on the walls as if tomorrow will never come.

After substantial restoration work, the **third floor** now houses an important collection of paintings (from the late 16th–19th centuries) amassed by local antiques dealer Professor Esidio Martini and bequeathed to the city, as well as the magnificent 18th-century pharmacy, moved from near San Stae and full of its original porcelain and glass vessels.

Campo San Barnaba E7

Vaporetto *Ca' Rezzonico.*

From the *vaporetto* stop Ca' Rezzonico, Calle di Traghetto leads back to this picturesque *campo*, charmingly bordered by its own eponymous canal. The area is best known in the city's annals for its resident patrician 'Barnabotti', *see* box.

San Barnaba E7

Campo San Barnaba; **vaporetto** *Ca' Rezzonico.* **Open** *7.30–12 and 3–7;* **adm** *free.*

The quarter's rather unprepossessing 18th-century church has a 14th-century campanile, an intimate Veronese (*The Holy Family*) and a *trompe l'œil* ceiling painting by Constantino Cedini.

Ponte dei Pugni D7

Rio San Barnaba; **vaporetto** *Ca' Rezzonico.*

Briefly follow the Rio San Barnaba westwards, passing the picturesque greengrocer's barge; the bridge alongside is the Ponte dei Pugni ('of fists'), where, before the days of parapets, the rival Nicolotti and Castellani (*see* p.169) would meet in the middle to punch it out, the losers tumbling into the canal. There are several bridges named Ponte dei Pugni, but this is the only one with marble footprints in the pavement marking the places where the contestants stood.

Campo Santa Margherita D7

Vaporetto *Ca' Rezzonico/San Basilio.*

Campo Santa Margherita, lined with houses from the 14th and 15th centuries, is Dorsoduro's morning marketplace and evening meeting-place. Although the **church** has been closed since Napoleon, its rows of weird masks and dragons have been transplanted to an old house and an amputated campanile on the north side of the *campo*; the church building has been abandoned since its last tenant, a cinema, left.

The isolated building near the centre is the **Scuola dei Varotari**, or 'Tanners' Guild', with a

---

The Barnabotti

In the last days of the Republic, impoverished patricians flocked to the cheap housing in the parish. The hotter bloods among them were always ready to stir things up against the government, and kept the Council of Ten's spies on their toes; others, resigned to their lot, made do on the meagre stipend supplied by the State (on the condition that they didn't marry and make any little Barnabotti). Some found employment at the Ridotto as bankers, etc. – jobs that the Senate decreed could only be held by Barnabotti. Others begged in the crimson silken robes that, as patricians, they were required to wear, and not a few travellers remarked on the elegance of Venice's paupers. Creating a class of idle gentry was probably not the intention of the law that forbade patricians from working in crafts or trades, but it was their discontent that worked as a slow cancer in the State, and in the end caused many to hail Napoleon as their liberator.

---

relief of the Madonna della Misericordia protecting the tanners, so worn that it could be anyone under her mantle.

Scuola dei Carmini D7

Campo dei Carmini, **t** *041 528 9420;* **vaporetto** *Ca' Rezzonico/San Basilio.* **Open** *Mon–Sat 9–6 (winter 9–4), Sun 9–1;* **adm** *€5 (sometimes also open for concerts).*

Built on a design by Longhena in the 1660s (his hand is best seen in the façade facing the Rio Terrà), the Scuola dei Carmini (one of the six Scuole Grandi) has a beautiful split stair and a ground floor entirely decorated with 18th-century *chiaroscuri*. In the 1740s, Giambattista Tiepolo was paid 400 *zecchini* to paint the upstairs hall ceiling; he made it one of his best and brightest works, nine paintings centred on the *Virgin in Gloria*. The symbolism is somewhat obscure. In the centrepiece, the Virgin is presenting a scapular to St Simeon Stock. Who, or when, or why this occurred is beyond the reach of our meagre scholarship. The other eight scenes feature female allegories and angels. Some of these are handing out scapulars; one miraculously catches a pious workman who has just fallen off the scaffolding of a church. You'll probably notice that most of these angels and allegories are showing off a good bit of leg, just to 'increase the faith'; they're some of the swellest gams on display in any Italian church, and a strong argument for those who maintain that the major purpose behind late Baroque ceiling painting was to get divine skirts to fly up. Beneath this unforgettable ceiling, which has just been restored after part of the central panel fell down when termites ate away the border, there's only timid and undistinguished 18th-century painting, filling large expanses of the main hall and adjacent rooms.

Carmini D7

Campo dei Carmini; **vaporetto** *Ca' Rezzonico/ San Basilio.* **Open** *Mon–Sat 2.30–5;* **adm free.**

This church has a basilican interior from the 14th century and a nave decorated with gilded Aztec cigar-store Indians; on closer inspection these are painted wooden figures of kings and warriors carved in the 17th and 18th centuries, strangely illuminated by the fluorescent tapers before them. The sculptural decoration, also of gilded wood, is of the same period, as are the paintings forming a frieze on the history of the Carmelite order. None of it is grade A art, but the total effect has a monumental if quirky charm.

The Carmini does have one major painting: Cima da Conegliano's *Nativity* on the second altar on the right, set in a fine landscape bathed by golden Veneto light. In the left side of the nave is a bronze plaque with a relief of *The Deposition*, a rare work by the Sienese sculptor-architect, Francesco di Giorgio Martini, with a portrait on the right of Duke Federigo of Montefeltro and his famous broken nose; the women in the scene resemble the Furies in a Greek tragedy. The second altar on the left has Lorenzo Lotto's *St Nicholas of Bari* (Santa Claus to us),

with an eerie landscape beneath the saints. Near the door, under a canvas by Padovanino, is a bench carved with pagan grotesques.

As you leave the Carmini, take a brief stroll down Calle della Pazienza to see its Gothic **side door** (across from the Scuola), decorated with a collage of Byzantine odds and ends.

SAN SEBASTIANO AND AROUND

San Sebastiano C8

Fondamenta San Sebastiano, **t** *041 275 0462;* **vaporetto** *San Basilio.* **Open** *Mon–Sat 10–5, under restoration;* **adm** *€2.*

Built to thank St Sebastian for delivering the city from the plague of 1464, this was the parish church of Veronese, who lived around the corner. Thanks to its prior, who was also from Verona, he was given the chance to decorate it, which he did from 1555 to 1560 and in the 1570s, managing to create a thematically unified interior – and, this being Veronese, one that blurs the boundaries of art and reality. Among his visual tricks are the frescoed loggia, partially made from real stone and wood, and the archer, above one side of the nuns' choir, shooting Sebastian – on the other side of the nave.

The **ceiling**, which Veronese painted after his first work in the sacristy, depicts the story of Esther in three panels: *The Repudiation of Vashti, Esther Crowned by Ahasuerus* and *The Triumph of the Mordecai.* The unusual Old Testament theme was used for its symbolic reference to the Virgin Mary. Vashti was the repudiated queen of Persia (Eve), Esther a Jewish girl chosen as the new queen (Mary), who helped to free her cousin Mordecai and his followers (redeeming mankind). The jewel-like colours lend a glittering sumptuousness to Veronese's monumental architectural perspectives and illusionism; note how he paints the central figures of each panel at an angle to get maximum sideways illumination (most notably the

Mordecai, where the spectator's angle of vision is from under the horses' hooves). This ceiling, with the surrounding decorations added by his brother Benedetto, met with great success and brought Veronese his second commission, the wall frescoes in the **upper choir** with the *Martyrdoms of St Sebastian*. One of Diocletian's centurions turned Christian, Sebastian survived his first martyrdom of arrows, only to rebuke the emperor and be martyred again, this time with blows.

Veronese designed the organ and painted its luminous panels; he also painted the altarpiece on the **high altar**, of the *Virgin and Child in Glory with Saints*, and the remarkable scenes flanking it in the choir, of *SS. Mark and Marcellinus Led to Martyrdom and Comforted by Sebastian* on the left and the *Martyrdom of St Sebastian* on the right. These are quintessential Veronese, full of action, stormy skies and big dogs, all done in magnificent costumes, set before a monumental, imaginary Rome. In the **chapel** to the left of the high altar, decorated in 1512 with blue and yellow majolica tiles from Urbino, are the tombs of Veronese (Paolo Caliari, d. 1588, with a bust) and his brother Benedetto (d. 1598).

There are even more Veroneses: a *Crucifixion* with the three Marys at the foot of the Cross, on the third altar on the right, set in an enormous monument designed by Sansovino for the Bishop of Cyprus. In the second chapel on the left, the *Baptism of Christ* is mostly by Veronese's workshop, while the third altar on the left, the *Virgin and St Catherine and Friar* is believed to be one of his first works in Venice, as are the ceiling panels in the sacristy (door below the organ).

Among the wall paintings here are works by Palma Vecchio, Bonifazio de' Pitati (the 'other' Veronese) and Tintoretto (*Punishment of Snakes*). A few other artists managed to get their brushes in as well: the 83-year-old Titian, who used big brushstrokes to paint the altarpiece of *St Nicolas* (first on the right), and, near it, Paris Bordone's dark and strange *Jonah and the Whale*.

Angelo Raffaele C7–8

Campo Angelo Raffaele, t 041 522 8548; vaporetto San Basilio. Open Thurs–Tues 8.30–12 and 4–6; adm free.

The sprawling hulk of the Angel Raphael's church looms forlornly over the Fondamenta del Soccorso, with a façade sprouting a five-year shadow of stubbly weeds, along with a thriving fig tree on the cornice. Raphael and his dog appear in a 16th-century relief over the portal. The sole reason for entering this gloomy church, built in 1618, is to take a look at the **organ parapet**, painted with a visionary, impressionistic scene of *Tobias and the Angel* (1753) by Gian Antonio Guardi, where material forms are dissolved into quick, free brushstrokes.

Palazzo Ariani C7

Fondamenta Briati; vaporetto San Basilio.

This is one of the rattiest, most unprettified corners of Venice, long a neighbourhood of fishermen, dock workers and sailors, and also one old palace, the Gothic Palazzo Ariani, with a lovely six-light window facing the intersection of Rio di San Sebastiano.

In the derelict *campo* behind Angelo Raffaele, there is a pretty Istrian stone **wellhead**, one of the few with a story: the well below was dug with funds left in Marco Ariani's will; he died of the plague of 1348, convinced that it was caused by contaminated water.

Santa Maria del Soccorso C7

Fondamenta del Soccorso; vaporetto San Basilio. Open irregular hours; adm free.

At this small church, you can pay your respects to the celebrated courtesan-poetess Veronica Franco (*see* box), who in 1519 retired here to found her asylum for less fortunate prostitutes. Though not as talented as the courtesan Gaspara Stampa of the previous generation, her *Terze Rime* earn her a place among Renaissance poets still in print.

Venetian Women – Honest and Not So Honest

Women in Venice lived in purdah-style seclusion until the 18th century. Before then, the most celebrated were prostitutes, whose wit, education and sophistication were much sought after in the Renaissance: Venice's courtesan culture rates with those of ancient Greece and medieval Japan. In the lusty 16th-century dawn of tourism, Venice had 11,654 registered tax-paying prostitutes, dressed in red and yellow 'like tulips'; there was even a guide book, listing addresses and prices. Two were as celebrated for their poetry as for their charms: the 'new Sappho', the beautiful **Gaspara Stampa** (1523–54), considered one of the best and most original of Renaissance women poets, who wrote elegant verses of burning passion, and **Veronica Franco** (1546–91), a more worldly, narrative poet who repented in later life.

Then there were honest women such as **Marietta Robusti** (1556–90), Tintoretto's talented daughter, who married a man who confined her to painting portraits of his colleagues. She is stifled even posthumously, for none of her works is on public display. A patrician's daughter, **Elena Lucrezia Corner Piscopia**, became the first woman to earn a university degree (a doctorate of philosophy, at Padua, in 1678).

The next century produced Contessa-cum-courtesan **Marina Querini-Benzon**, who inspired Venice's most famous love song, *La Biondina in Gondoleta* – the model for America's beloved blonde in a convertible. She was painted by Longhi and her wit was much admired by Stendhal. She remained frisky enough to have a fling with Byron in her 60s, when she was tremendously fat owing to an inordinate love for polenta, which she kept tucked in her bodice for convenient nibbling whenever she felt peckish – hence her nickname *Fumetta* or 'Little Smoke'. She was last seen dancing with the poet Ugo Foscolo around Napoleon's Liberty Tree in the centre of Piazza San Marco.

San Nicolò dei Mendicoli B7

Campo San Nicolò; vaporetto Santa Marta/ San Basilio. **Open** *Mon–Sat 10–12; adm free.*

From Fondamenta Barbarigo, turn right at a wide lane called Riello and then left at the Rio delle Terese. One of Venice's most ancient churches, San Nicolò 'of the beggars' was founded in the 7th century, even before the Venetians staged their phony theft of Santa Claus' relics from Myra. Rebuilt again and again, and restored most recently in 1977 by Venice in Peril, it has a Renaissance porch full of old architectural fragments, a detached Veneto-Byzantine campanile, and a sweet golden honey interior, embellished with wood sculptures, paintings by Alvise del Friso, and on the ceiling, a *tondo* of *St Nicholas in Glory*, framed with a perspective border by Francesco Montemezzano. The gilded wooden statue of the saint on the altar is attributed to a follower of Bartolomeo Bon. Inside the main portal is a detailed model of the church's appearance centuries ago, apparently made from sheets of Styrofoam insulation. In a way this little church was the St Mark's of this side of the Grand Canal. The inhabitants of these *sestieri* were known as the 'Nicolotti', and in this church they elected their 'Doge dei Nicolotti', who would lead them in all their races, regattas, games and general punch-ups against the other half of the population, called the 'Castellani' after their headquarters in Castello.

ALONG THE ZATTERE

This long quay facing the Canale della Giudecca is named after the wooden rafts that once lined the waterfront, used for unloading timber, salt, building materials, etc.

Gondolas

The gondola, Venice's most enduring symbol, was first mentioned during the reign of Vitale Falier, way back in 1094. It took another five or six hundred years or so to evolve into its present form, perfectly adapted to Venice's unique environment of narrow, shallow canals that often intersect at right angles: it has a flat underside and, unlike any other vessel, an asymmetrical hull, 24cm wider on the left than the right, so that it tends to lean on the right, creating a pivot that helps the gondolier posed on the stern manoeuvre the craft with one long oar.

A gondola measures precisely 10.87m in length, and 1.42m maximum width. It is built out of eight different woods – fir, cherry, mahogany, larch, walnut, oak, lime and elm – that must be seasoned in the dockyard, or *squero*, a word believed to be derived from the Greek *eskàrion* for shipyard. It is then carefully hand-crafted, and given the traditional ornaments: a *forcola*, or walnut oarlock; the peculiar-shaped *ferro* on the prow, its six divisions said to represent Venice's *sestieri*, its double curve said to symbolize the tilde-shaped Giudecca, and the blade, said to represent in one go the Rialto Bridge and the ducal bonnet; also mandatory are two brass sea-horses. The whole is painted black, still obeying sumptuary laws of 1562, which sought to limit the vast sums noble families were spending to tart up their carriages – note the brightly coloured gondolas in Carpaccio's paintings. Most of these had the now vanished *felze*, wooden shelters that permitted a legendary amount of hanky-panky, as Byron apparently knew all too well:

And up and down the long canals they go
And under the Rialto shoot along,
By night and day, all paces, swift and slow,
And round the theatres, a sable throng,
They wait in their dusk livery of woe,
But not to them do awful things belong,
For sometimes they contain a deal of fun,
Like mourning coaches when the funeral's
    done.

In the 18th century there were 14,000 gondolas; today there are less than 500, all nearly exclusively used in the tourist trade. Every few weeks in hot weather they gather so many weeds on the bottom that they have to be cleaned. An unlucky gondola will become so warped in five years that it's only fit for ferrying passengers across the Grand Canal (*traghetto*), and when it fails there it is burned in the glass furnaces of Murano. So if 55 minutes in a gondola seems dear, figure in the expense, the maintenance and lifespan of the average gondola, and the brief season in which a gondolier makes his living.

In the 14th century, each gondolier belonged to one of 16 *traghetti*, or landings, which had their own constitution and laws and clubhouse, formerly clustered along the Zattere. Much has been written on their strange cries, almost never heard today: '*Premi!*' they would cry if they wanted to pass on the left, or '*Stali!*' to pass on the right, and '*Sciar!*' if they were about to stop. Back in 1858 their haunting yodels in the night inspired Wagner to incorporate the sound as the long horn note that begins Act Three of *Tristan and Isolde*.

Gondoliers were quick to quarrel, with hot-blooded insults such as 'You Son of a Cow!', 'Spy!' or 'Assassin!'; and 'The Madonna of your *traghetto* is a whore not worth two candles!' or 'Your saint is a rascal who can't even make a decent miracle!' – insults that grew ever more vicious the further apart they were. For the Venetians, as Montesquieu said, were the best people in the world, and almost never came to blows. Modern gondoliers are especially genteel; most are Communists, and many are very good-looking. Venetians lately have been more upset than usual over the neglect and clownishness of the Rome government. When the prime minister and other big shots came to Venice for a festival a few years ago, the gondoliers to a man refused to carry them. Which proved, at least to the leader writer of *Il Gazzettino*, that 'the Venetians still have backbone'.

The rafts have been replaced with café and pizzeria platforms built out on to the water, fine places to linger and watch the *vaporetti* buzzing like dragonflies between the freighters and tankers ploughing their way to Marghera (*see* box, p.218).

Campo di San Trovaso E9

Vaporetto Zattere.

Set back from the Zattere and *vaporetto* stop is this little *campo* with its church and picturesque boatyard.

At No.1083, stop to have a look at the **reliefs** embedded in the wall, a grotesque face and a blacksmith scene over the door, with Cupid bringing arrows to the forge. An even older Byzantine bas-relief is embedded in the side of the 15th-century **Palazzo Nani** ('of the dwarfs'), just across the bridge.

Squero di San Trovaso E9

Campo di San Trovaso; vaporetto Zattere.

Cross the bridge that leaves the *campo*, and turn right down the Fondamenta Nani for the best view of the irresistible Squero di San Trovaso, or gondola boatyard (*see* box, opposite), its row of beached gondolas made picturesque by its old wooden balcony covered with geraniums.

San Trovaso E8

Campo di San Trovaso; vaporetto Zattere. Open Mon–Sat 3–6; adm free.

This church has two façades, either of which seems more fitting for a public market or 19th-century factory. The church was Santi Gervasio e Protasio before the Venetians got hold of the saints and merged them into a single unit. The church held a special place in the city as neutral ground between the Nicolotti and Castellani factions, where they would come together to meet, marry, baptize and bury (each side using its own door).

Originally founded in the 10th century, former San Trovasi churches on this site have burnt down twice and caved in once already; this, the fourth version, is true to its factory façades, and is rather dark and fairly functional within.

If it has reopened, look in the **Cappella della Grazie**, just to the right of the (south) door, to see a lovely bas-relief of angels on the altar by the unknown Renaissance 'Master of San Trovaso'; in the chapel exactly opposite is Michele Giambono's *San Crisogono*, a charming work reminiscent of Carpaccio's *St George*. Tintoretto painted some of his last works for the church, nearly all completed by his son Domenico: a *Last Supper* in the left transept, and by the high altar, the *Adoration of the Magi* and *Expulsion from the Temple*.

Santa Maria della Visitazione E9

Fondamenta Zattere ai Gesuati; vaporetto Zattere. Open Mon–Sat 9–12 and 3–6, Sun 3–6; adm €2.

This 'original' Gesuati was deconsecrated long ago, and now serves as part of an art and craft school for orphans. The entrance is through the school, just right of the façade, and usually you can just walk in and have a look around.

The confusion about the name is considerable. The order of the Gesuati, founded in the 14th century, built this church and monastery in 1524. Upon their dissolution in 1668, the Dominicans snatched up the property and later built another church, the other 'Gesuati' just down the Zattere.

Mauro Codussi was at least partially responsible for the façade, a plain but distinguished Renaissance construction; note the *Bocca del Leone* on the right of the façade, this one designated to receive gripes about hygiene and to tell tales on people tossing rubbish in the canals. Inside is a genuine surprise, a wooden ceiling painted by Umbrian or Tuscan artists of the 1500s. The central medallion, a *Visitation*, shows the gentle colours of Umbrian *cinquecento* art; surrounding it are panels with excellent portraits of prophets and saints. These works are almost unique in Venice; the only other central Italian art in Venice is in the Palazzo

Cini (*see* p.162). After a few days of Tintoretto and Titian, a comparison with painting more in touch with the sources of the Renaissance will prove enlightening.

Gesuati E9

*Fondamenta Zattere ai Gesuati; **vaporetto** Zattere. **Open** Mon–Sat 9–6, Sun 1–6; **adm** €2.*

Just down the Zattere stands the other Gesuati, Santa Maria del Rosario, with a façade that echoes Palladio's Redentore across the water. Built between 1726 and 1743 by Giorgio Massari, the interior is also an 18th-century compliment to Palladio, sceno-graphic in its illumination and the plasticity of its walls. Giambattista Tiepolo frescoed the ceiling with the *Life of St Dominic*, the stern saint being hauled up by angels to his heavenly reward amid suitably soaring perspectives; Tiepolo also painted the first altar on the right, the *Virgin in Glory with three female saints*, well lit in front with a rather haughty Virgin in the background.

The other paintings, including a Tintoretto *Crucifixion* and Piazzetta's *Three Saints*, and even the altar for all of its pounds of lapis lazuli, are sombre fare compared to the large *Madonna and Child* dolls in a little chapel on the left, dressed on feast days in dazzling jewels and costumes (including, it is rumoured, a pair of proper lace knickers for the *Bambino*).

Rio Terrà Antonio Foscarini E9–F8

***Vaporetto** Zattere/Accademia.*

Alongside the Gesuati is the pretty Rio Terrà Antonio Foscarini, which cuts through to the Ponte dell' Accademia, and is named after the unfortunate patrician who lost his head. It is one of the few *calli* in Venice planted with plane trees.

The Eastern Zattere

The Incurabili F9

*Fond. Zattere ai Gesuati; **vaporetto** Zattere.*

Further east along the Zattere, past the house that Ruskin rented in Venice (now a hotel), the large classical building adorned with two stone heads is the Incurabili, one of Venice's four main hospitals, designed by Antonio da Ponte. Built for victims of syphilis (a gift from the New World along with tobacco and potatoes), it had a girls' orphanage added in the late 16th century, which became, like La Pietà (*see* p.144), an important conservatory, famous for its choir. Sansovino added an oval church for its concerts, but it was demolished by the Austrians in 1831; today the Incurabili is used as a children's home.

Santo Spirito G9–10

*Fond. Zattere ai Gesuati; **vaporetto** Zattere. **Open** Mon–Sat 9–12 and 4–6; **adm** free.*

Further up the Zattere is the Renaissance façade of Santo Spirito, where fans of Giovanni Buonconsiglio come to see his painting of the *Redeemer and Saints*.

Magazzini del Sale G9–10

*Fond. Zattere ai Gesuati; **vaporetto** Zattere.*

These are the salt warehouses, where the Republic stored the most precious commodity of its Lagoon. Not so many years ago, salt was a state monopoly in Italy and sold only in tobacco shops, and the old salt signs they sometimes preserve are the last reminders of what was once a very, very serious economic and political issue. Most of the salt came from pans near Chioggia, though the Venetians imported it from as far away as the Balearic islands. Every grain of the 44,000 tons of salt that could fit in the salt warehouses was governed by the Salt Office, which issued licences to the exporters stating both the price and purchaser. Today the heirs of Venice's great sea captains – members of the local rowing club – use the warehouses as a boatyard.

San Polo and Santa Croce

THE FRARI AND AROUND 176
I Frari 176
Scuola Grande di San Rocco 179
San Rocco 181
San Pantalon 181
Casa Goldoni 182
San Giovanni Evangelista 182
Scuola Grande di San Giovanni Evangelista 182

SAN POLO AND AROUND 184

RIALTO 184
Ponte di Rialto 184
Rialto Markets 185
San Giacomo di Rialto 186

NORTH OF THE FONDAMENTA DEL VIN 186

CA' PÉSARO AND AROUND 187
Ca' Pésaro 187
Santa Maria Materdomini 187
San Cassiano 188
San Stae 188
Palazzo Mocenigo 189
Fondaco dei Turchi/Natural History Museum 189
San Giacomo dell'Orio 190

WESTERN SANTA CROCE 190
San Simeone Piccolo 190
San Simeone Profeta 191
San Nicolò da Tolentino 191

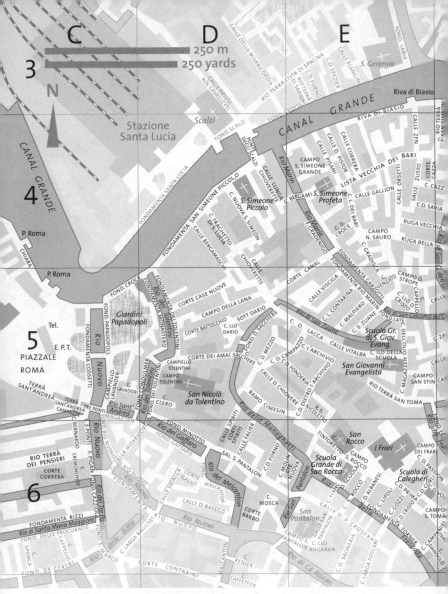

1 Lunch

Da Ignazio, *Calle del Saoneri*, **t** *041 523 4852*; **vaporetto** San Tomà. **Open** Sun–Fri 12–3 and 7–10. **Expensive**. Cosy fish trattoria.

2 Coffee and Cakes

Rizzardini, *Campiello dei Meloni*; **vaporetto** S. Silvestro. **Open** Wed–Mon 7am–9.30pm. Traditional Venetian cakes.

3 Drinks

Ruga Rialto, *Calle del Sturion*; **vaporetto** S. Silvestro. **Open** daily 11–2.30 and 6–12. Right near the market, with good *cicheti*.

Highlights

Medieval Venice: The art-filled Frari, p.176

Renaissance Venice: Tintoretto's master-pieces in the Scuola di San Rocco, p.179

Baroque/Rococo Venice: The extraordinary ceiling in San Pantalon, p.181

Indoor Venice: The beauties of Nature, in the Fondaco dei Turchi's Natural History Museum, p.189

Decadent Venice: The light-up plastic gondolas, in the Rialto markets, p.185

Pigeon Venice: The striking egg-shaped dome on San Simeone Piccolo, p.190

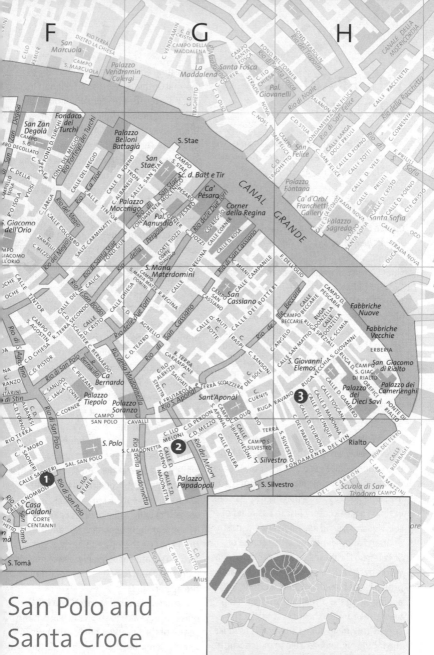

San Polo and Santa Croce

San Polo has withstood the test of time
well: its Rialto markets are still busy, even if
the wares have changed somewhat since the
Middle Ages; its church of the Frari, one of
Venice's big three, is still run by the
Franciscans; and its Scuola di San Rocco is
one of the great sights in Italy, guaranteed to
make you dizzy.

Santa Croce has fared less well: not only is
it missing its church, but much of it has been
turned into the likes of Piazzale Roma,
freight yards, the prison, and other ordinary
bits that all cities need. But any city would
be proud of Santa Croce's pretty little centre,
Campo San Giacomo dell'Orio, and its collection of intriguing minor churches.

THE FRARI AND AROUND

This small area in the heart of San Polo encompasses the greatest concentration of Venetian art after the Accademia.

I Frari E6

Campo dei Frari, t 041 522 2637; vaporetto San Tomà. Open Mon–Sat 9–6, Sun 1–6; adm €2.

Santa Maria Gloriosa dei Frari was the chief Franciscan rival to the Dominican Santi Giovanni e Paolo, on the other side of town; from St Mark's campanile the two stand above the higgle-piggle of Venice like a pair of brick bookends. The original Frari, founded in 1250 (just after St Francis' death), was no sooner completed in 1330 than the current Gothic pile started to rise right next to it. Based on a design by Friar Scipione Bon, it wasn't completed until 1469.

The Exterior

For Venice, the exterior is very severe, showing only a hint of the native delight for decoration. Venice's second tallest campanile is its most memorable feature, though there are some good carvings that liven up its stark exterior: a 15th-century Tuscan bas-relief of the *Madonna, Child and Angels* on the north door, and another nearby with a statue of St Peter; on the west side the Gothic door has works by the school of Bartolomeo Bon and others by Alessandro Vittoria. A Gothic edging along the cornice, like dripped icing on the cake, unites the mass of bricks; the curved 'crowning', added afterwards to make the façade higher, was a bid to match Santi Giovanni e Paolo. Around the left side, near the door, you'll see some small plaques marking the level of the *acqua alta* of 20 August 1902 – that was a bad one; the plaques are almost three feet high.

The Interior

The long cruciform interior is pinned together by wooden tie beams, which visually not only unite the vast space, but add an interesting abstract quality to the run-of-the-mill Gothic aisle bays and ceiling. On ground level, the eye is drawn through the arch of the monks' choir in the nave to Titian's vividly coloured *Assumption* in the sanctuary. The plain brick walls are covered with works of art and monuments ranging from the sublime to the ridiculous, beginning (inside the front portal) with the very vertical **Tomb of Pietro Bernardo** (d. 1538) [1], believed to be one of Tullio Lombardo's last works, but lacking the 800-stanza heroic poem that the deceased specified in his will. The other monument on this wall, the **Tomb of Procurator Alvise Pasqualino** (d. 1528), is by Lorenzo Bregno.

Both of these men ordered tombs long before they died; a sound policy, seeing the monument Titian got (the second altar on the right). It is a tradition in Italy to give the greatest artists the most unartistic memorials, and the **Tomb of Titian** [2] is even worse than Michelangelo's in Florence. Titian died in his 90s in the plague of 1576, and was the only casualty of that epidemic to get a church burial, owing to his fame; the massive inanity piled on top of his presumed burial place was added in the 19th century. The first altar, to the right, is dedicated to St Anthony of Padua; it has attracted some unusual ex-votos, including a pair of brass epaulettes left by some grateful general or bandmaster. The third altar (to the left of Titian) is graced by Vittoria's statue of *St Jerome*, one of his finest works, and said to be a likeness of Titian at the age of 93.

The newly restored **Monks' Choir** [3], the only one in Venice to survive in place in the centre of the nave, was built in the 1460s, and has a marble choir screen by Bartolomeo Bon and Pietro Lombardo, but even more impressive are its three tiers of monks' stalls, carved by Mauro Cozzi and decorated with intarsia designs. In the **right transept** are four markedly diverse tombs: first, the **Tomb of Iacopo Marcello** (d. 1484) [4], a fine piece of Renaissance quirkiness attributed to Giovanni Buora; it is followed by the hyper-florid Gothic terracotta **Tomb of Beato**

I Frari

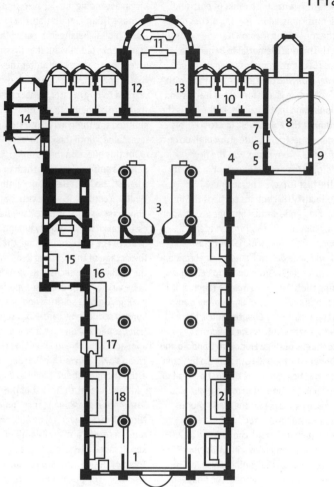

1 Tomb of Pietro Bernardo
2 Tomb of Titian
3 Monks' Choir
4 Tomb of Iacopo Marcello
5 Tomb of Beato Pacifico
6 Memorial to Benedetto Pésaro
7 Monument to Paolo Savelli
8 Sacristy
9 Chapter House

10 Chapel of St Massimiliano Kolbe
11 Titian's *Assumption of the Virgin*
12 Tomb of Doge Nicolò Tron
13 Tomb of Doge Francesco Foscari
14 Cappella Corner
15 Cappella Emiliani
16 Monument of Bishop Jacopo Pésaro
17 Tomb of Doge Giovanni Pésaro
18 Tomb of Canova

Pacifico [5] by Tuscans Nanni di Bartolo and Michele da Firenze, with ranks of *putti* and angel musicians, and sweeping arches rather like the tops of San Marco. Over the sacristy door, the marine **Memorial to Benedetto Pésaro** [6] commemorates a Venetian *capitano del mar* who died in Corfu in 1503, with reliefs of Ionian island fortresses (Lefkas and Kefalonia) and battle galleys. To the left is the **Monument to Paolo Savelli** (*c.* 1405) [7], his wooden equestrian statue stuck high up on a shelf; Savelli, from Rome, was the first *condottiere* to earn a monument in the city, and the first to have a horse under him.

The **Sacristy** [8] contains perhaps the most compelling and spiritual altarpiece Giovanni Bellini painted, his 1488 *Triptych of the Madonna and Child, with SS. Nicholas, Peter, Mark and Benedict*, still in its original frame, in the place Bellini intended it to be seen. Sharing the sacristy is a marble tabernacle by Tullio Lombardo; if it's open, another door leads down into the **Chapter House** [9], housing a 17th-century clock and the **Sarcophagus of Doge Francesco Dandolo and his Dogaressa**, topped with a fresco by Paolo Veneziano, believed to be the first portrait of a doge painted from life. From the chapter house you can look into the Frari's monumental Palladian cloister.

The first chapel in the **choir** has an altarpiece by Bartolomeo Vivarini (*Madonna, Child and Saints*, 1482), notable also for the original frame; in the second, the **Chapel of St Massimiliano Kolbe** [10], are two 14th-century wall tombs, the one on the left of a knight, Duccio degli Uberti. The next chapel, nearest the high altar, belonged to the Florentines, who hired Donatello to make its rustic but gilded wooden *Statue of John the Baptist* in 1438, his earliest work in the Veneto, and, like many of his Baptists in Florence, one who obviously lived on locusts.

But who is that hot number in the red dress floating over the high altar? Titian's enormous ***Assumption of the Virgin*** [11], painted in 1516–18, was the painter's first public commission in Venice. It caused a sensation for its extraordinary colour and revolutionary spiralling composition of the Virgin ascending into Heaven, and did much to make Titian's reputation, the way the *David* did Michelangelo's. For all that, the Frari monks didn't want it at first, graciously accepting the work only after they heard that Emperor Charles V, Titian's great patron, wanted to buy it. Later Franciscans, sharing the taste of their 16th-century predecessors, shuffled the thing away into storage, where it remained until this century.

But this questionable *Assumption* has perhaps suffered more at the hands of its friends. 'The Most Beautiful Painting in the World' according to some critics of generations past – such a tribute itself betrays the essential kitsch sensibility lurking at the heart of the work and the age that created it, the dotage of the expiring Renaissance. After the Bellini in the sacristy its virtues seem mere virtuosity, and its big-eyed, heaven-gazing Virgin as spiritual and profound as a Sunday school holy card. Pious sentimentality, especially on such a grand scale, rarely appears elsewhere in Venetian art or even in Titian's own *œuvre*. One wonders what the artist thought about it in his old age.

In the chancel, to the left of the *Assumption*, the Renaissance **Tomb of Doge Nicolò Tron** (d. 1473) [12] by Antonio Rizzo offers a serene and lovely antidote with its Renaissance allegories. To the right is the **Tomb of Doge Francesco Foscari** (d. 1457) [13], who wore the ducal bonnet the longest, reigning 34 years before the Senate pressured him to retire; he died a week later of a broken heart. Among the chapels to the left of the sanctuary the third contains the **grave of Claudio Monteverdi** (1567–1643), marked by a plain slab; the crowded scene that shares the chapel with him was begun by Alvise Vivarini and finished by Marco Basaiti. The fourth chapel, the **Cappella Corner** [14] in the left transept, is usually locked, but you can see through the grille Bartolomeo Vivarini's crystal clear painting of *St Mark Enthroned with Four Saints*, an early Renaissance Tuscan Tomb of Federico Corner, and Sansovino's broken but beautiful marble

St John on the font. Don't miss the carved wooden bench back in the transept, a masterpiece of Gothic tracery.

Continuing down the left aisle, a door leads into the **Cappella Emiliani** [15], with its numerous statues by the 15th-century school of Jacobello Dalle Masegne; next to it is the fine **Monument of Bishop Jacopo Pésaro** (d. 1547) [16], and Titian's *Madonna di Ca' Pésaro*, commissioned in 1519 by the same bishop. This painting, nearly as revolutionary in its time as the *Assumption*, had a more lasting influence on Venetian art, especially in its diagonal composition. Titian's wife Celia modelled for the Madonna, and paying her homage below are members of the Pésaro clan, including the Bishop (kneeling on the left); some Turks he captured in the Levant are dragged into the scene as well.

There's no known reason, though, for the ungainly, ragged Moors created to hold up the next monument, the dreadful **Tomb of Doge Giovanni Pésaro** (d. 1659) [17], though the sculptor, a certain Melchiorre Barthel, at least carved pillows for them to make the load lighter. Of all the stupefying tombs in the Frari, this one takes the cake. It rises nearly to the church's roofline, with decomposing bodies on top to add an endearing Hallowe'en note, together with some funhouse dragons and skeletons.

Next comes the **Tomb of Canova** [18], with a nearly full-sized pyramid, its door left ajar (a conceit taken from ancient Roman funeral steles); the ensemble, including sorrowful mourners and a sad, crouching winged lion, was designed by the sculptor as a tomb for Titian, but ended up being executed after his death as his own memorial, although only his heart is buried here.

The State Archives E6
Campo dei Frari. **Open** *only for exhibitions.*
The adjacent monastery and Palladian cloister have, since the early 1800s, housed the State Archives of Venice. The Republic left behind 45 miles of files (about the distance from here to Vicenza) beginning in the 9th century, covering every aspect of Venetian

life from important state secrets down to reports prepared by spies and busybodies on which patricians were gambling or whoring too much: a horde of paper occupying 300 rooms. Two or three times a year exhibitions are held here, based on archival material.

Scuola Grande di San Rocco E6

Campo San Rocco, t 041 523 4864, w www.sanrocco.it; vaporetto San Tomà; wheelchair accessible. **Open** *9–5.30; adm €5.50.*

'Venice's Sistine Chapel' was painted by Tintoretto over a 23-year period; like Michelangelo, he worked alone without assistants; like Michelangelo he created a visionary cycle of paintings from the depths of the imagination.

Founded in 1478, the Scuola di San Rocco was dedicated to caring for the ill, especially those ill with plague. Bartolomeo Bon the Younger designed the new confraternity's headquarters, though it was hardly completed when the Venetians nabbed the relics of St Roch from Montpellier. With subsequent outbreaks of plague, donations poured in, hoping to secure Roch's aid, but also so enriching the Scuola that Bon's building was given a beautiful, lively façade by Scarpagnino in 1549. To embellish the interior, a competition was held for the Scuola's inaugural painting. Four artists were asked to bring a preparatory sketch to the judges on a certain day, but Tintoretto won the contest by a blatantly unfair trick: rather than make a mere sketch, he finished a painting, and rigged it up behind a curtain where the winning picture was destined to be hung, unveiling it with a flourish and offering it as a gift to the confraternity. To the outrage of the other competitors, the judges accepted this *fait accompli*, and commissioned more works from him up until 1585, when he had covered nearly every square inch with an awesome 54 paintings.

Tintoretto strove to depict even the most conventional subjects from a fresh point of

Scuola Grande di San Rocco: Chapter House

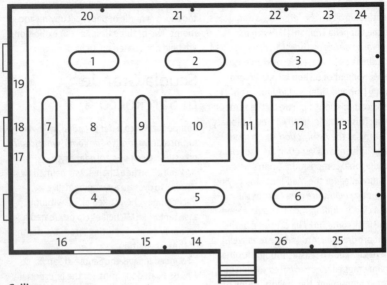

Ceiling

1 God appearing to Moses
2 Vision of Ezekiel
3 Elisha Feeding the Multitude
4 Moses and the Pillar of Fire
5 Jacob's Ladder
6 Elisha Fed by an Angel in the Desert
7 Adam and Eve
8 Moses Bringing Forth Water from the Rock
9 Jonah Emerging from the Whale
10 The Miracle of the Brazen Serpent
11 The Sacrifice of Isaac
12 The Fall of Manna in the Desert
13 The Passover

Walls

14 Ascension
15 Christ at Bethesda
16 The Temptation of Christ
17 San Rocco
18 Vision of San Rocco
19 San Sebastiano
20 Adoration of the Shepherds
21 Baptism of Christ
22 Resurrection
23 Christ in the Garden of Gethsemane
24 Last Supper
25 Miracle of the Loaves and Fishes
26 Resurrection of Lazarus

view, often working out his compositions in his little box-stages, with wax figures and unusual lighting effects. But unlike the virtuoso theatrics of the Baroque, Tintoretto's fireworks come entirely from within the subjects, and ignite their spiritual meanings. Vertigo is not an uncommon response.

To follow the development of Tintoretto, begin where he did, upstairs in the **Sala dell'Albergo**, just off the main hall. In the middle of the ceiling is his prize-winning panel, the *Glory of St Roch*, though it has

since been completely overpowered by the vast *Crucifixion* (1565), the greatest and most engrossing work in the cycle, where the noble sacrifice is the central drama of a cosmically busy human world. When you can draw your eye away, there are more Tintorettos on the opposite wall: *The Way to Calvary, Christ Crowned with Thorns* and *Christ before Pilate*. The easel painting of *Christ Bearing the Cross* (1510), long attributed to Giorgione, is now generally thought to be a Titian, and was venerated as a holy picture in the church of San Rocco, while the Pietà is believed to be by a pupil of Giorgione.

Tintoretto frescoed the adjacent **Chapter House** (*see* plan), in an intense period between 1575–81, with a programme of Old Testament scenes on the ceiling. The three dominant panels are the stunning *Moses Bringing Forth Water from the Rock*, *The Miracle of the Brazen Serpent*, and *The Fall of Manna in the Desert*. All the smaller paintings are just as remarkable; the only works not by Tintoretto are the *chiaroscuro* panels along the sides repainted for some reason in the 1770s.

Lining the walls are New Testament scenes, if anything even more dizzyingly conceived. The satirical allegorical carvings on the benches and *trompe l'œil* bookcases beneath them were added in the late 17th century by Francesco Pianta as an antidote to the mystically feverish paintings; Tintoretto himself, holding a bunch of brushes, represents Painting (near the high altar), while the comical figure of the cloak-and-dagger Spy (Curiosity) is perhaps the most endearing piece of sculpture in Venice.

If you have the time, you can follow the other allegories conveniently listed by Pianta himself by the main entrance. Other works asking for your attention are the easel painting by the altar: Titian's *Annunciation*, Tintoretto's *Visitation*, and Giambattista Tiepolo's *Abraham and the Angels* and *Hagar and the Angels*, the last works acquired by the Confraternity in 1785.

The last set of paintings Tintoretto did for the Scuola are downstairs, but, as you descend Scarpagnino's grand staircase, take a look at the two large canvases commemorating the end of the 1630 plague, by Antonio Zanchi and Pietro Negri, Tintoretto-esque paintings that more than anything bring out the unique qualities of the real thing. The paintings devoted to the life of the *Virgin* in the **Ground Floor Hall** (1583–7) were executed in Tintoretto's last years, when (unlike Michelangelo) he mellowed enough to take in landscapes – and few by any artist can match the luscious charm of *The Flight into*

Egypt, or the autumnal essences in the *Mary Magdalene* and *St Mary in Egypt*, both shown reading books. But he never compromised on the blasts when the subject was of blasting importance: *The Annunciation* startles the viewer as much as Mary, and the *Massacre of the Innocents* is aptly horrible and confusing.

San Rocco E6

*Campo San Rocco; **vaporetto** San Tomà. **Open** Mon–Fri 7.30–12.30, Sat and Sun 7.30–12.30 and 2–4; **adm** free.*

This church was built by Bartolomeo Bon in 1489 but rebuilt in 1725, with an ornate façade (1771). On either side of San Rocco's main door are refined rococo statues that could audition for parts in a Christmas pantomime: *David with Goliath's Head* and *St Cecilia* (1743) by Giovanni Marchiori. If you're lucky enough to find it open, the first altar on the right has Sebastiano Ricci's *Miracle of S. Francesco di Paola*, and the first on the left Pordenone's *SS. Christopher and Martin*. Most mesmerizing, though, is Tintoretto's series on the life of St Roch, a postscript to the masterpieces in the Scuola di San Rocco: *St Roch Taken to Prison* and the recently restored *St Roch Cures Victims of the Plague* are the best.

San Pantalon E6

*Campo San Pantalon; **vaporetto** San Tomà. **Open** Sun–Fri 4–6; **adm** free.*

From Campo San Rocco, walk along Calle Fianco della Scuola to the Rio della Frescada. Cross the bridge, and turn left on Calle dei Preti, only to take the next unmarked right for San Pantalon. Its unfinished façade is a slightly outrageous gift that someone forgot to wrap, for inside it contains *The Miracles and Apotheosis of San Pantalon*, the most extraordinary *trompe l'œil* ceiling in Italy.

This was the life's work of Gian Antonio Fumiani – literally, since he died in 1704, falling off the scaffolding after 24 years on the job. Rather than paint in fresco, Fumiani used 60 panels, which all put together make not one of the world's greatest paintings, but certainly one of the largest.

San Pantalon, martyred under Diocletian, was a healer like St Roch, and as such was very popular in plague-torn Venice. One of his miracles was the subject of Veronese's last paintings *St Pantalon Healing a Child* (1587), in the second chapel on the right; it is sombre, twilit and melancholy in tone, and you can sense Veronese's foreboding of his own death (and perhaps not a whole lot of confidence in Pantalon's ability to do anything about it). Another painting to look for is in the chapel to the left of the high altar: Antonio Vivarini and Giovanni d'Alemagna's glossy *Coronation of the Virgin*, in an elaborate tabernacle.

Around San Pantalon

As you leave the church, turn left for **Campiello da Ca' Angaran** (E6), which preserves something you'll probably never see in any other tiny square in Italy, or anywhere else: a rondel in bas-relief from the 12th century, portraying a Byzantine emperor, holding a sceptre and a symbol of the world he still pretended to rule.

To escape the labyrinth from here, retrace your steps by the side of San Pantalon along Calle San Pantalon, turning right in Calle Crosera, left in Calle Marconi, and right down Fondamenta Frescada to Calle Campaniel; from here Calle di Traghetto leads down to the San Tomà *vaporetto* stop.

Campo San Tomà E–F6

Vaporetto San Tomà.

The blank façade of **San Tomà** (*permanently closed*) was reputed to front the biggest batch of relics in all Christendom, including a record 12 intact bodies. Opposite the pathetic church is the old School of the Shoemakers, or **Scuola dei Calegheri** (now a public library), its façade bearing a charming but badly worn relief by Pietro Lombardo of *St Mark Healing the Cobbler Ananias*.

Casa Goldoni F6

Palazzo Centanni, Calle di Nomboli, t 041 523 6353; vaporetto San Tomà. Open April–Oct Mon–Sat 10–5, Nov–March Mon–Sat 10–4; adm €2.50.

Here Carlo Goldoni, the King of Venetian Comedy, was born in 1707, just in time to chronicle Venice's twilit play days. The palace (now completely restored) predates Goldoni by a good three centuries, and has one of the city's most delightful Gothic courtyards. If you're a student of Venetian theatre, an art descended directly from the Commedia dell'Arte, Goldoni's house is a goldmine of lore, with first editions of plays by unknown Venetians, playbills, engravings of early sets, a puppet theatre and 18th-century paintings, including a rollicking kitchen scene.

San Giovanni Evangelista E5

Campiello della Scuola; vaporetto San Tomà. Open Mon–Fri 9–12 and 4–6; adm free.

This is no place to look for art (there is a mild Tintoretto *Crucifixion* to the right of the altar), but a great place if you're in need of a kitten: the parishioners run a sort of cultural exchange programme involving tourists and Venetian strays. The church is also the local headquarters of the cult of Kaiser Karl, a rather shadowy international effort to transform the last of the Austrian emperors into a saint. Instructions on praying for his cause are posted near the entrance. San Giovanni also has a famous 1760 organ.

Scuola Grande di San Giovanni Evangelista E5

Campiello della Scuola, t 041 718 234; vaporetto San Tomà. Open by appt only (but try ringing the bell).

The Scuola Grande di San Giovanni Evangelista is one of the six 'grand' confraternities of Venice, founded in 1261. Its little Renaissance courtyard is one of the prettiest

The Scuole Grandi

One of the most amazing facts about Venice is that the people, completely shut out of power by the 1297 'Locking' of the *Maggior Consiglio*, never revolted in the 500 years that followed. There were occasional riots, especially by the seafarers in the Renaissance, who were universally mistreated and often cheated. But by and large, the Venetians lived much better and with more security than their mainland counterparts. When Napoleon barged in on the scene to introduce the democratic joys of the French Revolution, it was ironically the people who wept, whereas many patricians were so relieved they danced with the soldiers.

The secret of Venice's popular success was a precocious sense of social justice. Venice's merchant aristocrats, who never claimed any kind of divine right or natural superiority, knew the best way to retain their monopoly of power and their profits was to devote themselves to the public good: the only real privilege a patrician had was to serve the state. All the classes mingled together in the streets and at festivals, with no signs of deference beyond the requirements of common courtesy. There were even laws that *doubled* the punishment when a patrician committed a crime against a commoner. Europe's other aristocrats thought their Venetian cousins were bonkers.

The most important factor in maintaining social stability actually cost the patricians very little in time or money: they encouraged co-operative, independent guilds and confraternities (*scuole*), just when many European princes were trying to limit them, the way modern politicians try to bust up unions. At the fall of the Republic, there were over 300 of these corporations: six *Scuole Grandi*, or large religious and charitable confraternities

(like San Rocco); large, politically influential guilds like the glass-makers and arsenal workers; the club-like *scuole* for foreigners (like San Giovanni degli Schiavoni); down to the humble fruiterers' guild, whose members had the privilege of annually presenting the Doge with their finest melons.

The *scuole* were the backbone of everyday life in Venice, 'republics within the Republic'. Each had its own constitution, a body of electors, a senate (*banca*) and doge (the *gastaldo*); each decided what was best for the trade or society and its members. They regulated pay, settled quarrels, controlled and maintained the standards of Venetian crafts, promoted the best craftsmen and supervised the selection of apprentices. Long before Marx's 'from each according to his abilities, to each according to his needs', Venice was paying workers at the same job a different wage, depending on whether they had a wife or children to support. Each member paid dues according to his earnings and in return had access to the guild hospital and guild school for his children, was given a pension in his old age, and knew that the *scuola* would support his wife and children if he couldn't. Many a member left the confraternity a tidy sum in his will, often to beautify the church or guild hall – today among the finest things to see in Venice. Some even loaned the Republic money in times of need.

One of the first things Napoleon did was suppress the *scuole*; to his ideal of a modern, central government, they seemed like medieval anachronisms. It was like pulling the rug out from under the people, who at one blow lost their security and their chance to control their own affairs, and it wasn't long before a third of the Venetian workforce had to turn to the modern, central government dole.

in Venice, to which a number of artists contributed over the years. The Scuola has a lovely marble portal and screen delicately carved by Pietro Lombardo in 1481, with floral designs and a fierce eagle, along with a

doorway by Mauro Codussi and a 16th-century bas-relief of the hooded confraternity members praying all in a row.

It's worth the trouble of arranging a visit here just to see the **double ramp stairway** by

Mauro Codussi, a bravura Renaissance work, cascading in sophisticated rhythms past domes and barrel vaults. Most of the best paintings commissioned by the Scuola, from Carpaccio and Gentile Bellini, have been shuttled over to the Accademia – these are the scenes celebrating the miracles of a piece of the True Cross, the Confraternity's most prodigious relic, still behind the grille in the oratory on the first floor. It used to go for an annual outing through Venice, and dull indeed was the year that it didn't drive out a demon at the very least.

SAN POLO AND AROUND

Campo San Polo F5–G6

Vaporetto *San Silvestro/San Tomà.*

Campo San Polo is vast and lively, full of children playing, old men sunning themselves and, in summer, a 2,000-seat outdoor cinema showing Italian-dubbed films every evening (€5). Overlooking the action are several interesting palaces, which once faced a small curving canal since filled in: the **Palazzo Tiepolo** by Giorgio Massari, covered with masks, and its red neighbour, the **Palazzo Soranzo**, once the residence of the nobleman who adopted Casanova as his son, and now the Institute of Chinese Language and Literature. Just off the *campo*, past Palazzo Soranzo, Calle Bernardo is named after **Ca' Bernardo**, one of Venice's most beautiful Gothic palaces, overlooking the canal.

San Polo F6

*Campo San Polo; **vaporetto** San Silvestro/San Tomà. **Open** Mon–Sat 10–5, Sun 1–5; **adm** €2.*

Founded in 837, the church of San Polo has a number of interesting details on its **exterior**, from its great plaited Gothic doorway and rose window attributed to Bartolomeo Bon to the hungry Romanesque lions under the detached 14th-century

campanile. The **interior** has been much altered throughout the centuries, especially in 1804, when it was given a set of neoclassical columns to support its ship's keel roof. Inside is Tintoretto's darkest and most violent *Last Supper* (on the left), where Christ is shown literally leaping up from the table. Equally extraordinary in its own way is Giandomenico Tiepolo's *Via Crucis* series in the **Oratory of the Crucifix**, entered under the organ (but watch out for the imperious sacristan). Giandomenico got the commission in 1749, at the tender age of 20, and filled it with a certain amount of piety and an even greater amount of precocious pre-*paparazzi* interest in Venetian high society; the paintings look remarkably like snapshots.

Ponte delle Tette G5

Vaporetto *San Silvestro/San Tomà.*

From Campo San Polo, follow Calle Bernardo north past the palace, turn right on to Calle di Cristo and cross the bridge into Calle di Chiesa, then turn second right down Ramo d'Agnello, over the first bridge and on down Calle d'Agnello. At Rio di San Cassiano you'll be at the Ponte delle Tette, a favourite of all who dally in Venetian street names; this one means 'Bridge of Breasts', apparently after the courtesans who used to display them in the windows back in the 16th century when this was the red light district. These days the biggest things in the windows are geraniums.

RIALTO

Ponte di Rialto H5

Vaporetto *Rialto.*

The earliest version of this famous bridge goes back to 1173, a simple pontoon bridge built on a string of boats. The first real bridge came in the 13th century, and it was burned during the insurrection of Baiamonte Tiepolo. Later incarnations were rickety-looking wooden structures; you can see the last of them in Carpaccio's paintings in the Accademia, with a narrow wooden draw-bridge at the centre to allow the passing of sailing ships – and to cut communications when brawls between the city's rival factions got out of hand.

The stone bridge, one of Venice's eternal symbols, was planned as early as 1524, but not begun until 1588. The state held a competition for the design, a prestigious commission that attracted some of the finest architects of the Renaissance – even Michelangelo submitted a proposal. Classically minded critics since have often regretted that Palladio's design was not chosen; pictures of this survive, a truly ghastly Behemoth covered with Palladian temples and dripping with statues that would have looked as jarringly out-of-place here as a modern glass skyscraper.

Instead, the prize went to the suitably named Antonio da Ponte. The state councillors chose well, as they always did in their more grandiose undertakings: their little-known architect gave them the most Venetian of all possible bridges. Avoiding the architectural dogmas of the late Renaissance, he followed the steeply angled silhouette of the earlier bridge, covering it with slanted arcades that conceal rows of shops. The whole manages the difficult trick of harmonizing perfectly with all the buildings along the Canal, Byzantine, Gothic and Renaissance.

Rialto Markets H5

Vaporetto Rialto. Open Mon–Sat 7–1 (fruit and veg), Tues–Sat 7–1 (fish, on Ruga degli Specializi).

I will buy with you, sell with you, talk with you, walk with you, and so following; but I will not eat with you, drink with you, nor pray with you. What news on the Rialto?
        Shylock, The Merchant of Venice

The housewives and elderly gents who gravitate here for their daily shopping are continuing one of Venice's oldest traditions. The Rialto markets have been the city's

centre of trade – and, as such, the heart of the Republic's mercantile empire – since the 11th century. When Venice's first bank, the Banca Giro, was opened in the 1100s others quickly followed, making the Rialto the medieval equivalent of Wall Street, Europe's most glittering and powerful exchange, controlling the commercial links between East and West; in its houses incredible fortunes were gambled, won, or lost. 'All the gold of the Orient passes through the hands of the Venetians,' grumbled one commentator. And so it did until 1499, when news of Vasco da Gama's voyage around the Horn caused several banks instantly to fail. Those that survived saw their establishments burn to the ground in the great fire of 1514.

The northern edge of the markets, along the Grand Canal, is occupied by the lively neo-Gothic halls of the fish market, or **Pescaria** built in 1907 to replace an iron shed. Behind it is teeny Calle dei Beccarie ('Butchers'); beyond Campo Beccarie lies a maze of even narrower lanes where sugar was once sold for its weight in gold, and pepper and spices for only slightly less. On the Grand Canal, the porticoed **Fabbriche Vecchie** were built after the fire by Scarpagnino, continued by Sansovino's curving **Fabbriche Nuove di Rialto** (1554), now the assize courts. The **Erberia**, the fruit and vegetable market that fills most of the space between Campo San Giacomo and the Grand Canal, adjoins the white **Palazzo dei Camerlenghi** (1528) next to the Rialto Bridge on the sharp curve of the Grand Canal. This was the treasury of the Republic, a well-proportioned building built by Guglielmo dei Grigi of Bergamo, the only one in Venice where each façade is given equal attention. **Ruga degli Orefici** is the raucous main thoroughfare, leading up to the bridge; even though the golden treasures of the East have given way to tourist trinkets, the street and its rows of open-air stands cannot help keeping something of its old colour.

On the south side of Ruga degli Orefici is Scarpagnino's **Palazzo dei Dieci Savi**, home of the Serenissima's financial ministers. From here, the **Fondamenta del Vin** (H6) – a good name for a street packed with restaurants and cafés – runs along the Grand Canal, with occasional views of the same over the heads of the gawkers and waiters and gondoliers.

San Giacomo di Rialto H5

Campo S. Giacomo, t 041 522 4745; vaporetto Rialto. Open Mon–Sat 10.30–12 and 4–5.30; adm free.

Tradition has it that San Giacomo di Rialto, fondly known as San Giacometto, was the first church built in what is now Venice, perhaps as early as the 5th century. In 1097 it was rebuilt in conjunction with the markets, and then fiddled with in 1531 and 1601 to make a stylistic collage that from the outside makes the whole church look like an over-grown mantelpiece clock. Around the apse the 12th-century legend reads: 'Around This Temple Let the Merchant's Law Be Just, His Weight True, and His Covenants Faithful'.

The **clock**'s 24-hour face has shown the wrong time ever since its installation in the 14th century; its hands get stuck in the same place for so long that art historians have dated scenes of Venice by the time shown on it. The five-columned **porch**, a type once common in Venetian churches, is the only original one left in the city; the little bell tower over the clock is Baroque. The Veneto-Byzantine interior is a miniature mixture of basilica and a Greek cross, decorated with six ancient Greek columns, topped with foliage added in 1097; Alessandro Vittoria contributed the statue of *St James with Angels* for the main altar.

Campo San Giacomo H5

The church *campo*, with its Renaissance arcades, makes an elegant ensemble. The shabby planks and pipes also conceal the 16th-century granite figure of the **Gobbo di Rialto**, the 'hunchback' upon whose shoulders the decrees of the Republic were read to the public; criminals were made to run naked through a gauntlet of blows from Piazza San Marco to safety at the Gobbo's feet.

San Giacomo Elemosinario H5

Vaporetto Rialto. Closed for renovation until 2003/4.

This is a venerable church rebuilt by Scarpagnino, but preserving its Greek cross plan. If restoration work has been completed, see Titian's *Patron Saint Distributing Alms* (1545) on the high altar, and from the same year, in the chapel to the right, Pordenone's *Santi Catherine, Roch and Sebastian*, a painting Venetian in its colouring but quirky Tuscan Mannerist in its composition. The paintings in the cupola are also Pordenone's.

NORTH OF THE FONDAMENTA DEL VIN

San Silvestro G–H6

Campo San Silvestro; vaporetto San Silvestro. Open Mon–Sat 7.30–11.30 and 4–6; adm free.

At the end of the Fondamenta del Vin, Sottoportico Traghetto (near the *vaporetto* stop) leads to the undistinguished neoclassical church of San Silvestro, most noted for its painting of *St Thomas à Becket Enthroned with Angels* (1520, Gerolamo Santacroce).

Campo San Silvestro G6

Facing the church is the **Palazzo Valier** (No.1022) where Giorgione lived, and in 1510 died of the plague contracted from his mistress.

Sant'Aponal G5

Campo Sant'Aponal; vaporetto San Silvestro.

The deconsecrated brick Gothic church of Sant'Aponal (Apollinare) has a tabernacle over the portal bearing 1294 reliefs of the Crucifixion; the base of its Romanesque campanile once had the oldest known relief of the Lion of St Mark (since pensioned off to

Bianca Capello

An exceptional Venetian beauty, Bianca eloped to Florence in 1563 with Pietro Bonaventura, a humble bankers' clerk, an impetuous act of love that called down the full fury of the unsentimental Senate. The young couple were sentenced to death *in absentia*, and forgotten until it was discovered that Bianca had abandoned her clerk in favour of a much more palatable catch: the Grand Duke of Tuscany, Francesco de' Medici, who ignored his dumpy Habsburg duchess for her more dazzling charms. Diplomacy at this stage was a delicate affair, but as soon as his wife died and the Grand Duke married Bianca, Venice promptly proclaimed her 'the adopted and beloved daughter of our Republic'. But the Republic fell discreetly silent when Francesco and Bianca suddenly died of poison – ironically, for the Grand Duke's hobby, as a weekend alchemist, was brewing poisons from crates of scorpions.

the Correr Museum). And don't bother looking in; the interior is entirely filled with metal shelves, containing all the city's marriage records.

One file a little thicker than the others (if the records go back that far) would be that of **Bianca Capello** (*see* box, above). Her **house** is just around the corner from the church; take Calle del Ponte Storto (left of the church façade) up to the 'crooked' bridge, Ponte Storto; hers was the house overlooking it, the one with the neoclassical busts at the head of narrow Rio Sant'Aponal.

CA' PESARO AND AROUND

Ca' Pésaro G4

*Fondamenta Ca' Pésaro; **vaporetto** San Stae.*

One of Venice's grandest Baroque palaces, Longhena's Ca' Pésaro is vast enough to be used for major exhibitions and to shelter two museums.

Museum of Modern Art

*Ca' Pésaro ground floor, t 041 524 0695. **Open** Tues–Sun 10–5; **adm** €6.50.*

Founded to hold works purchased by the city at the Biennale, the museum also contains a fair if not wildly inspiring sample of contemporary Italian art – Giorgio Morandi, Filippo de Pisis, Manzu, and many lesser lights, interspersed by token foreigners. The most uncanny is Gustav Klimt's *Salome*, a Madonna/sorceress dream girl for psychoanalysts, the embodiment of Freud's 'Eros and Thanatos'. The 19th-century Italian art, from artists little known outside Italy, comes as a pleasant surprise, especially the works of sculptor Medardo Rosso of Milan, and Venetian painters Giacomo Favretto, Gugliemo Ciardi, master of luminous lagoon-scapes, and Francesco Hayez.

Museum of Oriental Art

*Ca' Pésaro top floor, t 041 524 1173. **Open** Tues–Sun 9.15–2; **adm** €2.10.*

After the First World War, Austria, in reparation for damage caused by its incendiary bombs, tried to make amends by giving Venice a higgledy-piggledy collection of screens, lacquer boxes, weapons, kimonos, armour, etc. amassed by a 19th-century Marco Polo, Count Enrico di Bourbon Parma.

Palazzo Agnusdio G4

*Fondamenta Pésaro; **vaporetto** San Stae.*

Just behind the Ca' Pésaro is the 14th-century Palazzo Agnusdio, named after its Byzantine *patera* of the Lamb of God. The palace has an ogival five-light window with reliefs of the Annunciation.

Santa Maria Materdomini G4

*Campo Santa Maria Materdomini; **vaporetto** San Stae. **Open** Mon-Fri 10–12; **adm** free.*

From the *vaporetto* stop, Fondamenta Pesaro leads into Calle del Tiozzi, then take the very next right, Corte del Tiozzi and walk under the Sottoportico del Fenestrer.

An early 16th-century church of uncertain paternity (Mauro Codussi or Giovanni Buora), with an Istrian stone façade, Santa Maria Materdomini has a cool grey and white Renaissance interior with half-moon clerestory windows and its own Tintoretto, *The Invention of the Cross*, to the left of the main altar. Its subject is the medieval *Legend of the Holy Cross* (*see* Sant'Alvise in Cannaregio, p.207), only with an eccentric Tintorettonian twist – who the lady with the newly made cross in her lap might be (St Helen?) is anyone's guess. The glaringly anachronistic bishop and Turk in the assemblage do their best to look nonchalant. On the first altar on the right are *Three Saints*, sculpted by Lorenzo Bregno in 1524, who is responsible for most of the carving in the church; Bonifazio's *Last Supper*, opposite the Tintoretto, also merits a look, as does the *Martyrdom of St Christina* by Vincenzo Catena, one of the favourite paintings of the Venetians, who love its sweet little angel holding the millstone.

Campo S. Maria Materdomini G5

Just opposite the church is the entrance to the charming *campo*, which, with its old well-head and houses, wears the Middle Ages like a worn, but very comfortable pair of shoes.

San Cassiano G5

*Campo San Cassiano; **vaporetto** San Stae. **Open** Tues–Sat 9–12 and 5–6; **adm** free.*

Campo San Cassiano once held the first public opera house in the world, opened in 1637 while Monteverdi was *maestro di cappella* at St Mark's. Nowadays the focal point, such as it is, is this lacklustre, façade-less old church, another reincarnated in the 17th century (except for its detached medieval campanile). The **interior** has more than a touch of Great Auntie, with its chandeliers and pillars wrapped in flocked fabric, but it also has a startling masterpiece by Tintoretto: a dynamic *Crucifixion*, composed as if the viewer were just under the cross,

looking up as the Roman soldier climbs the ladder to nail on the sign reading INRI. Two other Tintorettos (*The Descent into Limbo* and *The Resurrection*) that keep it company have suffered from an unhappy restoration, although in the former the painter's usual flair for drama finds expression in the fury of Christ bursting out of the tomb (€0.50 for the light). The chapel to the right of the altar contains a more typical *Crucifixion* by Palma Giovane, and Leandro Bassano's *Announcement of the Birth of St John the Baptist*, with quirky rows of Venetian heads underneath.

San Stae G4

*Campo San Stae; **vaporetto** San Stae. **Open** Mon–Sat 10–5, Sun 1–5; **adm** €2.*

Non-Venetians call him San Eustachio, or St Eustace, and his church, one of the landmarks along the Grand Canal, was built in the 17th century, though the exuberant façade was added later in 1709, by Domenico Rossi, and decorated with saints who perform daredevil circus acts on the high trapeze of a bracket over the door. The interior, bright, bright white and grey after a recent restoration, is still used for mass in winter, though in summer it's given over to exhibitions. All the year round, however, you can see the slab in the floor marking the last resting place of **Doge Alvise Mocenigo II** (d. 1709) who paid for the façade, but chose the Latin epitaph, 'Name and ashes buried together with vanity'. The chancel resembles a gallery of small 18th-century paintings. Two of the best hang in the lower left row: the *Martyrdom of St James the Great* by Piazzetta; *St Peter Freed from Prison* by Sebastiano Ricci; and, opposite, Giambattista Tiepolo's *Martyrdom of St Bartholomew*.

On the left side of the nave, if there's no exhibition on, you'll see the **Monument of Antonio Foscarini** (*see* box), with an inscription from the Republic noting that he was mistakenly executed for treason in 1621.

Butting up to the church's east flank is one of the most endearing (and smallest)

Antonio Foscarini

Foscarini was a dashing patrician who served as ambassador to England, but got into trouble for being far too chummy with the English and was recalled, and imprisoned for three years under suspicion of treason. When he was finally cleared of the charge and released, Foscarini secretly paid frequent visits to the Palazzo Mocenigo-Nero, then the residence of Lady Arundel, wife of one of the most powerful nobles in King James' court. Renewed accusations of treason reached the Council of Ten, who acted swiftly; Foscarini was captured, questioned, and executed within 12 days.

The first hint that justice had miscarried was when Lady Arundel immediately demanded an audience with the doge (and became the first woman granted one), declaring that neither she nor her household were involved in any plot.

Further investigations revealed that Foscarini's visits to the Palazzo Mocenigo-Nero were of an amorous nature, and that he had gallantly died with the secret; his real crime was having enemies in the stodgy Venetian bureaucracy. The Council of Ten executed his accusers, and tried to make posthumous amends with a state funeral and this inscription. Venice's critics sometimes accuse her of not doing enough for Foscarini's memory, but then again, how many governments, even these days, would have publicly admitted to a mistake in the first place?

buildings on the Grand Canal, the **Scuola dei Battiloro e Tiraoro** (the Guild headquarters of the goldsmiths), built in 1711 and also used now for exhibitions.

Palazzo Mocenigo G4

Salizzada San Stae, t 041 721 798, vaporetto San Stae. Open Tues–Sun 10–4; adm €4.50.

The Mocenigos owned several *palazzi* in Venice and gave the city several doges; this splendid palace, with its salon typically running the whole length of the building,

has been turned into a small museum of 18th-century noble Venetian life and costume, with stockings, corsets and silks.

Fondaco dei Turchi/ Natural History Museum F4

Salizzada dei Fondaco dei Turchi, t 041 275 0206; vaporetto Riva di Biasio. Closed for major restoration; due to reopen 2004.

Located in another landmark on the Grand Canal (*see* p.235), this is good fun, and nature's quiet reminder in the world's most beautiful city that its creatures are all masterpieces in their own way – even the sponges, from the delicate little Basket of Venus to the mighty Elephant Ear Sponge. There's a Japanese crab, the *Macrocheira kaempferi*, that could play a villain's role in a James Bond film; incredible bugs, scorpions and centipedes (more in the Vincent Price vein); beautiful butterflies, beetles and bees; and a collection of things you'd probably never pondered before, like the embryos of the shark and ray, complete with photos of a shark giving birth on an Egyptian ship, or the 'Monstrous Chimera', a strange fish with peculiar sex organs.

The Venetian natural habitat is explored in one section, with models of **lagoon craft** (including a pre-Roman boat found in the muck) and fishing nets, lagoon birds and 'Life on a *Bricole*' which shows all the tiny creatures and algae who have made those wooden posts their special home.

The museum is especially proud of its **Dinosaur Room**, with finds from the 1973 Ligabue Sahara expedition, starring a 35ft-long fossil, the largest ever discovered of the crocodile's ancestor, the *Sarcosuchus imperator*, and the complete skeleton of a never-before-seen reptilian biped, the *Ouranosaurus nigeriensis*, as well as a clutch of fossilized dinosaur droppings.

These are followed by lovely shells, stones, minerals and more fossils, and trophies and photos bagged on various safaris.

San Zan Degolà F4

*Campo San Giovanni Decollato; **vaporetto** Riva di Biasio. **Open** 10–12 and for concerts; **adm** free.*

Behind the Fondaco, the church of San Zan Degolà (Venetian for 'Beheaded John') has been deconsecrated for over 100 years, but if you get in, take a look at the 13th-century frescoes in the left apse.

San Giacomo dell'Orio F4

*Campo San Giacomo dell'Orio; **vaporetto** Riva di Biasio/San Stae. **Open** Mon–Sat 10–5, Sun 1–5; **adm** €2.*

Perhaps 'of the laurel', from '*alloro*', this is not the most prepossessing Venetian church from the outside, but well worth a look within. Founded in the 9th century, this church and its campanile were rebuilt in 1225 to house a pair of columns, one a massive and rare piece of *verde antico* (in the right transept) that the Venetians plundered from Byzantium. Crowned by a magnificent, nearly seaworthy 14th-century ship's keel roof – built to limit the church's weight on the swampy ground – it is another Old Curiosity Shop of Venetian memories, beginning with a quatrefoil stoup of Greek marble and, in the right transept, a wall of the original church, embedded with sculptural bits from Venice's sedimentary past.

A sombre *Madonna* by Lorenzo Lotto presides over the high altar, with Lorenzo Veneziano's crucifix and two marble crosses in the Lombardo style, and Lombardesque red and green geometrical patterns continued around the sanctuary. On the pier to the left of the altar, there's an unusual *Virgin Annunciate*, one hand raised in friendly greeting, the other holding a spindle; still to the left of the altar are two large black and white 13th-century frescoes of *Daniel*, perhaps, and *David*.

Although the gate of the **old sacristy** on the far left is usually locked, you can look through the bars to see its numerous Palma Giovanes and Buonconsiglio's *Three Plague Saints*. The left transept has a Veronese on the altar, where you'll find the light switch to illuminate its saints and rain of *putti* bearing martyrs' palms; on either side are Palma Giovane's *Scenes from the Life of St Laurence*, on the right presenting the Roman authorities with the 'treasures of the church' that they had demanded (he brought them his poor and wretched); on the left Laurence is toasting on the grill for his brave gesture.

If the sacristan is about, he'll open the **new sacristy**, with Veronese's *The Doctors of the Church and Faith*, and Francesco Bassano's *St John the Baptist*, who is preaching to the Bassano family and Titian (on the far left, in a red hat).

WESTERN SANTA CROCE

San Simeone Piccolo D4

*Campicchio da Comare; **vaporetto** Ferrovia. Currently **closed** for restoration.*

At the ranch-style **Stazione di Santa Lucia** (1955), passengers waiting for trains lounge about on the steps and wonder about the odd little green eggcup of a church across the Grand Canal, next to the **Ponte Scalzi**, the bridge of the 'barefoot friars', rebuilt in its current form in the 1930s.

The church looks, in fact, like many a Temple to Divine Reason proposed during the French Revolution. This, however, is San Simeone Piccolo (1718–38), designed by Giovanni Scalfarotto, who introduced neoclassicism to Venice. Though inspired by the Pantheon, with its classical porch and round plan, Scalfarotto perched a Salute-type dome on top, a charming farewell note to Venetian architecture.

As Rudolf Wittkower wrote: 'This blending of the Pantheon with Byzantium and Palladio is what one would expect to find in 18th-century Venice, and that it really happened is almost too good to be true'.

San Simeone Profeta (San Simeone Grande) E4

Campo San Simeone Profeta; **vaporetto** *Ferrovia.* **Open** *Mon–Sat 8–12 and 5–6;* **adm** *free.*

Back towards the Ponte Scalzi, turn right at Calle Lunga; near the end, take the last left, at unmarked Calle Bergami, and continue straight over the canal for San Simeone's big brother. Famous paintings in this bright and cosy church include a Palma Giovane over the altar and a *Last Supper* by Tintoretto near the door, a typically startling composition, with the Apostles all the complete Renaissance gentlemen, and the table set at an angle to the viewer. Even better is the 14th-century *Effigy of San Simeone* by an obscure artist named Marco Romano, laid out in full *rigor mortis* in the chapel to the left of the altar; if it's very quiet, they say, you can hear his death rattle. Perhaps it helps if you think hard about the thousands of victims of the 1630 plague buried beneath your feet under the church floor, or remember that San Simeone Profeta was once the parish of a pork butcher called Biasio, the original Sweeney Todd. Biasio would stuff his celebrated *squazzeto alla Boechera* with the flesh of little boys, an adventure in commercial cannibalism that makes old-school Venetians shudder every time they walk along the Riva di Biasio, skirting the Grand Canal to the north.

San Nicolò da Tolentino D5

Campo Tolentini; **vaporetto** *Piazzale Roma.* **Open** *Mon–Sat 9.30–11 and 5–6.30;* **adm** *free.*

The striking Corinthian porch of San Nicolò da Tolentino looms like a Roman ruin over the Fondamenta dei Tolentini. Commonly called the Tolentini, this church was designed by Andrea Tirali (1716) and inspired by Palladio's Villa Malcontenta. Under the porch you can see a cannonball embedded in the façade, a souvenir left by the Austrians in the siege of 1849. The equally Palladian **interior**, by Vincenzo Scamozzi (1591), is partly disguised by the rococo stuccoes added by a 17th-century pastry chef-cum-artist, perhaps to compensate for lopping off the dome. The Tolentini witnessed a number of Venetian dramas, the most glorious when Francesco Morosini, after his 1685 bravura reconquest of the Morea, dedicated to the church the banner he had captured from a Turkish general with its three dangling horsetails; the most inglorious occurred in February 1789, when the unloved Doge Paolo Renier was secretly buried here in the middle of the night so as not to interrupt Carnival with a tedious state funeral.

The Tolentini's prize artwork is *St Jerome Visited by an Angel* by Johann Lys (1628) to the left of the sanctuary. Lys, from northern Germany, was very young and soon to die in the plague of 1630, but he holds a special place in Venetian art as the primary exponent of the free brushstrokes and disintegration of form, the link between the late styles of Titian and Tintoretto and the Guardi brothers. The left wall of the sanctuary itself is occupied by the rollicking proto-rococo **Monument to Patriarch Francesco Morosini** (d. 1678), by Genoese sculptor Filippo Parodi, a tomb that doubles as a remarkable piece of theatre with its voluminous draperies. In the right aisle you'll find two good works by Bonifazio de Pitati, the lesser known of Venice's 'Veroneses': the *Banquet in the House of Herod* and *Decapitation of the Baptist*. The facile, unstoppable Palma Giovane painted all the chapels on the left. San Nicola's adjacent convent is now home to the University's Institute of Architecture.

Around San Nicolò da Tolentino

Spare a moment for a brief diversion south along Fondamenta dei Tolentini (to the right of the church) to **Fondamenta Minotto** (D6) for a look at an exceptionally lovely canal, and above it some of Venice's most remarkable chimneypots. Then circle around the left side of the church, by way of Campazzo dei Tolentini and Corte dei Amai; cross the bridge and turn right on **Ramo Cimesin** (D5), a rare Venetian lane between walled gardens.

Giardini Papadopoli C–D5

Vaporetto Piazzale Roma.

Just west across the Rio da Tolentini is this small patch of rare green park, on the site of the original church of Santa Croce, of which the only thing remaining is a stretch of wall on Fondamenta Croce, next to the Grand Canal.

Just south of the park is the **Tre Ponti** bridge, with a view of 12 other bridges.

Piazzale Roma C5

Vaporetto Piazzale Roma.

This windy great *piazza* is Venice's busy transport hub, with underground and multi-storey car parks and the main bus station to Mestre, the mainland and Chioggia.

Eastern Cannaregio

CA' D'ORO AND AROUND 196
Ca d'Oro/Franchetti Gallery 196
Strada Nuova 196

SANTI APOSTOLI AND AROUND 197
Santi Apostoli 197
Around Santi Apostoli 197

TWO RENAISSANCE CHURCHES 198
Santa Maria dei Miracoli 198
Around Santa Maria dei Miracoli 198
San Giovanni Grisostomo 198
Around San Giovanni Grisostomo 199

CAMPO DEI GESUITI 199
Gesuiti 199
Oratorio dei Crociferi 200
Fondamenta Nuove 200

Eastern Cannaregio

Originally a reedy cane (*canna*) swamp, the *sestiere* of Cannaregio is the largest in Venice, so big that we've split it into two separate chapters.

This section east of the Canale di Misericordia, closer to Piazza San Marco, was a high-rent district, with fancy *palazzi* and churches, ranging from the cool Renaissance perfection of Santa Maria dei Miracoli to the Baroque extravagances of the Gesuiti. Marco Polo lived here, and also Titian; as an added plus it has some of the most perfect canal views in all Venice.

1 Lunch

Vini da Gigio, *Cannaregio 3628A, Fond. San Felice, t 041 528 5140; vaporetto Ca' d'Oro. Open Tues–Sun 12–2.30 and 7.30–10.30. Expensive. Booking essential*. Small restaurant with views over the canal, one of the best places to eat in Venice. Has the feel of an old *bacaro*, with its low, beamed ceilings and rustic tiled floors. The wine list features 600 labels.

2 Cakes to Go

Puppa, *Cannaregio 4800, Calle del Spezzier, t 041 523 7947; vaporetto Ca' d'Oro. Open Tues–Sun 7.30–1 and 3.30–8*. Small *pasticceria* with wonderful cakes, but to take away only.

3 Drinks

Algiubagiò, *Cannaregio 5039, Fondamenta Nuove, t 041 523 6084; vaporetto Fond. Nuove. Open daily 7am–8.30pm; closed Jan*. Right by the *vaporetto* stop for the islands, this bar, with its large terrace overlooking the lagoon and super-friendly staff, is good for a drink, snack or light meal.

Highlights

Medieval Venice: The Gothic fairy palace of the Ca' d'Oro, p.196

Renaissance Venice: Santa Maria dei Miracoli, the jewel in Venice's Renaissance crown, p.198

Baroque/Rococo Venice: The Gesuiti for a blast of excess, Jesuit-style, p.199

Indoor Venice: The Franchetti Gallery, with its beautiful interior and beautifully displayed collection of art, p.196

Decadent Venice: The wistful Fondamenta Nuove, overlooking the cemetery island of San Michele, p.200

Pigeon Venice: Marco Polo's old haunts, in the Corte dei Milion, p.199

CA' D'ORO AND AROUND

Ca' d'Oro/ Franchetti Gallery H4

Calle di Ca' d'Oro, **t** *041 523 8790;* **vaporetto** *Ca' d'Oro.* **Open** *Mon 8.15am–2pm, Tues–Sun 8.15am–9.15pm;* **adm** *€3.*

Marino Contarini, a procurator of San Marco (the Venetian equivalent of a prince), purchased a Veneto-Byzantine palace on this site to match his newly elected dignity, and hired Marco d'Amadio to redesign it and Matteo Raverti to rebuild it in Venice's unique brand of fairytale Gothic. Raverti used Lombard craftsmen, but many of the finest touches on the Ca' d'Oro are by Giovanni and Bartolomeo Bon. Finished in 1434, it was known as the 'Golden House' because of the golden pinnacles along the roof, while the intricate floral tracery on its main façade was dazzlingly illuminated with vermilion and ultramarine.

The original gold is now long gone, and the next owners didn't always keep the old place up, most notoriously the 19th-century ballerina Maria Taglioni. In this century Baron Giorgio Franchetti bought the palace and filled it with his **art collection**, which he left to the State in 1916. After restoration, the lovely courtyard was salvaged, with its fine open stair and well-head with allegories of virtues by Bartolomeo Bon. Inside, however, the restorers were guilty of overkill, blasting away all the old palatial clutter, making the walls plain white like any new art gallery.

Upstairs, the first exhibit, set in its own little marble shrine, is Andrea Mantegna's grimacing, unfinished *St Sebastian*, one of the artist's last paintings (1506). Sebastian here looks like a hedgehog. Sculpture lines the walls of the *portego*, or main hall, with its loggia overlooking the Grand Canal: a charming double portrait bust called *The Young Couple* by Tullio Lombardo, bronze reliefs by Andrea Briosco, a lunette of the

Virgin and Child by Sansovino, and a 16th-century English alabaster relief of the *Life of St Catherine*, one of many that made their way to Italy. In the little rooms to the right of the *portego*, look for the fine collection of Renaissance bronzes, statuettes and medals by Pisanello and the Mantuan Pier Alari Bonacolsi, known as 'L'Antico' for his classical style. A carved 16th-century ceiling survives in one room, overlooking two of Carpaccio's paintings on the *Life of the Virgin* from the Scuola degli Albanesi. On the left side of the *portego* are paintings by non-Venetians, among them a minuscule *Flagellation* by Luca Signorelli and the *Coronation of the Virgin* by Andrea di Bartolo.

The beautiful 15th-century **stairway** in carved wood was brought here from another palace; it leads up to a collection of minor works by major artists, such as Tintoretto, Titian, Van Dyck, Pordenone, and some good sculptures by Vittoria. One room has a fine coffered ceiling from a palace in Verona; another contains the ghosts of Giorgione and Titian's exterior frescoes from the Fondaco dei Tedeschi, including a once-juicy pink nude by Giorgione, now bleached into a cartoon character. The two fine views of Venice in the same room are by one of the Guardi brothers, most likely Francesco.

Strada Nuova G3–H4

The Strada Nuova, running behind the Ca' d'Oro, is one of Venice's busiest shopping streets, bulldozed through the little alleyways in 1871 to provide a fast track from the Rialto Bridge to the railway station.

If you turn left (west) from the Ca' d'Oro, towards the station, you'll come to **San Felice** (H4), a 1532 church of simple design, with Tintoretto's armed *St Demetrius* on the third altar on the right. Digress briefly up the porticoed **Fondamenta di San Felice**, a fine stretch of canal with one of the narrowest palaces in Venice and the last bridge in the city without parapets. Two hundred years ago, when street lighting was practically non-existent, nearly all the bridges were just as precarious, and, although the natives could get around like cats, foreign visitors stuck to their gondolas or hired lantern-bearers to keep from tumbling in the canals.

Pause on the bridge after San Felice for the view of the lovely 15th-century **Palazzo Giovanelli** (G–H3), with its striking corner windows. It's now an auction house, and you may want to take advantage of any pre-sale viewings to see the well-preserved interior, with its delightful neo-Gothic stair.

If you turn right (east) on the Strada Nuova from the Ca' d'Oro you'll come to **Santa Sofia** (H4), a little church hidden by houses; inside are four statues of saints, brought here from the former church of the Servi, generally attributed to the workshop of Antonio Rizzo. In Campo Santa Sofia, overlooking the Grand Canal with a view of the Rialto markets, the **Palazzo Sagredo** (H4) is perhaps too embarrassed to let visitors in to see the most ridiculous ceiling in Venice – a *Fall of Giants* (1734) by genre painter Pietro Longhi.

SANTI APOSTOLI AND AROUND

Santi Apostoli I4

Campo di Santi Apostoli, t 041 523 8297; vaporetto Ca' d'Oro. Open Mon–Sat 7.30–11.30 and 5–6; closed Sun; adm free.

Santi Apostoli's bustling *campo* was one of the first of the Rialtine islets colonized in the Dark Ages, and this church went up soon after, though it has been rebuilt several times since and was given its tall, landmark campanile in 1672. The star attraction inside is on the right, the Renaissance **Cappella Corner** by Mauro Codussi, dedicated to the family of Caterina, Queen of Cyprus, who was buried here before being transferred to San Salvatore. Giambattista Tiepolo's 1748 *Communion of Santa Lucia*, on the chapel's altar, is rated among that artist's most spiritual works; Tullio Lombardo is given credit for the tomb of Caterina's father Marco (d. 1511),

and for the marble relief of St Sebastian's head (located among the detached 14th-century frescoes in the chapel to the right of the high altar). In the chapel to the left of the altar is Francesco Maffei's brightly coloured *Guardian Angel*, a popular subject during the terrors of the Counter-Reformation, when people really needed one, and a 15th-century Tuscan relief of the *Madonna and Child*.

Around Santi Apostoli

From the bridge spanning the Rio dei Santi Apostoli (to the right of the church façade) you have a good view of the Veneto-Byzantine **Palazzo Falier** (I5) with its portico, begun in the 13th century; this was the family home of the traitor Doge Marin Falier, deprived of his head in 1355. Its neighbour to the west, facing the Grand Canal, is the **Ca' da Mosto** (H5), whose most famous resident, Alvise da Mosto (d. 1483), enjoyed a happier fate as the man who discovered the Cape Verde islands while in the employ of the Portuguese king Henry the Navigator. Ca' da Mosto later became the Leon Bianco Inn, the equivalent of the Ritz of Venice from the 16th to the 18th century.

From Santi Apostoli, walk all along its flank to its apse and along Calle di Manganer to Campiello di Cason and Calle di Malavasia; the *palazzo* just before Ponte San Canzian was once the **Ca' Strozzi** (I4), a possession of the famous Florentine Renaissance family. Later it belonged to two antiquarians, Amadeo Svayer and David Weber, who covered it inside and out with their collections. All that is left are the fragments of ancient **Greek reliefs** on the side facing the bridge. The first one, a battered figure and a wheel, would have been a scene of Hades carrying off Persephone in his chariot. Over the bridge is **San Canciano** (I5, *closed*), a yawner rebuilt in the 18th century. Adjacent, Campiello B. Crovato gives into Campo Santa Maria Nova. In neighbouring Campiello S. Maria Nova, note the fellow holding a solar disc, 16th-century classicizing on the façade of the Gothic **Palazzo Bembo-Boldù** (I5).

TWO RENAISSANCE CHURCHES

Santa Maria dei Miracoli I5

Campo dei Miracoli, **t** *041 275 0462;* **vaporetto** *Rialto.* **Open** *Mon–Sat 10–5, Sun 1–5;* **adm** *€2.*

The chief jewel in Venice's Renaissance crown is Santa Maria dei Miracoli, prettily rinsing her skirts in the canal. The miracles in the name of this church come from a popular wonder-working painting that once had a shrine in the neighbourhood. It received enough donations to afford a proper, if small, church to shelter it, and one was designed by Pietro Lombardo and his sons, Tullio and Antonio, in 1481–9. But the real miracle is the church itself – the perfect expression of Venice's half-archaic brand of Renaissance, bending the classical laws to its own decorative ends. With a façade topped by a Mauro Codussi-style half-circle crowning, the church is covered inside and out with a pearly sheath of rich marbles like St Mark's – one tradition says that it got all the leftovers. The Lombardi embellished it with their trademark discs and geometric designs in porphyry or green serpentine marble, not to mention some of the most masterful stone-cutting in Venice, beginning with the angels on the façade, believed to be by Pietro Lombardo himself.

The glory of the luxuriant grey and pink **interior** is the exquisite carving on the pillars of the *barca*, or nuns' gallery, at the entrance, where the sculptors' fancy was given free rein to frolic among the delightful motifs of a Renaissance spring. These gallery carvings are attributed to the three Lombardi; the statues on the balustrade in front of the raised altar are by Tullio, and the reliefs of children and mermaids under the great arch are believed to be by Antonio. The miraculous painting (by Nicolò di Pietro) is still in place, and may have to be called upon to do its stuff to protect the church from damage

inside the marble walls caused by a recent over-hasty restoration. The raised choir and altar, with stairs leading to a small crypt, is an anachronistic feature, common in medieval churches throughout central Italy but surprisingly rare in Venice, where it is the only way to have a crypt at all, or at least one above the water line. Have a look at the barrel-vaulted ceiling before you go, decorated with 50 fine Renaissance portraits of the prophets and other Old Testament figures by Pier Maria Pennacchi.

Around Santa Maria dei Miracoli

From behind Santa Maria Miracoli, Ponte Maria Nova and, to its right, Ponte del Piovan cross the forking Rio di Ca' Widmann in a setting almost too bijou to be real. The lanes lead straight on to Santi Giovanni e Paolo (*see* p.136); instead take the first left (under the arches, just after Ponte del Piovan) to the next bridge, the Ponte Widmann. From the bridge you can see the **Palazzo Widmann-Foscari** (J4–5), with a façade by Longhena, embedded with Byzantine *paterae*; this was the headquarters of one of Venice's later noble and wealthiest families. The neighbouring **Palazzo Loredan** is noted for its 16th-century doorway.

San Giovanni Grisostomo I5

Campo San Giovanni Grisostomo, **t** *041 522 7155;* **vaporetto** *Rialto.* **Open** *Mon–Sat 8.30–12 and 3.30–5, Sun 3.30–5.30;* **adm** *free.*

This fine Renaissance church that takes up much of its *campo* is the last work of Mauro Codussi (finished in 1504), following the lines of his famous San Michele, only perhaps less skilfully. In form it is a square with a compact Greek cross inscribed within, perhaps as a nod to its namesake, the 'golden-mouthed' bishop of Constantinople; even the plaster has a red-gold tint, thanks to the addition of brick dust. Harmoniously proportioned and well articulated inside, with its vaulting and domes, the church contains its equal in art: on the right, the last work of another great Venetian, Giovanni Bellini's *Sts Christopher, Jerome and Louis of Toulouse* (1513, painted at the age of 82) and, on the high altar, Sebastiano del Piombo's *Seven Saints* (1508–11), one of his greatest works though too dirty to really appreciate; some art historians have detected the helping brush of the elusive Giorgione, especially in the figures of St John the Baptist and St Liberale. The marble altar on the left, by Tullio Lombardo (1502), shows *The Coronation of the Virgin*, where you can see how the sculptor concentrated his attention on the figure of Mary to the detriment of the bland Apostles.

Around San Giovanni Grisostomo

Take a brief detour down Calle della Stua, a small alley at the far end of Campo San Giovanni, to the left; at the end, on the Grand Canal, is the little **Campiello del Remer**, with a palace adorned by some fine Byzantine capitals and arches, plus a view across the water to the **Palazzo dei Camerlenghi** (I5) (Venice's Treasury).

Returning to Campo S. Giovanni, **Calle dell'Uffizio della Seda** (behind the church, at

Marco Polo

At the 1298 Battle of Curzola, Marco Polo was taken prisoner by the Genoese, and spent his time in the clink dictating the saga of his 17 years at the court of Kublai Khan to his cellmate, Rusticiano da Pisa. The resulting *Description of the World* was known, at least in Venice as '*Il Milion*', the million standing for the vast number of Polo's exaggerations and tall tales, though Polo's book was for a long while Europe's most accurate account of the East. There is some suspicion, however, that the Venetians were on to something: some scholars now believe Polo never went anywhere, but cribbed his book out of the *Historia Mongolorum*, written in the mid 13th century by Fra Giovanni di Pian di Carpine, a Franciscan missionary sent to China in 1225.

No.5864) was once the headquarters of silk workers and merchants from the Tuscan city of Lucca. From here, Calle del Teatro leads around to the **Teatro Malibran** (I5), built in the 17th century as the Teatro San Giovanni Grisostomo, but renamed after a famous singer of the 1830s, then rebuilt in the 1920s. Its Veneto-Byzantine arches are believed to have belonged to the family home of Marco Polo.

The pair of enclosed courts adjacent to the theatre recall 'Mr Million': the **Corte Prima del Milion**, and beyond it, the picturesque **Corte Seconda del Milion**, with its collage of architectural fragments from the 11th to 15th centuries, and a lovely Byzantine arch.

CAMPO DEI GESUITI

Gesuiti J3

Campo dei Gesuiti, t 041 528 6549; vaporetto Fondamenta Nuove. Open daily 10–12 and 5–7; adm free.

The Jesuits, banned from the Republic in 1606 for supporting the Pope during the Great Interdict, were permitted to return to the Republic only in 1657 – a permission subject to a review every three years. Because the city had forbidden the construction of new churches, the Order purchased the former church of the Crociferi and demolished it, hiring Domenico Rossi to design a new one (1715–29). After the charms of Santa Maria dei Miracoli, the Gesuiti has the sad air of a fat, overdone girl who can't get a date, no matter how much money her parents lavish on her appearance; the parents in this case were the Manin family (who also produced Venice's equally unloved last doge). They paid Giambattista Fattoretto for a façade larded with saints and angels, pinned to the wall with bars, wearing iron haloes that bleed rust over the white marble.

The Jesuits were convinced that the glory and richness of this world could bring the faithful closer to that of the next: Baroque architecture, after all, started out as the 'Jesuit style'. This style of ecclesiastical theatre, which delighted in *trompe l'œil* (as in the remarkable ceiling of San Pantalon) here reaches new heights of mouldering excess; what at first sight looks like green and white damask along the walls, curtains around the pulpit, and grandmotherly carpeting leading up to the high altar – is all really marble, carefully carved to resemble swags of fabric. Under the Jesuitical gold and cream stucco frosting, the eye is drawn to the unutterably grotesque *baldacchino* over the high altar, with fat twisted macaroni columns of *verde antico* and a huge dome and marble globe. The Manin family financed it as a tribute to themselves (something that, for a high altar, could happen only in Venice); many of them are buried underneath.

The only work of art that can top the interior decoration is one inherited from the previous church: Titian's restored *Martyrdom of St Lawrence* (1558, first altar on the left, lighting best around noon), one of his finest religious works, a revolutionary night scene of the Saint roasting on a Roman gridiron, lit and composed with a Tintoretto-esque touch. At the time of writing the church was covered in scaffolding, undergoing some sorely needed restoration work.

Oratorio dei Crociferi I3

Campo dei Gesuiti, t 041 270 2464; vaporetto Fondamenta Nuove. Open April–Oct Fri 10–12.30, Sat 3.30–7.30, Nov–March by appt only; adm €2.

On the left of the Gesuiti, this little Oratory was part of the Crociferi church, demolished by the Jesuits. Founded by Doge Ranier Zeno in the 13th century, the Oratory was devoted to charity, its chief moments illustrated in glowing colours by Palma Giovane between 1583 and 1591. The events in themselves lack the drama of some of Venice's other altruistic organizations, but the younger Palma, whose paintings elsewhere are often workmanlike

rehashes of Tintoretto, manages to convert them into charming images.

Fondamenta Nuove I2–L5

Vaporetto Fondamenta Nuove.

Unfortunately the construction of this 'new' quay in 1589 meant the demolition of a row of pleasure gardens, one of the most beautiful belonging to Titian, who lived and entertained his buddies Sansovino and Aretino and Europe's VIPs in this neighbourhood for half his lifetime (a plaque on the flats at Calle Larga dei Botteri 5179 marks the site of his small estate). He was living here when invited to Augsburg to paint Emperor Charles V, news that spread like wildfire through Venice and led to a siege of buyers outside his door, prepared to buy anything from the brush of the master – the 16th century saw the beginning of modern art marketing, as well as of modern artistic egos. But although the Venetians admired Titian, they thought he was untrustworthy for hanging around Aretino and mercenary because of his calculating interest in money.

Stripped of their gardens, the *fondamenta* has the dusty air of never having found its proper destiny; only one major palace was built, the austere **Palazzo Donà** (J3), begun in 1610 by the intellectual Doge Leonardo Donà, at the corner of the Rio dei Gesuti (No.5038). Just beyond are the landing stages for *vaporetti* sailing to San Michele's cemeteries (the floating citadel of cypresses that lies straight ahead, Murano just beyond) and Burano and the mainland port of Treporti.

If it's a clear winter's day, you should be able to see the outlines of the Dolomites, hovering like the mountains in a Chinese painting, sometimes made unnaturally sharp and clear by an optical illusion – a view that helped soothe Titian's longing for his native Cadore. On the *fondamenta* itself, there's little else to see, though if you continue east to the Rio dei Mendicanti, the border of Cannaregio, there's a *squero* (gondola building yard) that may be 300 years old.

Western Cannaregio

AROUND MADONNA DELL'ORTO 204
Madonna dell'Orto 204
Fondamenta Gasparo Contarini 205
Campo dei Mori 205
Campo dell'Abbazia 206
San Marziale 206
Fondamenta degli Ormesini 207
Sant'Alvise 207

SAN MARCUOLA AND AROUND 207
San Marcuola 207
The Casino 208
La Maddalena 208
Paolo Sarpi Statue 208

THE GHETTO 209
Campo Ghetto Nuovo 210
Museo Comunità Israelitica/Ebraica 210
Ghetto Vecchio 210

CANALE DI CANNAREGIO TO THE STATION 210
Canale di Cannaregio 210
San Giobbe 210
Palazzo Labia 212
San Geremia e Lucia 212
Lista di Spagna 213
Scalzi 213

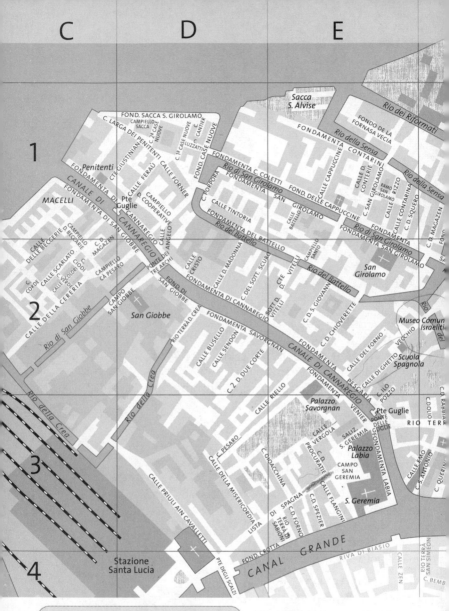

C   D   E

1

Sacca
S. Alvise

FOND. SACCA S. GIROLAMO
CAMPIELLO
SACCA
C. LARGA DEI PENITENTI
C. 24 CASE
NUOVE
C. CANTIERI
FONDO DE LA
FORNASA VECIA
Rio dei Riformati

Penitenti
CTE GIUSTINIAN PENITENTI
CALLE FERAÙ
CALLE FORNER
C. CASE NUOVE
LUZZATTIER CASE NUOVE
C. PORPORA
FONDAMENTA C. COLETTI
Rio di San Girolamo
FOND. DELLE CAPPUCCINE
RAMO SAN GIROLAMO
FONDAMENTA CONTARINI
Rio della Sensa

FONDAMENTA DI CANNAREGIO
CAMPIELLO D. COOPERATIVE
CALLE D. COOPERATIVE
FONDAMENTA SAN GIROLAMO
CALLE TINTORIA
CALLE D. CONTERIE
CALLE D. SQUERO
Rio della Sensa

CANALE DI CANNAREGIO
FONDAMENTA DI SAN GIOBBE
MACELLI
Pte
Guglie
CALLE FERAÙ
CAMPIELLO
CA' PESARO
CALLE TRE ARCHI
PONTE TRE ARCHI
CALLE D. MADONNA
Rio del Battello
FONDAMENTA DEL BATTELLO
CAMPIELLO
SANTO
San
Girolamo
C. D. MAGAZEN
FONDAMENTA SAN GIROLAMO

2

CALLE DELLE BECCERIE D. BECCERIE
CAMPIELLO D. BECCARIE
C. D. MAGAZEN
CALLE SCARLATO
CALLE CIODI
CALLE CERDOLOR
CAMPIELLO
CA' PESARO
CAMPO
SAN GIOBBE
San Giobbe
FOND. DI SAN GIOBBE
CALLE CRISTO
FONDAMENTA DI CANNAREGIO
Rio del Battello
CTE VITELLI
CTE VITELLI
C. DEL SOTT. SCUOLA
C. D. S. GIOVANNI
Rio del Battello
C. D. CHIOVERETTE
CALLE DEL FORNO
CALLE DEL GHETTO
Museo Comun
Israeliti
Scuola
Spagnola

CALLE DELLA CERERIA
C.
CORDE
Rio di San Giobbe
CAMPO
SAN GIOBBE
RIO TERRÀ D. CREA
CALLE BUSELLO
CALLE SENDON
FONDAMENTA SAVORGNAN
C. 2 D. DUE CORTE
CANALE DI CANNAREGIO
FONDAMENTA
PESCARIA
VECCHIO
POZZO
C. D. RABBIA
C. D. POZZO

3

Rio della Crea
Rio della Crea
CALLE PRIULI A IN CAVALLETTI
CALLE DELLA MISERICORDIA
CALLE RIELLO
CALLE PESARO
Palazzo
Savorgnan
CALLE
VENIER
Pte Guglie
PONTE
DELLE
GUGLIE
RIO TERRÀ
CALLE EMO
C.S ANTONIO
C. QUERINI

4

Stazione
Santa Lucia
PTE DEGLI SCALZI
CALLE DELLA MISERICORDIA
C. ODOACCHINA
DI SPAGNA
C. D. PROCURATIE
CALLE VERGOLA
SALIZ. S. GEREMIA
C. D. FORNO
C.D. SPEZIER
CAMPO
SAN
GEREMIA
Palazzo
Labia
FONDAMENTA LABIA
S. Geremia
CALLE FLANGINI
CALLE PROCURATIE
LISTA
FOND. GROTTA
C. D. FORNO
RIO TERRÀ SABBIONI
CANAL GRANDE
RIVA DI BIASIO
RIO TERRÀ SAN SIMEON
CALLE ZEN
C. BEMBO

---

1 Lunch

Anice Stellato, *Fondamenta della Sensa*,
t 041 720 744. **Open** *Tues–Sun 12.30–2 and
7.30–10*. **Moderate**. Friendly *bacaro; see p.276*.

2 Coffee

Caffè Costarica, *Rio Terrà San Leonardo*.
Open *Tues–Sun 7.30–1 and 3.30–8*.
Atmospheric coffee shop, *see p.278*.

3 Drinks

Paradiso Perduto, *Fond. della Misericordia*.
Popular late-night bar, *see p.283*.

Highlights

Medieval Venice: Madonna dell'Orto,
the city's most beautiful Gothic church,
p.204

Renaissance Venice: Pietro Lombardo's
sanctuary in San Giobbe, p.210

Baroque/Rococo Venice: The wonderful
Tiepolos in the ballroom of the Palazzo
Labia; try to get there for a concert, p.212

Indoor Venice: The Museo Comunità
Israelitica, and the synagogues, in the
Ghetto, p.210

Decadent Venice: Playing the roulette tables in the Casino, p.208

Pigeon Venice: The shabby razzle-dazzle along the Lista di Spagna, p.213

Western Cannaregio

West of the Canale di Misericordia is the Cannaregio of the cramped bittersweet confines of the Ghetto, and the tarnished tourist tinsel of the Lista di Spagna; like any part of Venice it has its share of good, or at least interesting, churches. But best of all is the Cannaregio in between, still wrapped in the silence that once enveloped the rest of Venice. Crumbling and piquant, it offers one of your best chances to see the city behind the glitz; here children play tag on the bridges on the broad *fondamenta*; shirts, sheets and some amazing examples of Italian underwear flutter gaily overhead; old men and cats soak up the sun in front of unnamed bars. The cavernous, narrow lanes of Venice spread into broad parallelograms in northern Cannaregio, of long straight lanes and canals, horizons and horizontals open to the setting sun.

AROUND MADONNA DELL'ORTO

Madonna dell'Orto H2

*Campo Madonna dell'Orto, **t** 041 719 933; **vaporetto** Madonna dell'Orto.* **Open** Mon–Sat 10–7, Sun 1–5; **adm** €2.

The most beautiful Gothic church in Venice, Madonna dell'Orto was built by Fra Tiberio of Parma in the mid-14th century and originally dedicated to the giant saint Christopher, the patron of the boatmen who used to sail from here to the north lagoon. Before long, though, Christopher was upstaged by the miracles performed by an equally large and rather ungainly statue of the *Madonna* by Giovanni de' Santi in a nearby vegetable garden (*orto*). Eventually the *Madonna* came out from the cabbages for a place inside the church, which was altered in the early 1400s and rededicated.

A 15th-century Istrian stone statue of *St Christopher Carrying Baby Jesus*, by Tuscan sculptor Nicolò di Giovanni, still holds pride of place over the doorway (a late work of Bartolomeo Bon); he keeps company with two rows of Apostles (by the Dalle Masegne brothers) in niches along the cornice. The distinctive onion dome on the campanile was added in the Renaissance.

The Madonna dell'Orto was Tintoretto's parish church, and he and his talented children, Domenico and Marietta, are buried within. There's a rather dubious tradition that he was forced to take refuge in its sanctuary after adding cuckold's horns to a portrait he had made of a doge. The furious doge, the story goes, would only forgive the painter on the condition that he fill the church with art, which Tintoretto did with his usual demonic speed in only a few months, to the doge's chagrin (even Aretino once suggested that he ought to change his *prestezza del fatto*, or 'quickness of the deed', into *pazienza del fare*, or the 'patience of the doing'. But if it was quick work, it was cheap; he only asked for his expenses). In the 1860s the church suffered a misguided restoration that destroyed its once-celebrated organ. Some of the damage was corrected in the 1930s, and much of the rest tidied up after the 1966 flood, an early effort of the Venice in Peril Fund.

The **interior** is fairly traditional Gothic, culminating in a vaulted apse. The first altar on the right glows with Cima da Conegliano's *St John the Baptist and Saints* (1493) standing in a ruined classical pavilion, with a brown city in the background, more Tuscan than Venetian in its austerity.

After the fourth altar is a pair of organ doors where Tintoretto painted his delightful *The Presentation of the Virgin at the Temple* (1552), a compositional cousin to Titian's in the Accademia, though very different in light and colouring, with the child Mary lit in a kind of holy spotlight.

Further up, the **Cappella di San Mauro** contains the enormous stone statue of the Madonna that gave the church its name.

Tintoretto lies under a simple slab in the chapel to the right of the choir, the site of two of his more mastadonic works: *The Making of the Golden Calf* (with a self-portrait, fourth from left, holding up the calf) and a *Last Judgement* that gave Ruskin's wife Effie such a bad case of heebie-jeebies that she refused to ever return to the church. Back in the apse are Tintoretto's less harrowing *Vision of the Cross to St Paul* and *Beheading of St Paul*, flanking an *Annunciation* by Palma Giovane; Tintoretto also painted four of the five *Virtues* in the vault (the painter of the centre one is unknown). In the left aisle, the Contarini chapel has two busts of family members by Vittoria (in the centre) and another Tintoretto, *St Agnes Raising Licinius*. At the end, in the elegant Cappella Valier (1526) is Giovanni Bellini's 1478 *Madonna* set in a sculpted tabernacle.

Campo Madonna dell'Orto H2

Local kids play Venetian court football in **Campo Madonna dell'Orto**; on the left they bounce the ball off the 16th-century **Scuola dei Mercanti** (G–H2, Merchants' Guild), and hope the ball doesn't fall into the canal or hit one of the jet-black outboard hearses usually moored by the bridge.

Fondamenta Gasparo Contarini H2

Extending to the east of Campo Madonna dell'Orto, Fondamenta Gasparo Contarini passes the **Palazzo Mastelli** (across the canal), whose magpie builders adorned the long wall of its façade with everything from a Roman altar (on the corner column with the ox heads), to a marble relief of an Eastern merchant with a camel carrying a heavy load – which lends the palace its more popular name, Palazzo Camello. Unlike its fellows in the neighbourhood, it faces north, and was the home of the three Mastelli brothers, 12th-century merchants from the Peloponnese.

Further down the *fondamenta* stands the 16th-century **Palazzo Contarini dal Zaffo**, a gloomy enough place, though the ghost legends are attached to the pleasure pavilion in its garden, the so-called **Casino degli Spiriti** (*see* box). The palace is now home to a charitable organization, and what the nuns do with the old casino is hard to tell.

The large basin here is the **Sacca della Misericordia** (drab or colourful, depending on

---

A Ghost Story

A traditional rendezvous for the odd tryst or noisy orgy, the **Casino degli Spiriti** is supposedly haunted by the screams and rattling chains of the damned souls of its old sinners. The most celebrated spirits belonged to a pair of lovers worthy of Boccaccio. The wife of a rich nobleman was having an affair with his best friend. The husband found out and raised the roof, and in grief and chagrin the best friend died. A few days later the sorrowing lady also determined to die, and asked to be brought to the Casino degli Spiriti; her last wish was that her wake be kept by only one of her serving maids. Yet as the little maid watched over the bier, in walked the 'ghost' of the lover, who picked up the 'corpse' and ordered the maid with her candle to lead them outside, whereupon the poor girl fainted in fright, and could recall nothing more.

---

which boats happen to be moored there), with a view over the funeral island of San Michele.

Campo dei Mori G–H2

Vaporetto Madonna dell'Orto.

This elongated residential square earned its name for its quaint **statues of three 'Moors'**, popularly believed to be the Mastelli brothers, Rioba, Sandi and Afani, residents of the 'Camel' palace. The brothers may have became 'Moors' because of their Peloponnesian homeland (the Morea), or from their trade with the East.

One of the brothers, in a turban and standing on a fragment of a Roman altar, is by himself on the Fondamenta dei Mori, at No.3399, decorating the façade of **Tintoretto's house** (H2); the painter lived here from 1574 until his death in 1594. In the early years he was plagued by slanders written by Aretino, who often came to Cannaregio to visit Titian. Tintoretto took as much as he could bear before he invited the writer in for a free portrait. Aretino came eagerly enough, then sat perfectly still as the painter measured his features with a loaded pistol before sending him off. The warning was heeded, and Aretino changed the poison in his pen to honey. A fourth 'Moor' in the corner of the square, with a metal nose, is Sior Antonio Rioba, once the source of much malicious fun (being sent to visit him was an initiation ritual for any greenhorn in Venice). He was also, like the statue of Pasquino in Rome, made to sign any satirical verse that was likely to get the author in trouble; denunciations could be left at his feet.

Besides the Moors, the *campo* has another indignant **plaque** for the 14 victims of an Austrian zeppelin attack in 1917.

Campo dell'Abbazia H3

Vaporetto Madonna dell'Orto.

If you take the Fondamenta dei Mori east from the Campo dei Mori, you'll come to the Ponte Muti, crossing a boatyard, or *squero*; then head straight along the Rio della Sensa, along the brick-paved Sottoportico dell'Abbazia to this slice of concentrated Cannaregio: open, uncluttered, a hodge-podge of styles, a shadowy portico, a wide and straight canal, all a bit down at heel.

In its day the **Misericordia** church (or Santa Maria di Valverde) was the parish of the six *scuole grandi*; its now deconsecrated church, founded in the 10th century, was rebuilt in the 13th, and given an inoffensive Baroque façade in 1651 by Clemente Moli, a follower of Bernini. It's the kind of bland façade that would help people forget the murder that took place here in the 18th century, when a jealous priest slipped a poet a poisoned Host after he caught him with his mistress.

At a right angle to the church is the Gothic **Scuola Vecchia della Misericordia**, built in 1308 with a pair of white rabbit-ear pinnacles and a curved crown roof (*at the time of writing it was covered in scaffolding*). Most of its ornate, canopied doorway by Bartolomeo Bon is in the Victoria and Albert Museum, although two angels and an inscription survive in the architrave. When the Confraternity moved to its new quarters, this building was given to the guild of silk weavers. If it's open (*no set hours*), you can see the old cloister between the church and Scuola; the whole complex is now used as a restoration centre.

A wooden bridge to Campo dell'Abbazia crosses over to the Fondamenta della Misericordia, address of the **Scuola Nuova della Misericordia**, a large building designed by Sansovino in 1534, its interior finished 50 years later, but the façade still lacking its costly marble sheathing. Its grand Renaissance salons are now home to an athletic association; not content with gobbling rebounds off the side of San Marziale (*see* below) the local sportsmen seem to be turning Sansovino's huge main hall into a basketball arena.

San Marziale H3

Campo San Marziale, off Fondamenta della Misericordia; vaporetto San Marcuola or Ca' d'Oro. Open Mon–Sat 4–6; adm free.

Although most of the changes imposed on this medieval church rebuilt in the 17th century have not been to the church's advantage (no other church in Venice has a basketball hoop fixed to it), it has held on to its ceiling frescoes by Sebastiano Ricci (1700–1705), early works by this gallant and colourful if not very demanding knight of the brush; in the centre the subject is the *Glory of St Martial*, too grimy to really appreciate, while at the sides are paintings referring to the miraculous icon of the Virgin carved from a tree trunk in the 15th century, which still occupies the second altar on the left.

Across the nave, there is a painting of *St Martial* by Tintoretto, of interest only as an example of botched restoration. The **chapel** around it is florid Baroque to match the ceiling; even better is the high altar, with a unique sculptural frame designed by an unknown berserker of the 18th century. In it all pretence of architecture and structure disappears, giving way to a free-form composition of angels, saints and clouds, floating around a giant golden globe and crown.

Fondamenta degli Ormesini F–G2

From San Marziale, continue east up the Fondamenta della Misericordia to the Fondamenta degli Ormesini ('of the dealers in ormesin', a delicate fabric made in the Persian city Ormuz), a long straight walk. Originally an outlying section of muddy swamps, this area was drained in the 11th and 12th centuries into three canals (Sensa, Misericordia and Madonna dell'Orto) laid out in a regular plan and making one of the most serene places in Venice to watch a sunset. Equally straight lanes and canals were cut to the north, opening up views of the lagoon.

Sant'Alvise G1

Fondamenta dei Riformati; ***vaporetto*** *Sant'Alvise.* ***Open*** *Mon–Sat 10–5, Sun 1–5;* ***adm*** *€2.*

This church, tucked away in the open outer reaches of northern Cannaregio, is a prime candidate for the title of 'loneliest church in Venice'. When this island was reclaimed in the 14th century, a doge's daughter named Antonia Vernier had a vision of St Louis of Toulouse and founded a monastery in his name (*Aloisius* in Latin, hence *Alvise* in Venetian). Its brick Gothic façade of 1388 is so severe it hurts: 'OW –!' says its peephole rose window and doorway. Behind it stands an equally severe little campanile; yet seen in the evening light Sant'Alvise takes on a rare beauty in its un-Venetian simplicity.

Nor is the **interior** any less stern: rearranged in the 17th century, it features an early version of a *barca*, or 'nuns' choir', hanging over the door, with wrought iron grilles over the windows to preserve the nuns' anonymity. Sant'Alvise's weightiest art is by Giambattista Tiepolo: *The Crown of Thorns* and *Flagellation* (both 1738–40) on the right wall, and the enormous, sceno-graphic *Road to Calvary* (1743) in the choir, a composition inspired by Tintoretto. The *trompe l'œil* ceiling, with a huge building rising up in crazy perspective, is a joint effort by two obscure 17th-century painters, Antonio Torri and Paolo Ricchi.

To the left of the entrance are eight charm-ingly naïve panels of Old Testament scenes in tempera that are known as the 'baby Carpaccios' thanks to the overheated brain of Ruskin, who considered them precocious works by the Renaissance master (Carpaccio would have been about eight when they were painted). More solid art scholars assign the paintings to Carpaccio's master, Lazzaro Bastiani, or more likely to his workshop.

Ruskin's favourite was the second panel, *Solomon and the Queen of Sheba* with its scene of the medieval *Golden Legend of the Holy Cross* – the bridge in the picture is made of a tree that St Michael gave to Seth to plant over the tomb of Adam, and the Queen of Sheba is warning Solomon not to cross it, for she has had a prophetic dream that it would some day bring about the end of the Jews. Solomon listens to her advice and goes on to bury the beam, but it is dug up and shaped into the Cross.

Another of the panels is *Joshua at the Walls of Jericho*, a ripping subject but one that painters rarely cared to tackle.

SAN MARCUOLA AND AROUND

San Marcuola F3

Campo San Marcuola; ***vaporetto*** *San Marcuola.* ***Open*** *Mon–Sat 8–12 and 5–7, Sun 8–1 and 4.30–8;* ***adm*** *free.*

With its unfinished corrugated grey façade, this church is one the Grand Canal's few sore thumbs. Although its name sounds like an affectionate diminutive of San Marco, it is actually Venetian for Santi Ermagora e Fortunato, two early martyrs, a remarkable transformation that even the Venetians themselves can't account for.

Rebel Priest Paolo Sarpi

Although Paolo Sarpi (d. 1623) was a Servite priest at the Convent of Santa Maria dei Servi (which stood near his statue until it was demolished in 1812), he has always been an 'honorary saint' for Protestants – while he was alive there was even speculation that Venice would join in the Reformation.

Sarpi, a close friend of Doge Leonardo Donà, was his chief advisor during the Great Interdict of 1606, arguing always for a strict separation of Church and State (Venice was in the doghouse with the pope for insisting on trying priests guilty of secular crimes in a secular court, and also for limiting the amount of money its religious houses could send to Rome). While the rest of Europe watched, Paul V excommunicated the whole Republic; but, with the attitude that St Mark was just as good as St Peter, Venice didn't budge – when one priest declared that the Holy Spirit had moved him to obey the Interdict, the Council of Ten's answer was that the Holy Spirit had moved them as well – to hang any priest who refused to say Mass. Thanks to the good offices of the French the Interdict was lifted, and although a face-saving gesture was made to Rome by handing over two convicted priests (not to the pope, but to the French), Venice conceded nothing, and kept right on taxing monasteries and trying priests in courts.

Paul V could not forgive Sarpi for forever defusing the chief weapon of the papal arsenal, and six months after lifting the Interdict he sent three hired assassins to do him in. They ambushed him where his statue now stands, plunging a dagger into his cheekbone. Sarpi could still make a pun: 'I recognize the *stylum* [style, and sharp instrument] of the Roman Curia,' he said.

After a miraculous recovery, Sarpi was given a pension by the Senate and he went on to live for a further 22 years, advising the Republic on spiritual matters and providing a living symbol of religious freedom and tolerance during the darkest days of Italy's Counter-Reformation.

The church was designed by Giorgio Massari in the 18th century and contains statues by Gianmaria Morleiter. Every Venetian church has its quirk: in San Marcuola it's two pulpits, facing each other across the nave as if set up for theological debate. A wildly rococo canopy hangs over the altar. To the right there's a copy of Tintoretto's *Washing of the Feet*.

The Casino F3

Palazzo Vendramin-Calergi, Canal Grande, t 041 529 7111, w www.casinovenezia.it; vaporetto San Marcuola. Open daily 11am–2.30am; over-18s only; adm €5.

Ponte Storto ('crooked bridge') leads from behind San Marcuola to the land entrance of the Palazzo Vendramin-Calergi, with a plaque recording the death here of Richard Wagner in 1883. This palace is now the year-round home of Venice's casino.

La Maddalena G3

Campo della Maddalena; vaporetto San Marcuola. Usually open for weddings only.

This peculiar small round church was built by neoclassical architect Tommaso Temanza in 1760, round and domed like the Pantheon. Temanza was primarily a scholar and apparently a dabbler in the same undercurrent of esoteric Masonry as George Washington, Mozart and lots of others, judging by the 'eye of God' symbol over the main door, the inscription over the door, and perhaps also the dedication to Mary Magdalen. The original art was probably just as provocative, but has all but disappeared from the church's hexagonal interior.

Paolo Sarpi Statue G3

Campo Santa Fosca; vaporetto San Marcuola/Ca' d'Oro.

From the Maddalena, turn right over Ponte Sant'Antonio, back into the bustling Strada Nova. Few in the thundering herd pause in front of the otherwise lacklustre church of

Santa Fosca (G3, straight ahead) to ponder the **statue of Fra Paolo Sarpi**, the only great intellectual Venice produced, a friend of Galileo, discoverer of the contraction of the iris, historian of the Council of Trent and one of the things every visitor would have sought out 50 years ago (*see* box).

THE GHETTO

In the bad old days two massive doors on Calle del Porton ('of the big door'), just on the south side of the Ponte degli Ormesini, would seal in the residents of the world's first **ghetto** (*see* box), where the houses loom

The Jews in Venice

One of Venice's Jewish historians, Elia Capsali, wrote: 'Having heard that the Germans were approaching Padua, like thorns in our eyes and prickles in our hearts, the majority of Jews hurried to escape to Venice. They took their money and came, for they feared for their very lives.' Capsali was writing in 1508 about the approach of Emperor Maximilian's troops, in the War of Cambrai. So many refugees swelled Venice's Jewish population that in 1516 the Senate decreed they should be isolated in one place, on an island known as the Ghetto Nuovo.

The word 'ghetto' derives from the foundry (*geto*) that occupied the island until 1390, when it was moved to the Arsenale; and the word came to be pronounced with a hard 'g' thanks to its first German residents. The name was quickly borrowed for similar segregated neighbourhoods all over Europe, perhaps because it's poignantly apt in Hebrew (where the root for 'cut off' sounds very similar). And cut off its residents were, from midnight to dawn, on an island surrounded by a moat-like canal, all its watergates locked and patrolled by a miniature Christian navy whose wages were levied from the Jews. And although there were no restrictions in the daytime, the Church insisted the Jews wear distinctive badges.

As bad as it was, the Republic seemed like a bed of roses compared to many states, and was one of the few places in Counter-Reformation Italy where Jews could live in peace; Venetian law specifically protected them and forbade preachers from inciting mobs against them – a common enough practice during the Counter-Reformation. Unfortunately, this treatment had little to do with any precocious concept of human rights: Jews in Venice were blackmailed for their security. Like most governments, Venice's exploited the Jews mercilessly, while their legal activities were limited to the rag trade, medicine and money-lending. Stalls were set up in the *campo*, known by the colours of their receipts, and some of the fittings of the red **Banco Rosso** still survive under the brick portico at No.2912.

But the Venetians were also receptive to the culture and learning in the Ghetto, and had plenty of empathy for the Jews, whose tradition-bound mercantile society, halfway between Western and Eastern cultures, was similar to their own. Its salons were among the most fashionable in the city; in autumn people would come to see it, white as snow with goose down plucked from the main ingredient of the season's religious feasts. And there was money left for each new wave of immigrants to build a sumptuous synagogue, locally known as *scuole*.

To cope with the influx of refugees, the Ghetto was expanded twice, in 1541 into the adjacent Ghetto Vecchio (the old foundry, around Campo delle Scuole) and in 1633, into the Ghetto Nuovissimo (Calle Farnese). Even so, to squeeze in a population that once numbered 5,000, the houses of the Ghetto are the tallest in Venice, some rising seven storeys, with cramped low ceilings, eerily presaging the ghetto tenements of centuries to come. When Napoleon threw open the gates in 1797, it is said the few impoverished residents who remained were too weak to leave (although they recharged quickly; 50 years after Napoleon, it was a Jew named Daniele Manin who led the revolt against Austria).

over the water like a wall. Today the Ghetto remains the centre of the Jewish community in Venice, even if its 500 members now live all over the city: a nursing home, nursery school, library, and kosher restaurant are to be found here.

Campo Ghetto Nuovo F2

Vaporetto Ponte Guglie/San Marcuola.

The *campo* is the evocative if melancholy and claustrophobic heart of the quarter. Compressed by water on all sides, some of the first 'tower blocks' ever built rise high here, plus the community museum, and seven **bas-reliefs** by Arbit Blatas in memory of 202 Holocaust victims.

Museo Comunità Israelitica/ Ebraica F2

Campo Ghetto Nuovo, t 041 715 359; vaporetto Ponte Guglie/San Marcuola. Open June–Sept Sun–Fri 10–7, Oct–May Sun–Fri 10–4.30, guided visits on the half-hour summer 10.30–5.30, winter 10.30–3.30, closed Sat; adm €3.

This museum opened in 1953 to display 17th- and 18th-century ritual objects – exotic *Rimmonim* (Torah finials) made in Turkey and Venice, old marriage contracts painted on parchment, prayer shawls, etc.

Upstairs you can visit the elegant **Scuola Grande Tedesca** (1528), the first one built in the Ghetto, by German Jews.

The optional tour also gets you into the synagogues in the Campiello delle Scuole: the lavish **Scuola Spagnola** (for the Spanish congregation, redesigned by Longhena) and the equally de luxe **Scuola Leventina** (1538, for Levantine Jews).

Ghetto Vecchio E2

From Campo Ghetto Nuovo, take the Ponte del Ghetto Vecchio (from the west side of the *campo*) and continue south straight through Campiello delle Scuole to reach the street marked simply Ghetto Vecchio.

You can recharge a slumping calorie count at No.1143, a traditional **Jewish baker's**. Above No.1131, an early 18th-century stone **plaque** warns converted Jews of punishments ranging from the lash to the gallows for returning to the Ghetto.

CANALE DI CANNAREGIO TO THE STATION

Canale di Cannaregio C1–E3

Just the other side of the the arch of the Ghetto's Campiello delle Scuola is the broad, sun-drenched *fondamenta* of one of Venice's main arteries, the Canale di Cannaregio, originally the mainland entrance to the city before the construction of the railway bridge to the south.

On the *fondamenta* is the former **French Embassy** (No.967) where Jean-Jacques Rousseau lived and worked as a secretary to the ambassador between 1743 and 1744. (Despite its setting in Venice, Rousseau manages to make this chapter the dullest in his *Confessions*, whining that he did all the ambassadorial work, although the truth was he was sacked after 10 months. His few sordid visits to the ladies were just as inept – and described down to the smallest painful detail). At the far northwest end of the canal you can see Andrea Tirali's **Ponte dei Tre Archi** (D2), the only bridge in Venice to boast more than a single arch.

San Giobbe D2

Campo San Giobbe; vaporetto Tre Archi. Open daily 10–12 and 4–6; adm free.

Job, the man who bore all, was canonized in the Eastern Church and in Venice for his hoped-for efficacy against the plague.

This church, founded by Doge Cristoforo 'Othello' Moro for the Franciscan Observants, dates back to the 1450s, but was remodelled soon after by Pietro Lombardo, who added its fine doorway, with statues in the lunette of *SS. Job and Francis*, and above, *Saints Louis of Toulouse, Anthony and Bernardino* (the patron saint of advertising, who preached here and is the co-dedicatee). Inside, over the second altar is a *Vision of Job* in the marble frame of Bellini's great *Madonna Enthroned*, unfortunately removed to the Accademia, for it depicts the Virgin seated in the sanctuary of this very church. The grandiose **Monument of the Ambassador Paulmy d'Arge** (d. 1651),

though cut in half in 1935, retains a pair of the ugliest, baldest cauliflower-eared lions in all Italy. In contrast with these shabby cats, the **sanctuary** is a sublime grey and white Renaissance vision by Pietro Lombardo, decorated with elegant carvings and the tomb slab of *Cristoforo Moro* (d. 1471) and his *Dogaressa*. The first chapel on the left was designed by Lombardo's Tuscan contemporaries for homesick silk workers from Lucca, with Della Robbia rondels.

A door on the right leads into the sacristy, passing by way of a *Nativity* (c. 1530), the only

Lion Fever

The Venetians were hardly the only people in the world to adopt the lion as their sign, although theirs is a winged lion with a book. This of course symbolizes St Mark, but no one really knows why. Some say Mark 'roared like a lion' when he preached, or that lion cubs open their eyes after three days, the same period as the Resurrection, or that the Christians endowed each of the four Evangelists with a key astronomical constellation. The inscription in the lion's book, *Pax tibi, Marce, Evangelista meus* are the words the angel used to greet Mark in his Venetian dream. But it's the sheer number of lions that makes Venice really stand apart: there are at least a couple of thousand in the city itself and perhaps twice as many in the lands once ruled by the Republic.

The bookish lion is first believed to have made its appearance on the standard of Doge Pietro Orseolo II, when he conquered Dalmatia in the year 1000. The oldest lion to survive dates from the 13th or early 14th century. It was embedded in the base of the campanile of Sant'Aponal (now removed to the Museo Correr store rooms), a disembodied owl-like creature, with staring eyes, pin curls and a kind of pie pan about his head, claws digging into a closed iron-bound book. But Venice, unlike other states, had no interest in standardizing their symbol, although there were two favoured poses: the standing lion (*en passant*), or the upper torso

(*sejent erect*), usually emerging from the sea, known in Venetian dialect as the *leone in molea*, 'lion in a soft shell' (because its wings are folded back like a pair of crab pincers). Each new member of the Venetian pride had to depend on the talent or attitude of the artist, and some, especially in the provinces, are among the funniest things in Italy: Chioggia still smarts over its puny 'Cat of St Mark'.

Venetian lions reached their peak in the Middle Ages and Renaissance, when they were as proud and brave as the Venetians themselves (see the regal Foscari lion on the Palazzo Ducale's Porta della Carta). In the Republic's death throes, in the 17th and 18th centuries, the lions responded by becoming twisted, clumsy and grotesque, reaching an incomparable nadir in the ghastly caricature of an animal in S. Giobbe. By the end of the Republic, a general lion revulsion set in, encouraged by Napoleon, who changed the inscription in the lion's book from '*Pax tibi, Marce*' to 'The Rights and Dignity of Man'. 'At last, he's turned the page,' quipped a gondolier. A general lion massacre took over a thousand victims in Venice itself; many lions you see today are reproductions from the 19th century.

Smaller felines have generally fared better, ever since Petrarch spent time in Venice in the company of a stuffed cat called the Laura II: there are moves afoot to declare the city officially 'the stray cat capital of the world'.

painting left in Venice by Gian Girolamo Savoldo, an artist who spent most of his career in the city, pioneering *tenebroso* night scenes that anticipate the Bassani and Caravaggio. The sacristy preserves a wooden ceiling of the 1500s, a portrait of Cristoforo Moro, and a triptych of the *Annunciation, St Michael and St Anthony* by Antonio Vivarini and Giovanni d'Alemagna.

Along Fondamenta di San Giobbe and Fondamenta Savorgnan

Back at the Canale di Cannaregio, a turn to the left on the **Fondamenta di San Giobbe** continues to the **Macelli Pubblici** (C1), or 'slaughterhouse', a site for which Le Corbusier designed a hospital in 1964 (though it was rejected by an architectural review board and never built, and even Le Corbusier agreed they were right).

Across the canal from the slaughterhouse is the locked-up **Ricovero Penitenti** (C1), a convent where Venice's prostitutes once came for a five-year reform course, far from the bright lights of the Ponte delle Tette, Venice's red light district in the 16th century.

Heading southeast along the Canale di Cannaregio, the **Fondamenta Savorgnan** approaches the vast 17th-century **Palazzo Savorgnan** (E2–3), Venetian headquarters of a Friulian dynasty of great wealth and impeccable service to the Republic, with a small, quiet public garden. South of this is the very busy **Ponte delle Guglie** (1580, named after the four obelisks, or 'needles' on its parapets).

Over the bridge, **Rio Terrà S. Leonardo** (E–F3) is often crowded with market stalls.

Palazzo Labia E3

Campo San Geremia, t 041 781 277; vaporetto Ponte Guglie/Ferrovia. Open by appointment only, Wed–Fri 3–4pm; adm free.

Phone as far in advance as possible to see the dazzling interior of the Palazzo Labia, with its ballroom of extraordinary ceiling frescoes by Giambattista Tiepolo. RAI, Italy's state radio and television, which now owns the building, uses the ballroom to record concerts once or twice a week; the tickets are free, but again you have to ring in advance to get one.

This *palazzo* (1750, with its main façade on the Canale di Cannaregio) has always had something about it that's sent its residents over the top (perhaps because it was designed in part by Alessandro Tremignon, the architect of San Moisè). It was built for a fabulously wealthy and slightly dotty Spanish family who paid their way into the Golden Book (*see* p.37) and then paid Giambattista Tiepolo to fresco their ballroom with *The Life of Cleopatra* (1745–50), obviously a family role model in extravagance. Along with Gerolamo Mengozzi-Colonna's fine *trompe l'œil* architectural frescoes, they are a sheer delight, sensuous and lavish in their illusionist perspectives.

The very thin line in Venice between the real and illusionary inspired one of the Labias, at a legendary party, to toss the family's gold dinner service out of the window into the canal, a memorable occasion for his pun: '*L'abbia o non l'abbia, sarò sempre Labia*' ('Have it or not, I'll always be a Labia'). Nets hidden in the canal, however, made sure that the Labias kept it.

San Geremia e Lucia E3

Campo San Geremia; vaporetto Ferrovia. Open daily 7.30–12 and 3–6.30; adm free.

Though not much of a looker from the outside, 18th-century San Geremia e Lucia with its hoary 11th-century campanile improves within. Unlike most churches, the focal point here is not the high altar but the **Cappella Santa Lucia**, where St Lucy's mummy was moved in 1863, after her church was demolished to make way for the train station. It was only one of Lucy's many moves, as the recent paintings around her altar attest. Lucia was a maiden of Syracuse, in Sicily, who was martyred in 304 or 310 during Diocletian's persecutions, and buried

Santa Lucia

The association of Lucia with lux or *luce* (light) went naturally with her appointed Feast Day, 13 December, close enough to the winter solstice to latch several old pagan holidays on to her name, especially in Scandinavian countries.

From light, Lucia became associated with eyesight, and she has been portrayed in much religious art holding a pair of eyes on a tray like two sunny-side-up eggs. And as many myths are believed to have been derived from misinterpreting drawings, so a whole legend has grown up that she was martyred by having her eyes pulled out, or that she pulled them out herself to keep from marrying a pagan cad.

in Syracuse's catacombs. In 1038 the Byzantines took her to Constantinople; in 1204 the Venetians, who simply couldn't pass up a good saint, brought her to Venice. She was stolen again from this church in 1981 by an unknown party, but miraculously was rediscovered on her feast day (*see* box).

Campo San Geremia E3

Campo San Geremia was once a favourite venue for bullfights; on one memorable occasion, the mighty patrician Girolamo Savorgnan joined the toreadors and neatly decapitated two sharp-horned bulls with single strokes of his sword to the admiring cheers of the Spanish ambassador.

Lista di Spagna D–E3

In its more dignified heyday, the tawdry and unabashedly touristy Lista di Spagna led to the Spanish Embassy (now the regional offices of the Veneto, opposite Hotel Continental) instead of to a soggy slice of pizza.

In 1618, when Venice was the European capital of intrigue and espionage, the Spanish Ambassador, the Marquis of Bedmar, masterminded a comic plot involving spies and a ruse to bring in a Spanish army, a few men at a time, in civilian clothes. Thanks to a

patriotic prostitute, the Ten sniffed out the plot, resulting in the arrest and execution of 300 people, including many down and out patricians whose services were for sale.

Scalzi D3–4

Fondamenta degli Scalzi, t 041 715 115; vaporetto Ferrovia. Open Mon–Sat 9.30–12 and 3.30–6, Sun 3.30–5.20; adm free.

Right before the Lista di Spagna ends at the station, eternally obscured by a wall of African pedlars, this church was built in the 1670s by Gerolamo Cavazza, a *nouveau riche* celebrating his recent admission to the Golden Book (*see* p.37).

The Carmelite Scalzi ('barefoot', though they wore sandals) were a prestigious religious order, and although Cavazza flamboyantly financed them (74,000 ducats, he boasted), the friars could have spent it better than on the petrified operetta stuck on Giuseppe Sardi's perilous façade – the figure of *Hope* has already fallen off and broken into bits. Letting Baldassare Longhena follow his fancy in the interior wasn't a good idea, either, resulting in gloomy, opulent, overpopulated Baroque encrustations from the dark side of his imagination (shadows he managed to keep out of his masterpiece, La Salute).

In 1915 an Austrian bomb addressed to the train station fell through the Scalzi's roof, turning the church's prize work, Giambattista Tiepolo's celebrated buoyant ceiling of *The Miracle of the House of Loreto*, into a million-piece jigsaw puzzle. The largest fragments have been preserved in the Accademia, which also has a study of the work – a Baroque version of Dorothy's twister-blown house in *The Wizard of Oz*. The house was the Virgin Mary's, which according to legend miraculously picked itself up and flew to Dalmatia, and later took off again to settle at Loreto, near Ancona, where you can see it today. In its place is Ettore Tito's modern *Council of Ephesus*.

The second chapel on the right bears a stone marked: '*Manini Cineres*', all that marks the passing of the last doge, the weak and melancholic Ludovico Manin (d. 1802). The chapel's ceiling, *Santa Teresa in Glory*, is one of Tiepolo's less exalted works. Altogether this is the spookiest church in Venice, with an ambience that can be matched only by the major basilicas of Rome and Naples. The filthy Baroque ensemble entertains a chorus of odd women whenever the church is open, chanting prayers in loud metallic voices, often with an audience of snoring railroad workers.

The Lagoon

ISLANDS IN THE SOUTH LAGOON 217
San Giorgio Maggiore 217
The Giudecca 220
The Lido 222
From the Lido to Chioggia 223
Smaller Islands in the South Lagoon 225

ISLANDS IN THE NORTH LAGOON 225
San Michele: the Island of the Dead 225
Murano 226
Burano 229
San Francesco del Deserto 230
Torcello 230
Cavallino and Jesolo 232
Smaller Islands in the North Lagoon 232

The Lagoon

Venice's Lagoon is one of its wonders, a desolate, often melancholy and strange, often beautiful and seductive 'landscape' with a hundred personalities. It is 56km long and averages about 8km across, adding up to some 448 sq km; half of it, the Laguna Morta ('Dead Lagoon'), where the tides never reach, consists of mud flats except in the spring, while the shallows of the Laguna Viva are always submerged, and cleansed by tides twice a day. To navigate this treacherous sea, the Venetians have developed highways of channels, marked by *bricole* – wooden posts topped by orange lamps – that keep their craft from running aground. When they were threatened, the Venetians only had to pull out the *bricole* to confound their enemies; and as such the Lagoon was always known as 'the sacred walls of the nation' (*see* box, below).

Once, the major islands (39 in all) were densely inhabited, each occupied by a town or at least a monastery. Now all but a few have been abandoned; many a tiny one, with its forlorn, vandalized shell of a building, has been overgrown with weeds. There are a wide range of plans to bring them back to life, though most seem to wither on the vine of Italian bureaucracy. If you think you have a good idea, take it up with the Revenue Office (Intendenza di Finanza).

The Creature from the Lagoon

The city of the Venetians, by divine providence founded in the waters and protected by their environment, is defended by a wall of water. Should anybody in any manner dare to infer damage to the public waters he shall be considered as an enemy of our country... This act will be enforced forever.

16th-century edict

Unfortunately Venice's 'forever' ended with the 20th century. A lagoon by its very nature wants to turn into land or sea, but Venice went to great lengths to artificially preserve its 'sacred wall' just as it was. Post-war Italian governments blithely ignored all the lessons from the past. New islands were made of landfill dredged up to deepen the shipping canals, upsetting the delicate balance of Lagoon life; outboards and vaporetti churn up the gook from the Lagoon and canal beds, and send corroding waves against Venice's buildings. Purists fight, without any notable success, to ban all motor boats, for these affect the tide, and increase the number both of acque alte and of unnaturally low tides (now infrequent) that embarrassingly expose Venice's under-things – and let air in where it was never supposed to go, accelerating the rot.

Then there are the ingredients in the water itself. The Lagoon is a messy stew of more than 50 years' worth of organic waste, phosphates, agricultural and industrial by-products and sediments – a lethal mixture that local ecologists warn will take a hundred years to purify, even if by some miracle pollution is stopped now. It's a sobering thought, especially when a handful of Venetians still remember when even the Grand Canal was clean enough to swim in.

And then, more recently, the Lagoon started sprouting the kind of blooms that break a girl's heart – algae, 'green pastures' of it, choking its fish and stinking out many tourists in the summer. No one was sure if the algae epidemic wasn't just part of a natural cycle; after all, there's an ancient church on one Lagoon island called San Giorgio in Alga (St George in Algae). Crops of algae are on record in the 1700s and 1800s and at the beginning of the 20th century, at times when the water temperatures were abnormally high because of warm weather.

But other statistics are harder to reconcile to climatic cycles: since 1932, 78 species of algae have disappeared from the Lagoon, while 24 new ones have blossomed, mostly microalgae thriving on the surplus of phosphates. These chemicals have been banned in the Lagoon communities – and just coincidentally, since then, algae counts have gone down.

ISLANDS IN THE SOUTH LAGOON

San Giorgio Maggiore J10–K11

Vaporetto no.82 (from San Zaccaria).

The islet of San Giorgio Maggiore, the most prominent landmark across the Bacino San Marco from the *piazza*, has been home to a Benedictine monastery since 982 AD.

A major restoration project in the 16th and 17th centuries endowed it with its present buildings by Palladio and Longhena, creating a major Late Renaissance and Baroque architectural showcase. All fell into decline in the 19th century, when Napoleon suppressed the monastery and confiscated its property and artworks; in compensation, with a keen sense of the absurd, he made the itty-bitty island a free port (you can still see its twin Lilliputian lighthouses designed by a professor of architecture for the occasion). And although only a handful of monks linger on to maintain the church, most of the complex has been beautifully restored as part of the **Giorgio Cini Foundation**, established by Count Vittorio Cini as a memorial to

Mordor-on-the-Lagoon

For a view of a slightly different Venice, stand on the Zattere, across the broad Giudecca Canal from Palladio's Church of the Redentore, and look towards the west. Over at the far end of the Giudecca you'll see such classics of Venetian architecture as the old Venezia Brewery, the Women's Prison and the massive brick Victorian hulk called the Mulino Stucky, a flour factory built in the 1890s by a German architect; it is abandoned now, one of the most awkward and unloved landmarks of the city. On the horizon, the steel and concrete skyline of Marghera closes the view down the canal: tall smokestacks in *parfait* stripes, glittering oil tanks and refinery towers, the perfect arch of a pipeline crossing high over a canal.

Shelley and Keats, one supposes, would faint in dismay. John Ruskin would alternately thunder and weep. And almost every writer since, it seems, has saved up some venom for Marghera and Mestre, malignant as Tolkien's Mordor and the blight on their city of dreams, a sleazy imposition by some itchy-palmed tycoon on the forlorn *Serenissima*. From some newspaper features, you might imagine that this little patch of dark satanic mills was magically apported here from the Ruhr valley by an evil sorcerer. Imposition, though, is not exactly the correct word, for almost all of these modern atrocities were the work of Venetians.

One of the chief conspirators was a certain Count Volpi di Misurata, a local promoter

who had many chances to do favours for his home town as Mussolini's finance minister in the 1920s (the Fascists were never unpopular in Venice). Mussolini himself was against the road causeway, but the Venetians managed to get it built anyhow. The authors of the wacky planning schemes that occasionally surface, intending to bring cars into the city or to fill in half the lagoon for new development, are inevitably Venetians, and since the war Venetians have voted with their feet and shown us their new idea of how a city should look – shapeless concrete Mestre.

Mestre and Marghera are Venice too, as much as Piazza San Marco and the Rialto. The real Venice is a hard-working port city of some 340,000 souls, with all of the common reflexes and attitudes of modern port cities; it just happens to have an extremely unusual *centro storico*, one that creates unique problems in transport and economic efficiency. In matters of aesthetics, it is as tenacious as a bulldog about preserving the past, and pathetically lazy about improving the present. Its people aren't at all interested in the *Death in Venice* complex of jaded foreigners: they want to earn an honest living. Look at that view of Marghera again: not so awful after all, perhaps – a colourful piece of abstract art, one of the more fantastical apparitions of the enchanted lagoon. It is beginning to look rather *Venetian*. And it will look even better when they get all the pollution control equipment installed.

---

his son, who died in a plane crash in 1949. The Foundation is dedicated to the arts and the sciences of the sea (it's the Foundation's ship you may see occupying most of the harbour of the old free port) and holds frequent conferences and special exhibits.

San Giorgio Maggiore J10

Isola di San Giorgio Maggiore; **vaporetto** *San Giorgio.* **Open** *daily 9.30–12.30 and 2.30–6.30;* **adm** *free to church, €3 to campanile.*

Palladio's church, like St Mark's Campanile, is such an integral part of Venice that many

visitors, having seen it painted on a hundred pizza parlour walls, look at it without really seeing it. Its importance in the history of architecture is in Palladio's solution to the Renaissance problem of sticking a classical temple façade on a church with naves and side chapels. The dissenting opinion, as usual most thunderously expressed by Ruskin, is that the problem was ridiculous to begin with and the result couldn't be 'more childish in conception, more servile in plagiarism', etc. But even if, like Ruskin, you find the façade, a white mask of recycled classicism stuck on good red brick, ridiculous, it's hard to deny that its colour and clean lines are effective where they are, hanging between the water and sky, bathed by a diaphanous, ever-changing light as magical as the variations in Monet's series on the cathedral of Rouen.

The **interior** is equally white and clear of cluttering detail, but as theatrical as the façade in its play of light and shadow. To compensate for the exceptional length of the nave and aisle, Palladio subtly raised the height of the floor near the high altar. On the entrance wall is the **Tomb of Doge Leonardo Donà** (d. 1612), the great humanist and friend of Galileo and Sarpi, who calmly snapped his fingers at the Great Interdict of 1606. Above the first altar on the right, Jacopo Bassano's dark *Adoration of the Shepherds* is illuminated entirely (and rather alarmingly) by the Child; the 15th-century wooden *Crucifix* on the next altar is equally unnerving in its vivid agony. The painting over the third altar, with its striking diagonals, is from the workshop of Tintoretto. The **high altar**, black in contrast with the whiteness, is topped by a statue of *Christ* with a triangular halo standing on a globe. On either side of the chancel hang the two masterpieces of Tintoretto's old age, *The Fall of Manna* and an extraordinary and dynamic *Last Supper* (1594).

In the choir behind the altar, *Scenes from the Life of St Benedict* (1590s) are told with Counter-Reformation fervour in the carvings on the wooden stalls and lectern. On the balustrade are two bronze saints, *George and Stephen*, by Nicolò Roccatagliata (1593); the latter's body was brought to this church from Constantinople in 1100, and on Christmas Eve all Venice would sail over in fairy-lit boats to pay homage to his relics. From the choir a door on the right leads into a corridor containing the **Monument to Doge Domenico Michiel** (d. 1130), proudly described as the 'Terror of the Greeks' and the 'Lament of Hungary'; at the end is the **Cappella dei Morti**, or 'Chapel of the Dead', containing Tintoretto's last painting, rather appropriately a *Deposition*, completed by his son Domenico. The photograph here is of

Carpaccio's *St George Slaying the Dragon* – a later variation on the canvas in San Giorgio degli Schiavoni, more autumnal in tone, though the dragon's appetite, judging from the leftovers, is as fierce as ever. The original is housed in a locked room where the Conclave of 1799–1800 (on the run from Napoleon) met to elect Pius VII.

The Campanile

Left of the choir you'll find the lift up to San Giorgio's campanile. Although its forerunner collapsed in 1791, as all Venice's belltowers seem cursed to do sooner or later, the replacement offers a view rivalled only by the one from St Mark's, and includes a bird's-eye view into the cloisters of the monastery.

Monastery/Fondazione Giorgio Cini J10

Isola di San Giorgio Maggiore, t 041 528 9900; vaporetto San Giorgio. Open Mon–Fri by appointment only; adm free.

Always the most important of several Benedictine houses in the Lagoon, San Giorgio was noted for its scholarship, thanks to Cosimo de' Medici, who in 1433 spent his brief exile from Florence here in the company of his favourite architect, Michelozzo. The two busied themselves building and endowing the monastery's first library, later demolished in the 16th-century rebuilding plan. The first cloister, or **Cloister of the Cypresses**, was designed by Palladio and, as has been noted, looks more like a palace courtyard than a religious cloister. The **Library**, by Longhena, with elegant 17th-century wood shelving by Francesco Pauc, separates it from the second, or **Cloister of the Laurels**, by Andrea Buora. Adjacent to the latter is Palladio's first work for the Monastery, the magnificent **Refectory** (1559–63, now a conference hall); it was from here that Napoleon pinched Veronese's *Marriage at Cana*, now in the Louvre. Don't miss the **Grand Staircase** (1643) that Longhena built off Palladio's cloister, a theatrical masterpiece in a limited space that was very avant-garde in its day, and inspired many a northern Italian architect.

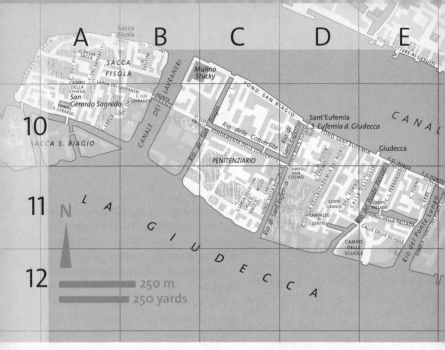

The Giudecca A9–I12

Vaporetto no.82.

The beautiful painting of Venice in the Bodleian Library's *Codex of Marco Polo* shows a Lagoon full of swans and the Giudecca like a rocky desert, populated only by lions. No one is even sure if this long, tilde-shaped series of suburban islets was named after Venice's Jews, forced to live here before being removed to the Ghetto, or for its more rumbustious nobles, exiled here in the 9th century, far from the action on the Rialto. For many centuries it was a little garden oasis, until the 1800s, when it became a little Industrial Revolution oasis. Although many of its factories are now abandoned, it is still famously the home of Fortuny fabrics. A few trendy touches have accompanied the **Cipriani Hotel** (I11), Venice's most glamorous, and property prices on the main *fondamenta* are going up as speculators capitalize on the fabulous view. The island is also regaining a little of its old independence with its own new bank and small grocery store. For the most part, the Giudecca is still a place where the Venetians go about their daily business with a little more room than the centre affords; some even have flower gardens, an extraordinary luxury in Venice.

Calle di Michelangelo (H11) is the only street that crosses the width of the Giudecca; from its far end you can see the Lido. To the west down the picturesque **Calle della Croce** (G11) lies the 'Garden of Eden' (named after the Englishman who planted it), but there's no public access.

Le Zitelle I11

Giudecca; vaporetto Zitelle. Open Sun am for Mass only; adm free.

At the eastern end of the island, near the Cipriani, is the church of Le Zitelle ('the old maids', 1582), built to Palladio's design after his death. The old maids in question lived in a benevolent hostel for the poor (on either side of the church) and helped support themselves by making Venice's most rarefied, delicate lace, *punto in aria*.

Inside, the Zitelle is built on a square plan with rounded corners for better acoustics; the girls from La Pietà (*see* p.144) used to perform here. The neo-Venetian Gothic house with the large arched windows, which you can't help but notice to the right of the Zitelle, was built in 1910 as a studio by a painter named Mario de Maria. Another artist named Michelangelo spent a few months in a nearby villa, sulking during his exile from Medici-ruled Florence in 1529.

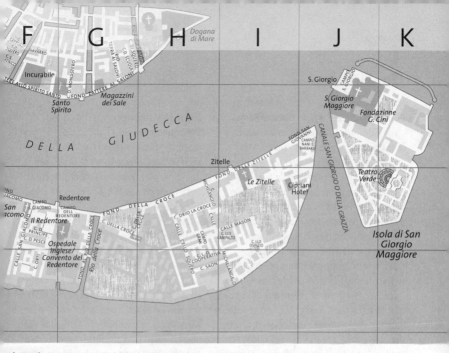

Il Redentore G11

Giudecca, **t** *041 523 1415;* ***vaporetto*** *Redentore.*
Open *Mon–Sat 10–5, Sun 1–5;* ***adm*** *€2.*

A short walk down the *fondamenta* stands
the Giudecca's chief attraction, the church of
the Redentore, built in thanksgiving after the
end of the savage plague of 1575–6 that
killed 46,000 Venetians. Palladio was chosen
to design a votive church by the doge and
Signoria, who vowed to pay an annual
pilgrimage on the third Sunday in July for the
Festa del Redentore (see p.301). Of all
Palladio's churches, the Redentore, consecrated in 1592, is the most successful and
harmonious, the simple geometric triangles
and rectangles of its façade composed in
fine-tuned proportions; like Palladio's
Venetian villas it is set atop a wide flight of
stairs. The **interior**, at first glance a simple
rectangular nave leading back to an apse,
actually opens up into curves on three sides
crowned by a beautiful dome, the whole
effect 'like a bubble structure softly blown
from a tube', as Michael Levey put it. This is
where the Signoria gathered for the service.
Unfortunately it's all become a bit dingy, and
the dome area is apt to be roped off. On
request, the sacristan will open the sacristy,
where Alvise Vivarini's *Madonna with Child*

holds pride of place among dusty paintings
and some wax effigies from the 1700s.

Sant'Eufemia D10

Giudecca; ***vaporetto*** *Sant'Eufemia.* ***Open*** *daily
9–12 and 6–7;* ***adm*** *free.*

The last church on the Giudecca is also the
oldest, founded in the 9th century on a basilican plan like Torcello's, and rebuilt in the
same form in the 11th century. Like all the
churches facing Venice, it has a classically
inspired façade, Doric this time, pasted on in
the 1500s, while inside some of its Veneto-
Byzantine capitals keep company with rococo
glitz and plush fittings added 700 years later.
The first chapel on the right contains the
church's one notable painting, the 1480 *San
Rocco and the Angel* by Bartolomeo Vivarini.

Western Giudecca

Weedy, seedy **Campo San Cosmo** (D11), just
inland from Sant'Eufemia, is one of the most
remote corners in Venice, and the last square
to keep its 19th-century earth paving. The
Mulino Stucky (B–C9) is a massive neo-
Gothic abandoned flour mill. There isn't
much use continuing west of the Mulino
Stucky to **Sacca Fisola** (A9–B10), a landfill
island covered with modern flats, unless you
fancy a swim at the municipal pool.

The Lido Off maps

Vaporetto nos.1, 6, 12, 14 (to San Nicolò), 51, 52, 61, 62; bus A, B and 11 from Piazzale Roma.

The Lido – *the* Lido that gives its name to countless bathing establishments, bars, arcades and cinemas all over the world – is one of the long spits of land, or *lidi*, that form the protective outer barrier of the Lagoon. For most of its history it was a wild sandy place, a place to go riding, as Byron did daily to cure his urban claustrophobia, and a place to store the French Crusaders in 1202.

In the 18th century, the only people who swam off the Lido were courtesans, whose lascivious beach parties were one of Venice's tourist attractions. In 1857, the first reputable bathing establishment was opened, and by the early-20th-century seaside holidays on the Lido were the rage. On its 12km of beach, the world's poets, potentates and plutocrats spent the halcyon days before the First World War in palatial hotels and villas, making the Lido the pinnacle of Belle Epoque fashion, so

brilliantly evoked in Thomas Mann's novel and Visconti's film version of *Death in Venice*. And even though families with their trunks and maids no longer descend on the Lido for the entire summer, it's still a popular enough place, the playground of the Venetians and their visitors, where they can drive their cars, go riding, play tennis or golf, or parachute out of aeroplanes. It is also expensive and overcrowded.

The free beach, the **Spiaggia Comunale**, is on the north part of the island, a 15min walk from the *vaporetto* stop at San Nicolò (go down the Gran Viale and turn left on the Lungomare d'Annunzio), where you can hire a changing hut and frolic in the fine sand and not-so-fine sea. If, upon landing at the San Nicolò stop, you walk north instead of east, you will soon pass the little church of **San Nicolò**, where the doge, in his role as bridegroom of the sea, would meet the patriarch for some mumbo-jumbo over the fake relics of Santa Claus, or St Nicholas of Myra (*see* box). Though it was founded in 1044, there's

The Invasion of the Body Snatchers

Long before sci-fi there were the Venetians, whose ghoulish mania for stealing the corpses of saints is one of the odder perversities that criss-cross their history. Of course they had nothing to do with the origins of the cult of relics: credit for that goes mostly to Pope Gregory the Great in the 6th century, who for the glory of the Roman Catholic Church shamelessly exploited the superstitions of his age by putting the papal seal of respectability on the cult of relics, miracles and saints. Praying to or, better yet, owning a bit of a saint was like having a hot-line to him or her in Heaven. For centuries mouldering bones and withered cadavers (some kept 'uncorrupted' with arsenic and wax) were the greatest status symbol a city could hope for, and competition for the ones deemed most influential was intense. A prime candidate for sainthood, like Catherine of Siena, would scarcely breathe her last before the relic-mongers started

pulling apart her anatomy (Venice, a bit slow off the mark that time, only managed to come away with a foot).

But on the whole the Venetians were without parallel in this Hallowe'en treasure hunt; no other people went about it with so much freebooting enthusiasm or so much encouragement from the State. The reason isn't hard to seek: as a new, self-made city Venice needed relics to gain the respect of and outdo its rivals. It also needed all the ju-ju it could muster against the plague.

By 1519, the *Serenissima* had snatched 55 intact saintly bodies and hundreds of smaller relics: a veritable *cordon sanitaire* of saints, as H.V. Morton called it, including some of Heaven's biggest celebrities: Saints Lucy, Zacharias, Helen, Isidore, John the Almsgiver, Donato and the proto-martyr Stephen, this last brought from Byzantium in 1105 and carried in state on the shoulder of the doge himself. The most celebrated and valuable haul of all, though, was the first: the theft from Alexandria in 828 of the relics of nothing very compelling about it, if there ever was; if the body snatchers had grabbed the real bones it would have been far more grand. But near here, looking north towards the **Porto di Lido** (the most important of the three *porti*, or sea entrances to the Lagoon, where the doge tossed his gold ring to the waves) is the mighty octagonal **Fortezza di Sant'Andrea** on the island of Le Vignole, built in 1543 by Venice's fortifications genius Sammicheli. In times of danger, a chain was extended from the fort across the channel. The Lido was also the site of Venice's first **Jewish cemetery**, founded in 1386. From the San Nicolò stop, follow Via Cipro. This passes a small **Catholic cemetery**, where Protestant headstones from a graveyard, now under the airport runway, have been deposited.

Buses from the *vaporetto* stop will take you down Lungomare Marconi to the centre of Lido swish. *Death in Venice* was set and filmed in the **Grand Hotel des Bains**, just north of the **Palazzo del Cinema**, where Venice hosts its Film Festival (*see* p.301).

From the Lido to Chioggia Off maps

***Buses/ferries** (line 11) from the Lido's **vaporetto** landing run all the way south to Chioggia, following the line between the sea and Lagoon. Schedules change, but the bus usually leaves once an hour; count on half a day to get to Chioggia, walk around (and perhaps have lunch) and return to Venice. You can return to Venice by the same route or take the dismal shorter **bus** ride to Piazzale Roma.*

This is a fine excursion when you need a rest for aching feet or a brain too saturated by art and churches.

After the Lido, the bus passes through **Malamocco**, a tranquil fishing village named after the first capital of the Lagoon townships, a nearby islet that lost its status after Pepin and the Franks nabbed it in 810. The capital moved to the Rialto, leaving the original Malamocco to sink poetically into the sea during a mighty storm in 1106.

St Mark, the Apostle of the Italians, a caper plotted down to the last detail. When the Apostle was lifted from his tomb, it is said, such a sweet smell spread over Alexandria that everyone knew 'Mark was stirring' and rushed to see his tomb, but the Venetians fooled them with a substitute body. They got their prize past Egyptian customs – as depicted on the mosaics of St Mark's – by hiding it in a barrel of pickled pork.

Nabbing the remains of S. Roch (San Rocco), one of the key 'plague saints', was another coup. Before becoming a pile of desirable relics, Roch was a young nobleman of Montpellier who gave his fortune away to the poor, then made a pilgrimage to Rome. City after city he passed through was stricken by plague. He rendered what assistance he could to the sufferers he found, until on his way back home he himself was stricken with a horrid ulcer on his thigh. He retreated to a cave so that no one else had to hear his groans, while his faithful dog brought him food and licked his wound.

Roch recovered but was so changed by his sufferings that when he returned home, claiming to be Roch, he was arrested as a spy and thrown in prison. After languishing for five years he died. His gaolers found his cell flooded with light, and there was a note saying that he would help anyone stricken with plague who called upon his name. Some Venetians disguised as pilgrims stole his body from Montpellier in 1485, before he was even canonized.

There was even a sham heist: the robbery in 1087 of St Nicholas from Myra, in Anatolia. Word of Venice's intention to steal the relics had leaked to rival Bari, whose merchants beat the Venetians to the precious body (for Nicholas, better known in the West as Santa Claus, was the patron saint of sailors). But the Venetians proved to be very poor losers. Instead of admitting defeat, they contrived a fake body and built a church to St Nick on the Lido, for centuries pretending in the face of all fact that it sheltered the real McCoy.

Next is the small resort of **Alberoni**, home of the Lido Golf Course and the ferry to cross over the Porto di Malamocca for the island of **Pellestrina**, an island reef even thinner than the Lido. It has two sleepy villages, **San Pietro in Volta** and **Pellestrina**, where the *murazzi*, or sea walls, begin, the last great public works project of the Republic's *Magistrato alle Acque*. Built in response to increased flooding in the 18th century, the 4km-long *murazzi* are constructed of huge white Istrian blocks and built, as their plaque proudly states: '*Ausu Romano – Aere Veneto*' ('With Roman audacity and Venetian money'). From 1782 until 4 November 1966 they succeeded in holding back the flood.

Chioggia Off maps

Chioggia, the dusty, southernmost town on the Lagoon, is one of the most important fishing ports on the Adriatic, a kind of working-class Venice where the canals and streets are arrow-straight; where the sails of the fishing fleet are painted with brightly coloured pictures and symbols. The morning **fish market** (*open Tues–Sun 7–12*) is one of the wonders of Italy. The Chioggians have a not entirely undeserved reputation for grumpiness, a temperament that is hardly improved when the uppity Venetians call their little lion up on its column in the **Piazzetta Vigo** (where the ferry deposits you) the 'Cat of St Mark'. Goldoni was amused enough by it all to make the town the

---

Abandoned and Hospital Islands

The small islet of **La Grazia**, near San Servolo, in the 13th century a stopover for pilgrims travelling to the East, is now a hospital for infectious diseases. To the south, **San Clemente**, long a monastery, has another hospital, for chronic mental diseases.

Further south is the **Lazzaretto Vecchio**, dedicated to St Mary Nazaretum (Nazareth), a 13th-century asylum for poor and sick pilgrims. In 1423 it became Europe's first public hospital for contagious diseases, its principal task to isolate plague victims. In time 'Nazaretum' was corrupted to 'Lazzaretto' – the name given to all such hospitals and quarantine islands in Europe. In the 20th century the island became a military garrison, and now the huts are used as a home for stray dogs.

Among the islands currently in a state of limbo are **Sant'Angelo delle Polveri**, first a women's convent and then a gunpowder factory that blew up in 1689 when struck by lightning; its last residents, the military, abandoned it in 1946. Then there's **Sacca Sessola**, an artificial island made of material dredged to make a commercial port for Venice in 1870. It was a tuberculosis hospital until 1980. Between Sacca Sessola and San Giorgio Maggiore flow the deep currents of a canal, making it the ideal place to execute death sentences by drowning, especially discreet ones ordered by the Ten; hence its name, Orfano Canal, or 'orphans' canal'.

Santo Spirito, a monastery since the 12th century, was given a major boost in the 16th century when Sansovino designed its church and Titian punted out to paint some of its ceiling frescoes. The Order was suppressed in 1656, and in 1965 the city council purchased it; badly vandalized, it waits, 'in a dramatic condition of decay' with only a few flakes of colour left from Titian's brush.

Further south lies the island of **Poveglia** (a corruption of *popilia*, or poplars), which once boasted a thriving salt and wine economy. From the 9th century, it was inhabited by retired servants of the doge, who had their own government, run by a ducal chamberlain; according to legend, the residents of Poveglia led the fight against Pepin when he tried to approach the Rialto. In the War of Chioggia it wasn't so lucky, and was converted to a fortress, suffering such damage that it never regained its population.

One last little island, **San Giorgio in Alga** ('St George in Algae'), was a monastery until Napoleon; it suffered further indignities under the Austrians, and has been abandoned ever since.

setting of one of his comedies, *Le Baruffe Chiozzotte*. Almost nothing remains of medieval Chioggia, thanks to the blockade and siege of Genoa's fleet in the 1380 War of Chioggia. But if you take the first bridge left from the port and continue straight, you will reach the church of **San Domenico**, which boasts Carpaccio's last painting, *St Paul*. The town's other churches are strung out along the main street, the Corso del Popolo – the fish market is just beyond a large 14th-century grain warehouse, the **Granaio**, with a relief of the *Madonna* on the façade by Sansovino. Further up the Corso, past a couple of low-key churches, is the **Duomo**, or cathedral, built by Longhena after the 14th-century orginal, except for the campanile, burned in 1623. In the chapel to the left of the altar are some murky 18th-century paintings of martyrdoms, one attributed to Tiepolo.

And when you've had your fill of fish and the locals, you can stroll along the long bridge (or catch the bus at the Duomo) for a swim among the vivacious Italian families at Chioggia's Lido, **Sottomarina**.

Smaller Islands in the South Lagoon Off maps

San Lazzaro degli Armeni
Vaporetto no.20 from San Zaccaria at 3.10pm. Guided tour begins daily at 3.25; adm €6.

One of the smaller islands just west of the Lido, with its landmark onion-domed campanile, this was Venice's leper colony in the Middle Ages, and was long deserted when in 1715 it was given to the Armenian noble and monk, Manug di Pietro, expelled from the Morea by the Turks. The Armenian colony in Venice already dated back to the 13th century, and their presence is maintained by these islanders, the Mechitarist Fathers of the Armenian Catholic Church; San Lazzaro is one of the major centres of Armenian culture. Its monks are noted linguists and its famous polyglot press is able to print in 32 languages – one of the last presses to remain in a city celebrated for its publishing. It was the only island monastery

to survive Napoleon – apparently thanks to an Armenian in the French bureaucracy.

The fathers will take you on a guided tour of San Lazzaro and its amazing library, with books dating back to the 5th century (the Armenians, after all, were the first nation to convert to Christianity, around the year 300). Elsewhere are oddities such as a statue of Napoleon's son, the King of Rome, and a room of Byron memorabilia (Byron spent a winter visiting the fathers). The fathers offer inexpensive prints of Venice for sale; otherwise, they would appreciate a donation.

San Servolo
t 041 526 8546, w www.centroeuropeomestieri.com; vaporetto no.20 from San Zaccaria.

Another islet just west of the Lido, San Servolo was originally a Benedictine monastery, and from 1725–1978, an insane asylum. It is now home to a centre for ancient crafts, the **Centro Europeo di Venezia per i Mestieri della Conservazione del Patrimonio Architettonico**, which runs two-week foundation courses open to anyone and three-month courses open to artisans and architects working with stone, wood, plaster, fresco and metals.

ISLANDS IN THE NORTH LAGOON

San Michele: the Island of the Dead L1–M3

Vaporetti nos.41 or 42 from San Zaccaria or Fondamenta Nuove.

All Venetians eventually take that last gondola ride to San Michele, Venice's walled cemetery island, where the massive cypresses shoot up like the pinnacles of a secret evergreen metropolis. The first church was built on the island in the 10th century, and from 1212 to 1810 it belonged to a Camaldolesian monastery that produced many scholars, most notably the cosmographer Fra Mauro (d. 1459), *see* box, p.226.

Fra Mauro

Fra Mauro was of such international renown as a cosmographer that King Alfonso V of Portugal commissioned a world map. All of his works have been lost, sadly, save his celebrated map in the Biblioteca Nazionale Marciana – the most accurate in showing the dimensions of the world of 1459. When Fra Mauro presented this map to a senator, the senator was enraged to find that the city was so small. Mauro tried to explain: compared to the vast extent of the world, Venice was indeed quite tiny. The senator listened to his reasoning, then ordered him as a patriotic son of the Republic: '*Strenze el mondo, e fé Venezia più grande!*' ('Make the world smaller and Venice bigger!').

San Michele L1

*Isola di San Michele; **vaporetto** San Michele. **Open** daily 7.30–12 and 3–4; **adm** free.*

Next to San Michele's *vaporetto* stop is Mauro Codussi's first work in Venice, the church of San Michele (1469), revolutionary not only in its style (an adaptation of the local Gothic tri-lobed church) but in its use of white Istrian stone in its façade, which soon became the rage in Venice. (If the front door isn't open, go under the gateway to the right, under the carving of *St George and the Dragon*, and cross the pretty cloister to the church's second entrance.) Another famous Venetian friar, Fra Paolo Sarpi (d. 1623, *see* p.208), is buried under the lozenge by the front door; his remains were relocated here when his monastery San Servolo was demolished in 1828. San Michele's interior, with its muddly proportions, lacks the conviction of the façade, and is shown up by the domed, hexagonal **Cappella Emiliana** off to the left of the nave, a pale marbled Renaissance gem, designed in 1530 by Guglielmo dei Grigi.

The Cemetery L2

*Isola di San Michele; **vaporetto** San Michele. **Open** April–Sept daily 7.30–6, Oct–March daily 7.30–4; **adm** free.*

The cemetery is joined from the cloister of the church. As in any Italian *campo santo*, the deceased, depending on the station they attained in life, are installed in detached houses, villas, or council flats; here though, after 10 years, the lease is up (unless you pay extra) and the bones are shipped out to an ossuary to make room for a new tenant. Signs indicate the way to the '*Acattolica*' section to the left of the first hemicycle, where Time and Neglect have staged a trial run for the Judgement Day. But here lie the cemetery's foreign celebrities: **Serge Diaghilev** (1872–1929), whose burial was marked by a devotee leaping into the open tomb, and Diaghilev's favourite composer, **Igor Stravinsky** (1882–1971), who died in New York but requested to be buried here, in the Russian Orthodox section; the Venetians were so pleased that they gave him a doge-like funeral in Santi Giovanni e Paolo. In the Protestant section you can find the quiet, rather neglected tombs of two writers who were certainly cranky and unpleasant enough in life, Baron Corvo and Ezra Pound. To get to these you must pass through a section of children's tombs. Venice traditionally had one of the highest birthrates in Italy, perhaps because the mortality rate historically has been high; when a child died, parents comforted themselves with the thought that they would serve as advocates for the family in Heaven.

Murano Off maps

*Vaporetto nos.41 or 42 from S. Zaccaria or Fond. Nuove, 12, 13 or 14 from Fond. Nuove; or the DM, a fast route from Tronchetto, Piazzale Roma and Ferrovia. Murano has six stops including **Colonna, Faro** and **Museo**.*

In 1291 all of Venice's glass furnaces were moved to the ancient island city of Murano, the better to control the risk of fire and industrial espionage. For Venice made the finest glass in Europe – transparent crystal, spectacles, blown-glass mirrors and coloured glass and beads – and it held on to its secrets until the early 17th century. To meet the demand for *cristallo di Venezia* the kilns burned day and night, and the glass workers laboured in shifts in the searing heat, except in August and September, when they relaxed at bullfights and 'other rowdy sports'.

But the glassmakers had other compensations. Even more than the *arsenalotti* they were treated with kid gloves, as the aristocrats of Venetian artisans, ennobled, they claimed, by the French King Henri III on his way from Poland to France. Murano was permitted to govern itself as a kind of autonomous republic of glass, with a population of 30,000, minting its own coins, policing itself, even developing its own 'Golden Book', whose enlistees built solid palaces along Murano's own Grand Canal. Patricians and humanist scholars from Venice retreated here to summer villas with luxuriant summer gardens, where they strolled under the trees like the ancient Greeks discussing art and philosophy in their academies. In 1376 a law was passed declaring that any male child of a patrician and a glassblower's daughter could sit in the *Maggior Consiglio*; other laws were passed to discourage glassmakers from being tempted abroad and divulging their secrets (their families would be imprisoned, and assassins employed by the Ten would be set on their trail – though these stories were mostly bluster, for there are historical references to Murano glassblowers living quite openly in other cities).

The biggest diaspora of glassblowers occurred in the 1600s; the Republic didn't pay them well enough, compared to the offers of others. An even worse blow was the immediate popularity of Bohemian cut crystal in the 1670s. The ensuing glass crisis was only resolved when Murano learned to make cut glass as well. The death of the Republic set off another decline, and only towards the end of the 19th century were the forges stoked up again on Murano.

Visitors to the museum are more than welcome (it's traditional – medieval pilgrims sailing out of Venice for the Holy Land chronicled glass tours) but in exchange you have to take the solemn tour through the showroom, where you may feel as if you've gone through the Looking Glass the wrong way, with the Mad Hatter in charge of colour.

Vaporetto stop Colonna is at one end of Murano's main glass bazaar (*see* 'Shopping', pp.289–90), the **Fondamenta dei Vetrai**. Across the *fondamenta* stands an isolated medieval **campanile**; its church, like 15 others on Murano, was demolished after 1797. Murano's palaces suffered the same fate, but around the corner from San Pietro Martire and beyond the Ponte Vivarini, there's an exception, the **Palazzo da Mula**, a 14th-century palace altered in the 16th century to make a pleasure villa.

San Pietro Martire Off maps
Fondamenta dei Vetrai; vaporetto Colonna.
Open 9–12 and 3–6; adm free.

The Fondamenta dei Vetrai runs the length of the canal as far as Gothic San Pietro Martire, one of Murano's three surviving churches. Well worth a visit, it is the home of Giovanni Bellini's restored 1488 *Madonna with St Mark, St Augustine and Doge Barbarigo*, a beautiful, serene painting complete with angel musicians playing some celestial soul music that perhaps only the Bellinis of this world can hear. Veronese's *St Jerome* may be seen over the sacristy door; the sacristy itself has a collection of 17th-century wood panels carved with a rather unexpected crowd of Roman and Greek emperors, gods, philosophers and villains. But most winsome are the local touches – the Murano chandeliers, the 15th-century frescoes of Dominican saints in the nave, the glass-doll *Madonna and Child*, covered with the candles and flowers of the devout, and on the first altar to the right, another *Madonna*, very much like a primitive idol.

Museo Vetrario Off maps
Fondamenta Giustinian 8, t 041 739 586;
vaporetto Museo (nos.41/42). Open April–Oct Thurs–Tues 10–5, Nov–March Thurs–Tues 10–4; adm €4.

The Ponte Vivarini crosses Murano's own Grand Canal, where Fondamenta Cavour leads around 17th-century **Palazzo Giustinian**, built for the bishops of Torcello, and for more than a hundred years the seat

Heart of Glass

Ever since the Syrians invented glass-blowing in the 1st century, the craft has always had a certain air of magic to it, an alchemical process that transforms sand with fire and air into something hard and clear. The magical aspect was the key of Werner Herzog's 1970s film *Heart of Glass*, in which the entire cast of non-actors played their roles while under hypnosis. The plot centred around a German glass-manufacturing family, who had forgotten the ancestral secret of making a rare ruby crystal; there are fascinating scenes of men blowing glass before infernal kilns.

The Romans were the first in Europe to refine this alchemy into art. Among those who took refuge from the Huns in the Lagoon, there must have been a Roman glassblower or two, even though the first Venetian document to mention one dates from the 980s. The fragments of glass that survive from that period are simple and utilitarian. In the 12th century Murano invented a process of producing glass panes from blown cylinders, which brought Venetian glass its first fame, a technological breakthrough that opened up the façades and let light into the cramped, courtyard-less Venetian palaces. Perhaps the most beautiful products of this functional period are the transparent glasses and lamps, as clear as rock crystal (hence the name 'crystal'), a technique invented in the 1450s, just in time to illuminate so many Renaissance paintings.

At this stage the only way to add colour to glass was through lead enamel or *smalto*, melted over the glass or mosaic *tesserae*. But a revolution occurred on Murano in the early 15th century when Angelo Barovier (1405–60), a member of one of Venice's most venerable glass-making dynasties, began to make glass in colours. The ancient Roman technique called *murrine* was rediscovered, enabling glassmakers to create designs by laying cold pieces of different coloured glass together and firing them together in the kiln. The famous Barovier nuptial cup, with its couple bathing in a fountain, is a superb example of the new art.

After that there was no going back – beginning in the 16th century Murano became a laboratory for ever more elaborate designs and techniques: *vetro a filigrana*, the most original technique from Murano, consisting of thread-like rods of white glass 'woven' on to the surface in free-form patterns; *vetro lattino* or milk glass, imitating Chinese porcelain; *vetro a ghiaccio*, with a rugged, ice-like surface made by suddenly dropping the temperature in the glass process; *vetro graffito*, with designs scratched on the surface with a diamond; *vetro a pettine* ('combed glass') or *vetro a penne* with a wavy design; or the very difficult to make *venturina* or *stellaria* glass, shot through with shiny copper crystals. Murano also learned how to make coloured glass that looked so much like semi-precious stones that in the early 1600s a law had to be passed banning the manufacture of false gems. You'll see examples of these revived traditional techniques on a stroll down Murano's glass canal; many factories make souvenirs you can take home without any embarrassment.

In the 19th century, when the entire industry was in decline, Murano's glass-makers stayed alive by producing tons of glass beads for European colonialists to trade to the natives in Asia and Africa – a compromise from which their art has never really recovered. Today, in Murano, collecting dust beside a filigree glass bowl, stands the most lurid, simpering green clown in the hemisphere; chandeliers dangling glass flowers of death glow overhead. Glossy scorpions and pyramids seem to be fashionable.

Pondering the range of kitsch belched from Murano's kilns, you begin to suspect that the whole island has been hypnotized, like Herzog's glassblowers, for the past hundred years. But alchemy, like most enchantments, is out of fashion these days, or seems forbidden, and it's really not suprising to see monsters in glass as well as in every other aspect of modern life.

of the glass museum, where you can learn something of Murano's livelihood. The **first floor** contains ancient Roman glass; examples range from the 1st–3rd centuries AD and include many cinerary urns found in Yugoslavia. Upstairs, beyond the 19th-century mosaics of *Garibaldi* and *Vittorio Emanuele II*, the multilingual description of ancient and modern glassmaking and its styles is a good background to the glass displayed: medieval, utilitarian pre-1400s fragments, and some of the earliest surviving Murano glass, including the famous blue **Barovier nuptial cup** (1480), with its scene of merry frolicking in a basin; some of the earliest 'Murano crystal', and an example of the lamps that were painted by *quattrocento* artists. Simplicity and elegance went by the board in the 1500s, as the glassmakers indulged, and probably helped create, a taste for the extravagant and bizarre, reaching a kind of kitsch epiphany in a model of a garden made entirely of glass.

Santi Maria e Donato Off maps
Fondamenta Giustinian; vaporetto Museo. ***Open** daily 9.30–12 and 4–7; adm €2.*

Just beyond the glass museum is one of the finest Veneto-Byzantine monuments in Venice, a contemporary of St Mark's Basilica, with a beautiful arcaded apse reflected in the canal – altogether far too over-restored by the Austrians, according to many critics. Over the door, there's a good lunette of the *Virgin*, and inside, an outstanding 12th-century mosaic pavement (only St Mark's Basilica has another as fine), incorporating pieces of ancient Murano glass, with geometric figures encircling scenes straight from the Middle Ages: two roosters bearing a fox on a pole, an eagle capturing a lamb, griffins, and other less explicable symbols. On the wall there's a fine 12th-century Byzantine mosaic of the *Virgin*, and some of the capitals are from the same period. To the left there's a large painted relief of *San Donato of Euboea*, the church's other titular saint, with a flock of midget donors gathered below. His relics were part of an 1125 Venetian

relic-raid (*see* p.222) led by Doge Domenico Michiel, but in this case the holy raiders outdid themselves, bringing home not only San Donato's bones but those of the dragon the good bishop slew with a gob of righteous spit; you can see four hanging behind the altar. In an old wall by the campanile are the bas-reliefs of a war memorial.

Burano Off maps
Vaporetto no.12 from Fondamenta Nuove.

Burano is the Legoland of the Lagoon, where everything is in brightly coloured miniature – the canals, the bridges, the leaning tower, and the houses, painted with a Fauvist sensibility in the deepest of colours. Traditionally on Burano the men fish (and there's a fair collection of *trattorie* where you can sample the catch, at prices that would be a bargain in Venice) and the women make Venetian point, 'the most Italian of all lace-work', beautiful, intricate and murder on the eyesight. Burano is literally draped with the stuff, although beware! In among the real articles is much that is machine made or imported.

In the sacristy of the church of **San Martino** (of the tipsily leaning campanile) in Piazza Galuppi, look for Giambattista Tiepolo's *Crucifixion*, which Mary McCarthy aptly described as 'a ghastly masquerade ball'.

Scuola dei Merletti Off maps
*Piazza Galuppi, t 041 730 034. **Open** April–Oct Wed–Mon 10–5, Nov–March 10–4; adm €4.*

You can watch the women make lace here, though '*scuola*' is misleading – no young girl in Burano wants to learn such an excruciating art, and their mothers may well be the last generation to make lace. But you never know; the school was originally founded in 1872, when lacemaking had declined so drastically that only one woman remembered the stitches.

Mazzorbo Off maps
You can cross the bridge to the island of Mazzorbo (ancient *Majourbium*), another island once famous for its gardens and villas,

and one that even in the 18th century could still boast a dozen churches. Now it has mostly empty space to offer between its scattered cottages, though students of residential architecture may be interested in the island's new communal houses designed by Giancarlo De Carlo, inspired by the traditional houses of Burano (and painted bright blue too, to make the *Buranelli* feel at home). On Mazzorbo's southern end is its one surviving church, **Santa Caterina**, a medieval effort rebuilt in the 15th century.

San Francesco del Deserto Off maps

From Burano (*see* above) you can hire a *sandolo* (small gondola) to this islet some 20 minutes to the south. On this islet St Francis is said to have founded a chapel in 1220, when his boat ran aground on his return from the East. Not long after, the island was given to Francis' followers, who founded a **monastery** (*open 9–11 and 3–5.30; donations welcome*). The friars were forced out to make room for a military depot in 1806, but were welcomed back in 1856, but it's not the buildings you'll remember (though there's a lovely 14th-century cloister) but the love of nature evident in the beautiful gardens.

Torcello Off maps

Vaporetto no.12 Murano/Mazzorbo/Burano line from Fondamenta Nuove, 35–40mins.

Of all the possible destinations hidden among the shadows and shallows of the Lagoon, this one is the real treasure. At first the Torcello stop looks unpromising, a concrete pier and a wilderness beyond. But take the only path, down a jungly canal that was once a busy urban *fondamenta*, pass the solitary old 'Devil's bridge', and you'll finally arrive at a *piazza* that contains two of the most remarkable churches in all Italy, and very little else.

Torcello was the heir of *Altinum*, and may have settled some refugees from it as early as the 5th century. The big exodus, however, came in 639, when the Altinese finally found life with the Lombards too expensive and too dangerous. According to the legend their bishop, Paolo, was commanded in a vision to ascend the city's tower and look. He saw certain stars rising over this lonely island, and led the people of *Altinum* there to their new home. The town developed quickly, and for the first few centuries it seems to have been the real metropolis of the Lagoon. Its cathedral, founded in 639 and rebuilt about 1008, is the oldest building in the Lagoon and still one of the most impressive. At its height, Torcello was said (probably with a modicum of medieval exaggeration) to have 20,000 inhabitants, and, even long after the refounding on the Rialto, Torcello continued as the commercial centre of Venice.

It was no war or other disaster but only the fickle Lagoon itself that ruined Torcello. The gradual silting up of the island's approaches doomed its trade, and also created malarial marshes. The population gradually drifted off to Venice proper. As they had done in *Altinum* a thousand years before, they came back for the building stone; after a few centuries' service as a quarry, Torcello today is nearly picked clean and has fewer than 30 inhabitants. But for the *piazza* in the centre it would be impossible to guess that this was ever anything more than overgrown farmland.

Santa Maria Assunta Off maps

No longer functioning as a cathedral, though Mass is celebrated every Sunday during the summer. Open daily April–Oct 10.30–5.30, Nov–March 10–5; adm €3, campanile €2.

On Torcello's *piazza*, the most imposing building is the basilica. More than St Mark's, or any other Venetian building, this one shows the difficult balance between Byzantine and Italian styles that was sought in local architecture on the threshold of the Middle Ages. In form it is much more Italian, a typical Latin three-aisled basilica; such details as the blind arcading on the façade and apses and the massive, square campanile, a prototype for many later ones in

Venice, suggest that it is the work of Lombard masons. There are some unusual features: stone shutters on stone hinges, over the side windows, and a baptistry set squarely in front of the main portal – only the foundations survive today.

Inside, the mood shifts abruptly towards the east, with an exquisite 13th-century **mosaic of the *Madonna and Child*** in the apse, a severe but compelling figure with the deepest Byzantine eyes, alone on a broad gold ground. Beneath, there is a mosaic row of the 12 apostles, and below that a marble veneer facing in symmetrical patterns. The Roman sarcophagus near the high altar was recycled for the remains of St Heliodorus, first bishop of *Altinum*; to the left, the foundation stone of the original cathedral bears an inscription from 639 AD, the oldest in Venice.

There is more fine work in every corner of the cathedral: an intricate coloured marble pavement, and beautiful capitals on the nave columns that seem to have come from ancient *Altinum* but are really originals from the 11th century. Between two of these columns, on the right side of the nave, a wooden trap door allows a peek at a small segment of the original mosaic flooring. Another series of mosaics, in the right transept, shows four angels supporting a crown and the lamb, representing Christ; below, Christ appears with the Archangels Michael and Gabriel. Some of the best work is around the iconostasis (altar screen) and pulpit: early fragments taken from the original cathedral, like the relief of the two peacocks sipping from the fountain of life (an allegory of the Eucharist). Look carefully and you will find some genuine oddities – on the left side, *Ixion*, grandfather of the centaurs from Greek mythology, stretched on his wheel. More wheels appear on the opposite side of the screen, winged wheels said to represent *Occasion*, the counterpart to Fortune, the chance that can be seized.

Best of all is the spectacular **Apotheosis of Christ and the Last Judgement** covering the entire west wall, the largest and most memorable mosaic in Venice. Probably begun in the 12th century, the work was heavily restored in the 19th. Few mosaics reveal with such candour the Byzantine mixture of intel-lectuality and imagination; it's an ensemble of obsessive organization, with hosts of angels and devils in tidy symmetry.

It is divided into six levels:

1 On top, the *Crucifixion*, with the Virgin and St John.

2 *The Descent into Hell*, with Jesus flanked by Michael and Gabriel (like all Byzantine archangels, they wear the dress of high offi-cials at the court in Constantinople). Jesus treads under blue demons, and welcomes Adam from the tomb. The shower of broken locks and keys is another common Byzantine image for the Last Day, when all earthly bonds are loosed.

3 *Christ in Glory*, in His mandorla, with the Virgin, Baptist, Apostles and Saints.

4 *The Beasts and Fishes Give up their Human Prey* to the call of angelic music; also the mystic *etoimasia*, the *Preparation of the Throne*. Ancient Greek art sometimes portrayed the same empty throne as a symbol of Zeus, only with a pair of thunder-bolts on it instead of the Gospels.

5 *Michael Weighs the Souls in a Scale* (more ancient symbolism; this was the job of Minos and Rhadamanthys in antiquity, and trace-able to Egypt). The virtuous elect look up with expectant faces, while angels cast down the damned (many princes and clerics among them, along with Muslims in turbans) to the blue demons. The devil himself appears.

6 On the left, *Mary Comforts the Children* while St Peter (with banner) guards the *Gates of Paradise*; right, the interesting *Tortures of the Damned*: fire, dismember-ment, water and hunger, with serpents floating through the eye-sockets of floating skulls.

After lengthy and superb restoration, the Basilica's **campanile**, discreetly set apart in its overgrown garden, is open for a pre-lunch clamber. Since the restorers thought to put in ramps rather than stairs, it's a relatively untaxing climb, and well worth it for the views over the varying greens of Torcello.

Santa Fosca Off maps

Open *daily 10–12.30 and 2–5; **adm** free.*

On the other side of the cathedral stands the 11th-century Santa Fosca. This church was never really completed, and whatever internal decoration it ever had is gone. Nevertheless, the plain shell of it is the most elaborate work of late Byzantine architecture in existence, a lovely and unique conception. As in so many other churches, beginning with the Hagia Sophia itself, it takes a central Greek plan and elongates one side to form a nave with three apses; the front and sides are graced by an arcaded porch, and surmounted by a low cylindrical dome. Like all the best medieval buildings, this one was built by constructive geometry: both in the plan and the elevation its architects employed the proportions of the 'Golden Section' of the ancient Greeks.

Santa Fosca was intended as a *martyrion*, a small church in honour of the saint, whose remains were buried here. The ensemble of the lost baptistry, cathedral and *martyrion* were symbolically meant to recall the circle of birth, life and death, as pretty a conceit for a monumental centre as any town ever had.

Attila's Seat Off maps

You may snap your sweetheart's picture in **Attila's Seat**, in the centre of the *piazza*, just as Venice tourists have been doing for generations. The connection of this rugged old throne with the Hunnish supremo sounds suspiciously as if it were dreamed up by someone sprung from generations of tour guides. Some scholars believe that the throne, if it has any history at all, was used by Torcello's consuls in open-air assemblies.

Museo dell'Estuario Off maps

Palazzo del Consiglio, t 041 730 761. **Open** *Tues–Sun 10–12.30 and 2–5 daily; **adm** €2.*

In this pleasant grab-bag, you'll find architectural fragments from the 6th–12th centuries, a pair of *bocche di leone* (the long arm of the Ten reached even here), a lovely

6th-century marble holy-water stoup from Murano, and a few gilded silver reliefs from the cathedral altarpiece – Napoleon stole the rest of them. Upstairs, among big soppy canvases from followers of Veronese, there's the cathedral's original door key, Byzantine ceramics, coins and jewellery, Byzantine and Cretan-Venetian icons from the 1400s, and a big jolly *cinquecento St Christopher* with fish swimming around his toes.

Cavallino and Jesolo Off maps

*For **Punta Sabbioni**, take **vaporetto no.14**, which goes to the Lido and San Zaccaria. **Treporti** is the last call on line 12, connecting Torcello, Burano, Murano to Venice. **Buses** connect the Jesolo with Punta Sabbioni to coincide with the ferries.*

The Litorale del Cavallino, the 10km peninsula that protects the northern part of the Lagoon, was long known as a semi-wild place of beach, sand dunes and pine forests. There's still some of that left, among the 35 camping grounds, hotels and restaurants. There are two ports on the *litorale*: **Punta Sabbioni** and **Treporti**. **Lido di Jesolo** is a far more developed and densely packed resort, seeing some six million tourists a year, though the number has fallen off because of the dirty sea – a disaster the hoteliers have tried to stave off by adding pools.

Smaller Islands in the North Lagoon Off maps

These have played a much smaller role than the islets to the south, though green **Sant'Erasmo** (*vaporetto* no.13), still with a few hundred inhabitants and with lovely country walks, and its tiny neighbour, **Le Vignole** (*vaporetto* no.13), are Venice's kitchen gardens and suppliers of produce in the Rialto markets. **San Giacomo in Paluda** (St James in the Bog), now a ruined ghost island, was originally a rest stop for pilgrims, a monastery until the 1400s, then a leper colony, and a Franciscan monastery.

A Grand Canal Tour

GIARDINI PAPADOPOLI TO THE CASINO 234

THE CASINO TO PONTE DI RIALTO 235

RIALTO TO CA' FOSCARI 238

CA' FOSCARI TO ACCADEMIA 239

ACCADEMIA TO SAN MARCO 240

A GRAND CANAL TOUR

It may be a cliché to sail down the Grand Canal in a gondola at twilight with your own true love, but it's one of the most unforgettable clichés in which you could ever indulge. Although the gold and frescoes have long ago worn off the fantasy façades of its palaces, the *Canalazzo*, as the Venetians call it, has not entirely lost the colour of past ages. It has simply become a little more prosaic, chock-a-block with grunting *vaporetti*, private boats, and the workaday barges, carrying lettuces, bath-tubs, cartons of Coca-Cola and sides of beef all over Venice. In this city of water we offer a tour instead of a walk – if not a gondola, take the slowpoke no.1 *accelerato* – arranged from north to south. You could do this trip in an hour and a half or so; or you could make a day of it, stopping for lunch at one of the three mid-way points suggested below, and hopping off to visit any of the major museums and churches along the way.

Start: Piazzale Roma *vaporetto* stop (line 1).
Finish: Piazza San Marco.
Journey time: The trip takes 1hr 30mins if you stay on the boat.
Suggested day: Any day, even a wet one.
Lunch and drinks stops: Choose one of the following mid-way stops; all the restaurants are within 10mins' walk of the *vaporetto* stop; *see* pp.268–9 for a map showing their location. At Ca' d'Oro *vaporetto* stop: Alla Vedova, *see* p.277; Casa Mia, *see* p.277; Ai Promessi Sposi, *see* p.276. At **Rialto** *vaporetto* stop: Bancogiro, *see* p.274; Alla Madonna, *see* p.274; All'Arco, *see* p.275; Ai Do Mori, *see* p.275; Ruga Rialto, *see* p.275. At **San Tomà** *vaporetto* stop: Trattoria San Tomà, *see* p.274; Da Ignazio, *see* p.274; Alla Patatina, *see* p.275.
Museum stops: Natural History Museum, p.189; Galleria Franchetti, p.196; Museo dei Settecento, p.165; Accademia, p.158; Peggy Guggenheim Collection, p.163; Salute, p.163.

Giardini Papadopoli to the Casino

Great thoroughfares often seem to meet bad ends: Fifth Avenue comes to grief among junkyards and gasworks over the Harlem River; the Champs-Elysées leads only to the nightmare of La Défense. The Grand Canal's shabby demise comes at its northern end, among the causeways, the docks of the Tronchetto, and the colossal parking garages of Piazzale Roma.

The first sight is the **Giardini Papadopoli [1]**, which despite its greenery tends to blend in with its surroundings; still visible from the canal is the memorial to the 'inventor of modern hydraulic principles'. After that comes the **railway station**, built in the style of the fancier American suburban super-markets of the 1950s. Beyond it, snack-stands and African pedlars line the left bank leading towards the **Lista di Spagna** (*see* p.213). From here, no more embarrassments, as the Grand Canal comes into its own.

On the right bank, opposite the station, stands the 18th-century **Palazzo Diedo [2]**, once the home of Angelo Emo, the last admiral of Venice. To the left of it, the peculiar egg-cup church is **San Simeone Piccolo [3]**, one of the youngest of Venetian churches, completed in 1738 (*see* p.190). Next you approach the Ponte degli Scalzi, built in 1934, one of only three bridges to knot the two halves of the city together. The mouldering hulk to the left before the bridge is the **Scalzi [4]** church (*see* p.213) built for the Reformed (or *scalzi* – shoeless) Carmelites in the 1640s. To the right, the **Rio Marin** is one of the busiest canals, a shortcut to San Marco; after it, also on the right, you'll catch a glimpse of the long **Campo San Simeone Profeta** (*see* p.191). The next canal is to the left: the **Canale di Cannaregio**. On the corner is the addition to the back of **San Geremia e Lucia [5]** (*see* p.212), built to hold the relics of Santa Lucia, brought here in the 1860s when her own church was demolished for the station.

Here the canal grows more colourful, with a number of ancient palaces, Veneto-Byzantine and Gothic. To see the best example of the genesis of the former style, wait until two more canals pass on the right. At the corner before the second stands the monumental **Fondaco dei Turchi [6]**, with its arcades of round arches, a work of the 12th–13th centuries built for the Palmieri family, and passing through many owners thereafter. In 1453, the last ambassador from Constantinople sojourned here; ironically, after 1621 the palace was occupied by his Turkish successors. It served as the head-quarters for Ottoman merchants in Venice until 1838, and was tidily over-restored by the Austrians to house the city's Natural History Museum (see p.189).

Across the little canal, **Rio Fontego dei Turchi**, the rugged old building with the Lion of St Mark was a public granary, the **Deposito del Meglo [7]**.

Opposite, the Casino (see p.208) keeps its quarters in the **Palazzo Vendramin-Calergi [8]**, one of the most impressive on this stretch of the canal. A Renaissance building with Corinthian columns, it was designed by Mauro Codussi, and completed by the Lombardi in 1509, one of the first to forsake the old Gothic style for Renaissance classicism; death in Venice came for Richard Wagner here in December 1883.

The Casino to Ponte di Rialto

The next quarter-mile or so, as far as the Rialto markets, is one of the high-rent squares on Venice's Monopoly board, lined with imposing palaces on both sides.

On the Right

Next to the granaries are the 17th-century **Palazzo Belloni-Battaglia [9]**, a sickly-sweet *torte* in overwrought Baroque by Longhena, architect of the Salute; the late Renaissance **Palazzo Tron [10]**; then two 15th-century Gothic palaces, the **Palazzo Duodo [11]** and **Palazzo Priuli-Bon [12]**, the creamy white

façade of **San Stae [13]**, on its canalside *campo* (see p.188), and next to it one of the most charming buildings on the canal, the **Scuola dei Battiloro e Tiraoro [14]** (gold-smiths and jewellers) – not as old as it looks, but an eccentrically retro building of 1711. Its neighbour is the 17th-century **Palazzo Foscarino-Giovanelli [15]**, home of the poor diplomat Antonio Foscarini, unjustly executed by the republic for treason (see San Stae, where his memorial and the State's apology can be seen). Next is one of the grandest of all Baroque palaces, the **Ca' Pésaro [16]**, Longhena's last work, and now the home of the Museum of Modern Art (see p.187). The third palace after this is the **Palazzo Corner della Regina [17]** (rebuilt 1724), the birthplace of Caterina Cornaro, Queen of Cyprus; then **Casa Favretto [18]**, a fine Gothic-Byzantine building with some parts as old as the 11th century; three more buildings down comes the **Palazzo dei Brandolin [19]**, another 15th-century Gothic home, and the last palace before the Fondamenta dell'Olio and the striking neo-Gothic fish market. From the canal, some of the busy life of the **Rialto markets** (see p.185) can be seen, though much is blocked out by the two ungainly market buildings: the **Fabbriche Nuove [20]** and Sansovino's **Fabbriche Vecchie [21]**. After them are the outdoor fruit and vegetable markets, and then the building that was once Venice's treasury, the 16th-century **Palazzo dei Camerlenghi [22]**.

On the Left

After the Casino and its adjacent garden, the second palace is the 15th-century Gothic **Palazzo Erizzo [23]**, and the third the Renaissance **Palazzo Soranzo [24]**, a work of Sante Lombardo; to the right of the narrow Rio della Maddalena, the **Palazzo Barbarigo [25]** is one of the last to retain some traces of its exterior frescoes, once a common feature of canal-front mansions. Just before the next side canal on the left, the 16th-century **Palazzo Gussoni-Grimani della Vida [26]** once sported a full set of these frescoes by

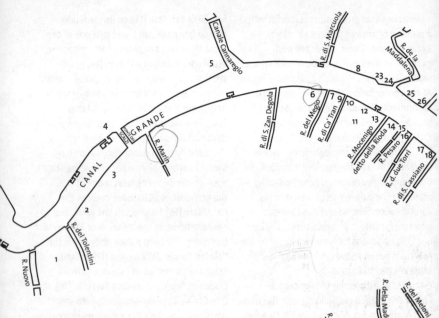

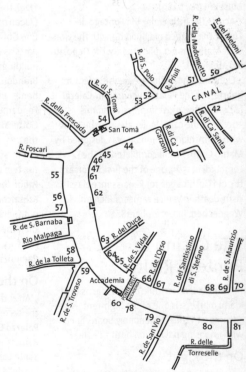

1 Giardini Papadopoli
2 Palazzo Diedo
3 San Simeone Piccolo
4 Scalzi
5 Palazzo Labia a San Geremia
6 Fondaco dei Turchi
7 Deposito del Megio
8 Palazzo Vendramin-Calergi
9 Palazzo Belloni Battaglia
10 Palazzo Tron
11 Palazzo Duodo
12 Palazzo Priuli-Bon
13 San Stae
14 Scuola dei Battiloro e Tiraoro
15 Palazzo Foscarino-Giovanelli
16 Ca' Pésaro
17 Palazzo Corner della Regina
18 Casa Favretto
19 Palazzo dei Brandolini
20 Fabbriche Nuove
21 Fabbriche Vecchie
22 Palazzo dei Camerlenghi
23 Palazzo Erizzo
24 Palazzo Soranzo
25 Palazzo Barbarigo
26 Palazzo Gussoni-Grimani della Vida
27 Ca' d'Oro
28 Palazzo Pesaro-Rava
29 Palazzo Sagredo
30 Palazzo Foscarini

31 Palazzo Michiel dalle Colonne
32 Palazzo Michiel del Brusa
33 Ca' da Mosto
34 Palazzo Lion-Morosini
35 Fondaco dei Tedeschi
36 Palazzo Dolfin-Manin
37 Palazzo Bembo
38 Palazzo Loredan
39 Palazzo Farsetti
40 Palazzo Grimani
41 Palazzo Corner-Contarini dei Cavalli
42 Palazzo Benzon
43 Palazzo Corner-Spinelli
44 Palazzo Mocenigo
45 Palazzo Contarini delle Figure
46 Palazzo Nani-Mocenigo
47 Palazzo Lezze
48 Palazzo Barzizza
49 Palazzo Businello
50 Palazzo Dona
51 Palazzo Bernardo
52 Palazzo Barbarigo della Terrazza
53 Palazzo Pisana della Moretta
54 Palazzo Marcello dei Leoni
55 Ca' Foscari
56 Palazzo Giustiniani
57 Ca' Rezzonico
58 Palazzo Loredan
59 Palazzo Contarini degli Scrigni
60 Accademia
61 Palazzo MoroLin
62 Palazzo Grassi
63 Ca' del Duca
64 Palazzo Falier
65 Palazzo Giustiniana-Lolin
66 Palazzo Cavelli Franchetti
67 Palazzo Barbaro
68 Casetta delle Rose
69 Ca' Grande/Palazzo Corner
70 Palazzo Minotto
71 Santa Maria Zobenigo
72 Palazzo Gritti-Pisani
73 Palazzo Contarini-Fasan
74 Hotel Bauer-Grünwald
75 Ca' Giustinian
76 Capitaneria del Porto
77 Giardini Reali
78 Palazzo Contarini del Zaffo
79 Palazzo Barbarigo
80 Palazzo Venier
81 Palazzo Dario
82 Palazzo Salviati
83 Santa Maria della Salute
84 Dogana di Mare

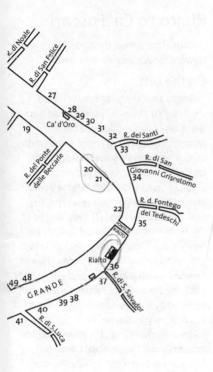

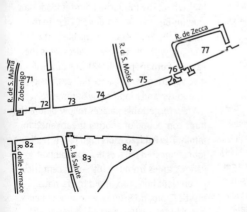

Tintoretto himself. After a long stretch of undistinguished palaces, mostly from the 1600s, you can't miss the spectacular **Ca' d'Oro [27]**, with the most fanciful and ornate façade of all Venice's Gothic palaces: this 'Golden House', completed about 1440, took its name from the heavy load of gilding that originally covered its columns and ornament. The home of the Contarinis, the great family that gave Venice eight doges, it was built over another palace that had belonged to the family of Carlo Zeno; some parts of this earlier work can still be seen. It now houses the Galleria Franchetti (*see* p.196).

After the Ca' d'Oro, a chorus of three more Gothic palaces compete for your attention: the **Palazzo Pésaro-Rava [28]**, the **Palazzo Sagredo [29]**, parts of which go back to the 1300s, and the 15th-century **Palazzo Foscari [30]**, on the right flank of the narrow Campo Santa Sofia. After these, the mood changes again with the late 16th-century **Palazzo Michiel dalle Colonne [31]**, so-called for its columned portico, and the **Palazzo Michiel del Brusà [32]**, an ancient palace rebuilt after a fire in 1774. With the **Ca' da Mosto [33]** on the corner of Rio di San Giovanni Crisostomo it is one of the oldest buildings on the canal, a typical 13th-century Veneto-Byzantine building with its narrow arches, with just a hint of the peak at the top that would later grow into the full pointed arch of the Venetian Gothic. One of the great old Venetian merchant-adventurers was born here in 1432: Alvise da Mosto, discoverer of the Cape Verde islands.

Heading into the bend of the canal before the Ponte di Rialto, after the tiny Campiello Remer comes another 13th-century building, the much-altered **Palazzo Lion-Morosini [34]**. Just before the bridge itself, the **Fondaco dei Tedeschi [35]**, austere without its once sumptuous frescoes by Giorgione and Titian, was one of the largest of the foreign merchants' *khans*, home not only to the many German and Austrian traders, but those from Hungary, Bohemia and all central Europe; its less glorious fate in the present is to be Venice's main post office. You now pass

under the **Rialto Bridge** (*see* p.185), the most photographed bridge in Europe.

Rialto to Ca' Foscari

South of the bridge, the canal is lined with crowded *fondamente* on both sides.

On the Left

Directly after the bridge you will see a short stretch of smaller *palazzi*, some from the 1400s or earlier and some modern reconstructions. Though none is noteworthy in itself, together they make up one of the loveliest building ensembles in Venice. Beyond these are the large **Palazzo Dolfin-Manin [36]**, a work of Sansovino, and the Gothic **Palazzo Bembo [37]**. Near the end of this *fondamenta* (the **Riva del Carbon**) are Venice's municipal buildings, including the 12th–14th-century **Palazzo Loredan [38]** and **Palazzo Farsetti [39]**. At the next canal on the left, is the Renaissance **Palazzo Grimani [40]**, designed by Michele Sammicheli in the 1560s and now used as law courts.

After the small canal (Rio di San Luca), the **Palazzo Corner Contarini dai Cavalli [41]** (1445), a late-Gothic palace, takes its name from the horses on the coats of arms. Just before the next canal is the **Palazzo Benzon [42]**, where the footloose Countess Marina Querini-Benzoni entertained Byron; to the right of the Rio Ca' Corner, the elegant building with the tri-lobed balconies is the **Palazzo Corner-Spinelli [43]**, one of the definitive Venetian Renaissance palaces, designed by Codussi and modified by Sammicheli.

A few forgettable palaces follow, before the huge compound of another great Venetian family. The **Palazzo Mocenigo [44]** is really four connected palaces in a row, built at various times from the 16th–18th centuries. Byron slept here, too, as did the famous mystic Giordano Bruno – who shocked or bored his Mocenigo host so seriously with his heretical opinions that Mocenigo turned him over to the Pope for burning in 1592. Next is the **Palazzo Contarini delle Figure [45]**, so-called from the caryatids on the façade (every palace of this prolific family has such an appellation, so we can tell one from the other); and then there follow two more Gothic palaces, the **Palazzo Nani-Mocenigo [46]** and **Palazzo Lezze [47]**.

On the Right

After the long Fondamenta del Vin, opposite the Palazzo Grimani are two 12th–13th-century survivals, the **Palazzo Barzizza [48]** and **Palazzo Businello [49]**. One street further down are two adjacent Gothic buildings both much altered and both called **Palazzo Donà [50]**; the one on the left is often referred to as '*alla Madonnetta*' after the early Renaissance Madonna set in a shrine on its façade.

After the next canal, the **Palazzo Bernardo [51]**, is also 15th-century Gothic; Francesco Sforza, future Duke of Milan, lived here in the 1450s while he was still a mercenary *condottiere* working for Venice.

After the broad entrance to the Rio di San Polo, the **Palazzo Barbarigo della Terrazza [52]** (1569) takes its name from its sumptuous roof garden; a famous collection of paintings, with most of Venice's Titians, was once kept here, but is now in the Hermitage in St Petersburg – in the sad days of the 1850s the Barbarigi had to sell the collection to the Tsar. Next, the **Palazzo Pisani della Moretta [53]** is a delicate Gothic confection, like so many of its fellows completely redone inside in the 18th century (and the best art here, an important Veronese, ended up in the National Gallery).

As far as Ca' Foscari, two canals down, the rest is of little interest, but you can see a few Byzantine and Gothic fragments incorporated into later buildings, like the venerable stone lions in front of the **Palazzo Marcello dei Leoni [54]**.

Ca' Foscari to Accademia

Here the canal becomes even wider and grander; nearly all of the family names represented on this stretch can be found at least once in the list of doges.

On the Right

Ca' Foscari [55] was built by the controversial Doge Francesco Foscari in 1437; he died here of a broken heart, not long after having been dismissed from office. One of the last great Gothic palaces, it was still thought one of the city's finest in the late Renaissance; Venice put up King Henry III of France here on his memorable visit in 1573.

Next, Bartolomeo Bon's **Palazzo Giustiniani [56]** (1452), built for the family that traced its origins back to Byzantine Emperor Justinian; palace-hopping Richard Wagner spent some time here in 1859, while he was working on *Tristan und Isolde*.

Thirty years later, Robert Browning was breathing his last, next door at the massive **Ca' Rezzonico [57]**. A work of Longhena, expanded in the 1740s, it is now the Museo dei Settecento (*see* p.165).

After two more canals, the next substantial Gothic palace is the 15th-century **Palazzo Loredan [58]**, later the Austrian Embassy and a nest of espionage and intrigues. To the left of the next canal, the **Palazzo Contarini degli Scrigni e Corfù [59]** is two palaces connected into one, half Gothic and half a 1609 work of Vincenzo Scamozzi.

The wooden **Ponte dell'Accademia**, with its single arch over the canal, has excited argument among Venetian and foreign aesthetes ever since it was built in 1932, replacing an iron bridge that was not much older, called the English Bridge by Venetians who saw it as an aberration of the Industrial Revolution. Behind it stands Venice's great art gallery, the **Accademia [60]** (*see* p.158).

On the Left

One palace before San Samuele is the odd 13-windowed **Palazzo MoroLin [61]**, designed by rococo painter Sebastiano Mazzoni. Its solemn block of a neighbour, **Palazzo Grassi [62]**, was built in 1748 by a wealthy family from Bologna who bought their way into the Golden Book of the nobility, and is now owned by Fiat and used for special exhibitions; it faces **Campo San Samuele** and its church (*see* p.132). Just before the next canal

(Rio del Duca), the **Ca' del Duca [63]** was built over an ambitious but never completed work of Bartolomeo Bon; after the canal are the 15th-century Gothic **Palazzo Falier [64]** and **Palazzo Giustinian-Lolin [65]**, another work of Longhena (1623).

Accademia to San Marco

On the Left

On this side of the bridge, narrow Campo San Vitale (San Vidal) opens up into the broad Campo Santo Stefano; bordering it, with Venice's most enviable canal-front garden, is the **Palazzo Cavalli-Franchetti [66]**, 15th-century Gothic prettified in the 1890s. Across the narrow Rio dell'Orso, the **Palazzo Barbaro [67]** was the home of the vain family who glorified themselves on the façade of Santa Maria Zobenigo. Among the next stretch of smaller houses, you'll be able to pick out the **Casetta delle Rose [68]** – a lovely place that was home to the sculptor Canova and later to Gabriele d'Annunzio.

You'll have no trouble finding the **Ca' Grande [69]**, (or **Palazzo Corner**), one of the real monsters of the canal, a magnificently gloomy pile that is considered one of the masterworks of Sansovino, completed in the 1560s; once the home of declining Venice's wealthiest family, it seems better fitted for its new job – home of the State Prefecture. Next to it there's the 15th-century Gothic **Palazzo Minotto [70]**. At the narrow Campo del Traghetto, peer through to the façade of the aforementioned **Santa Maria Zobenigo [71]** (*see* p.127).

To the right of the *campo*, the **Palazzo Gritti-Pisani [72]** has become the posh Gritti Palace hotel (*see* p.252). Five palaces down is the Gothic **Palazzo Contarini-Fasan [73]** (1475): imaginative tour guides used to tell the English this was the house of Othello's Desdemona. After the next canal comes the **Hotel Bauer-Grünwald [74]**, a 19th-century imitation of the old Venetian Gothic; next to it is the real thing, the 1474 **Ca' Giustinian [75]**. Here we are almost at Piazza San Marco; as the canal opens up into the Bacino San Marco you will see the 15th-century **port authorities**, the **Capitaneria del Porto [76]** and the **Giardinetti Reali [77]**.

On the Right

The second palace after the Accademia is the **Palazzo Contarini dal Zaffo [78]**, a fine work of the late 1400s decorated after the style of the Lombardi. After Campo San Vio, the **Palazzo Barbarigo [79]** has mosaics from the 1880s (Venice still had a flourishing school of mosaicists at that time; their work, some good and some horrible, can be seen on churches across Italy).

There's no mistaking the canal's most peculiar landmark, the triumphantly unfinished **Palazzo Venier dei Leoni [80]**. Only the ground floor of this mid-18th-century palace was ever built. The resulting ranch-house effect attracted an American heiress, who lived here for 30 years; her excellent taste in modern art has provided the basis for the **Peggy Guggenheim Collection** (*see* p.163), one of the best of Venice's many museums. The second palace after it is another work influenced by the Lombardi, with a wealth of decoration in coloured marbles, the precariously leaning **Palazzo Dario [81]**. More modern mosaics can be seen on the **Palazzo Salviati** (1924) **[82]**, built by one of the Murano glass barons.

Now your *vaporetto* has reached the end of the canal and the ensemble of **Piazza San Marco**, **San Giorgio Maggiore** and the tip of the **Giudecca** comes into view. The last buildings on the canal contribute to the perfect crescendo climax of the trip: the great domed church of **Santa Maria della Salute [83]**, by Longhena (*see* p.163), and the golden ball of the 'Fortune' weathervane atop the **Dogana di Mare [84]** (*see* p.164), the old customs house of the republic.

Day Trips

VENETO VILLAS 242
Along the Brenta Canal 242
Villa Barbaro 243

PADUA 244

VERONA 247

12

Inland from Venice, the Veneto is lush and green, plush with art and architecture. The Bard may never have visited the cities where he set his plays, but there's something very Shakespearean about them – something gorgeous and poetic, full of character and Renaissance swagger. Thousands of villas and gardens, the country retreats of wealthy Venetians, give the Veneto a uniquely rarefied if often daydreamy distinction.

VENETO VILLAS

Along the Brenta Canal

Over the years, the river Brenta made itself universally detested by flooding the surrounding farmland and choking the Lagoon with silt, and in the 14th century the Venetians decided to control its antics once and for all. They raised its banks and dug a canal to divert its waters, and when all the hydraulic labours were completed in the 16th century they realized that the new canal was the ideal place for their summer *villeggiatura*; their gondoliers could conveniently row them straight to their doors, or, as Goethe and thousands of other visitors have done, they could travel there on the Burchiello, a water bus propelled by oars or horses. Over 70 villas and palaces sprouted up along this 'extension of the Grand Canal' and they were famous for summer parties.

La Malcontenta

Open May–Oct, Tues and Sat 9–12 or by appointment, t 041 520 3966; adm €8; guided tours.

Sailing up from Venice, the first sight is Palladio's temple-fronted Villa Foscari, better known as La Malcontenta, built in 1560 and as striking as it is simple. Viewed from the canal, it is a vision begging for a Scarlett O'Hara to sweep down the steps – not surprising, as the villa was a favourite model for American plantation-builders. Inside are some suitably delicate frescoes by Zelotti, Bernardino India and Battista Franco, one of which shows a sad woman – a possible source of the villa's name, although others say the unhappy one was the beautiful La Foscarina, who hated being cooped up here by her husband, far away from the fleshpots of Venice. Descendants of the original Foscari now own La Malcontenta, and have restored it beautifully.

Villa Nazionale (Villa Pisani)

Strà, t 049 502 074. Hour-long guided tours June–Sept Tues–Sun 9–6, until 7.30pm in Aug; Oct–May Tues–Sun 9–1.30; adm €5.

'If you've got it, flaunt it,' was the rule in Venice, especially in the 1700s, when one of the grandest villas in all Italy went up at Strà: the Villa Nazionale (or Pisani), enlarged by Alvise Pisani, scion of the fabulously wealthy banking family, to celebrate his election as doge in 1735. The new doge had

Getting There

In *The Merchant of Venice* Portia left her villa at Belmont on the Brenta Canal and proceeded down to Fusina to save Antonio's pound of flesh. For about the same price you can trace her route on the stately, villa-lined Brenta in a motorized version of the original public canalboat, the *Burchiello*, or on the simpler craft of *I Battelli del Brenta*; both make the day-long cruise (including stops) Mar–early Nov, Tues, Thurs and Sat from Venice, and Wed, Fri and Sun from Padua.

Burchiello, *at Siamic Express, Via Trieste 42, Padua,* **t** *049 660 944.*

I Battelli del Brenta, *Via Pellizzo 34, Padua,* **t** *049 876 0233,* **f** *049 807 2830,* **w** *www. intercity.shiny.it/battellidelbrenta.*

You can also follow the Brenta on the half-hourly **bus** to Padua from Venice's Piazzale Roma. For La Malcontenta, however, you must take a different bus, no.53, from Piazzale Roma, which leaves only hourly.

Eating Out

Locanda alla Posta, *Via Ca'Tron 33, Dolo,* **t** *041 410 740. Open Tues–Sun.* **Expensive**. This restaurant has been around a long time: great fish, delicately prepared.

Nalin, *Via Nuovissimo 29, Mira,* **t** *041 420 083. Open Tues–Sat and Sun lunch, closed Aug.* **Moderate**. One of the traditional places to round off a Brenta Canal excursion, with a lovely poplar-shaded veranda. The emphasis is on Venetian seafood, finely grilled.

served as Venice's ambassador in Paris; he suggested that something in the Versailles mould might just do, complete with *parterres* and canals, and hired an architect with the delicious name of Frigimelica Preti to do the job. The villa was completed in 1760, but only after the original plans were scaled down (!). The Pisani sold their brick and mortar dream of grandeur to Napoleon, who gave it to his stepson and viceroy in Italy, Eugène Beauharnais. In June 1934 Mussolini chose it as the stage for his first meeting with Hitler, where he strutted about in full fig, offering the Führer tips on how to deal with Austria and those pesky socialists. Although most of the villa has been stripped of its decoration, the ballroom makes up for the boredom with one of Tiepolo's most shimmering frescoes (the last he painted before leaving for Madrid), depicting, what else, the *Apotheosis of the Pisani Family*, who float about on clouds, hobnobbing with virtues and allegories of the continents. Son Giandomenico painted the chiaroscuro Roman scenes along the gallery. The vast park (the *parterres* were replaced in the 1800s with an English-style garden) contains the stables, a veritable equine Ritz, as well as innumerable pavilions and an expert-level box maze, planted in 1721.

Villa Contarini

Piazzola sul Brenta, **t** *049 559 0238.* **Open** *daily 9–12 and 3–6;* **adm** *€5.50.*

Built in 1414, this villa was greatly enlarged in 1564 by Palladio for Marco Contarini, a Procurator of the Republic; later residents added the 17th-century *barchesse*, adorned with the full whack of Palladian statues and balustrades, on grounds that include an arcaded hemicycle, park and lake. The interior is more elaborate than the average villa as well, featuring special Music and Listening Rooms with excellent acoustics. Villa Contarini had an interesting career in the 19th century, when it was purchased by Silvestro Camerini, who made Piazzola into a model industrial/agricultural estate. In fact, one of its main products, jute, was still being processed in the 1960s.

Villa Barbaro

Masèr, **t** *0423 923 004.* **Open** *Mar–Oct Tues, Sat, Sun and hols 3–6; Nov–Feb Sat, Sun and hols 2.30–5;* **adm** *€8.*

One villa, north of Padua, is not on the Brenta canal excursion, but is worth making the effort if you've fallen in love with Palladio. This unique synthesis of two great talents, Palladio and Veronese, was created in

Getting There

Frequent **buses** from Treviso (which is a 20min **train** journey from Venice, €1.80) serve Masèr for the Villa Barbaro.

Eating Out

Da Bastian, *Via Cornuda, Masèr,* **t** *0423 565 400.* **Open** *Fri–Wed lunch, closed Wed eve and Thurs.* **Moderate.** Just up the road from Palladio's villa, dine in enchanting surroundings, where the pâté, risotto, Venetian-style snails and desserts are renowned.

Al Ringranziamento, *Via San Pio X 107, Cavaso del Tomba,* **t** *0423 543 271.* **Open** *Tues eve–Sun, closed Mon, and Tues lunch.* **Expensive.** Just north of Masèr, you can eat at this romantic restaurant, where the creative chef is a master at concocting delicious dishes.

1568 for two great patrons, the Barbaro brothers, Daniele and Marcantonio.

Palladio used the Temple of Fortuna Virilis in Rome as his inspiration for the central residence, while the *barchesse* are graceful wings with dovecotes rising at the ends, each with a sundial, forming the five-part profile that would inspire countless buildings (including the United States' Capitol). The horses frisking about the front lawn add to the patrician dignity, while the reliefs on the central pediment – the double-headed eagle of Byzantium (Aquileia, in this case) and two men astride dragons or sea monsters – add an air of mystery. Emblems like this were the rage in the Renaissance, full of puns and allegorical references for those in the know.

Palladio taught Veronese about space and volume, and nowhere is this so evident as in these ravishing, architectonic *trompe-l'œil* frescoes, which repopulate the villa with the original owners and their pets, lingering as if the villa lay under the same spell as Sleeping Beauty's castle. Signora Barbaro and her sons gaze down from painted balconies; a little girl opens a door; a dog waits in a corner; painted windows offer views of imaginary landscapes; the huntsman in the far bedroom is Veronese, gazing across the row of rooms at his mistress.

The back garden is taken up with a **nymphaeum**, guarded by giants sculpted by Marcantonio Barbaro. The striking, if crumbling **Tempietto**, just across the road, is a miniature Barbaro pantheon designed by Palladio in 1580, inspired by his favourite building, Bramante's Tempietto in Rome.

PADUA (PADOVA)

Padua refuses to be overshadowed by Venice, and can rightly claim a place among Italy's most interesting and historic cities. Its university, one of the oldest in Europe, was attended by Petrarch, Dante and Galileo; its churches, under the brushes of Giotto, Altichiero, Giusto de' Menabuoi and Mantegna, were virtual laboratories in the evolution of fresco. But above all, Padua attracts pilgrims of a more pious nature; its exotic, domed mosque of a basilica is the last resting place of St Anthony of Padua.

If Venice proves too expensive, it would be perfectly feasible to sleep in Padua and see Venice by day.

Cappella degli Scrovegni

Piazza Eremitani 8, **t** *049 201 0020,* **w** *www.cappelladegliscrovegni.it.* **Chapel open** *by appt only, summer 9am–10pm, winter 9–6, museum open Tues–Sun 9–6; adm €5.15; visits to the chapel timed, book 3 days in advance.*

It's a short walk from the station to the jewel in Padua's crown: Giotto's extraordinary frescoes (1304–7) in the Cappella degli Scrovegni. In sheer power and inspiration, the cycle was as revolutionary as Michelangelo's Sistine Chapel: a fresh, natural, narrative New Testament cycle, with three-dimensional figures solidly anchored in their setting. Giotto's sons worked at his side, and were visited by Dante during work.

In the adjacent convent, Padua's vast **Museo Civico** combines archaeology (coins,

vases, and funerary stelae from the 6th to
1st centuries BC) with acres of fine art. Here
you'll find Giotto's *Crucifixion*, works by
Guariento, founder of the medieval Paduan
school, and others by nearly every Venetian
who ever applied brush to canvas: Bellini,
Tintoretto, Titian, Vivarini, Veronese, Tiepolo
and others down the line. The small
Renaissance bronzes were a speciality of
Padua, especially those by Il Riccio.

Eremitani

Piazza Garibaldi 9, t 049 875 6410. **Open**
*Mon–Sat 8–12.30 and 4–6; Sun 9.30–12 and
4–6; adm free.*

Next to the museum, the church of the
Eremitani (1306;) was shattered in a
Second World War air raid, but what could
be salvaged of the frescoes has been
painstakingly pieced together, most importantly Mantegna's **Ovetari chapel** (1454–7).

Santa Sofia

Via Santa Sofia. **Open** *Mon–Sat 7.30–12 and
4–7, Sun 8–12.30 and 4.30–6; adm free.*

Padua's oldest church, 9th-century Santa
Sofia, to the east, has a lovely Veneto-
Byzantine apse and a precious polychrome
Pietà by Egidio da Wienerneustadt.

The Carmine

Open *daily 8–12 and 4–7.30; adm free.*

The quarter to the west of the Eremitani,
Borgo Molino, was once an 'island' cut off
by the Bacchiglione. Its centrepiece, the
Carmine, was rebuilt as the headquarters of
a confraternity by Lorenzo da Bologna in
1494; the **Scuola del Carmine** has an interior

Getting There

Padua is easily reached by **train** from Venice (30mins), leaving Stazione Santa Lucia every half-hour or so.

There are also **buses** from Venice's Piazzale Roma every half-hour, arrving at Padua's bus station in the Piazzale Boschetti (**t** 049 820 6844), a 10min walk from the train station.

Tourist Information

In the train station, t 049 875 2077. **Open** Mon–Sat 9–7, Sun 9–12.

Galleria Pedrocchi, t 049 876 7927. **Open** Mon–Sat 9–12.30 and 3–7.

Piazza del Santo, t 049 875 3087. **Open** April–Oct Mon–Sat 9–6, Sun 9–12.
e info@turismopadova.it
w www.turismopadova.it

Where to Stay ✉ 35100

****Donatello, Via del Santo 102, **t** 049 875 0634, **f** 049 8675 0829. **Expensive**. By the basilica of Sant'Antonio: Gattamelata points right to it. Rooms are air-conditioned.

****Grande Italia, Corso del Popolo 81, **t** 049 876 111, **f** 049 875 0850. **Expensive**. A beautiful Liberty building, opposite the railway station.

***Al Cason, Via Paolo Scarpi 40, **t** 049 66236, **f** 049 875 4217. **Moderate**. Cheaper and near the station.

***Leon Bianco, Piazzetta Pedrocchi 12, **t** 049 875 0814, **f** 049 875 6184. **Moderate**. Small and cosy and right in the heart of Padua.

Ostello Città di Padova, Via Aleardi 30, **t** 049 875 2219, **f** 049 654 210. **Cheap**. Pleasant, clean, and city-run; IYHF cards required. Take bus 3, 8 or 11 from the station to Prato della Valle.

*Pavia, Via del Papafava 11, **t** 049 661 558. **Cheap**. Deservedly popular, clean, central and friendly.

Sant'Antonio, Via S. Fermo 118, **t 049 875 1393, **f** 049 875 2508. **Cheap**. Between the station and centre by the Porta Molino, providing a friendly, family atmosphere.

Eating Out

La cucina padovana features carni di cortile: chicken, duck, pheasant, goose and pigeon.

Antico Brolo, Corso Milano 22, **t** 049 664 555. **Closed** Mon and Sun lunch, some of Aug. **Expensive**. Not far from the historic centre and occupying an elegant 15th-century building. There's a garden for outdoor dining on Veneto and Emilian specialities. There's a good pizzeria down in the old wine cellar where you'll spend a lot less.

La Corta Dei Leoni, Via Pietro D'Abano 1, **t** 049 815 0083. **Closed** Sun eve, Mon; wheelchair accessible. **Moderate**. For a truly sumptious meal in a walled courtyard in the historic centre. The seasonal menu is changed weekly, while the wine list reflects the best Italy has to offer. Specialities include lardo di colonata (wafer-thin lard, spiced and salted) and scaloppa di rombo con finocchi gratinati.

Bastioni del Moro, Via Bronzetti 18, **t** 049 871 0006. **Open** Mon–Sat. **Cheap**. This serves delicious gnocchi beyond Padua's western walls (take Corso Milano). The tourist menu is cheap, though prices soar if you order fish.

Bertolini, Via Antichiero 162, **t** 049 600 357. **Open** Sun–Fri. **Cheap**. This has been a favourite for 150 years; go for the hearty vegetarian dishes and home-made desserts.

with cinquecento frescoes by Domenico Campagnola and Stefano dall'Azere.

Piazza Cavour

A short walk from the Eremitani takes you to the historic heart of Padua. You'll see a stylish Egyptian-revival mausoleum with columned stone porches; this is the **Caffè Pedrocchi** (Piazzetta Pedrocchi, open Tues–Sun 9.30–12.30 and 3.30–7; adm €2), built in 1831 by Giuseppe Japelli, and famous in its day for never closing (it had no doors) and for the intellectuals and students who came here to debate. You can still get a coffee, as well as visit the upper floor. Also in the piazza, the **Palazzo del Bo'** (Via VII Febbraio 2, open for guided tours March–Sept Tues, Thurs and Sat 9, 10,11, Mon, Wed and Fri 3, 4 and 5; adm €3) was the seat of the University of Padua, where Galileo delivered his lectures from an old wooden pulpit.

The Medieval Civic Centre

To the west are the bustling market squares of **Piazza delle Erbe** and **Piazza delle Frutta**, separated by the massive **Palazzo della Ragione** (*closed for restoration*).

Padua's **Duomo** is rather neglected, but the **baptistry** (*open 9.30–1 and 3–6, adm €2*) was beautifully frescoed by Florentine Giusto de' Menabuoi in the 1370s, its awesome, chilling dome painted with a multitude of saints.

Basilica di Sant'Antonio

Piazza del Santo, t 049 878 9722. Open daily 7.30–7; adm free.

Below the commercial heart of Padua, an exotic, fantastical cluster of seven domes rises up around a lofty cupola, two campanili and two minarets: this is the Basilica di Sant'Antonio, begun in 1232, the same year that St Anthony was canonized. Inside, pilgrims queue patiently to press their palm against his tomb; no one pays much attention to the 16th-century marble reliefs lining his chapel, but they are exquisite: the fourth and fifth are by Sansovino, the sixth and seventh by Tullio Lombardo, and the last by Antonio Lombardo. The high altar is the work of Donatello and his helpers (1445–50), while the great Paschal Candelabrum is the masterpiece of Il Riccio. In the ambulatory, don't miss the treasury of gold reliquaries, one containing Anthony's tongue and larynx, found extraordinarily intact when his tomb was opened in 1981.

In front of the basilica, a bit lost among the pigeons and souvenirs, is Donatello's **statue of Gattamelata** (1453), the first large equestrian bronze since antiquity.

VERONA

The gorgeous rosy-pink city curling along the banks of the Adige has evocative streets and romantic *piazzas*, sublime art, magnificent architecture, romantic associations with Juliet, and all the gnocchi you can eat.

The first thing most people see, whether arriving by rail or road, is Sammicheli's Renaissance gate, the **Porta Nuova**, at the head of the Corso Porta Nuova. This avenue leads straight under another gate, Gian Galeazzo Visconti's **Portoni della Brà**, and into the heart of tourist Verona: the large, irregular **Piazza Brà**, the favourite promenade of the Veronese and tourists.

Arena

Piazza Brà, t 045 800 3204. Open Tues–Sun 8–7; adm €3.10; for opera information call t 045 805 1811, w www.arena.it.

Built in the 1st century AD and, after the Colosseum, the best-preserved amphitheatre in Italy, the elliptical Arena seats 25,000. Dressed in pink and white marble, the Arena is lovely enough to make one almost forget the brutal sports it was built to host. During the Middle Ages, Verona kept up Roman traditions by using it for public executions; in the Renaissance it hosted knightly tournaments, and in the Baroque era it was used for bull-baiting. Since 1913, the death and mayhem has been purely operatic.

Museo Lapidario Maffeiano

Piazza Brà/Via Roma, t 045 590 087. Open Tues–Sun 9–2; adm €2.

Established in 1714, this was one of the first museums in the world dedicated to ancient inscriptions. It houses an incredible collection, including some beautiful Roman funeral reliefs, depicting a couple as their children wished them to be remembered.

Piazza delle Erbe, Piazza dei Signori and the Scaliger Tombs

From Piazza Brà, Via Mazzini is the most direct route to the core of medieval and Roman Verona, the **Piazza delle Erbe**. The market square still fulfils its original purpose. A colourful panoply of buildings encases the square, including the 12th-century **Torre de Lamberti**, 275ft high, reached by a lift from the courtyard of the **Palazzo della Ragione** (*open Tues–Sun 9–6; adm*). The striped *palazzo* has a lovely Romanesque-Gothic courtyard, the Cortile del Mercato Vecchio, which forms a pretty setting for a series of free summer classical/jazz/blues concerts.

From Piazza delle Erbe, the Arco della Costa leads into stately **Piazza dei Signori**, the civic centre of Verona, presided over by a grouchy statue of Dante (1865). Behind Dante, the **Loggia del Consiglio** (1493) is the city's finest Renaissance building, decorated with yellow and red frescoes. The crenellated **Tribunale** (law courts), formerly a Scaliger palace, has a portal by Sammicheli; in the courtyard, and in adjacent Via Dante, you can peer down through glass into Verona's Roman streets, revealed in the 1980s **Scaliger excavations**. The underground corridors are used for photo exhibitions (*open Tues–Sun 10–6.30*).

The arch adjoining the Tribunale leads to the grand Gothic pantheon of the della Scala, the **Scaliger Tombs** or Arche Scaligere (*open Tues–Sun 9–6; adm €2.80*), which Ruskin considered the crowning achievement of Veronese Gothic. Don't miss the crowned dogs next to Cangrande's effigy, standing like firemen holding up ladders.

Casa di Giulietta
*Via Cappello 23, near Piazza delle Erbe, **t** 045 803 4303. **Open** Tues–Sun 9–6.30; **adm** €3.*

Although the association is slim (the 13th-century house was once an inn called 'Il Cappello', reminiscent of the dal Cappello family, the original of the Capulets), it was restored on the outside in 1935 to fit the Shakespearian bill, with lovely windows and *de rigueur* balcony.

Sant'Anastasia
*Piazza Sant'Anastasia. **Open** Mon–Sat 9–6, Sun 1–6; **adm** free.*

North of the Scaliger Tombs, it's hard to miss Verona's largest church, begun in 1290 but never completed. The interior is beautiful, but, just coming in from the bright sun, many people start at what appears to be two men loitering under the holy water stoops; these are the Gobbi, or hunchbacks. The three naves are supported by massive marble columns and decorated by an all-star line-up of artists: there's the beautiful Fregoso altar by Sammicheli), and excellent frescoes by Verona native Altichiero from 1390, in the Cavalli Chapel in the right apse. The next chapel has 24 terracottas by Michele da Firenze on the Life of Jesus; paintings by the school of Mantegna fill the Pellegrini chapel and, to the left of the high altar opposite a large 15th-century *Last Judgement*, the tomb of Cortesia Serego (1429) has an equestrian statue by Tuscan Nanni di Bartolo and frescoes by Michele Giambono. Best of all, in the sacristy, there's a fairytale fresco, *St George at Trebizond* (1438) by Pisanello.

Galleria d'Arte Moderna

Via Piana, t 045 800 1903. Open Tues–Sun 9–7 for the permanent exhibition, 9–10 for the summer exhibitions; adm €3.

The medieval Palazzo Forti which once lodged Napoleon now houses the modern art gallery, where frequent exhibitions share the walls with Italian masters of the 19th and 20th centuries.

Duomo

Piazza Duomo, t 045 595 627. Open 10–5.30, Sun 1.30–5.30; adm €2.

Verona's cathedral was consecrated in 1187, Romanesque at the roots and Renaissance in

Getting There

Verona is accessible by **train** from Venice, 1hr 45mins. The station, **Porta Nuova**, is a 15min walk south of Piazza Brà, along Corso Porta Nuova; alternatively, **city buses** nos.71 or 72 link the station with Piazza delle Erbe and Piazza Brà.

Tourist Information

Opposite Palazzo Barbieri, *Via degli Alpini 9, t 045 806 8680 (next to the Arena). Open summer daily 9–6, winter Mon–Sat 9–6.*

Porta Nuova station, *t 045 800 861. Open summer daily 9–6, winter Mon–Sat 9–6.*

e iatbra@tiscalinet.it

w www.tourism.verona.it

Verona urban (ATM) and APT buses offer an ***Invito a Verona*** pass (available at the bus depot, tourist office or museums, €11.50) from mid-June–Oct, a daily or weekly scheme that includes unlimited travel and museum admissions.

Note that most sights are closed on Mondays.

Eating Out

The Veronese have long gastro-memories. They've been fond of potato gnocchi (served with melted butter and sage) since the late 16th century.

Arche, *Via delle Arche Scaligere 6, t 045 800 7415. Open Mon eve–Sat. Very expensive.* Run by the same family for over 100 years, and located near the Scaliger tombs. The freshest of fish is brought in daily from Chioggia.

Il Desco, *Via dietro San Sebastiano 7, t 045 595 358. Open Mon–Sat. Very expensive.* This king of the Veronese restaurant scene occupies a 15th-century palace, not far from the Ponte Nuovo.

Bottega del Vino, *Via Scudo di Francia 3, t 045 800 4535. Open Wed–Mon. Expensive.* A century-old restaurant, preparing traditional recipes using organically grown ingredients, and pasta made on the premises.

I Dodici Apostoli, *Corticella San Marco 3, t 045 596 999. Open Tues–Sat. Expensive.* An even older favourite, located a couple of streets from Piazza delle Erbe, offering a traditional Renaissance setting.

Maffei, *Piazza delle Erbe 38, t 045 801 0015. Open Tues–Sat. Expensive.* Another beauty, both ancient and elegant, which serves a melt-in-the-mouth cheese flan and risotto.

Greppia, *Vicolo Samaritana 3, t 045 800 4577. Open Tues–Sun, closed June. Moderate.* Near Juliet's house, serving traditional and Veronese favourites in a quiet little square.

Alla Pergola, *Piazzetta Santa Maria in Solaro 10, t 045 800 4744. Open Thurs–Tues, closed Aug. Moderate.* A traditional and reliable old favourite, housed in a deconsecrated medieval church off Via Garibaldi.

Antico Cafè Dante, *Via Fogge 1. Open Mon–Sat 10–6. Cheap.* Stop for a coffee at this historic café.

its windows and octagonal crown. Inside, there's the beautifully carved Tomb of St Agatha (1353) in the Cappella Mazzanti, and an *Assumption* by Titian in the first chapel on the left.

Veronetta

The north bank of the Adige, locally known as 'Veronetta', was the part of the city that remained in Austrian hands until 1866. If you cross over the Ponte Garibaldi, just down from the Duomo, the first landmark is the large dome of **San Giorgio in Braida** (1477) to your right. Follow the Adige down to **Santo Stefano** (*open 8.30–12 and 4.30–7; adm free*), an important palaeo-Christian church, pieced together in the 12th century from 5th–10th-century columns and capitals.

In ancient times, the citizens of Verona would trot over the Ponte Pietra to attend the latest plays at the picturesque **Teatro Romano** (*open summer 9–7, winter 9–3 adm €2.50*). A lift goes up to the **Archaeology Museum** (*open Tues–Sun 9–3.30; adm €3*), occupying a convent built on top of the theatre, with bronzes, busts and mosaics.

San Fermo Maggiore

*Stradone San Fermo. **Open** Mon–Sat 10–1 and 1.30–4, Sun 1.30–4; **adm** €2.*

From Piazza delle Erbe, Via Cappello/Leoni leads past the picturesque ruins of the 1st-century BC **Porta dei Leoni** (incorporated into a building), marking the beginning of the Roman *cardo maximus*. This leads to the splendid vertical apse of San Fermo Maggiore, an architectural club sandwich: it consists of two churches, one built on top of the other. The Romanesque bottom was begun in 1065 by the Benedictines, while the upper Gothic church, with its attractive red and white patterns, was added by the Franciscans in 1320, along with the façade.

The upper church is covered with a lovely wooden ceiling of 1314 and fine 14th-century frescoes. The first chapel on the right has a fresco by Stefano da Verona; in the right transept the Renaissance Cappella Alighieri has a pair of tombs by Sammicheli; and the

left transept has good frescoes on the *Life of St Francis* by Liberale da Verona. The Cappella delle Donne contains one of Caroto's best altarpieces (*Madonna and Saints*, 1528) and a beautiful tomb, the Monumento Brenzoni (1439) by Florentine Nanni di Bartolo).

Castelvecchio

From Piazza delle Erbe, Corso Porta Bórsari leads through the twin-arched **Porta dei Bórsari** to **Corso Cavour**, one of Verona's most elegant thoroughfares, embellished with palaces from various epochs. The best is Sammicheli's refined if unfinished **Palazzo Bevilacqua** (1588, No.19), with its ornate, rhythmic alteration of large and small windows, columns and pediments.

Cangrande II's fortress of **Castelvecchio** (1355) has weathered centuries of use by other top dogs, from the Venetians to Napoleon and the Nazis, to become Verona's excellent civic **museum of art** (*open Tues–Sun 9–7; adm €3*). Beyond the collection of old town bells and detached frescoes wait excellent 14th-century paintings. The museum is especially rich in lovely Madonnas.

Basilica of San Zeno Maggiore

*Piazza San Zeno, t 045 800 6120, a 15min walk from Castelvecchio or bus 32 or 33 from Corso Porta Borsari. **Open** summer Mon–Sat 9–6, Sun 1–6, winter Mon–Sat 9–5; **adm** €2.*

This is one of the finest Romanesque buildings anywhere. First built in the 4th century next to a Benedictine monastery, the basilica took its present form between 1120 and 1398. For centuries San Zeno was the symbol of Veronese liberty, the custodian of its *carroccio* or war wagon.

The rich **façade** of San Zeno has a perfect centrepiece: a 12th-century rose window, the *Wheel of Fortune* by Maestro Brioloto. The vast **interior**, divided into three naves by Roman columns and capitals, has a beautiful Gothic ceiling, 13th- and 14th-century frescoes and, on the altar, the magnificent triptych *Madonna, Angels and Saints* (1459) by Andrea Mantegna. Also spare a glance for the handsome **cloister**, completed in 1313.

Where to Stay

San Marco 252

Castello 256

Dorsoduro 258

San Polo and Santa Croce 259

Cannaregio 260

The Lagoon 261

Hostels 262

Camping 262

Self-Catering 262

For hundreds of years it was the Senate's policy to lodge guests free of charge in the best palaces in the city, and if they insisted on staying in an inn, the Senate made sure the grub was as lousy as the bed. This magnanimity probably had as much to do with the desire to spy on the guest as the fact that hosts were exempt from the restrictions of the sumptuary laws; a guest meant they could dress up in forbidden jewels and serve extra courses at dinner.

Well, in this city where change is slow, you can still stay in a palace and flaunt every sumptuary law left on the books – for a pound of flesh (blood included this time). Even the cheap hotels charge about 30% more than you'd pay on the mainland, but if you're really counting the kopecks you can stay in Padua's municipal hostel or in Mestre and commute to Venice. Still, this is never as much fun as trying to find your hotel in the labyrinth after dark.

Not surprisingly, the most charming hotels in such a popular city are no secret, and to get a room in any of them, you need to book several months in advance (remember to request a room with a view). The best means is to ring the hotel and make arrange-ments to pay a deposit directly, which insures your booking, though if you cancel your reserva-tion the hotel will keep the deposit unless another agreement has been reached. Booking via the internet is another possibility (and means you can check out what the hotel looks like), but on the whole discounts are not given for online bookings, nor can you bargain.

If you're coming in the summer without reservations, take pot luck with the tourist office's free hotel-finding service in the train station or Piazzale Roma.

Perhaps the most relaxed and serendipitous *sestiere* for sleeping, containing, by Venetian standards, many of the most pleasant 'economy' hotels, is Dorsoduro.

Price Categories

As with restaurants, hotel prices in Venice are much higher than anywhere else in Italy. Rates quoted are for a standard double room in high season, but prices vary enormously depending on the time of year and the day of the week. High season runs from about Easter to mid-November, with the exception of July/ August, plus New Year and any Italian holidays (*see* p.89). In some places, prices will be almost halved out of season. There is also room for negotiation within high season at some hotels; some places will give a discount for last-minute bookings, so always ask (not usually true of luxury hotels).

The price categories below are for a double room with bath in high season. For rooms without private baths, subtract 20–30%. For a single, count on paying 70% of a double; to add an extra bed in a double room will add 33% to the bill. Taxes and service charges are included in the given rate.

luxury	€400 and over
very expensive	€300–400
expensive	€200–300
moderate	€100–200
inexpensive	under €100

San Marco

Luxury

Europa e Regina*** H8
San Marco 2159, Corte Barozzi, **t** *041 240 0001,* **f** *041 523 1533,* **e** *europaregina@westin.com,* **w** *www.westin.com;* **vaporetto** *Vallaresso.*
Across the Grand Canal from the Salute, this old hotel is nicely renovated and has large rooms; 20 have views of the Grand Canal, others look out on to a quiet garden courtyard. There are pretty, high-ceilinged reception rooms and a majestic Venetian drawing room furnished with every amenity. Cots, babysitting service; phones, TV and air-conditioning in all rooms.

Gritti Palace*** G8
San Marco 2467, Campo Santa Maria del Giglio, **t** *041 794 611,* **f** *041 520 0942,* **e** *grittipalace@ starwoodhotels.com,* **w** *www. starwood.com/grittipalace;* **vaporetto** *Santa Maria del Giglio;* wheelchair accessible.
The 15th-century Grand Canal palace that belonged to the dashing Doge Andrea Gritti has been preserved as a true Venetian fantasy and an elegant retreat, with one of the finest dining terraces on the canal. The staff are particularly cordial and the atmosphere, though grand, is unusually welcoming. For a real splurge do as Somerset Maugham did and stay in the Doge Suite. Or, even more sumptuous, the Hemingway (a mere €3,450, and that's not including tax). Cots, babysitting service; phones, TV and air-conditioning in all rooms.

Very Expensive

Concordia** I7
San Marco 367, Calle Larga San Marco, **t** *041 520 6866,* **f** *041 520 6775,* **e** *venezia@hotelconcordia.it,* **w** *www.hotelconcordia.it;* **vaporetto** *San Marco.*
The only hotel overlooking Piazza San Marco has a touch of Hollywood in some of the furnish-ings. Stairs up to reception put paid to disabled access. Cots, babysitting service; phones, TV and air-conditioning in all rooms.

Kette** H8
San Marco 2053, Piscina San Moisè, **t** *041 520 7766,* **f** *041 522 8964,* **e** *info@hotelkette.com,* **w** *www.hotelkette.com;* **vaporetto** *San Marco;* wheelchair accessible.
The Kette has been upgraded to 4-star status. The 63 elegant rooms have pale striped walls, *mezzacrona* beds and smart bathrooms; colour schemes are dusty pink and green. Public rooms on the ground floor have been expanded and there are now conference facilities. Cots, babysit-ting service; phones, TV and air-conditioning in all rooms.

Monaco e Grand Canal** H8
San Marco 1332, Calle Vallaresso,
t 041 520 0211, f 041 520 0501,
e mailbox@hotelmonaco.it;
vaporetto Vallaresso; wheelchair
accessible
A medium-sized hotel in an 18th-
century palace overlooking the
mouth of the Grand Canal, near
Piazza San Marco. Rooms have a
view of the canal or garden at the
back; the restaurant has a canalside terrace; and the garden
terrace is another plus. Cots,
babysitting service; phones, TV
and air-conditioning in all rooms.

Very Expensive

Panada** I7
San Marco 646, Calle Specchieri,
t 041 520 9088, f 041 520 9619,
w www. hotelpanada.com;
vaporetto San Marco.
On a relatively quiet, narrow street
very near Piazza San Marco, this
old building has pleasantly renovated Venetian-style rooms. All
have bath, some of them Jacuzzis
(and the added delight of
windows – a rare feature in
Venetian hotel bathrooms). Prices
are at the top of this price band,
but there are good off-season
discounts. Cots, babysitting
service; phones, TV and air-conditioning in all rooms.

San Molsè** H8
San Marco 2058, Piscina San Moisè,
t 041 520 3755, f 041 521 0670,
e info@sanmoise.it, w www.
sanmoise.it; vaporetto Vallaresso.
A major overhaul of this quiet
hotel has swept aside the rather
cloying Venetian style in favour of
a cleaner look. Most bathrooms
have a tub. Book well ahead for a
room overlooking the canal; there
is a little terrace outside on the
calle. Cots, babysitting service;
phone, TV and air-conditioning.

Expensive

Centauro** H7
San Marco 4297, Campo Manin,
t 041 522 5832, f 041 523 9151,
w www.hotelcentauro.com;
vaporetto Rialto.

This friendly hotel was undergoing restoration work on its top
floor as we went to press, and
there were plans to overhaul the
first floor. One of the older inns in
Venice, it still has some rooms
with original, typically Venetian,
mosaic flooring. The atmosphere
is pleasingly old fashioned, the
staff very courteous. Cots, babysitting service; phones, TV and
air-conditioning in all rooms.

Flora** H8
San Marco 2283A, Calle Larga XXII
Marzo, t 041 520 5844, f 041 522
8217, e info@hotelflora.it, w www.
hotelflora.it; vaporetto Vallaresso.
This delightful little hotel seems
to be in just about every guide
book there is, so you need to book
early to snare one of the typically
Venetian rooms (the rest are
comparatively spartan and
cramped); the best are those
facing the garden on the ground
floor and those on the corners of
the building. The garden makes a
magical breakfast setting in warm
weather. Cots, babysitting service;
phones, TV and air-conditioning.

San Zulian** I7
San Marco 534, Calle San Zulian,
t 041 522 5872, f 041 523 2265,
e info@hotelsanzulian.com,
w www.hotelsanzulian.com;
vaporetto San Marco; wheelchair
accessible.
Situated in a typical back street in
the centre of town, this hotel has
an airy reception hall with stylishly spare décor and a calm white
and grey colour scheme. The 22
rooms are furnished in unfussy
Venetian style and have smart
marble bathrooms. Cots; phone,
TV and air-conditioning.

Moderate

Bel Sito e Berlino** G8
San Marco 2517, Campo Santa
Maria del Giglio, t 041 522 3365,
f 041 520 4083, e belsito@iol.it,
w http://users.iol.it/belsito/;
vaporetto Santa Maria del Giglio.
Closed Nov.
A charming and comfortable 34-
room hotel overlooking the ornate

façade of Santa Maria del Giglio.
All rooms have private bath,
phone, TV and air-conditioning,
cots and a babysitting service.

Do Pozzi** G8
San Marco 2373, Via XXII Marzo,
t 041 520 7855, f 041 522 9413,
e info@hoteldopozzi.it,
w www.hoteldopozzi.it; vaporetto
Vallaresso/Santa Maria del Giglio.
With 29 rooms on a charming
little square where tables are set
out for breakfast or a drink, this
friendly hotel is very appealing.
Rooms on two of the three floors
have been recently renovated, and
there are some in a nearby
annexe. Public rooms are
furnished in traditional Venetian
style, but bedrooms are more
modern. A discount is offered at
nearby restaurant Da Raffaele.
Cots, babysitting service; phones,
TV and air-conditioning.

Gallini** G7
San Marco 3673, Calle della Verona,
t 041 520 4515, f 041 520 9103,
e hgallini@tin.it; vaporetto
Sant'Angelo.
The décor in this hotel makes no
concessions to contemporary
trends: browns predominate, and
the furniture is largely no-frills
light wood. But many of the
rooms are very spacious, and
those on the top floors have
marvellous views. The place is
spotless and the management are
charming; a large black cat seems
to rule the roost. Bearers of this
guide will be given a discount. All
room have phones, and some have
TV and air-conditioning; there are
six without a bath.

Locanda Art Déco** F7
San Marco 2966, Calle delle
Botteghe, t 041 277 0558, f 041 270
2891, e info@locandaartdeco.com,
w www.locandaartdeco.com;
vaporetto San Samuele.
This delightful 7-room *locanda*
opened in 2001; the stylish, light
rooms are dotted with Art Deco
furniture. Bathrooms are pale pink
marble, and there's a particularly
romantic attic room. In high
season, minimum 3-night stay at

H I J K L M N O

Venice Hotels

500 m
500 yards

N

S. Michele

Gesuiti

7

SS.
Apostoli

8

Rio dei SS. Apostoli

FONDAMENTA NUOVE

S. Ferce

ADA NUOVA

d'Oro

SS. Giovanni
e Paolo

9

12

10

CHIA

PONTE DI RIALTO

DEL CARBON

45

CAMPO S.
BARTOLOMEO

S. Lio

13

S.
Salvador

SALIZZADA
S. LIO

CAMPO S.
MARIA
FORMOSA

S. Maria
Formosa

11

Rio di S. Francesco

14

MERCERIE

FUGA GIUFFA

CALLE DEI FABBRI

FUSSERI

17

18

15

16

CAMPO SS
FILIPPO E
GIACOMO

20

Rio del Vin

S. Giorgio
dei Greci

Rio di S. Lorenzo

Scuola di
S. Giorgio
degli Schiavoni

ARSENALE

Canale delle Galeazze

ARCO

39

St
Mark's

19

PIAZZA S.
MARCO

22

23

21

S. Zaccaria

CASTELLO

8

Pal.
Ducale

30

29

28

27

26

24

Giardini
Reali

RIVA DEGLI SCHIAVONI

32

31

S. Moisè

Maria
ella
ute

Dogana
di Mare

25

VIA GIUSEPPE GARIBALDI

Canale di San Marco

S. Giorgio
Maggiore

S. Giorgio
Maggiore

Giardini
Biennale

FONDS.
GIOVANNI

66

FOND. S. ZITELLE

65

Le Zitelle

SQUERO

Map Key

55	Accademia
58	Agli Alboretti
8	Ai Santi Apostoli
47	Ai Tolentini
59	American
56	Antica Locanda Montin
34	Bel Sito e Berlino
1	Bellini
25	Bucintoro
26	Ca' del Dose
52	Ca' Foscari
57	Ca' Pisani
63	La Calcina
14	Caneva
7	Casa Boccassini
2	Casa Carettoni
50	Casa Peron
22	Casa Verardo
43	Centauro
66	Cipriani
19	Concordia
13	Da Bruno
49	Dalla Mora
30	Danieli
35	Do Pozzi
21	Doni
6	Eden
32	Europa e Regina
48	Falier
36	Flora
23	Fontana
11	Foresteria Valdese
42	Gallini
33	Gritti Palace
4	Guerrini
51	Hotel Iris
64	Istituto Canossiano
37	Kette
41	Locanda Art Déco
10	Locanda La Corte
5	Locanda del Ghetto
16	Locanda Remedio
53	Locanda San Barnaba
28	Londra Palace
9	Malibran
45	Marconi
60	Messner
27	Metropole
31	Monaco e Grand Canal
65	Ostello di Venezia
18	Panada
54	Pausania
24	La Residenza
20	Rio
3	Rossi
61	Alla Salute da Cici
46	San Cassiano
40	San Fantin
39	San Gallo
38	San Moisè
17	San Zulian
12	Santa Marina
29	Savoia e Jolanda
62	Seguso
15	Silva
44	Sturion

weekends, but rates are lower mid-week and *much* lower off season. All rooms have phone, TV and air-conditioning.

San Fantin** G7
San Marco 1930A, Campiello Fenice, t/f 041 523 1 401; vaporetto Vallaresso.
Just round the corner from La Fenice in a quiet little *campo*, this simple hotel is out of a time - warp, with a reception area a bit like your granny's parlour, dated in a rather refreshing way. The 14 rooms (two without a bath) are pleasant and the place is spotless. All rooms have phone and TV.

San Gallo*** H7
San Marco 1093A, Campo San Gallo, t 041 522 7311, f 041 522 5702, e sangallo@hotelsangallo.com, w www.hotelsangallo.com; vaporetto Vallaresso.
A door in a rather shabby building and a steep flight of steps lead to this friendly, 12-room hotel with its attractive breakfast room/reception area. Some rooms are heavily Venetian, others a little sparer. Several are big enough for one or two extra beds, a couple of others are tiny. There is a pretty roof terrace. Cots; TV, phone and air-conditioning.

Castello

Luxury

Danieli***** J8
Castello 4196, Riva degli Schiavoni, t 041 522 6480, f 041 520 0208, e danieli@luxurycollection.com, w www.luxurycollection.com; vaporetto San Zaccaria; wheelchair accessible.

The largest and most famous hotel in Venice, set in the Gothic palace of the ducal Dandolo family, was transformed into a hotel in 1822. Nearly every room has some story to tell, and you can add your own in a beautiful setting of silken walls, Gothic stairs, gilt mirrors and oriental rugs. The 'new' wings, much vilified since they were built in the 1940s, are comfortable but lack the charm and stories. The biggest problem the Danieli has to contend with is noise; avoid a room on the Riva unless you are desperate for views of the Lagoon. Cots, babysitting service; phones, TV and air-conditioning in all rooms.

Londra Palace**** K8
Castello 4171, Riva degli Schiavoni, t 041 520 0533, f 041 522 5032, e info@hotelondra.it w www.hotelondra.it; vaporetto San Zaccaria; wheelchair accessible.
This hotel, made by linking two palaces together, has been a favourite of Russian composers, from Tchaikovsky, who composed his Fourth Symphony in room 108, to Stravinsky. Smaller than most hotels in this class, it has its own luxurious restaurant – Les Deux Lions – a cool, elegant lobby in which to retreat from the bustle of the Riva, and a stunning roof terrace. Cots, babysitting service; phones, TV and air-conditioning in all rooms.

Metropole**** K8
Castello 4149, Riva degli Schiavoni, t 041 520 5044, f 041 522 3679, e venice@hotelmetropole.com, w www.hotelmetropole.com; vaporetto San Zaccaria; wheelchair accessible.
A luxurious hotel with a hip, slightly decadent feel to it. Situated on the Riva, it not only has great views over the water to San Giorgio Maggiore, but also a fantastic, quiet garden for cooling off. Furnishings are sumptuous and romantic, with lots of brocade in rich colours, chandeliers, wonderful antiques (some of

which are for sale) and heavily scented fresh flowers. Cots, babysitting service; phones, TV and air-conditioning in all rooms.

Very Expensive

Santa Marina**** I5
Castello 6068, Campo Santa Marina, t 041 5239202, f 041 520 0907, e info@hotelsantamarina.it, w www.hotelsantamarina.it; vaporetto Rialto; wheelchair accessible.
After a long renovation programme, the Santa Marina now has several rooms in the neighbouring building and 4-star status. Comfortable, with smart public rooms and elegant bedrooms, it is situated on a pretty, quiet *campo*. Cots (€20 extra), babysitting; phone, TV and air-conditioning in all rooms.

Savoia & Jolanda**** J8
Castello 4684, Riva degli Schiavoni, t 041 520 6644, f 041 520 7494, e info@savoiajolanda.com, w www.hotelsavoiajolanda.com; vaporetto San Zaccaria.
Another fine, characteristic Venetian hotel near the centre, though it's not too noisy. The best of the 80 rooms have terraces, and there's a restaurant. Cots, babysitting service; phones, TV and air-conditioning in all rooms.

Expensive

Da Bruno*** I6
Castello 5726A, Salizzada San Lio, t 041 5230452, f 041 52 5324, e reception@hoteldabruno.it, w www.hoteldabruno.it; vaporetto Rialto.
A clean and well-run hotel not far from the Rialto bridge, with 32 bedrooms decorated in a restrained, traditional style. Rooms are on the small side, but very pleasant; all have phone, TV and air-conditioning.

Locanda Remedio*** J7
Castello 4412, Calle del Remedio, t 041 520 6232, f 041 5210485, e hotelremedio@libero.net; vaporetto San Zaccaria.

Under new (and youthful) ownership, this hotel reopened in mid-2002 after a complete revamp. The décor – a heady mix of traditional and modern Venetian styles, with elaborate fabrics, rich colours, marble, and gold paint – will not be to everybody's taste, but the Remedio certainly represents good value for such luxury. Cots; phone, TV and air-conditioning in all rooms.

Moderate

Bucintoro** M8
Castello 2135, Riva degli Schiavoni, t 041 522 3240, f 041 523 5224, e pensionebucintoro@tin.it; vaporetto Arsenale.
An old-fashioned, family-run *pensione* right by the *vaporetto* stop, with wonderful views across St Mark's basin from nearly all the modest yet faultlessly clean rooms (the ones at the corners of the building are the best), which are flooded with watery light. There are a few rooms without a bath.

Ca' del Dose K8
Castello 3801, Calle del Dose, t/f 041 520 9887, e info@cadeldose. com, w www.cadeldose.com; vaporetto Arsenale.
One of the new generation of good-value *affitta camere* or small B&Bs in Venice. Just off the Campo Bandiera e Moro, it has six comfortable rooms furnished stylishly with dark parquet floors and elegant fabrics. One very large room at the top of the house has a private terrace. Cots; phone, TV and air-conditioning in all rooms.

Casa Verardo*** J7
Castello 4765, Ponte Storto, t 041 528 6138, f 041 523 2765, e info@casaverardo.it, w www. casaverardo.it; vaporetto San Zaccaria; wheelchair accessible.
A delightful, recently renovated hotel in a quiet corner with rooms in two adjoining *palazzi*. The atmosphere is cool and elegant, yet prices are very reasonable, especially in the original building. The newest rooms are quite

smart, with beamed ceilings, parquet floors and elegant fabrics. One tiny (and very romantic) room has its own terrace. Cots; phone, TV and air-conditioning in all rooms.

Doni* J7
Castello 4656, Calle del Vin, t/f 041 522 4267, e Albergodoni@libero.it; vaporetto San Zaccaria.
A basic but clean little family-run hotel on a pretty canal; the best rooms (larger with creaky old wooden floors and overlooking the water) are the three without a bath.

Fontana** J7
Castello 4701, Campo San Provolo, t 041 522 0579, f 041 521 0533, e Htlcasa@gpnet.it, w www. hotelfontana.it; vaporetto San Zaccaria.
A very friendly, family-run hotel with 15 light and airy rooms; the quietest overlook a pretty garden, but all have nice views. Furnishings are a mix of old and new, but the overall feel is old-fashioned. Phone and TV in all rooms.

Locanda La Corte*** J5
Castello 6317, Calle Bressana, t 041 241 1300, f 041 241 5982, e info@ locandalacorte.it, w www. locandalacorte.it, vaporetto Rialto.
This very pleasant hotel is set on a small canal (five rooms have canal views and are more expensive than the rest) and has a lovely inner courtyard. All 18 rooms are decorated in restful pale greens and creams, with traditional furnishings and beamed ceilings; many look on to the courtyard. There is an internet point for guests' use. Cots, babysitting service; all rooms have phone, TV and air-conditioning.

La Residenza** L7
Castello 3608, Campo Bandiera e Moro, t 041 528 5315, f 041 523 8859, e info@venicelaresidenza.com, w www.venicelaresidenza.com; vaporetto Arsenale.
Located in the lovely Gothic Palazzo dei Badoari-Partecipazi in a quiet square between San

Marco and the Arsenale. The public rooms are flamboyantly decorated with 18th-century frescoes, antique furniture and paintings; the bedrooms have all been done up and are decorated in a uniform traditional style. Breakfast is served at little tables scattered around the sitting room. Cots; all rooms have phone, TV and air-conditioning.

Rio** J7

Castello 4356, Campo SS Filippo e Giacomo, t 041 523 4810, f 041 520 8222, e info@aciugheta-hotelrio. it, w www.aciugheta-hotelrio.it; vaporetto San Zaccaria.

Under the same ownership as the Aciugheta restaurant (*see* p.271), this little hotel offers a new take on traditional Venetian style – at least in half of its rooms, which boast contemporary colours, headboards, light fittings and clean lines. Breakfast is served at the Europa bar in the *campo*. All rooms have phone, TV and air-conditioning; seven don't have a bath.

Silva* J6

Castello 4423, Fondamenta del Remedio, t 041 522 7643, f 041 528 6817, e albergosilva@libero.it; vaporetto Rialto/San Zaccaria.

A delightful bargain on one of Venice's most photographed little canals , between the San Zaccaria *vaporetto* stop and SantaMaria Formosa. No lift, no disabled access and no a/c, but pleasant, spick and span rooms all with telephone and half with bath. Some family rooms available, as well as cots. Very agreeable atmosphere and friendly staff.

Inexpensive

Caneva* I6

Castello 5515, Ramo dietro la Fava, t 041 522 8118, f 041 520 8676; vaporetto Rialto.

Stands between the Rialto and San Marco on a quiet canal. Rooms are simply furnished but well kept. All rooms have phone, half have a/c and half have baths.

Dorsoduro
Expensive

American*** F9

Dorsoduro 628, Fondamenta Bragadin, t 041 520 4733, f 041 520 4048, e reception@hotel american.com, w www. hotel american.com; vaporetto Accademia.

An elegant, traditional hotel that has undergone extensive renovation, this overlooks the lovely San Vio canal (the best rooms, with windows on two sides, are 201 and 202). There's a pretty first-floor breakfast terrace and an internet point for guests' use. Staff are very friendly. Cots, babysitting service; phone, TV, air-conditioning and well-equipped new bathrooms in all rooms.

Ca' Pisani**** E9

Dorsoduro 979A, Rio Terrà Foscarini, t 041 240 1411, f 041 277 1061, e info@capisanihotel.it, w www.capisanihotel.it; vaporetto Accademia; wheelchair accessible.

Located in a 17th-century *palazzo* just behind the Zattere, the Ca' Pisani flies in the face of Venetian hotel tradition by being designer-minimalist. Original 1930s pieces (beds, mirrors, wardrobes, chests) are scattered throughout and blend well with contemporary pieces and a colour scheme where silver, orange, grey, pale violet and browns dominate. There is a roof terrace, Turkish bath and basement wine bar, and not a scrap of flock wallpaper in sight. Cots, babysitting service. All rooms have phone, TV, air-conditioning and modem ports.

Pausania*** D7

Dorsoduro 2824, San Barnaba, t 041 522 2083, f 041 522 2989, e pausaniahtl@hotmail.com; vaporetto Ca' Rezzonico.

Just up the canal from the last floating vegetable shop in Venice, this traditional hotel is in an old *palazzo* in a quiet corner of Dorsoduro. The courtyard has an old well and an ancient stone staircase leading to some of the rooms, and there is a pretty garden. Cots, babysitting service; phone, TV and air-conditioning in all rooms.

Moderate

Accademia*** E8

Dorsoduro 1058, Fondamenta Bollani, t 041 521 0188, f 041 523 9152, e pensioneaccademia@ flashnet.it; vaporetto Accademia.

A charming 17th-century villa just off the Grand Canal with gardens and a gondola landing. Once home to the Russian Embassy, it has 17 individually furnished rooms; many are gems and all have views of the canal or gardens. Extraordinarily popular, even by Venetian standards, so book months in advance. Off-season discounts. Cots, babysitting service; all rooms have phone, TV and air-conditioning.

Agli Alboretti** F9

Dorsoduro 884, Rio Terrà Foscarini, t 041 523 0058, f 041 521 0158, e alboretti@gpnet.it, w www.aglialboretti.com; vaporetto Accademia.

A warm welcome and genuine family atmosphere awaits you at this modest but cosy hotel. Bedrooms are mostly simple and modern, with the odd antique. There is a comfy sitting room on the first floor and a wonderful terrace at the rear. The family's restaurant next door is excellent. Cots and babysitting service.

Alla Salute da Cici** G9

Dorsoduro 222, Fondamenta Ca' Balà, t 041 523 5404, f 041 522 2272, e hotel.salute.dacici@iol.it; vaporetto Salute. Closed Dec and Jan.

A well-scrubbed, friendly, family-run hotel in an old *palazzo*, prettily located in a quiet corner of the city with some of its 50 rooms overlooking a lovely little canal. There is a lovely garden for breakfasts. All rooms have phone and TV.

Antica Locanda Montin* D8
*Dorsoduro 1147, Fondamenta di
Borgo, t 041 522 7151, f 041 520
0255, e locandamontin@libero.it;
vaporetto Accademia/Zattere.*
One of the last old-fashioned
Venetian hostelries, with 10 char-
acter-filled rooms, a bohemian
atmosphere and an infamous
arty restaurant. All rooms have
a phone.

La Calcina*** E9
*Dorsoduro 780, Fondamenta delle
Zattere, t 041 520 6466, f 041 522
7045, e la.calcina@libero.it,
w www.lacalcina.com; vaporetto
Zattere/Accademia.*
La Calcina has several things
going for it: the wonderful
floating terrace where breakfast,
drinks and light meals are served;
the views over the water to the
Giudecca; the traditional *altana* or
roof terrace, which can be
privately booked; the very reasonable prices; and the airy and
uncluttered interior. Some beautifully furnished suites and
apartments. All rooms have phone
and air-conditioning.

Locanda San Barnaba*** E7
*Dorsoduro 2486, Calle del
Traghetto, t 041 241 1233, f 041 241
3812, e info@locanda-sanbarnaba.
com, w www.locanda-sanbarnaba.
com; vaporetto Ca' Rezzonico;
wheelchair accessible.*
An elegant new hotel in a 16th-
century *palazzo* down a quiet
alley. The 13 rooms and suites have
dark parquet floors, white walls, a
mix of antiques and painted furniture, and elegant fabrics; the look
is refreshingly uncluttered. Rooms
look on to the pretty garden or
over the canal; several have frescoes. There is also a roof terrace.
Cots, babysitting service. All
rooms have phone, TV and air-
conditioning.

Messner** G9
*Dorsoduro 216, Fondamenta Ca'
Balà, t 041 522 7443, f 041 522 7266,
e messner@doge.it, w http://
home. venere.it/venezia/messner/;
vaporetto Salute; annexe is
wheelchair accessible.*

A nicely modernized hotel next to
Alla Salute da Cici (*see* p.258) and a
couple of minutes from the
Salute, with many multiple-
bedded rooms suitable for
families. Great showers, and
phone, TV and air-conditioning in
all rooms. The annexe round the
corner has some cheaper rooms.
There is also a budget restaurant,
but the coffee is awful. Cots,
babysitting service.

Seguso** F9
*Dorsoduro 779, Zattere, t 041 528
6858, f 041 522 2340; vaporetto
Zattere.*
With its cluttered, old-fashioned
feel, welcoming atmosphere (it's a
bit like an old aunt's house), cosy
sitting room, reasonable prices
and lovely setting, the Seguso is
very popular, so book well ahead.
The tiny front terrace (where
breakfast is served in summer)
looks over the Giudecca canal, as
do the best bedrooms. Some
rooms are quite small and not all
have their own baths; all have a
phone. Cots and babysitting
service. Half board is obligatory in
high season.

Inexpensive

Ca' Foscari* E7
*Dorsoduro 3887B, Calle della
Frescada, t 041 710 401, f 041 710
817, e valtersc@tln.lt; vaporetto
San Tomà.*
Hidden in a tiny lane near San
Tomà, this has a friendly family
atmosphere and 11 nice, quiet,
clean rooms, five with bath.

San Polo and
Santa Croce

Very Expensive

Marconi*** H6
*San Polo 729, Riva del Vin, t 041 522
2068, f 041 522 9700, e info@hotel-
marconi.it, w www.hotelmarconi.
com; vaporetto Rialto.*
In a 16th-century palace a hop and
a skip from the Rialto bridge. The
35 rooms are in the typical
Venetian style with all mod cons;

book months in advance for the
two overlooking the Grand Canal.
Phone, TV and air-conditioning in
all rooms; cots, babysitting service.

San Cassiano*** G4
*Santa Croce 2232, Calle della Rosa,
t 041 524 1768, f 041 721 033,
e cassiano@sancassiano.it,
w www.sancassiano.it; vaporetto
San Stae.*
The 14th-century Ca' Favretto that
houses this hotel is on the Grand
Canal, right opposite the Ca' d'Oro;
six or seven of the best rooms
enjoy the view, as do the pretty
little waterside terrace and the
breakfast room. The ground-floor
public rooms have a faded
grandeur; the bedrooms, while
comfortable, are less interesting.
All have phone, TV and air-conditioning. Cots and a babysitting
service are available.

Moderate

Falier** D6
*Santa Croce 130, Salizzada San
Pantalon, t 041 710 882, f 041 520
6554, e reception@hotelfalier.com,
w www.hotelfalier.com; vaporetto
Piazzale Roma/San Tomà.*
A reasonably priced and more-
than-pleasant little hotel, with
some elegant new rooms on the
second floor and a lovely, wisteria-
bedecked terrace where you can
collapse after a hard day's sight-
seeing.All rooms have phone, TV
and air-conditioning.

Hotel Iris** E6
*San Polo 2910A, Calle del Cristo,
t 041 522 2882, e Htliris@tin.it;
vaporetto San Tomà. Closed Jan.*
The clean, pleasant rooms in this
hotel have been recently redeco-
rated; one has a pretty ceiling
fresco and is really quite elegant.
All rooms have phone and TV.

Sturion*** H6
*San Polo 679, Calle dello Sturion,
t 041 523 6243, f 041 522 8378,
w www.locandasturion.com,
e info@locandasturion.com;
vaporetto Rialto.*
A beguiling, eccentric choice, this.
is one of the lowest-priced hotels
on the Grand Canal, perhaps

because of the three-flight walk up to reception (precluding disabled access). Book well ahead for one of its 11 fine, mosaic-floored, brocaded rooms. Only two have canal views, but all have phone, TV and air-conditioning. There's also an internet point for guests' use.

Inexpensive

Ai Tolentini* D5
Santa Croce 197/G, Calle Amai, t 041 275 9140, f 041 275 3266, e *aitolentini@tiscalinet.it;* **vaporetto** Piazzale Roma.
Convenient for the station but off the normal tourist trail, this quiet hotel has seven simple but spotless and reasonably light and spacious rooms. All rooms have TV.

Casa Peron* D6
Santa Croce 84, Salizzada San Pantalon, t 041 711 038, f 041 710 021, e *casaperon@libero.it;* **vaporetto** San Tomà. No cards.
A simple, friendly hotel with 11 rooms in all shapes and sizes. The fairly basic furnishings are brightened up by cheerful bedspreads. Two rooms have little terraces, and some have air-conditioning.

Dalla Mora* D6
Santa Croce 42, Salizzada San Pantalon, t 041 710 703, f 041 723 006, e *hoteldallamora@libero.it;* **vaporetto** San Tomà.
A simple but inviting 14-room hotel down a narrow alleyway just off the *salizzada*, which ends in a canal. Four rooms have views over the water, two have air-conditioning.

Cannaregio

Expensive

Ai Santi Apostoli*** H4
Cannaregio 4391, Strada Nova, t 041 521 2612, t 041 521 2611, e *aisantia@tin.it*, w www.veneziaweb.com/santiapostoli; **vaporetto** Ca' d'Oro. **Closed** 2 weeks in Aug and mid-Dec–March.
Discreetly hidden behind an elegant green door on the third

floor of an old *palazzo* on the Grand Canal, this was one of the first upmarket 'locanda' hotels in Venice. The feel is that of a hospitable private home, with a comfy sitting room overlooking the water and filled with interesting objects, books and magazines. Rooms are individually furnished with a mix of old and new (the best – and most expensive – being the two overlooking the canal). All have phone, TV and air-conditioning, and cots are available.

Bellini**** D3
Cannaregio 116, Lista di Spagna, t 041 524 2488, f 041 715 193, e *reservation@bellini.boscolo.com*, w www.boscolohotels.com; **vaporetto** Ferrovia.
The best hotel within a cuckoo's spit of the train station, though those on this kind of budget may not want to be in the scruffy Lista di Spagna. However, the Bellini is a snazzy place with loads of marble, Murano chandeliers and damask on the walls, and some rooms at the front have little terraces with canal views. All rooms have phone, TV and air-conditioning, and cots and a babysitting service are available.

Casa Carettoni*** D3
Cannaregio 130, Lista di Spagna, t 041 716 231, f 041 275 0973, e *info@anticacasacarettoni.com*, w www.anticacasacarettoni.com; **vaporetto** Ferrovia.
The Casa Carettoni has moved up in the world and now positively sparkles, with a modern take on trad style (light and airy with lots of gleaming marble and white paintwork). Cots, babysitting service; phone, TV and air-conditioning in all rooms.

Locanda del Ghetto*** F2
Cannaregio 2892, Campo del Ghetto Nuovo, t 041 275 9292, f 041 275 7987, e *ghetto@veneziahotels.com*, w www.veneziahotels.com; **vaporetto** San Marcuola/Guglie; wheelchair accessible.
A delightful new hotel offering a high standard of accommodation

for the price, and a pretty canal-side breakfast room. Right by the synagogue (one room has a beamed ceiling that was part of the 16th-century version), it has nine stylish bedrooms with honey-coloured parquet floors, pale gold fabrics, smart furniture and excellent bathrooms. Two have terraces overlooking the *campo*; all have phone, TV, air-conditioning and modem ports. Cots are available.

Moderate

Casa Boccassini* J4
Cannaregio 5295, Calle del Fumo, t 041 522 9892, f 041 523 6877; **vaporetto** Fondamenta Nuove.
In a quiet neighbourhood well away from the crowds, this is something of a find. The basic but clean-as-a-whistle rooms have the odd antique piece to add character, and there is a pleasant breakfast room and sitting area, though it's the delightful garden filled with shrubs, flowers and trees and hung with coloured lights that is the real attraction. All room have a phone; three don't have a bath.

Eden*** G3
Cannaregio 2357, Campiello Volto Santo, t 041 524 4003, f 041 720 228, e *hotel.eden@libero.it*, w www.htleden.com; **vaporetto** San Marcuola.
An exceptionally friendly, pleasant little hotel in a tiny *campiello* off busy Santa Maddalena. The 12 quiet, comfortable rooms are done out in fresh colours and pretty floral fabrics; all have orthopaedic mattresses. The sitting and breakfast rooms are equally cheerful, but you can have breakfast in your room for no extra charge. All rooms have phone, TV and air-conditioning, and a babysitting service is offered.

Guerrini ** E3
Cannaregio 265, Lista di Spagna, t 041 715 333, f 041 715 114; **vaporetto** Ferrovia.
In a quiet cul-de-sac next to Campo San Geremia, off the

garish Lista, this simple and clean hotel is one of the best near the station. Its bright rooms have painted furniture and tiled floors. All rooms have phone and air-conditioning; seven without bath.

Malibran*** I5

Cannaregio 5864, Corte del Milion, t 041 522 8028, t 041 523 9243, e info@hotelmalibran.it, w www.hotelmalibran.it; vaporetto Rialto.

Right beside the restored Teatro Malibran, this has a marvellously old-fashioned feel to it. Rooms have pretty painted furniture and candlewick bedspreads. A few bathrooms have been updated, and there are plans to modernize extensively, but let's hope they don't spoil it. The Malibran has its own restaurant, and you can stay on a half- or full-board basis for a very reasonable charge. All rooms have phone, TV and air-conditioning, and cots are available.

Inexpensive

Rossi* E3

Cannaregio 262, Lista di Spagna, t 041 715 164, f 041 717 784, e rossihotel@interfree.it; vaporetto Ferrovia.

A budget choice just opposite the Guerrini (*see above*), the Rossi has 14 basic but clean rooms and a rustic breakfast room. All rooms have phone and air-conditioning, 10 have a bathroom.

The Lagoon

Luxury

Cipriani***** I10

Giudecca 10, Fondamenta San Giovanni, t 041 520 7744, f 041 520 3930, e info@hotelcipriani.it, w www.orientexpresshotels.com; vaporetto hotel boat leaves from Vallaresso stop; wheelchair accessible.

For more than two decades this villa isolated in a lush garden on the eastern tip of the Giudecca, linked day and night to Piazza San Marco by private motor launch,

has been one of Italy's (if not the world's) most luxurious hotels. No place will pamper you more, anywhere. An Olympic pool, tennis courts, a beauty parlour, Jacuzzis in the bathrooms, three restaurants and live music in the evening; prices vary. The suites in the exclusive annexe, Palazzo Vendramin, are exquisitely furnished and have arched windows framing Piazza San Marco across the Lagoon. Cots, babysitting service; all rooms have phone, TV, air-conditioning and modem port.

Des Bains**** Off maps

Lido, Lungomare Marconi 17, t 041 526 5921, f 041 526 0113, w www. sheraton.com, e reso78.desbains@ starwoodhotels.com; vaporetto Lido. Closed Dec–mid-March.

A grand old luxury hotel in a large park designed for dalliance. Thomas Mann stayed here on several occasions, and had Aschenbach sigh his life away on the private beach. Now part of the Sheraton empire, it has a salt-water swimming pool, two tennis courts, a private pier and a motor-boat service into Venice. There are 190 large rooms, a Liberty-style salon and a breeze-filled veranda dining room. Service is faultless. All rooms have phone, TV and air-conditioning, and cots and a babysitting service are available.

Westin Excelsior***** Off maps

Lido, Lungomare Marconi 41, t 041 526 0201, t 041 526 7276, e reso77. excelsior@westin.com, w www. westin.com; vaporetto Lido. Closed mid-Nov–mid-March.

An immense fantasy confection built in 1907, with majestic Moorish archways and Alhambra-style extravagance. Try to get a room during the film festival to ogle the stars. A private beach, a swimming pool, *cabanas* more comfortable than some bedrooms on the Grand Canal, seven tennis courts, three restaurants, a night-club with a retractable roof, and a private launch service to Venice are a few of its amenities. All rooms have phone, TV and air-

conditioning, and cots and a babysitting service are available.

Expensive

Locanda Cipriani*** Off maps

Torcello, Piazza S. Fosca, t 041 730 150, f 041 735 433, e brass@ locandacipriani.com, w www. locandacipriani.com; vaporetto 12 to Torcello. Closed Jan.

There are only six rooms in this famous yellow-painted, green-shuttered country house hotel, basking in the most rural and tranquil spot of the whole comune of Venice. Some have views over the hotel's blissful garden; you can sleep where Hemingway wrote his Venice novel, *Across the River and Into the Trees* – standing up because of haemorrhoids. All the rooms are spacious and fresh. The restaurant (*see p.278*) serves delicious seafood with all the Cipriani trimmings. All rooms have phone, TV and air-conditioning.

Quattro Fontane**** Off maps

Lido, Via delle Quattro Fontane 16, t 041 526 0227, f 041 526 0726, e info@quattrofontane.com, w www.quattrofontane.com; vaporetto Lido. Closed Nov–March.

The best of the smaller hotels, Quattro Fontane is the former seaside villa of a Venetian family. Its white stucco, mock-Tyrolean exterior, dark shutters and cool, walled-in courtyard are inviting and tranquil; the public and private rooms, including the restaurant, are comfortable and individually decorated with antiques and mementos. It even has its own tennis court near the beach and Casino. Book as early as possible. All rooms have phone, TV and air-conditioning, and cots and a babysitting service are available.

Villa Mabapa***** Off maps

Lido, Riviera San Nicolò 16, t 041 526 0590, f 041 5269 441, e info@ villamabapa.com, w www. villamabapa.com; vaporetto Lido; wheelchair accessible.

Set in a peaceful garden over-looking the lagoon, this villa was a holiday home in the 1930s. The best bedrooms are on the first floor and are traditionally furnished; others are in a rather dull annexe. In summer meals are served on a lovely terrace from which you can watch the spectacular sunsets. Phone, TV and air-conditioning in all rooms; cots, babysitting service.

Inexpensive

Al Raspo de Ua* Off maps
Burano, Via Galuppi 560, **t** *041 730 095,* **f** *041 730 397;* **vaporetto** *Burano.*
These five rooms above one of the most popular restaurants in Burano have recently been modernized, but the modest prices still make it a bargain. The rooms are cheerful if simply furnished, and very clean. Al Raspo offers a chance to get to know Burano after the tourists have caught the last *vaporetto* back to the big city. All rooms have phone, TV and air-conditioning.

Hostels

The tourist office at San Marco keeps a constantly updated list of all inexpensive hostel accommodation in Venice.

Foresteria Valdese K6
Castello 5170, Calle della Madonetta, **t/f** *041 528 6797,* **e** *veneziaforesteria@chiesavaldese. org,* **w** *www.chiesavaldese.org/ venezia;* **vaporetto** *San Zaccaria.* **No cards.**
An old *palazzo* converted into a dormitory/*pensione* by the Waldensians; one room is an inexpensive self-catering flat for up to six people. Check in is 9am–1pm and 6–8pm. Doubles cost €54, beds in dorms with bath €22; breakfast included.

Istituto Canossiano E11
Giudecca 428, Fondamenta del Ponte Piccolo, **t/f** *041 522 2157;* **vaporetto** *Palanca.*
In a similar location to the youth hostel below, this women-only hostel is run by nuns who may initially seem rather severe but are actually totally charming. Basic rooms are multi-bedded (eights and up) and the place is spotless. The rate of €13 per person per night includes sheets and showers. There is a 10.30pm curfew (10pm in winter) and the doors are locked between 9am and 3pm.

Ostello di Venezia H11
Giudecca 86, Fondamenta delle Zitelle, **t** *041 523 8211,* **f** *041 523 5689;* **vaporetto** *Zitelle.*
One of the most strikingly located youth hostels in Italy, right on the Giudecca Canal, with views of San Marco. No phone reservations; to be assured of a place in July or August, write well in advance. At other times, you can chance it and book in person any day after 6pm (doors open for queueing at midday). It's members only, but cards are sold at the door. Doors are open 7–9.30am and 1.30–11pm (curfew is 11.30pm). Rates are €16 a head, including breakfast.

Camping

Booking ahead is advisable in the Italian holiday season (July and August). For a list of campsites in the Venice area and information, call Assocamping, **t** *041 968 071,* **f** *041 537 1106,* **e** *assocamping@cavallino.net,* **w** *www.cavallino.net.*

Fusina** Off maps
Via Moranzini 79, **t** *041 547 0055,* **f** *041 547 0050,* **e** *info@camping-fusina.com,* **w** *www.camping-fusina.com,* **bus** *no. 1 from Mestre station (last stop).* **Open** *year-round.*

At least 1,000 places. Venice is 20 minutes away by boat; *vaporetto* 16 from San Zaccaria runs every hour (until 11pm in the summer; there's a more skeleton service off season). It has a restaurant, pizzeria, bar, breakfast bar, public Internet and email terminals, and a marina with slip access so you can yacht off to Greece, leaving your car at Fusina. Tents are €4, plus €6 pp; campers/car s plus a tent are €13 per night, then €6pp. There are also small self-catering bungalows for rent.

Serenissima** Off maps
Via Padana 334, Oriago, Mira, **t** *041 920 286,* **f** *041 920 286,* **e** *campingserenissima@shineline.it,* **w** *www.campingserenissima.com.* **Open** *April–Oct.*
Three hundred camping places and 60 bungalows just off the Brenta Canal; bus 53 connects with Venice every half-hour.

Self-Catering

If you mean to spend a week or more in Venice, consider renting a self-catering apartment. Firms that offer them include:

Carefree Holidays
Zurich House, East Park, Crawley, West Sussex RH10 6AJ, **t** *(01293) 552277,* **w** *www.carefree-italy.com.*

Interhome
383 Richmond Road, Twickenham, TW1 2EF, **t** *(020) 8891 1294,* **w** *www.interhome.co.uk.*

Vacanze in Italia
Manor Court Yard, Bignor, Pulborough, West Sussex, RH20 1QD, **t** *(01798) 869 426,* **f** *(01798) 869 014,* **w** *www.indiv-travellers.com.*

Venetian Apartments
408 Parkway House, Sheen Lane, London SW14 8LS, **t** *(020) 8878 1130,* **f** *(020) 8878 0982,* **w** *www.venice-rentals.com.*

Eating Out

San Marco 266

Castello 270

Dorsoduro 273

San Polo and Santa Croce 274

Cannaregio 276

The Lagoon 278

Of the panoply of pleasures that were celebrated in Venice in the past, food and drink were naturally an important part, so much so as to encourage gastronomic voyeurism; there are paintings of lavish feasts in theatres, with a full audience on tap to watch the nobility dine in style. There are tales of the legendary Doge, Andrea Gritti, of Henry VIII-ish appetites, eating himself to death, and others of entire table settings, including the napkins, sculpted of sugar. Quantity and style were more important than quality, which is rarely mentioned: the wine, especially the swill in the cheap inns or *Malavasie*, is condemned, even by English visitors, for its 'pall'd disgustful Taste'; the bread, 'Even when fresh [...] could be so dry and solid that you had to take a hammer to it', and most damning of all is the shocking fact that Venetian housewives not only did not make their own pasta (either they were too lazy or were simply having too much fun to bother) but they purchased it already boiled from the shop. Heresy comes in many forms, but in a land governed by the *al dente* convention, that takes the cake.

Unfortunately, the taint of heresy lingers in many of Venice's restaurants. If the pasta isn't already boiled, it might have been improved if it had. Nowhere on the entire Italian peninsula can you, without any luck, dine so poorly so often; even paying more offers no protection from the heavy-handed Venetian cook. Use the listings below as a guide through the labyrinth of indigestion; most of the restaurants included have a history of being decent to good, so chances are they still will be when you plump for a meal.

Venetian Cuisine

Good Venetian cuisine is based on fish, shellfish and rice, often mixed together in a succulent seafood risotto. Popular antipasti include *sarde in saor*, or marinated sardines, *prosciutto San Daniele*, a delicious raw ham cured in Friuli, oysters from Chioggia, or any possible hot or cold seafood delicacy. *Risi e bisi* (rice and peas, cooked with ham and Parmesan) is perhaps the best known Venetian first course, while the local pasta dish of choice is *bigoli in salsa*, a kind of spaghetti topped with butter, onions, and anchovies or sardines. There are various very palatable *risotti*: *di mare*, with seafood; or *in nero*, with cuttlefish cooked in its own ink; or *alla sbirraglia* (with vegetables, chicken and ham). Venetian fish soup, *brodetto*, is usually prepared with tomatoes and garlic. For *secondo*, liver (*fegato alla veneziana*) with cornmeal polenta (or *tecia*, but a lead weight on the stomach by whatever name) shares top billing with grilled scampi, *baccalà mantecato* (salt cod), Sile eel, cuttlefish in its own ink (*seppie alla veneziana*), *fritto misto* (Adriatic mixed fry) and, for a big splurge, lobster (*aragosta*). Bitter red *radicchio* (chicory) from Treviso is a favourite side-dish, often in salads. Top it all off with a *tiramisù*, a traditional Veneto chilled dessert of layered sponge fingers, with *mascarpone* sugar and raw egg, coffee and a sprinkling of cocoa powder. For more menu items, *see* the glossary in **Language**, p.304.

Wine

The wines, at least, will almost always compensate for the cuisine. Most of what you'll see in Venetian restaurants comes from the surrounding three regions of Venetia: the Veneto, Friuli-Venezia Giulia and Trentino-Alto Adige, which together produce nearly half Italy's wines, and many of her best. Most Italian wines are named after the grape and the district they come from. If the label says DOC (*Denominazione di Origine Controllata*) it means that the wine comes from a specially defined area and was produced according to a certain traditional method. Some of the Veneto's wines may already be familiar, especially Verona's red *Bardolino* and *Valpolicella* and white *Soave* and *Bianco di Custoza*. Others, like the dry or sweet bubbling white or rosé *Prosecco* of Conegliano, or the splendid array of wines from Friuli (whites *Tokai*, *Pinot Bianco* and *Pinot Grigio*, and reds *Refosco* and *Cabernet*) and Trentino-Alto Adige (*Riesling*, *Silvaner* *Chardonnay*, *Pinot Grigio* and *Gewürztraminer*) still seem to be Italian secrets. The province of Venice produces three DOC wines, centred around the village of Pramaggiore: the refined white *Tocai di Lison*, with an almond and peach bouquet, and two reds: hardy *Cabernet di Pramaggiore*, a fine companion to polenta and strong meat dishes and the softer, smoother *Merlot di Pramaggiore*, so light that the locals even serve it with fish.

Eating Out

Breakfast

Breakfast coffee in the hotels is overpriced and, in some establishments, tastes as if it were brewed with *eau de Lagoon*, so you may want to do as the Venetians do and grab a quick stand-up breakfast in a bar or *pasticceria* of coffee (usually a *cappuccino* or *caffè latte*) and a warm *cornetto* ('horn', like a croissant, filled or empty) or a *brioche* (a sweet bread roll with chocolate inside). You can stop for refills as often as necessary, though around noon it's time to move on to an *aperitivo*: a Campari, some kind of vermouth (Italians prefer something bitter, to whet the appetite) or perhaps a fruit juice.

Lunch

Most restaurants open at 12 for *pranzo* and stop serving at around 2.30 or 3. This is traditionally the biggest meal of the day for Italians, though these days many people prefer to grab a quick meal in a cafeteria-buffet, *tavola calda* (a selection of hot, prepared foods), or a *bacaro* (bar) that serves *cicheti* (often delicious two-bite snackerels for €1 each) rather than commute home to Mestre. But most will have some form of pasta (rather than in the evening, when it tends to sit on the all-important stomach), a salad or vegetable, wine or water, and fruit, followed by a coffee, perhaps '*corretto*' (corrected with brandy or grappa) in a nearby bar (the stomach bunch will have a *digestivo* to aid gastric action, perhaps an Amaretto, a Strega (made from saffron), a Fernet-Branca (made from mysterious herbs) or a Scotch.

Snacks

Venetians feeling peckish between 5pm and dinnertime indulge in a beer and *tramezzini*, finger sandwiches that come in a hundred varieties (prawns, spinach and cheese, asparagus tips, etc.), side stepping the ones that have been sitting pre-prepared for hours. Takeaway slices of pizza are popular and good everywhere in Italy save, with rare exceptions, Venice.

Dinner

Venetians eat dinner (*cena*) fairly early by Italian standards – restaurants begin opening to accommodate German tourists at 6pm and close at 10 or 11pm (*see* p.272, 'Late-night Food', for some exceptions). A plate of antipasti, or a salad and a pizza, is a popular (and economical) supper, or you can order the works. Flasks of the house wine, usually from Verona or Friuli, help fill out the evening. Last stop: another *bacaro*, another coffee (to help you sleep!).

Prices

Venice's restaurants are usually more expensive than the mainland norm; the few approaching great status tend to be very much more (not altogether because they batten off tourists – transport and handling charges add

30% to the cost of food). Even the moderate ones may give you a surprise at *conto* time with their service and cover charges. If you're watching expenses, pizza is a reliable standby, and not bad if it's freshly made.

Although neither price nor décor have anything to do with the quality of the food, generally the fancier the fittings, the fancier the *conto* at the end. When you eat out, mentally add to the bill the bread and cover charge (*pane e coperto*, €1–3.50, depending on the fanciness quotient) and a 15% service charge. This is usually included in the bill (*servizio compreso*); if it says *servizio non compreso* you'll have to do your own arithmetic (doubling the inevitable tax charge is a good rule of thumb). And an additional small tip is expected for good service.

Finally, note that when a restaurant advertises a fixed-price menu (*menu turistico*), you won't see a trace of it inside – memorize what you want before you go in. Also, many of the places that take food seriously offer a *menu degustazione* – a set-price gourmet meal that allows you to taste whatever seasonal delicacies the chef has whipped up. Both are cheaper than if you had ordered *à la carte*. When you leave a restaurant you are given a receipt, which by law you must hold on to until you're 60m from the door or risk an ambush from the not-very-vigilant tax police.

Price Categories

The prices listed below are for an average meal (two courses, dessert and wine) per person. If you order seafood or truffles, the price will be considerably higher; with some discretion (and drinking the house wine only) it could be considerably less. In the summer, you would do well to book in the better restaurants.

We haven't included a price band for the snacks and *cicheti* sections, as in these establishments you can spend anything

from €1 for a deep-fried crab claw to €25 for a full meal. A word of caution: while *cicheti* cost very little individually (often there are no price labels – staff miraculously remember what you had), the bill soon mounts up if you pile your plate with a lot of tempting goodies.

very expensive	over €50
expensive	€35–50
moderate	€25–€35
cheap	under €25

Cafés, *Gelaterie* and *Bacari*

Cafés and *Gelaterie*

What skill the Venetians may lack in the kitchen, they have made up for by introducing the perky joys of caffeine to the West back in 1640. Like Coca-Cola, *kahvé* was initially regarded as medicine and sold only in pharmacies, until 1720, when Europe's first 'boutique of coffee' was opened in Piazza San Marco, with the proud name of *Venice Triumphant*, modelled by its founder, Floriano Francesconi, on the houses in Istanbul. Like many innovations, coffee houses were once very *risqué*; Bach's light-hearted *Kaffee Kantata* is a dialogue between a young lady who wants to go to a café and her father, who forbids it. And if he were Venetian, he would have had good cause, for they were the favourite rendezvous for extra-marital shenanigans. Perhaps this is why, to this day, you always pay double the price for sitting down. Nowadays, the steam-hissing machine dragons provide most of the thrills.

Some cafés are combined with *pasticcerie*, though don't expect too much from Venetian cakes (*see* 'Cake Crumbs', p.266). Other cafés combine with *gelaterie*.

Bacari

Many Venetians forgo the sweets altogether, and even begin the day with a glass of white wine and a savoury snack, a ritual to be repeated as often as possible

Cake Crumbs

You can usually judge a place by its cakes. Take the sensuous if somewhat Cartesian rows of tarts and éclairs in a French pâtisserie, or the anal-retentive, not-a-crystal-of-sugar-out-of-place perfection in Austria, or the comfortably plump pies and buns at the British baker's, or the American chain doughnut shops that sell 50 varieties 24 hours a day, or the Turk's predilection for exotic delights made of roses, quinces, almonds and pistachios with names like 'Nipples in Honey' or 'Lady's Thighs'.

And Venice? If this is your first trip, close your eyes and play psychogeographic-pastriologist for a moment. Imagine what awaits you in the most beautiful city in the world, a centre of culture and delicate refinement, midway between the East and West, in close historical contact with the luscious Austro-Hungarian apricot and poppy-seed strudel culture and the lavish chocolate-and-cream traditions of Northern Italy and Switzerland, not to mention the honey-laden walnut confections of Greece, and the sinful masterpieces of Turkey. Just imagine it. Venetian pastries must be nothing less than an elegant, delicate synthesis of ingredients and cultures as sublime and fantastical as St Mark's.

Now open your eyes and look in the window of the typical Venetian *pasticceria* and what do you see? Spotted shoe soles called *panserotti* or *zaletti* made of yellow maize flour and laid out to dry in the sun; lengths of coarse braided rope called *kranz* with sultanas and whole almonds wedged in the cracks; miniature sarcophagi (*alleanza alla frutta*), filled with chunks of mummified candied fruit in Murano-glass colours; iron rings for mooring boats (*bussolai Buranei*); and crumbling bricks called *pan di Dogi* rejected on the building site of the Great Pyramid. Not to mention a vile assortment of dehydrated brownish balls, possibly rolled by dung beetles.

What does it all mean? Could Venice really be a very simple, and rather humble place behind its complex façades? In many ways it is. But all sugar psychology aside, these inept cakes support a great historical truth: Venetians can't cook.

during the day (they even swallow the wine in one go, the way most Italians drink their coffee). If a Venetian invites you to duck in the shade ('*andemo al ombra*'), it means a wine stop, which is especially nice in a *bacaro* (old-fashioned wine bar) or *osteria*, or in an *enoteca*, which stocks a wide variety of vintages. These usually offer snacks, or **cicheti** – mussels, pickled onions, artichoke hearts, vegetables cooked in oil, or a bit of cuttlefish. These titbits are also popular fare for a *giro de ombra* (a Venetian pub crawl).

San Marco

Restaurants

Very Expensive

Antico Martini H7
San Marco 1983, Campo San Fantin, t 041 522 4121, w www.anticomartini.com; vaporetto S. Maria del Giglio/ Sant'Angelo. Open Thurs–Mon 12–2.30 and 7–11.30, Wed 7–11.30pm; closed Tues.
Once a Turkish coffeehouse, this classic on the Venetian restaurant scene has been run by the Baldi family since 1921 and serves traditional dishes, both local and otherwise. There's a weekly changing menu, as well as various set '*menu dégustazione*'. Dishes might include *pâté de foie gras*, *tagliolini* with asparagus and basil, duck breast with truffles, and John Dory with artichokes. It's just a shame that the elegant atmosphere has been temporarily compromised by the Fenice building works opposite.

La Caravella H8
San Marco 2397, Via XXII Marzo, t 041 520 8901, w www.hotel saturnia.it/caravella; vaporetto S. Maria del Giglio/Vallaresso. Open daily 12–3 and 7–11.
For sheer variety of seasonal and local dishes (including gilthead with thyme and fennel), few restaurants can top this merrily corny repro of a dining hall in a 16th-century Venetian galley. There's an elegant, colourful courtyard for summer eating.

Harry's Bar H8
San Marco 1323, Calle Vallaresso, t 041 528 5777, w www.cipriani. com; vaporetto Vallaresso. Open daily 12–3 and 7–10.30 (bar opens 10.30am). Booking advised.
Like riding in a gondola, a visit to Harry's is something you should do at once during a visit to Venice, though you'll need to save up to do it. And despite the crowds of tourists who pour in to sip a Bellini, the atmosphere is great, especially on the ground floor with its buzzy bar. The food is reliable but not particularly exciting: risottos, *carpaccios*, squid stew with polenta.

Trattoria Vini da Arturo G7
San Marco 3656, Calle degli Assassini, t 041 528 6974; vaporetto Rialto/Sant'Angelo. Open Mon–Sat 12–2.30 and 7–10.30. No cards.
In an infamous little street near La Fenice, this is a tiny trattoria that marches to a different drum from most Venetian restaurants, with not a speck of seafood on the menu. Instead, try the *pappardelle al radicchio* or Venice's best steaks; its tiramisù is famous. There are also good vegetarian options.

Expensive

Le Bistrot de Venise H7
San Marco 4685, Calle dei Fabbri, t 041 523 6651, w www.bistrotde venise.com; vaporetto Rialto. Open daily 12 noon–12.30am.
This cosy restaurant presents poetry readings, live music and other cultural events as well as

specializing in historical Venetian dishes which, reflecting the city's multicultural past, is full of unusual herbs and spices. The menu, complete with helpful notes on the origins of each dish, features such choices as sardines stuffed with tomato and asparagus, nettles and tomato, tagliatelle with pheasant and wild asparagus sauce, and spicy Turkish spiced rice pudding.

Osteria San Marco H7
San Marco 1610, Frezzeria, t 041 528 5242; vaporetto San Marco. Open Mon–Sat 12.30–2.30pm and 7.30–10.30pm; closed Jan.

The unadorned white walls, exposed brickwork and plain wooden tables in this stylish new *osteria/enoteca* offer a reprieve from the tourist tat that surrounds it. The food is interesting too: scallop salad with artichoke hearts, ravioli stuffed with ricotta and mint and served with a lamb sauce, gnocchi with crab and rosemary, guinea fowl with balsamic vinegar, and fillet steak cooked with coffee (an ancient recipe). You can have a snack and a glass of wine all day.

Moderate

Osteria ai Assassini G7
San Marco 3695, Rio Terrà dei Assassini, t 041 528 7986; vaporetto San Marco. Open Mon–Fri 12–2.45 and 7–10, Sat 7–10. Outside seating.

The menu at this popular *osteria* on a quiet street north of La Fenice changes daily: fish features on Thursdays and Fridays, the rest of the week is for carnivores. The ambiance is rustic (low ceilings, wood panelling and brickwork) and lively, and the place is full of Italians. Snack on *cicheti* if you're not up for a whole meal.

Cheap

Rosticceria San Bartolomeo I6
San Marco 5424, Calle della Bissa, t 041 522 3569, vaporetto Rialto; wheelchair accessible. Open daily 9.30am–9.30pm.

Honest cooking for honest prices in a no-frills trattoria with an even cheaper glass-fronted snack bar downstairs. Takeaways available.

Snacks, Light Meals and *Cicheti*

Al Bacareto F7
San Marco 3447, Calle della Botteghe, t 041 528 9336; vaporetto Sant'Angelo/San Samuele. Open Mon–Fri 12–3 and 7–10.30, Sat 12–3; closed Aug. Booking advised. Outside seating.

A popular, traditional *bacaro* serving traditional *bacaro* fare: a huge variety of excellent *cicheti* at the bar (don't miss the fried sardines or deep-fried meatballs with spinach), to be accompanied by an *ombra*, plus more substantial dishes at the tables. There's a small terrace too.

Bar al Teatro H7
San Marco 3464, Campo San Fantin, t 041 522 1052; vaporetto Santa Maria del Giglio/Sant'Angelo. Open Tues–Sun 7.30am–midnight. Outside seating.

Although it's a little forlorn these days because of the temporary abandonment of La Fenice next door, this famous bar has excellent *tramezzini* and *piadine*. If you can't bear having to stand, have a pizza (or more) in the dining room in the *campo*.

Caffè Città di Torino H6
San Marco 459, Campo San Luca, t 041 522 3914; vaporetto Rialto. Open 10am–1am.

From about 11pm, this café transforms itself from a pedestrian snack bar into Torino Notte, a trip-hop-acid-jazz joint with its logo laser-lit across the *campo*.

Al Volto H6
San Marco 4081, Calle Cavalli, t 041 522 8945; vaporetto Rialto. Open Mon–Sat 10–2.30 and 5–10.

A cosy little *bacaro* near Campo San Luca. In warm weather you can sit outside for a snack and a drink, or go for one of the handful of daily dishes such as *bigoli in salsa* or *calimari in umido*.

Vino Vino G7
San Marco 2007A, Calle del Caffettier, t 041 523 7027, w www.vinovino.co.it; vaporetto S. Maria del Giglio/ Sant'Angelo. Open Wed–Mon 10.30am–midnight; closed Tues.

A pleasant little wine bar near La Fenice, offering some 350 wines from all over Italy and further afield. You can choose from snacks at the bar or eat reasonably priced meals in the adjoining room.

Cafés and Gelaterie

Bar All'Angolo F7
San Marco 3464, Campo Santo Stefano, t 041 522 0710; vaporetto Sant'Angelo. Open Sun–Fri 6.30am–midnight; till 9.30pm in winter; closed Sat. Outside seating.

A crowded bar serving snacks, *piadine*, *tramezzini* and an interesting selection of toasted sandwiches.

Caffè Florian I8
San Marco 56/59, Piazza San Marco, t 041 520 5641, w www.caffeflorian.com; vaporetto Vallaresso. Open daily 10am–midnight; closed Wed in winter. Outside seating.

Florian's has a charming and cosy 18th-century décor of mirrors and frescoes put up in a nostalgic mood in the 1850s (it was actually founded in 1720), and every Venetian learns to take coffee here rather than at Quadri (*see* below). The thimblefuls of espresso are good, if outrageously costly, and be warned that sitting on the outside terrace when there is live music carries an extra charge of €4.50 per head whether or not you are interested in listening to the music.

Gran Caffè Lavena I7
San Marco 133, Piazza San Marco, t 041 522 4070, w www.venetia.it/ lavena; vaporetto San Marco. Open daily 9.30am–midnight.

Excellent coffee in this café dating from 1750, with a beautiful setting, fewer tourists and less stinging prices.

H I J K L M N O

500 m
500 yards

N

S. Michele

Gesuiti 16

17 ~277

Telei

15

13

O
11
12 SS.
Apostoli
14

d'Oro

19

18

20

58

RIALI

21 CAMPO S.
BARTOLOMEO

S. Lio

22

SS. Giovanni
e Paolo

23

24

CAMPO S.
MARIA
FORMOSA

SALIZZADA
S. LIO

29

28

27

26 25

Rio di S. Francesco

ARBON

S.
Salvador

DEI FABBRI

MERCERIE

S. Maria
Formosa

LUCA GIUFFA

Scuola di
S. Giorgio
degli
Schiavoni

Canale delle Galeazze

53

52

SAN MARCO

30

CAMPO SS
FILIPPO E
GIACOMO

33

ARSENALE

39 38

St
Mark's

31

Rio di S. Lorenzo

Rio dei Greci

S. Giorgio
dei Greci

CASTELLO

42

PIAZZA S.
MARCO

40

Pul.
Ducale

32

37

S. Zaccaria

34

oise

41

Giardini
Reali

36

RIVA DEGLI SCHIAVONI

35

101

gana
Mare

VIA GIUSEPPE GARIBALDI

Canale di San Marco

99 100

S. Giorgio
Maggiore

98

S. Giorgio
Maggiore

Giardini
Biennale

FONDS
GIOVANNI

97

FOND. D. ZITELLE

Le Zitelle

Map Key

31	Al'Aciugheta	85	Gobbetti
86	Ai 4 Feri	29	Il Golosone
59	Ai Do Mori	38	Gran Caffè Lavena
12	Ai Promessi Sposi	39	Gran Caffè Quadri
16	Algiubagiò	41	Harry's Bar
95	Altanella	94	Harry's Dolci
4	Anice Stellato	100	Hostaria Da Franz
70	Antica Birraria La Corte	84	L'Incontro
3	Antica Mola	57	Alla Madonna
24	Antica Trattoria Bandierette	30	Marchini
44	Antico Martini	25	Alla Mascareta
60	All'Arco	26	Al Mascaron
48	Al Bacareto	96	Mistra
58	Bancogiro: Osteria da Andrea	93	Nico
47	Bar All'Angolo	61	Al Nono Risorto
45	Bar al Teatro	101	Alla Nuova Speranza
88	Bar alla Toletta	51	Osteria ai Assassini
90	Bar da Gino	18	Osteria Boccadoro
52	Le Bistrot de Venise	72	Osteria alla Patatina
89	Al Bottegon	67	Osteria al Postali
81	Il Caffè	42	Osteria San Marco
54	Caffè Città di Torino	22	Osteria di Santa Marina
5	Caffè Costarica	77	Al Pantalon
40	Caffè Florian	46	Paolin
74	Caffè dei Frari	13	Pizzeria La Perla
98	Caffè Paradiso	64	Al Prosecco
8	La Cantina	15	Puppa
43	La Caravella	66	Il Réfolo
28	Cip-Ciap	79	Ribò
97	Cipriani	32	Alla Rivetta
7	La Colombina	71	Rizzardini
34	La Corte Sconta	23	Rosa Salva (Castello)
35	Al Covo	53	Rosa Salva (San Marco)
17	Da Alvise	21	Rosticceria San Bartolomeo
37	Da Bonifacio	56	Ruga Rialto
80	Da Codroma	14	Il Sole Sulla Vecia Cavana
69	Da Fiore	78	Sottosopra
73	Da Ignazio	27	Alle Testiere
33	Da Remigio	76	Tonolo
87	Da Toni	11	Trattoria Casa Mia
1	Dal Mas	91	Trattoria ai Cugnai
36	Danieli Terrace	75	Trattoria San Tomà
83	Il Doge	99	Trattoria da Tosi
63	Easy Bar	50	Trattoria Vini da Arturo
19	Enoteca Boldrin	62	Vecio Fritolin
6	Enoteca Due Colonne	10	Alla Vedova
20	Fiaschetteria Toscana	9	Vini da Gigio
2	Gam-Gam	49	Vino Vino
68	Ganesh	55	Al Volto
82	Gelateria Causin	92	Alle Zattere
		65	Alla Zucca

Gran Caffè Quadri I7
San Marco 120, Piazza San Marco. t 041 522 2105, w www.quadri venice.com, **vaporetto** Vallaresso. **Open** daily 9am–midnight; closed Mon in winter. Outside seating.

Another of Venice's historic coffee-houses, Quadri fell from grace during the Second World War, when the Austrians hung out here. It's an elaborate confection of stucco and mirrors. The food in the gorgeous restaurant upstairs is good. There's a charge for music on the terrace.

Marchini I7
San Marco 676, Calle Spadaria, t 041 522 9109, w www.golosessi. com; **vaporetto** San Marco. **Open** Mon–Sat 9am–8pm.

The smell of chocolate as you enter Pasticceria Marchini is almost overwhelming; it has a mouth-watering range of chocolates, cakes and pastries, all of them beautifully presented, including the prize-winning Torta del Doge.

Paolin F8
San Marco 2962, Campo Santo Stefano, t 041 522 5576; **vaporetto** San Marco. **Open** 9.30–midnight daily; closed Thurs in winter. Outside seating.

Coffee and legendary pistachio ice-cream.

Rosa Salva H7
San Marco 4589, Campo San Luca, t 041 522 5385; **vaporetto** Rialto. **Open** daily 7.40am–8.30pm.

This branch of the famous cake shop is less atmospheric than the one in Castello (see p.272), but the cakes and ice cream are still unmissable. Try the zaleto, a traditional cake made with polenta flour.

Castello

Restaurants

Very Expensive

Al Covo L8
Castello 3968, Campiello della Pescaria, t 041 522 3812; **vaporetto** San Zaccaria. **Open** Fri–Tues 12.45–2pm and 7.30–10pm; closed Wed, Thurs and 20 Dec–20 Jan. Booking advised. No cards.

One of those 'elegant-rustic' places offering exquisitely cooked, simply served dishes in calm surroundings. You'll get a hefty bill at the end, but it's probably worth it (there's a cheaper deal at lunchtimes). The fare includes bigoli in an onion and anchovy sauce, taglierini with scallops, dorade with tomato and mint, and an excellent *frittura mista*.

Danieli Terrace J8
Hotel Danieli, Castello 4196, Riva degli Schiavoni, t 041 522 6480, w ww.starwoodhotels.com/danieli; vaporetto San Zaccaria; wheelchair accessible. Open daily 12.30–2.30 and 7–10.30. Booking required. Outside seating.
The Danieli Terrace is renowned for its classic cuisine (try the *spaghetti alla Danieli*, prepared at your table) and perfect service in an incomparable setting overlooking Bacino San Marco.

Hostaria da Franz O9
Castello 754, Fondamenta San Giuseppe, t 041 522 0861, w www.hostariadafranz.com; vaporetto Giardini. Open daily 12.30–2.30 and 7.30–10.30; closed Jan. Booking advised. Outside seating. No Diner's Club.
This fine restaurant in the eastern reaches of Castello is well worth the fairly hefty outlay. Eat in the intimate, elegant dining room or outside on the enchanting canalside terrace. The traditional fish dishes (with creative twists) prepared by Franz contain only the freshest ingredients: giant prawns are marinated in citrus fruits, ravioli are stuffed with fish, and sea bass is prepared with fresh herbs. Eels are a speciality; Franz

Pigeon Venice

Tucked away where tourists never venture, good value for money, traditional style – the Venice of locals and pigeons – are: **Al'Aciugheta**, Castello, p.271; **Ai Do Mori**, San Polo, p.275; **All'Arco**, San Polo, p.275; **Al Bacareto**, San Marco, p.267; **Al Bottegon**, Dorsoduro, p.273; **Da Codroma**, Dorsoduro, p.273; **Enoteca Due Colonne**, Cannaregio, p.278; **Easy Bar**, Santa Croce, p.276; **Gam-Gam**, Cannaregio, p.277; **Ganesh**, San Polo, p.275; **Mistra**, Giudecca, p.279; **Osteria ai Assassini**, San Marco, p.267; **Rosticceria San Bartolomeo**, San Marco, p.267; **Trattoria dai Tosi**, Castello, p.272.

prepares them to a secret recipe. The wine list is excellent.

Expensive

La Corte Sconta L7
Castello 3886, Calle del Pestrin, t 041 522 7024; vaporetto Arsenale. Open Tues–Sat 12.30–2 and 7–9.45; closed Sun and Mon, and mid-July–mid-Aug. Booking essential.
It's worth leaving the beaten track for La Corte Sconta's superb seafood, but be sure to book well in advance. The danger of opting for the '*degustazione antipasti*' (a vast selection of superb fishy hors-d'œuvres) is that you surely won't have room for any of the delicious main dishes, such as *tagliolini* with lobster, *gnocchetti* with fresh anchovies and mushrooms, black *tagliolini* with scallops and artichokes, and John Dory in a sweet and sour sauce ('*agrodolce*'). The rustic but uncluttered décor is a breath of fresh air. Highly recommended.

Al Mascaron J6
Castello 5225, Calle Lunga Santa Maria Formosa, t 041 522 5995; vaporetto Rialto. Open Mon–Sat 12–3 and 7–11; closed Jan. Booking essential.
A favourite Venetian *osteria*, now somewhat spoilt by too many tourists, but nonetheless full of atmosphere and serving good food. Wine is served out of huge containers in the front room and the atmosphere is noisy and unpretentious. Traditional Venetian specialities – both fish and meat – are served at marble-topped tables. Liver, as well as the more usual sardines, is served *in saor*, that is with pine nuts, raisins and marinated onions.

L'Osteria di Santa Marina I5
Castello 5911, Campo Santa Marina, t 041 528 5239, w www.osteriadisantamarina.it; vaporetto Rialto. Open Mon 7.30–9.30pm, Tues–Sat 12.30–2.30 and 7.30–9.30; closed 2 weeks Jan and 2 weeks Aug. No Diner's Club or AmEx.
For something a little different from Venetian standards: scampi

in saor are given a twist with the addition of leeks and ginger; *baccalà mantecato* is presented in the form of a terrine with polenta; and a creamy bean soup is garnished with rosemary flavoured fresh tuna. The *fritto* of scampi, calamari and vegetables and the fish kebabs are delicious.

Da Remigio K7
Castello 3416, Ponte dei Greci, t 041 523 0089; vaporetto San Zaccaria. Open Mon 12.30–2.30, Wed–Sun 12.30–2.30 and 7.30–10; closed Tues, most of Jan, 2 weeks July/Aug. Booking essential.
Between the Arsenale and San Marco, this classical Venetian trattoria, considered to be among the best by locals, serves the freshest of fish dishes. Antipasti consist of an array of weird and wonderful shellfish and wriggly things; *tagliolini* are served with crab, and the catch of the day is grilled, roast in the oven or baked in a salt crust. The squid stew is exceptionally tasty and the *fritto misto di mare* perfectly crisp and light.

Alle Testiere J6
Castello 5801, Calle del Mondo Nuovo, t 041 522 7220; vaporetto Rialto. Open Mon–Sat 12–2 and 7–10.30; closed first 3 weeks Aug, first 2 weeks Jan. Booking essential.
A tiny *osteria* between Campo Santa Maria Formosa and Rialto, with seating for just 20. If you're lucky enough to secure a table, the unusual fish-based fare at lunch and dinner includes delicious and varied antipasti, *gnocchetti* with baby squid or scampi and rocket, monkfish tails with capers, and turbot with red radicchio. Home-made puds. *Cicheti* and wine are also served.

Moderate

Al'Aciugheta J7
Castello 4357, Campo SS Filippo e Giacomo, t 041 522 4292, w www.aciugheta-hotelrio.it; vaporetto San Zaccaria. Open daily noon–midnight.

Late-night Food

Not a late-night city, Venice's main late-night refuelling points tend to be snack bars or *gelaterie*, though some restaurants stay open until midnight or 1am. Try the following, which go on serving until at least 11pm: **Ai Promessi Sposi**, Cannaregio, p.276; **Al' Aciugheta**, Castello, p.271; **Antica Mola**, Cannaregio, p.277; **Bar al Teatro**, San Marco, p.267; **Bar alla Toletta**, Dorsoduro, p.273; **Le Bistrot de Venise**, San Marco, p.266; **Il Caffè**, Dorsoduro, p.273; **Caffè Città di Torino**, San Marco, p.267; **Da Codroma**, Dorsoduro, p.273; **La Colombina**, Cannaregio, p.277; **Easy Bar**, Santa Croce, p.278; **Florian**, San Marco, p.267; **Alla Mascareta**, Castello, p.272; **Osteria al Postali**, Santa Croce, p.275; **Quadri**, San Marco, p.270; **Il Refolo**, Santa Croce, p.275; **Ruga Rialto**, San Polo, p.275; **Sottosopra**, Dorsoduro, p.273; **Vino Vino**, San Marco, p.267. Venice's last ice-cream cones are served at 3am on the Lido at the **Maleti**, p.279.

There are two sides to the 'Little Anchovy': on the left is a fairly standard pizzeria/trattoria with a large terrace on the *campo*, serving good, reasonably priced food; on the right is a much more 'genuine' wood-panelled *osteria* where locals come for good *cicheti* and a glass of wine.

Antica Trattoria Bandierette K5
Castello 6671, Barbarie delle Tolle, t 041 522 0619, w www. bandierette.it; vaporetto Fondamenta Nuove. Open Mon–Sat 12–2 and 7–10; closed 2 weeks in Aug, 2 weeks in Dec.
A lively seafood restaurant with plenty of Italians in among the tourists. Specialities include *spaghetti ai gamberoni e radicchio rosso* and *capesante al forno* (roast scallops).

Alla Nuova Speranza O8
Castello 145, Campo Ruga, t 041 528 5225; vaporetto San Pietro di Castello. Open daily 12–3 and 7.30–11. Booking required for dinner. Outside seating. No cards.

This simple, friendly trattoria in the nether reaches of eastern Castello has a TV at one end of the wood-panelled room, sells football coupons from a little booth at the other, and gets packed with local workmen at lunchtime. Fill up on great-value seafood: fat *capparossoli* (clams) sautéed in garlic and wine or tossed into spaghetti or monkfish. The tourist menu is good value at €15. If you want dinner, you need to book or the cook will go home early!

Alla Rivetta J7
Castello 4625, Ponte San Provolo, t 041 528 7302; vaporetto San Zaccaria. Open Tues–Sun 11.30–11; closed Mon and 15 July –15 Aug.
Students, locals and tourists alike pile into this cosy neighbourhood trattoria, which is always full and often noisy. Try the excellent '*fritto misto*'.

Trattoria dai Tosi O9
Castello 738, Secco Marina, t 041 523 7102; vaporetto Giardini. Open Thurs–Tues 12–2 and 7–10; closed Wed and 2 weeks Aug.
There's a real neighbourhood buzz to this trattoria/pizzeria far from the tourist drags. The above-average pizzas cooked in a wood oven are a real bargain, but the full menu (Venetian standards) is good value too. Very popular, so book before tramping out here.

Snacks, Light Meals and *Cicheti*

Cip-Ciap J6
Castello 5799, Calle del Mondo Nuovo (no phone); vaporetto Rialto. Open Wed–Mon 9am–9pm.
This small takeaway pizza joint sells a good range of excellent pizzas-by-the-hefty-slab and a choice of *tortina rustica* – filling, rustic savoury tarts stuffed with various appetising ingredients (try *tortino* filled with *provolone* cheese and rocket).

Alla Mascareta J6
Castello 5183, Calle Lunga Santa Maria Formosa, t 041 523 0744; vaporetto Rialto. Open Mon–Sat 6pm–1am.

This *enoteca* has an exceptional wine list (some 400 labels) and a wonderful choice of cheeses, hams and salamis.

Ristorante-Bar-Caffè Paradiso N10
Castello 1260, t 041 523 1166; vaporetto Giardini. Open Tues–Sun 10am–6pm.
In the yellow pavilion in the Public Gardens, just south of Giardini Biennale. Sit at the top for the snacks and a classic view of Venice's front door.

Cafés and Gelaterie

Da Bonifacio J7
Castello 4237, Calle degli Albanesi, t 041 522 7507; vaporetto San Zaccaria. Open Fri–Wed 7.30am–8.30pm; closed Thurs and Aug. No cards.
A squeeze of a pastry shop (there's hardly room even to perch) with a constant flow of locals. Excellent pastries, delicious little *pizzette* with various toppings to accompany an *aperitivo*, and home-made biscuits in cellophane packaging (a good going-home gift).

Il Golosone I6
Castello 5689, Salizzada S. Lio, t 041 523 9386; vaporetto Rialto. Open daily 8am–1am.
Known for pastries, *panini* and fresh fruit shakes as well as ice-cream.

Rosa Salva J5
Castello 6779, Campo Santi Giovanni e Paolo, t 041 522 7949; vaporetto Fondamenta Nuove. Open daily 8.30–8.30. Outside seating. No cards
There are several branches of this famous *pasticceria* in Venice, but this one is the best, thanks to its wonderful old-fashioned feel and its handful of quiet tables with a side view of the church. The coffee is excellent, as are the pastries and ice cream (home-made): try the unusual and delicious steamed *budino* with semolina and raisins, or the liquorice ice cream. There's

another branch in Campo S. Luca, near Piazza San Marco (see p.270).

Dorsoduro

Restaurants

Moderate

L'Incontro D7
Dorsoduro 3062, Rio Terrà Canal, t 041 522 2404; vaporetto Ca' Rezzonico. Open Tues 7.30–10.30, Wed–Sun 12.30–2.30 and 7.30–10.30; closed Mon, Jan and 2 weeks Aug; July and rest of Aug open evenings only. Booking advised.
An unusual restaurant for Venice on two counts: the food is Sardinian, and there's no fish. Succulent meat dishes include fillet of veal with mustard sauce, and carpaccio of goose breast with pine nuts and parmesan, but non-carnivores should be happy with Sardinian pasta dishes such as *orecchiette* with asparagus, and *trofie* with mixed vegetables. An excellent choice.

Trattoria ai Cugnai F9
Dorsoduro 857, Piscina del Forner, vaporetto Accademia, t (041) 528 9238. Open Tues–Sun 12–2.30 and 7–10.30; closed Mon.
Cosy little meat and fish restaurant, popular with the locals. The teeny garden has canaries and a view into the kitchen.

Alle Zattere E9
Dorsoduro 795, Rio Terrà Foscarini, t 041 520 4224; vaporetto Accademia. Open Mon and Wed–Sun 12–3 and 7–10.30; closed Tues and mid Nov–early Jan.
A decent trattoria/pizzeria with a big floating terrace on the Giudecca canal.

Cheap

Ai 4 Feri D8
Dorsoduro 2754, Calle Lunga San Barnabà, t 041 520 6978; vaporetto Ca' Rezzonico. Open Mon–Sat 12–2.30 and 7.30–10.30. No cards.
A new *osteria* run along tradi-tional lines, with excellent *cicheti* and full meals at honest prices: try the pumpkin soup, the spaghetti

with artichokes and shrimps, some simply grilled fish, the *seppie* with polenta or the fresh tuna '*in saor*', a speciality of the house. Highly recommended.

Da Toni C8
Dorsoduro 1642, Fondamenta San Basegio, t 041 528 6899; vaporetto San Basilio. Open Tues–Sun 7am–8pm; closed 3 weeks Aug. No cards.
Well off the tourist beat, this simple local trattoria harks back to pre-commercial days. Scallops with parsley, garlicky sea snails, risotto with scampi and rocket, and excellent grilled monkfish are among the fishy options on offer.

Al Pantalon E6
Dorsoduro 3958, Calle del Scalater, t 041 710 849, w www.osteriaal pantalon.it; vaporetto San Tomà. Open Mon–Sat 10–3 and 6–10; closed 3 weeks Aug.
Venetians and tourists alike pile into this popular rustic *osteria* near the Frari. Run by the same team as Alla Patatina (see p.275) and, like many eateries of its kind, it has *cicheti* at a front counter and tables in an adjoining room.

Snacks, Light Meals and *Cicheti*

Al Bottegon E8
Dorsoduro 992, Fondamenta Nani, t 041 523 0034, vaporetto Zattere. Open Mon–Sat 8.30–2.30 and 3.30–8.30, Sun 8.30–2.30. Closed 2 weeks Aug. No cards.
This wonderfully old-fashioned wine shop just along from the San Trovaso boatyard hasn't changed for 50 years. Shelves of wines from all over Italy fill two rooms, and wine by the glass and snacks are served from a long counter. No seating.

Da Codroma C7
Dorsoduro 2540, Fondamenta Briati, t 041 524 6789; vaporetto Ca' Rezzonico. Open Mon–Sat 8am–midnight; closed 3 weeks Aug. No cards.
At lunchtime, the long communal tables at this cosy, wood-panelled

osteria are packed with students from the nearby university filling up on tasty *panini*, excellent *tramezzini* and *piadini* or the hot dish of the day. It's no less popular in the evenings, when the atmos-phere is smoky and laid-back.

Sottosopra E6
Dorsoduro 3740, Campo San Pantalon, t 041 528 5320; vaporetto San Tomà. Open Mon–Sat 7pm–1am.
Cocktails, music and snacks.

Cafés and Gelaterie

Bar da Gino F9
Dorsoduro 853A, Piscina Venier, t 041 528 5276; vaporetto Accademia. Open Mon–Sat 6.30am–8pm; closed 3 weeks Aug. Outside seating. No cards.
A lively, friendly neighbourhood bar full of locals. Excellent sandwiches.

Bar alla Toletta E8
Dorsoduro 1191, Calle della Toletta, t 041 520 0196; vaporetto Accademia. Open Mon–Thurs 7am–9pm, Fri–Sun 7am–1am; closed 2 weeks Jan and 2 weeks July.
This popular bar, enlivened by background jazz, does a roaring lunchtime trade in excellent *tramezzini* and 'toasts', but it's also a good place for a coffee.

Il Caffè D7
Dorsoduro 2963, Campo Santa Margherita, t 041 528 7998; vaporetto Ca' Rezzonico. Open Mon–Sat 8am–2am. Outside seating. No cards.
With tables on bohemian Campo Santa Margherita, this is popularly known as Caffè Rosso because of its red paint and red plastic chairs outside. The cosy interior is dominated by a huge Art Deco coffee machine, and hip back-ground music makes for a mellow atmosphere. Cakes, *tramezzini* and other snacks are all good. If the time is right, go for a 'spritzer' *aperitivo*. Equally popular as a nightspot.

Il Doge D7

Dorsoduro 3058, Campo Santa Margherita, t 041 523 4607; vaporetto Ca' Rezzonico. Open daily 10.30am–midnight. No cards.

Lively *gelateria* known for its buzzy atmosphere.

Gelateria Causin D7

Dorsoduro 2996, Campo Santa Margherita (no phone); vaporetto Ca' Rezzonico. Open Mon–Sat 8.30–7.30. Outside seating.

The Causin family have been making ice cream since 1928, and their *caffè/gelateria* is reassuringly old-fashioned. The choice of flavours is interesting rather than overwhelming.

Gobbetti D7

Dorsoduro 3108B, Rio Terrà Canal, t 041 528 9014; vaporetto Ca' Rezzonico. Open daily 7.45am–8pm. No Diner's Club or AmEx.

A small *pasticceria* with excellent cakes. Try the Venetian version of pumpkin pie, *crostata di zucca*.

Nico E9

Dorsoduro 922, Fondamenta Zattere ai Gesuati, t 041 522 5293; vaporetto Zattere. Open June–Sept daily 7.30am–11pm, Oct–May daily 8am–9.30pm. No cards.

Generally considered to win the ice-cream war. The late-night queues are a testament to its popularity.

Tonolo E6

Dorsoduro 3764, Calle San Pantalon, t 041 523 7209; vaporetto San Tomà. Open Tues–Sun 8am–8.30pm; closed Mon, and Sun in July; closed Aug. No cards.

A contender for Venice's best pastry-purveyor, and good value.

San Polo and Santa Croce

Restaurants

Luxury

Da Fiore F5

San Polo 2202a, Calle del Scaleter, near Campo San Polo, t 041 721 308; vaporetto San Stae. Open Tues–Sat 12.30–2.30 and 7.30–

10.30; *closed Sun and Mon, early Jan and Aug. Booking essential for dinner.*

This deceptively simple restaurant is considered by many to be the best in Venice. The menu is based on market availability, but classics of Venetian cuisine (like *bigoli in salsa*) appear regularly alongside interesting variations such as thyme-flavoured scallops '*gratinati*', sardine and caper '*involtini*', ravioli stuffed with fish and asparagus, and '*tagliata*' of fresh tuna with rosemary. Leave room for the sinful hot chocolate '*tortino*' with coffee sauce.

Expensive

Da Ignazio F6

San Polo 2749, Calle dei Saoneri, t 041 523 4852; vaporetto San Tomà. Open Sun–Fri 12–3 and 7–10; closed Sat and 3 weeks July–Aug. Booking advised.

This cosy, traditional trattoria has been serving classic Venetian fish dishes for more than 50 years, but you can also taste such oddities as *moeche* (small, soft-shelled crabs eaten whole), *castraure* (spring artichokes) and *sparesee* (wild asparagus). Or go for the delicious spaghetti with *vongole veraci* (giant clams). There is a pretty courtyard.

Trattoria San Tomà E6

San Polo 2864A, Campo San Tomà, t 041 523 8819; vaporetto San Tomà; wheelchair accessible. Open daily 12–3 and 7–10.30; closed 15 Nov–15 Dec. Outside seating.

The outside tables on the quiet little *campo* or in the rear garden make up for the largely overpriced and average food at this trattoria/pizzeria. Venetian standards and pizzas (also to takeaway) plus paella.

Vecio Fritolin G5

Santa Croce 2262, Calle della Regina, t 041 522 2881, w www.veciofritolin.com; vaporetto San Stae/Rialto. Open Tues–Sat 12–2.15 and 7–10.15pm, Sun 12–2.15.

A calm, civilized restaurant where the delightful owner, Irina, will greet you and guide you through

the menu. The day's catch is cooked without fuss and beautifully presented on wide plates; you might find baby shrimp on a bed of sautéed artichoke hearts; green *tagliolini* with nettles; courgette flowers and shrimp; steamed fillet of turbot with asparagus in a buttery vinegarette. Highly recommended.

Moderate

Antica Birraria La Corte F5

San Polo 2168, Campo San Polo, t 041 275 0570, w www.antica birrarialacorte.com; vaporetto San Silvestro; wheelchair accessible. Open daily 12–2.30 and 7.30–10.30pm; closed Mon in winter and 2 weeks Nov. Outside seating.

A new-ish restaurant/pizzeria catering for a hip, young crowd and boasting décor (exposed brick, steel, zinc and copper plate) that wouldn't be out of place in New York or London. In warm weather there are tables in the courtyard and on the lovely *campo*. Food is of the 'modern *osteria*' type: antipasti, pasta, rice dishes, big salads, pizzas, fish and grilled meats. There are some ethnic and veggie dishes too, and you don't have to eat a full meal.

Bancogiro: Osteria da Andrea H5

San Polo 122, Campo Giacometto, t 041 523 2061; vaporetto Rialto. Open Tues–Sat 10.30–3 and 6.30–12, Sun 10.30–3; closed Mon. Booking essential.

This modern *osteria* opened in summer 2000 and enjoys a fabulous position overlooking the Grand Canal. In the street-level bar, excellent wines and snacks are served; above, on a sort of mezzanine, those who have booked can choose from a menu of creative dishes such as fish salad with apple and mandarin, roast fresh tuna with pine nuts and coriander and gratin of steamed vegetables flavoured with coriander, all at very reasonable prices.

Ganesh E5

San Polo 2426, Rio Marin, t 041 719 804; vaporetto Biasio. Open daily 12.30–2 and 7–11; winter closed Wed. Outside seating.

There is room for just three tables on the pretty canalside terrace of Venice's only Indian restaurant. The cooks are Indian, but the food, while perfectly decent, is geared towards rather unadventurous Italian tastebuds. Occasional live music.

Alla Madonna H5

San Polo 594, Calle della Madonna, t 041 522 3824; vaporetto Rialto/San Silvestro. Open Thurs–Tues 12–3 and 7–10.30; closed Wed and Jan.

This traditional trattoria is in lots of guidebooks but attracts plenty of locals too, with its reasonable prices. Waiters in white jackets serve grilled or fried eel (*anguilla*) from the lagoon, *seppioline* with polenta and *tartufi di mare* (sea urchins). No bookings taken.

Al Nono Risorto G5

Santa Croce 2337, Calle della Regina, t 041 524 1169; vaporetto San Stae. Open Mon, Tues, Fri–Sun 12.30–2.30 and 7–11, Thurs 7–11; closed Wed and Jan. Booking advised at weekends. Outside seating. No cards.

This restaurant/pizzeria gets packed with a lively young crowd who come to hang out, eat reasonably priced pizza, listen to live jazz and enjoy the pretty garden in warm weather. The full restaurant menu features such dishes as tagliatelle with prawns and artichoke hearts, and monk-fish with polenta or potatoes.

Ribò D6

Santa Croce 158, Fondamenta Minotto, t 041 524 2486. vaporetto Piazzale Roma/San Tomà. Open Tues–Sun 12.30–2.30 and 7–10.30.

The young new owners of this small restaurant have favoured a clean, elegant and modern look, and food to match: the menu changes monthly, but expect the likes of *carpaccio* of octopus with shallot vinegar, risotto with

scampi and asparagus, tuna steak with fresh herbs, and tempura of scallops. There's a delightful garden for warm weather.

Cheap

Il Réfolo F4

Santa Croce 1459, Campo San Giacomo dell'Orio, t 041 524 0016, w www.dafiore.com; vaporetto Riva di Biasio. Open Wed–Sun 9am–1am; closed Tues, and Dec and Jan. Booking advised. Outside seating.

A modern new pizzeria run by the same team behind the legendary Osteria da Fiore (*see* p.274). Eat sandwiches and snacks in the large bar area or sit at one of a few tables in the adjacent room for excellent pizza (not easy to find in Venice). Outside there are tables on a pretty canal.

Alla Zucca F4

Santa Croce 1762, Ponte del Megio. t 041 524 1570; vaporetto San Stae. Open Mon–Sat 12.30–2.30 and 7–10.30. Booking advised. Outside seating. No cards.

'The Pumpkin' has something of the feel of a 1970s veggie restaurant: wood panelling, plain tables, friendly, 'earthy' staff. The menu has a strong emphasis on non-meat dishes (such as penne with gorgonzola and pine nuts), but there is plenty for carnivores too and the odd 'exotic' dish such as Venezuelan beef with rice and beans.

Snacks, Light Meals and *Cicheti*

Ai Do Mori H5

San Polo 429, Calle dei Do Mori, t 041 522 5401; vaporetto Rialto. Open Mon–Sat 8.30–8.30; closed 3 weeks Aug. No cards.

This historic '*locale*' occupies a long, rather gloomy, wood-panelled room hung with copper pans. There's nowhere to sit, so punters (a mix of locals and clued-up foreigners) prop up the bar. A good selection of wine, plus *cicheti* and snacks such as *tramezzini*.

All'Arco H5

San Polo 436, Calle dell'Ochialer, t 041 520 5666; vaporetto San Silvestro/Rialto. Open Mon–Sat 7am–5pm. Outside seating. No cards.

This tiny, authentic *bacaro* hidden away in the warren of narrow alleys around the Rialto markets is only open during the day, but it's worth seeking out for its excellent *cicheti* and Venetian atmosphere. Hang out at the bar or sit down at one of the few outside tables.

Osteria Alla Patatina F6

San Polo 2741A, Ponte San Polo, t 041 523 7238, vaporetto San Tomà. Open Mon–Fri 9–3 and 5–9.30; Sat 9.30–2; closed 2 weeks Aug.

Popular with students and locals thanks to its low prices, this lively little *osteria* owes its name to the wonderful home-made potato chips that, among other excellent *cicheti*, weigh down the bar counter (full meals are also available).

Osteria al Postali E4

Santa Croce 821, Rio Marin, t 041 715 156; vaporetto Riva di Biasio. Open Mon–Sat 8.30pm–2am. Music, visual projections, and crêpes until 1am.

Al Prosecco F4

Santa Croce 1503, Campo San Giacomo dell'Orio, t 041 524 0222; vaporetto Riva di Biasio. Open Mon–Sat 8–8 (to 11 in summer; closed 1st week July, Aug and Jan. Outside seating. No cards.

With its tables on a quiet little *campo*, this is a good place for imbibing light, fizzy *prosecco* wine, a coffee and an *aperitivo*, and for munching on good *cicheti*.

Ruga Rialto H5

San Polo 692, Calle del Sturion, t 041 521 1243; vaporetto San Silvestro. Open daily 11–2.30 and 6–12. No Diner's Club.

An animated *osteria* with a crowded, smoky front bar area where you can drink and graze on *cicheti*, and several spacious rear rooms where you can sit down to a good-value full meal.

Cafés and *Gelaterie*

Caffè dei Frari F6
San Polo 2564, Fondamenta dei Frari, t 041 524 1877; vaporetto San Tomà. **Open** *Mon–Sat 8.30am–9.30pm. No cards.*
Atmospheric little café-bar opposite the Frari church.

Easy Bar G5
Santa Croce 2119, Campo Santa Maria Materdomini, t 041 524 0321; vaporetto San Stae. **Open** *Fri–Wed 7.30am–1.30am; closed Thurs and Jan. Outside seating. No cards.*
A relaxed, studenty neighbourhood hangout serving coffee and cakes in the morning, lunchtime snacks such as *tramezzini, piadine* and *bruschette*, and late-night drinks. There is Stream TV for football fans. No smoking 12–3pm.

Rizzardini G6
San Polo 1415, Campiello dei Meloni, t 041 522 3835; vaporetto San Silvestro. **Open** *Wed–Mon 7am–9.30pm; closed Tues and Aug. No cards.*
An invitingly old-fashioned pastry shop and *caffè* (it first opened for business in 1742) with traditional Venetian cakes and biscuits, including marzipan cake and a mean-looking strudel.

Cannaregio

Restaurants

Very Expensive

Fiaschetteria Toscana I5
Cannaregio 5719, Salizzada San Giovanni Crisostomo, t 041 528 5281; vaporetto Rialto. **Open** *Mon 12.30–2.30, Wed–Sun 12.30–2.30 and 7.20–10.30; closed Tues and 21 July–21 Aug. Booking essential.*
This not in the least bit Tuscan restaurant is usually full of well-heeled foreigners attracted by the elegant atmosphere, very good food (which includes meat as well as fish) and fabulous wine list. Sole is served *in saor*, and scallops with almonds, while *foie gras* is

marinated in *picolit, gnocchetti* are served *gratinée* with scampi and porcini mushrooms, duck breast is flavoured with balsamic vinegar, and turbot comes with artichokes.

Il Sole Sulla Vecia Cavana I4
Cannaregio 4624, Rio Terrà SS Apostoli, t 041 528 7106, w www.isolevenezia.it; vaporetto Ca' d'Oro. **Open** *Tues–Sun 12–2.30 and 7.30–10.30; closed Mon, and 2 weeks Aug, 2 weeks Jan.*
Both traditional and more creative dishes are served at this elegant restaurant, all beautifully presented. The seafood salad with 'pearls' of melon and cucumber makes for an unusual antipasto; follow this with '*margherite*' (a kind of ravioli) stuffed with sea bass, and wonderful Sicilian-style tuna steaks seared on the grill and served with capers, tomato and oregano. Some meat dishes also feature on the menu.

Expensive

Osteria Boccadoro J5
Cannaregio 5405A, Campiello Widman, t 041 521 1021, w www.osteriaboccadorove.org; vaporetto Fondamenta Nuove; wheelchair accessible. **Open** *Tues–Sun 12.30–2.30 and 8–11.30. Outside seating.*
A tiny modern *osteria* run by an enthusiastic young team, with tables on pretty Campiello Widman and an internal courtyard. Background jazz and 'modern rustic' décor make for a mellow atmosphere. The short menu might included sautéed, marinated mussels, gnocchi with mussels, and grilled tuna or John Dory with artichokes. Ingredients are of the highest quality.

Vini da Gigio H4
Cannaregio 3628A, Fondamenta San Felice, t 041 528 5140; vaporetto Ca' d'Oro; wheelchair accessible. **Open** *Tues–Sun 12–2.30 and 7.30–10.30; closed Mon, 3 weeks Jan/Feb and 3 weeks July/Aug. Booking essential.*
This small restaurant with views over the canal is considered to be one of the better places to eat by

local foodies and is always crowded. Though it has moved up in the world in recent years, it still has the feel of an old *bacaro*, with its low, beamed ceilings and rustic tiled floors. Food – fish, game and meat, various kinds of raw, marinated fish, fish soup, a superb *baccalà mantecato* (creamed stockfish), sautéed scallops, duck from the lagoon ('*masorini*') – remains faithful to Venetian traditions, and the superb wine list features some 600 labels from both Italy and beyond.

Moderate

Ai Promessi Sposi I4
Cannaregio 4367, Calle dell'Oca, t 041 522 8609; vaporetto Ca' d'Oro. **Open** *Thurs–Tues 9am–midnight; closed Wed. Outside seating. No cards.*
This down-to-earth bar/trattoria has changed hands, and the food has taken a turn for the better. You can still fill up for a reasonable price, however, and the 'Menu Veneziano' is particularly good value at €20. Meals are served all day, but there's also an eye-catching range of *cicheti* as you walk in. *Pasta e fagioli* soup is served Burano-style with chunks of eel, while the *fritto misto* (from the island of Erasmo) contains vegetables.

Anice Stellato F2
Cannaregio 3272, Fondamenta della Sensa, t 041 720 744; vaporetto Ponte Guglie/ Sant' Alvise. **Open** *Tues–Sun 12.30–2 and 7.30–10; closed Mon and 3 weeks Aug/Sept. Booking advised.*
This new generation, family-run *bacaro*/trattoria is near the remote church of Sant'Alvise but it's worth the trek. Traditional dishes are enlivened by the odd creative twist – try spaghetti with *caparossoli* (local clams) or with sardines and balsamic vinegar, bean soup with crustaceans, tagliatelle with scampi and courgette flowers, dorade flavoured with curry, or salmon with aniseed and potatoes – and served in a youthful, friendly atmosphere.

Vegetarian Restaurants

Fishy Venice has no actual vegetarian restaurants, but there are many places offering vegetarian options. And of course there are always vegetarian antipasto, pasta and pizza dishes to be had almost everywhere, and snacks will present no problem either. The Italian for 'I am a vegetarian; I do not eat meat or fish (or eggs)' is 'Sono vegetariano/a; non mangio ne carne, ne pesce (ne uova).'

The following offer vegetarian options: **Antica Birraria La Corte**, San Polo, p.274; **Gam-Gam**, Cannaregio, p.277; **Al Gatto Nero**, Burano (also has gluten-free choices), p.279; **Trattoria Vini da Arturo**, San Marco, p.266; kosher **Alla Vedova**, Cannaregio, p.277; **Alla Zucca**, Santa Croce, p.275.

La Colombina G3
Cannaregio 1828, Campiello del Pegolotto, t 041 275 0622, w www.lacolombina.it; vaporetto San Marcuola; wheelchair accessible. Open Wed–Mon 6pm–2am; closed Tues and 10–25 Aug. Booking advised. Outside seating.
With its yellow walls hung with modern art, young management and late-night jazz, this restaurant really stands out from the crowd. The excellent meat, fish and vegetable dishes are based on traditional Venetian cuisine but have a creative slant and are complemented by a fine wine list. There are a few tables on the campiello.

Gam-Gam E2
Cannaregio 1122, Sottoportico di Ghetto Vecchio, t 041 715 284, w www.jewishvenice.org; vaporetto Ponte Guglie. Open Mon–Thurs and Sun 12–10, Fri 12–sunset; closed Sat. Outside seating. No cards.
This modern kosher bar and restaurant by the entrance to the ghetto has tables on the busy Cannaregio canal. Dishes include an excellent choice of antipasti (including hummous, baba ganoush and tasty salads), fish,

meat and vegetable couscous, shwarma and latkes. The odd Italian dish is thrown in too, and there are vegetarian options.

Trattoria Casa Mia H4
Cannaregio 4430, Calle dell'Oca, t 041 528 5590; vaporetto Ca d'Oro. Open Wed–Mon 12–2 and 7–10; closed Tues. Outside seating.
This busy, friendly trattoria/pizzeria has very reasonable prices and is generally filled with locals. There are a few tables in the courtyard at the back.

Alla Vedova H4
Cannaregio 3912, Ramo Ca d'Oro, t 041 528 5324; vaporetto Ca d'Oro. Open Mon–Wed and Sat 11.30–2.30 and 6.30–10.30, Sun 6.30–10.30; closed Thurs, Fri and Aug. Booking essential.
One of the oldest and best-known bacari in Venice (it now doubles as a trattoria), where locals crowd round the bar to eat a selection of excellent cicheti (including wonderful spicy polpette or meatballs) while hungrier punters join a relaxed crowd of tourists at wooden tables in the adjoining room. The same family has run the place for some 130 years, and the décor and atmosphere have been carefully preserved. Dishes might include tagliatelle with duck, fritto misto and fegato alla veneziana, and vegetarian options are available. Highly recommended.

Cheap

Antica Mola F2
Cannaregio 2800, Fondamenta degli Ormesini, t 041 717 492; vaporetto Ponte Guglie/ Ferrovia. Open daily 8am–midnight; closed Aug. Outside seating.
All the old favourites – fish, risotto, zuppa di pesce – and tables by the canal, though it can be touristy.

Da Alvise J4
Cannaregio 5045, Fondamenta Nuove, t 041 520 4185, w www.daalvise.com; vaporetto Fondamenta Nuove. Open Tues–Sun 12–2 and 7–10; closed Mon and Jan. Outside seating.
This new pizzeria/restaurant has a great setting on the Fondamenta

Nuove and tables overlooking the lagoon. Fresh herbs grow in pots on the terrace. Pizzas are good and reasonably priced; you'll spend more if you order fish.

Pizzeria La Perla I4
Cannaregio 4615, Rio Terrà dei Franceschini, t 041 528 5175; vaporetto Ca' d'Oro. Open Tues–Sun 12–2 and 7–10; closed Mon and Aug.
The Alpine-look wooden tables here are always crowded with locals drawn by some of the best pizzas in Venice (though let's face it, there's not much competition).

Snacks, Light Meals and Cicheti

Algiubagiò J3
Cannaregio 5039, Fondamenta Nuove, t 041 523 6084, w www.algiubagio.com; vaporetto Fondamenta Nuove. Open daily 7am–8.30pm; closed Jan. Outside seating.
Right by the vaporetto stop for the islands, this bar, with its large terrace overlooking the lagoon and super-friendly staff, is good for a drink, snack or light meal: apart from the usual selection of panini and tramezzini, there are pasta dishes and salads. A little way east along the water is an ice cream and takeaway pizza outlet owned by the same guys.

La Cantina H4
Cannaregio 3689, Strada Nova, t 041 522 8258; vaporetto Ca' d'Oro. Open daily 10am–9pm; closed 21 July–7 Aug and 1–15 Jan. Outside seating. No cards.
A small, busy wine bar where the choice of wines reflects the owners' enthusiasm for Friuli whites and robust Piemonte reds. Snacks include cheeses, salamis, hams and lots of vegetables.

Enoteca Boldrin I5
Cannaregio 5550, Salizzada San Canciano, t 041 523 7859; vaporetto Ca' d'Oro/Rialto. Open Mon–Sat 9.30am–9pm; closed 21 July–4 Aug.
A barn of a place, but a useful address for a cheap meal (there is

a self-service system) – hot dishes include pastas and lasagne. Or eat a sandwich washed down by a glass of wine or a beer.

Enoteca Due Colonne F3
Cannaregio 1814C, Rio Terrà del Cristo, t 041 524 0453; vaporetto San Marcuola. Open Sun–Fri 7.30am–8.30pm; closed Sat, 2 weeks Aug. No cards.
A fun, noisy, no-frills bar full of Venetians, serving *cicheti, panini* and a wide variety of drinks.

Cafés and *Gelaterie*

Caffè Costarica F3
Cannaregio 1337, Rio Terrà San Leonardo (no phone); vaporetto Ponte Guglie. Open Mon–Sat 9.30–1 and 4–7.
This no-frills but atmospheric shop adorned with sacks of coffee, grinders and old espresso machines is one of Venice's oldest coffeehouses and sells a vast selection of coffee and tea. In warm weather, try the refreshing *frappé* (iced coffee). No seating; you stand at the bar to drink.

Dal Mas D3
Cannaregio 150A, Lista di Spagna, t 041 715 101; vaporetto Ferrovia. Open Wed–Mon 7.30am–9pm; closed Tues and July.
Standing out among all the plastic-looking fare available at

Decadent Venice

Decadence, in eating, means pushing the boat out, following in the footsteps of film stars and luxuriating in the kind of food and service that might usually be the sole preserve of those who devote their lives to pleasure and leisure.

In Venice, save up and try: **Caffès Florian, Quadri** and **Lavena** in Piazza San Marco, p.267 and p.270; **Cipriani**, Giudecca, p.278; the **Danieli Terrace**, Castello, p.271; **La Favorita**, Lido, p.278; **Da Fiore**, San Polo, p.274; **Harry's Bar**, San Marco, p.266, **Locanda Cipriani**, Torcello, p.278; **Osteria da Franz**, Castello, p.271.

the bars along the touristy Lista di Spagna, the home-made cakes and pastries at this *pasticceria* are probably the nearest decent sugar fix to the station.

Puppa I4
Cannaregio 4800, Calle del Spezier, t 041 523 7947; vaporetto Ca' d'Oro. Open Tues–Sun 7.30am–1pm and 3.30–8.30pm. Cash only.
Small *pasticceria* with wonderful cakes. Take-away only.

The Lagoon Restaurants

Very Expensive

Cipriani I10
Giudecca 10, t 041 240 8507, w www.orient-expresshotels.com; vaporetto Zitelle (but hotel boat from Vallaresso vaporetto stop is free to restaurant clients); wheelchair accessible. Open daily 12–2.30 and 8–10.30; closed Nov–March. Booking advised. Outside seating.
A meal in the main restaurant of the legendary Hotel Cipriani may not be the ultimate gastronomic experience, but it certainly holds its own with romance and atmosphere, especially in summer when tables are laid on a magical terrace and a piano tinkles in the background. The wide variety of dishes, both local and otherwise, are all well prepared and exquisitely presented: try the interesting array of antipasti to start, the fillet of John Dory in a potato crust and served with asparagus, and the duck breast with polenta soufflé. Note that children under eight aren't allowed in at dinner. For a less wallet-busting (and far less romantic) experience, come for lunch at the Cip's club.

La Favorita Off maps
Lido, Via F. Duodo 33, t 041 526 1626; vaporetto Lido. Open Tues 7.30–10.30, Wed–Sun 12.30–2.30 and 7.30–10.30; closed Mon and mid Jan–mid Feb. Booking advised. Outside seating.
One of the best places to eat on the Lido, this restaurant serves traditional fish dishes, including

caparossoli (clams) marinated in garlic and parsley or tossed with *tagliolini*, fillet of John Dory cooked with vegetables, and a light and fragrant *frittura* of scampi and calamari. There's an excellent-value fixed menu.

Harry's Dolci D10
Giudecca 773, Fondamenta San Biagio, t 041 522 4844; vaporetto Sant'Eufemia/Redentore. Open Wed–Sun 12–3 and 7–11; closed Mon, Tues and Nov–March. Booking advised. Outside seating.
It sounds like a coffee and cake shop, but Harry's Bar's baby brother is actually a restaurant decked out like a trattoria, with tiled walls and wooden tables. The excellent food is similar to that at Harry's Bar, but prices are considerably lower. The views across the canal from the wide windows (or, better still, the waterside terrace) are stunning.

Locanda Cipriani Off maps
Torcello, Piazza Santa Fosca 29, t 041 730 150, w www.locanda cipriani.com; vaporetto 12. Open Wed–Mon 12–3 and 7–9; closed Tues.
In spite of the high prices and merely average food, Locanda Cipriani (a distant relation of the Hotel Cipriani) is an idyllic place to eat, as Hemingway and Chaplin discovered in their time. The restaurant, situated off sleepy Torcello's main square, is rustic and cosy, but it's best to come in warm weather so you can eat on the lovely vine-covered terrace. If you can't be bothered to go back to the mainland, there are six elegant bedrooms above the restaurant (*see* p.261).

Expensive

Ai Pescatori Off maps
Burano, Via Galuppi 371, t 041 730 650; vaporetto 12; wheelchair accessible. Open Thurs–Tues 12–3 and 6–9; closed Wed and Jan.
A deservedly popular haunt where you can try the old standby, *risotto di fagioli* (beans), or *anguilla in brodo di branzino* (eel in sea bass sauce; order it in advance).

Altanella E11
Giudecca 268, Calle delle Erbe, t 041 522 7780; vaporetto Sant'Eufemia/ Redentore. Open Wed–Sun 12.30–2 and 7.30–9; closed Mon, Tues and 6 Jan–carnival. No cards.
A delightful old seafood restaurant with an attractive setting on the Rio del Ponte Longo and a sideways glimpse of the Giudecca canal. The fresh grilled fish is superb, and the *risotto di pesce* and *fritto* are worth the trip alone.

Busa alla Torre Off maps
Murano, Campo Santo Stefano 3, t 041 739 662; vaporetto La Colonna. Open daily 11.30–3.30. Outside seating.
Tucked away in a corner of Campo Santo Stefano, this small red-painted building with its green awning houses one of the best places to eat on Murano. Lele (the larger-than-life owner) presides over the restaurant, where you can pick your way through a *granseola* (huge spider crab) and move on to a fine *fritto misto*.

Garibaldi Off maps
Chioggia, Via San Marco 1924, Loc. Sottomarina, t 041 554 0042, bus 11 from Lido or Piazzale Roma; wheelchair accessible. Open Tues–Sun 12.30–2.30 and 7.30–10.30; closed Mon and Nov. Booking advised. Outside seating.
Situated on the Sottomarina, Chioggia's popular lido, Garibaldi is often bursting with Italian families tucking into the freshest of fish, simply grilled or prepared with a touch of fantasy (try scampi marinated in citrus fruit, *tagliolini* with scallops and *calamaretti*, or *gambas* in a red radicchio sauce. Home-made desserts.

Al Gatto Nero Off maps
Burano, Fondamenta della Giudecca, t 041 730 120, w www.gattonero.com; vaporetto 12; wheelchair accessible. Open Tues–Sun 12–3 and 7–9.30; closed Nov and last week Jan. Booking advised.
The traditional dishes in this attractive little trattoria far from

the daytripping crowds are prepared with the freshest ingredients. Try *tagliarini* with *granseola* crab, *risotto alla buranella*, eel or monkfish cooked on an iron skillet, or delicious deep-fried *mazzancolle* (a type of shrimp). The owner's art collection adorns the walls and you eat from plates that the family has painted with scenes of the island. Book ahead for a table on the pretty terrace. Vegetarian and gluten-free menus are available.

Osteria Penzo Off maps
Chioggia, Calle Largo Bersaglio 526, t 041 400 992; bus 11 from Lido or Piazzale Roma. Open Mon 12–2.30, Wed–Sun 12–2.30 and 7.15–10.30 (open daily June–Aug); closed Tues and Christmas–New Year. No cards.
In the old town near the Vigo column, this was once a simple *bacaro*. Now you can sit comfortably with locals and eat traditional dishes such as black *tagliolini* with scampi and tomato sauce, scallops with porcini mushrooms and radicchio, and an excellent *fritto misto*.

Moderate

Mistra G12
Giudecca 212A, t 041 522 0743; vaporetto Redentore. Open Mon 12.30–3.30, Wed–Sun 12.30–3.30 and 7.30–10.30; closed Tues and Jan. Booking advised.
Way beyond the imagination of most tourists, this first-floor trattoria among boatyards on the south side of Giudecca island has watery views. Specialities are fish and dishes from Liguria (so expect lots of pesto).

Snacks, Light Meals and *Cicheti*

Bar Trento Off maps
Lido, Via San Gallo 82, t 041 526 5960, w www.lidovenezia.it/bartrento; vaporetto Lido. Open Mon–Sat 8am–9pm (meals served 12–2.30); closed 2 weeks Dec. Outside seating. No cards.
Near the casino, this is a cheap and cheerful place to eat, and is

unfrequented by tourists – a rare occurrence on the Lido. Stand at the bar and graze on excellent traditional *cicheti*, or sit down for a meal, including salt cod cooked in various ways (especially on Fridays), risottos, pasta with fish sauce, *pasta e fagioli*, *fegato alla veneziana* and fish of the day.

Al Ponte del Diavolo Off maps
Torcello, 10/11 Fondamenta Borgognoni, t 041 730 401; vaporetto 12. Open Mon–Fri 12–3.30, Sat 7–10.30pm.
A vogueish place to eat on Torcello; primarily a lunchtime spot because of its exquisite garden and the problem of evening mosquitos. The *fritto misto* is as light and tasty as you'll get anywhere; desserts are outstanding.

Cafés and Gelaterie

Gelateria Bar Maleti Off maps
Lido, Gran Viale 47, t 041 242 8133; vaporetto Lido. Open daily 10am–3am.
Venice's last ice-cream cones are served up at 3am.

Mestre

Restaurants

Very Expensive

Dall'Amelia Off maps
Mestre, Via Miranese 113, t 041 913 955, w www.boscaratoristotazione. it; bus 7 from Piazzale Roma; wheelchair accessible. Open Thurs–Tues 12–2.30 and 8–10.30; closed Wed.
An elegant and highly regarded restaurant that lures gourmets across the big bridge. Dishes are based on traditional recipes of the region, with the addition of the odd creative dish, and fish is brought in daily from the market at Chioggia. Try scallop and porcini salad with rocket, wholewheat *bigoli* with shellfish, *tagliolini gratinée* with sole and *sformato* (flan) of prawns and courgette.

Expensive

Darsena Off maps
*Mestre, Via Forte Marghera 183,
t 041 531 8420, **bus** 12 from Piazzale
Roma. **Open** Mon 7.30–10, Tues–Sat
12.30–2.30 and 7.30–10; closed first
3 weeks Jan and 15–30 July.*
Don't be put off by the appearance of this restaurant among the boatyards on the edge of Mestre – the generous mixed fish antipasto is fantastic and the *spaghetti alle vongole* and other traditional fish dishes are excellent. You choose your fish from a large tank.

Moderate

Le Bronse Off maps
*Mestre, Via Terraglietto 23, t 041
534 6740; **bus** 8 from Mestre. **Open**
Tues–Sun 12.30–2.30 and 8–10.30;
closed Mon. Booking advised.*

An excellent-value little trattoria with no written menu which has just taken up residence at the Sporting Club in Mestre. The dishes, based on seasonal ingredients, might include chestnut flour tagliatelle with wild mushrooms, rabbit cooked in balsamic vinegar, and lamb cutlets cooked in white wine. Good home-made desserts that are worth leaving room for.

Osteria da Mariano
Off maps
*Mestre, Via Spalti 49, t 041 615 765,
bus 2, 4 from Piazzale Roma. **Open**
Mon–Sat 7.45am–3.30pm and
5–8.30pm; closed Aug.*
This traditional *osteria* near the 'centro storico' of Mestre serves cheeses, meats ands *cicheti*,

accompanied by a wide variety of wines. More substantial fare is also available.

Osteria La Pergola Off maps
*Mestre, Via Fiume 42, t 041 974 932,
train to Mestre. **Open** Mon–Fri
12–2.30 and 8–10.30, Sat 8–10.30;
closed Sun, and Sat in winter..*
A simple, unfussy trattoria not far from the station, with surprisingly inventive cooking and very reasonable prices. Dishes are meat and vegetable based: *garganelli* with gorgonzola, *pitacchios* and cognac, rabbit with fresh herbs, veal cooked in citrus and ginger, and sinful pannacotta with strawberry sauce . The wine list is excellent.

Nightlife and Entertainment

Late Bars and Clubs 282

Music 283

Cinema 284

Theatre 284

Dance 285

Gambling 285

Here they are getting dressed while the rest of world is going to bed, it was said – and if all were right with the world, Venice would still be a real blow-out after dark, the one city in the world where you could dress up outrageously, catch a gondola with your sweetheart and dance under the fair lights in the company of a Casablanca mix of people from all over the world, gathered in the eternal capital of romance and pleasure. But the sad truth is that the Venetians and most of their visitors tuck themselves in early like old biddies. The locals are content with a twilight *passeggiata* to Campo San Bartolomeo, Riva degli Schiavone, Piazza San Marco, or to their neighbourhood *campo*, for a chat with friends and an *aperitivo* before heading home to dinner and the dubious delights of Italian TV, while the more hot-blooded amphibians may go to the clubs or bars in Mestre or Marghera.

Visitors who aren't ready for bed at 10pm are left to become even poorer at in Venice's gambling haunts (see p.285), though you may spend less more memorably on a moonlit gondola ride (€75 per hour), or you can do as most night owls do – wander about. Venice is a different city at night, when the *bricole* lights in the Lagoon are a fitting backdrop for a mer-king's birthday pageant. For all that, there are things to do after hours on the magic Lagoon.

Listings Information

For listings in the entire Veneto region (Verona's Arena, most notably, has summer opera, major rock and jazz concerts, and other blockbusters) check the newspapers (*Il Gazzettino* or *La Nuova*) or the monthly *Marco Polo* magazine. Note that concerts nearly always mean classical music. Pick up a copy of the hotel association's free Italian/English booklet, *Un Ospite di Venezia*, published fortnightly in summer and monthly off season, with its calendar of what's on. A quarterly free leaflet called *Bussola*, published by the Province of Venice, is available at tourist offices. Another free publication to look out for is *Pocket Venice*, also quarterly.

Late Bars and Clubs

There are a few oases in Venice's clubbing desert. On a good night, any can be fun; on a bad night, they'll be almost empty or dominated by posing androids squeezed into £400 designer pants. We refuse to be responsible for what you find (try ringing ahead), but the following is a fairly comprehensive list.

Note that the following venues reviewed in the Eating Out chapter also have a nightlife scene: **Le Bistrot de Venise** (San Marco, see p.266), **La Colombina** (Cannaregio, see p.277), **Easy Bar** (Santa Croce, see p.276), **Harry's Bar** (San Marco, see p.266), **Alla Mascareta** (Castello, see p.272), **Al Nono Risorto** (Santa Croce, see p.275), and **Ruga Rialto** (San Polo, see p.275).

Bacaro Jazz I5
San Marco 5546, Salizzada del Fontego dei Tedeschi, *t* 041 528 5249; *vaporetto* Rialto. **Open** Thurs–Tues 11am–2am.
A brightly lit, wood-panelled, lively bar where you can eat and drink until late to the accompaniment of jazz and blues sounds and the occasional live act.

Caffè Blu D6
Dorsoduro 3778, Salizzada San Pantalon, *t* 041 710 227; *vaporetto* San Tomà. **Open** Mon–Fri 8.30am–2am, Sat 5pm–2am.
A crowded, smoky bar serving snacks and Guinness and Harp on tap. From October until April, there is live music (blues, Latin, jazz) on Friday evenings, and drinks are half-price during happy hour (8.30–9.30pm). Board games are supplied to accompany afternoon tea.

Il Caffè D7
Dorsoduro 2963, Campo Santa Margherita, *t* 041 528 7998; *vaporetto* Ca' Rezzonico. **Open** Mon–Sat 7am–1.20am.
This café-by-day (see p.273) becomes an open-air nightspot after dark.

Casanova Disco E3
Cannaregio 158A, Lista di Spagna, *t* 041 275 0199; *vaporetto* Ferrovia. **Open** daily 9pm–4am.
Near the station, a large classic 'disco' with pop, rock and chart music and some house nights.

Da Codroma C7
Dorsoduro 2540, Fondamenta Briati, *t* 041 524 6789; *vaporetto* San Basilio. **Open** Sun–Fri 8am–midnight.
This popular student eaterie and drinkerie (see p.273) turns into a crowded nightspot with live music (jazz and blues) on Tues.

Al Delfino Off maps
Lido, Lungomare Marconi 96, *t* 041 526 8309. **Open** until 2am.
An 'American bar' with music, snacks and late-night billiards.

The Fiddler's Elbow H4
Cannaregio 3847, Campiello Testori, *t* 041 523 9930; *vaporetto* Ca' d'Oro. **Open** daily 5pm–1am.
An Irish pub behind Palazzo Fontana serving Guinness on tap and piped Irish music. They do have live concerts in summer in the *piazza* outside.

Iguana H3
Cannaregio 2515, Fondamenta della Misericordia, *t* 041 713 561; *vaporetto* San Marcuola. **Open** Tues–Sat 6pm–2am.
A Latin club where you can drink great cocktails (happy hour is 7–9), eat spicy food and dance to Latin sounds. Live music Tues.

Margaret Duchamp D7
Dorsoduro 3019, Campo Santa Margherita, *t* 041 528 6255; *vaporetto* Ca' Rezzonico. **Open** daily 9am–2am (winter closed Tues).
A designer 'disco bar' (as it calls itself); one of the few in Venice

and frequented by a trendy mix of black-clad Venetians and foreigners. Open until the wee hours (2am), it serves sandwiches and snacks and a range of beers.

L'Olandese Volante I6
Castello 5658, Campo San Lio, **t** *041 528 9349;* ***vaporetto*** *Rialto.* **Open** *Mon–Sat 10am–midnight.*
'The Flying Dutchman' is a current favourite for young trendies and one of Venice's answers to a pub, open late with snacks.

Paradiso Perduto G2
Cannaregio 2540, Fondamenta della Misericordia, **t** *041 720 581,* ***vaporetto*** *San Marcuola.* **Open** *Thurs–Tues 7pm–2am; closed 2 weeks Aug.*
The city's best-known and most popular late-night bar/restaurant with inexpensive though variable food, and a relaxed, bohemian atmosphere popular with a mix of locals and English visitors; live concerts (jazz and roots music), parties, art exhibitions.

Piccolo Mondo E8
Dorsoduro 1056, Calle Contarini-Corfù, **t** *041 520 0371;* ***vaporetto*** *Accademia.* **Open** *Tues–Sun 10pm–4am.*
The Piccolo Mondo is tiny and rather sleazy, but it's one of the few real clubs in Venice.

Sound Code Off maps
Mestre, Via delle Industrie 32, **t** *041 531 3890;* ***bus*** *from Piazzale Roma, 10mins.* **Open** *Fri and Sat until 4am.*
The best disco within spitting distance of Venice.

Teranga Off maps
Mestre, Via della Crusca 34, **t** *041 531 7787;* ***bus*** *82.* **Open** *Fri and Sat 9.30pm–4am.*
A popular and lively club playing mainly African sounds and with regular live music. Membership required (about €10).

Vitae H6
San Marco 4118, Calle Sant'Antonio, north off Calle Teatro, **t** *041 520 5205;* ***vaporetto*** *Rialto.* **Open** *Mon–Fri 9am–1am, Sat 3pm–1am.*
Small, smoky and crowded, this bar with designer décor and loud,

laid-back music is especially popular at cocktail hour, when the 'spritz' (white wine, campari and a dash of soda) flows. Summer nights see Venice's hip crowd spill on to the street outside. Salads and pastas are served at lunch.

Music
Piano, Jazz and Blues, Rock

Some of the above bars and clubs also have regular live music spots. See also Teatro Toniolo under Theatre (below).

Cipriani Hotel I10
Giudecca 10, Fondamenta San Giovanni, **t** *041 520 774;* ***vaporetto*** *hotel boat from Vallaresso.* **Open** *daily 7pm–2am.*
The Cipriani has two piano bars: the San Giorgio (7–10pm) and Bar Gabbiano (from 10pm). In the latter the pianist also sings, and you can dance if you so desire.

Linea d'Ombra H9
Dorsoduro 12, Punta della Dogana, **t** *041 528 5259;* ***vaporetto*** *Salute.* **Open** *Mon, Tues, Thurs–Sat 8pm–2am.*
A tinkling piano and very occasional concerts.

T.A.G. Club Off maps
Mestre, Via Giustizia 19, **t** *041 921 970,* **w** *www.v4u.it/tag;* ***train*** *to Mestre.* **Open** *Wed–Sat 10pm–5am.*
An excellent little club in Mestre with live blues, jazz and rock.

Al Vapore Off maps
Marghera, Via Fratelli Bandiera 8, **t** *041 930 796;* ***train*** *to Mestre.* **Open** *Tues–Sun noon–3pm and 6pm–2am.*
This small venue near Mestre station is very popular for its excellent live jazz and blues concerts featuring both known and lesser-known names.

Classical Music and Opera

Although it's no longer bubbling over with effervescent home-grown talent on the level of

Summer Nights
A suggestion for after-dinner activities on a warm Venice night: go to **Florian's** (*see* p.267) in Piazza San Marco for an *aurum*, a cup of coffee or delicious hot chocolate while listening to the band, though be aware that this will set you back around €4 per person on top of what you pay for food and drink. It finishes at 12.30 sharp.

For something livelier, walk through **Campo Santo Stefano** (F7–8) (which tends to be at its best rather earlier, around 7–9pm) and then over the Accademia bridge and through Dorsoduro to the roomy **Campo Santa Margherita** (D7), which young Venetians tend to use as their late-night *salotto*. There are plenty of bars and cafés where you can have a drink inside or out, and there are good *gelaterie* (*see* p.274).

Goldoni or Vivaldi, Venice at least holds its own in the highbrow league.

There are plenty of groups in Venice playing regular concerts of mostly Venetian Baroque music (featuring plenty of Vivaldi) throughout the year. Standards vary enormously, as many of these concerts are geared towards tourists, but if you're lucky you will catch a top-notch Baroque orchestra playing on original instruments. Some groups perform in period costume (the all-female Putte di Vivaldi, the Musici Veneziani and the Orchestra di Vivaldi, for example) complete with powdered wigs; standards are likely to be lower.

If you're in search of a top-quality concert, look out for the **Ensemble Accademia di San Rocco** (**t** *041 962 999,* **w** *www. musicinvenice.com*), who perform regularly on original instruments from April to November at the Scuola Grande di San Rocco; the **Collegium Ducale** (**t** *041 523 2381*); and the **Venetia Antiqua Ensemble** (**t** *041 962 999*). The latter two also both perform on period instruments, often at the churches of Santa Maria Formosa, Santo Stefano and San Giacometto.

Apart from the venues listed (see also 'Theatres'), regular concerts are held at the following **churches** and *scuole*: La Pietà (Vivaldi's church, see below), I Frari (see below), Scuola Grande di San Rocco, Scuola Grande di San Giovanni Evangelista, Santa Maria Formosa, San Bartolomeo, San Giacometto and more. Look out for posters, flyers in hotels and bars, and notices in the local press.

See also **Teatro Toniolo** under Theatre (below).

For festivals featuring classical music, see Festivals (p.299). The **Biennale** now runs a performing arts programme during the summer, with music, theatre and dance events, staged mostly in the new **Teatro Tese** and the **Teatro Piccolo Arsenale** (both situated within the Arsenale complex, **t** *041 521 8711*, **w** *www.labiennale.org*).

La Fenice G7
t *041 786 511*, **e** *fenice@interbusi ness.it*, **w** *www.teatrola fenice.it*.
PalaFenice, *Tronchetto island*; *vaporetto Tronchetto or special vaporetto from Vallaresso*.
Teatro Malibran, *Cannaregio 5850*, *Campo del Milion*, **t** *041 786 601*, *vaporetto Rialto*.
Until restoration work at La Fenice is completed (see p.126), the resident orchestra and chorus perform at two venues: the **PalaFenice**, a vast tent on Tronchetto used mainly for opera and other large productions (including ballet and concerts); and the beautifully restored **Teatro Malibran** (see p.199), used for both smaller operas and concerts. Events take place year-round apart from August, and there's a mix of productions.

I Frari E6
San Polo, Campo dei Frari, **t** *041 522 2637*; *vaporetto San Tomà*.
From May–July and Sept–Oct, regular concerts Fridays at 9pm in this huge church.

Fondazione Querini-Stampalia J6
Castello 4778, Campiello Querini-Stampalia, **t** *041 271 1411*; *vaporetto Rialto/San Zaccaria*.
Recitals and other cultural events are held at this museum (see p.141).

Palazzo delle Prigioni J7–8
Riva degli Schiavoni, **t** *041 984 252*, **w** *www.concertinvenice*; *vaporetto San Zaccaria*.
The Collegium Ducale ensemble (see above) promotes and plays some 70 concerts a year in the ex-prison next to the Palazzo Ducale. The main season runs from January to May but concerts are also held through the summer. The repertoire is Venetian Baroque and classical.

La Pietà K7–8
Castello, Riva degli Schiavoni, information and tickets, **t** *041 523 1096*; *vaporetto San Zaccaria*.
You have to pay for your music, usually above the odds, and sometimes for less than riveting performances, in Vivaldi's lovely rococo church (see p.144), though the acoustics are well-nigh perfect and it's still quite an experience.

Cinema

Outside the week of the Film Festival (see p.301; now one of the most important in Europe, usually late August or early September for 12 days at the **Palazzo del Cinema** on the Lido, **t** *041 521 8711*, **w** *www. labiennale.org*), Venice's cinemas rarely show anything you can't see back home in English rather than dubbed into Italian; you'll find it nigh-on impossible to find a *versione originale* (*vo*) film if your Italian isn't up to it.

The exceptions, mostly under the auspices of the **Cinema Club** (**t** *041 524 1320*), are listed in *Un Ospite* and occur at the following cinemas:

Cinema Accademia d'Essai E8
Dorsoduro 1018, Calle Gambara, **t** *041 528 7706*, *vaporetto Accademia*.

Giorgione Movie d'Essai I4
Cannaregio 4612, Rio Terrà dei Franceschi, **t** *041 522 6298*, *vaporetto Ca' d'Oro*.
Original-language films are shown here on Tuesdays.

Theatre

For obvious reasons, Italian theatre is of limited interest to most foreign visitors to Venice, but the theatre scene is active and Italian-speakers can enjoy anything from classic Goldoni and other mainstream productions at the Teatro Goldoni to some fairly wild avant-garde productions at the tiny Teatro Fondamenta. The latest arrivals on the scene are the now Biennale-administered open-air Teatro Tese and the Teatro Piccolo Arsenale, both located within the vast Arsenale.

L'Avogaria C7–8
Dorsoduro 1617, Corte Zappa, **t** *041 520 6130*; *vaporetto San Basilio*.
An experimental theatre founded by the great director Giovanni Poli, specializing in obscure plays from the 15th century on.

Teatro Fondamenta Nuove I2
Cannaregio 5013, Fondamenta Nuove, **t** *041 522 4498*; *vaporetto Fondamenta Nuove*.
Notable for its contemporary dance events, this former workshop has a full programme of experimental theatre and dance, film, workshops and related events.

Teatro Goldoni H6
San Marco 4650B, Calle del Teatro, **t** *041 240 2011*, **w** *www.teatro stabileveneto.it*; *vaporetto Rialto*.
Italian classics (Goldoni, Pirandello and so on) in a beautiful state-run theatre. Big-name directors and actors appear regularly; there are some concerts too.

Teatro Toniolo Off maps
Mestre, Piazzetta Battisti 1, **t** *041 274 9070*, **w** *www.comune. venezia.it/teatrotoniolo*; **bus** *2, 7 from Piazzale Roma*.
This partially restored theatre (work was still ongoing as we

went to press, with possible scheduling repercussions) opened in 1913 and specializes in 20th-century Italian theatre. Also look out for big-name jazz, soul and roots music performances, dance and high-quality chamber music.

Dance

Classical ballet is staged as part of the La Fenice season at **PalaFenice** (*see* above) while fans of more contemporary productions should look into the programmes at the **Teatro Fondamenta Nuove** and the **Teatro Toniolo** (*see* below).

Gambling

The Casino on the Lido is now closed.

Casinò di Venezia F3
Cannaregio 2040, Ca' Vendramin-Calergi, **t** *041 529 7111,* **w** *www. casinovenezia.it;* **vaporetto** *San Marcuola.* **Open** *all year daily 11am–2.30am (gaming tables start up at 3pm);* **adm** *€5.*
Fabulously situated on the Grand Canal, the casino offers blackjack, chemin de fer, French roulette and more, as well as slot machines. Jackets are obligatory for men.

Shopping

Antiques 287

Arts 287

Books 287

Clothes and Accessories 288

Crafts and Hobbies 289

Food and Drink 289

Glass and Ceramics 289

Homewares 290

Jewellery 290

Lace 290

Markets 291

Masks and Costumes 291

Paper and Stationery 291

Wood 291

Since the Middle Ages, Venice has been one of Italy's top cities for shopping, whether you're looking for tacky bric-a-brac (just walk down the Lista di Spagna, the Riva degli Schiavoni or through the Rialto) or the latest in hand-crafted Venetian design.

Many Venetian shops neither have nor display a name, and many of those listed below will be mere addresses. But they are no less interesting for that.

Shops are generally **open** Mon–Sat 8–1 or 9–1 and 4–7.30, although many tourist shops have longer hours. Many shops are closed on Monday mornings (except grocers). Markets and grocers tend to close on Wednesday afternoons.

Antiques

Antichità E8
Dorsoduro 1195, Calle Toletta, t 041 522 3159; vaporetto Accademia/Ca' Rezzonico.
A squeeze of a shop packed with beautiful antique glass beads, jewellery, lace, children's clothes, and bits and pieces.

Anticlea J7
Castello 4719A, San Provolo, t 041 528 6946; vaporetto San Zaccaria.
A small shop selling antique beads, lace and glass.

Antonietta Santomanco della Toffola H7
San Marco 1504, Frezzeria, t 041 523 6643; vaporetto San Marco.
Russian and English silver, prints, antique jewellery and glass.

Bastianello Arte I6
San Marco 5042, Campo San Bartolomeo; vaporetto Rialto.
Western and oriental antiques, as well as Art Nouveau and jewellery.

Giancarlo Ballarini F7
San Marco 3174, Calle delle Botteghe; vaporetto Sant'Angelo/ San Samuele.
Restoration/antique shop; the owner has a good eye for the more florid styles.

Pietro Scarpa H8
San Marco 1464, Campo San Moisè; and San Marco 2089 Calle Larga XXII Marzo; vaporetto San Marco.
The shops resemble museums; the second one sells old drawings.

Unnamed Shop I6
Castello 5672,Salizzada San Lio; vaporetto Rialto.
Prints of Venice, old clocks, and other curious odds and ends.

Unnamed Shop C7
Dorsoduro 2609, Fondamenta del Soccorso; vaporetto San Basilio.
A real 'Old Curiosity Shop', with everything from Baroque clocks to bills printed by the 1848 revolutionary government.

Xanthippe E7
Dorsoduro 2773, Campo San Barnaba, t 041 528 5348; vaporetto Ca' Rezzonico.
A cosy, highly eclectic shop near Ca' Rezzonico, specializing in the 19th-century and Art Deco Venetian glass, with unusual styles such as Piedmontese Biedermeier.

Arts

Madera E7
Campo San Barnaba, Dorsoduro 2762, t 041 522 4181, w www. maderavenezia.it; vaporetto Ca' Rezzonico.
The contemporary *objets* in this small design shop are all handmade using traditional methods, mostly by young Italian artisans. Jewellery made of Venetian glass beads, beautifully turned wood bowls and utensils, the odd handbag, cushions, slate boards, and a selection of Japanese-inspired ceramics.

Sabbie e Nebbie F6
San Polo 2768A, Calle dei Nomboli, t 041 719 073; vaporetto San Tomà.
An interesting little shop with a carefully chosen mix of Japanese ceramics, ethnic papers, ceramics by Italian designers, and beautiful silk scarves by Tess Blondell.

Books

Fantoni Libri Arte H6–7
San Marco 4119, Salizzada di San Luca, t 041 522 0700; vaporetto Rialto.
Monumental display of monumental art, architecture and photography books.

Filippi I–J6
Castello 5763, Calle del Paradiso, t 041 523 6919; vaporetto Rialto.
The city's best selection of Italian books about Venice – folktales, dialect, theatre, costumes, the navy, etc., including many facsimiles of antique books from the days when Venice was one of Europe's chief printing centres.

Libreria Cassini H8
San Marco 2424, Calle Larga XXII Marzo, vaporetto San Marco.
Has old prints, antique books and rare editions.

Libreria Goldoni H6
San Marco 4742, Calle dei Fabbri; vaporetto Rialto.
Venice's largest general bookstore, with eveything you might want for holiday reading.

Libreria alla Toletta E8
Dorsoduro 1214, Calle Toletta, t 041 523 2034; vaporetto Accademia.
This large bookshop occupies several adjoining buildings and offers up to 25% discount on a large part of its stock, which covers local history, art, architecture, children's books, cookery, and includes some English titles.

The Museum Shop F9
Dorsoduro 710, Fondamenta Venier dei Leoni, t 041 240 5410; vaporetto Accademia. Closed Tues.
Situated next to the Guggenheim Museum, this shop sells a fine selection of art and photography books, children's books in English, jewellery, Illy coffee cups, gifts and postcards. Profits go towards maintaining the museum.

Punto Libri D6
Santa Croce, Salizzada di San Pantalon; vaporetto San Tomà.
Art and architecture books.

Sangiorgio H8
*San Marco 2087, Calle Larga XXII Marzo; **vaporetto** San Marco.*
Books in English, especially about Venice, and some hefty art tomes.

Sansovino H7
*San Marco 84, Bacino Orseolo (just outside the Procuratie Vecchie); **vaporetto** San Marco.*
Large collection of art and coffee-table books, and lots of postcards.

Unnamed Shop E6
*San Polo 3951, Calle Crosera, near the Frari; **vaporetto** San Tomà.*
Good selection of books on art, crafts and music.

Clothes and Accessories

Most of the big-name **designer boutiques** (Gucci, Prada, Versace, Louis Vuitton, Armani) are clustered around the outskirts of Piazza San Marco, along streets such as Mercerie, Frezzeria, Calle dei Fabbri, Calle Larga XXII Marzo and Salizzada San Moisè. Most Venetians buy their clothes at the **COIN** department store, while most tourists buy their 'Vuitton' and 'Prada' handbags from the streetsellers paving the way to Piazza San Marco along Calle Larga XXII Marzo. Their first offer will be about three times what you should end up paying.

Camiceria San Marco H8
*San Marco 1340, Calle Vallaresso; **vaporetto** San Marco.*
Men's shirts and ladies' dresses made to order in 24hrs.

COIN I5
*Cannaregio 5787, Fontego Salizzada San Giovanni Grisostomo, **t** 041 520 3581; **vaporetto** Rialto. **Open** daily.*
Good department store with stylish fashions (their Koan line is particularly interesting), bright furnishings and excellent, well-priced household items.

La Coupole H8
*San Marco 2031, Calle Larga XXII Marzo; **vaporetto** San Marco.*

Fashions by maverick Italian and French designers; the sister shop, **La Fenice** (Frezzeria 1674), stocks more everyday designers.

Emilio Ceccato H5
*San Polo, Sottoportico di Rialto; **vaporetto** Rialto.*
The place to buy gondoliers' shirts, jackets and tight trousers.

Hibiscus G5
*San Polo 1060, Ruga Rialto, **t** 041 5208989; **vaporetto** San Silvestro.*
Beautiful garments and accessories in silk in a range of colours; raw silk jackets, bags and scarves, and a range of original jewellery.

Kalimala I6
*Castello 5387, Salizzada San Lio, **t** 041 528 3596; **vaporetto** Rialto.*
Beautiful and practical handmade leather goods; chunky bags, luggage, belts, and accessories.

Jade Martine H7
*San Marco 1645, Frezzeria, **t** 041 521 2892; **vaporetto** San Marco.*
Expensive designer underthings.

Laura Biagiotti H8
*San Marco 2400A, Calle Larga XXII Marzo; **vaporetto** San Marco.*
Designer clothes in larger sizes.

Missoni H8
*San Marco 1312, Calle Vallaresso; **vaporetto** San Marco. **Open** daily.*
Beautiful knitwear.

Pinco Pallino I6
*Castello 5641, Campo San Lio, **t** 041 523 5500; **vaporetto** Rialto.*
Beautifully made but bizarre shoes and bags in a great range of colours decorated with ornaments or with leather cut-outs.

Prénatal I5
*Cannaregio 5783, **t** 041 522 1593, Salizzada San Giovanni Grisostomo; **vaporetto** Rialto.*
Casual, low-priced maternity and baby clothing.

Risuola Tutto di Giovanni Dittura F8–9
*Dorsoduro 871, Calle Nuova Sant'Agnese, **t** 041 5231163; **vaporetto** Accademia. **Open** daily.*
The best selection of brightly coloured velvet slippers with cord and rubber soles, and cheaper

than in the markets. Giovanni Dittura also sells other styles of slipper and repairs shoes.

Rolando Segalin H7
*San Marco 4365, Calle dei Fuseri, **t** 041 522 2115; **vaporetto** San Marco/Rialto. **Open** Mon–Fri and Sat am.*
'Il Calzolaio di Venezia' stocks fabulous handmade shoes in his shop, which range from the sublimely elegant to the extraordinarily eccentric.

Trois G8
*San Marco 2666, Campo San Maurizio, **t** 041 522 2905; **vaporetto** Santa Maria del Giglio.*
A Venetian institution, with Fortuny fabrics made to traditional specifications on the Giudecca.

Venetia Studium H8 / I6
*San Marco 2403, Calle Larga XXII Marzo 2403; San Marco 723, Merceria San Zulian, **t** 041 522 9281; **vaporetto** Santa Maria del Giglio/San Marco.*
Pleated silk Fortuny scarves, Fortuny lamps, pochettes, cushions, waistcoats and drawstring bags.

Vogini H8
*San Marco 1257a, Calle Larga XXII Marzo 1300, **t** 041 522 2573; **vaporetto** San Marco.*
The greatest name in Venetian leather, with articles by Venetian designer Roberta di Camerino.

Shoes

La Fenice H8
*San Marco 2255, Calle Larga XXII Marzo, **t** 041 523 1273; **vaporetto** San Marco.*
Posh shoes by French and Italian designers.

Mario Valentino H7–8
*San Marco 1255, Calle dell' Ascensione; **vaporetto** San Marco.*
The Neapolitan designer's sought-after shoes.

No Name Cobbler I–J6
*Castello 5268, Calle delle Bande; **vaporetto** Rialto.*
Atmospheric, old-fashioned shoe repair shop.

Crafts/Hobbies

Cartoleria Accademia E8
Dorsoduro 1044, Rio Terrà della Carità, t 041 520 7086; vaporetto Accademia.
Jam-packed with paints, paper, easels, etc. for those who want to make their own souvenirs.

Mosaics

Mosaics are one of the oldest Venetian crafts, but hard to carry home. If you've been smitten by the wonders in St Mark's, you can buy some glass or gold tesserae to try making your own mosaics.

Arte del Mosaico L6
Castello 4002, Calle Frizzo; vaporetto Celestia.

Donà Ugo e Figlio Off maps
Murano, Fondamenta di Vetrai 61; vaporetto line 12.

Unnamed Shop E2
Cannaregio 1045, Campiello del Battello; vaporetto Ponte Guglie.

Food and Drink

Bottiglieria Colonna I6
Castello 5595, Calle de la Fava, just off Campo San Lio, t 041 528 5137; vaporetto Rialto.
This is a serious, no-frills wine and spirits shop.

Caffè Costarica F3
Cannaregio 1337, Rio Terrà San Leonardo; vaporetto Ponte Guglie.
Open Mon–Sat 9.30–1 and 4–7.
Espresso subscriptions or gift packs for Java junkies.

Cantinone già Schiavi E8
Dorsoduro 992, Fondamenta Priuli; vaporetto Zattere.
A fine old wine shop with plenty to choose from.

Il Melograno D7
Dorsoduro 2999, Campo Santa Margherita, t 041 528 5117; vaporetto Ca' Rezzonico.
Tisanes, herbal lotions and potions including the wonderful L'Erbolario bath and skin products.

Panificio Volpe E2
Cannaregio 1143, Calle Ghetto Vecchio, t 041 715 178; vaporetto Ponte Guglie.
Traditional Jewish pastries; gazelle's horns full of almond paste, tiny sugar paste candies that look like solar disks, and Aman's ears, the favourite sweet of King Assuero of Babilonia.

Pantagruelica E7, D10
Dorsoduro 2844, Campo San Barnabà, t 041 523 6766; vaporetto Ca' Rezzonico; and Giudecca 461, Fondamenta Sant' Eufemia, t 041 523 1809; vaporetto Sant'Eufemia
Maurizio is passionate about food and where it comes from. So all his stock of cheeses, hams and salamis, pastas, rice, preserves, wines, bread, oils and vinegars is carefully sourced and much of it is organic. He is to be found at the Dorsoduro shop; the Giudecca also sells beauty products.

Il Pastaio H5
San Polo 219, Calle del Varoteri, Rialto markets; vaporetto Rialto.
Pasta in a score of colours and shapes, including tagliatelle made with cuttlefish ink or curry.

Pastificio Artigiano H4
Cannaregio 4292, Strada Nuova; vaporetto Ca' d'Oro.
Paolo Pavon's half-century of experience has gone into creating Venice's tastiest and most exotic pastas; for kicks, take home a bag of *pasta al cacao* (chocolate pasta), *pasta al limone* (lemon) or beetroot, garlic, mushroom...

Rizzo Pane F7
San Marco, Calle delle Botteghe, (just off Campo F. Morosini); vaporetto Sant'Angelo/Accademia.
Everything you need for a picnic.

Sacchi F3
Cannaregio 1815, Rio Terrà San Leonardo; vaporetto Ponte Guglie.
Possibly the best fruit and veg shop in Venice, with a spectacular and mouthwatering display.

Supermercato Punto D7
Dorsoduro 3114, Rio Terrà Canal; vaporetto Ca' Rezzonico.

One of the few supermarkets in the *centro storico* of Venice, Punto sells food, drink and most things you would expect to find in a (smallish) supermarket.

Unnamed Boat D7
Dorsoduro, Ponte dei Pugni; vaporetto Ca' Rezzonico. **Open** Mon–Sat am; closed Sat pm, Sun.
Near Campo San Barnabà, this boat houses the last floating greengrocer's in Venice.

Unnamed Shop E2
Cannaregio 1143, Ramo Ghetto Vecchio; vaporetto Ponte Guglie.
Kosher wines.

Unnamed Shop F3
Cannaregio 1563, Rio Terrà San Leonardo; vaporetto Ferrovia.
A wonderful, bright sweet shop crammed full of pure tooth decay.

Vini D7
Dorsoduro 3664, Campo Santa Margherita; vaporetto Ca' Rezzonico/San Basilio. **Open** Mon–Sat 9am–1pm and 5–7.30pm.
Bring empty bottles to this shop and have them filled with a selection of wines on tap. Good value.

Glass and Ceramics

Arca F4
Santa Croce 1811, Calle Tintor; vaporetto Riva di Biasio.
Modern, intensely coloured ceramic tiles, vases, plates and pendants.

CAM Off maps
Murano, Piazzale Colonna 1/b; vaporetto line 12.
One of the largest selections of glassware on Murano (from the tiniest objects to tables and giant sculptures). Exceptionally friendly, informative and unpushy.

Carlo Moretti Off maps
Murano, Fondamenta Manin 3, t 041 739 217; vaporetto line 12.
Glassblower Moretti makes contemporary glasses, jugs and plates, some of which have become collector's items.

Domus Vetri d'Arte Off maps
Murano, Fondamenta Vetrai 82;
vaporetto line 12.
A small shop with an unusually
tasteful selection of glassware by
some top Italian designers.

Guido Farinati F4
Santa Croce 1658, Campo San
Giacomo dell'Orio, t 041 721 1OO;
vaporetto Riva di Biasio.
Fine leaded glass.

Paolo Rossi J7
Castello 736, Campo San Zaccaria;
vaporetto San Zaccaria.
Reproductions of ancient decorative glass at reasonable prices.

Pauly I7
San Marco 4391, Calle Larga San
Marco, t 041 709 899; *vaporetto*
San Marco.
Classic blown glassware.

Rigattieri G7
San Marco 3532/6, Calle dei Frati;
vaporetto Sant'Angelo.
The sort of emporium that does a
good line in wedding lists, with
traditional Bassano ceramics,
table ornaments and glassware.

San Vio F8–9
Dorsoduro 669, Campo San Vio
669; vaporetto Accademia.
Bowls, plates, vases and jewellery
in handsome, striking, modern
designs by two young sisters. Not
a flounce, twirl or toucan in sight.

Ta 'Kala' H4
Cannaregio 4391, Strada Nuova,
near Campo Santi Apostoli;
vaporetto Ca' dOro.
Ceramic figurines, puppets, glass
jewellery and trinkets, some of
them quite original.

Unnamed Shop H8
San Marco 1470, Salizzada San
Moisè; vaporetto San Marco.
Murano's most ambitious
creations, including life-size
toucans, abstract pieces, and
chandeliers. Astronomical prices.

Homewares

Domus H6
San Marco 4746, Calle dei Fabbri,
t 041 522 6259; *vaporetto* Rialto.
Excellent all-round kitchen shop.

Rubelli H7
San Marco 1090, Campo Sangallo,
t 041 523 6110; *vaporetto* Rialto.
Damasks, velours and brocades in
the rich colours of the *cinquecento*,
many with an Imperial Russian
and Byzantine touch.

Unnamed Shop D6
Santa Croce 154, Fondamenta
Minotto; vaporetto Piazzale Roma.
Gold and brass items, including
Venetian doorknockers.

Jewellery

Jewellers are concentrated in
Piazza San Marco and on the
Ponte Rialto.

Codognato H7–8
San Marco 1295, Calle dell'
Ascensione, t 041 522 5042;
vaporetto San Marco.
One of the oldest jewellers in
Venice, with rare pieces by
Tiffany and Cartier, and Art
Deco baubles.

Gualti D7
Dorsoduro 3111, Rio Terrà Canal,
t 041 520 1731, w www.gualti.it;
vaporetto Ca' Rezzonico.
The simple white interior of this
small shop perfectly sets off
Gualti's designs. Delicate, ethereal
and, above all, highly original
brooches, earrings and bracelets
look extraordinarily fragile but are
in fact made from tough mixed
synthetic resin and tiny crystal
beads. Also elegant satin shoes.

Missiaglia I7
San Marco 125, Piazza San Marco,
near Quadri; vaporetto San Marco.
Some of the most elegant work by
Venetian gold and silversmiths, as
well as necklaces, etc.

Nardi I8
San Marco 69/71, Piazza San Marco
69–71, next to Florian; vaporetto
San Marco.
One of Venice's luxury establishment jewellers, celebrated for its
series of 'Othellos', elaborate
jewelled pieces of carved ebony,
each unique; also clocks, frames
and other glittering dust-magnets.
Past customers include Grace Kelly,
Liz Taylor and Barbara Hutton.

Perle e Dintorni G7, I6, I4
San Marco 3740, Calle della
Mandola, t 041 520 5068;
vaporetto Sant'Angelo; *San Marco*
5468, Calle della Bissa, t 041 522
5624; *vaporetto* Rialto; *Cannaregio*
5622, Campo Santi Apostoli, t 041
520 6969; *vaporetto* Rialto.
Glass beads to buy individually or
have made into necklaces or
bracelets in a couple of hours,

Rose Douce I5
Cannaregio 5782, Salizzada San
Giovanni Grisostomo, t 041 522
7232; *vaporetto* Rialto.
Coloured glass chalices from
Murano and coffee cups made
from *murrine*, the tiny glass
Venetian beads. Necklackes made
from very old Venetian pearls and
thousands of large and small
vases in filigreed glass, in milk
glass or with gold leaf.

Lace

This is fiendishly hard to avoid
on Burano, though beware – the
bargains you find are probably
neither handmade nor Buranese.
Pick up a lace connoisseur's eye at
the Lace School.

Annelie D8
Dorsoduro 2748, Calle Lunga San
Barnabà, t 041 520 3277; *vaporetto*
Ca' Rezzonico. *Closed* Sat pm.
Full of exquisitely worked lace
blouses, towels, bedlinens, hand-
kerchiefs, lavender bags and baby
clothes, both new and antique.

Cenerentola F6
San Polo 2600A, Rio Terrà dei
Nomboli, t 041 523 2006; *vaporetto*
San Tomà.
The lampshades here are all
made with precious antique
fabrics or with embroidered
initials that come from bed linen
made in Venice in the 1800s. Also
a great selection of antique laces
and edgings.

La Fenice Atelier G7
San Marco 3537, Campo Sant'
Angelo, t 041 523 9578; *vaporetto*
Sant'Angelo.
A small boutique which
produces its own exquisite bed

linens, towels and nightwear in superb silks, satins and cotton lawn. Items are decorated with lace and embroidery. There is also a made-to-measure service.

Jesurum I7
San Marco 60/61, Piazza San Marco, t 041 522 9864; vaporetto San Marco.
A vast quantity of lace (table-cloths, lingerie, etc.) on display in a former 12th-century church, plus an array of swimming costumes and summery togs.

Markets

Campo San Maurizio G8
A week before Easter and Christmas, and third week of Sept.
A flea market appears periodically in this square, in the heart of the principal antiques area.

Rialto Markets H5
Open Mon–Sat 7–1 (fruit and veg), Tues–Sat 7–1 (fish, on Ruga degli Specializi).
The Rialto area is home to Venice's major markets, selling everything under the sun on the bridge and in all the streets to the north. There is a fish market, and fruit and veg, in the Peschiera, Fabbriche Vecchie and Fabbriche Nuove, *see p.185.*

Rio Terrà San Leonardo F3
Daily
Clothes, fish and food.

Masks and Costumes

Giorgio Clanetti (Laboratorio Artigiano Maschere) K5
Castello 6657, Barbaria delle Tole, t 041 522 3110; vaporetto Ospedale.
A long and well-deserved reputa-tion for traditionally crafted masks. Rarely open, so call ahead.

Mondonovo D7
Dorsoduro 3063, Rio Terra Canal; vaporetto Ca' Rezzonico.
Some of the best masks in town: camels, sphinxes, moonfaces and everything else.

Papier-mâché J6
Castello 5175; Calle Lunga Santa Maria Formosa; vaporetto Rialto.
An emphasis on exquisite, delicate paintwork and masks decorated in the style of Kandinsky.

Tragicomica F6
San Polo 2800, Calle dei Nomboli; vaporetto San Tomà.
Very well regarded by other young mask-makers, with an extraordi-nary variety of wonderfully shaped masks and costumes.

Paper and Stationery

Alberto Valese-Ebrû F7
San Marco 3471, Campo Santo Stefano; vaporetto Accademia.
Alberto Valese fuses Persian and Italian styles in his paper-making; he also makes silk ties and paints masks. Paper designs range from marble and hieroglyphs to stun-ning renditions of Venice's most beautiful architectural façades. Folding waste-paper baskets, pencil-holders and every sort of covered book and folder.

Carta da Casetti G9
Dorsoduro 364, t 041 523 2804, w www.cartadacassetti.yahoo.it; vaporetto Salute.
Tucked away in a tiny *piazzetta* between the Salute and the Guggenheim, Franco Cassetti's paper shop is worth seeking out for his original designs. Sheets of paper or original gifts; CD holders, folders, bound books, photos frames, lampshades and all sorts of boxes. Refreshingly different.

Legatoria Piazzesi G8
San Marco 2511, Campiello Feltrina, t 041 522 1202; vaporetto Santa Maria del Giglio.
'The Oldest Paper Shop in Italy' sells all sorts of gifts and papers.

Paolo Olbi G7
San Marco 3652, Calle della Mandola (near Campo San Angelo); vaporetto Sant'Angelo.
Exquisite handmade paper, blank books and photo albums. Also leather-bound.

Il Pavone F9
Dorsoduro 721, Fondamenta Venier dei Leoni, t 041 5234517; vaporetto Accademia.
Paper products covered in unusual designs made on the premises by the owner. Bound books and other gift items; ex-libris, pens, inks, silk ties, and aprons.

Wood

Dalla Venezia Angelo F5
San Polo 2204, Calle Scaleter; vaporetto San Stae.
Knick-knacks in a range of woods – pencil-holders, candlesticks, spinning tops and, Angelo's speciality, handmade wooden spheres.

Franco Furlanetto F6
San Polo 2768, Calle dei Nomboli; vaporetto San Tomà.
A workshop for 'remi e forcole' where you can buy gondola oars and oar-locks (more like beautiful sculptures than anything remotely practical).

Livio de Marchi F7
San Marco 3157, Salizzada San Samuele; vaporetto San Samuele.
Internationally renowned for everyday objects sculpted in natural wood – clothes hanging on pegs, benches in the form of giant paintbrushes, desks made from piles of oversized wooden books.

La Scialuppa F6
San Polo 2695, Calle Seconda dei Saoneri; vaporetto San Tomà.
A little shop where Gilberto Penzo canes beautiful *forcole* (gondola oar-locks made of walnut); pick up little make-your-own gondola kits, replicas of Venetian guild signs or a marine ex-voto painted on wood.

Sports and Green Spaces

Spectator Sports 293

Activities 293

Green Spaces 294

Until the refined and dandified 18th century, sport in Venice long had a rough-and-tumble character – bullfights, cudgel and fist-fights, *calcio* (a nearly-free-for-all kind of football) and fencing were favourites, although duels went out of fashion when the first to draw faced the death penalty. In the 1960s people still swam in the Lagoon and Grand Canal. Nowadays most Venetians are content with the considerable exercise they get by just walking.

But boating and regattas (from *riga*, or starting line) understandably remain Venetian passions. There are traditional regattas for gondolas and rowing crews, and at the other extreme, the *Serenissima* Offshore Gran Prix for European Formula One motor boats in the first week of June; contestants begin at Jesolo and zip along the sea coast off the Lido. For all these, *see* the calendar of events in **Festivals**, pp.300–301.

Spectator Sports
Football

Stadio P.L. Penzo Q11
Sant'Elena Island, t 041 958 1000, w www.veneziacalcio.it; vaporetto Sant'Elena.
The orange/black/green-clad team AC Venezia are still in Serie A. Home matches take place on alternate Sundays at 3pm from September to June. Tickets are available at the ground, and from ACTV and Vela public transport offices, e.g. in Piazzale Roma and Calle dei Fuseri in San Marco.

Activities
Cycling

Giorgio Barbieri Off maps
Lido, Via Zara 5, halfway along the Gran Viale, t 041 526 1490; vaporetto Lido. Open daily March-Oct 8.30–7.30. Rates €3/hr, €9/day.
Rent a bike, or a wonderfully touristy tricycle with a canopy, to explore the length of the Lido.

Flying and Parachuting

Aero Club G. Ancillotto Off maps
Lido, t 041 526 0808, w aeroclubvenezia.com; vaporetto Lido.
A flying school that also offers excursion flights over Venice.

Nicelli Airport Off maps
Lido, t 041 526 0823; vaporetto Lido.
A favourite for parachuting. It often holds international team competitions.

Golf

Alberoni Golf Course Off maps
Lido, Via del Forte Alberoni, t 041 731 333, w digilander.iol.it/circologolfvenezia; vaporetto Lido. Open Oct–March Tues–Sat 8.30–6; April–Sept Tues–Fri 8.30–6, Sat and Sun 8.30–8. Rates Tues–Fri €50/day, Sat & Sun €60/day.
This course on the southern tip of the Lido is rated among the best in Italy. Non-members are permitted, but need proof of membership of another club.

Gyms

Palestra Club Delfino E9
Dorsoduro 788A, Zattere, t 041 523 2763, w www.palestraclub-delfino.com; vaporetto Zattere. Open Mon–Fri 9–9, Sat 9–12. Rates €13/day, €44/week, €112/month.
All the latest machinery, classes and personal trainers, and, to recover from it all, sauna, solarium, steamroom, hydrotherapy and massage.

Wellness Centre K7
Castello 3697, Calle della Pietà, t 041 523 1944; vaporetto San Zaccaria. Open Mon, Wed, Fri 8am–9pm; Tues and Thurs 9am–9pm; Sat 9–1. Rates €16/day.
Provides a range of weight machines and others, with a personal trainer if required. Cardio fitness, body-building, etc.

Horseriding

Circolo Ippico Veneziano Off maps
Lido, Ca' Bianco, t 041 526 8091; vaporetto Lido. Rates €116 for 5 lessons including membership and insurance.
Ride on the Lido as Byron did, though it's no longer a romantic, hooves-in-the-dunes affair.

Jogging and Running

Joggers need to choose their routes carefully if they don't want to end up running an obstacle race. The most obvious places for a good flat run are the Zattere (the south side of Dorsoduro), the Giardini Pubblici (*see* p.294), and the Lido.

Venice Marathon
Sunday in late Oct, t 041 940 644, w www.venicemarathon.it.
Starting at the Villa Pisani in Strà (*see* p.242), the marathon runs along the Brenta Canal, over the big road bridge and into Venice, finishing on the Riva degli Schiavoni.

Rowing

Foreigners can try their luck in Venice's many regattas, especially the Vogalonga Marathon on Ascension Day. Finding a boat to hire for a holiday row is quite a bit harder; try one of the rowing clubs:

Canottieri Bucintoro H9
Dorsoduro, Punta della Dogana, t 041 522 2055; vaporetto Salute.

Canottieri Francesco Querini L5
Cannaregio 6576, Fondamenta Nuove, t 041 522 2039; vaporetto Ospedale.

Canottieri Diadora Off maps
Lido, Ca' Bianco, t 041 526 5742; vaporetto Lido, then bus B.
Lessons available on Venetian rowing for beginners.

Sailing and Boating

Compagnia della Vela I8
San Marco, near the Giardinetti Reali, t 041 520 0884; vaporetto San Marco.
Sailing lessons for adults and children as young as seven, as long as they know how to swim.

Courses and Lessons

The following offer sailing courses and lessons leading to a motorboat pilot's licence:

Base Mare 21 Off maps
Mestre, Punta San Giuliano, t 041 531 1523.

Il Sesante Off maps
Mestre, Via Felisati 71, t 041 940 287.

Swimming

Despite reports about toxic by-products, people still swim off the Lido (the public beaches are at San Nicoló in the north, Murazzi and Alberoni in the south). The other alternative is the public pool:

Piscina Comunale Sacca Fisola B10
Sacca Fisola Island, by the bridge from the Giudecca, t 041 528 5430. **Open** *Mon and Thurs 10.30–noon and 1–2.30, Tues and Fri 10.30–noon and 6.30–7.15, Wed 2.15–5, Sat 2.45–5 and 6.30–8, Sun 3–6.* **Rates** *€4.50.*
Venice's only public pool.

Tennis

Venice's tennis courts are concentrated on the Lido.

Tennis Club Lido Off maps
Lido, Via San Gallo 163, t 041 526 0954; vaporetto Lido. **Rates** *€7/hr per person.*
Has seven clay-courts.

Tennis Club del Moro Off maps
Lido, Via Ferruccio Parri 6, t 041 770 801; vaporetto Lido. **Rates** *€5–€8.50 depending on court.*
Has grass, clay and indoor courts, plus a gym.

Green Spaces

Fairly obviously, the capital of stone and water is not very well off for parks and green spaces. If you tire of brick and stone, the best thing to do is take a boat to any of the outlying islands – **Lido** (*see* p.222), **Torcello** (*see* p.230), **Burano** (*see* p.229), the south side of **Giudecca** (*see* p.220) and especially **Sant'Erasmo** (*see* p.232).

Giardini Papadopoli C–D5
See p.192.

Giardini Pubblici (Biennale) N10–O11
See pp.153–4.

Giardinetti Reali I8
See p.116.

Isola di San Pietro O8–P9
Castello; vaporetto Giardini; see pp.152–3.
A quiet place, with a green space in front of the church.

Parco Savorgnan E2
Palazzo Savorgnan, Cannaregio 349, Fondamenta Venier; vaporetto Ponte Guglie.
A small, pretty garden hidden behind this 17th-century *palazzo.*

Sant' Elena P9–Q10
Castello; vaporetto Sant'Elena; see p.154.
This island at the far eastern end of Castello is quiet, green and open, and contains the **Parco delle Rimembranze** with a kids' play area (swings, etc.) and roller skating rink.

Children's and Teenagers'Venice

Children 296

Teenagers 298

> ## Make Walking Fun!
> It can be tiring and boring for children to have to walk so much everywhere. Set the challenge of giving your kids the map for a morning and let them lead you where they will without getting lost. Or try this game: on four pieces of paper, write Left, Right, Straight Ahead, and Backwards.
> At each junction, get the child to select one of the pieces, and follow the instruction. You can make up your own extra rules: e.g. you will stop for a drink at the fifth café you encounter; if you come across a museum you could have two more pieces of paper with Go In and Don't Go In; you could assign points for every bridge you actually cross, etc.

Children

Like all Italians, Venetians are very fond of children, sometimes poignantly so, because there are so few around in the old city. There is little for kids to do in Venice, and few open places to play; families who can usually move to Mestre. On the other hand, most children do enjoy visiting Venice – all those boat rides, canals and bridges (and no cars to watch out for!).

All the walking, however, tires young children easily, and adults, too, as the steps on the bridges render prams and pushchairs more of a nuisance than a help. If your tot is too big to fit comfortably into a back carrier, think again about your mother's offer to baby-sit.

Nappies, formula and other baby paraphernalia are available in pharmacies (though note that food and nappies cost less in supermarkets).

Children under one metre tall go free on *vaporetti*.

Activities

There's no way you're going to get away without taking your kids on a gondola ride, but if money is

tight try the **gondola-*traghetti*** that make the short crossings over the Grand Canal at various points (*see* p.80). Our **Grand Canal Tour** (pp.233–40) uses the no.1 *vaporetto* line to *palazzo*-spot along the whole length of the canal. See how many can be notched up...

The patterned pavement in the *campo* in front of Santa Maria della Salute is great for playing follow-the-lines tag.

You can feed the pigeons in **Piazza San Marco**; vendors in the square sell bags of corn.

Most offspring under 10 will give their parents a decent interval in **St Mark's** (*see* p.98), but for good behaviour in other churches and museums you may have to barter away an afternoon on the **Lido**, to swim or just run in the sand and build castles. **Bikes**, and fun **tricycles with canopies**, can be hired to explore the whole length of the Lido (*see* p.293).

Watching a crew dredge a canal is almost as good as watching the **Murano glass-blowers** (*see* p.226) or the **Burano lace-makers** (*see* p.229).

Despite reports about toxic by-products, people still **swim** off the Lido (the public beaches are at San Nicoló in the north, Murazzi and Alberoni in the south). The other alternative is the public pool:

Piscina Comunale Sacca Fisola B10
Sacca Fisola island, by the bridge from the Giudecca, **t** *041 528 5430.* **Open** *Mon and Thurs 10.30–noon and 1–2.30, Tues and Fri 10.30–noon and 6.30–7.15, Wed 2.15–5, Sat 2.45–5 and 6.30–8, Sun 3–6.* **Rates** *€4.50.*

Lagoon Trip Off maps
Diporto Velico di Sant'Elena, **t** *041 523 1927; or Diporto Velico di San Giorgio,* **t** *041 521 0723.*

Go on a trip around the lagoon in a traditional flat-bottomed wooden sailing boat; explore the smaller islands, see fishermen at work, and observe everyday life on the water.

Babysitting

Babysitting services are offered in many hotels. Where available, they are listed in the individual hotel reviews in the 'Where to Stay' chapter.

Eating Out

The majority of restaurants don't officially provide children's portions, but most places will be happy to whip up a *pasta al pomodoro* for kids if there is nothing else on the menu that appeals. Pizzas are obviously a good option too (*margherita* – just tomato and mozzarella – is about as plain as they come), and bread and cake shops are full of tempting snacks. And then there's the ice cream...

Entertainment and Festivals

Carnevale
10 days before Shrove Tues, in Feb.
Carnival presents lots of entertainment for children; during the four-week run up, especially at weekends, kids dress up in costume and parade around the place, throwing '*coriandoli*' or confetti and squirting shaving foam. At Carnival itself, young visitors can dress up in costumes like the Italian kids and get sick on fritters and other sticky sweets. During Carnival, there is Antico Salone 'La Bauta' in Campo San Polo, with workshops and shows for kids; mask-making workshops, a puppet theatre, mime shows and acrobats.

Feast of the Redentore
3rd Sat and Sun in July
See p.301; there's a fireworks display at 11pm.

Funfair
Riva degli Schiavoni, all January.

Regatta delle Befana
6 Jan
The Befana is the kind witch who brings good kids toys on Epiphany (and bad ones lumps of coal).

Regata Storica
1st Sun in Sept
A splendid pageant of historic vessels and crews in Renaissance costumes and races by a variety of rowers down the Grand Canal.

St Martin's Day
11 Nov
This revival of a popular fair in the streets of Venice is always liked by children.

Further Reading

Venice for Kids by Elisabetta Pasqualin (2000, Fratelli Palombi) is a good all-round guide.

Museums and Attractions

There are usually special 'family days' in all civic museums on alternate Sundays between March and August. Call **t** 041 274 7607 for dates and a programme of events.

Ca' Rezzonico E7
*Fondamenta Rezzonico, **t** 041 241 0100; **vaporetto** Ca' Rezzonico. Open Wed–Mon 10–5; adm €6.50. Bookshop and café.*
This museum of 18th-century life may have enough gold and glitter to catch children's attention, especially the lavish ballroom. They will also like the reproduction pharmacy and puppet theatre.

La Fenice G7
*Campo San Fantin, **w** www.teatro-lafenice.it; **vaporetto** Santa Maria del Giglio. Due to reopen 2004.*
Although it's obviously not possible until the theatre is rebuilt, a tour of front and backstage usually fascinates, with the contraptions and pulleys used for scenery changing ably demonstrated.

Natural History Museum F4
*Salizzada dei Fondaco dei Turchi, **t** 041 275 0206; **vaporetto** Riva di Biasio. Closed for major restoration; due to reopen 2004.*
Plenty of bugs, beetles, crabs and dinosaurs, plus models of lagoon craft from the past.

Naval Museum M8
*Campo San Biagio, **t** 041 520 0276; **vaporetto** Arsenale. Open Mon–Fri 8.45–1.30, Sat 8.45–1; adm €1.55.*
With its ships' models and cannons, model of the doge's barge and memories of naval battles, this should please boys; non-tomboy girls may like the iridescent **shell collection** on the third floor.

St Mark's I7
*Piazza San Marco, **t** 041 522 5205; **vaporetto** San Marco; wheelchair accessible from Piazzetta dei Leoncini. Open Mon–Sat 9.30–5, Sun and hols 2–4.30; adm free.*
Besides boat rides, Italian ice cream and feeding the vultures in St Mark's Square, most kids in Venice like to climb the **clock tower** and watch the clock mechanism working, and to climb up to the porch to see the life-sized **bronze horses**.

Squero di San Trovaso E9
*Campo di San Trovaso; **vaporetto** Zattere.*
Visit the gondola workshop at the corner of Rio di San Trovaso and Rio Ognissanti.

Parks

Giardini Pubblici N10–O11
This has a small children's playground, with swings. *See pp.153–4.*

Parco delle Rimembranze P12
*Isola di Sant'Elena, Castello; **vaporetto** Sant'Elena.*
With a kids' play area (swings, etc.) and roller skating rink. See p.154.

Shops

Bambolandia G6
*San Polo 1462, Calle Madonetta, **t** 041 520 7502; **vaporetto** San Silvestro. Open Mon–Sat 10–12 and 2–6.*
At the foot of the bridge that leads from Campo San Polo towards the Rialto is this amazing shop which sells antique toys and toys made with traditional techniques. Most visitors here are nostalgic adults rather than children, as these are really collectors'

The Ice Cream Trail

Il Doge D7
*Dorsoduro 3058, Campo Santa Margherita, **t** 041 523 4607; **vaporetto** Ca' Rezzonico. Open daily 10.30am–midnight. No cards.*
Lively *gelateria* known for its buzzy atmosphere.

Gelateria Causin D7
*Dorsoduro 2996, Campo Santa Margherita (no phone); **vaporetto** Ca' Rezzonico. Open Mon–Sat 8.30–7.30; closed Sun.*
The Causin family have been making ice cream since 1928, and their *caffè/gelateria* is reassuringly old-fashioned.

Il Golosone I6
*Castello 5689, Salizzada S. Lio, **t** 041 523 9386; **vaporetto** Rialto. Open daily 8am–1am.*
Known for pastries, *panini* and fresh fruit shakes as well as ice cream.

Nico E9
*Dorsoduro 922, Zattere ai Gesuati, **t** 041 522 5293; **vaporetto** Zattere. Open June–Sept daily 7.30am–11pm, Oct–May daily 8am–9.30pm. No cards.*
Generally considered to win the ice-cream war. The late-night queues are a testament to its popularity. Coffee, snacks and tables overlooking the Giudecca.

Paolin F8
*San Marco 2962, Campo Santo Stefano, **t** 041 522 5576; **vaporetto** San Marco. Open 9.30–midnight daily; closed Thurs in winter. Outside seating.*
Legendary pistachio ice cream.

items. There are dolls in all shapes and sizes, soft toys, puppets, board games, wooden constructions, mini theatres, and stamps.

Città del Sole Off maps
Mestre, Via Palazzo 50.
If you're serious about toys, you have to go to the mainland: this national chain specializes in quality kids' stuff from many countries.

Emporio Pettenello D7
*Dorsoduro 2978, Campo Santa Margherita, **t** 041 523 1167; **vaporetto** Ca' Rezzonico.*

An old-fashioned, low-ceilinged and rather ramshackle shop that feels as if it hasn't changed for years, Pettenello's toy emporium is stuffed with toys and games.

Signor Blum D8
*Dorsoduro 2840, Calle Lunga San Barnaba, **t** 041 522 6367; **vaporetto** Ca' Rezzonico.*
Beautiful jigsaw puzzles and brightly painted wooden toys.

Views

Campanile I7
*Piazza San Marco, **t** 041 522 4064; **vaporetto** San Zaccaria/San Marco. Lift **open** 9–7 daily, **adm** €6.*
A striking view; Venice looks surprisingly canal-less from here.

San Giorgio Maggiore J10
*Isola di San Giorgio Maggiore; **vaporetto** San Giorgio. **Open** daily 9.30–12.30 and 2.30–6.30; **adm** free to church, €3 to campanile.*
The campanile of this church has an even more amazing view.

Teenagers

Older children often like the **Doge's Palace** (*see* p.108), especially the Secret Itinerary (*see* p.112), the odds and ends in the **Museo Correr** (*see* p.118), and the Carpaccios in the **Scuola di San Giorgio degli Schiavoni** (*see* p.146).

Beaches, on the whole, are a real teenager hang-out in Italy in the summer. While their parents laze in the sun, teenagers will congregate in the various bars , which often have slot machines, etc. Try **Lido di Jesolo** (*see* p.232) and **Alberoni** (*see* p.224).

Activities

Aero Club G. Ancillotto
Off maps
*Lido, **t** 041 526 0808, **w** www.aero clubvenezia.com; **vaporetto** Lido.*
A flying school that offers excursion flights over Venice.

Stadio P.L. Penzo Q11
*Sant'Elena island, **t** 041 958 1000, **w** www.veneziacalcio.it, **vaporetto** Sant'Elena.*

Home matches on alternate Sundays at 3pm Sept–June. Tickets available at the ground, and from ACTV and Vela public transport offices, e.g. in Piazzale Roma and Calle dei Fuseri in San Marco.

Eating Out

Teenagers will enjoy spending an evening in lively **Campo Santa Margherita** (D7), full of young locals, with bars and cafés where you can have a drink inside or out, and excellent *gelaterie* (*see* p.296). They may also find it cool that you can still eat ice cream at midnight.

McDonald's H4, I7
*Cannaregio 3362, Strada Nuova, **t** 041 522 2969; and San Marco 656, Calle Larga San Marco, **t** 041 528 5258.*
In case they're tired of pasta.

Festivals and Events

Venetians, once entertained by a full calendar of state pageants, religious feast days, lotteries, itinerant jugglers and universal singing in the streets and gondolas, nowadays get by with a lot less. The big events – Carnival, the Film Festival, the Biennale – are international and have little spontaneity outside of the controversy and disputes they inevitably engender. And after the fireworks everyone goes to bed.

Tourist offices (see p.92) and websites will have additional information and precise dates.

All **regattas** are organized by Ufficio Regate (**t** 041 274 7735) and take place on Sundays (few have fixed dates). All involve various kinds of boats – gondolas and others – and specify the use of one or two oars. There are races for various classes – young gondoliers, master gondoliers, women, and so on. All events are accompanied by music, traditional crafts for sale, food and drink stalls and the like.

January
New Year
1 Jan
New Year's Day on the beach, Lido. Swimmers take a morning dip in the sea. Food and drink available.

Regatta delle Befana
6 Jan
The Befana is the kind witch who brings good kids toys on Epiphany (and bad ones lumps of coal).

February
Carnevale
10 days before Shrove Tues
Venice's renowned Carnival, founded back in 1094, was revived in 1979 after several decades of dormancy. It packs in the crowds, but still faces an uphill battle against the inherent Italian urge to make everything *bellissima* – at the expense of any serious carousing. In 1993 new ground was broken in the commercialization of the Carnival when Italy's premier media magnate Silvio Berlusconi, now prime minister,

undertook to finance the entire event in return for world TV rights. Inevitably enough, the modern version is in tame contrast to the rollicking carnival of the 18th century, ruled by the *commedia dell'arte* characters of Arlecchino (or Harlequin, a servant from Bergamo), Senor Pantalone (a rich and pedantic old Venetian merchant, constantly being cuckolded) and Zany Corneto ('Zany' or 'Zanni' is Venetian for Gianni, the name for porters; it is from this madcap character that the English word is derived). Nowadays masks are worn for the 10 days before Lent, not for any high jinks but for the sake of cutting a dash and posing for photographs. In response, the art of making the masks has been revived in little workshops all over the city. The city sponsors events such as celebrity performances at La Fenice (*still closed*), Renaissance carnival madrigals and *commedia dell'arte* performances. But the down-side is that the Carnival is no longer really a Venetian festival; in fact most Venetians clear out of the city and leave it all to the tourists. If you want a really good Carnival, go to Cadiz.

March
Su e Zo per i Pontli
4th Sun of Lent
A running race (the name means 'Up and Down the Bridges').

April
Feast of St Mark
25 April (public holiday)
Men send their beloved a single rose; there's also a gondoliers' regatta and the Lion of St Mark golf championship.

May
Sagra della Sparesea
1 May (May Day public holiday).
Asparagus festival at Cavallino.

La Sensa
40 days after Easter Day, on a Sun
In 1988 Venice revived its ancient marriage-to-the-sea ceremony, La Sensa (see p.150, **Castello**), with

the mayor playing the role of the Doge in a replica of the *Bucintoro*, all of which is as corny and pretentious as it sounds.

Vogalonga
Sun after La Sensa
The 'long row' covers 33km around the lagoon, the Cannaregio Canal and the Grand Canal. You can take part if you have a rowing boat (*call* **t** 041 521 0544).

Regatta of the Maritime Republics
Every 4th year (next is 2003), on a Sun in late May/early June.
A race between Venice and old rivals Pisa, Genoa and Amalfi.

St Erasmus
Sun in late May/early June (depends on date of Easter)
Patron saint's festival. A regatta takes place, and there is an exhibition of local arts and crafts, games, and dancing in the square.

June
Biennale
June–Sept, in odd-numbered years; **t** 041 521 8711
Founded in 1895, the Biennale is the most famous contemporary art show in the world. It takes place every other year in the pavilions of the Giardini Pubblici, where the various nations' pavilions are arranged as at a World's Fair, among groves of huge, perfect lime trees. The permanent buildings, although modest, are often of some interest in themselves, such as those of the Netherlands, by *de Stijl* architect Gerrit Rietveld, Finland, designed by Alvar Aalto, and Austria, by Josef Hoffmann. The show has also now taken over the Arsenale as extra exhibition space (*see* p.148). The uneven quality of the exhibits ('Nothing more than black holes,' fumed one art critic) and the recent spate of scandals has stripped away some of the Biennale's gloss. Who actually gets exhibited is decided by bureaucratic bodies in each country. Naturally there is a good deal of politicking in the larger

countries, and merit is not always the prime consideration. Perhaps the most exciting thing about the Biennale is the range of fringe exhibits by unknowns that are shown all over Venice to coincide with the main event.

Serenissima Offshore Gran Prix
1st week June

Fr European Formula One motor boats; contestants begin at Jesolo and zip along the sea coast off the Lido.

Feast of San Pietro di Castello
Sun of 3rd week in June
Feast of San Pietro on the island of San Pietro on the eastern end of Castello; regatta for young gondoliers.

July

Murano Regatta
Sun in early July
On the island of Murano.

Feast of the Redentore
3rd Sat and Sun in July
Venice's most exciting festival is also the one best loved by the Venetians themselves. Now a time of tremendous unification and unquashable exuberance in the city, the Redentore celebrates the end of the plague of 1576. In its prayers for deliverance from the epidemic, the Senate vowed to build a church (Palladio's Il Redentore, on the Giudecca) and to cross over the canal on a bridge of boats to attend mass there on its feast day, the third Sunday in July. Nowadays the streams of pious Venetians flock over to the Giudecca by way of a Bailey bridge (pontoon) built overnight by the army and dismantled less than 48 hours later. Most of the excitement happens on the Saturday night, when Venetians set sail in the evening for a picnic on the water, manoeuvring for the best views of an utterly incandescent

11pm fireworks show over the Lagoon. For landlubbers (and there are thousands of them) the prime viewing and picknicking spots are towards the eastern ends of either the Giudecca or the Zattere.

Sagra del Peocio
Mid-July
Mussel festival in Alberoni.

Feast of the Madonna dell'Apparizione
5 days in late July/early Aug
Regattas, dancing, fireworks and a traditional pilgrims' parade on the island of Pellestrina.

August

Feast of San Rocco
16 Aug
A religious festival in the Campo and church of San Rocco. The Scuola is open free of charge for the day.

Venice Film Festival
Late Aug/early Sept
The Venice Film Festival unreels in the grand Palazzo del Cinema and in the Astra Cinema on the Lido. Besides the thrill of seeing your celluloid heroes in the flesh, you can get in to see some of the films, although you should arrive at the cinemas early as the tickets are sold only on the day of their showing, and be prepared to put on the dog. Venice is generally ranked second after Cannes on the European circuit, and the festival's equivalent of the Oscar, the *Leone d'Oro*, is proudly flaunted by every winner's publicity machine. For information, call t 041 521 8711.

September

Regata Storica
1st Sun in Sept
A splendid pageant of historic vessels and crews in Renaissance costumes and races by a variety of rowers down the Grand Canal –

the race between gondoliers, who have special racing gondolas for the occasion, is the most intensely fought.

Burano Regatta
3rd Sun in Sept
On the island of Burano.

October

Wine-harvest festival at Sant'Erasmo
1st weekend in Oct
The first tasting of the new wine on the island of Sant'Erasmo, plus food stalls.

Venice Marathon
Last Sun in Oct
Starting at the Villa Pisani in Strà, the marathon runs along the Brenta canal, over the big road bridge and into Venice, finishing on the Riva degli Schiavoni. For information, call t 041 940 644 or see w www.venicemarathon.it.

November

St Martin's Day
11 Nov
Revival of a popular fair in the streets of Venice. Good for kids.

Feast of Santa Maria della Salute
21 Nov
Another holiday celebrating the end of a plague (1631), with a bridge of boats over to Santa Maria della Salute. This ceremony is notable not for its fireworks but for the chance it affords to see Longhena's unique basilica with its doors thrown open on to the Grand Canal.

Giornate Wagneriane
Nov–Dec, t 041 523 2544
A series of fine concerts, lectures and other peripheral events focusing on the works of Wagner.

December

Premio Venezia
The international piano competition reaches its final stages.

Language

Pronunciation 303

Basic Vocabulary 303

Navigating Venice 304

Eating Out 305

The fathers of modern Italian were Dante, Manzoni and television. Each played its part in creating a national language from an infinity of regional and local dialects; the Florentine Dante, the first to write in the vernacular, did much to put the Tuscan dialect into the foreground of Italian literature. Manzoni's revolutionary novel, *I Promessi Sposi*, heightened national consciousness by using an everyday language all could understand in the 19th century. Television in the last few decades has performed an even more spectacular linguistic unification; although many Italians still speak a dialect at home, school and work, their TV idols insist on proper Italian.

Italians are not especially apt at learning other languages. English lessons, however, have been the rage for years, and at most hotels and restaurants there will be someone who speaks some English. In small towns and out-of-the-way places, finding an Anglophone may prove more difficult. The words and phrases below should help you out in most situations, but the ideal way to come to Italy is with some Italian under your belt; your visit will be richer, and you're much more likely to make some Italian friends.

See pp.64–5 for of historical, artistic and architectural terms.

Pronunciation

Italian words are pronounced phonetically. Every vowel and consonant is sounded. Most consonants are the same as in English, exceptions are the **c** which, when followed by an 'e' or 'i', is pronounced like the English 'ch' (*cinque* thus becomes cheen-quay). Italian **g** is also soft before 'i' or 'e' as in *giro*, or jee-roh. **H** is never sounded; **r** is trilled, like the Scottish 'r'; **z** is pronounced like 'ts' or 'ds'. The consonants **sc** before the vowels 'i' or 'e' become like the English 'sh'; **ch** is pronouced like a 'k' as in Chianti; **gn** as 'nya' (thus *bagno* is pronounced ban-yo);

while **gli** is pronounced like the middle of the word 'million' (Castiglione, pronounced Ca-stil-yohn-ay).

Vowel pronunciation is as follows: **a** is as in English father, **e** when unstressed is pronounced like 'a' in fate as in *padre*, when stressed it can be the same or like the 'e' in pet (*bello*); **i** is like the 'i' in machine; **o** like 'e', has two sounds, 'o' as in hope when unstressed (*tacchino*), and usually 'o' as in rock when stressed (*morte*); **u** is pronounced like the 'u' in June.

The stress usually (but not always!) falls on the penultimate syllable. Beware of the **Venetian dialect/accent** where vowels and consonants are often slurred into a porridge of 'u's, 'v's, 'x's (pronounced 'sh') and 'z's (e.g. San Zanipolo for Santi Giovanni e Paolo).

Basic Vocabulary

Common Expressions
yes/no/maybe *sì/no/forse*
I don't know *Non lo so*
I don't understand (Italian) *Non capisco (italiano)*
Does someone here speak English? *C'è qualcuno qui che parla inglese?*
Speak slowly *Parla lentamente*
Could you assist me? *Potrebbe aiutarmi?*
Help! *Aiuto!*
Please *Per favore*
Thanks (very much) *(Molte) grazie*
You're welcome *Prego*
It doesn't matter *Non importa*
All right *Va bene*
Excuse me *Mi scusi*
Be careful *Attenzione!*
Nothing *Niente*
It is urgent! *E urgente!*
How are you? *Come stai? (informal) / sta? (formal)*
Well, and you? *Bene, e tu? (informal) / Bene, e Lei? (formal)*
What is your name? *Come si chiama?*
Hello *Salve or ciao (both informal)*
Good morning *Buongiorno (formal hello)*
Good afternoon (also evening) *Buonasera (formal hello)*

Goodnight *Buonanotte*
Goodbye *ArrivederLa (formal) / Arrivederci (informal)*
What do you call this in Italian? *Come si chiama questo in italiano?*
What? *Che cosa?*
Who? *Chi?*
Where? *Dove?*
When? *Quando?*
Why? *Perché?*
How? *Come?*
How much? *Quanto?*
I am lost *Mi sono smarrito/a*
I am hungry *Ho fame*
I am thirsty *Ho sete*
I am sorry *Mi dispiace*
I am tired *Sono stanco/a*
I am sleepy *Ho sonno/a*
I am ill *Mi sento male*
Leave me alone *Lasciami in pace*
good *buono/bravo*
bad *male/cattivo*
It's all the same *Fa lo stesso*
slow *lento/piano*
fast *rapido*
big *grande*
small *piccolo*
hot *caldo*
cold *freddo*
up *su*
down *giù*
here *qui*
there *lì*

Shopping, Service and Sightseeing
I would like ... *Vorrei ...*
Where is/are?... *Dov'è/Dove sono?...*
How much is it? *Quanto viene questo?*
open *aperto*
closed *chiuso*
cheap *a buon mercato*
expensive *caro*
bank *banca*
beach *spiaggia*
bed *letto*
church *chiesa*
entrance *entrata*
exit *uscita*
hospital *ospedale*
money *soldi*
museum *museo*
newspaper (foreign) *giornale (straniero)*
chemist *farmacia*
police station *commissariato*

policeman *poliziotto*
post office *ufficio postale*
sea *mare*
shop *negozio*
telephone *telefono*
tobacco shop *tabacchaio*
WC *toilette/bagno*
   men *Signori/Uomini*
   women *Signore/Donne*

Time

What time is it? *Che ore sono?*
month *mese*
week *settimana*
day *giorno*
morning *mattina*
afternoon *pomeriggio*
evening *sera*
today *oggi*
yesterday *ieri*
tomorrow *domani*
soon *fra poco*
later *più tardi*
It is too early *È troppo presto*
It is too late *È troppo tardi*

Days

Monday *lunedì*
Tuesday *martedì*
Wednesday *mercoledì*
Thursday *giovedì*
Friday *venerdì*
Saturday *sabato*
Sunday *domenica*

Months

January *gennaio*
February *febbraio*
March *marzo*
April *aprile*
May *maggio*
June *giugno*
July *luglio*
August *agosto*
Septem ber *settembre*
October *ottobre*
November *novembre*
December *dicembre*

Numbers

one *uno/una*
two *due*
three *tre*
four *quattro*
five *cinque*
six *sei*
seven *sette*
eight *otto*
nine *nove*
ten *dieci*

eleven *undici*
twelve *dodici*
thirteen *tredici*
fourteen *quattordici*
fifteen *quindici*
sixteen *sedici*
seventeen *diciasette*
eighteen *diciotto*
nineteen *diciannove*
twenty *venti*
twenty-one *ventuno*
twenty-two *ventidue*
thirty *trenta*
thirty-one *trentuno*
forty *quaranta*
fifty *cinquanta*
sixty *sessanta*
seventy *settanta*
eighty *ottanta*
ninety *novanta*
hundred *cento*
one hundred and one *cent'uno*
two hundred *duecento*
thousand *mille*
two thousand *duemila*
million *milione*
billion *miliardo*

Transport

airport *aeroporto*
bus stop *fermata*
bus/coach *autobus/pulmino*
car *macchina*
customs *dogana*
port *porto*
port station *stazione marittima*
railway station
   stazione (ferroviaria)
seat (reserved) *posto (prenotato)*
ship *nave*
taxi *tassi*
ticket *biglietto*
train *treno*
train/platform *binario*

Navigating Venice

corte a blind alley
fondamenta a street that runs
   along a canal or along the
   lagoon banks
piscina an old turning basin for
   boats that has been filled in to
   become a square (Latin for pool
   or reservoir)
ramo a street branching off
   another street, often with the
   same name

rio a canal; the status of *canale* is
   reserved for the Grand Canal
   and a few others
rio terrà a filled-in canal
riva or **molo** a quay
ruga an old word for an important street

Street Talk

If you want to pretend you're in
the Venice of the old days, there's
one clue that will help make the
place come to life: the smaller
streets were generally named (in
Venetian dialect) after the trade or
whatever other sort of enterprise
went on there, and they have
conserved the names to this day.
Some of the most common are:
bareteri capmakers
beccarie butchers
caffetier coffee house
calderer coppersmith
calegheri shoemakers
carbon coal barges (on a canal)
carrozzer carriage-maker
   (amazingly, Venice supported
   quite a few until the 17th
   century)
cason police prison
cerchieri coopers
corrazzeri armourers
diamanter diamond-cutters
fabbri smiths
formagier cheesemonger
forner baker
frezzeria arrow factory
fruttarol fruiterer
luganegher pork-butcher
malvasia seller of malvasia wine
mandoler almond-seller
marangon ship's carpenter
margaritera glass bead-maker
   (a Latin word that survived only
   in Venice)
mendicoli beggars
muneghe nuns
murer builder
piovan parish priest
remer oar-maker
ridotto gambling house
spezier apothecary
squero boat-yard
stagneri tinsmiths
strazzarol ragman
tentor dyer
testari silk-weavers
veriera glazier

sacca a basin on the city's edge; Venice being man-made, these can be rectangular, like the Sacca della Misericordia

salizzada a word from the old days meaning a paved street

sottoportego (sottoportico) an arcade or archway under a building.

strada street/road

Travel Directions

I want to go to... *Voglio andare a...*
How can I get to...? *Come posso arrivare a ...?*
The next stop, please *La prossima fermata, per favore*
Where is ... /where is it? *Dove ... / Dov'è?*
How far is it to ...? *Quanto siamo lontani da ... ?*
What is the name of this station? *Come si chiama questa stazione?*
When does the next train leave? *Quando parte il prossimo treno?*
From where does it leave? *Da dove parte?*
How long does the trip take? *Quanto tempo dura il viaggio?*
How much is the fare? *Quant'è il biglietto?*
Have a good trip! *Buon viaggio!*
near *vicino*
far *lontano*
left *sinistra*
right *destra*
straight ahead *sempre diritto*
forward *avanti*
back *indietro*
north *nord/settentrionale (the North of Italy)*
south *sud/mezzogiorno (the South of Italy)*
east *est/oriente*
west *ovest/occidentale*
around the corner *dietro l'angolo*
crossroads *bivio*
square *piazza*

Eating Out

Antipasti
antipasto misto mixed antipasto
bruschetta toast with garlic and tomatoes
carciofi (sott'olio) artichokes (in oil)
crostini liver pâté on toast
frutti di mare seafood

funghi (trifolati) mushrooms (with anchovies, garlic and lemon)
gamberi ai fagioli prawns with beans
mozzarella (in carrozza) cow or buffalo cheese (fried with bread in batter)
olive olives
prosciutto (con melone) raw ham (with melon)
salame cured pork
salsiccia sausage

Minestre e Pasta
These dishes are the principal first courses (*primi piatti*) served throughout Italy.
agnolotti meat-filled pasta
cacciucco spiced fish soup
cappelletti small ravioli, often in broth
crespelle crêpes
fettuccine long strips of pasta
frittata omelette
gnocchi potato dumplings
minestra di verdura thick vegetable soup
minestrone soup with meat, vegetables and pasta
orecchiette ear-shaped pasta, often served with turnip greens
panzerotti ravioli filled with mozzarella, anchovies and egg
pappardelle alla lepre flat pasta ribbons with hare sauce
pasta e fagioli soup with beans, bacon and tomatoes
pastina in brodo tiny pasta in broth
penne all'arrabbiata pasta tubes in spicy tomato sauce
polenta cake or pudding of corn semolina, fried, baked or grilled
risotto (alla Milanese) rice cooked with stock, saffron and wine
spaghetti all'Amatriciana with tomatoes, bacon and garlic, plus pecorino cheese
spaghetti alla Carbonara with bacon, eggs and black pepper
al pomodoro with tomato sauce
al sugo/ragù with meat sauce
alle vongole with clam sauce
stracciatella broth with eggs and cheese
tagliatelle flat egg noodles

tortellini al pomodoro/ panna/ in brodo stuffed rings of pasta filled with meat and cheese, served with tomato sauce, cream, or in broth
vermicelli very thin spaghetti

Second Courses: *Carne* (Meat)
abbacchio milk-fed lamb
agnello lamb
anatra duck
animelle sweetbreads
arista pork loin
arrosto misto mixed roast meats
bistecca alla Fiorentina Florentine beef steak
bocconcini veal mixed with ham and cheese and fried
bollito misto stew of boiled meats
braciola pork chop
brasato di manzo braised beef
bresaola dried salt beef served with lemon, olive oil and parsley
capretto kid
capriolo roe buck
carne di castrato/suino mutton/ pork
carpaccio thin slices of raw beef served like *bresaola*
cassoeula winter stew with pork and cabbage
cervello (al burro nero) brains (in black butter sauce)
cervo venison
cinghiale boar
coniglio rabbit
cotoletta (alla Milanese/alla Bolognese) veal cutlet (fried in breadcrumbs/with ham and cheese)
fagiano pheasant
faraona (alla creta) guinea fowl (in an earthenware pot)
fegato alla veneziana liver and onions
involtini rolled slices of veal with filling
lepre (in salmi) hare (marinated in wine, herbs etc)
lombo di maiale pork loin
lumache snails
maiale (al latte) pork (cooked in milk)
manzo beef
osso buco braised veal knuckle with herbs
pancetta bacon

pernice partridge
petto di pollo (alla Fiorentina/ Bolognese/Sorpresa) boned chicken breast (fried in butter/with ham and cheese/ stuffed and deep fried)
piccione pigeon
pizzaiola beef steak with tomato and oregano sauce
pollo (alla cacciatora/alla diavola/ al Marengo) chicken (with tomatoes and mushrooms cooked in wine/grilled/fried with tomatoes, garlic and wine)
polpette meatballs
quaglie quails
rane frogs
rognoni kidneys
saltimbocca veal scallop with prosciutto and sage, cooked in pieces of beef or veal, usually stewed
stufato beef braised in white wine with vegetables
tacchino turkey
vitello veal

Pesce (Fish)
acciughe or **alici** anchovies
anguilla eel
aragosta lobster
aringhe herrings
baccalà salt cod
bonito small tuna
branzino sea bass
calamari squid
conchiglie scallops
cefalo grey mullet
cozze mussels
datteri di mare razor (or date) mussels
dentice dentex (perch-like fish)
fritto misto mixed fish fry, with squid and shrimp
gamberetto shrimp
gamberi (di fiume) prawns (cray-fish)
granchio crab
insalata di mare seafood salad
lampre lamprey
merluzzo cod
nasello hake
orata/dorata gilthead
ostriche oysters
pesce azzuro various small fish
pesce S. Pietro John Dory
pesce spada swordfish
polipo octopus
rombo turbot

sarde sardines
seppie cuttlefish
sgombro mackerel
sogliola sole
squadro monkfish
tonno tuna
triglia red mullet (*rouget*)
trota trout
trota salmonata salmon trout
vongole small clams
zuppa di pesce mixed fish in sauce or stew

Contorni (Side Dishes, Vegetables)
asparagi (alla Fiorentina) asparagus (with fried eggs)
broccoli (calabrese, romana) broccoli (green, spiral)
carciofi (alla giudia) artichokes (deep fried)
cardi cardoons, thistles
carote carrots
cavolfiore cauliflower
cavolo cabbage
ceci chickpeas
cetriolo cucumber
cipolla onion
fagioli white beans
fagiolini French (green) beans
fave broad beans
finocchio fennel
funghi (porcini) mushroom (boletus)
insalata salad
lattuga lettuce
lenticchie lentils
melanzane (al forno) aubergine/ eggplant (filled and baked)
patate (fritte) potatoes (fried)
peperonata stewed peppers, onions and tomatoes
peperoni sweet peppers
piselli peas
pomodoro tomato
porri leeks
radicchio red chicory
ravanelli radishes
rapa turnip
sedano celery
spinaci spinach
verdure greens
zucca pumpkin
zucchini courgettes

Formaggio (Cheese)
Bel Paese soft, white cow's cheese
cacio/caciocavallo pale yellow, often sharp cheese

fontina rich cow's milk cheese
groviera mild cheese
gorgonzola soft blue cheese
Parmigiano Parmesan cheese
pecorino sharp sheep's cheese
provolone sharp, tangy cheese; dolce is more mild
stracchino soft white cheese

Frutta (Fruit, Nuts)
albicocche apricots
ananas pineapple
arance oranges
banane bananas
cachi persimmon
ciliege cherries
cocomero watermelon
composta di frutta stewed fruit
dattero date
fichi figs
fragole (con panna) strawberries (with cream)
frutta di stagione fruit in season
lamponi raspberries
macedonia di frutta fruit salad
mandarino tangerine
mandorle almonds
melograna pomegranate
mele apples
melone melon
more blackberries
nespola medlar fruit
nocciole hazelnuts
noci walnuts
pera pear
pesca peach
pesca noce nectarine
pompelmo grapefruit
pignoli pine nuts
prugna secca prune
susina plum
uve grapes

Dolci (Desserts)
amaretti macaroons
cannoli crisp pastry tube filled with ricotta, cream, chocolate or fruit
coppa assorted ice cream
crema caramella crème caramel
crostata fruit flan
gelato (produzione propria) ice cream (homemade)
granita flavoured ice, usually lemon or coffee
Monte Bianco chestnut pudding with whipped cream

panettone sponge cake with candied fruit and raisins
panforte dense cake of chocolate, almonds and preserved fruit
Saint Honoré meringue cake
semifreddo refrigerated cake
sorbetto sorbet
spumone a soft ice cream or mousse
tiramisù mascarpone, coffee, chocolate and sponge fingers
torrone nougat
torta tart
torta millefoglie layered custard tart
zabaglione whipped eggs, sugar and Marsala wine, served hot
zuppa inglese trifle

Bevande (Beverages)
acqua minerale con/senza gas mineral water sparkling/still
aranciata orange soda
birra (alla spina) beer (draught)
caffè (freddo) coffee (iced)
cioccolata (con panna) hot chocolate (with cream)
latte (magro) milk (skimmed)
limonata lemon soda

sugo di frutta fruit juice
tè tea
vino (rosso, bianco, rosato) wine (red, white, rosé)

Cooking Terms
affumicato smoked
ai ferri grilled
al forno baked
alla brace braised
arrosto roasted
costoletta/cotoletta chop
filetto fillet
forno oven
fritto fried
ghiaccio ice
limone lemon
magro lean meat/or pasta without meat
mostarda sweet mustard sauce, served with meat
olio oil
pane (tostato) bread (toasted)
panini sandwiches
panna fresh cream
pepe pepper
peperoncini hot chilli peppers
salmi wine marinade
salsa sauce

Miscellaneous
aceto (balsamico) vinegar (balsamic)
aglio garlic
bicchiere glass
burro butter
cacciagione game
coltello knife
conto bill
cucchiaio spoon
forchetta fork
marmellata jam
miele honey
piatto plate
prezzemolo parsley
rosmarino rosemary
sale salt
salvia sage
senape mustard
tartufi truffles
tazza cup
tavola table
tovagliolo napkin
tramezzini finger sandwiches
in umido stewed
uovo egg
zucchero sugar

Index

Numbers in **bold** indicate main references. Numbers in *italic* indicate maps.

Accademia 158–62, 239
accommodation *see* hotels; where
    to stay
addresses 77–8
admission prices 82
Agnadello, battle of 44
air travel 72–3, 76–7
Ala Napoleonica 117
Alaric the Goth 28
Albanian community 128
Alberoni 224
Aldine Press 128, 129
Aldus Manutius 128, 129
d'Alemagna, Giovanni 60
Alexius IV 36
algae invasion 53, 216
Anafesta, Paoluccio 29
Angelo Raffaele 168
antiques 287
Antonello da Messina 60, 66
Arab corsairs 31
Archaeology museum 119–20
Archaeology museum
    (Verona) 250
Arena (Verona) 247
Aretino, Pietro 129, 130, 205–6
Arsenale 34, **148–9**
art and architecture **56–70**
    architectural terms 64–5
    Baroque 63
    directory of artists 66–70
    Gothic 58–60
    High Renaissance 61–3
    International Gothic 60
    19th and 20th century 65–6
    preservation of 66
    Quattrocento 60–1
    Rococo Revival 63–4
    Veneto-Byzantine art 57–8
art shops 287
Artiglierie 148
Ateneo Veneto 126
Attila the Hun 28, 42
Attila's Seat 232
Austrian rule 51, 52

babysitting services 296
bacari 265–6
    see also food and drink
Bacino Orseolo 127
Baiamonte Tiepolo 37, 124
ballet 285

Banco Rosso 209
banks 88
Barbari, Jacopo de' 66
Barbaro villa 243–4
Barnabotti 166
Baroque art and architecture 63
bars 282–3
Basaiti, Marco 66
Bassano, Francesco 66
Bassano, Jacopo 62, 66
Bastiani, Lazzaro 66
Battista, Giovanni 67
Bauer-Grünwald hotel 240
beaches 222
Bella, Gabriel 66
Bellini, Gentile 60, 66
Bellini, Giovanni 60, 66
Bellini, Jacopo 60, 66
Biblioteca Nazionale Marciana
    118–19
Biennale 65
Black Death 38
Blue Venice card 82
blues music 283
boat hire 80
boating 294
body snatching 222–3
Bon, Bartolomeo 59, 66
Bon, Giovanni 59, 67
Bonifazio de'Pitati 67
bookshops 287–8
Bordone, Paris 67
Borgia family 43
Bragadin, Marcantonio 45, 136, **138**
breakfast 264
Brenta Canal 242–3
Brustolon, Andre 64
Brustolon, Andrea 67
Burano 229–30
buses and coaches 74, 80
buying a property 94
Byron, Lord 53

Ca' Angaran 182
Ca' Bernardo 184
Ca' di Dio 149
Ca' del Duca 240
Ca' Foscari 239
Ca' Giustinian 240
Ca' Grande 240
Ca' Malpiero Trevisan 141
Ca' da Mosto 197, 238

Ca' d'Oro 59, **196**, 238
Ca' Pésaro 187, 235
Ca' Rezzonico 165, 239, 297
Ca' Strozzi 197
Cabot, Giovanni and Sebastiano
    151
cafés 265
    see also food and drink
cakes and tarts 266
Calendario, Filippo 67
Calle dell'Uffizio della Seda 199
Campanile 114–15, 298
Campiello da Ca'Angaran 182
Campiello del Remer 199
Campo dell'Abbazia 206
Campo Bandiera e Moro 145
Campo delle Gatte 147
Campo Geremia 213
Campo dei Gesuiti 199–200
Campo Ghetto Nuovo 210
Campo Madonna dell'Orto 205
Campo Manin 129
Campo dei Mori 205–6
Campo San Barnaba 166
Campo San Bartolomeo 125–6
Campo San Cosmo 221
Campo San Fantin 126
Campo San Giacomo 186
Campo San Margherita 166
Campo San Maurizio 128
Campo San Polo 174–5, 175, **184**
    food and drink 174, 274–6
    where to stay 259–60
Campo San Salvatore 124–5
Campo San Samuele 132, 239
Campo San Silvestro 186
Campo San Simeone Profeta 234
Campo San Tomà 182
Campo di San Trovaso 171
Campo San Zaccaria 143–4
Campo Santa Maria Formosa
    141–2
Campo Santa Maria
    Materdomini 187–8
Campo Sant'Angelo 131
Campo Santo Stefano 130
Canale di Cannaregio 210
Canaletto, Antonio 64, 67
Candiano IV, Pietro 31
Cannaregio
    eastern **194–200**, *195*
    food and drink 194, 202, 276–8

Cannaregio (cont'd)
  highlights 194–5, 202–3
  western **202–14**, 202–3
  where to stay 260–1
Canova, Antonio 64, 67
Capello, Bianca 187
Capitaneria del Porto 240
Cappella degli Scrovegni (Padua) 244–5
Carmagnola 41
Carmine (Padua) 245–6
Carmini 167
Carnival 49, 296
Carpaccio, Vittore 61, 67, 161, **162**
Carrà, Carlo 67
Carriera, Rosalba 64, 67
cars 74, 77, 80
Casa Favretto 235
Casa di Giulietta (Verona) 248
Casa Goldoni 182
Casa Magno 130
Casa di Risparmio 129
Casetta delle Rose 240
Casino de Caffè 116
Casino degli Spiriti 205
casinos 50, 127, 208, 285
Castagno, Andrea del 67
Castello **134–54**, 134–5
  food and drink 134, 270–3
  highlights 134–5
  where to stay 256–8
Castelvecchio (Verona) 250
Caterina Cornaro, queen of Cyprus 43, 125, 197
Catherine of Siena 137–8
Cavallino 232
cemeteries 223, 225, 226
Centro Europeo 225
ceramics shops 289–90
Charlemagne 30
Charles VIII of France 43
chemists 87
children **296–8**
Chioggia 38–9, 224
Chioggia war 38–9
Chirico, Giorgio de 67
churches
  etiquette 86
  opening hours 89
  services 90
  tickets 82–3
Cima da Conegliano 60, 67
cinema 284
Cini family 162, 217–18
Cipriani Hotel 220
classical music 283–4
climate 83
clothes shops 288

clubs 282–3
coaches and buses 74, 80
Codussi, Mauro 61, 67
coffee culture 117
Colleoni, Bartolomeo 139–40
Comunità Israelitica 210
Conservatory of Music 131
Constantinople 35–6, 42
consulates 86
Contarini, Andrea 130
Contarini villa 243
Corderie 148
Corner, Elena Lucrezia 169
Correr museum 118
Corte Corner 131
Corte Nuova 147
Corte Prima del Milion 199
Corte Seconda del Milion 199
costumes 291
Council of Ten 37
craft shops 289
credit cards 88
crime 83–4
Crivelli, Carlo 67
Crusades 34–5
customs formalities 76
Customs House (Dogana di Mare) 164–5
cycling 293
Cyprus 43, 45

Dalmatian community 146
dancing 285
Dandolo, Enrico 35, 36
Dante 37
Dark Ages 29–30
day trips **242–50**
  Padua 244–7, 245
  Verona 247–50, 248
  villas 242, 242–4
De Pisis, Filippo 67
debit cards 88
Deposito del Megio 235
Diaghilev, Serge 226
Diedo, Ludovico 137
Diocesano museum 120
directory of artists 66–70
disabled travellers 84–5
discount cards 82
Dogana di Mare 164–5, 240
doges 40–1, 110
  elections 34, **35**
  tombs 136–9, 176–9, 188, 219
Doge's Palace 38, **108–14**
Donà, Leonardo 219
Donatello 67
Doria, Andrea 45

Dorsoduro **156–172**, 156–7
  food and drink 156, 273–4
  highlights 156
  where to stay 258–9
Duomo (Chioggia) 224
Duomo (Verona) 249–50
duty-free allowances 76

electricity 85
embassies 86
  French embassy 210
emergencies 86–7
Emo, Angelo 47
entertainment **282–5**
entry formalities 76
Erberia 185
Eremitani (Padua) 245
estate agents 93
Estuario museum (Torcello) 232
etiquette 86
euro 88
Eurotunnel 74
excursion boats 79

Fabbriche Nuove 185, 235
Fabbriche Vecchie 185, 235
Falier, Marin 38
fax machines 90
Feast of the Marys 153
Fenice, La 126, 297
ferries 74
festivals 296–7, 300–1
  Carnival 49, 296
  Feast of the Marys 153
  La Sensa 150
fish market (Chioggia) 224
Flabanico, Domenico 34
floods 53, 54
Florian's 117
flying 293
Fondaco dei Tedeschi 238
Fondaco dei Turchi 189, 235
Fondamenta Gasparo Contarini 205
Fondamenta Minotto 191–2
Fondamenta Nuove 200
Fondamenta degli Ormesini 207
Fondamenta di Rimedio 142
Fondamenta San Felice 196–7
Fondamenta San Giobbe 212
Fondamenta Savorgnan 212
Fondamenta della Tana 151
Fondamenta del Vin 186
Fondazione Giorgio Cini 219
Fondazione Querini-Stampalia 141–2
food and drink **264–80**, 268–9
  Brenta Canal 243, 244

food and drink (cont'd)
  cakes and tarts 266
  Cannaregio 194, 202, 276–8
  Castello 134, 270–3
  for children/teenagers 296, 298
  coffee culture 117
  Dorsoduro 156, 273–4
  ice cream 297
  Lagoon 278–9
  late-night food 272
  menu decoder 304–7
  Mestre 279–80
  Padua 246
  restaurant opening hours 89
  San Marco 97, 122, 266–70
  San Polo 174, 274–6
  Santa Croce 174, 274–6
  shopping 289
  tipping in restaurants 91
  vegetarians 277
  Venetian cuisine 264
  Verona 249
  wine 264
football 293
Forni Pubblici 149
Fornovo, battle of 43
Fortezza di Sant'Andrea 223
Fortuny museum 128–9
Foscari, Francesco 40
Foscarini, Antonio 188–9
Francesco di Giorgio Martini 67
Franchetti Gallery 196
Franco, Veronica 169
Franks 30, 34
Frari 176–9, 177
French embassy 210
French wars 43–4
Frezzeria 127
Fumiani, Gian Antonio 63

Gaggiante 148
Galleria dell'Accademia 158–62,
  239
Gambello, Antonio 67
gambling 50, 127, 208, 285
gardens see parks and gardens
Gattamelata 41
gay Venice 86
gelaterie 265
  see also food and drink
Genoese Wars 36–9
Gesuati 171–2
Gesultì 199–200
ghetto 209–10
Giambono, Michele 60, 67
Giardinetti Reali 116, 240
Giardini Papadopoli 192, 234
Giardini Pubblici (Biennale) 153–4

Giorgio Cini Foundation 217–18
Giorgione 61, 67–8
Giotto di Bondone 68
Giovane, Palma 63
Giudecca 218, 220–1, 220–1, 240
glass and ceramics shops 289–90
glassblowing 226–7, 228
Gobbo di Rialto 186
Goldoni, Carlo 125, 182
golf 293
gondolas 79–80, 170
Gothic art and architecture 58–60
Granaio 224
Grand Canal 234–40, 236–7
Grand Hotel des Bains 223
Grazia, La 225
Greek community 145
Greek-Gothic wars 29
Grimani, Marino 154
Guardi, Francesco 64, 68
Guardi, Gian Antonio 64
Guariento 68
Guggenheim collection 66, 163,
  240
guided tours 80
gyms 293

health 86–7
Henry III of France 45–6
history 28–54
  Austrian rule 51, 52
  Black Death 38
  building Venice 56–7
  chronology 32–3, 40–1
  Crusades 34–5
  Dark Ages 29–30
  decline 46–51
  foundation of the city 25–9
  French wars 43–4
  Genoese Wars 36–9
  life in Venice 48–50, 54
  locking of the Consiglio 37, 124
  sack of Constantinople 35–6
  Turkish Wars 42, 44–5, 46
  Wars of Italy 43, 44
homeware shops 290
horseriding 293
hostels 262
hotels 252–62, 254–5
  Bauer-Grünwald 240
  Cannaregio 260–1
  Castello 256–8
  Cipriani Hotel 220
  Dorsoduro 258–9
  Grand Hotel des Bains 223
  Lagoon 261–2
  opening hours 89
  Padua 246

hotels (cont'd)
  San Marco 252–6
  San Polo 259–60
  Santa Croce 259–60
  Verona 249
  see also where to stay

ice cream 297
Icone museum 145
Incurabili 172
insurance
  motor 74
  travel 86–7
International Gothic art and
  architecture 60
internet access 87
Isola di San Pietro 152, 152–4
Isola di Sant'Elena 154

Jacobello del Fiore 60, 68
jazz music 283
Jesolo 232
jewellery 290
Jews 209
  cemetery 223
job hunting 94
jogging 293
Julius II 43–4

La Fenice 126, 297
La Grazia 225
La Maddalena 208
La Malcontenta 242
La Pietà 144
La Salute 163–5
La Sensa 150
La Zecca 119
lace 290–1
Lagoon 30, 216–32, 217
  boat trips 296
  Burano 229–30
  Cavallino 232
  Chioggia 38–9, 224
  food and drink 278–9
  Giudecca 218, 220–1, 220–1, 240
  Jesolo 232
  Lido 222–3
  Mazzorbo 229–30
  Murano 226–9
  San Francesco del Deserto 230
  San Giorgio Maggiore 217–19
  San Lazzaro degli Armeni 224
  San Michele 225–6
  San Servolo 225
  Torcello 57, 230–2
  where to stay 261–2
language 303–7
  street names 78

Lapidario Maffeiano (Verona) 247
late-night food 272
Law, John 127
Lazzaretto Vecchio 225
Le Court, Juste 68
Le Vignole 232
Le Zitelle 220
League of Cambrai 44
left-luggage offices 77, 79, 87
Legend of St Ursula 161, **162**
Leopardi, Alessandro 68
Lepanto, battle of 45
lesbian Venice 86
Lido 222–3
Lido di Jesolo 232
life in Venice 48–50, 54
lion symbol 211
Lista di Spagna 213, 234
locking of the *Consiglio* 37, 124
Lombardo, Antonio 61, 68
Lombardo, Pietro 61, 68
Lombardo, Tullio 61, 68
Lombards 29
long-stay accommodation 93–4
Longhena, Baldassare 63, 68
Longhi, Pietro 64, 68
Loredan, Leonardo 43
Lorenzo Veneziano 60, 68
lost property 77, 79, 87
Lotto, Lorenzo 62, 68
Lucia, Saint 213
Lys, Johann 63, 68

Macelli Pubblici 212
Maddalena, La 208
Madonna dell'Orto 204–5
Maffei, Francesco 68
Magazzini del Sale 172
Maggior Consiglio 35, 37, 124
Malamocco 223
Malcontenta, La 242
Manin, Daniele 52, 129
Manin, Ludovico 47
Mansueti, Giovanni 68
Mantegna, Andrea 60, 68
maps 78
Marciano museum 102–3
Marco Polo 199
Marco Polo airport 76
Marghera 52, 218
Mark, Saint 30, 223
markets 185–6, 224, 291
Masegne, dalle, Jacobello and Pier Paolo 68
masks 291
Massari, Giorgio 64, 68
Mauro, Fra 225, **226**
Mazzoni, Sebastiano 68–9

Mazzorbo 229–30
media 87–8
Mehmet the Conqueror 42, 43
menu decoder 304–7
Mercerie 124–6
Mestre 218
  food and drink 279–80
Michiel, Domenico 219
Michiel II, Vitale 35
Misericordia 206
Mocenigo, Giovanni 136
Mocenigo I, Alvise 136
Mocenigo, Pietro 136
Mocenigo, Tommaso 40
Modern Art museum 187
Modern Art museum (Verona) 249
Molo 116
Monastery Giorgio Cini 219
money 88
Morandi, Giorgio 69
Morosini, Francesco **46**, 130, 191
mosaics 289
motoscafi 78
Mulino Stucky 221
Murano 226–9
museums
  Accademia 158–62, 239
  Archaeology (Verona) 250
  Archeologico 119–20
  Arte Moderna (Verona) 249
  Ca' d'Oro (Franchetti Gallery) 196
  Ca' Pésaro (Modern Art/Oriental Art) 187
  Ca' Rezzonico (Museo dei Settecento) 165, 239, 297
  Comunità Israelitica 210
  Correr 118
  Diocesano 120
  Estuario (Torcello) 232
  Fortuny 128–9
  Franchetti Gallery 196
  Icone 145
  Lapidario Maffeiano (Verona) 247
  Marciano 102–3
  Modern Art 187
  Natural History 189, 297
  Naval History 149–51, 297
  opening hours 89
  Oriental Art 187
  Peggy Guggenheim collection 66, **163**, 240
  Querini-Stampalia 141–2
  Raccolta d'Arte Vittorio Cini 162
  Settecento 165
  Vetrario (Murano) 227, 229
music 283–4

Napoleon Bonaparte 47, 51
Narentine pirates 31
Natural History museum 189, 297
Naval History museum 149–51, 297
newspapers 87
Nicholas, Saint 223
nightlife **282–5**
Normans 34

Old Woman with a Mortar 124
opening hours 88, 89
opera 283–4
  La Fenice 126, 297
Orange Venice card 82
Oratorio dei Crociferi 200
Orfano Canal 225
Oriental Art museum 187
Orseoli dynasty 31, 34
Orso Ipato, Orso 29
Ospedaletto 140
Ottoman empire 42, 44–5, 46

packing 89
Padua 244–7, *245*
palazzi
  Agnusdio 187
  Ariani 168
  Barbarigo 235, 240
  Barbarigo della Terrazza 239
  Barbaro 240
  Barzizza 239
  Belloni-Battaglia 235
  Bembo 238
  Bembo-Boldù 197
  Benzon 238
  Bernardo 239
  Brandolin 235
  Businello 239
  Camerlenghi 185, 199, 235
  Cavalli-Franchetti 240
  Cinema 223
  Cini 162
  Contarini del Bovolo 129
  Contarini dal Zaffo 205, 240
  Contarini delle Figure 238–9
  Contarini degli Scrigni e Corfù 239
  Contarini-Fasan 240
  Corner 240
  Corner Contarini dai Cavalli 238
  Corner della Regina 235
  Corner Spinelli 238
  Dario 240
  Dieci Savi 185–6
  Diedo 234
  Doge's Palace 38, **108–14**
  Dolfin-Manin 238

palazzi (cont'd)
Donà 200, 239
Ducale 38, **108–14**
Duodo 235
Erizzo 235
Falier 197, 240
Farsetti 130, 238
Foscari 238
Foscarini-Giovanelli 235
Franchetti 130
Giovanelli 197
Giustinian-Lolin 240
Giustiniani 239
Grassi 132, 239
Grimani 238
Gritti Badoer 145
Gritti-Pisani 240
Gussoni-Grimani della Vida 235, 238
Labia 212
Lezze 239
Lion-Morosini 238
Loredan 130, 198, 238, 239
Marcello dei Leoni 239
Mastelli 205
Michiel dalle Brusà 238
Michiel dalle Colonne 238
Minotto 240
Mocenigo 189, 238
Moro-Lin 239
Morosini 130
Nani 171
Nani-Mocenigo 239
Patriarcale 116
Pésaro degli Orfei 128
Pésaro-Rava 238
Pisani 131
Pisani della Moretta 239
Priuli 141
Priuli-Bon 235
Sagredo 197, 238
Salviati 240
Savorgnan 212
Soranzo 184, 235
Tiepolo 184
Tron 235
Valier 186
Vendramin-Calergi 208, 235
Venier dei Leoni 240
Vitturi 141
Widmann-Foscari 198
Palladio 63, 69
Palma, Giovane 69
Palma Vecchio 62, 69
Paolo Veneziano 60, 69
paper and stationery shops 291
parachuting 293
parking 77

parks and gardens 294, 297
Giardinetti Reali 116, 240
Giardini Papadopoli 192, 234
Giardini Pubblici (Biennale) 153–4
Parodi, Filippo 69
Participazio, Angelo 30
passports 76, 84
Peggy Guggenheim collection 66, **163**, 240
Pellestrina 224
Pescaria 185
photography 89
Piazza San Marco **96–120**, *96–7*
food and drink 97, 122, 266–70
highlights 97, 122
St Mark's Basilica 34, 56, 58, 59, **98–108**, *105*, 297
San Marco **122–32**, *122–3*
where to stay 252–6
Piazzale Roma 192
Piazzetta, Giambattista 63, 69
Piazzetta dei Leoncini 116
Piazzetta San Marco 115–16
Piazzetta Vigo 224
Piero della Francesca 69
Pietà, La 144
Pisanello (Antonio Pisano) 69
Pisani, Vettor 38–9
Pisani villa 242–3
Piscina San Samuele 131
police 83–4
Polo, Marco 199
Ponte dell'Accademia 239
Ponte, Antonio da 69
Ponte delle Guglie 212
Ponte della Paglia 116
Ponte dei Pugni 166
Ponte Rialto 125, **184–5**, 238
Ponte dei Sospiri 116
Ponte Storto 208
Ponte delle Tette 184
Ponte dei Tre Archi 210
Pordenone 69
Porto di Lido 223
post offices 90
Poveglia 225
practical A–Z **80–94**
Prigioni 116
Procuratie 117
prostitution 45, 169
public transport 78–9
Punta Sabbioni 232

Quattrocento 60–1
Querini, Francesco 131
Querini-Benzon, Marina 169
Querini-Stampalia museum 141–2

Raccolta d'Arte Vittorio Cini 162
radio 88
railways 73–4, 77, 234
rainfall 83
Ramo Cimesin 192
Redentore, Il 220
Regata delle Befana 296
Regata Storica 296–7
relics of saints 222–3
religious affairs 90
Renaissance art and architecture 61–3
renting flats 93
residency 93
restaurants *see* food and drink
Rialto 30, 125, **184–6**, 235
Rialto bridge 125, **184–5**, 238
Ricci, Sebastiano 63, 69
Ricovero Penitenti 212
Ridotto 127
Rio Fontego dei Turchi 235
Rio Marin 234
Rio Riello 151
Rio Terrà Antonio Foscarini 172
Rio Terrà S. Leonardo 212
Riva del Carbon 130, 238
Riva degli Schiavoni 116, 144
Rizzo, Antonio 61
Rizzo (Bregno), Antonio 69
Robusti, Marietta 169
Roccatagliata, Nicolò 69
Roch, Saint 223
rock music 283
Rococo Revival 63–4
Rolling Venice card 82
Rossi, Domenico 64, 69
Rossi, Giustina 124
rowing 293
Ruga degli Orefici 185
running 293

Sacca Fisola 221
Sacca della Misericordia 205
Sacca Sessola 225
sailing 294
St George 162
St Mark's Basilica 34, 56, 58, 59, **98–108**, *105*, 297
altar of the Sacrament 106
altar of St James 106
Ascension dome 106
Baptistry 103
Cappella della Madonna dei Máscoli 108
Cappella di Madonna di Nicopeia 107
Cappella di San Clemente 106–7
Cappella di Sant'Isidoro 107

St Mark's Basilica (cont'd)
Cappella Zen 103
Loggia 102
Museo Marciano 102–3
Pala d'Oro 107
Pentecost dome 103
Sanctuary 106
Treasury 106
salt trade 28
salt warehouses 172
Salute, La 163–5
Sammicheli, Michele 69
San Barnaba 166
San Bartolomeo 125–6
San Basso 116
San Benedetto 129
San Canciano 197
San Cassiano 188
San Clemente 225
San Domenico 224
San Fantin 126
San Felice 196
San Fermo Maggiore (Verona) 250
San Francesco del Deserto 230
San Francesco della Vigna 147–8
San Giacomo Elemosinario 186
San Giacomo dell'Orio 190
San Giacomo in Paluda 232
San Giacomo di Rialto 186
San Giobbe 210–12
San Giorgio in Alga 225
San Giorgio in Braida (Verona) 250
San Giorgio dei Greci 145
San Giorgio Maggiore 217–19, 298
San Giovanni in Brágora 144
San Giovanni Crisostomo 198–9
San Giovanni Evangelista 182
San Giuseppe airport 76–7
San Giuseppe di Castello 154
San Lazzaro degli Armeni 224
San Lio 142
San Lorenzo 147
San Luca 130
San Marco 122–32, 122–3
food and drink 97, 122, 266–70
where to stay 252–6
San Marcuola 207–8
San Margherita 166
San Martino 149, 229
San Marziale 206
San Maurizio 128
San Michele 225–6
San Moisè 127
San Nicolò 222
San Nicolò dei Mendicoli 57, 169
San Nicolò da Tolentino 191
San Pantalon 181–2
San Pietro di Castello 152–3

San Pietro Martire 227
San Pietro in Volta 224
San Polo 174–5, 175, 184
food and drink 174, 274–6
where to stay 259–60
San Rocco 181
San Salvatore 125
San Samuele 132
San Sebastiano 167–8
San Servolo 225
San Silvestro 186
San Simeone Piccolo 190, 234
San Simeone Profeta 191
San Stae 188–9, 235
San Tomà 182
San Trovaso 171
San Vitale 131
San Zaccaria 142 3
San Zan Dégola 190
San Zanipolo 136–9, 137
San Zeno Maggiore (Verona) 250
San Zulian 124
Sansovino, Jacopo 63, 69
Santa Caterina 230
Santa Croce 174–5, 175, 190–2
food and drink 174, 274–6
where to stay 259–60
Santa Fosca 209, 232
Santa Maria Assunta 230–2
Santa Maria della Fava 142
Santa Maria Formosa 58, 141
Santa Maria Gloriosa dei Frari
176–9, 177
Santa Maria Materdomini 187–8
Santa Maria dei Miracoli 198
Santa Maria del Rosario 172
Santa Maria della Salute 163–4,
240
Santa Maria del Soccorso 168
Santa Maria della Visitazione 171 2
Santa Maria Zobenigo 127–8, 240
Santa Sofia 197
Santa Sofia (Padua) 245
Sant'Alvise 207
Sant'Anastasia (Verona) 248–9
Sant'Andrea 223
Sant'Angelo 131
Sant'Angelo delle Polveri 225
Sant'Antonin 146–7
Sant'Antonio (Padua) 247
Sant'Aponal 186–7
Sant'Elena 154
Sant'Erasmo 232
Sant'Eufemia 221
Santi, Andriolo de' 69–70
Santi Apostoli 197
Santi Geremia e Lucia 212–13, 234

Santi Giovanni e Paolo 59, 136–9,
137
Santi Maria e Donato 229
Santo Spirito 172, 225
Santo Stefano 130–1
Santo Stefano (Verona) 250
Sardi, Giuseppe 70
Sarpi, Paolo 46, 208
statue 208–9
Scaliger tombs (Verona) 248
Scalzi 213–14, 234
Scamozzi, Vincenzo 70
schools 94
scuole 183
Albanesi 128
Battiloro e Tiraoro 189, 235
Buona Morte 126
Caleghori 182
Carmini 166–7
Leventina 210
Merletti 229
Nuova della Misericordia 206
San Giorgio degli Schiavoni 146
San Giovanni Evangelista 182–4
San Marco 140
San Nicolò dei Greci 145
San Rocco 179–81, 180
San Teodoro 124
Spagnola 210
Tedesca 210
Varotari 166
Vecchia della Misericordia 206
Sebastiano del Piombo 70
Second World War 52
self-catering accommodation 262
Selva, Gian Antonio 65, 70
Sensa, La 150
Serrata 37, 124
Settecento museum 165
Sforza, Francesco 41
shoe carving 131
shoe shops 288–9
shopping 287–91
with children 297–8
markets 185–6, 224, 291
opening hours 89
tobacconists 91
useful phrases 303–4
VAT refunds 88–9
weights and measures 85
slave trade 29–30
smoking 90–1
snacks 265
Sottomarina 224
Spiaggia Comunale 222
sports 293–4
Squero di San Trevaso 171
Stampa, Gaspara 169

State Archives 179
stationery shops 291
Stazione Santa Lucia 77
Strada Nuova 196–7
Stravinsky, Igor 226
street numbering 77–8
students
  courses 91
  Rolling Venice card 82
  studying in Venice 93–4
  travel discounts 72, 82
Suleyman the Magnificent 44
Surian, Giacomo 130
swimming 294, 296

taxes 88–9
Teatro alle Tese 148
Teatro Malibran 199
Teatro Romano (Verona) 250
teenagers **298**
telephones 91
television 88
temperature chart 83
tennis 294
theatre 50, 148, 199, 250, 284–5
tickets and passes 78, 82
Tiepolo, Giambattista 64, 70
Tiepolo, Giandomenico 64
Tiepolo uprising 37, 124
time 91, 304
Tintoretto 62, 70
  house 205–6
tipping 91
Titian 61, 70
  tomb 176
tobacconists 91
toilets 92
Torcello 57, **230–2**
Torre dell'Orologio 116–17
Torri dell'Arsenale 148–9
tour operators 75
tourist information 92

traghetti 80
trains 73–4, 77, 234
travel **72–80**
  air travel 72–3, 76–7
  boat hire 80
  cars 74, 77, 80
  coaches and buses 74, 80
  disabled travellers 84–5
  duty-free allowances 76
  entry formalities 76
  Eurotunnel 74
  excursion boats 79
  ferries 74
  gondolas 79–80, 170
  guided tours 80
  insurance 86–7
  lost property 77, 79, 87
  packing 89
  public transport 78–9
  street numbering 77–8
  for students 72, 82
  tickets and passes 78, 82
  tour operators 75
  trains 73–4, 77, 234
  useful phrases 304
  water-taxis 79
  women travellers 93
traveller's cheques 88
Tre Ponti 192
Treporti 232
Trevisa airport 76–7
Tura, Cosmè 70
Turkish Wars 42, 44–5, 46
Two Columns 115–16

Uskoks 44

vaporetti 78
Vasco da Gama 43
VAT refunds 88–9
vegetarians 277
Venetii 28

Veneto-Byzantine art 57–8
Venier, Francesco, tomb 125
Verona 247–50, *248*
Veronese 63, 70
Verrocchio, Andrea del 70
Vetrario museum (Murano) 227, 229
Via Giuseppe Garibaldi 151
villas *242*, 242–4
visas 76
Visconti, Gian Galeazzo 39
Vittoria, Alessandro 63, 70
Vittorio Emanuele II monument 144
Vivarini family 60, 70

Wagner, Richard 208
Wars of Italy 43, 44
water-taxis 79
waterfront 116
websites 92
weights and measures 85
when to go 83
where to stay **252–62**, *254–5*
  camping 262
  hostels 262
  renting flats 93
  self-catering 262
  see also hotels
wine 264
women travellers 93
women in Venice 169
woodwork 291
working in Venice 93–4

Zattere 169, 171, 218
Zecca, La 119
Zeno, Carlo 39
Ziani, Sebastiano 35
Zitelle 220

No more
excuses –
just go!

flying visits
ITALY
*great getaways by
budget airline*

CADOGANguides

flying visits
FRANCE
*great getaways by
budget airline, train & ferry*

CADOGANguides

flying visits
SPAIN
*great getaways
by budget airline & ferry*

CADOGANguides

Flying Visits make
travel simple

CADOGANguides
well travelled well read

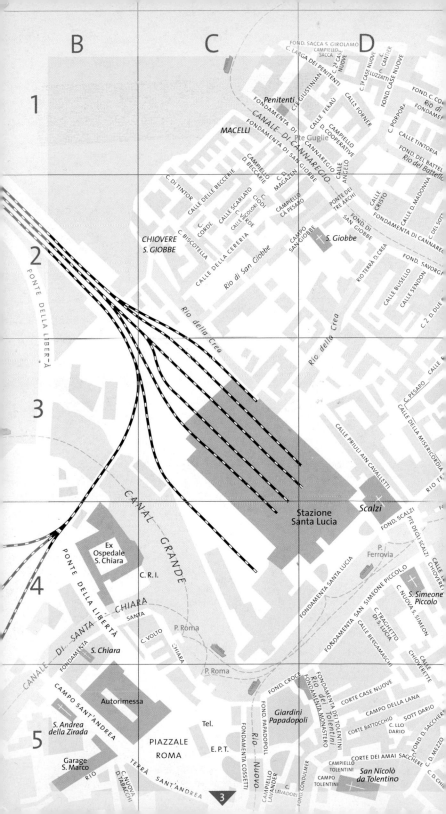

Venice Street Maps

Key

			Vaporetto Routes
i	Information		Park
★	Place of Interest		Canal
M	Metro Station		Place of Interest
			Public Building

N

━━━━━ 500 m
━━━━━ 500 yards

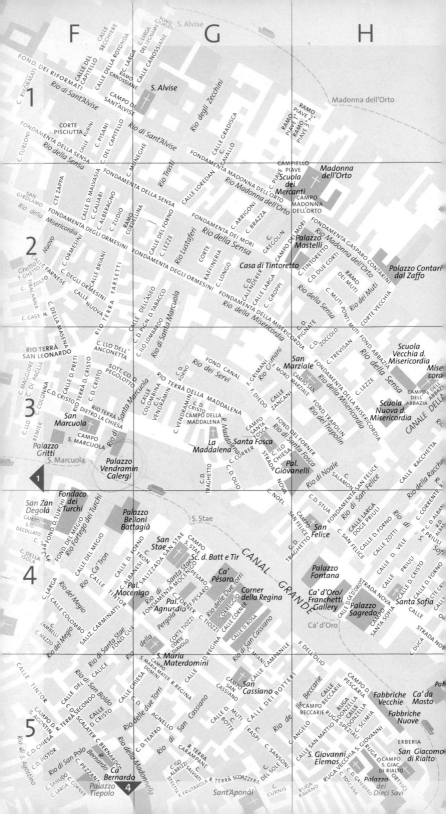

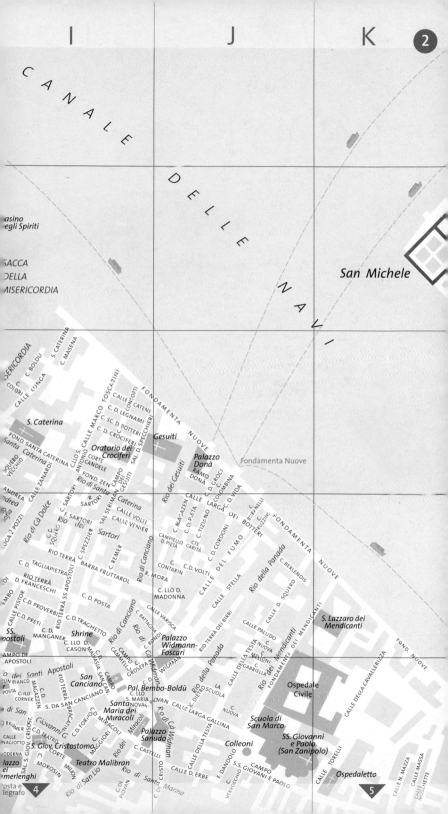

CANALE

DELLE

NAVI

asino
egli Spiriti

SACCA
DELLA
MISERICORDIA

San Michele

ERICORDIA

S. Caterina

S. CATERINA
C. BOLDU
C. MASENA
C. C. COLORI C. UNGA
CALLE UNGA

FOND. SANTA CATERINA
Santa Caterina
SQUERO VECCHIO

ANDREA
ndrea
glia

FOSCARINI
CALLE MARCO
CLLO S.
C. SC. D. BOTTERI
C. D. CROCIFERI
ANTONIO CORTE CANDELE

CONSORTI
C. D. CATENE
C. D. LEGNAMI

FONDAMENTA NUOVE

Oratorio dei
Crociferi

Gesuiti

CALLE ZANARDI
FOND. ZEN CAMPO DEI GESUITI
SAL. D. SPECCHIERI

Palazzo
Donà
RAMO
DONÀ

Fondamenta Nuove

LUGA 2 POZZI
CALLE
Rio di Cà Dolce

C. D. SARTORI
F. SARTORI
C. D. SQUERO
SAL SERIMAN
CALLE VENIER

CAMPO
Santa Caterina
Rio di Santa

C. SPEZZIER
C. REMER
Rio di Canciano

Rio dei
Sartori

CALLE VOLTI

Rio di R. MORA

RIO TERRÀ
BARBA FRUTTAROL

C. D. TAGLIAPIETRA
RIO TERRÀ
D. FRANCESCHI

C. D. POSTA

C. D. TRAGHETTO

Rio di Canciano
Rio di Ca' Widman

CALLE VARISCA

C. BATAGGIA

EMBO
CALLE PISTOR C. D. PROVERBI

C. D.
PRETI
C. D.
MANGANER

Shrine
C. LLO D.
CASON

C. D. POSTA

SS.
ostoli

AMPO DI
APOSTOLI

o dei Santi Apostoli
UN BIANCO
POSTA
C. ILO
CORNER

San
Canciano

RIO TERRÀ SS APOSTOLI

C. D.
MAGAZEN SAN CAN

RIO TERRÀ
CAMPIELLO
CAMPIELLO
MAVASIA SAN CAN

C. GROSERA

Rio di Ca' Widman

Palazzo
Widmann-
Foscari

CALLE STELLA
Rio della Panada

C. BERLENDIS

CALLE D. SQUERO

FONDAMENTA NUOVE

S. Lazzaro dei
Mendicanti

di San
REMER
CALLE
NAGIOTTO
ODERNA
lazzo
ei
merlenghi

S. Giov. Cristostomo
SAL S. GIOV CRISOST.
C. D. TEATRO
CORTE
C. DI MOROSIN
Teatro Malibran

C. D.
FORIGO
C. MILON

C. D. MAGGIORI
Santa
Maria dei
Miracoli

S. DA SAN CANCIANO

Pal. Bembo-Boldù
S. MARIA
NOVA
C. D. CASTELLI
Palazzo
Sanudo

Rio dei Miracoli

Rio di San Lio

C. DI
PIOVAN

C. DI
CRISTO

Rio di Santa Marina

PIOVAN CALLE LARGA GALLINA
CALLE DELLA TESTA NUOVA
C. DIETRO SCUOLA
C. LARGA GALLINA

CALLE DELLA TESTA
F. DANDOLO

S.S. GIOVANNI E PAOLO
CAMPO
SS. GIOVANNI E PAOLO

Colleoni

C.
NUOVA

Scuola di
San Marco

SS. Giovanni
e Paolo
(San Zanipolo)

Ospedaletto

RIO TERRA DEI BIRRI
CALLE PALUDO
RIO TERRA DELLA PANADA
C. GABRIELLA
C.
MARCONI

Rio dei Mendicanti
FONDAMENTA DEI MENDICANTI

Ospedale
Civile

FOND NUOVE

CALLE DELLA CAVALLERIZZA

CALLE TORELLI

CALLE N. MAZZA
CALLE MASSA
CALLE MOLINETTE

C. VERROCCHIO
CALLE D. ERBE

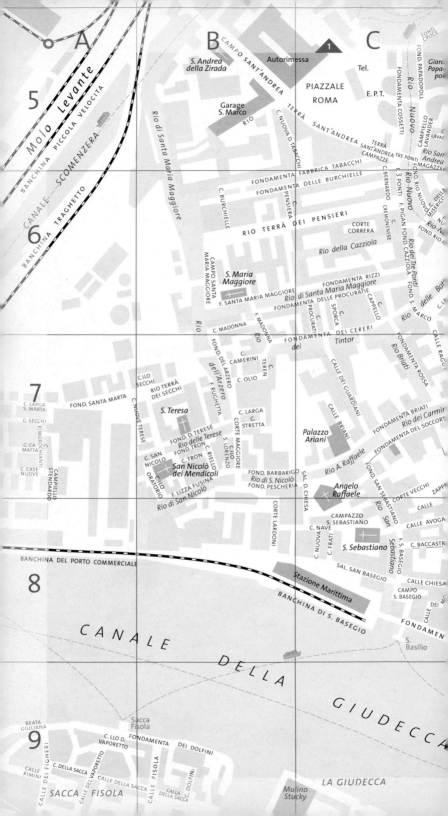

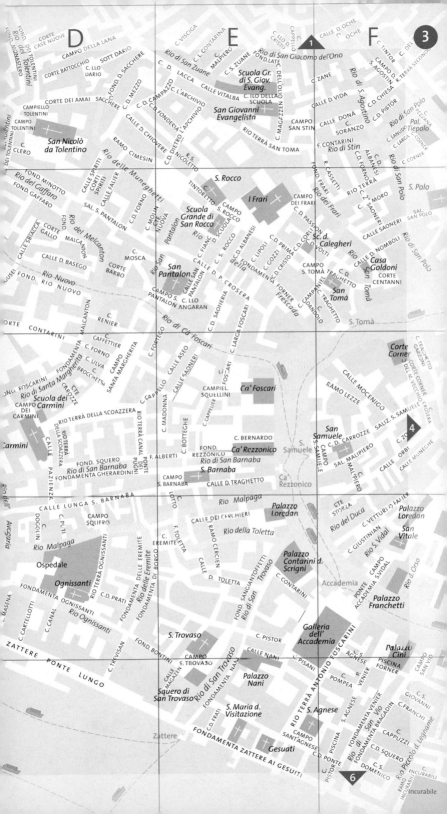

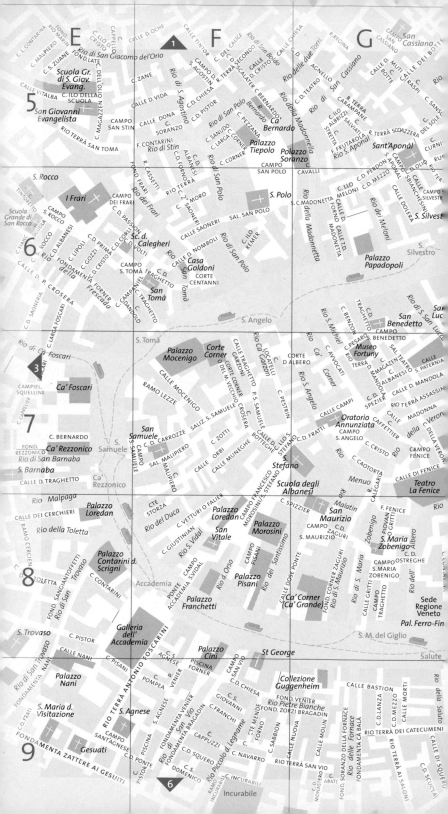

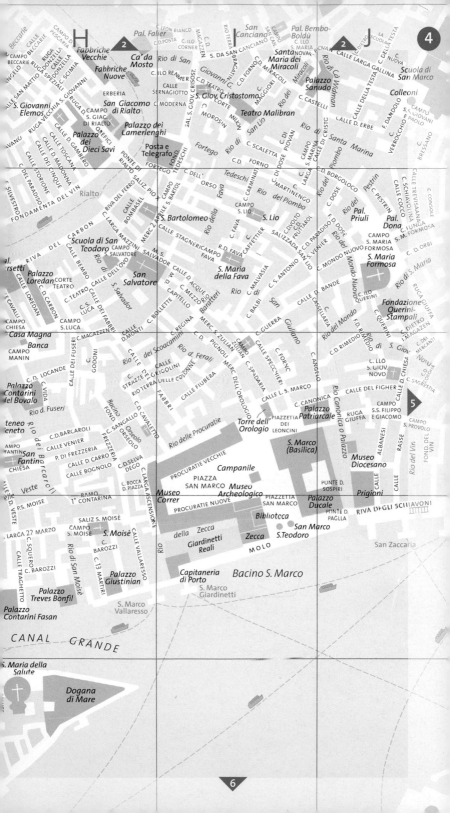

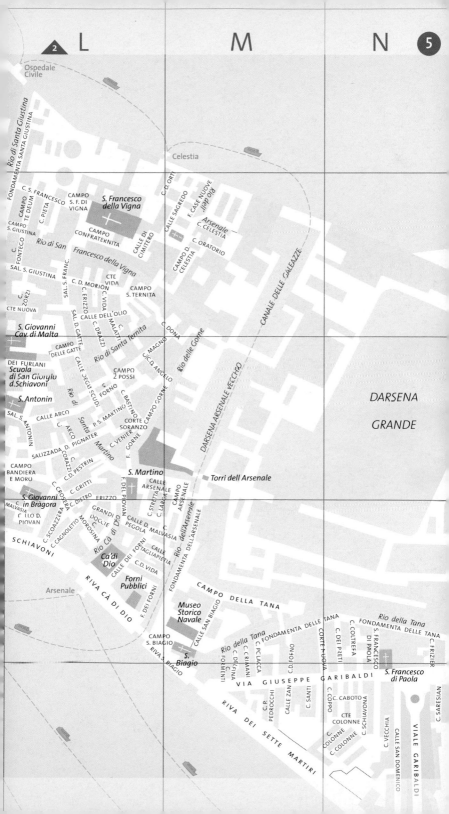

Ospedale
Civile

Celestia

Rio di Santa Giustina
FONDAMENTA SANTA GIUSTINA
C. S. FRANCESCO
CAMPO
TE DEUM
C. PIETA
CAMPO
S. GIUSTINA
C. FONTEGO
SAL. S. GIUSTINA
C. ZORZI
CTE NUOVA

CAMPO
S.F. DI
VIGNA

S. Francesco
della Vigna

CAMPO
CONFRATERNITA

Rio di San
Francesco della Vigna

SAL. S. FRANC.

C. D. MORION

CTE
VIDA
C. VIDA

CAMPO
S. TERNITA

CALLE DI
CIMITERO

C.D. ORTI

CALLE SAGREDO

F. CASE NUOVE
RIO PIO SAGREDO

Arsenale
C. CELESTIA

C. ORATORIO

CAMPO D.
CELESTIA

CANALE DELLE GALEAZZE

S. Giovanni
Cav di Malta

CAMPO
DELLE GATTE

SAL. D. GATTE

C. ERIZZO

CALLE DELL'OLIO

C. DRAZZI

C. D. MALATTI

Rio di Santa Ternita

C. DONA

C. MAGNO

C. C. ANGELO

Rio delle Gorne

DARSENA ARSENALE VECCHIO

DEI FURLANI
Scuola
di San Giorgio
d.Schiavoni

S. Antonin

SAL. S. ANTONIN

CALLE ARCO

Rio di

C. ARCO

Santa Martino

CALLE DEGLI SCUDI

CAMPO
2 POSSI

C. FORNO

C. BASTION

P.S. MARTINO

CORTE
SORANZO

C. VENIER

F. GORNE

C. D. PIGNATER

SALIZZADA D. PIGNATER

CORAZZI

C.D. PESTRIN

CAMPO GORNE

DARSENA

GRANDE

CAMPO
BANDIERA
E MORO

S. Giovanni
in Bràgora

MALVASIA

C. ILO D.
PIOVAN

C. GRITTI

C. DIETRO ERIZZO

C. CROSERA

C. SCOAZZERA

C. CAGNOLETTO

MOROSINA

GRANDI D.
DOCLIE

F. DEL PIOVAN

CALLE D. MALVASIA

S. Martino

CALLE
ARSENALE

C. STRETTA

C. LABIA

CAMPO
ARSENALE

Rio dell'Arsenale

Torri dell'Arsenale

FONDAMENTA DELL'ARSENALE

SCHIAVONI

Arsenale

RIVA CÀ DI DIO

Rio Cà di Dio

Ca'di
Dio

CALLE DEI FORNI

CALLE D.
PEGOLA

CALLE
TAGLIAPIETRA

C.D. VIDA

Forni
Pubblici

F. DEI FORNI

Museo
Storico
Navale

CAMPO
S. BIAGIO

RIVA S. BIAGIO

CALLE SAN BIAGIO

S.
Biagio

CAMPO DELLA TANA

Rio della Tana

C. FOMENTI

C. DELFINA

C. CRIMANI

C. PCLACCA

FONDAMENTA DELLE TANA

C.D. FOENO

CORTE NUOVA

C. DEI PRETI

C. COLTREFA

S. FRANCESCO
DI PAOLA

Rio della Tana
FONDAMENTA DELLE TANA

C. FRIZIER

S. Francesco
di Paola

RIVA DEI SETTE MARTIRI

VIA GIUSEPPE GARIBALDI

C.P.
PEDROCCHI

CALLE ZAN

C. SANTI

C. COPPO

C. CABOTO

CTE
COLONNE

C.
COLONNE

C. COLONNE

C. SCHIAVONA

C. VECCHIA

CALLE SAN DOMENICO

VIALE GARIBALDI

C. SARESIAN

H **I** **J** **6**

CALLE
LARGA 22 MARZO
SALIZ S. MOISÈ
CAMPO
S. MOISÈ
C. SQUERO
C. BAROZZI
CALLE TRAGHETTO
C. 13 MARTIRI
C. BAROZZI
Rio di San Moisè
S. Moisè
C. BAROZZI
CALLE VALLARESSO
Rio della Zecca
Biblioteca
Zecca
San Marco
S. Teodoro
Giardinetti
Reali
MOLO
4

Palazzo
Treves Bonfil
Palazzo
Giustinian
Capitaneria
di Porto
Bacino S. Marco

Palazzo
Contarini Fasan
S. Marco
Vallaresso
S. Marco
Giardinetti

CANAL   GRANDE

S. Maria della
Salute
FOND SALUTE
Dogana
di Mare

CANALE DI S. MARCO
5

S. Giorgio
CAMPO
S. GIORGIO

S. Giorgio
Maggiore

FOND. SAN GIOVANNI
CAMPO
NANI E
BARBARO

CANALE SAN GIORGIO O DELLA GRAZZA

Zitelle
FONDAMENTA DELLE ZITELLE
Le Zitelle
Cipriani
Hotel

C. MICHELANGELO

DELLA   CROCE
C. DELLA
CROCE
CALLE DRIO LA CROCE
CALLE
C. CAMPO
DI MARTE
CAMPO DEL
GRAN
CAMPO DEL GRAN
RAMO
D. GRAN
CALLE MASON
C. 4ª CAMP.
C. 3ª CAMP.
C. 2ª CAMPALTO
C. LLO
CAMPALTO
C. 1ª
CAMPALTO
C. LLO
OSPIZIO
CALLE DELLO SQUERO
R.D. SQUERO
C. L. D. COOPERATIVA
CALLE SAON
C. OSPIZIO
MICHELANGELO

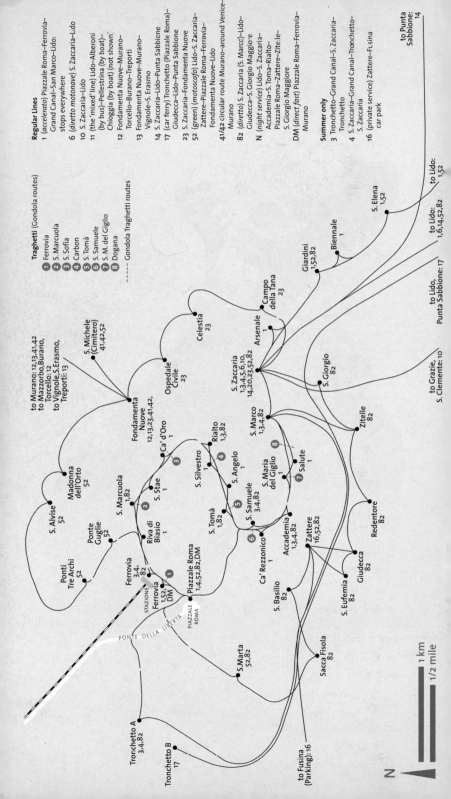

Regular Lines

1 (*accelerato*) Piazzale Roma–Ferrovia–Grand Canal–San Marco–Lido: stops everywhere
6 (*diretto motonave*) S. Zaccaria–Lido
10 S. Zaccaria–Lido
11 (the 'mixed' line) Lido–Alberoni (by bus)–Pellestrina (by boat)–Chioggia (by boat) (not shown)
12 Fondamenta Nuove–Murano–Torcello–Burano–Treporti
13 Fondamenta Nuove–Murano–Vignole–S. Erasmo
14 S. Zaccaria–Lido–Punta Sabbione
17 (car ferry) Tronchetto (Piazzale Roma)–Giudecca–Lido–Punta Sabbione
23 S. Zaccaria–Fondamenta Nuove
52 (green) (*motoscafo*) Lido–S. Zaccaria–Zattere–Piazzale Roma–Ferrovia–Fondamenta Nuove–Lido
41/42 circular route Murano–around Venice–Murano
82 (*diretto*) S. Zaccaria (S. Marco)–Lido–Giudecca–S. Giorgio Maggiore
N (*night service*) Lido–S. Zaccaria–Accademia–S. Toma–Rialto–Piazzale Roma–Zattere–Zitelle–S. Giorgio Maggiore
DM (*direct fast*) Piazzale Roma–Ferrovia–Murano

Summer only

3 Tronchetto–Grand Canal–S. Zaccaria–Tronchetto
4 S. Zaccaria–Grand Canal–Tronchetto–S. Zaccaria
16 (private service) Zattere–Fusina car park

Traghetti (Gondola routes)

1 Ferrovia
2 S. Marcuola
3 S. Sofia
4 Carbon
5 S. Tomà
6 S. Samuele
7 S. M. del Giglio
8 Dogana

----- Gondola Traghetti routes